A COMMENTARY ON
Plutarch's
Life of Agesilaos

For my wife

A COMMENTARY ON
Plutarch's
Life of Agesilaos

Response to Sources in the Presentation
of Character

D. R. SHIPLEY

CLARENDON PRESS · OXFORD
1997

Oxford University Press, Great Clarendon Street, Oxford OX2 6DP

Oxford   New York

Athens Auckland Bangkok Bogota Bombay
Buenos Aires Calcutta Cape Town Dar es Salaam
Delhi Florence Hong Kong Istanbul Karachi
Kuala Lumpur Madras Madrid Melbourne
Mexico City Nairobi Paris Singapore
Taipei Tokyo Toronto Warsaw
and associated companies in
Berlin Ibadan

Oxford is a trade mark of Oxford University Press

Published in the United States
by Oxford University Press Inc., New York

British Library Cataloguing in Publication Data
Data available

Library of Congress Cataloging in Publication Data
A commentary on Plutarch's life of Agesilaos : response to sources
in the presentation of character / D. R. Shipley.
Includes bibliographical references.
1. Plutarch. Agesilaus. 2. Agesilaus II, King of Sparta.
3. Greece—History—Spartan and Theban Supremacies, 404–362 B.C.—
Historiography. 4. Greece—History—Spartan and Theban
Supremacies, 404–362 B.C. 5. Sparta (Extinct city)—Historiography.
6. Greece—Kings and rulers—Biography. 7. Sparta (Extinct city)—
History. 8. Biography as a literary form. 9. Plutarch—Technique.
I. Plutarch. Agesilaus. II. Title.
PS4369.A43S48   1997   938'.906'092—dc21   97-15113
ISBN 0-19-815073-3

1 3 5 7 9 10 8 6 4 2

Typeset by Regent Typesetting, London
Printed in Great Britain on acid-free paper by
Bookcraft (Bath) Ltd., Midsomer Norton

PREFACE

THE interpretation of the complex and varied works of Plutarch continues. It 'has long been pursued, but has in some senses hardly begun'[1] even now. In the *Lives* he plays the roles of 'the moral biographer, the historian and the literary artist'.[2] Rhetorical analysts have concluded that 'classical historiography'—even Thucydides' 'scientific history'[3]—is 'primarily a rhetorical genre and is to be classified (in modern terms) as literature rather than as history'.[4] How, then, do we read Plutarch's *Lives*?

The past cannot be revisited by the historian; the only evidence available is the fragmentary record which the past has left behind, literary, documentary, numismatic, archaeological remains—the 'Visible Past'[5] that has survived into the present. One can read and handle this material, but it is not itself history: the 'Mute Stones Speak'[6] only in the words of the author: history is concerned with revealing the *invisible past*, that is its *significance*, which is in the mind and in the present time.

Historical writing is essential to historical understanding;[7] the end of the task is the verbal account, 'History as Text',[8] and so is unavoidably a work of effective language—rhetorical. Rhetoric— the art of composition and presentation—is an indispensable tool without which the historian cannot write even the most straight- forward meaningful account of events. The criticism that it is rhetorical cannot be fatal, if we wish to know about the past. The rhetorical work becomes a history if it communicates to the reader the ordering and linking of the past events that the historian's studies and expertise have created, for it is only when the written history is being conned with understanding that it has any signifi- cant existence, a coherent interpretation by the reader of the events connected in meaningful discourse.

Two functions the biographer shares with the historian are rele- vant to the form of the present commentary on Plutarch's *Life of Agesilaos*. First is his analytical technique, involving assumptions, judgements, and generalizations, of selecting what is considered relevant from the vast but already incomplete web of data that is available in the record. The second is the synthetical function of composition. The ability to show the unassailable truth about the events of the past, untainted, as it were, by his own or his predecessors' mental processes—to achieve, in a word, objectivity—is hardly to be expected beyond the assembly of documentary evidence in the form in which it exists. Writing about the past involves the construction of a set of ideas concerning the evidence which establishes connections, causes, and consequences and offers the reader the means of understanding these. These functions are subjective in the sense of bringing intellect, experience, and imagination to bear on the explication of the historical evidence selected as relevant.

The elements of interpretation, organization of the narrative, and its ornamentation—which the critics denigrate as rhetoric—are in a sense a creative fiction; and sometimes the persuasive presentation may be suspected as designed to mislead. 'But rhetoric in the wide sense, that is, all that is implied by textuality, is as much a part of all but the most technical historical writing as it is of literature itself.'[9] These are matters of form. The content is properly evaluated using other criteria. It is to content that the term 'scientific history' should be applied,[10] for it is in the treatment of evidence that Thucydides in his *Preface* (i. 21) claimed to be exceptional. The scientific element consists in the intellectual rigour of the process of conceptualization of the subject matter *before* composition begins.

The biographer's work, like the historian's, is not just about facts: it, too, is a piece of literature concerned with the past. But the conflict of art and reality in creating an account of a man's life from birth to death makes greater artistic demands on the biographer: for the historian chooses not only his own starting and finishing points, but also the thematic parameters which impose, as it were, the organic beginning, middle, and end on the otherwise ongoing series of events.[11] On the other hand, the biographer has the advantage that the organic core, at least, of the *Life* clearly lies between the natural limits of a lifespan.[12] He focuses more narrowly on his chosen individual in the chosen context (public life etc.) by further selecting from the historical record the actions he considers relevant to the display of the subject's qualities and achievements in the context of the *Life*, his moral role. His illustrations and assessments of character largely account for the wide interest in biography through the ages. The work's impact and acceptability will be determined by the readers' attitude to the author's intellectual, political, moral, and aesthetic stance, and by the quality of his presentation.

The biographer's presentation of moral values is given coherence and focus by selection and creative manipulation: a rhetorical representation, not the reality, and therefore in a sense a false image, though intended not to deceive but to portray what he believes to be the truth, where the plain factual account, only 'what happened', can have no moral content. The incomplete historical narrative is filled out to make it serviceable as a moral tool where historical truth is not available: reality—the living subject—is remote in space and time, but his actions reveal character, inherited and inculcated. Inculcation, the concern of the moral biographer, begins with presentation of examples. But Plutarch saw that presentation was not paramount. As in visual art, so in biography, the mind as well as the eye must be engaged: literary representation of virtuous action—image rather than reality—will attract the reader, but in the development of character the formative agent is the intellect (*Per.* 1. 3–4; cf. 2. 3). Clearly Plutarch expected attentive readers to make the effort to transform the images of virtue into the reality of moral traits in their own characters.[13] Plutarch's conceptualization of the moral and historical significance of Agesilaos' handling of the affairs of Sparta during his reign is proof of the intellectual rigour of his analysis of the varied evidence and justifies serious consideration of his work.

'Literature and history must go together':[14] the responsible reader appreciates and evaluates both.[15] The present commentary aims to elucidate Plutarch's roles as moral biographer, historian, and artist by studying his treatment of his sources, and is a historical commentary only in that sense. It shows that Plutarch presents a study of Agesilaos' reign in Sparta which illuminates, modifies and supplements other extant historical accounts with an independent, penetrating and balanced analysis of some of the historical and moral issues of the period.

It is a pleasure to thank Professor J. F. Lazenby of the University of Newcastle, who inspired and supervised my Ph.D. thesis, completed in 1990, the source of this commentary, and Dr A. J. S. Spawforth of the University of Newcastle, and Dr S. J. Hodkinson of the University of Manchester, my examiners, for

their subsequent guidance, encouragement, and helpful suggestions. Other members of Classics Departments, especially Mr J.
Longrigg and Dr A. Laird, of the University of Newcastle, and
Dr J. L. Moles, of the University of Durham, have also given generously of their time on occasions when I needed further help and
advice on their specialist subjects and I very much appreciate their
kindness in discussing my work. I was privileged to use the facilities of the Libraries of Newcastle and Durham Universities and of
the Bodleian and Ashmolean Libraries in Oxford, and thank the
Librarians for their prompt and willing assistance in locating and
obtaining the books and periodicals I needed. Topographical work
in Thessaly, Boiotia, the Attic frontier area, and the Peloponnese,
and exploration in Asia Minor of routes from Ephesos and of the
countryside between the valleys of the Rivers Maiandros and
Hermos, were made possible through the hospitality of the British
School at Athens and its Library, and the many kindnesses of the
Director, Dr H. W. Catling, and of Mrs Catling, and the school
staff in 1986 and 1987. The American School of Classical Studies
and the Gennadion Library at Athens most generously granted
me access to all their Library accommodation and facilities and I
enjoyed valuable contacts with their staffs and members.

The task of preparing my thesis for publication has been a long
one, involving rewriting, enlargement, and refinement. I benefited
very greatly from the comments, suggestions, and invaluable
advice of the Readers of the Oxford University Press and its copy-
editor, who traditionally remain anonymous: my privilege
deserves more fully to be acknowledged than that allows. My debt
to the works of many scholars is evident in every chapter and in
my Bibliography, notably Professors J. Buckler and R. J. Buck for
Thebes and Boiotia; above all, for seminal inspiration, Dr P. A.
Cartledge of Clare College, Cambridge, on Sparta and Lakonia,
Dr C. B. R. Pelling of University College, Oxford, on Plutarch
and biography, and for kindly allowing me to see some of his
unpublished work, and Dr S. Hornblower of Oriel College,
Oxford, on Greek history and historiography and Dr L. A.
Holford-Strevens for personal communications. These many con-
tributors combined greatly to advance and transform my work and
I thank them all, and the Senior Editor, Classics, sincerely for
their generosity. I am grateful also to my son, Graham Shipley,
who has read and commented upon successive versions, and

compiled the General Index. The misconceptions and imperfections that remain are entirely my responsibility. It remains for me to express my appreciation to Dr T. E. Duff of the University of Reading for allowing me to read his Ph.D. (Cantab.) thesis before publication, and to Mr David Taylor, of the Department of Archaeology, University of Nottingham, for the realization of the maps from the author's sketches.

Finally, my studies would not have been possible without the support of my wife. I am grateful to her for her patience, encouragement, and help.

CONTENTS

LIST OF MAPS

NOTE ON REFERENCES

References to Plutarch's *Agesilaos* and *Pompey* are numbered as in Budé (1973). I use 'ch.' and 'chs.' to refer to chapters of *Agesilaos*. The texts of the Loeb Classical Library are used for references to his other *Lives*, to *Moralia*, Xenophon, Diodoros, and Pausanias, and of standard editions for other works. The Persian monarch is referred to as King. Cross-references to the Introduction are to sections A–F and their subsections. A translation of Plutarch's *Agesilaos* is published in Penguin Classics, *The Age of Alexander*; several *Lives* and sources are translated in *Plutarch on Sparta* and elsewhere in the series.

NOTE ON TEXT

The lemmata follow the text of R. Flacelière and É. Chambry, *Plutarche: Vies*, viii (Paris, 1973). However, in addition to minor variations in punctuation and paragraphing, I have adopted readings suggested there in square and angle brackets, except in the following respects.

(i) At ch. 9. 6 I have bracketed ἀντὶ δειλῶν ὁπλιτῶν, perhaps imported, with variations, from *Mor.* 209 b: ἀντὶ δειλῶν καὶ πλουσίων.

I have bracketed, with Cobet (1878), τοὺς βουλομένους στρατεύεσθαι, οἱ δὲ μὴ βουλόμενοι ἱππεύειν. Thus I adopt the reading of Bos (1947), 71: ἐμισθοῦντο γὰρ οἱ μὴ βουλόμενοι στρατεύεσθαι τοὺς βουλομένους ἱππεύειν.

At 11. 9, I have adopted the conjecture of Reiske (1774–82): Οὐδέν, ἔφη, ⟨δεινὸν⟩ πείθειν ὑμᾶς ἐκεῖνον.

At 11. 10 I have adopted Cobet's conjecture, ἄν for αὖ.

At ch. 21. 2 I have filled the lacuna with ⟨καὶ τὰ νεώρια⟩, adapted from Xenophon, *Hellenika*, iv. 4. 19.

(ii) I have adopted the spelling -νικ- rather than -νεικ- in φιλονικία and its cognates at chs. 2. 2, 4. 4, 5. 5, 5. 7, 7. 4, 11. 6, 18. 4, 23. 11, 26. 6, 33. 2, 34. 2, and *Comp.* 1. 3.

The Greek text is reproduced from *La Vie d'Agésilas* (1973) by kind permission of © Les Belles Lettres, Paris, and the editors and translators, Robert Flacelière and Émile Chambry.

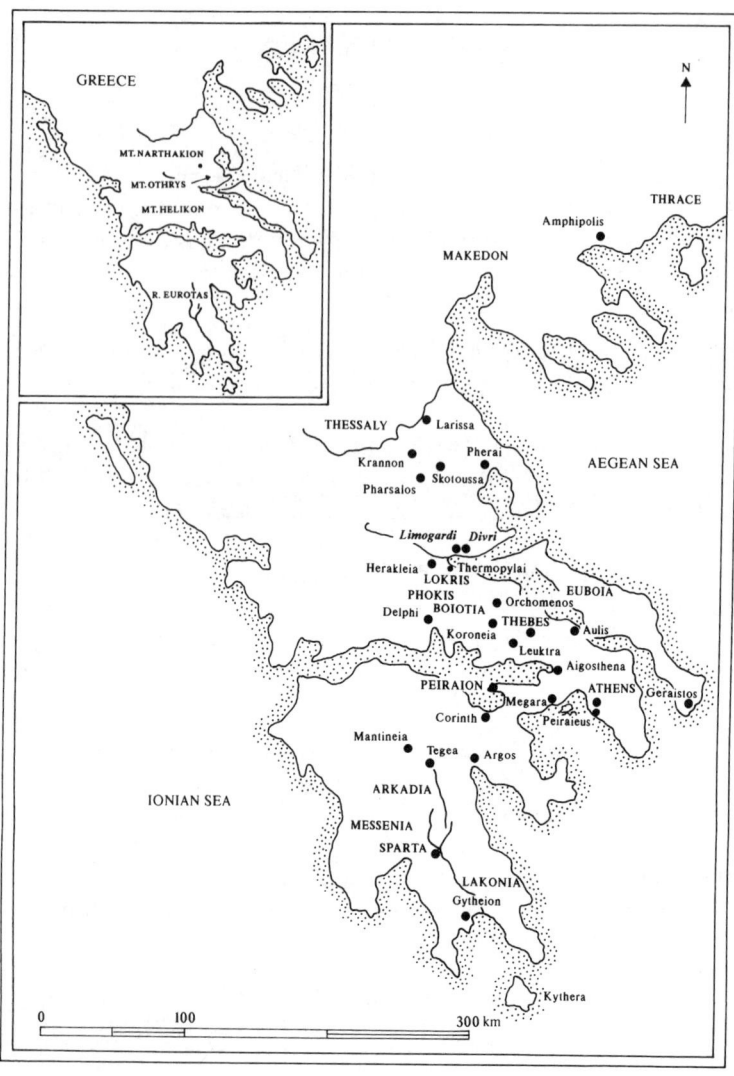

MAP I. Greece

INTRODUCTION

A. The *Life of Agesilaos* in the Life of Plutarch

Plutarch is thought to have been born about AD 45 and, until his death in about AD 120, lived at Chaironeia in Boiotia, the area where much of the interest in *Agesilaos* lies.[1] He was at Athens for part of his rhetorical and philosophical education, and studied with the Egyptian Platonist Ammonios, who may have been a valuable consultant for Agesilaos' Egyptian episode (chs. 36–40: *Them.* 32. 5; *De adul. et am.* 70 E; *Quaest. Conv.* iii. 1, 2, viii. 3, ix; *De E apud Delph.*; *De def. or.*).[2] His was one of the leading local well-to-do families, from whom no doubt he inherited the humane but broadly aristocratic outlook characteristic of his works. He made several visits abroad, to Asia, Egypt, and, as a member of diplomatic embassies, to Italy and Rome, gaining contacts and experience which afforded him the confidence to write authoritatively about the distinguished men who became the subjects of his *Lives*. He returned home without pretentiousness, as did Agesilaos (*Dem.* 2; below, ch. 19. 6). There he took part in municipal affairs, established a school, and succeeded to one of the two permanent priesthoods at Delphi. He had a fortunate married life and was devoted to his wife and children, although some of the latter died young. These, among the known details of Plutarch's life, inform much of his literary work. His appreciation of family values and his interest in public life, in religion, and in the education and development of the young, are especially relevant to his biography of the Spartan king Agesilaos.

About half of his literary work survives, including forty-six of the *Parallel Lives* and four other biographies for which he is now best known.[3] His main writing was done in his later lifetime which, like that of Tacitus (*Agricola*, 3. 1), saw the renaissance of free expression under Nerva, Trajan, and Hadrian, and the increasing political and social unity of the Greek and Roman worlds. However, the past political difficulties in both worlds[4] are underlying themes in *Agesilaos* and its pair, *Pompey*. In these

Lives, as in others, Plutarch regrets the decline in standards of public behaviour from what he saw as the high ideals of earlier times (ch. 33. 2, 3–4; *Pomp.* 70. 1; cf. *Lyk.–Num.* 4. 8; *Phok.* 3. 2–3; *Lys.–Sull.* 1. 2–3, 3. 5).[5] Thus *Agesilaos* and *Pompey* involve an element of political analysis as well as the study of the personal characteristics of the two men.[6] Plutarch's writings reflect his outlook and his experience as a Greek, a Boiotian, a citizen active in the affairs of Chaironeia, a family man and a scholar. Active, too, in the affairs of Delphi, in the world of the Roman empire, and in the wider context of the west and the east which was so important to the Greek and Roman nations, he held equestrian status, *ornamenta consularia*, and imperial, perhaps honorific, offices.[7] What he made of Agesilaos in the light of this experience it is the purpose of this commentary to elucidate.

B. PLUTARCH'S CONCEPTUAL FRAMEWORK[8]

1. *Literature and History*

The evidence for Plutarch's conceptual framework for his biographies as character studies and for their relationship to history and literature is in his works. The exemplary moral, that is protreptic, purpose of the *Lives* was to encourage admiration and imitation of good characters by displaying virtuous actions directly and by examining also bad and blameworthy lives (*Aem.* 1. 4, *Alex.* 1. 2–3, *Dtr.* 1. 6), thus complementing and continuing the intentions of the theoretical moral and philosophical works, now known to us as *Moralia*, with studies of individual statesmen drawn from history (*Aem.* 1. 5, 5. 10).[9] Plutarch displays character indirectly, too, in passages of 'characterization by reaction'[10] that allow him to present judgements not on his own authority but on that of one or more of his characters.[11] He records the response of an observer, Lysander, to portray Agesilaos' natural modesty (ch. 2. 1); the devotion of Antony's wounded troops to portray his popular leadership (*Ant.* 43. 1–2); the fine imposed by the ephors to condemn Agesilaos' growing political power (ch. 5. 4); the disgust of decent people to condemn Antony's debauchery and extravagance (*Ant.* 9. 5–6). The device is used by Homer, who asserts Helen's beauty by its impact on the Trojan elders (*Il.* iii.

156–8), and by Thucydides, who uses the confusion of the participating sailors to characterize the great battle at Syracuse (vii. 71.
3); Plutarch warns against the rhetorical technique of orators who
attribute their false accusations to others (*Mor.* 57 B).[12]

The literary qualities of Plutarch's *Lives* are visible in small-
scale features and in larger-scale structures. The former include a
clear but ornate style of writing and of linguistic usage—ornamentation by quotation, metaphor, simile, anecdote, variation, and
rhetorical figures. Among the latter are *synkrisis* (B.2(*a*) below),
digression, ring composition, and chiastic and other word-
patterns, often at key points in the narrative: in *Agesilaos*, there
are more than 150 chiastic patterns and many pairs of parallel
words and phrases. Plutarch creates suspense, dramatic tension,
thematic climax; sustains moral seriousness, emotional impact,
narrative interest; and projects a humane and delicate personality.
His allusions to ideas and attitudes familiar to us from the works
of earlier authors manifest significant literary continuity and
affinity with the past in his thinking.

As history the *Lives* present problems of accuracy. Recognizable
sources provide factual content, but Plutarch selects events and
judges their significance for his own purposes.[13] The way his
narratives are directed—here, his interpretation of the life of
Agesilaos—reveals an independent and penetrating mind, but he
justly uses an appropriate phrase, such as 'it is said', to indicate
judgements and information, including the anecdotal, for which
he cannot—or does not—give clear definition or supporting
authentication (F.4 below). In the particular 'conceptual framework' which may be identified in his *Agesilaos*, Plutarch presents
not only a valid account of Agesilaos' character and reign, but also
an interpretation of Spartan morality and history which is especially significant in the larger context of the fourth century.

(*a*) *Biography*. The subjects of biographies have not always been
people: in the ancient world '*Βίος*' was a word also used for the life
of a country by writers such as Dikaiarchos (F.3(*e*) below), who
were interested in antiquarian erudition as well as individuals.[14]
Plutarch displays antiquarian interest in *Agesilaos* (chs. 1, 5, 19,
30), but the object of attention and assessment is the city of Sparta
of Agesilaos' lifetime, which features almost as much as Agesilaos
himself. Indeed, the five Spartan *Lives*, *Lykourgos*, *Lysander*,

Agesilaos, Agis, Kleomenes, together present—perhaps unintentionally—a Spartan cycle (see below, D.3, E.3(*e*), and the Epilogue). Plutarch's moral and aesthetic stance is that of the earlier period portrayed in his *Lykourgos*; a stance adjusted in the light of his reading of the political and philosophical writings of Plato and Aristotle, and of his own experience as a Greek in the Roman empire.[15] He indicates the longer Spartan perspective lightly at the start by tracing Agesilaos' family back as far as his grandfather (ch. 1. 1), and more significantly at the end by referring to Agis IV (*c.*244–241), the fifth Eurypontid king in descent from Agesilaos—significantly, because he credits Agis with attempting to restore to Sparta its lost 'Lykourgan' standards (ch. 40; *Agis*, 4–5).

(*b*) *Ideology*. Plutarch's commitment to Spartan ideology may not be accepted as historically legitimate by some modern historians, who demand, in the words of John Tosh (1991, 131), a 'dispassionate, "passive" observer', but his balanced judgements contributed greatly to the inspiration of philo-Laconism in European, and later in American culture. His ideals and interests centre in Greece and in leaders of the Greek *poleis*, though he sees them imaged in Rome too. While he is less concerned to approve forms of government than the quality of the ruler or the lawgiver, his preference here is for Sparta and Lykourgos, a preference shared with Aristeides, Agis IV, Phokion, but not Philopoimen and Aratos;[16] Athens and Athenian statesmen and the Boiotian Epameinondas are also prominent, and Numa, who avoids Sparta's militarism (*Lyk.–Num.* 1. 2–4).[17] To the ancient Spartan regimen of Lykourgos he attributes 'the pursuit of wisdom', φιλοσοφεῖν, in the context of practical politics and concise—*laconic*—discourse, the ideal of a harmonious society (*Lyk.* 19–20, 31. 1–2), and the establishment of the system of education (ἀγωγή), inculcating frugality, obedience, and devotion to the service of the state. Plutarch praises Agesilaos for adhering to the practice of obedience and moderation; but he indicates inadequate intellectual education in Sparta among Lykourgos' successors who failed to provide guiding principles for the control of excess, for the interpretation of ordinary moral values like justice, and for the exercise of power in accordance with those values; and he blames Agesilaos for misreading the true interest of his city.

Plutarch recognized and praised Lykourgan standards in the *Lives* of other statesmen. Numa shared Lykourgos' love of wisdom, his justice and his mildness (δικαιοσύνη καὶ πρᾳότης), and saw the potential of inculcating such an ideal life in Rome. (*Num.* 20. 3–8; cf. *Lyk.* 28. 6.) Solon of Athens was a philosopher with a moderate attitude to wealth, though he could not adopt all Lykourgos' measures (*Sol.* 2–3, 22. 2). In the *Moralia* Plutarch's standards are those of the *Lives* and his illustrations are often taken from them. The purposes and the values of the two sets of works are almost inseparable,[18] the *Lives* offering clear models for imitation of the ethical principles discussed in the essays, such as respect for elders, *laconic* discourse, frugality (*Mor.* 788–9, 510 E, 809 A–B).[19] And Spartan *Lives*—and his *Sayings*, if Plutarchan, as those incorporated in the *Lives* are—were frequently also used to warn (*Sol.* 16. 1–2, *Lyk.–Num.* 2. 2–5, *Lys.* 17. 4, *Mor.* 239 F). *Agesilaos* reflects Plutarch's consistent moral position and protreptic purpose.

(*c*) *Creative writing.* Judged only by the relationship between writer and reader, ancient biography and historiography can be compared to the modern historical novel, the television documentary, and reports compiled by war correspondents, in the way they mix fact and fiction. These modern productions knowingly use fictional or 'misappropriated' material.[20] Plutarch uses no conscious fictionalizing, but 'creative reconstruction' from other sources and situations to fill out his narrative—e.g. of early childhood (ch. 2); to bridge chronological gaps (chs. 21. 3–22. 1; cf. Xen. *Hell.* iv. 5. 2–6); to enhance a description (Xen. *Hell.* vi. 5. 28: women had never seen an enemy; ch. 31. 6: they had never seen the smoke of an enemy's fires).[21] Plutarch judged himself no historian—largely for rhetorical reasons[22]—yet one may argue that he incorporates some of the more important elements of a modern work of history, such as taking a critical and independent approach to the sources and arguing an original thesis. He has combined shrewd and thoughtful analysis both of Agesilaos' domestic and public life and of the Spartans' regimen and behaviour during his reign; and in presenting a favourable illustration of Lykourgan virtues, together with expressions of regret for their eventual neglect, he has also revealed his view of the moral principles to be valued in his own times and for the future.

Moreover, his account of Agesilaos' character contains elements of a psychological exploration of the man's motivation (chs. 7. 4; 15. 5; 18. 4; 40. 2), his personality (chs. 2. 3–5; 22. 2; 25. 11; 35. 5; 36. 5, 10–11, 38. 6–39. 2), and his responses to emotional stimulus (chs. 6. 11; 11. 2, 6–10; 13. 2–3; 23. 11; 28. 2). By introducing these elements into his narrative he implants in readers the impulse towards enlightenment, involving them in his inquiry, ἱστορία, in the areas of private and public morality (*Per.* 2. 2–3). It is a convincing psychology, though undeveloped by modern standards as regards individual personality, 'personhood',[23] and along with the historical and literary elements it, too, contributes to the complex conceptual framework of Plutarchan biography.

2. *Plutarch's Technique*

(*a*) Synkrisis: *the comparative method.* Plutarch composed his parallel *Lives* in pairs, each containing the biographies of one Greek and one Roman.[24] Elsewhere he states that his aim in pairing these *Lives* by a regular comparative method, *synkrisis*,[25] was to achieve a clearer understanding of character (*Mor.* 243 B–D).[26] Illumination by the drawing of comparisons is an ancient technique,[27] observed for example in Herodotos' work, in the way he sets the Greek in contrast with the non-Greek. In Thucydides' history Athens is set in contrast with Sparta, the fate of Pausanias with that of Themistokles (i. 128–38). These are implicit comparisons, but each hero of Isokrates' and Xenophon's biographies is contrasted explicitly with a king of Persia (*Euagoras*, 37–8, *Agesilaos*, 8. 6–9. 5).[28] The technique was developed in rhetorical education (Quintilian, *Inst.* 2. 4. 21),[29] and may be illustrated from Cicero's oratory (*de imperio Cn. Pompei*, 9–10, 20–50): the superiority of the generalship of Pompey is implied by a comparison with that of Lucullus, and Cicero's own praise of Lucullus is favourably compared with that of Lucullus' own supporters; he tactfully demonstrates that Pompey conducted his campaign in Spain more effectively than Lucullus conducted his against Mithridates; he compares the delay of Lucullus' pursuit by the treasure Mithridates left behind him with Medea's delaying her pursuers by scattering her brother's remains; then he compares their operations directly.

(*b*) *The* Prooimia: *Introductions to the* Lives. Each of Plutarch's *Lives* has a *prooimion*, a prologue, which serves primarily to catch the reader's interest. The *prooimia* have been classified as either 'formal' or 'integrated'.[30] Thirteen pairs have 'formal' openings, located in the first *Life* of the pair. They chiefly explore Plutarch's biographical purposes, methods, and practice, sometimes with regard to both *Lives* in the pair, sometimes with more general historiographical relevance, informing the reader's generic expectations of utility and truth;[31] they also name the pair and list similarities that justify the pairing. Neither *Alexander* nor *Nikias*[32] is an exception here, for in *Alexander* Plutarch implies similarities with Caesar by mentioning those that he has excluded—'their greatness and their struggles' (1. 3)—and in *Nikias* there is a brief list—'Sicilian disaster alongside Parthian' (1. 1). The latter is surely diagnostic, for Nikias, faulted for hesitancy, and Crassus, for greed, die on the only extended campaigns reported, tragically after recovering their spirits.

Plutarch continues these formal *prooimia* with introductory personal details relevant only to the current *Life*. Personal details form the 'integrated' openings, with no mention here of the pair or biographical method. Integrated proems introduce the other nine leading *Lives*, including *Agesilaos*, and the twenty-four *Lives* (including *Kleom.–Grac.*) that complete the pairs. These details bring a *Life* into focus and create immediate interest. Plutarch often gives family history at this point; in four of these *Lives* the father's name is mentioned at the beginning of the proem, in others at the point where the account of the life opens. A striking feature is the importance assigned to the influence of the subject's mother and her family (*Thes.* 3. 4–4. 1, *Rom.* 2. 2–3. 3, *Sol.* 1. 2, *Kim.* 4. 1, *Per.* 3. 1–2, *Alk.* 1. 1, *Dem.* 4. 2, *Cic.* 2. 1–2, *Alex.* 2. 1–3. See below, ch. 1. 1).[33]

(*c*) *Character, career, choices.* (i) Erbse's study of some of these *prooimia* showed that Plutarch's purpose is accomplished by portraying 'the conspicuous similarities of character and career' which the pair displays.[34] Further study of the formal proems clarifies Plutarch's procedure and suggests an enlargement of Erbse's two categories. In the introduction to *Demosthenes–Cicero*, analysed by Erbse,[35] Plutarch says that these two men had many similarities in their natures, which shaped their characters—

ambition, love of liberty, lack of courage—and many similarities
of fortune, which shaped the circumstances they faced in their
careers: their small beginnings as orators, the loss of their
daughters, their exile and death, and the loss of liberty by all the
citizens (*Dem.* 3. 3–5). In this passage Plutarch identifies two
categories that determine men's characters and the shaping of
their lives: nature and fortune. However, another item—their
opposition to tyrants, listed by Plutarch among their 'fortunes'—
does not fit neatly into this or the other category.

In other formal introductions three conceptual categories are
involved. They are readily discernible at *Phokion*, 1. 2, 3. 1–5.
Phokion and Cato have similar natures and fortunes, both are
virtuous men who live in calamitous and corrupt times, but their
virtues carry on the unequal struggle against these adverse
fortunes through political actions. Detailed treatment of character
is normally delayed to the epilogue which this pair lacks; placed
here it sharpens the distinction between nature, fortunes, and the
third category: the struggle.

The three are expressed in more self-explanatory terms at *Dion*,
1. 2–3, 2. 1–3: Dion and Brutus follow Platonist philosophical
principles requiring power and good fortune to be used with
wisdom and justice if political actions are to be seen as noble as
well as great. Plutarch asserts similarity in their virtues, in many
of their actions, and in their *fortunes*, the last being alike more 'in
chance events'—their early death, the failure of their purposes, the
divine warnings they received—'than in their deliberate choices',
the third category, represented by political *actions*.[36] The three
categories in *Dion* are thus: (1) qualities bestowed by nature, that
is to say character; (2) fortunes, the events through which the men
lived, resulting from chance; and (3) deliberate choices, the
characteristic responses to the chance factors. Accordingly, in
Demosthenes, Plutarch compares the pair's actions (chosen opposition to tyrants) in the context of their fortunes and of their virtues.

(ii) The three categories, though often discernible, are not consistently differentiated in Plutarch's terminological usage; nor,
perhaps, in real life. His method was more flexible in this as in
other areas (see B.2(*b*) above, and E.3(*c*) below), and should not be
expected to conform to precise rules. The distinction between
characters and chosen actions can be an awkward one, as in the
case of Demetrios and Antonios. The two men's similar natures

(φύσεις)—their vices—determine their chosen actions, 'womaniz-
ing, drinking, fighting': and, of course, their characters are
revealed by these actions; their fortunes—conquests and disasters
—depend also on their choices: their deaths, though in similar
circumstances (the one in captivity, the other on the brink of
captivity), reflect their different characters in the choice each made
(*Dtr.* 1. 7–8, *Dtr.–Ant.* 6. 2). The ignominy of the men's last
chosen actions is not left to emerge in the narrative, but is
suggested in the introduction; in order, perhaps, by anticipating
the ultimate censure of their deaths, to remind the reader that
these are not positive *Lives*.

A *Life* is compounded of these three categories. The categories
are not set out systematically in each formal preface, but the
principle can be identified in twelve of the thirteen. (*Nik.* 1. 1
refers only to chance events, 'what happens to them', τὰ παθήματα;
cf. *Nik.–Crass.* 3. 7, 5. 1.) Expressions for chance events in the
Lives are τὰ συμπτώματα, ἀνελπίστως ('unlooked for'), and
παραλόγως ('contrary to all reckoning'). Chosen actions are indicated by αἵρεσις ('choice'), τὰ πράγματα and τὰ πολιτικά ('acts of
policy'), ὠφελιμώτατοι πατρίσι or ἀναπνοὴ ταῖς πατρίσι ('benefit or
respite for the fatherlands').

C. The Pairing of *Agesilaos* and *Pompey*

Although not announced in a formal proem to *Agesilaos*, the first
of this pair of *Lives*, there are general and particular similarities in
the *Lives* themselves which justify the pairing. Yet the similarities
are not sustainable.[37]

1. *Similarities and Differences*

(*a*) *Fortunes*. In general, Agesilaos and Pompey had similar
career curves: they rose to the highest powers in their states
and finally declined, having experienced in between a series of
successes and reverses. Both were supreme military commanders,
led armies and navies representing the greatest Greek and Roman
powers of their times (*Pomp.* 25. 1–3, 25. 6, 30. 1–2; chs. 10. 9, 40.
3), and often dominated political life (*Pomp.* 22. 1; chs. 20. 6, 21.
1). Both conducted campaigns in the east (*Pomp.* 30. 1–42. 7; chs.

6. 4–16. 1) and met their deaths after going to Egypt (*Pomp.* 79.
4–5; ch. 40. 3). But Agesilaos was born into a royal family, able to
maintain a dominant position despite opposition, in a city which
could still benefit from the admired Lykourgan 'constitution', and
after the Peloponnesian war became the potential hegemon of
Greece; Pompey's city suffered from civil wars, corrupting political competition, and struggles for power between generals.[38]

There are similarities also in particular situations, but major
divergences again appear. Both were called upon to be saviours of
their countries (*Pomp.* 59. 1–2; chs. 15. 2, 31. 4): Pompey could
not raise troops willing to meet Caesar, Agesilaos had to restrain
the Spartans as Epameinondas approached. Each is compared
with Alexander (*Pomp.* 46. 2; ch. 15. 4): it would have been better
for Pompey to have lived no longer, having enjoyed fortunes like
Alexander's at a young age; regrettably it was left for Alexander to
do what Agesilaos might have done. After their deaths, both
received makeshift disposal: Agesilaos' body was preserved in
melted wax because honey was not available, but it was brought
home ceremonially; Pompey's pyre was built from the remains
(λείψανα) of a small fishing-boat on the beach and his remains (also
λείψανα, a striking example of pathos) were buried privately
(*Pomp.* 80. 3, 80. 10; ch. 40. 4). *Pompey* ends tragically with the
punishment of the assassins and Caesar's belated sympathy, while
at the end of *Agesilaos* Plutarch records that the line of kings continued down to Agis, fifth in descent from Agesilaos: the tragedy
was not his death on the way home from Egypt, but his decision to
go there (ch. 36. 1–5).

(*b*) *Actions.* Plutarch shows Agesilaos and Pompey in similar
situations, but their chosen actions are not similar. Both gave up
power when they might have been least expected to do so (*Pomp.*
43. 1, cf. 21. 5–7; ch. 15. 1): Pompey was thought to be intending
to march on Rome and secure his own sole rule, Agesilaos was
intending to march further east and dethrone the King of Persia;[39]
Pompey then suddenly disbanded his army, Agesilaos obediently
began—and completed—the march home to help Sparta (*Pomp.*
43. 3; ch. 15. 5). Each is called his country's healer (ἰατρός): but
after his election as sole consul, Pompey only celebrated his
wedding and failed to remedy his ailing high command, Agesilaos
adjudicated wisely as νομοθέτης, legal officer or 'lawgiver', on the

survivors of Leuktra (*Pomp.* 55. 4, 67. 8; ch. 30. 2–5). Both men decided to go to Egypt (*Pomp.* 76. 7–77. 1; ch. 36. 1) and died abroad (*Pomp.* 79. 5; ch. 40. 3): Pompey had been defeated by Caesar and was fleeing in uncertainty (*Pomp.* 72–6), Agesilaos believed it was in Sparta's interest that he should undertake mercenary service with a rebel against the King of Persia (ch. 36. 1).

(*c*) *Natures.* Divergences soon appear in their shared individual characteristics.

(i) Plutarch attributes to both men a simple lifestyle and a harmonious attitude to people (*Pomp.* 1. 4, 2. 11, 18. 3; chs. 1. 2, 1. 5, 2. 1–5): Pompey suffers through association with the lavish camp-life of his luxurious friends, Agesilaos gains from his own continuing moderation and from the contrast with the luxurious lifestyles of his eastern enemies (*Pomp.* 72. 5–6; chs. 9. 8, 12. 2). The Roman's style is, of course, not as spare as Agesilaos' is said to be; although it is moderate at first (*Pomp.* 40. 8), Pompey does not maintain it unchanged, unlike Agesilaos after his success (*Pomp.* 40. 9; ch. 19. 5, 36. 8–10).

(ii) Friendship and kinship have implications for the political lives of both men (see E.4–5 below). They have strong personal relationships: Agesilaos enjoys companionship with young men as well as with his family (chs. 11. 6–10, 13. 3–4, 20. 7–9, 25. 11), Pompey is a ladies' man (*Pomp.* 2. 5, 53. 2); but only Pompey is distracted from public duties by infatuation, even to the extent of tampering with a jury (*Pomp.* 2. 10, 30. 7, 48. 8, 55. 4, 55. 7), and there is insincerity in some of his pledges of friendship (*Pomp.* 70. 7). Agesilaos advances members of his family (chs. 10. 11, 21. 1), as does Pompey (*Pomp.* 11. 2); Agesilaos makes a mistake (ch. 10. 11), but Pompey abuses his position to influence elections in favour of friends (*Pomp.* 22. 2, 53. 1). Pompey has critics (*Pomp.* 29. 1, 44. 5, 49. 1, 53. 1, 55. 4, 55. 6, 55. 8), Agesilaos too; but in exerting his influence Agesilaos can plead the city's interest (chs. 23. 7, 25. 9), and the critics can be confounded (ch. 21. 2).

(iii) Both are credited with the quality of πρᾳότης. This is essentially the restraint of excessive feelings.[40] It ensures that in his youthful training Agesilaos is motivated by a sense of honour rather than fear, despite his disability; in the end he endures the abuse of the Egyptians, knowing that his opportunity will come (chs. 2. 2, 39. 2); but he crucially lacks restraint towards Thebes (chs. 6. 11, 22. 6, and 28. 2). Pompey's πρᾳότης, linked with τὸ ἥμερον, 'mildness', gives Tigranes confidence in surrendering to him (*Pomp.* 33. 2; cf. 36. 3), but it means that he will not restrain or punish his friends' wrongdoings (*Pomp.* 39. 6; cf. 60. 8),[41] and in his intimate personal relationships he supinely suffers insult and abuse (*Pomp.* 60. 8; cf. 15. 4, 40. 6).[42] Agesilaos does not criticize friends who are in the wrong, and wins their loyalty by helping them: this is not weakness, however, but a deliberate and consistent policy of increasing his political influence (chs. 5. 2, 20. 6).[43] Pompey suffers when πρᾳότης is attributed to others: Caesar serves as a foil, for his troops remain composed and motionless, while Pompey's men are unsteady and noisy (*Pomp.* 68. 7, 69. 6); but when Agesipolis, the young regal colleague of Agesilaos, plays little part in public affairs, Agesilaos takes advantage of his natural πρᾳότης in the process of eliminating political opposition (ch. 20. 7–9).

(iv) The predominant quality in *Agesilaos*, referred to eighteen times, is φιλοτιμία, 'love of honour'.[44] It is often to be translated as 'ambition'. Early on, Plutarch attributes misguided forms of φιλο-τιμία to Alkibiades, who wants to be the father of Spartan kings, and to Lysander, who is becoming a rival to Agesilaos; and he draws the moral that excess of φιλοτιμία, displayed here even by Agesilaos, does more harm than good (chs. 3. 2, 7. 4, 8. 5–6). Excess of φιλοτιμία, indeed, brings trouble upon his city and him-self because of his attitude to Thebes (ch. 23. 11); but he later renounces it in order to save Sparta (ch. 33. 2). It occurs only six times in *Pompey*, three times with reference to other men. Pompey's ambition is specifically tainted with selfishness. He incurs Sulla's displeasure by asking for a triumph when neither consul nor quaestor (*Pomp.* 14. 1), and although he is said not to wish to become a senator before the proper age, it is only because he aims to achieve 'outstanding esteem by being exceptional' (τὸ ἔνδοξον ἐκ τοῦ παραδόξου (*Pomp.* 14. 9)—a play on words in Greek). Yet Plutarch claims honourable standards for Pompey, and rejects the accusation that he acquired his command in Egypt by under-hand means, on the ground that his φιλοτιμία was not evil or servile (*Pomp.* 49. 14). He is, however, shown to be ambitious for personal acclaim in reaching all parts of 'Ocean' and in celebrating three triumphs (*Pomp.* 45. 7), but above all, perhaps, in his aim for power: the Roman empire is not big enough to be shared between two men (*Pomp.* 38. 4–6, 53. 10). Pompey is accused of φιλοτιμία despite his dissimulation (*Pomp.* 30. 8), and it renders him liable to divine retribution (*Pomp.* 38. 1).

However, φιλοτιμία is not always a pejorative term,[45] and the translation 'ambition' is then inappropriate (see on ch. 2. 3). It denotes motivation towards patriotic achievement, not only in Plutarch's Spartans, but invariably, in *Hellenika*, for Xenophon too: in leading Spartans, Kallikratidas and Peisander (i. 6. 5, iii. 4. 29), and in others, Pharnabazos of Persia, Lykomedes of Mantineia (iv. 1. 37, vii. 1. 23), even Epameinondas of Thebes (vii. 5. 19); poor-quality Spartan cavalry (πονηρότατον) at Leuktra specifically lacked it (vi. 4. 11). Agesilaos displays φιλοτιμία prominently, but as a theme in the *Life* Plutarch presents it very differently from Pompey's ambition. He approves of the φιλοτιμία institutionalized in Sparta by the constitution of Lykourgos (ch. 5. 5); it is to be based on 'good actions' (*Agis*, 2.1). Agesilaos displays it in combating his lameness, in keeping Sparta free from anything petty or mean, and in supporting competitive games for the young (chs. 2. 3, 11. 5, 21. 7). Other Spartans perform similarly: the bodyguard of fifty, the young king Agesipolis, and the mothers of the dead of Leuktra (chs. 18. 5, 20. 9, 29. 7). When motivated by φιλοτιμία in its institutionalized form, Agesilaos is always pursuing the best Spartan interest as he—sometimes mistakenly—sees it, and thus evokes no reference by Plutarch to the desire for personal acclaim that he attributes to Pompey (*Pomp.* 38. 4–6): Agesilaos' purpose in wishing to march further east is a military one (ch. 15. 1).

Both men are anxious to further their own reputations at the expense of others. Crassus in Spain and Metellus in Crete have almost completed their missions when Pompey arrives for the final stages and robs them of the credit (*Pomp.* 21. 3, 29. 6); in Asia Minor Agesilaos fears that credit for any successes will be given to Lysander instead of himself (ch. 7. 4); but he is in command, and there is no cheating. The reason why credit was important to a Spartan was not political so much as social, manifested in the characteristic talk in *syssitia* and public gatherings (*Lyk.* 18, 24–5). Nevertheless, motivated by φιλοτιμία, he disgraces himself by mercenary service in Egypt (ch. 36. 3–5).

(v) These key-words determine character only in context, for

they have positive and negative values. Plutarch's protreptic purpose requires the reader to identify these, and he adds definition:
by denoting excess: ἐκμελὴς φιλοτιμία (Lys. 23. 5), ὑπερβάλλων τῇ
φιλοτιμίᾳ τὸν καιρόν (ch. 8. 6); or by linking words of significant
import: φιλοτιμία brings glory, ἔθαψε λαμπρῶς καὶ φιλοτίμως
ἅπαντας (Pomp. 39. 2), or punishment, πάθος νεμεσητὸν ὑπὸ φιλοτιμίας ἔπαθε (Pomp. 38. 1); πρᾳότης indicates co-operation,
εὐπείθεια καὶ πρᾳότης (ch. 2. 2), or political inactivity, φύσει πρᾷος
καὶ κόσμιος (ch. 20. 7).[46]

(vi) The key to political and military wisdom is the ability to
perceive and exploit the καιρός, 'moment', 'opportunity'.[47]
Pompey's restoration of the tribunate exploits the political καιρός
to show his gratitude to the people (Pomp. 21. 7–8), but on
another occasion a remark is inopportune (Pomp. 47. 8). While
Agesilaos is also criticized for not recognizing the true requirements of the καιρός (chs. 35. 6, 36. 4), he seizes advantageous
opportunities as general, once at the cost of abandoning his
principles as friend (chs. 13. 6, 34. 6, 37. 2, 39. 2).

The two words καιρός and πρᾳότης are crucial for the final contrast between Agesilaos and Pompey. Agesilaos displays πρᾳότης in
dealing with the young pharaoh Nektanebo at the end of his
career, and then restores his reputation for generalship by exploiting the καιρός he has been awaiting. Caesar is again a foil: the
πρᾳότης of his troops puts Pompey at a disadvantage, and the
realization that Caesar has taken the advantage (καιρός) against
him produces the tactical error which deprives his soldiers of their
driving force at the start of the battle (Pomp. 68. 7, 69. 6).
Plutarch's verbal parallels between the two Lives at these critical
points sharply contrast Agesilaos' steady nerve with Pompey's
instability—perhaps his fatal flaw, ultimately proved in the closing
stages of his final engagement (Pomp. 72. 1–3). In Agesilaos and
Pompey generally the understanding of one Life 'is not especially
enhanced by its pair';[48] but here, perhaps, the parallel is meant to
be noticed (ch. 39. 4).

2. The Portrait of Pompey[49]

The similarities between Agesilaos and Pompey are far outweighed by the differences that emerge, and almost all of these tell
in favour of Agesilaos. They do not, of course, represent the whole

portrait in *Pompey*, which, for the reader, despite the selective
method of the formal *synkrisis*, will count against the whole
portrait in *Agesilaos* (cf. D.2 below). In the first twenty of the
eighty chapters of *Pompey*, where favourable notices outnumber
the unfavourable, Plutarch describes him as attractive and
successful in ways which are not relevant to any direct comparison
with Agesilaos. But attitudes change, with the entry of suspicion
and fear (*Pomp.* 21. 5), vocal critics (*Pomp.* 29. 1–3, 30. 6–31. 7),
and divine displeasure (*Pomp.* 38. 1), until the ruin becomes
irreversible, explicitly at *Pomp.* 46. 2–4. By contrast, the downturn
in *Agesilaos* starts only in the second half, when, at the Corinthian
Heraion, Agesilaos' pride is about to be punished (ch. 22. 3).
Criticism of Pompey increases through his *Life*, so that the divergences pointed out above do not misrepresent Plutarch's interpretations, for he gives explicit clarification in the imaginary words
composed for Kratippos (*Pomp.* 75. 5) which suggest that Pompey
would have been no better than Caesar if he had defeated him.[50]
Plutarch then hints (*Pomp.* 76. 9) that Pompey was being led on
his last journey by a δαίμων—a parallel with *Agesilaos* at ch. 30. 1,
where the Spartans realize that they had failed to heed the warning
of τὸ δαιμόνιον.[51] Criticism of Agesilaos, however, is relieved by
frequent hints of commendation (chs. 6. 7, 14. 1–4, 36. 1).

Pompey is seen here 'as a man to whom things happen—and he
lets them',[52] while Agesilaos is a man of initiative, single-mindedly
pursuing the best interest of Sparta (cf. ch. 23. 7). The essential
difference between the two men lies here: the unstable Pompey is
outmanoeuvred (*Pomp.* 51. 1), allows himself to be used by others
(*Pomp.* 47. 9, cf. 46. 8), and is at last totally deranged (*Pomp.* 72.
1), but when the determined Agesilaos accepts subservience it is
contrary to his nature and he is deliberately waiting to seize his
opportunity (ch. 37. 2): he has undertaken mercenary service in
Egypt—despite the cost to his reputation (ch. 36. 2)—out of the
conviction that it is a service that Sparta needs (chs. 36. 5, 40. 2).
Both men are flawed and experience failure and decline, and
Plutarch criticizes them for what are perhaps their main characteristics: Pompey for his personal moral weakness and political
failings,[53] which cause the tragedy of death and disgrace (*Comp.* 3.
7, 5. 2); Agesilaos for his excessive exercise of typically Spartan
moral qualities and his misguided understanding of the true
interest of Sparta—prompted by his self-indulgent policies

towards Messenia and Thebes—which destroy the Spartan
hegemony (*Comp.* 1. 7, 3. 2). This is not the whole of Plutarch's
judgemental material, but it indicates that this pair of *Lives* does
not belong to a series of positive characters and is not a simple
model for emulation (*Per.* 2). But neither do these *Lives* provide
the reader with the negative moral examples of recklessness or
conspicuous evil advertised at *Demetrius*, 1. 4–7.

3. *The Absence of a Formal* Prooimion *to* Agesilaos–Pompey

Declining career-curves seem to be the main determining factor
which led Plutarch to form this pair, and it is perhaps not surprising that he did not give prominence to similarities in the usual
formal proem, for they are rarely sustained for long. Each *Life* in
this pair is full of complexities, and not all its details are capable of
direct comparison with those of the other *Life*. The total effect of
the two completed narratives, however, suggests a comparison
which Plutarch surely did intend his readers to make. These two
men were in positions of power and able to influence affairs, yet
they failed to control the destinies of their countries successfully,
and failed mainly for different reasons: Pompey because of
personal weaknesses, Agesilaos because he could not see that the
Spartan virtues and principles that were his strength were not
suited to international imperialism.

The usual 'auffällige Ähnlichkeiten im Charakter und im
Lebenslauf' (see B.2(*c*) above) do not constitute the full
significance of these *Lives*. Plutarch's portrait of the whole man is
of interest for itself, but the Rome and the Sparta where the two
men lived and failed are also portrayed, as in a βίος of their own,
with self-destructive flaws. He regrets that both Romans and
Greeks engaged in conflicts among themselves instead of uniting
in crusades among barbarians; Agesilaos was deprived of leading
Greeks poised for the war (ch. 15): Pompey and Caesar were leading blind and frenzied Romans to 'civil' conflict (*Pomp.* 70. 2).
Plutarch reveals dissatisfaction with the corruption and clumsi-
ness of Roman political life, in which Pompey had to play his part:
in contrast he approves of the Sparta of Lykourgos, but regrets
that in Agesilaos' reign the Spartans did not maintain their high
standards. Plutarch had reasons for omitting the formal *prooimion*
here. Compared with the pairing of founders (*Thes.–Rom.*), law-

givers (*Lyk–Num.*), reformers (*AKl.–Gr.*), defenders of liberty (*Dem.–Cic.*), Platonists (*Dion–Brut.*), lost causes (*Phok.–Cato Min.*), great vices (*Dtr.–Ant.*), and destructive ambitions (*Lys.–Sull.*), the parallels here, though sometimes striking, were transient.

D. THE FORMAL COMPARISON

Plutarch clarifies his ultimate judgements of the lives of his chosen pairs in an epilogue, or *Comparatio*, in all but four cases.[54] His method is to select similar situations with which chance confronted each of the pair and, in a point-by-point comparison, to observe their divergent responses or choices.[55] The tone of the present *Comparatio*, which may be considered under twelve headings, is largely hostile to Agesilaos and harsher than that in the *Life*, and contradicts the generally unfavourable impression of Pompey given in his *Life*; the crude judgement in Pompey's favour obtained from the score may be reckoned as 7–5.[56] All twelve headings point to the differing characters of the two men. Ten involve ethical choices; one (5) is a pragmatic choice, one (7) is a pragmatic achievement.

1. Agesilaos–Pompey: *the* Comparatio

(*a*) *Both came to power and fame.* In the *Life* (chs. 3. 4–4. 1) Plutarch arranges the arguments in favour of Agesilaos' accession with great cumulative effect, presenting the Spartans with logical justification for their decision. He withholds authorial comment at this point and his account of Agesilaos' reign proceeds, as the reign itself does, without exposure of its defective legitimacy. That exposure comes about when the Spartans themselves are made aware that the doom-laden oracular prophecy is being fulfilled (ch. 30. 1). At *Comp.* 1. 1 Plutarch indicates that the accession was improper, which seems to be closer to the truth. He reinforces this judgement at *Comp.* 2. 2, where he makes the shrewd observation, not found in other sources, that even if Latychidas were ineligible, the oracle required that his place should not be taken by the lame Agesilaos: other members of the family were eligible.

Pompey first takes command of an army he has raised privately (*Pomp*. 6. 5), and this 'choice' of action is legitimated because he is assisting Sulla's fight 'against tyrants' (*Comp*. 1. 2). He is criticized for illegal election to the consulship after the downturn (*Pomp*. 55. 5).

(*b*) *Both were helped by a benefactor*. At *Comp*. 1. 3–4 the ingratitude manifested in Agesilaos' removal of Lysander's privileges is added to the criticisms made in the course of the quarrel in the *Life* (chs. 7–8), and serves here to contrast Pompey's more lasting gratitude to Sulla, even beyond death (*Pomp*. 13. 1–3, 15. 4).

While ingratitude may be relevant to Plutarch's presentation of the quarrel where his literary purpose is to reveal blemishes in Agesilaos' character, it does not necessarily penetrate to the truth, or provide a historical interpretation of the departure of Lysander or his later denigration (see below, chs. 8, 22): he continued to serve Agesilaos honourably in Asia Minor and it is, perhaps, significant that on his return the ephors gave him command in Boiotia (Xen. *Hell*. iii. 5. 6).

(*c*) *Both transgressed justice over others' illegalities*. At *Comp*. 1. 6 the criticism of Agesilaos' decision ('choice') to support Phoibidas and Sphodrias by arranging their escapes from justice repeats the criticism of Agesilaos' personal motives made in the *Life* (chs. 23–5). No source reveals privileged access to information about discussions and negotiations at the level where policy decisions were made, but Plutarch implicates Agesilaos in the initiation of the seizure of the Kadmeia, perhaps interpreting Xenophon's admission (*Hell*. v. 2. 32) that Agesilaos defended Phoibidas on the ground that the action was in the interest of the state. Plutarch now explicitly asserts (*Comp*. 1. 7) Agesilaos' responsibility for the war which ensued from Sphodrias' raid into Attic territory, and his assertion seems to be justified; he thus differs from Xenophon, who attempts unfairly to lay the blame for the outbreak of hostilities on the Athenians' military preparations (*Hell*. v. 4. 34).

Plutarch relieves Pompey of responsibility for the harm he did to the Romans 'out of respect for others or want of perception'. This conflicts with the attitude expressed in the *Life* (*Pomp*. 39. 6, 67. 7–8): in public affairs concessions should be followed by assertion of authority (*Per*. 15. 2; cf. *Phok*. 2. 4–5).[57]

(*d*) *Both brought about disaster*. At *Comp*. 2. 1 Pompey's failures are assigned to chance, unforeseen by the Romans; Agesilaos' to choice of action: his accession is now criticized for the further point that he led the Spartans to disregard the oracle concerning his lameness. Whereas Lysander interpreted χωλὴ βασιλεία as 'lame monarchy' (ch. 3), Plutarch here refers to 'lame king', as the Spartans did when they acknowledged that they had caused divine displeasure by ignoring the warning (ch. 30. 1).[58]

Plutarch also reports suspected illegalities in the procedures surrounding Pompey's inheritance (*Pomp.* 4. 1–6), although the state is not involved. The state *is* involved in the nemesis incurred by Pompey later (*Pomp.* 38. 1) when his excessive φιλοτιμία is threatened with divine retribution. These considerations do not vitiate Plutarch's main contention that Agesilaos was knowingly at fault; the nature of oracular utterances leaves their interpretation to a human agency.

(*e*) *Both disregarded the laws of the state.* At *Comp.* 2. 3 Plutarch reconsiders the treatment of the τρέσαντες, 'runaways' (ch. 30. 2), shamed survivors of Leuktra. The designation of Agesilaos' choice to allow the laws to sleep for a day as a σόφισμα (political 'skill' or 'trick') is ambiguous, evoking both commendation because of the element of σοφία ('wisdom') and suspicion because of its connection with σοφιστής ('sophist'), which acquired its pejorative sense from the distortion of sophistic principles to justify amoralism.[59] Plutarch's relations with sophists were hostile, so Philostratos tells us (*Ep.* 63); he commends their skills and acclaims an earlier Philostratos, a sophist, the ablest impromptu speaker of his day (*Ant.* 80. 3), but he withholds recognition of their philosophical wisdom, the essential part of education (*Them.* 2. 4–5, *Tim.* 6. 1–2, *Brut.* 1. 3, *Mor.* 451 c).

Plutarch indicates political approval of the σόφισμα by a comparison with Pompey's contravention of his own laws (*Comp.* 2. 3), no doubt a reference to the case of Plancus (*Pomp.* 55. 8–9). Full approval would be inconsistent with his expressed view of deception (*Phil.* 13. 6; see E.6 below) and with his general attitude to true Spartan values. Here he compromises, for the strictest ethic (cf. Cato Minor at *Phok.* 3. 1) is impracticable even for divine government (*Phok.* 2. 5); 'political skill' devises the σόφισμα but concedes the philosophical ideal, lacking in Spartan education. The word is carefully chosen: the device worked well, but to ignore the law was to risk weakening Sparta's reputation, which rested largely on the Lykourgan tradition of respect for law.

(*f*) *Both served the state.* Plutarch commends Agesilaos' obedience to the state and his renunciation of fame and power in order to serve its best interest; in contrast he condemns Pompey, whose concern for the state was secondary to his own advancement (*Comp.* 2. 5). Obedience, inculcated by the ἀγωγή and combined with powers of leadership, made Agesilaos, in Plutarch's exaggerated phrase, 'uniquely qualified' for the kingship (ch. 1). The interest of the state is, in political terms, capable of definition only by the government of the day; obedience to it was the most valuable factor in the Spartan constitution.

(*g*) *Both had success in war.* At *Comp.* 3. 1 Pompey's military resources, victories, and trophies far outnumber those of Agesilaos. Yet Plutarch will soon supplement the numerical criterion with another (*Comp.* 3. 4).

(*h*) *Both made terms with enemies.* At *Comp.* 3. 2–3 Plutarch's views of Agesilaos' treatment of Thebes are the same as those found in the *Life* (chs. 18. 9, 27. 7), and are totally opposed to those of Xenophon; for while Xenophon shared the hatred for Thebes which he repeatedly attributes to Agesilaos, Plutarch lays the blame for the decline of Sparta on Agesilaos' determination to crush Thebes and dominate Messenia (*Comp.* 3. 2), contrasting Pompey's generous treatment of the cities in Sicily and his former enemies, the pirates (*Pomp.* 10. 2, 28. 5–6).

(*i*) *Both faced a threat to their city.* At *Comp.* 3. 4 Plutarch's strongest commendation of Agesilaos' military leadership is accorded to his successful defence of Sparta in the years after Leuktra (*Comp.* 3. 5, 4. 7; cf. chs. 31–2, 34. 5). On the other hand, his strongest condemnation of Pompey here is for abandoning Rome to Caesar (*Comp.* 3. 6–7), confirming his statement at *Pomp.* 61. 6–7 that people loved the general but blamed his generalship. Caesar and Cicero faulted him for his departure from Italy, too (*Pomp.* 63. 1–2).

(*j*) *Both faced superior enemy strength.* At *Comp.* 4. 1 Agesilaos is said to have shown good generalship when he avoided confrontation with superior force: he engaged Tissaphernes before his cavalry reached Sardis and held back at Sparta against Epameinondas (chs. 10. 3, 31. 4). Plutarch's claim that Agesilaos was undefeated is consistent with his own narrative, apart from the uncertain result at Koroneia, but not with Xenophon's account, which records reverses in Asia Minor (*Hell.* iii. 4. 13, iv.

1. 19); whether or not Epameinondas[60] was aiming for the capture of Sparta, the city was not taken (ch. 31. 4). Only Pompey's final defeat on the Pharsalian plain is relevant (*Pomp*. 68–72).

(*k*) *Both faced pressure of opposition.* At *Comp*. 4. 3–11 Plutarch assigns the longest continuous passage of the *Comparatio* to what seems to be his most serious criticism of Pompey, which corresponds to the comment in the *Life* at *Pomp*. 72. 1. Pompey surrendered to the opposition over his conduct of the war despite the presence and support of Rome's governing officials and his past successes in campaigning, while Agesilaos with commendable persistence followed his own 'counsels' (ch. 39. 2). The contrast is pointed up by the use of λογισμοί (*Comp*. 4. 8), the word used originally in criticizing Pompey for abandoning his own 'best counsels' (*Pomp*. 67. 7). Plutarch refuses to transfer the blame to Scipio, the father-in-law, for deceiving him: Pompey should not have let that happen.[61]

(*l*) *Both arrived finally in Egypt.* At *Comp*. 4. 11 Plutarch appears to indicate that his assessment of the two men is now complete. But the *Comparatio* ends with perhaps its harshest criticism of Agesilaos, matching that at chs. 35. 5–36. 6, in which his last campaign, that in Egypt, is condemned. Its intention was neither honourable nor necessary, for it was undertaken only to obtain money, which was to be used only to make war on other Greeks (*Comp*. 5. 1); its execution was marred by breach of trust in deserting allies and going over to the other side (*Comp*. 5. 2).

The Egyptian episode has positive importance for the *Life*, since there Agesilaos finally demonstrates his Spartan asceticism and reasserts the quality of his generalship (chs. 36. 7–11, 39. 7–10); yet there is no reference to that here. The explanation for this lack of balance may lie more in *Pompey* than in *Agesilaos*, for the pathos worked out at length in the closing chapters devoted to Pompey's last actions (*Pomp*. 73–80) could not be sacrificed. The comparison with Agesilaos favours Pompey partly because of the sympathy evoked by his tragic situation: he is in flight—yet this was caused by his own lack of judgement (*Pomp*. 67. 7); his trust is betrayed, and the advice he has acted upon is leading him into danger rather than to safety—but he discovers this only when it is too late to turn back (*Pomp*. 78. 3). Plutarch's main criticism of Agesilaos is that he undertook the mercenary enterprise because he did not heed Lykourgos' warning that Sparta should avoid imperial ambitions.

2. *The* Comparatio *as a Final Judgement*

Scholars have identified *synkrisis* as comparison both of *Life* with *Life* and of character with character within a *Life* (cf. the explicit τῷ Καλλικρατίδᾳ παραβαλλόμενος at *Lys.* 7. 3). The *Lives* are presented in pairs and ancient readers trained in rhetoric could be expected to be alert to the intentions of the author, though ancient 'books' did not allow easy cross-reference from one to another. Instead of linear exposition of character and the idea that Plutarch intended a series of positive and negative *Lives*, which is less in vogue, we may regard the two individuals' actions as open to our assessment successively throughout the narrative—the purpose *is* protreptic—and to contribute to our total view at the end. We may then be surprised by the Plutarchan formal *Synkrisis* which by its final treatment (*Comp.* 5) favours neither man strongly: readers must judge for themselves.[62]

Successful comparison requires a degree of equality.[63] The *Comparatio* omits overt reference to the admired elements of the constitution of Lykourgos which could not be matched on the Roman side, for Plutarch could not approve of the very different principles which determined the workings of the Roman constitution in Pompey's time, permitting personal aggrandizement and the manipulation of formal state procedures. These constitutional aspects—their βίος—appear in scattered references in both *Lives*, and Plutarch's intention is clearly not to summarize in the *Synkrisis*. In their *Lives* neither Agesilaos nor Pompey is presented as having a positive influence on future history. This is reserved for Epameinondas and Caesar, though with only limited effect. Lasting influence belongs to Sparta and the Lykourgan ideal, and that is portrayed not in the *Synkrisis*, but in the *Life*, where Plutarch praises Sparta's traditions, and shows that Agesilaos at times resisted their decline and upheld the standards; and he saved Sparta in war. Hence the *Life* is less hostile to Agesilaos.

Plutarch's admiration of Lykourgan Sparta contrasts with his disapproval of the corruption at Rome. Yet Pompey's indecisiveness is not responsible for introducing the corruption, which

Plutarch attributes to the lack of an educational system in the constitution (*Lyk.–Num.* 4. 2–5; cf. *Phil.* 1. 4). He suggests that Rome was not worse off because of Pompey's deficiencies of character and defeat (*Pomp.* 75. 5; C.2 above). Despite the qualities and achievements for which Agesilaos deserved and received Plutarch's admiration, Sparta suffered because of his mistakes. His strong position and his single-mindedness render him responsible for the decline in the observance of vital Lykourgan values. Ultimately he undermined the standards, and in the *Synkrisis* he carries responsibility for their decline and the loss of Sparta's reputation. The final judgement could not praise Agesilaos. Hence the formal *Synkrisis* is less favourable to him.

The deficiencies which Plutarch stresses are sufficient to indicate the different reasons why each man failed. Plutarch regrets their failures and ends with the sadness appropriate to their decline. The contrasting factors of shame and tragedy come together appropriately in the Egyptian conclusion. The sad tone of its ending suggests an explanation of the *Comparatio* as a final judgement of the pair. The *Lives* have set the two men in the contexts of the tragic situations in their states. The decline of Rome and Pompey was due to the inevitable frailty of the human condition, their 'nature'; the decline of Lykourgan Sparta was due to human error, Agesilaos' 'choices and actions' (B.2(*c*) above). It is an irony that Pompey's *Life* ends in his tragedy, while Agesilaos dies enjoying recent success and fame.[64]

3. *The Spartan Series*

There is a *Synkrisis* attached to each of the other four Spartan *Lives*. Two of these evince a rather different attitude from that of the respective *Life*. Lykourgos' political benefit to Sparta in his *Life* is replaced by his impact on the individual: his resort to violence (*Comp.* 1. 4, 2. 3, 4. 8), his treatment of the Helots (*Comp.* 1. 4–5), and his effect on women's morals (*Comp.* 3). Lysander's introduction of wealth (*Lys.* 2. 4, 16. 1–17. 6) and his harshness (χαλεπότης, *Lys.* 19) towards enemies in the *Life* are replaced by his personal virtues: mildness (πραότης) in planned reforms (*Comp.* 2. 1–2) and indifference to riches (*Comp.* 3. 1, 4–5).[65] On Agis and Kleomenes, Plutarch's *Comparatio* remains consistent. In the *Lives* they attempted to restore Lykourgan standards in

Sparta,[66] but the former was defeated by opposition, the latter, emulating Lykourgos, resorted to violence, and met violence. In the *Synkrisis*, Agis failed through lack of courage, Kleomenes through rashness (*Comp.* 4. 1). Both in their *Lives* and in the *Synkrisis*, Plutarch stresses their personal qualities: there was now no secure Lykourgan basis for a political comparison. The *Synkrisis* is a judgement between paired characters; the *Life* places actions in a political context—and Plutarch's ideal was the Spartan context. Sparta ceased to embody the ideal; it was left for him to resuscitate its values and offer extrinsic reasons for its decline.

E. Plutarch's Themes in the *Life*

Xenophon's *Agesilaos* separates the chronological sections from a *catalogue raisonné* on the theme of Agesilaos' virtues. In Plutarch's *Agesilaos* the chronological narrative provides a framework for a broad thematic trail of significant historical and biographical events which the author offers to the reader who wishes, in Thucydides' phrase (i. 22. 4), 'to understand clearly' the lessons of this part of Sparta's past. It is evident that in responding to Xenophon and other sources Plutarch recognized themes which he understood to explain Sparta's decline. These themes emerge repeatedly in the episodes of the *Life*.

1. *The Decline of Sparta*

Although the character of Agesilaos is interesting to Plutarch for its own sake, it is also important for its bearing on the eclipse of Sparta as a power in the Greek world during his reign (ch. 26).[67] Xenophon, Plutarch's main source, does not directly address the cause of the decline of Sparta. In *Agesilaos* he may perhaps, by asserting Agesilaos' ἀρετή at his accession and afterwards, be rebutting charges made against him after his death that he had been responsible for the military failure.[68] In *Hellenika*, later, the charge may have been against his piety, whether concerning Diopeithes' oracle or for other reasons (cf. F.2(*a*) below, and ch. 3).[69] It is less clear that Agesilaos would have needed defending against a charge of collaborating with Persia as *philobarbaros*, though it is possible that his enemies interpreted in that way his manipulation of the King's Peace in Sparta's favour.[70] Where Xenophon offers an explanation of a reverse, it is in terms of divine displeasure, which is an explanation used by Plutarch too, crucially when Agesilaos' anger against Thebes forebodes retribution at Leuktra.

Plutarch's concern is rather with the disregard of the parts of the Lykourgan constitution to which he attributes the admired qualities of the traditional Spartan way of life. The influence of wealth, Aristotle's diagnosis, is noted as a cause of Sparta's decline by Plutarch in *Lysander* and *Agis*, but in this *Life* it is only Agesilaos' resistance to this influence that is significant. He is also aware of Sparta's shortage of citizens, stressed by Aristotle, but he does not dwell on it here (ch. 30. 5). Aristotle's fundamental criticism of the Spartan constitution was its concentration on military virtue, which he regarded as being designed for the domination of others rather than for the good of the governed and the survival of the state (*Pol.* 1324^{b}8, 1333^{b}14, and 1333^{b}38–1334^{a}10).[71] According to Plutarch, however, although Lykourgos indeed prescribed the regimen for the good life, and included provision for security, he advised against the imperialist use of military power (chs. 26, 27; *Lyk.* 13. 6, 31. 1; D.1(*l*) above; E.2(*a*) below); failure to adhere to his principles is his key to Sparta's decline (*Lyk.–Num.* 4. 8). Xenophon's *Lak. Pol.* (if it is by Xenophon)[72] emphasizes and admires the provisions for developing Sparta's military power, organization, and battle-drill (*Lak. Pol.* 1. 1–2, 11–13), and producing resourceful fighting men (2. 7; cf. *Agesilaos*, 1. 5), physically fit for soldiering (4. 7), pursuing valour and glory (9. 2). Agesilaos' hegemonic aims accord with the way Xenophon presented Lykourgan ideology, rather than with Plutarch's non-hegemonic principle of security combined with citizens' well-being, here and at *Lykourgos*, 31. 1; though at *Lak. Pol.* 14, in a more Plutarchan spirit, Xenophon criticizes contemporary Spartans for abuse of Lykourgan hegemony and disregard of Lykourgan well-being, for which Agesilaos was largely responsible. Plutarch's ideological consistency is illustrated from another *Life*: 'Did not Rome make her great advance through warfare? That is a question requiring a lengthy answer for men who define "advance" in terms of wealth, luxury, and empire rather than safety, restraint, and an honest independence' (*Lyk.–Num.* 4. 7).

Plutarch's main thrust is to identify failure of character, and he finds it in both the man and his city. He points to Agesilaos' individual weaknesses, as in his judgement that he was at times excessively φιλότιμος and φιλοπόλεμος, but the deeper malaise is in the whole body of citizens. At the beginning of the reign, as it turned out, they disregarded guidance in choosing their king, subsequently joined him in his unjust judgements and policies, and continued to trust him even when he was seen to have been discredited. The Spartans shared with the rest of Greece the propensity to wasteful internecine strife, but their special problem was their failure to develop in their education a critical intellectual attitude to their traditional values—a problem that was also addressed by Plato's Socrates, as in the doubtfully Platonic *Menexenos* (cf. E.7 below).[73] The link between ancient Greek values and philosophic training is made explicit at *Philopoimen*, 1. 4. In this *Life* Plutarch does not draw these conclusions in a final analysis, but sets the individual continually in the broad context of his time and place; his biographical approach thus provides a historical perspective, and reveals social, political, and military factors which contributed to the failure of the Spartan hegemony in Agesilaos' reign. His explanation is complex and cannot be reduced to a single thematic uniformity; it will be seen to be presented cumulatively in the succession of circumstances and crises which the narrative unfolds.

2. *Militarism*

Militarism—belligerent activity for its own sake—is to be distinguished from wars for the defence and control of material resources and lines of supply—the policing function.[74]

(*a*) Sparta was not established as a militarist state but its military organization served to acquire and defend its vital material needs in the fifth century and before. Aristotle links the Spartan (Lykourgan) system of laws exclusively with military valour and military conquest (*Pol.* 1271[b]1–3) and again (*Pol.* 1333[b]14–23) judges that it was wrong to *admire* the constitution so framed, for it failed.[75] He believed that the Spartans aimed from the start to obtain material goods by military superiority (*Pol.* 1334[a]40–b1), and the series of Spartan chariot victors beginning *c.*548 shows that wealth was being accumulated.[76] Plutarch recognizes the Spartans' mistake in following an imperialist policy, but he does not attribute it to Lykourgos. The thrust of the reforms was not military (*Lyk.* 5. 2–16. 4), although discipline and courage were stressed for boys of seven years (*Lyk.* 16. 5) and from that age their training as warriors intensified until at maturity they lived as in a military camp (*Lyk.* 24. 1). Plutarch attributes the development of Sparta's superior fighting strength to the Lykourgan system of training, but he insists that it was intended for virtue, concord, and defence, not for imperial conquest (*Lyk.* 31. 1). Later, he records that military activity brought the proceeds of tribute and plunder to the state, though he does not explain that Sparta needed money to take over the leadership left vacant by the defeat of Athens in the Peloponnesian war (*Lys.* 17. 4).

(*b*) Plutarch's analysis of this issue is not given separately but develops in the relevant episodes as they occur (cf. ch. 33. 3–4, *Lys.* 18. 1–5). In early wars the Spartans made Helots their slaves and acquired land from the Arkadians by conquest under Soös (*Lyk.* 2. 1), dated before 895; Spartans were active under King Theopompos (*Lyk.* 30. 3), *c*.720–675; and defeated Argives, *c*.545, and Athenians, 424 (*Lys.* 1. 1–2); but Plutarch sees no imperialism here. Antalkidas' grievance that Agesilaos, who waged wars repeatedly against the same enemy, broke a rule attributed to the Third Rhetra (*Lyk.* 13. 5–6; *Mor.* 213 F), has no precedents reported by Plutarch from the time of Lykourgos. He reports the foreign enterprises of individual generals in the Peloponnesian war: Gylippos with the Sicilians, Brasidas with the Chalkidians (*Lyk.* 30. 5; cf. *Lys.* 1. 1, 16. 1–2); that Brasidas was hostile to peace because of what he achieved in war (*Nik.* 9. 2) and died in Thrace (*Lyk.* 25. 5, *Nik.* 9. 3) in 422; that Lysander won unprecedented power in Asia Minor (*Lys.* 5. 3, 7. 2, 11. 6–7), in Greece (*Lys.* 13. 3, 18. 2), in Thrace (*Lys.* 16. 1), and again in Asia Minor (*Lys.* 19. 2–20. 3; cf. ch. 7. 1). For Plutarch imperial conquest (ἀρχαί, δυναστεῖαι βίαιοι, ch. 33. 4; cf. *Lys.* 5. 3–4) began only long after Lykourgos.

(*c*) The defence of Sparta had always involved a preference for action beyond its frontiers, as the anecdotes boast (ch. 31. 7–8). Lysander's installation of governors and garrisons was a development, by sea as well as land, of the earlier colonizing of Herakleia in 426. The growth of Theban influence after the Peloponnesian war posed a threat to Sparta's communications with the north to which Agesilaos responded aggressively. He clearly interpreted

Sparta's interest in terms of hegemony rather than defence of its frontiers (ch. 33. 4), and may have hoped that the expedition to Asia Minor would secure financial resources as well as control of the Hellespont (Xen. *Hell.* i. 1. 35). He was determined to eliminate obstacles—the Thebans and their allies—and tried to do so both by direct military confrontation and by diplomatic manoeuvres in enforcing the Peace of Antalkidas (chs. 22–3, 26–8). He refused to accept the failure of the policy at Leuktra which had resulted in the loss of Messenia (ch. 35. 4), and undertook the Egyptian expedition in the hope of obtaining the resources needed to finance a restoration of Sparta's military power.

Agesilaos was, for Plutarch, a true Spartan following Lykourgos' principle when he defended his city (ch. 33. 2), but not when he flouted it by his hostility towards Thebes (ch. 26. 5) and his misguided application of military supremacy to imperialist aims (ch. 33. 4). This was perceived in the second century by Polybios, a Greek historian from another 'remote' city, Megalopolis, one founded indeed after Sparta's defeat by Epameinondas to stand in the way of future imperialist expansion (ch. 34. 1); he criticized Agesilaos' unfriendly attitudes (ix. 23) and the misapplication of Lykourgos' provisions for Spartan security and harmony to establishing supremacy beyond the frontiers for which resources could not be provided (vi. 48–50). Plutarch's analysis is consistent, and although he does not address the causes and timing of Sparta's excessive concentration on military training, his narratives help to trace its later course and consequences.

3. Exceptional Spartans

The un-Spartan Spartan has been recognized in Brasidas, as portrayed by Thucydides. 'The antithesis of the conventional Spartan leader', both diplomatic and military, he showed remarkable flair for good and tactful personal relations, for determination and duplicity in war, and for imaginative independent decisiveness, though he was not always successful.[77] Agesilaos and Lysander are portrayed by Plutarch and Xenophon as exceptional, but each in his own way (ch. 4. 5; *Lys.* 8. 4).[78] This raises the question of how men could draw such different traits from their Spartan education, which generally produced uniformity.[79]

(*a*) Lysander's upbringing,[80] like Agesilaos', inculcated traditional qualities: indifference to money, obedience to custom, a spirit of patriotic competitiveness and φιλοτιμία, a desire for excellence (*Lys.* 2. 1–4).[81] Unusually for a competitive Spartan, a natural deference and tolerance of the arrogance of powerful men contributed much to his political skill (*Lys.* 2. 3, 4. 2); Agesilaos combined φιλοτιμία, unusually, with a nature that was humane and close to the people (ch. 1. 5), again in contrast with the harshness displayed by Lysander (*Lys.* 13. 5, 19. 1–4, 27. 2–28. 1).[82] Lysander exploited other un-Spartan Spartans (ch. 20. 3, *Lys.* 5. 3–4), and the Persian Kyros (*Lys.* 4. 4).[83]

Xenophon's portrayal of Lysander is unflattering by neglect (see below, on ch. 6. 2);[84] Plutarch's often unfavourable characterization in *Lysander* is more specific, yet reveals flair and talent. He reports his un-Spartan gratification of his friends' greed (*Lys.* 5. 4), statues at Delphi, altars and sacrifices dedicated to him, and a festival named after him (*Lys.* 18);[85] he repeats criticism of his underhand, sophistic methods (*Lys.* 7. 3) and condemnation of his disregard of the sanctity of oaths (*Lys.* 8. 3); he adds harshness in speech and a propensity to melancholy and anger (*Lys.* 22. 1, 24. 2, 28. 1), not offset, like Agesilaos', by humour (ch. 2). The most hostile criticism is that he established a personal supremacy over Greece by suppressing democracies and appointing friends as harmosts (governors), and that because of the cruelty of his conduct of affairs he brought Sparta's rule into disrepute (*Lys.* 13. 3–4).[86] The Spartans eventually called a halt (*Lys.* 14. 2), and blamed him for the decline of Sparta, caused by the great quantity of money he introduced from abroad (*Lys.* 17. 1, 17. 6).

(*b*) Like Xenophon, Plutarch uses his successor Kallikratidas as a foil, comparing Lysander adversely with him (*Lys.* 6. 6–7. 1, 7. 3). Xenophon throws doubt on Lysander's boast that he was master of the sea (*Hell.* i. 6. 2; cf. 6. 2–3), when he notes his numerical inferiority at Ephesos (*Hell.* i. 5. 15).[87] Even Kyros, to whom Lysander had returned his funds, repaid them to Kallikratidas after his naval success (*Hell.* i. 6. 17–18). Plutarch approves his panhellenic wish (on panhellenism see E.7 below) to end Greek competition for Persian support, and to foster hostility instead (*Lys.* 6. 7; Xen. *Hell.* i. 6. 7). Kallikratidas was worthy to compete in Spartan virtues with the finest of the Greeks; he dies in vain, not outstandingly successful but a true Spartan (*Lys.* 5. 5, 7. 1; *Lyk.* 30. 5; *Art.* 22. 2; *Hell.* i. 6. 33).[88]

Unlike Xenophon, Plutarch finds much in Lysander of which to approve. He recognizes his successes in a panhellenic context: providing the Spartans with funds and allies for war, winning the support of Kyros and of powerful men in the cities of Asia Minor, and making Ephesos prosperous (*Lys.* 3. 2–4, 4. 2, 5. 3; cf. 23. 1–3). He recognizes his military intelligence (διάνοια) in outwitting the Athenians at Aigospotamoi (*Lys.* 10. 1), and praises him for bringing the Peloponnesian war to an end—a divine act (*Lys.* 11. 6–7). At this time, too, although critics faulted his supposed further ambitions, his power was recognized and he was given unprecedented honours (*Lys.* 18. 2–3).

The death of Lysander at Haliartos, given only perfunctory treatment by Xenophon, is described with respect by Plutarch despite his sympathy for Thebes. He suggests no hatred of Thebans and no impatience or rivalry with Pausanias: the letter containing the final plan of action was intercepted, the city was saved, and Lysander fell beneath its walls (*Lys.* 28. 2–5).[89] Lysander exemplifies Spartan austerity in accepting poverty throughout his life, proving his virtue finally to the Spartans, who honour him for justice and financial integrity (*Lys.* 2. 4, 30. 2, 5). He devoted the moneys he received to maintaining his fighting force (*Lys.* 4. 4); the opposite is implied by the report of money deposited at Delphi (*Lys.* 18. 2), but it was mostly the surplus covered by Lysander's accounts (*Lys.* 16–17). He displayed his selfless pursuit of Sparta's interest, an important Spartan characteristic, after King Pausanias' Athenian settlement, motivated by jealousy, failed (*Lys.* 21. 1–4). The *Life* ends with the Spartans' indignation at his death: they showed respect for his unendowed daughters by fining their reluctant suitors (*Lys.* 30. 1, 30. 5).

(c) In the *Comparatio* Plutarch is ambivalent as he again brings out the complexity of Lysander's character. He is condemned for introducing a destructive attitude to wealth into Sparta (*Comp.* 3. 4–5) and for his pitiless Athenian settlement (*Comp.* 5. 4; cf. *Lys.* 14. 3–15). He is praised for the continued support he received from the Spartans (*Comp.* 1. 1, 1. 4, 5. 1), and for his attempted reform of the kingship; although at 25. 3 and 26. 2 he tried, as Ephoros reported, improperly to obtain the support of the oracles at Delphi, Dodona, and Ammon, he rejected the use of force and Sparta deserved to have the best possible rulers (*Comp.* 2. 1).[90] Lysander yields to Sulla in contests of war (*Comp.* 4. 1), but in service to the state, self-control, and moderation he takes first place; and he had fewer failings (*Comp.* 5. 1, 5. 5). The parallel closing remark in *Agesilaos–Pompey* (5. 2) draws attention to Agesilaos' betrayal of his employer in Egypt (D. 1(*l*) above).

Plutarch's treatment of Lysander in the two *Lives*, *Agesilaos* and *Lysander*, reveals flexibility in the censure and praise of this complex character:[91] truly Spartan 'in bravery, simplicity, and attitude towards money' yet un-Spartan in 'subservience and ability to manipulate those in power'.[92] He presents a dynamic Lysander who recognized Agesilaos' natural soundness, urged him to compete for the succession, and overcame an unfavourable oracle (chs. 2–3); he procured the campaign in Asia Minor for the benefit of Agesilaos and himself (chs. 6–8), and wielded influence and power there until Agesilaos reasserted himself. Even then, he won for Agesilaos the allegiance of the Persian Spithridates and his cavalry unit. And when at this point Plutarch records Lysander's plan to reform the Spartan monarchy for his own benefit, it is so that he can conclude the quarrel with blame given equally to the two men. He refers to the plot again (ch. 20) when Agesilaos discovers his hostile fraternity (ἑταιρία) in Sparta and a speech advocating constitutional change: however, Plutarch is showing only that Agesilaos used the information as a weapon against his opponents in Sparta; he was restrained from publishing it.

(*d*) The light in which Plutarch presents his material varies according to the context, and may be determined by his interpretation of the interactions between the characters as they view the situations in which they currently find themselves. He combines two biographical objectives: the explication of career-curves, accounting for decline by an appropriate character defect; and the moral protreptic, which, in the Spartan series, includes his favourable critique of Lykourgan qualities. Lysander's φιλοτιμία was overdeveloped in the ἀγωγή, perhaps because of his ambiguous status, *mothax* and Heraklid (*Lys.* 2. 1, 24. 4),[93] while the training in the simplicity of a Spartan lifestyle strengthened his natural and proper attitude to private wealth. Agesilaos' better start in life provided resistance to less desirable tendencies in the training, and he, too, retained his simplicity, rejected statues, and preserved a common touch, but lack of development of critical and intellectual faculties left him without the means to judge the true interests of his city, just as Lysander was unaware of the

effect of wealth on other Spartans. Lysander's career saw a tragic
unleashing of the destructive force of his own characteristics.[94]
Equally Agesilaos' manipulation of the Lykourgan system was
counter-productive.[95] In these two *Lives* the Spartan ἀγωγή, defective in intellectual content, generated the forces of the city's own
destruction: the creative individuality of Lysander, the reformer,
the stubborn manipulations of Agesilaos, the conformer.

(*e*) Agis IV (244–241), a descendant of Agesilaos, and
Kleomenes III (236–222), of the Agiad royal house (*Agis*, 3. 2–4),
were exceptional in their day, when Sparta was decadent (*Agis*, 5,
Kleom. 2. 1, 16. 4, *Mor.* 239 F–240 B). They attempted to revive
the ἀγωγή and other Lykourgan traditions (*Agis*, 6–13, *Kleom.* 3.
1–2, 10. 6–11. 3), by reform or revolution.[96] Both failed, and their
Lives complete the curve of the Spartan series. Each met death
heroically, and their friends and families, including many women,
were executed (*Agis*, 20, *Kleom.* 37–8). The tragedy closes with
'Sparta in an equal competition, the women's dramatic action
emulating the men's' (*Kleom.* 39. 1).

4. *Friendship and Agesilaos' Power-Base*

Friendship is a continuing theme in *Agesilaos*. Denoted by ἔρως
and its derivatives, it was part of Spartan education (ch. 20. 9; the
Spartans spoke of 'giving inspiration', *Kleom.* 3. 2).[97] First met
when Lysander was Agesilaos' ἐραστής, 'senior partner, lover' (ch.
2. 1 and n.) it recurs in his relationship with his colleague
Agesipolis (ch. 20. 7–9). Both associations were secured by the
natural restraint and discipline of the junior in the contexts of the
ἀγωγή and the συσσίτιον. Agesilaos' son Archidamos had a similar
friendship with Sphodrias' son Kleonymos (ch. 25. 1); and such
friendships occur with the sons of powerful men in Asia, one with
Spithridates' son and another with Pharnabazos' (chs. 11. 6–10,
13. 1–4), but an incapacitated 'friend' is abandoned in an emer-
gency (ch. 13. 6).

Public and private friendship is denoted by φιλία and its derivatives. Pharnabazos, Thrace, and Larissa are to be friends of
Agesilaos rather than enemies (chs. 12. 6, 16. 1–2, 16. 5); Thebes
is friend of Corinth (ch. 22. 6) and offers friendship to Agesilaos
(ch. 22. 1); Xenophon speaks of peace (*Hell.* iv. 5. 6, 9). Envoys of
Tachos and Nektanebo offer friendship at Sparta and Chabrias the

mercenary speaks of his employer Tachos as his friend (ch. 37. 4). Diplomatic contracts with Kotys (ch. 11. 1) and Pharnabazos (ch. 12. 6, 7, 9) are denoted by φιλία. Apollophanes (ch. 12. 1) and Pharnabazos' son (ch. 13. 1) are more formally ξένοι, but the King uses both ξενία and φιλία in his letter to Agesilaos (ch. 23. 10). In their quarrel the friends Agesilaos and Lysander breach the code (ch. 8. 2, 6), though Agesilaos regards it as flexible in writing to Hidrieus (ch. 13. 5). Informal relations appear in family and financial contexts (chs. 15. 8, 25. 11, 35. 6).

(a) The terms 'friends' and 'enemies' pervade Greek popular thought.[98] They are found in alliances between a dominant city and a subordinate city: transitivity is established, requiring the subordinate allies to have the same 'friends and enemies' and to go wherever they are led (Xenophon, *Hell.* ii. 2. 20, v. 3. 26; cf. Thuc. viii. 18, 37, 58). Equals promise only to come to each other's defence—'reciprocity'—with no obligation to harm each other's enemies (Thuc. v. 23).[99] The source of Plutarch's thought was no doubt the debate on the definition of justice as 'rendering help to friends and harm to enemies' (Plato, *Resp.* 332 A–D; cf. *Sull.* 38. 4, Xen. *Agesilaos*, 9. 7, 11. 10). Plato's discussion leads to an agreement that it is never just to harm any man (335 E).[100] Agesilaos modifies the popular principle so that he gives to unjust friends help they do not deserve and withholds from unjust enemies harm they do deserve. Thus he 'renders harm' to neither supporters nor opponents, ensuring their commitment to himself personally (ch. 5. 3). His defence of Phoibidas and Sphodrias illustrates this, and Plutarch reveals disapproval (chs. 23–5; cf. *Mor.* 807 F, 808 B). The wrongdoing friends should rather, perhaps, be redefined as more truly enemies and taken aside, admonished, and instructed (cf. Plato, *Ap.* 26). Careful definition of the terms of friendship is needed (id. *Resp.* 334 C; Arist. *EN* 1156[b]7–32); Plutarch advises caution in making and using friends (*Mor.* 94 D–F, 808 B–C). When there is a clash of moral principles, the study of philosophy (cf. ch. 37. 11) leads to greater discrimination between true friends and enemies.[101]

(b) The philosophical discussions of 'friends and enemies' refer to relations between equals, whether personal and family ties or alliances between nations, but Agesilaos places his acquired Spartiate friends—classed politically as ὅμοιοι ('peers')—into a subordinate relationship, as political supporters. They were not

subversive, like Lysander's alleged association of friends discovered by Agesilaos (ch. 20), but they are akin to the ἑταιρία,
political club, which developed from fifth-century social, com-
mercial, and religious associations:¹⁰² Spartiates were now bound
by personal allegiance to a powerful leader.

Archidamos' friendship with Sphodrias' son (ch. 25. 1) appears
to be a connection established between families for political
advantage; it was important for Agesilaos precisely because
Sphodrias was an opponent, although Plutarch does not make this
explicit.¹⁰³ Agesilaos' formal ξενία with the son of Pharnabazos, his
Persian opponent, obliged him to manipulate the rules of the
games at Olympia, possibly unjustly, and involved him in some
form of love-affair, ἐρωτικά (ch. 13. 1–4).

(c) The function of friends as political supporters and partisans
is important for Plutarch here. Lysander had φίλοι, partisans, in
Asia (chs. 6. 2–3, 7. 2, 8) and others in Sparta who formed a ἑταιρία
to assist in reforming the kingship (ch. 20. 3). His development of
influence before Agesilaos' reign is not recorded by Xenophon in
terms of friendship with individuals but as 'making Athens his
own' (Hell. ii. 4. 29). When the charge is brought against
Agesilaos as he builds his power-base, Plutarch adapts
Xenophon's phrase: 'he makes the state's citizens his own' (ch. 5.
1–4). Agesilaos brings a new relationship into politics which
weakens the Lykourgan constitution, designed to benefit the state:
now associates are benefiting a leader. In so far as Agesilaos
opposes subversive elements, it may be a necessary step, germane
to the survival of Spartan society whose structure was now less
secure—it was by such an influence that Lysander procured
Agesilaos' accession. Agesilaos' affability marked his early friendships, but in his pursuit of power Plutarch traces the unforeseen
destructive effects upon Sparta of Agesilaos' exploitation of otherwise acceptable institutions in the furtherance of unacceptable
influence.

The treatment of friendships in the Life reveals conflicts of
principle, between popular and Platonic morality, between the
interests of the individual and of society, and how those interests
are decided—by the society or by an individual ruler (cf. below,
5(c) and ch. 5. 1–3). Plutarch's protreptic purpose clearly requires
a rational rather than a popular judgement, and the wisest judgement benefits individual and society alike—including those in

error, by means of correction—and, in the long term, harms none.
For Plutarch's Sparta, Lykourgos provided the aim and the test,
survival and well-being, and also the means, the regimen. The
tension is there in other *Lives*: in *Aristeides* (2. 4), Themistocles
advantages friends over enemies, but in his own *Life* (5. 4) he
aspires to show no favour contrary to the law. Democratic Athens
exalted the *polis* over the individual, Sparta judged friends and
enemies by the city's interest. Plutarch judged a government not
by its ideology but by its quality. Practice varied: he judged
Agesilaos sometimes right, sometimes wrong, to put the *polis*
before himself in the matter of friends and enemies, or the reverse;
but since 'the interest of the *polis*' was precisely how Agesilaos
decided it, that was where he was sometimes mistaken. Plutarch,
with hindsight, could claim that Sparta's decline showed his criticism to be correct.

5. *Extending the Power-Base*

Plutarch's work on statecraft, *Political Precepts* (*Mor.* 798–825), is
set in his own time when Rome's authority was supreme and often
dire (*Mor.* 813 E–F, 814 E–F), and his statesmen appear largely, like
himself, as well-intentioned local administrators; their function
is to serve (*Mor.* 811 B–D; cf. 783 F, 797 E). He also mentions
earlier models, including Agesilaos and Phokion (*Mor.* 805 E–F,
807 E–808 A, 809 B, D, and *passim*); the philosophy complements
the moral intention of the *Lives* (B.1(c) above). The early development of a man's career is treated briefly: after training in oratory
(*Mor.* 804 C), he enters public life quickly with a daring success in
war, like Pompey, or in law, politics, or diplomacy (*Mor.*
804 C–805 E); or more securely, like Agesilaos, helped by a powerful adviser (*Mor.* 805 E–806 F). Much of the advice is directed
to those already established: how to maintain power by understanding the character of the citizens, and by the choice and
use of friends, avoiding participation with wrongdoers (*Mor.*
806 F–807 D, 814 C, 819 B–D, cf. 799 B; see E.4 above). The statesman is advised on decorous behaviour (*Mor.* 800 D, 801 A)[104]
which, together with the support of wise and powerful men, will
ensure that he is invited to hold office (*Mor.* 813 C, 819 C). Elective
offices are to be avoided (*Mor.* 813 C; on demagogues and democracy cf. 802 E, 827 A); effective leadership is based on patronage

(*Mor.* 814 C) and the support of the sound and worthy (σώφρων καὶ χρηστός: *Mor.* 807 A; cf. 812 C–D).

(*a*) Of the *Lives*, *Phokion* most intensely illustrates these aspects of the *Moralia*. Statesmanship, as a gift of god, works by concord, like god himself (*Phok.* 2. 5; *Mor.* 824 D). Phokion was virtuous (*Phok.* 1. 2, 3. 4; *Mor.* 800 B–D), and began his career, as recommended, slowly and securely, attaching himself to Chabrias, who advanced him to unelected commands (*Phok.* 6. 1–2; *Mor.* 805 E–F). He did not seek office too eagerly (*Phok.* 8. 1; *Mor.* 813 C), and gained the support of 'the best men' and the council of the Areiopagos (*Phok.* 16. 3; cf. φιλόκαλοι, at *Mor.* 806 C); and he benefited from useful friends (*Phok.* 14. 4, 17. 5, 21. 1, 28. 1–4, 30. 1–4; *Mor.* 814 C).[105]

Plutarch's accounts of how Agesilaos and others established their power-bases show that the routes to power were related to the distinctive *mores* of the particular city and times. Alkibiades and Demosthenes established themselves at democratic Athens through oratory (*Alk.* 10. 2, *Dem.* 6. 2); combined with Alkibiades' lifestyle, this made him appear 'tyrannical' (*Alk.* 16. 2, 16. 5). Alexander used the belief in his divinity to subjugate others (*Alex.* 28. 6; cf. *Arist.* 6. 2–4).[106] After his accession Agesilaos gained in power as king under the Spartan 'constitution' by holding military command. He then further secured his power-base, extending his influence informally outside the political constitution. He first won support among relatives by sharing the estate of his predecessor Agis, and then developed relationships with other Spartans in powerful offices by generous gifts or bribes (ch. 4. 3–6). He acquired influence among ordinary citizens, whether they were friends or opponents, by exploiting their misdemeanours (see C.1(*c*) and E.4 above); he did not copy Lysander's formal ἑταιρικά, political clubs (ch. 20. 3; *Lys.* 5. 3–4, 21. 1), but was accused of demagogy (ch. 5. 3).

(*b*) Kinship and friendship helped Pompey to power, too; while Agesilaos had the advantage of royal birth, though not the right of primogeniture, Pompey's father Strabo gave him the advantage of a military background, which he exploited in supporting and being supported by Sulla and the nobility (*Pomp.* 1. 1, 7–8, 11. 1–3, 16. 2; cf. *Mor.* 805 F, 806 C). His modest lifestyle brought him goodwill (*Pomp.* 18. 3). By restoring the tribunate (*Pomp.* 21. 7–8, 22. 3–4) he confirmed this popularity but antagonized the senate and aristocrats, who came to regard him as a tyrant when he was given far-reaching military powers (*Pomp.* 25. 3, 30. 3). He pleased his friends by tolerating their faults (*Pomp.* 39. 6), but weakened his reputation thereby (*Pomp.* 46. 3) and was forced into an association with Caesar (*Pomp.* 47. 6–7). He was reconciled with the senate (*Pomp.* 49. 6) but again drawn to Caesar (*Pomp.* 51. 5–6). In the end he fought—and died—on the side of the senate (*Pomp.* 59. 1–79. 6). Plutarch shows the inconsistencies and inconstancy of Pompey's career as he sought for support among the powerful factions, and summarizes the consequences at 46. 2: his successes made him odious, his failures were beyond remedy. There was no permanence in his power-base given the disturbed times he lived in (cf. *Phok.* 3. 3; see C.1(*a*) and 2 above).

(*c*) Another Greek and another Roman were rather more successful than Pompey. Caesar's first advance came from his forensic eloquence and his popular, friendly nature (*Caes.* 4. 4–5).[107] He espoused the Marian party and the people's cause, and on the popular vote and demonstrations of support, which he often won by generous spending on rewards and public entertainments, was elected to civic offices and to military commands (*Caes.* 5. 1–5, 8–9, 6. 3–7, 7. 2, 8. 5). Unlike Pompey he gave up a triumph, procured his and Crassus' friendship, and became consul (*Caes.* 14. 2). In Gaul his military achievements surpassed those of all others (*Caes.* 15. 2–4), and by effectively exploiting corruption among candidates at Rome (*Caes.* 28. 4) he was able to exercise great influence. Finally he defeated Pompey at Pharsalos (*Caes.* 42. 1–45. 9) and was made dictator for the second time (*Caes.* 51. 1). After his victory at Munda in Spain he became 'dictator for life' (*Caes.* 57. 1). He introduced valuable reforms but resentment grew among the senators and others (*Caes.* 59–62). His whole career was a consistent and single-minded struggle for popular power, but having achieved it he was assassinated (*Caes.* 66. 4–7, 69. 1).

Perikles, like Lykourgos, had the virtues of tolerance and justice, πρᾳότης καὶ δικαιοσύνη, unlike Agesilaos, whose sense of justice was explicitly flawed by his own and Sparta's self-interest (*Per.* 2. 4, *Lyk.* 28. 6; chs. 13. 5, 37. 11). He was rich, noble, and widely educated, yet politically he espoused the poor. Plutarch (*Per.* 9–16. 1) discusses Thucydides' judgement that his was not democratic rule but rule of the first citizen. He concludes that Perikles had exploited the democratic processes in securing his power-base, bribing the poor with their own public money and with the work he provided in adorning Athens; he then became aristocratic and monarchic in order to lead the city always for the best, either by persuasion or with a firmness like that of a doctor, ἰατρός, a term used also of Agesilaos and Pompey (see C.1(b) above). Plutarch thus confirms Thucydides' judgement. This power-base made Perikles pre-eminent for forty years (*Per.* 16. 2). In the closing summary he is, in contrast with Agesilaos, who also reigned for forty years, the defender and saviour of the constitution (*Per.* 39. 5).

(*d*) Plutarch's accounts show that Roman leaders courted ambitious individuals and conflicting institutions, and relied on military power and the personal allegiance of their troops. Pompey and Caesar show up the factional divisions of Rome and the consequent insecurity of their times. Perikles' support was not personalized and he managed to unite the Athenians, largely under the threat of war. Agesilaos' Sparta was a much smaller citizen community, also united under stable government against threats to its survival. Evidence was not available to Plutarch for a detailed consideration of Sparta's internal politics, but he shows that Agesilaos' inherited position as king and his increasing influence as he courted individuals gave him almost uninterrupted management of the city's affairs. Plutarch's fullest approval was reserved for the rule of a good king (*Num.* 6. 2–4, 20. 7, *Mor.* 790 A, 827 B–C).[108]

6. *Deception*

Perjury and deception generated for Plutarch a leading theme in the *Life*.

(*a*) The morality of deception of enemies is discussed by Xenophon at *Mem.* iv. 2. 15 and at *Agesilaos*, 1. 17, where the practice is proclaimed just, once a war has started. This is also the view of Agesilaos reported by Plutarch at ch. 9. 4. Indeed it was one of the chief qualifications for success[109] from Homer on, employed even by Zeus (*Il.* ii. 5–6). Plutarch's attitude is revealed in the *Life of Philopoimen*; deception was associated with ignoble cheating by Cretans (*Phil.* 13. 6)—foils to the creditable standards of other Greeks. Deception was thus a resource of those branded morally and ethnically inferior to the courageous users of military might (*Phil.–Fl.* 2. 2; but for Spartan celebration of success by deception see *Marc.* 22. 5; cf. ch. 33. 6). Yet Philopoimen adopted Cretan methods when necessary; any regret was outweighed by his superior performance, 'showing them as children' (*Phil.* 13. 6)—a phrase used by Xenophon when Agesilaos surpassed Tissaphernes in deception (*Agesilaos*, 1. 17; cf. *An.* ii. 5).

Deception in the form of surprise is also acceptable. It is exemplified by the unexpectedness of Philopoimen's attack on the Spartan forces of Nabis, and by the suddenness of his enemy's movements, and in the sequel by a change in tactical formation (*Phil.* 14. 4–5). Philopoimen, of course, benefited from his philosophical education, with its cumulative historical and military aspect (*Phil.* 1. 4), and that combination of the intellectual and the practical developed his ability to recognize and exploit an opportunity (the καιρός, 15. 2; cf. C.1(*c*) above, and Xenophon on the training of a general at *Mem.* iii. 1–5 and *passim*).

(*b*) Plutarch implies deception—not pejoratively—when Agesilaos' deformity is 'concealed' by his youthful appearance (ch. 2. 3). Unjust deception permeates the account of his accession: Agis was deceived by Alkibiades (ch. 3. 1) and by Timaia (ch. 3. 2); the Spartans were deceived by Lysander and by Agesilaos in the interpretation of Diopeithes' oracle (ch. 3. 4–9), as the citizens eventually realized (ch. 30. 1) and Plutarch confirms (*Comp.* 1. 2). Agesilaos increased his power surreptitiously by courting and manipulating friends (chs. 4. 5–6, 5. 1–5, 20. 6). After undermining Lysander's influence in the quarrel in Asia Minor, he deceived with perverted judgements on petitions and lawsuits (ch. 7. 5–7), as he did in the cases of Phoibidas and Sphodrias after their Theban enterprises (chs. 23. 11–26. 1). Deception was involved possibly at Olympia and in a letter to Hidrieus (ch. 13. 4–5); certainly at Chaironeia, when by ψευδαγγελία defeat at Knidos was announced as victory and thanksgiving sacrifices (εὐαγγέλια) were offered (ch. 17. 4–5). Agesilaos 'deceived' the laws by allowing them to sleep, and so saved the survivors of Leuktra from disgrace (ch. 30. 6). He deceived the rebellious soldiers and the people (ch. 32. 7–9, 12). He felt that he was deceived by Tachos over his command in Egypt, but then deceived him by his desertion, and Nektanebo by secrecy (chs. 37. 1, 10, 39. 2, 4).

The contrast between the practices of Agesilaos and

Tissaphernes epitomizes the two types of deception. Agesilaos' deception is expressed at Xenophon's *Agesilaos*, 1. 17 by ἀπάτη. This word is one of the main terms for stratagem, denoting 'the creative activity of changing an object or situation into something else',[110] and has both neutral and pejorative senses. Plutarch uses it when Agesilaos responds with ἀπάτη δικαία, 'justifiable deception' (ch. 9. 3): the war is in progress and there is no oath. Herein lies the difference between the two generals, for Tissaphernes' deception in asking the King for extra troops when he has sworn to a truce is unacceptable, because the war is not yet on, and it violates his oath (*Hell.* iii. 4. 11, *Agesilaos*, 1. 11–13). Xenophon seems to have intended the repetition of the word ἀπάτη to reflect Tissaphernes' own definition of his action as deceit (*Agesilaos*, 1. 15) rather than to place the two devices in the same moral category. Plutarch, too, after defining Tissaphernes' action as ἐπιορκία, 'perjury', uses the word ἀπάτη in reading his mind at ch. 10. 1, thus reflecting its use at ch. 9. 3 where the epithet δικαία ('just'), strongly oxymoronic, saves Agesilaos from the pejorative sense.

(*c*) The neutral sense of deception, expressed by the plural ἀπάται (ch. 38. 4), implies the 'unexpected'. The essential military categories of surprise are illustrated by Thucydides: τὸ αἰφνίδιον καὶ ἀπροσδόκητον καὶ τὸ πλείστῳ παραλόγῳ ξυμβαῖνον, 'sudden, unexpected action, contrary to every calculation' (ii. 61. 3). The causes of surprise progress in a rising series: speed of action, action mounted under cover (as foreseen by Demosthenes at Pylos because of obstructed visibility (iv. 29. 4); see below, on ch. 24. 5), and 'the incalculable' (as in the Athenian warning to the Spartans (i. 78)). The intellectual quality of this vocabulary is assured by the identity of the speaker, Perikles, himself chosen as ξυνετός, 'wise' (ii. 34. 6, 8).[111] Plutarch appropriately uses the rational verb παραλογίζεσθαι when Agesilaos exploits the element of 'surprise' (ch. 9. 4), and when he instructs the young Egyptian king Nektanebo in its acceptable use (ch. 38).[112]

Plutarch attributes to Agesilaos the idea of taking pleasure in deceiving enemies (ch. 9. 4). In this he follows, consciously perhaps, the thought of Xenophon (*Mem.* iv. 5. 10) on the pleasurable study of defeating them. Xenophon explains an underlying principle: since deception by an enemy is to be expected, it is culpable to be so deceived, while the bond of trust between friends vindicates a friend's victim; it is culpable to deceive a friend but not to deceive an enemy (*An.* vii. 6. 21 and *Agesilaos*, 11. 4).[113]

7. *Panhellenism*

Agesilaos began and ended his reign with campaigns at the eastern end of the Mediterranean and during it Persian influence at times inspired and resourced major military and political events.

(*a*) In Xenophon's *Hellenika*, soon after Agesilaos became king, Lysander, responding to a report of a new Persian fleet, suggested an anti-Persian expedition to Asia Minor—a panhellenist crusade.[114] No aims are stated, but Xenophon adds that Lysander privately wished to re-establish his deposed oligarchs there (iii. 4. 2). In Xenophon's *enkomion* Agesilaos himself proposed to go to Asia to make peace or, if not, to forestall a Persian attack on the Greeks; he also desired revenge at the enemy's cost, and to make Asia the prize (*Agesilaos*, 1. 8).

Plutarch, ignoring the panhellenist aspect, gives Lysander's private motive first (ch. 6. 2), and then his proposal for a defensive war: a war for Greece waged at the greatest distance, appropriate to Persia's more limited concern for western Asia Minor.[115] At *Lys.* 23. 1–2 advancement for Agesilaos is linked with the more aggressive motive. Here Plutarch introduces panhellenism in Agesilaos' dream at Aulis (ch. 6. 6), comparing his enterprise with Agamemnon's and requiring him to perform the same sacrifice (Eur. *Iph. Aul.* 89–93, 1580–3, 1592). Plutarch does not attribute to Agesilaos the intention to offer sacrifice at Aulis, as Xenophon does (*Hell.* iii. 4. 3). He implies divine intervention—the panhellenist dream—as the source of the instruction to sacrifice; the interruption by Thebans, which follows the violation of the shrine, Agesilaos regards as an ill-omen for the expedition (ch. 6. 11).

(*b*) Greek relations with Persia and individual Persians dominated policies in Agesilaos' reign, as in other times,[116] and were inconsistent and often ambivalent, hostile or friendly, determined by a city's material self-interest or designed for purposes of propaganda. Authorial intentions also vary: Agesilaos' own panhellenist motive suits Xenophon's encomium, and corresponds with the glorious conclusion to the campaign (*Agesilaos*, 1. 33–5); the end of the historical account (*Hell.* iv. 1. 41) leaves Agesilaos' desired achievement still only in prospect, but without the failure that a more ambitious initial expectation would have implied. While Xenophon allows Agesilaos political motivation in his relations with Pharnabazos (*Hell.* iv. 1. 35–6), Plutarch brings the anti-Persian idea into the early part of the *Life*, and retains it as a factor in the assessment of Agesilaos' reign: he deplores the internal wars that cause Agesilaos' recall from Asia (cf. *Kim.* 19. 2–3), and regrets that it is left for Alexander of Makedon to overthrow the Persian empire (ch. 15. 4).[117]

(*c*) The stances of Plutarch and Agesilaos stem from a long and varied history. Early contact between west and east in the Trojan war was not presented in terms of Greeks and non-Greeks; Homer's Trojans were morally equal to their foes, the collective name Hellas was not then in use (Thuc. i. 3), and Sappho's contemporary Asiatic friends were indistinguishable from Greeks. Archaic poets had contemporary themes recognizing Greeks and Others as different but not unequal:[118] the inferior non-Greeks of literature and art were at first mythical creatures such as centaurs.[119] The word 'barbarian' at first denoted only linguistic difference, but polarization of Greek and barbarian in the Persian wars gave the victors a sense of military superiority and ethnic unity.[120] The tragedians of the fifth century established Greek cultural and moral superiority among humans,[121] portraying the flaws of barbarian despotism, luxury, and emotional instability (cf. Hdt. ix. 82–3, 122).[122] The Panathenaic festival and the Parthenon embodied the panhellenic messages in metaphor and history,[123] with the metopes and frieze celebrating the victories of reason and order over chaos. The battle of the Athenians against the Amazons[124] is seen as symbolic, a 'parable' for Marathon.[125]

The growth of democracy and empire more specifically manifested the ideological and political superiority of Athens over the eastern tyrants or despotic kings,[126] though democracy itself is not much favoured in the historical and philosophical literature, even if Plato differentiated the tyrants he deplored from their oppressed subjects.[127] And in an earlier age, it was Kimon, not the democratic reformers, who upheld the panhellenic policy of friendship with Sparta and war against Persia. There were indeed barbarians who to some extent shared in noble traits. The Persian prince Kyros and the satrap Pharnabazos were treated with sympathy and admiration by Xenophon and others; the latter, by Plutarch, for his potential acceptability if fully converted to Hellenic culture (chs. 12–13. 4). In dealing with topics such as education, law, and estate management, Plato and Xenophon sometimes turned approvingly to Persian models.[128] And Herodotos revealed that the ethnic and geographic isolation of Skythians, which determined their traditions and customs, made them aware of their superiority to Greeks: they rejected foreign ways (iv. 76–80; cf. Persians at i. 135, Egyptians at ii. 79).

In an ironical supposed funeral oration of Aspasia, Plato questioned the sincerity of Athenian relations with Persia regarding the freedom of Greece (*Mx.* 239 A–46 A).[129] Socrates, in his parody of the oration, illustrated inconsistencies in Athenian policy with events as late as the Peace of Antalkidas—which he did not live to see: noble motives declared at 239 B repeatedly became self-interest (244–5 A, 245 D–6 A). Plato perhaps felt the shame, αἰσχύνη, which prevented Athens dishonouring the memory of Marathon, Salamis, and Plataia (245 A): the true Greek by nature hated barbarians, φύσει μισοβάρβαρος (245 D).[130] Plato's references to Persia and barbarians—often favourable, especially in early times, but often hostile (*Ll.* 692 C–701 E, esp. 694–5; *Phdr.* 258 B; *Alk.* I. 120–3)—reflect the even complexities of educated Athenian political and diplomatic experience already voiced in Xenophon's writings.[131] Propagandists such as Lysias and Isokrates, with their admired speeches at Olympia and political pamphlets, aroused no enthusiasm for the undertaking of any anti-Persian aggression after Agesilaos' return, indicating that it is misleading to take as the 'Greek' view what was said by the intellectuals at the expense of what was done by statesmen with the support of their citizens (cf. on ch. 23. 2–3).

(*d*) Panhellenism was not an Athenian preserve; indeed, as Sparta and others saw it, Athens perverted a panhellenic league into a tyranny over Greek cities. Even after the medism of Thebes, cities commissioned the Boiotian Pindar to celebrate eastern and western victories over non-Greeks. In the first *Pythian*, the victory of Hieron of Syracuse (d. 467/6) over the Phoenician and Etruscan fleets, in the battle of Cumae (474), is symbolized by the victory of Zeus over the Giants. Typhos stretches to the cliffs of Cumae from his burial-place under Etna: the foundation of the city Aitna by Hieron was honoured in the ode, and the triumph of order over chaos is associated with Greek victories over the attacks of other peoples as firmly as in the Parthenon frieze. The Spartans had headed the early hostility to Persia, assuming full command against Xerxes (Hdt. i. 152, vii. 159), but, victors in the Peloponnesian war through Persian support and money (Thuc. viii. 37, 84; Xen. *Hell.* i. 5. 3), they became liberators of Greeks, from Athenian imperialism and from Persian overlordship in Asia Minor (Xen. *Hell.* iii. 1. 3).

Panhellenist sentiments were exploitable for other purposes:[132] wars in the east were more profitable than wars between poorer Greek states (Hdt. v. 49; Xen. *Hell.* vi. 1. 12, vii. 5. 27),[133] and could, *c.*382, provide opportunities for the settlement of landless Greek mercenaries (Isok. 4. 36, 168; *Phil.* 96, 120–1; *Ep.* ix. 9). They developed and persisted as the propagandists' authorization for the hegemony of a current superpower, or of Athens and Sparta jointly (Ar. *Lys.* 1130–5; cf. Kallikratidas, E.3 above), if they would agree to abandon their war to face Persia instead. Xenophon used the idea in glorifying Agesilaos as μισοπέρσης, 'hater of Persians' (*Agesilaos*, 7. 7); and Plato (*Resp.* 469 B–470 C), Lysias (*Olympic*), Isokrates (*Philippus*), and Demosthenes (*Philippics*) advocated hostility towards Persia, Dionysios of Syracuse, or Philip of Makedon, either to advance the narrower interests of their own city (see below, chs. 5. 6–7, 8. 3, and 35. 4–6),[134] or to distract the Greeks from their internecine wars— without success.[135] The exploitation of panhellenism is here extreme: Dionysios of Syracuse was a Greek, however keen Lysias was to mention the King in the same breath; and whatever Demosthenes might say, the Makedonian royal family was Greek for the purpose of the Olympic Games and for Isokrates' war on Persia. It was, on the one hand, a threadbare cover for the self-interest of a state or faction (ch. 40. 2), yet on the other, a desperate attempt to end war. Plutarch held these conflicts responsible for the weakness that forced the Greeks to submit to Rome, though that submission, paradoxically, brought them liberation, too (*Flam.* 11. 4).

(*e*) Lysander's anti-Persian stance (ch. 6. 2–3) illustrates Spartan ambivalence: Sparta benefited from Kyros' Persian money (*Lys.* 4, 9), but after Kyros' death was called on to protect Greeks in Asia against Tissaphernes. Persian money was soon to be used to provoke the war against Sparta (ch. 15. 8; *Lys.* 27. 1; Xen. *Hell.* iii. 5. 1) in which Lysander died (ch. 8. 4). Reports of that war (ch. 15. 3) and later of the battle at the Nemea (ch. 16. 6) stir Plutarch and Agesilaos to anger and regret that Greeks are fighting Greeks, not Persians. Yet, in further Spartan ambivalence, Agesilaos relentlessly conducts wars against Thebes (ch. 26. 3), one of the evil acts of barbarism, βάρβαρα κακά, done by Greeks to themselves (ch. 15. 3); Plutarch approves of Lykourgos' warning against all hegemonic wars (*Lyk.* 31. 1).

(*f*) Agesilaos' mercenary service in Egypt to a rebel from the King, the final episode of the *Life* (chs. 36–40), is described by Xenophon as at least tangentially part of a creditable project with wider Greek significance, offering the chance to punish the King for his hostility and for recognizing the newly liberated Messene (*Agesilaos*, 2. 28–9); but refusal of recognition to Messene was only in Spartan self-interest: Plutarch refers to this panhellenic motive only to deny that it would be proper for a man over the age of eighty, though it would have been better than undertaking mercenary service to a barbarian in revolt (ch. 36. 1–4), only to finance war against Greeks (*Comp.* 5. 1).

(*g*) The Hellenizing of the east was not the single-minded aim of Alexander. His was rather a pragmatic policy of mixing races and cultures—adopting partly Persian dress, encouraging inter-marriage (*Alex.* 47. 5–8, 70. 3; but cf. 45. 1–4), and making appointments of Persians to imperial posts—in order to facilitate the management of his empire. Even his foundation of cities may have had economic rather than ideological aims.[136] In accommo-dating to Persian manners, one of his most un-Hellenic 'political' innovations was *proskynesis*, 'obeisance', regarded by Greeks as an admission of inferiority, a sign of subjection to monarchy, and a gesture appropriate to the worship of a god (*Alex.* 54. 3; Aeschylus, *Pers.* 499; Hdt. i. 134. 1, iii. 86. 2, vii. 136. 1; Isok. 4. 151). Also un-Hellenic were his hints—and possible demand for recognition—of his divinity (*Alex.* 27. 5–11, 28, 33. 1; *Mor.* 219 E; Aelian, *VH* ii. 19).[137] But his visits to Delphi and Troy (*Alex.* 14. 6–7, 15. 8–9) were typical panhellenic gestures, empty, or at best only part of the story, as was Agesilaos' conduct at Aulis (cf. (b) above, and see below, ch. 6. 6).

(*h*) Plutarch shared with Agesilaos the desire for the pan-hellenist crusade against Persia (chs. 15. 3, 16. 6), but he com-mends a notable corollary to the ideology in the speech made in Sparta by the Theban Epameinondas, 'not for the Thebans but for the whole of Greece as one', advocating just and lasting peace which would endure only when all were equal (ch. 27. 7). This sentiment is similar to Plutarch's apparent attitude to the possible Hellenizing of Pharnabazos' values (ch. 12. 7–9; see E.7 above), and contrasts with the alternative of Xenophon and Agesilaos giving priority to Spartan hegemony.

Peace was not brought to the Greek cities until 196, when, at the Isthmian Games, the Roman senate and Titus Flamininus proclaimed their freedom from the king of Makedon. The expressions of relief at the achievement which great Greeks themselves— including Agesilaos—had found impossible (*Flam.* 10–11) illustrate the intensity of the earlier extreme panhellenism. The anti-Persian project was still in mind in the unhappy report of the Roman civil wars (*Pomp.* 70. 2–5), where Plutarch seems to recall the earlier folly of the Greeks (ch. 15. 3).[138]

F. The Sources for Plutarch's *Agesilaos*

Plutarch's *Agesilaos* is unusual in that the main sources available to him are still available,[139] so that it provides an opportunity to compare what he may have read with what he wrote on the subject. The history of a period has often been written with a strong focus on a single powerful individual who seemed to determine the course of events (Polyb. ix. 23). Agesilaos' reign spanned approximately the first forty years of the fourth century BC, which is a period that can be defined by clear limits, starting when Sparta began to be closely involved in the affairs of Greeks and Persians in Asia Minor and ending when its influence was reduced to insignificance. Thus he and his city were central figures in historical accounts of an important period. Lives and characters now became the subject of separate biographical monographs: one encomium—perhaps *Agesilaos*, but it is not named—is attributed to the contemporary Xenophon by Dionysios of Halikarnassos (*Rh.* 9. 358; cf. D. L. 2. 57, and see below, 1). Xenophon, though Athenian, was an admirer of Sparta and friend and admirer of Agesilaos: perhaps the encomium was composed for a Spartan audience. Other authors, from less central Greek cities, were more independent, even hostile to Sparta, and although less of their work survives, much was available, directly or indirectly, to

Plutarch. He therefore was able to present a balanced account, although it is not possible to distinguish always his own judgements from those contained in his sources.

1. *Known Sources*

The main known sources used here by Plutarch are Xenophon's *Agesilaos* and *Hellenika*, iii. 3. 1–vii. 5. 27. Scholars have questioned whether Xenophon, the author of *Hellenika*, also composed *Agesilaos*, and if so which came first. Differences in the two compositions are explained variously as toning down, enhancement, or proof of a new author; comparisons of verbal similarities, synonyms, and stylistic features are inconclusive.[140] Given the relationship to Agesilaos claimed by the author (*An.* v. 3. 5, *Agesilaos*, 1. 1, 5. 6–7), it is not impossible that he was both the encomiast and the historian, and arguments to the contrary are not decisive. Plutarch used both works, and the question of authorship does not affect the study of his sources: since he acknowledges Xenophon's authorship (see 3. (*a*) below), the attribution was already firmly in place.

These works are not named here, but their use can certainly be identified, as can that of Ephoros for Lysander's attempted reform (ch. 20),[141] directly or indirectly, since he is named as source for the discovery of Lysander's speech (*Lys.* 30. 3). Diodoros (xiv. 79–xv. 93) covers the same period but is not named in any of the *Lives*; his account differs frequently from Xenophon's.[142] He often confirms Plutarch where Xenophon is silent, indicating, perhaps, only their use of the same sources: Lysander's proposed reform (xiv. 13. 2–8, cf. chs. 8. 3, 20. 3–5); Theban success at Koroneia (xiv. 84. 1–2, cf. ch. 18), and at Tegyra (MSS Tegea) (xv. 37. 1–2, 81. 2, cf. ch. 27. 4); the death of Kleombrotos at Leuktra (xv. 33. 3, 55. 5, cf. ch. 28. 8); Epameinondas as leader of the invasion of Lakonia (xv. 63. 4, cf. ch. 31. 1); the duration of Epameinondas' stay in Lakonia—85 days, 3 months (xv. 67. 1, cf. ch. 32. 13–14); the title 'Tearless Battle' (xv. 72. 3, cf. ch. 33. 5); Sparta's lone continuation of the war (xv. 89. 2, cf. ch. 35. 4); Agesilaos' appointment to the mercenary command only (xv. 92. 2, cf. ch. 37. 1); Nektanebo's revolt (xv. 92. 3–4, cf. ch. 37. 3; but 93. 2–6 confuses Tachos and Nektanebo); the details of the death and burial of Agesilaos (xv. 93. 6, cf. ch. 40. 3–4).

Direct or indirect use is possible of Nepos' *Life of Agesilaus* (or a common source); on Agesilaos' accession (I. I–4, cf. ch. 3, *Comp.* I. 2), and on his death (8. 6–7, cf. ch. 40. 4).[143] Chapters from the *Hellenica Oxyrhynchia*[144] dealing with Agesilaos in Asia Minor (VI. I–IX. I, XVI. I–XVII. 4) and the Corinthian war (XIII. I–XIV. 3) provide useful comparisons; e.g. Agesilaos' feelings for Megabates (XVI. 4; cf. ch. II. 6–IO). But Plutarch's omission of details of Agesilaos' eastward incursions or plans (XVI–XVII) suggests either that he failed to consult less accessible sources or that he thought the results too insubstantial. Pausanias' work indicates that he had other sources, now lost, which will have been available also to Plutarch.[145]

That Plutarch does not name his sources for the major narratives seems to indicate confidence in his presentation and a wish to appear autonomous, without imposing on the reader the need for prior knowledge of the other accounts. Sometimes a piece of evidence is given a named source which he seems already to be following, such as Xenophon at chs. 4. 2, 18. 2. He does not overtly strike a fresh note in order to divert his readers: if they are familiar with the earlier accounts, they will recognize that his changes stem from a new, balanced, approach to the subject.

2. *Xenophon*

(*a*) Despite its well-known deficiencies Xenophon's *Hellenika* is the only extant contemporary account of the period 4II–362, continuing and extending the work of Thucydides. Its character and intention are much disputed, but some features in which Plutarch would have special interest are clear: its attitudes, generally though not invariably favourable to Agesilaos and Sparta but hostile to Thebes, its selectivity in the omission or inclusion of events and personalities, and its reflections on divine intervention and responsibility, especially at Mantineia at the close (vii. 5. 26–7). Xenophon's encomium, whether written before or during the composition of *Hellenika*, has been seen equally as an apologia, responding to criticisms of Agesilaos (see on ch. 3. 9, 'The literary evidence', (*e*); cf. E.I above). That there were differing historical accounts and contemporary reports of criticisms of Agesilaos still available may be gathered from passages in Plutarch and Diodoros which can be attributed to Ephoros and to other fourth-century writers, now wholly or partially lost.[146]

Plutarch clearly recognized the difference between the genres to which Xenophon's two works belong. His *Agesilaos* belongs to neither, but incorporates the biographical element into the broader historical context of the period. He gives a plain statement of Agesilaos' accession (ch. 4. 1; cf. *Hell*. iii. 3. 4), but Xenophon uses the accession as proof of character—before the reign began (*Agesilaos*, 1. 5). At *Hell*. iii. 4. 26 Agesilaos accepted thirty talents from Tithraustes 'for the journey', but at *Agesilaos*, 4. 6, offered 'numerous gifts' if he would depart, he refused to enrich himself, preferring to take spoils. Plutarch was aware of both versions, but chose to omit the tempting sum and retained the necessary funding: Agesilaos, offered only an unspecified amount of 'money', refused to enrich himself, preferring spoils, and accepted the thirty talents for expenses (ch. 10. 6–8).

Plutarch's main use of Xenophon's encomium, only the first two chapters of which are in narrative form, is for the study of Agesilaos' character, treated thematically in the *catalogue raisonné* (3–11); he uses *Hellenika* mainly for the account of Agesilaos' career. Some details and events which Xenophon omitted from *Agesilaos*, often because they would be unsuitable in a eulogistic work,[147] are contained in *Hellenika*; but since Xenophon ends that work before the Egyptian campaign, Plutarch turns at that point either to his *Agesilaos* or to other sources.

(*b*) Plutarch's response to Xenophon in this *Life* is discussed throughout the present commentary, but a few instances will indicate the range. That he often follows Xenophon's language and phrasing very closely has been shown by comparisons of sample passages (chs. 6. 10, 10. 1–2; *Hell*. iii. 4. 4, iii. 4. 20, *Agesilaos*, 1. 28–9).[148] However, some of the passages also reveal and illustrate his thematic independence. Plutarch stresses that the disregard of local tradition at Aulis aroused Boiotian anger; Agesilaos departed distressed by the omen, not angry. At Ephesos Xenophon shows Agesilaos not practising deceit (*Hell*. iii. 4. 6, 12, *Agesilaos*, 1. 12, 16), but Plutarch states that he intended to deceive Tissaphernes in return for his deception (ch. 9. 3). Xenophon regularly suggests deficiencies in the Theban character: fear as their motive for devising Sphodrias' raid into Attika (*Hell*. v. 4. 20); incompetence during battle in Boiotia (v. 4. 40); hesitation after Leuktra and

before invading Lakonia (vi. 4. 20, vi. 5. 24). Such cases illustrate
Plutarch's judgemental independence—on Sphodrias' raid (ch.
24. 5), Agesilaos in Boiotia (ch. 26. 2–4), after Leuktra (ch. 29. 1),
in Lakonia (ch. 31.4). Plutarch was sensitive to aspersions on his
ancestors and in *De Herodoti malignitate* (*Mor.* 854 E–874 C)
objects to Herodotos' criticisms of various Greeks; Boiotians
occupy a small portion (*Mor.* 864 D–867 B), and there is prejudice, especially over Thermopylai (*Mor.* 864 E; Herod. vii. 222,
233).[149]

Xenophon's omissions from his account in *Hellenika* are sub-
stantial.[150] He does not, for instance, either record the victory of
the Thebans at Tegyra or mention Epameinondas until, at vii. 1.
42, he names him as the leader of the third invasion of the
Peloponnese; but Plutarch records the battle at Tegyra (ch. 27. 4;
cf. *Pel.* 16–17), tells us that Epameinondas was creditably involved
in peace negotiations at Sparta (ch. 27. 6) and later in the building
of Messene (ch. 34. 1), and alone describes Agesilaos' handling of
the τρέσαντες after Leuktra (ch. 30. 2–6, *Comp.* 2. 3).

(*c*) There are significant differences in the two authors' views of
the constitution of Lykourgos (see E.1 above) and their respective
attitudes towards Sparta's policy of hegemony. Plutarch presents
a balanced—perhaps more credible—account, measuring practice
against theory. Xenophon observed the system under which
Spartan affairs were conducted; he shared with Agesilaos a deep
hatred of Thebes and Boiotians (now Sparta's chief opponents),
welcomed their humiliations, and like Agesilaos disparaged their
abilities and actions (*Hell.* iv. 2. 18, vi. 5. 24, vii. 4. 35, 5. 1, 12; cf.
chs. 22. 2, 23. 11, *Comp.* 3. 1–2); he suggests (iv. 3. 19) that they
escaped to safety from the battle of Koroneia with losses; Plutarch
records that the Thebans withdrew in high spirits without being
routed (ch. 18. 9); and he implies divine punishment of Agesilaos'
overbearing treatment of Theban envoys, exposing his injustice
and possible complicity in the occupation of Thebes and the
incursion into Attica (chs. 22–4). Xenophon approves of
Agesilaos' expedition to Egypt, undertaken for monetary reward
in the service of Spartan interests, and explains away his desertion
of an employer as the means of gaining a more reliable friend for
the future (*Agesilaos*, 2. 31). Plutarch disapproves of the accumulation of funds for wars in Greece and condemns the desertion as
treachery (chs. 36. 1–4, 37. 10; *Comp.* 5. 2). Yet he is fairer than

Xenophon, in that he also justly honours Agesilaos and the Spartans (chs. 15–16, 28. 8; *Comp.* 4. 8).

Two final cases reveal and explain the fundamental independence of Plutarch's use of Xenophon. His interpretation of Agesilaos' accession as flawed is probably right (*Comp.* 1. 6; see below, ch. 3); Xenophon gives only a more superficial, perhaps the official, account (*Hell.* iii. 3. 1–4, *Agesilaos*, 1. 6), as he does of the trials of Sphodrias and Phoibidas (see below, chs. 23. 6–26. 1). Their judgements of Agesilaos' character also diverge: both stress his friendships, but whereas Xenophon eulogizes and emphasizes his resistance to powerful emotions (*Agesilaos*, 5. 3, 8. 1–3, 11. 4), Plutarch portrays both strong emotions and powers of restraint and self-control, and shows that Agesilaos exploited his capacity for friendship for political advantage (see E.4 above). It is not surprising that as criticism of Agesilaos grows and Thebes exerts greater influence, Xenophon provides a diminishing contribution to the record. From ch. 30 to the end Plutarch relies more and more on other sources, and on his own reflections, to make up for the silences and distortions of his main source.[151]

3. *Minor Sources*

For minor references Plutarch changes his practice and assumes that readers who wish can, given the author's name, identify his work.

(*a*) Xenophon's work is quoted at chs. 4. 2 (*Agesilaos*, 6. 4), 18. 2 (*Hell.* iv. 3. 16), 19. 7–9 (*Agesilaos*, 8. 7), 29. 2 (*Smp.* i. 1), 34. 4 (*Hell.* vii. 5. 10); and he is linked to Agesilaos at chs. 9. 2 (*An.*) and 20. 2, where he cannot be identified as the source.[152]

(*b*) Anecdotes come from Hieronymos (ch. 13. 7) and Theophrastos (chs. 2. 6, 36. 11): the former, a philosopher of Rhodes (*c*.290–230), is also mentioned at *Arist.* 27. 2; the latter, Aristotle's successor, and the author of *Characters*, also (for example) *Laws*, *Barbarian Customs*, and botanical works, is much quoted by Plutarch.

(*c*) Literary quotations come from Simonides, a lyric and elegiac poet from Keos, author of epigrams, epinikia, and an encomium commemorating the Spartans who fell at Thermopylai, in a dactylo-epitrite metre; either that or an epigram may be the source here (ch. 1. 3); from Timotheos, a dithyrambic poet from Miletos and a younger contemporary of Euripides who is said by Satyros (*Vita Euripidis, POxy.* 1176) to have collaborated with him over his *Persai*, a *nomos* or solo song to the cithara, and possible source here (ch. 14. 4);[153] and from Theopompos of Chios (ch. 31. 4), the fourth-century historian, student, contemporary with Ephoros, of Isokrates (*FGrH* 70 T 3a–c), and author of an account in twelve books, *Hellenika*, of events between 410 and 394, continuing Thucydides (Diod. xiii. 42. 5, xiv. 84. 6), and *Philippika*, in 58 books (Diod. xvi. 71).[154] Since Epameinondas' invasions of Lakonia (370–362) occurred before the accession of Philip in 360, the references at chs. 31. 4, 32. 14–33. 1 (see (*i*) and (*k*) below) may not be part of the main narratives.

(*d*) Homer is named at ch. 5. 6 (*Od.* viii. 77), but references to Euripides at ch. 15. 3 (*Tro.* 764) and Homer at chs. 9. 7 and 15. 7 (*Il.* xxiii. 296 f. and iv. 175) are not attributed.

(*e*) A reference to Dikaiarchos supports the complaint that Xenophon omitted women's names (ch. 19. 9), an omission which Plutarch makes good from his researches in another source, the Lakedaimonian archives (ch. 19. 10). A Dorian from Messana in Sicily and a contemporary of Theophrastos, Dikaiarchos was long resident in the Peloponnese, and was a student of Aristotle and the author of political, historical, philosophical, geographical, and other works, including Βίος Ἑλλάδος (*Life of Greece*).

(*f*) Kallisthenes, the authority for naming the Thespian Euthynos at ch. 34. 4, was a relative and student of Aristotle, the companion and historian of Alexander, mentioned also at *Arist.* 27. 2. He was the author of an account of events between 387 and 356 (Diod. xiv. 117. 8, xvi. 14. 4).

(*g*) A reference to Thucydides (v. 64) is used to distinguish between the two battles of Mantineia, in 418 and 362, but not to give authority to Plutarch's comment (ch. 33. 7).

(*h*) The speech used to incriminate Lysander is identified by naming Kleon of Halikarnassos as the author (ch. 20. 4; also at *Lys.* 25. 1; cf. 30. 3; Nepos, *Lys.* 3. 5).

(*i*) Independent but named judgements are quoted, of Agesilaos from Theopompos (ch. 10. 10), and of the Spartans from Erasistratos son of Phaiax (ch. 15. 7; see below).

(*j*) Supporting evidence on the father of Timaia's child (ch. 3. 2) comes from Douris, tyrant of Samos at about the end of the fourth century; he claimed descent from Alkibiades (*Alk.* 32. 2), was a student of Theophrastos, and wrote works on history, literature, and other subjects.

(*k*) Contrary evidence on the bribing of the Thebans by Agesilaos (chs. 32. 14–33. 1) comes from Theopompos. The authority of these two is questioned: of Douris[155] at *Per.* 28. 1–3, of Theopompos at ch. 33. 1.

(*l*) Evidence about the weapon which killed Epameinondas comes from Dioskourides, named as the author of a work on the Spartan constitution (*Lyk.* 11. 4) and perhaps a student of Isokrates.[156]

(*m*) The Lakedaimonian tradition was perhaps communicated to Plutarch orally by a contemporary, Kallikrates (ch. 35. 1–2).

(*n*) Plutarch's own opinions favouring Agesilaos and the Spartans are twice developed in conflict with apparently familiar remarks. One favoured Alexander (ch. 15. 4), from an old man of Corinth, Demaratos, who was with him at Persepolis (*Alex.* 37. 7). The other devalued the Spartans' private virtues (ch. 15. 7), from Erasistratos, son of Phaiax, an Athenian; his father was a rival of Alkibiades, but, in a minority view attributed by Plutarch to Theophrastos, nevertheless combined with him in the ostracism of Hyperbolos (*Alk.* 13. 1–5, *Nik.* 11. 7).[157]

(*o*) There are other possible minor sources: Ammonios, Plutarch's teacher (*Mor.* 385 B), for Egypt (chs. 36–40), though not named;[158] lists of victors for the repeat of the Isthmian Games (ch. 21. 5); Agesilaos' letters (chs. 13. 5 and 23. 10); oral communications from guides, temple officials, and local historians at Delphi and Chaironeia. Plutarch's own comments on topography add little to the scenes of action, but introduce legendary, historical, or religious topics of local interest, such as the trophy erected in front of the temple of Athena Itonia near Koroneia (ch. 19. 2; cf. *Per.* 18. 2).[159]

4. *Unattributed Comments*

Plutarch avoids indicating a source by using λέγεται ('he' or 'it is said') and λέγουσι ('they say') to introduce additional details, which may suggest to modern minds less authenticity but may, by modest disclaimer (εἰρωνεία), lightly reveal the thoroughness of his researches.[160]

(*a*) At ch. 8. 1 the verb, which is not used in the parallel passage

(*Lys.* 23. 7), destabilizes, perhaps, only the first sentence of the dialogue (*Hell.* iii. 4. 9 being the source only for what follows).

(*b*) No other source reports the gifts given by Xerxes to the Tralleis (ch. 16. 2).

(*c*) The Theban individuals involved with Sphodrias' raid into Attica at ch. 24. 6 are not named at *Hell.* v. 4. 20; Plutarch himself names them at *Pel.* 14. 1 as Pelopidas, a Boiotarch, not with Melon, as here, but with Gorgidas; later he speaks of οἱ περὶ τὸν Πελοπίδαν, 'those with Pelopidas' (*Pel.* 14. 2).

(*d*) A local witness may have reported that Sphodrias' men were frightened by a light at Eleusis (ch. 24. 7), though none is mentioned at *Pel.* 14. 3, and no fright occurs at *Hell.* v. 4. 21.

(*e*) Partisan witnesses, including Theopompos, disputed the reasons for the Thebans' departure from the Peloponnese (ch. 32. 13).

(*f*) The use of λέγεται at ch. 11. 5 seems to be exceptional: to indicate not a change of source at this point (cf. *Hell.* iv. 1. 28), but a move to a more subjective treatment of an emotional topic, Spithridates' departure.

(*g*) The verbs λέγεται and λέγουσι also introduce anecdotal material: Agesilaos' love of children (ch. 25. 11), his tricking of allied tradesmen (ch. 26. 7), his admiring remark about Epameinondas (ch. 32. 4), Antalkidas' retort to an Athenian (ch. 31. 7), and the controversial treatment of a brave Spartan (ch. 34. 11); the last reminiscent, perhaps, of a dilemma proposed in the Schools for rhetorical exercises.

(*h*) Other verbs possibly introduce Plutarch's own conjectures and inferences. He uses forms of δῆλον ἐποίησεν (chs. 2. 3, 23. 5), ἐδήλωσεν (ch. 13. 6), 'he made it clear', when action reveals character, and ὁ καιρὸς δηλοῖ (ch. 28. 7), 'the chronology shows', when he suggests that anger replaces reason; ἔοικε, 'it seems likely' (ch. 8. 7) when he suggests that Agesilaos and Lysander suffer the same temperamental affliction, and again (ch. 18. 5) when he suggests that it was his bodyguard that rescued the wounded Agesilaos. With δοκῶ, 'I think' (ch. 34. 8) Plutarch may suggest his own proposal of a Spartan location for what is reported by Polyainos at Gytheion (ii. 9); if the latter were true, it would be remote from Spartan observers in the city.

(*i*) Another verb, ὁμολογεῖται, 'it is agreed', or its participial form, lays down a consensus, of contemporaries or commentators,

which Plutarch will modify. At chs. 10. 10, 33. 2, the consensus of
commentators—Xenophon (*Agesilaos* 1. 36–8), and Theopompos
—and of all concerned, on Agesilaos' military superiority, is overtaken by Plutarch's moral, or political and moral, criteria; and
agreed success and ch. 33. 2, adapted from *Agesilaos*, 2. 24, is
qualified at §3. At ch. 24. 1, suspicion of responsibility is overtaken by agreement to the charge produced by subsequent actions,
whether it is taken as general public agreement or as Agesilaos'
tacit agreement, amounting to a confession.

(*j*) Unattributed comments are introduced by φασί, 'they say': a
commentator's gloss on the poet Simonides (ch. 1. 3), a gloss on
the bravery and death of Kleonymos (ch. 28. 8), and an uncomplimentary gloss on Antalkidas' behaviour (ch. 32. 1). For the
comments of philosophical authorities more appropriately,
perhaps, οἴονται, 'they think', is used; at ch. 5. 5 to report what is
presented as their general knowledge, and at ch. 5. 6 to introduce
an extract from an argument based on the applicability of the poet
Homer.[161]

TEXT AND COMMENTARY

PART I (chs. 1–3)

Early years to accession: the qualities of leadership

Xen. *Hell.* iii. 3. 1–4, *Agesilaos*, 1. 5; Nepos, *Agesilaus*, 1. 2–5; Paus. iii. 8. 7–10

1. Agesilaos' ancestry and training: Plutarch's verbal patterning

Plutarch's opening chapter aims to ensure that the reader continues reading.[1] The chronological sequences of biography may not always be interesting. The conflict between art and life makes it the most intransigent of literary forms. Peripatetic biography, the forerunner of Plutarch's ethical biography, choosing to display a man's virtues through his actions, worked to the fixed formula of 'an account of the life of a man from birth to death' to suggest authenticity.[2] Yet the work will be judged also by the artistic standards of other genres, which are not governed by the artless shape of real life. Here Plutarch preserves life's chronological progression, but meets the literary challenge, presenting the early biographical details and revealing his subject-matter in verbal patterns which lead indirectly to the approaching choice of the dead King Agis' successor (ch. 3).

The chapter has a five-part structure. The first two and last two parts are biographical, recording the developing stages of life— birth and early upbringing, and the resulting mature qualifications and characteristics. In the centre the chronological sequence is interrupted by an ornament, a quotation from Simonides. Within this elaborate structure, key words have special significance for this *Life*: there are references to Agesilaos by name, to 'law' (νόμος), to obedience (ἄρχεσθαι), to 'institutionalized education' (ἀγωγή), and to traits of character.

1 Ἀρχίδαμος ὁ Ζευξιδάμου βασιλεύσας ἐπιφανῶς Λακεδαιμονίων

κατέλιπεν υἱὸν ἐκ γυναικὸς εὐδοκίμου Λαμπιδοῦς, Ἆγιν, καὶ πολὺ νεώτερον ἐξ Εὐπωλίας τῆς Μελησιππίδα θυγατρός, Ἀγησίλαον.

Plutarch's use of family names advertises his concern for scholarly research and detailed knowledge. The birth of Agesilaos is stated not by simple fact but by his parentage, in the chronological context of the death of Archidamos, his father. His descent (ancestral γένος)[3] within a Spartan royal family is the most significant feature for the main theme, the account of his reign; that is, the part of his adult life following the death of his predecessor, Agis. His birth is not securely dated, but the date of his death (see below, ch. 40) may be fixed at 360/59 by the accession of Nektanebo II to the Egyptian throne.[4] If Agesilaos died at the age of 84 (ch. 40. 3), he was born in 445 or 444.[5]

Literary features

Literary—rhetorical—features here are the ornamental patterning of names and the naming of women. The placing of three proper nouns with alliteration, Archidamos, Agis, and Agesilaos,[6] gives the sentence a tripartite structure. The *Life* begins not with the name of the subject, as half the *Lives* do, but with the name and parentage of Agesilaos' father.[7] The name of his brother also precedes his own, which is the last word in the sentence and the seventh mentioned. This pattern establishes Agesilaos' juniority to his brother, and places the three men in the order of their succession to the throne: father, son, and brother, representing the indirect and delayed rise of Agesilaos.

Two parallel pairs of accusatives frame the names of the mothers of Archidamos' two sons, Lampido[8] and Eupolia. In identifying the wives of Archidamos, Plutarch evinces a personal interest in the women of the family, which contributes to the artistic ornamentation. Elsewhere in Greece the immediate significance of dedicatory and funerary inscriptions made some women's names available, but in Sparta the latter were perhaps restricted to those who died in childbirth (*Lyk.* 27. 2).[9] At ch. 19. 10 he refers to his researches on the subject in Spartan archives,[10] which gave him these names. Eupolia, though by implication here not as well-born as Lampido, and perhaps not so wealthy (Xen. *Agesilaos*, 4. 5; see below, ch. 4. 1), bears a name 'Well-Foaled' (πῶλος, a foal) which suggests an aristocratic horse-owning family.[11]

In Boiotia there was a tradition of literary interest in women as early as Pindar, who composed songs for girls' choral performances. Korinna was a Boiotian woman poet, and she mentions another, Myrtis.[12] This provides evidence of the education of women in Boiotia, for the composer may also have trained the performers.[13] Performances of this kind appear to have taken place at Sparta, too (*Lyk.* 14. 1): the Spartan—less likely Lydian—seventh-century poet Alkman was an early, if not the first, practitioner of the Partheneion, written for girls' choirs.[14] As further evidence of Boiotian interest in women, there are examples of female portraits on *stelai* and pottery from Boiotian artists.[15] Plutarch may be following this Boiotian tradition, but he may also have in mind Aristotle's remarks about the prominence and influence of Spartan women (*Pol.* 1269ᵇ12–1270ᵃ29), the *Sayings of Spartan Women*, and *Mulierum virtutes* (*Mor.* 240 c–263 c). His biographical interest attaches much importance to the family, and particularly to the formative influence and powerful connections of the mother, often more strikingly than to those of the father (see Introd., B.2(*b*), and below, on ch. 19. 7–9).[16] Xenophon shows less interest in women,[17] except in respect of their important role in the home (*Oik.* 3. 12–15), stressed also by Plutarch.

2 ἐπεὶ δὲ τῆς βασιλείας Ἄγιδι προσηκούσης κατὰ τὸν νόμον, ἰδιώτης ἐδόκει βιοτεύσειν ὁ Ἀγησίλαος, ἤχθη τὴν λεγομένην ἀγωγὴν ἐν Λακεδαίμονι, σκληρὰν μὲν οὖσαν τῇ διαίτῃ καὶ πολύπονον, παιδεύουσαν δὲ τοὺς νέους ἄρχεσθαι.

The law referred to here does not denote any known legislation. The meaning is 'customary practice', since the dual kingship, and the arrangements for its inheritance, were survivals from the distant past, perhaps from the unification of separate villages.[18] It was believed to be sanctioned by the Delphic Oracle (Hdt. 6. 51–2) and was being formalized and regulated by law in the sixth century (Hdt. 5. 75. 2). Lykourgos was regarded as the reformer of laws, not the founder of the kingship.

Plutarch moves on chronologically to the education of Agesilaos. Juniority to his half-brother is now said to have entailed participation in the training system (ἀγωγή) as an ordinary Spartan boy (ἰδιώτης); only the heir to the throne was exempt. Plutarch selects for mention the harsh, laborious upbringing (πολύπονον; cf. Thuc. ii. 39. 1, 4; Xen. *Lak. Pol.* 2. 2–6;

Arist. *Pol.* 1338ᵇ12) in the ἀγωγή that is significant for his adult
career and the inculcation of obedience[19] (ἄρχεσθαι; see note after
§5), crucial for the analysis of his character as king.

The ἀγωγή and the ἀγέλη

The Lykourgan educational system of Sparta is explained by
Xenophon (*Lak. Pol.* 2–3.) and by Plutarch (*Lyk.* 16. 4–17. 4).
Recent scholarship has corrected many misunderstandings
about the ἀγωγή and the Spartan way of life, and much that was
attributed to them has been discarded as mythical or of late date.[20]
Plutarch selects what he regards as the most significant features in
Agesilaos' upbringing.

The ἀγωγή was thought to have produced the superior soldiers
who maintained the Spartans' dominance over their subject
population. The Spartan boy was taken from his parents at the
age of 7 and enlisted into an ἀγέλη, 'troop' or 'pack'. From that
age he underwent junior warrior-training, supervised by older
boys and adults, learning the asceticism of diet, discipline, and
dress that would guide the rest of his life. He was led by the boy
in his group most outstanding in judgement and courage, and
was subject to punishment by an appointed warden, παιδονόμος, or
any other adult. He was encouraged to steal for survival and
trained to conquer in mock battles under the command of a
20-year-old youth, εἴρην (cf. Paus. iii. 14. 9–10). Plutarch
comments on the little attention paid to literacy, and Aristotle
criticizes the predominance of physical training (*Lyk.* 16. 6, *Pol.*
1338ᵇ11–27).

Supervision, training, and hardship intensified at 12 and continued until maturity (*Lyk.* 16. 6, 24. 1). 'Lykourgos wished by
educating them in this way to make the boys more resourceful in
getting supplies, and better at fighting' (*Lak. Pol.* 2. 7). Simplicity
and uniformity of dress are other aspects of their way of life
(Thuc. i. 6. 4). Social values, as well as military, were inculcated in
the ἀγωγή, and developed in the συσσίτιον, the 'mess',[21] to which
men of twenty years of age and over belonged, if they were
Spartiates and were admitted. For Plutarch the influence of
Lykourgos was directed to the character and self-fulfilment of
Sparta and the Spartans (*Lyk.* 31), not, as it was for the author
of *Lak. Pol.* (at 1. 1), to their power in Greece. Obedience

(ἄρχεσθαι), whether to law (νόμος), to elders, or to superiors, is regarded here as one of the chief values of the Spartan system.

3 διὸ καί φασιν ὑπὸ τοῦ Σιμωνίδου τὴν Σπάρτην προσηγορεῦσθαι δαμασίμβροτον, ὡς μάλιστα διὰ τῶν ἐθῶν τοὺς πολίτας τοῖς νόμοις πειθηνίους καὶ χειροήθεις ποιοῦσαν, ὥσπερ ἵππους εὐθὺς ἐξ ἀρχῆς δαμαζομένους.

The quotation from Simonides raises the question whether Plutarch relied on his own reading among the ancient authors or on extracts and collections already made by himself or others. With φασιν, 'they say', Plutarch refers to the reason given by commentators for Simonides' remark: it does not prove that he has not read the work from which he quotes. The quality and range of the references in the *Lives* indicate wide reading and study, even if he did not always have his own copy of his source beside him as he composed.[22]

The ornament does not disturb the chronology of the *Life*, for it names the city of Sparta as the scene, and characterizes it in a single word, δαμασίμβροτον, 'man-subduing'.[23] The quotation, a *chreia*,[24] introduces, from the evidence of the near-contemporary poet Simonides (c.556–468 BC), who knew Sparta as the system developed, literary validation for those features of the ἀγωγή selected by Plutarch for mention. However, he is still recording only what the poet chose to say, and, as a guest travelling around and commemorating his friends and their cities, Simonides, when in Sparta, would receive and repeat the formidable impressions of Spartan training that they wished the world to have, contributing to the Spartan myth; for some of their invincibility in war resulted from the reluctance of their enemies to risk challenging it. Aristotle may record the propaganda when he says that the Spartans were superior because they trained and their enemies did not (*Pol.* 1338[b]28), but the myth—and the training—ensured infrequent challenge (ch. 31. 3).

An ancient work formerly attributed to Plutarch, *De liberis educandis*, establishes, in general and for the Spartans, the principle of the effective formation of character by habituation and training in the ἀγωγή (*Mor.* 2 A–B, 3 A–B). Simonides' metaphor, δαμασίμβροτον, 'breaking' the Spartans, like horses, δαμαζομένους, suggests the violence of Poseidon, the god of earthquakes, δαμασίχθων, 'earth-subduing' (Bacchylides, 15. 19). The metaphors in the enclosed simile, πειθηνίους καὶ χειροήθεις, 'obedient to reins and accustomed to the hand', 'tamed', are milder. The laws to which the training in obedience, ἄρχεσθαι, is directed here seem to be the constitutional reforms attributed to Lykourgos (*Lyk.* 1; *Lak. Pol.* 1. 2). It is these provisions that won for the Spartans admiration in other parts of the Greek world and in other times for stable rule of law (εὐνομία: Thuc. i. 18. 1),²⁵ and Plutarch consistently commends the upholding of Lykourgan standards, blaming the decline of Sparta, which in the end marks Agesilaos' reign, on those who neglected them.

4 ταύτης ἀφίησιν ὁ νόμος τῆς ἀνάγκης τοὺς ἐπὶ βασιλείᾳ τρεφομένους παῖδας. Ἀγησιλάῳ δὲ καὶ τοῦθ' ὑπῆρξεν ἴδιον, ἐλθεῖν ἐπὶ τὸ ἄρχειν μὴ ἀπαίδευτον τοῦ ἄρχεσθαι.

The law referred to is not otherwise known. No doubt, when the system was being developed, kings, with their wealth, 'barbaric' funerals, and existing privileges, could ensure for themselves an institutionalized exceptionalism. The royal families may have asserted exclusive eligibility for the kingship by a separate upbringing for the king's heir, free from competitive assessment and supervision by their future subjects in the ἀγωγή: nor could one count on the reigning king's staying alive until his son had passed through.

The biographical sequence begun in the first section is resumed. Agesilaos' typical Spartan upbringing is significant, although it is an exaggeration to say that he was unique. Leonidas I, a younger son, also by a different wife (Hdt. v. 40. 2), became king (Hdt. vii. 204); and Kleombrotos, Agesilaos' co-king, succeeded his elder brother Agesipolis. The regal qualities which Agesilaos is assumed to have inherited are combined with the Spartan qualities he acquired in his upbringing. Agesilaos' name occurs three times in the chapter, with increasing prominence: as the last word in the first sentence, in the middle of the second sentence, and here with full prominence as the first word in its sentence, where his coming to power is implied. His reign is now established as the subject of the work.

Plutarch establishes the Spartan link of leadership, ἄρχειν, with obedience (ἄρχεσθαι). The repetition of a word in a different form is ornamental, but here Plutarch uses a combination frequently expressed (see note below, following §5). Both qualities were developed at Sparta in the ἀγωγή: obedience by the presence of supervisors at every stage (*Lak. Pol.* 2. 11), leadership by the competitive, hierarchic organization of boys, youths, and young men (cf. Xen. *Hell.* v. 4. 32, for παῖς, παιδίσκος, and ἡβῶν, the terms used of Sphodrias).

5 διὸ καὶ πολὺ τῶν βασιλέων εὐαρμοστότατον αὐτὸν τοῖς ὑπηκόοις παρέσχε, τῷ φύσει ἡγεμονικῷ καὶ βασιλικῷ προσκτησάμενος ἀπὸ τῆς ἀγωγῆς τὸ δημοτικὸν καὶ φιλάνθρωπον.

Plutarch further distinguishes Agesilaos among the kings as the most in harmony with his subjects because of a special combination of inherited and acquired qualities; to leadership and kingship, two natural qualities, are added two inculcated qualities, the public and private skills of getting on with others. Emphatically placed at the end of the chapter, these four qualities are programmatic for the analysis of Agesilaos' character that Plutarch offers. The essential Lykourgan simplicity, τὸ δημοτικόν, is also exemplified by the later Kleomenes III; it can develop into demagogy (ch. 5. 3, *Kl.* 13. 1–2). Most favourable is τὸ φιλάνθρωπον, although the word is used only once more, when Agesilaos fails to give any hint of future kindness (ch. 25. 6). This Greek virtue *par excellence*, inseparable from civilization, Hellenism, 'courtesy', is displayed in Agesilaos' dealings with important easterners (*Flam.* 5. 5, *Lys.* 27. 4; chs. 11–13, 39. 4–8, 40. 1–2).[26]

The author of *de Liberis educandis* gives an insight into a methodological concept important for the twofold basis of Plutarch's analysis of character, the one explicitly derived from nature and the other from training (*Mor.* 2 A–B). The two themes, Agesilaos' birth and upbringing, are brought together as the climax in the twofold catalogue of essential adult characteristics: a capacity for military and constitutional leadership inherited from his royal ancestors, and a capacity for social and cultural acceptability acquired in his education,[27] obedience, an acquired characteristic, having already been assigned to the training of the ἀγωγή (see above, §2). The element of inherited personality in leadership he would share with his royal ancestors, though it was also enhanced by training (ch. 20. 2); obedience makes him a royal 'exception'.

The distinction between inherited and formed characteristics—between nature (φύσις) and the rational or customary (λόγος, νόμος)—engaged attention in the fifth century and thereafter (Plato, *Ap.* 22 C; cf. *Chrm.* 157 E–159 A).²⁸ In the fourth century it was argued that man, being social by nature, survives only by accepting society's law (Lysias, *Epitaphios*, 17–19).²⁹ For the Stoics law becomes consistent with nature when these accord with divine reason.³⁰ For Plutarch, both elements in a man's character, his nature and his reason, can be developed by training. Competitiveness was inherited in Lysander's nature and was trained—excessively—in the ἀγωγή (*Lys.* 2. 2); and tolerance, πρᾳότης, which is a natural quality, is inculcated as in a young horse (*Lyk.* 30. 4, *Pomp.* 28. 5; see above, §3), or remains defective (*Cor.* 15. 3, 21. 1).³¹ The duality was resolved by regarding the inherited and acquired traits as embedded in the character of the developed individual to form his 'nature' (see below on Agesipolis, ch. 20. 7).³² In the perfectly educated man nature and reason are not in conflict, but complement each other.³³ They are in conflict in some *Lives*, and cause disaster (see below, chs. 7 and 28. 2; cf. *Pel.* 32. 6). For Plutarch, as for Aristotle, one reason for Sparta's decline was that the Spartan training did not provide a complete intellectual education, either for Agesilaos or for other Spartans (chs. 33. 3–4, 37. 11). Individual virtues, αἰδώς and σωφροσύνη, 'modesty and discretion', were inculcated (*Lak. Pol.* 2. 14, 3. 4),³⁴ but only to meet the state's requirements. Plutarch's moral essays suggest that what was missing was control for the dangerous limitations and excesses of a man's φύσις and ἦθος, 'disposition', which only the development of sound reasoning, λόγος, could ensure.³⁵

The rationale of ἄρχειν καὶ ἄρχεσθαι

The Lykourgan constitution sought to train Spartans to command and to obey, expressed by two parts of the same verb in Greek, 'to rule and to be ruled', ἄρχειν καὶ ἄρχεσθαι (ch. 20. 2), in both the military and the non-military aspects. Agesilaos displayed both qualities (*Mor.* 211 C; Xen. *Agesilaos*, 2. 16), as did the Dorian Herakleidai, the first kings of Argos, Messene, and Lakedaimon, who originated 'under oath the principle of reciprocal obligations of ruler and ruled' in Plato's *Laws* (684 A). The Spartan system, institutionalized in the ἀγωγή, brought up the citizens to obey authority and the laws, and to keep the laws unchanged (*Lyk.* 17,

13. 1, 29. 2, 5); Sparta won lasting admiration for the stable rule of law, εὐνομία (*Lyk.* 29. 6). The universal training of Spartiates ensured that the small community did not overlook any citizen source of strength in the struggle for survival; in the military command structure which impressed Thucydides, 'almost all were officers' (v. 66. 4).[36] Nevertheless, the supreme military command was held by the hereditary kings alone, most of whom had not been through the ἀγωγή and were without the formal training which Agesilaos had. But the efficiency of the army evidently did not depend heavily on the skills of the higher command;[37] one thinks of Plataia (Hdt. ix. 50–5, 71. 1). On the other hand, navarchs were not royal, apart from Latychidas II and Agesilaos (Hdt. viii. 131; ch. 10. 9).

The Spartan type of institutional training was not provided by other Greek *poleis* for their potential political and military leaders. Nor was institutional training in obedience provided except for citizens during military service, notably in Thebes and Boiotia (cf. Plato, *Prt.* 326 D for presumptions in the law as enforced by εὔθυναι, 'corrections'; Xen. *Hell.* vi. 5. 23, for general training of Boiotians in arms). Other political ideologies developed the idea of ruling and being ruled in other ways. Aristotle saw in it an element of necessity, or the law of nature, determined by status—king, statesman, husband, wife, child, slave—and corresponding to the virtues belonging to the two parts of the soul (*Pol.* 1259ᵃ37–ᵇ17, 1260ᵃ; cf. 1277ᵃ22–ᵇ16). He attributed these characteristics, as does Plutarch (*Mor.* 783 D, 816 F), to democracy,[38] in which citizens occupy the majority of offices and rule and are ruled in turn. The commander learns to lead soldiers through being taught obedience himself, with the laws as the main source of instruction (Xen. *Cyr.* i. 6. 20); the citizen is taught obedience by the good commander (*Lyk.* 30. 3; Plato, *Leg.* 942 C). Plato and Aristotle also recognized that the ruler learns to rule by being ruled, that the good commander and the good citizen must be capable of both, and that this is the essence of being the citizen of a *polis*-republic (*Leg.* 762 E, *Pol.* 1277ᵇ8–16, 1333ᵃ2–3; cf. *Mor.* 806 F).

In democracies such as Athens selection by lot for most offices spread participation widely, but election was retained for the public treasurers and the generalship (Arist. *Pol.* 1294ᵇ7–10, 1299ᵃ21). The benefits of full education, which counted for much in the emergence of politicians and generals, were confined to the families of men of landed property, οἱ καλοὶ κἀγαθοὶ ὀνομαζόμενοι, 'the men who are designated noble and good', who could afford it and whose background and administrative experience assisted in the development of natural and inherited qualities. Thus, as in oligarchies, the most powerful office-holders and leaders were generally elected from among this group—though the most 'democratic' of them were denied that status and designated 'demagogues' (Ps.-Arist. *Rh. Al.* 2. 14, 1424ᵃ17–20, 2. 18, 1424ᵃ40–ᵇ3).³⁹

The obedience of the individual is a continuing theme in the *Life*, but Plutarch's further concern is, at least implicitly, with the more general obedience of the Spartans collectively to the Lykourgan ideology itself and with the legitimacy of Agesilaos' regime within that ideology. The basis for the legitimacy and acceptance of rulers and the cohesion of the community varies among the Greek states. The early lawgivers, such as Solon in Athens, whether they were aristocrats, democrats, or anything else, had to deal with the clash of interests between rich and poor citizens, and with the consequent outbreaks of *stasis* in the struggle to maintain or increase their shares in what they saw as the good life. Their constitutional reforms were 'ideal' attempts to achieve stability and consensus in society by defining functional obligations and rights throughout the hierarchical structure of the state.⁴⁰ But political stability depended heavily on the majority's loyal acceptance of the ideology and continuity of ancestral power bases, indicated by the use of οἱ γνώριμοι, 'the notables', to distinguish them from ὁ δῆμος, 'the people' (Arist. *Pol.* 1291ᵇ18, 28–30).

The Spartans' obligation of loyalty to the city and their voluntary allegiance to the Lykourgan constitution were exceptional. Their lawgiver faced a different problem: the control of territory by a small élite after the annexation of Messenia. The Spartiates were to be 'political equals', οἱ ὅμοιοι, with common values and qualifications. They, or their record-keepers, believed that their constitution was sanctioned by the Delphic Oracle (πυθόχρηστοι νόμοι (*Lak. Pol.* 8. 5; cf. *Lyk.* 5. 3, Hdt. i. 65. 3), but in practice the Lykourgan regime was legitimated by the vital need for that united collectivism which would ensure the survival of their small community, surrounded by potential enemies, holding hegemony over subject peoples, and above all keep the helots down, if we are to believe Thucydides (iv. 80. 2). Acceptance of this system even meant that there was no need for formal political discussion or competition for privileged access to 'the good life' (*Lyk.* 6. 3, 25. 3), although these could occur informally in the συσσίτιον. Justice was defined as 'the interest of state' rather than in terms of individual rights: lawsuits were unknown (*Lyk.* 24. 4). At Athens, too, the need for stability and survival could at times override temporarily even 'the preservation of laws' (Euripides, *Supp.* 312–13; Thuc. iii. 47. 5; cf. ch. 30. 6), but 'the interest of state' was debated democratically.[41] Until the late fifth and early fourth centuries obedience to Lykourgan principles appears to have served the interests at least of the Spartiate citizens for whom they were instituted, and whose lives were dedicated to and depended on the solidarity first developed in the ἀγωγή.

Plutarch's interpretation of Sparta's problems during Agesilaos' reign is not based on changes in class or economic structures.[42] He shows that traditional adherence to Spartan ideology, designed for self-defence and survival, was exposed to danger by growing 'disobedience'—individual and collective disregard of two Lykourgan principles: competition among citizens and avoidance of imperialism. By courting friendship even with opponents Agesilaos undermined discipline, political equality, and loyalty to the state; by pursuing military hegemony he overstretched Sparta's resources.

2. Agesilaos' moral and physical qualities; his lameness[1]

In the first half of the chapter Plutarch turns back in time to set out the qualities developed in Agesilaos' character by the ἀγωγή. In the second half he assigns a prominent place, at the start of the *Life*, to the effect of Agesilaos' physical qualities on his early character.

Character in childhood

Whether and where details of Agesilaos' childhood adequate for purposes of biography were preserved, even for Xenophon, a contemporary enquirer, to discover, is a question which casts doubt on the accounts given. There would presumably be no documentary evidence at the time, and Xenophon would have to rely on the adult recollections of Agesilaos himself, and those of his family and friends who knew him as a child. The absence from the record of such anecdotal evidence indicates a contemporary lack of interest.[2] Plutarch, by recording the persistence of certain qualities into Agesilaos' old age, indicates that he is exploiting the final results of his character study. Xenophon's résumé at *Agesilaos*, 11 not only gives a convenient summary but asserts continuity from youth to old age (§§14–16). The traits that emerge from study of the mature actions of the man can be presented as already possessed by the child, and as the observations of Lysander at the time, filling gaps in the evidence with a continuous narrative, without fabricated material. The integration of traits in the ἀγωγή (§§2, 3 below) makes up the moral portrait of the boy, to be complemented by recording interrelated traits in the adult's developed character.[3]

Plutarch is presenting a model for imitation in his day and beyond (*Per.* 1–2, *Aem.–Tim.* 1. 1).[4] An attempt to portray a developing rather than a completely formed personality could blur the impact and confuse the reader. Plutarch was aware of the controversy among ancient thinkers about the possibility of changes in a man's personality or character during his lifetime, for he reports Theophrastos' indecision about it (*Per.* 38. 2). But childhood development was treated as a matter of character and intellect rather than of individual and personal selfhood,[5] and so as the concern of education. Adult behavioural variations are not so much a matter of development as responses to varying situations (see below, chs. 33. 2, 34. 6). For his purposes the biographer is predisposed 'to present a relatively static picture of a person's character' from childhood.[6] The formative influences recognized in the early chapters are reflected in Agesilaos' later struggles with features of his character (chs. 11. 6–10, 33. 2).

1 Ἐν δὲ ταῖς καλουμέναις ἀγέλαις τῶν συντρεφομένων παίδων Λύσανδρον ἔσχεν ἐραστήν, ἐκπλαγέντα μάλιστα τῷ κοσμίῳ τῆς φύσεως αὐτοῦ.[7]

As a boy, Agesilaos, though a younger son by a second marriage, was still a privileged person, a Heraklid and the son of a king, which would give him advantages in the competitive Spartan system. Thus he had a close association with another Heraklid,

Lysander, who, though perhaps suffering some temporary handicap of poverty and as a *mothax* (*Lys.* 2. 1; Phylarchos;[8] Aelian, *VH*
xii. 43),[9] underwent Spartan training and the citizenship (*Lys.* 2.
2), and rose to be appointed admiral in 407 (Xen. *Hell.* i. 5. 1).
Lysander in his early years showed, according to Plutarch (*Lys.* 2.
4), that he had acquired the tough and frugal characteristics traditionally admired by the Spartans. He was also clearly endowed
with special qualities of leadership, for he later became so powerful as to be thought to rival the kings (Xen. *Hell.* ii. 4. 29).

It was a general quality, 'the orderliness' of Agesilaos' nature,
which attracted Lysander and began the association (cf.
Agesipolis: ch. 20. 7; Pompey did not possess it: *Pomp.* 52. 3, 54.
5–6). In the rest of the first half of the chapter, by enlarging on the
idea of orderliness, Plutarch adds particular qualities to the
picture of the broad characteristics given in ch. 1. He presents
this orderliness as a balance between Agesilaos' competitive
excellences and his quieter or co-operative excellences,[10] and
increases the sense of authenticity here by using indirect characterization (see Introd., B.1). So it is the impact of Agesilaos'
personality on Lysander which provides the means to integrate
into the *Life* a description of his character at the boyhood stage, as
an explanation (γάρ, 'for') of that impact, thus creating an artistic
illusion that evidence is continually available at each stage.

On the relationship between ἐραστής and ἐρώμενος[11]

It is not known whether the senior partner (ἐραστής) chose the boy
or was chosen for him.[12] Pederastic relationships, which Plutarch
delays to the age of 12 (*Lyk.* 16. 6, 17. 1), were intended to
contribute to excellence (*Lak. Pol.* 2. 12–14). The ἐραστής[13] was a
young man above the age of 20 (ἡβῶν) and a member of a συσσίτιον
(if Plutarch's εὐδόκιμος, 'approved', entails the completion of the
ἀγωγή). There is no evidence—or reason to think—that the
ἐραστής courted a boy, his παιδικά (or ἐρώμενος), from his own
troop (ἀγέλη) but he could perhaps earlier be given some supervisory association with him.[14] It is possible that a youth was
normally introduced into the συσσίτιον of his 'senior',[15] having
attended occasionally as a 'junior'.[16] Political motivation for the
manipulation of such connections could occur in the choice of
either the senior or the junior partner if élite families wished to

exploit the institutionalized pederastic system[17] to their advantage (cf. the Sphodrias affair, ch. 25 below). If the connection with Lysander was planned, Agesilaos would perhaps go to his ἀγέλη, and Lysander to the συσσίτιον which Agesilaos, as half-brother of Agis II, would automatically be joining on attaining majority—the Royal Mess. Agesilaos' family background would ensure entry into élite circles, and though it did not guarantee that he would be leader of his group, it would mean that any qualities of leadership he displayed would be recognized, encouraged, and developed.

Because of the inevitable distance between the observer and the phenomenon, Greek pederasty, like the Spartan way of life, has lent itself to speculative interpretation of the various kinds of evidence. Not all of this is wholly compelling, since there was no ancient investigation of the subject that can be called thorough and objective. Writers often reflected traditional disparagement of remote or rival cities and peoples, such as Boiotians (Plato, *Smp.* 182 B; *Lak. Pol.* 2. 12), and this persisted into the second century AD in the fable of Babrius (*Fables*, 15), who disparaged a Theban as less eloquent than an Athenian despite his intelligence. Aristophanes' plays and Greek painted vases were often explicit on the subject, but as works of art they must be admitted to be distanced from life. They were intended to please, making the audience laugh or satisfying the owner's interest. References in legal and political speeches were intended to influence an audience or move a jury, rather than deal objectively with the truth. Plato's idea of a temporary pederastic love or desire (ἔρως) served to illuminate an early stage in the philosopher's education. Especially in *Symposium*, he presented the ideal of an emotional urge which could not be explained by reference to physical consummation, but was an ongoing, infinite dedication; and the attraction of Socrates to the handsome Charmides is not introduced for its own sake but to start the philosophical argument about whether physical excellence indicates mental excellence (*Chrm.* 155 D, 157 D–8 C). 'Any relationship between an older and a younger male in a Greek community had an educational dimension',[18] and especially in a military context there is an ideal element which transcends the physical.[19] The relationships encouraged in Sparta were open to possible fulfilment in other, even physical ways, though the comparative ethnographic evidence illuminates the origins rather than the practice of *rites de passage* in the Classical ἀγωγή. Their importance at Sparta was that they created political connections[20] and were conducive to hero-worship, acts of heroism, *esprit de corps*, and self-sacrificing devotion to the good of the state; and that this devotion was expected, implicitly, without any distractions from the collective purpose. The application to Spartans of the words εἰσπνεῖν (e.g. Aelian, *VH* iii. 12) and εἴσπνηλος (e.g. Theocr. 12. 13) points to the 'inspirational' function of their associations.[21] The subject recurs at chs. 13 and 20.

2 φιλονικότατος γὰρ ὢν καὶ θυμοειδέστατος ἐν τοῖς νέοις καὶ πάντα πρωτεύειν βουλόμενος, καὶ τὸ σφοδρὸν ἔχων καὶ ῥαγδαῖον ἄμαχον καὶ δυσεκβίαστον, . . .

This list of Agesilaos' traits corresponds with the two pairs of key qualities at the end of ch. 1: competitive and co-operative virtues. The five practical virtues of the man of action are part of the natural endowment of his royal birth. The basic quality, 'competitive', appears in the manuscripts of Plutarch and other authors in the spellings φιλονικ- and φιλονεικ- indifferently. He uses the word twelve times in *Agesilaos*: signifying desire for achievement, pre-eminence or victory at chs. 2. 2, 5. 7, 7. 4, 11. 6, 18. 4, 23. 11, 26. 6, 33. 2, 34. 2, *Comp.* 1. 3; in association with διαφορά, strife, at chs. 4. 4 and 5. 5. It is advantageous four times, and potentially harmful eight times; it is never said to be intrinsically evil, but it needs to be controlled, for the spirit of rivalry and competition always contains an element of strife. In Plutarch's philosophical discussion at ch. 5. 5, the instituted φιλόνικον, which Agesilaos removed by his abuse of friendship, matches by analogy the νεῖκος καὶ ἔρις, strife and rivalry, of the cosmic elements; and in the pejorative contexts the ever-present element of strife is taken to excess. When it is clustered with ὀργή, ἔριδες or δύσερις, and θυμός (chs. 18. 4, 26. 6, *Pomp.* 35. 2, 67. 9, *Phil.* 17. 4; cf. *Lyk.* 16. 5), the link with νεῖκος may be close, but this does not necessitate the spelling φιλονεικία, stressing 'contentiousness for its own sake': that is nowhere the required meaning here.

Two words denoting closely neighbouring qualities (πάθη), φιλονικία and φιλοτιμία, 'desire for achievement', are frequently found together (see below, §3, and chs. 5. 5, 7. 4, 23. 11, 33. 2; cf. *Phil.* 3. 1, *Phil.–Flam.* 1. 4). Plato, complaining that both, success and reputation, satisfy not reason but τὸ θυμοειδές, in its two senses, makes the instrument of the latter—the desire for honour—φθόνος, envy, and that of the former—the desire for victory—βία, violence (*Resp.* 586 C 9–D 1; cf. 581 A 10–B 2, 582 E, and see below, ch. 7. 4). The connection with νίκη rather than νεῖκος is thought primary, for νεῖκος, being an *es*-stem (cf. νεικέω, fut. νεικέσω), would have yielded *φιλονεικής and *φιλονείκεια.²² Lykourgos introduced rivalry amongst Spartan youth as at *Lak. Pol.* 4. 2 (cf. the 'battles and rivalries' instituted at *Lyk.* 16. 5, and ὑπέκκαυμα τῆς ἀρετῆς, 'the incentive to virtue', at ch. 5. 5); the associated strife, ἔρις περὶ ἀρετῆς, 'competition in excellence', was instituted to inculcate 'manliness', ἀνδραγαθία, not divisiveness for its own sake. Here, too, consistency with what follows suggests the positive 'desire to win' rather than 'strife for its own sake'; hence φιλονικότατος, not φιλονεικότατος, confirmed by the link with πρωτεύειν, and consistent with θυμοειδέστατος, 'high-spirited', opposite of ἄθυμος, rather than 'hot-tempered', opposite of πρᾷος (see below). 'Striving for victory' is relevant in the political struggles between kings and ephors (ch. 4. 4), and even in the extreme case of Agesilaos' attitude to Thebes (ch. 26. 6). The sense is always to be judged by the context, for both meanings were felt by Plutarch: he admired true Spartan qualities, but found them abused.

'The wish to take the lead' among the boys of his own age (cf. *Lyk.* 16. 5) also characterized Kyros of Persia (Hdt. i. 114–15), and ῥαγδαῖος is used of a soldier with the careless abandon of a man in poor health, for whom 'valour had a high value, life a low value' (*Pel.* 1. 2; cf. below, §3). A storm described as ῥαγδαῖος can incapacitate an army (*Tim.* 28. 4, *Alex.* 60. 4, *Dion*, 25. 6; cf. Arist. *Mete.* 349ᵃ6), and a man so described is exceptionally violent (*Tim.* 3. 6, *Alex.* 4. 8).

. . . εὐπειθείᾳ πάλιν αὖ καὶ πρᾳότητι τοιοῦτος ἦν οἷος φόβῳ μηδέν, αἰσχύνῃ δὲ πάντα ποιεῖν τὰ προσταττόμενα, καὶ τοῖς ψόγοις ἀλγύνεσθαι μᾶλλον ἢ τοὺς πόνους βαρύνεσθαι.

The six co-operative, quiet virtues correspond to the second pair of key qualities, those acquired in training. It is 'paradoxical' (πάλιν, 'on the other hand') that these should now be found in combination with the earlier qualities, but they needed to be inculcated and developed in the traditional activities of the ἀγωγή. 'Obedience' and 'gentleness' correspond to being 'rendered tame' like the young horse in ch. 1, and with 'the pained or distressed response to criticism' and 'a willingness to accept hardship' which distinguish Agesilaos from other Spartan kings. Plutarch details separately in these two lists the distinctive qualities to be desired respectively in the character of a king as general and as constitutional monarch: on the one hand the inherited, competitive virtues, the general's fighting efficiency, on the other hand the acquired, co-operative virtues, ensuring popularity through the avoidance of tyranny in the king's rule.

The quality of πρᾳότης features commonly among Plutarch's subjects (*Marc.* 3. 4), in a variety of senses,[23] not always in their own interests (*Agis*, 20. 4, 21. 3; cf. *Kl.* 1. 3). Essentially it is a deliberate composure or self-restraint (see Introd., C.1(c)(ii), (vi); *Mor.* 37 A, 458 C): Xenophon claims that Agesilaos was πρᾷος when enjoying good fortune, εὐτυχῶν (*Agesilaos*, 11. 2). Artaxerxes, the future Persian king, endured his parents' hostility to his bride (*Art.* 2–3, cf. 19). Lykourgos was πρᾷος, like the early king Charilaos (*Lyk.* 5. 5, 11. 3, 28. 6), and Sparta, taught by a poet Thales, taught others the well-ordered life, using the art of horsemanship, πρᾷον ἵππον παρασχεῖν (*Lyk.* 4. 1, 30. 4). Perikles was πρᾷος through philosophy (*Per.* 5. 1), while Agesipolis was φύσει πρᾷος (ch. 20. 7; cf. *Lyk.* 5.5), perhaps through complete habituation (*Mor.* 2 A–B, 3 A–B).[24] Agesilaos, faced with abuse in Egypt, exercises it successfully (ch. 39. 2). Here αἰσχύνη provides another constraint on Agesilaos' behaviour, as he fears loss of face (cf. chs. 11. 5, 24. 3, 38. 6); he must even honour his enemies when they succeed (ch. 5. 2).

3 τὴν δὲ τοῦ σκέλους πήρωσιν ἤ θ' ὥρα τοῦ σώματος ἀνθοῦντος ἐπέκρυπτε, καὶ τὸ ῥᾳδίως φέρειν καὶ ἱλαρῶς τὸ τοιοῦτο, παίζοντα καὶ σκώπτοντα πρῶτον ἑαυτόν, οὐ μικρὸν ἦν ἐπανόρθωμα τοῦ πάθους . . .

Plutarch, having described how Agesilaos was equipped for external relationships, completes the picture with Agesilaos' more private world, his mastery of the problems presented by his own person. Later (ch. 11. 6) Agesilaos' problem will be to control his emotions. The initial phrase introduces Agesilaos' physical disability, his lameness. In the circumstances, if the testing and exposure of infants took place in accordance with tradition, one may suppose it was not congenital or developed later as the limbs grew, but an adventurous youth, such as Agesilaos appears to have been, might easily sustain that sort of injury as the result of a boyhood accident.²⁵ Plutarch uses the lameness to reveal Agesilaos' inner spirit. The external qualities that enabled him to surmount his handicap are followed by the advantages which accrued to his character because of the handicap, advantages which others did not share. The perspective approaches that of the 'personality-viewpoint'²⁶ in which the author attempts to penetrate 'beneath the skin'. Plutarch does not suggest any self-doubt that might justify a study of psychological abnormality in Agesilaos,²⁷ but indicates the positive response of a powerful personality, which explains his popularity with ordinary people.

Plutarch's *Lives* generally do not refer to physical appearance: of those that do, most focus on defects and peculiarities to supplement disagreeable characteristics.²⁸ Here the defect is relevant to Agesilaos' eligibility as king (see below, chs. 3–4), not to any revulsion, as is made clear by the reference to 'his fine physical condition' which obscured the disability and helps to explain how he could match his fellows. Plutarch now concentrates on more private reactions, though these also determine external relationships, man to man. 'Patience' and 'cheerfulness' enabled Agesilaos not only to bear the affliction but largely to overcome the difficulty. Confirmed by Xenophon, the cheerfulness, ἱλαρότης, the opposite of σκυθρωπός, 'gloomy' (*Mem.* ii. 7. 12), and joined with 'optimistic and genial', εὔελπις καὶ εὔθυμος, made him good company, but it was an assumed appearance when he was fearful, φοβούμενος (*Agesilaos*, 8. 2, 11. 2), and somewhat subdued. Plutarch has the subdued sense: with πράως as the Spartans go into battle (*Lyk.* 22. 3); φιλανθρώπως, as Kleomenes receives petitioners 'courteously' (*Kl.* 13. 2); ἀλύπως, of enduring exile 'without pain' (*Kl.* 38. 4); and ἐπηρμένη, of Pompey's army 'elated' after success (*Pomp.* 8. 3). Here it takes two forms, 'playful actions' and 'verbal jesting'. Rough humour seems natural among groups of men, and both perpetrated and suffered stimulates comradeship, but the strict discipline of the *syssition* could have suppressed it as unruly; Lykourgos idealized and formalized it; the cult of laughter in Spartan society was institutionalized²⁹ as part of the training of the ἀγωγή and συσσίτιον, though Plutarch sees it as an emollient for the harsh discipline (*Lyk.* 25. 2). It seems to have had a therapeutic effect on Agesilaos, and to have strengthened his resistance to teasing.

. . . ἀλλὰ καὶ τὴν φιλοτιμίαν ἐκδηλοτέραν ἐποίει, πρὸς μηδένα πόνον
μηδὲ πρᾶξιν ἀπαγορεύοντος αὐτοῦ διὰ τὴν χωλότητα,

At this point Plutarch turns from the negative surmounting of
problems to the compensatory benefits for Agesilaos' character.
The disability induced a positive development[30] of his innate
φιλοτιμία.[31] The noun is often translated as 'ambition' (Xen. *Hell.*
iv. 1. 37; cf. ch. 12. 8), but this is generally inadequate to cover
Plutarch's several uses of this important word in *Agesilaos* and
other Spartan *Lives*. Excess and lack of φιλοτιμία are both
unacceptable (ch. 8. 6, *Lys.* 23. 5, *Agis*, 2. 2; cf. *Lyk.* 18. 2, *Lys.*
2. 2, *Kl.* 3. 1, Xen. *Hell.* vi. 4. 11). The various clusters it is
used in sometimes clarify its meaning but not always: cf. the
pejorative φιλοτιμία καὶ φιλαρχία (*Pomp.* 30. 8) with the approved
τὸ φιλότιμον καὶ φιλόνικον (ch. 5); and ὑπὸ τοῦ θυμοειδοῦς κρατοῦντος,
φιλονικίαι καὶ φιλοτιμίαι (Plato, *Resp.* 548 c) with §§2–3 here. In
Athens, Plato disapproves (*Resp.* 336 c 3, 347 b 2) and sometimes
Xenophon (*Mem.* i. 2. 14, ii. 3. 16), who, however, approves at
Sparta (*Hell.* i. 6. 5, *Agesilaos*, 10. 4); there, for Plato, it is unjust,
and the mark of timocracy (545 a 3, b 5), the target of his critique
(547–55).

In Spartans Plutarch condemns only its excess (ὑπερβάλλων) and
abuse (ch. 8. 6; cf. *Lys.* 23. 2, *Agis*, 2. 1, 2. 5). For him it was
deliberately introduced by Lykourgos to unite the citizens with
the fatherland, ὅλους εἶναι τῆς πατρίδος (*Lyk.* 25. 3); women
inspired the youth and were inspired (*Lyk.* 14. 3–4, *Agis* 7. 1–2).
Whereas the translation 'ambition' is appropriate in Xenophon
and Plato, where aims are criticized, in Plutarch's Sparta 'desire
for attainment' represents the spirit of the competitive regimen of
Lykourgos, who was perhaps associated with Iphitos in restoring
the Olympic Games (*Lyk.* 1. 1; but see Paus. v. 4. 5–6, 20. 1). Its
deeper significance can be appreciated in the context of the ἀγωγή.
The necessity to prove worth (ἀνδραγαθία) by competitive achievement, through endurance and enterprise, was an essential feature
of the ritual of supervision and assessment in the strenuous training characterized in ch. 1 (*Lyk.* 14. 3, *Agis*, 16. 3; Xen. *Lak. Pol.* 4.
2, *Agesilaos*, 9. 6, 10. 2).[32]

While acts of heroism and supreme effort were not exclusive to
Spartans, it was rare that individual material self-enrichment was
so strongly discouraged as it was traditionally at Sparta, where

service to the best interests of the state was substituted as the ideal (*Lak. Pol.* 4. 5). There is in the tradition no sign that the ambition of Lysander and Agesilaos contained any desire for personal wealth (*Lys.* 30. 5; Xen. *Agesilaos*, 8. 6–7). Desire for attainment, on the other hand, so strongly inculcated in the ἀγωγή, continued to be manifested in adult life in the paramount importance for a Spartan of being known to have acted in Sparta's best interest (cf. ch. 23). Plutarch recognizes, and conveys, the special nature of Spartan φιλοτιμία, notably in *Agesilaos* and *Lysander* (see Introd., C.1(*c*)(iii), E.1, E.3(*a*), and Xen. *Agesilaos*, 7. 1 for Agesilaos' refusal to make his disability an excuse for non-participation; cf. *Mem.* iii. 2. 3). He also recognized the strength of psychosomatic interactions in *Pelopidas*, where a physical change induces a corresponding change of spirit (*Pel.* 1. 3; see above, §2).

The last words of this section round it off in a ring structure by returning to the lameness which introduced it. This reference provides Plutarch with a bridge to the next topic, Agesilaos' refusal to permit a portrait to be made.

4 τῆς δὲ μορφῆς εἰκόνα μὲν οὐκ ἔχομεν (αὐτὸς γὰρ οὐκ ἠθέλησεν, ἀλλὰ καὶ ἀποθνήσκων ἀπεῖπε μήτε πλαστὰν μήτε μιμηλάν τινα ποιήσασθαι τοῦ σώματος εἰκόνα), . . .

By Suetonius' time descriptions of physical appearance had become a regular part of biography, but in Agesilaos' day the faithful representation of the features in statues and paintings was 'a thing of the future'.[33] Here the absence of a likeness makes description impossible, but Plutarch clearly did not wish to use Agesilaos' 'physical appearance as a guide to his moral personality'.[34] A representation in a portrait of, for example, πρᾳότης, '*deliberately displayed* composure', could be misleading. He shows, rather, the effect of Agesilaos' physical condition on the development of his character. The context links Agesilaos' refusal of a statue with a reluctance to have his disability portrayed, so that while he overcame the physical effects of his handicap, it may appear that he felt the mental effect more deeply; but statues need not be full-length. Plutarch reinterprets Xenophon, who suggests dislike of ostentation, and preference for spiritual memorials (*Agesilaos*, 11. 7). The display of any statue would be incompatible with Agesilaos' simple lifestyle and his φιλοτιμία: refusal would be in sympathy with the Roman Agricola, who dismissed the value of material images because of their lack of durability (Tacitus, *Agricola*, 46).

That a portrait of some kind was made of a king who died in war is suggested by Herodotos (vi. 58. 3). Agesilaos died abroad but not in war; his body was brought home to Sparta (ch. 40). A portrait statue of Lysander was set up in the treasury of the Akanthians at Delphi (*Lys.* 1); he was portrayed among Spartan dedications as being crowned by Poseidon after his victory over Athens at Aigospotamoi (Paus. x. 9. 7–8) even in his lifetime; and he was represented elsewhere as part of his deification and heroization. Lysander's growing personal constituency first gave rise to annoyance among his peers (*Lys.* 19. 1) and then to envy and fear among the kings (*Lys.* 21. 3)—Xenophon perhaps wrongly identifies only envy at *Hell.* ii. 4. 29—as they contemplated the projected Athenian settlement. The sudden transfer to Pausanias of the support of the majority of ephors which this caused, although Lysander had only recently been sent out as harmost, may have been a lesson which led Agesilaos to avoid such forms of ostentation throughout his career, as Plutarch continually points out.

. . . λέγεται δὲ μικρός τε γενέσθαι καὶ τὴν ὄψιν εὐκαταφρόνητος·

Plutarch uses an anonymous report of Agesilaos' small and unprepossessing stature, originating, perhaps, from Egypt, where reaction to his appearance gives only a distorted reflection of his character (ch. 36. 9). The antithesis between favourable and unfavourable impressions may sometimes, as in Homer, lead to a compliment: Τυδεύς τοι μικρὸς μὲν ἔην δέμας ἀλλὰ μαχητής (*Il.* v. 801). Here Plutarch interrupts the list of eulogistic descriptions with an adverse comment, perhaps to establish a balance before he resumes the positive description. Other qualities are attributed without naming any authority, but οὐκ ἔχομεν (§4 above) raises a doubt which needs to be removed; if λέγεται hides a known source here, Plutarch is being protective. The use of indirect characterization also allows him to remain uncommitted (cf. Nepos, *Agesilaus*, 8. 1).

5 ἡ δ' ἱλαρότης καὶ τὸ εὔθυμον ἐν ἅπαντι καιρῷ καὶ παιγνιῶδες, ἀχθεινὸν δὲ καὶ τραχὺ μηδέποτε μήτε φωνῇ μήτε ὄψει, τῶν καλῶν καὶ ὡραίων ἐρασμιώτερον αὐτὸν ἄχρι γήρως παρεῖχεν.

Plutarch again looks back in a ring structure to the characteristic good humour he mentioned earlier (§3); ἱλαρότης, 'jollity', recalls the adverb ἱλαρῶς, and παιγνιῶδες, 'playfulness', recalls the participle παίζοντα. These were used to mark the quality that enabled Agesilaos to counteract the physical problems of his disability. The same two qualities, reinforced by 'cheerfulness', τὸ εὔθυμον, are now instrumental in determining his reaction to the social disadvantages of his appearance. Plutarch ends the list with Agesilaos' avoidance of the irritability that might have been associated with the strains of his physical difficulties. These qualities assisted in the strengthening of his character: Plutarch now extends their relevance, in further ring structures, to the social factors introduced in the key words at the end of the first chapter, and to the topic introduced at the start of this chapter with the key word ἐραστήν, which has the same root as ἐρασμιώτερον, used here. All these qualities, given social significance, establish Agesilaos as a popular companion. That this popularity remained with him until old age suggests the larger context of a lifetime for all the traits of character attributed to him in his youth, and furnishes another contrast with Lysander, in his later years a man of 'atrabilious temperament' (*Lys.* 2. 3, citing Ps.–Arist. *Pr.* xxx. 1).

It may seem strange that such a harmonious and affable personality should emerge from the harsh discipline of the ἀγωγή, which inculcated the qualities of φιλοτιμία and φιλονικία (§§2–3) and which Agesilaos shared with Lysander (*Lys.* 2). Both men display these qualities and indifference to personal wealth in their service to Spartan interests. They also display divergent qualities, and would respond differently to the experience of the ἀγωγή; for while Agesilaos' nature is described as πρᾷος and κόσμιος (chs. 2, 39), Lysander's is severe, arrogant, and harsh (*Lys.* 19. 1, 22. 1, 28. 1), and while Lysander may have been a *mothax*, Agesilaos was certainly the son of the king; cf. Introd., E.3(*d*). Plutarch would perhaps attribute the difference to three factors which distinguish Agesilaos: a kindly nature; its enhancement by a cheerful response to disability, avoiding by anticipation possible embarrassment; and exploitation to his own advantage of the traditional humorous practices in the συσσίτια.

6 ὡς δὲ Θεόφραστος ἱστορεῖ, τὸν Ἀρχίδαμον ἐζημίωσαν οἱ ἔφοροι

γήμαντα γυναῖκα μικράν· Οὐ γὰρ βασιλεῖς, ἔφασαν, ἁμῖν, ἀλλὰ
βασιλείδια γεννάσει.

Theophrastos' anecdote reverts to the description of Agesilaos'
unimposing appearance (§4; cf. *Mor.* 1 D). Plutarch now reinforces
the earlier unfavourable judgement, but because it occurs in a
quotation the impression of impartiality is not impaired. Neither
author associates himself directly with the judgement, but the
ephors seem to believe that physical appearance does indicate
character. The story cannot refer to Agesilaos, who was not heir
to the throne (ch. 1 above). If Plutarch was aware of this dis-
crepancy, the transfer to Agesilaos fills a gap in the portrait with a
feature that he will have believed true.[35] The ephors were wrong.
Agesilaos was no βασιλείδιον, 'petty prince': his lack of height, like
his lameness, served, in Plutarch's estimation, greatly to enhance
his character and hence his standing among his peers; but the
feature needed evidential support.

3. Alkibiades at Sparta: the disputed succession[1]

The first major historical event in the *Life* is the accession of
Agesilaos as king, of which the ancient authorities give accounts
differing in important details.[2] Xenophon (*Agesilaos*, 1. 5) is
wholly eulogistic, recording an unexplained dispute over the
succession, decided on grounds of birth and merit (καὶ τῷ γένει καὶ
τῇ ἀρετῇ), perhaps 'but by merit too': he is most discreet here, and
alludes only in passing to the question of legitimacy. In his other
account (*Hell.* iii. 3. 1–4), the city rejected Latychidas, contending
as heir apparent, as of illegitimate birth, and chose Agesilaos as
king. Xenophon portrays a legitimate accession. Nepos (*Agesilaus*,
1. 2–5) and Pausanias (iii. 8. 7–10) suggest otherwise, implying
that Latychidas *was* the true heir of Agis. Plutarch (*Alk.* 23. 7–8)
presents Alkibiades' adultery with Agis' wife Timaia as a fact
reported to the king; Agis calculated that he could not be the
father, disowned the child, and thus disqualified him from the
kingship. Plutarch further reports (*Lys.* 22. 3–6) that Agis, having
disowned 'his reputed son', acknowledged him on his deathbed;

but although many Spartans inclined towards him, Lysander championed Agesilaos, and he became king.

Here Plutarch's account seems to indicate that Latychidas was Alkibiades' son and not the rightful successor to Agis. Thus the scene is set for the start of the new reign with the king and the citizens in harmony, as established above (ch. 1. 5); for, by a majority decision, the Spartans obtained political advantages yet maintained their traditional conservatism, observing to their own satisfaction, for the moment, certain relevant religious and other sanctions. The *Life* proceeds with the Spartans accepting the legitimacy of the accession of the king of their choice. Plutarch presents the Alkibiades connection at this point without rejecting it, but at *Comp.* 1. 2 (cf. ch. 30. 1) he accuses Agesilaos of wrongfully seizing the kingship. He does not pass judgement here, either because that is the obvious way to tell the story with some drama, or so that the reader approaches the sequel in possession of the same background of scandal as the Spartan 'judges'—the citizens (see below, §5)—may have had.

Two problems are discernible; the historical one of manipulation of the constitution at the time of the death of Agis, and the historiographical one of accretion of 'historical' evidence.

1 Βασιλεύοντος δ' οὖν Ἄγιδος ἧκεν Ἀλκιβιάδης ἐκ Σικελίας φυγὰς εἰς Λακεδαίμονα· καὶ χρόνον οὔπω πολὺν ἐν τῇ πόλει διάγων, αἰτίαν ἔσχε τῇ γυναικὶ τοῦ βασιλέως, Τιμαίᾳ, συνεῖναι.

Agis' reign began in 427 when Agesilaos was 17 or 18 years old. Alkibiades went to Sparta on the way back from Sicily in the twelfth year of Agis' reign, when Agesilaos was nearly 30, but the relevance of his presence is not yet made explicit. Thucydides mentioned the visit (vi. 88. 9), though not this episode.[3] The adultery of Alkibiades with Timaia—Plutarch again names the woman—is reported briefly at *Lys.* 22. 3. It is reported more fully, and initially as fact, at *Alk.* 23. 7–8, where Plutarch contrasts Alkibiades' wish for his descendants to be kings of Sparta with his assumed Lykourgan manners and support for Sparta (*Alk.* 23. 6). Now Plutarch presents the charge directly, giving it independent status; but even if the report is true, the charge is not evidence.

At *Alk.* 23. 7 Plutarch notes the further detail that Agis was away on campaign at the time, though that puts in doubt his presence at Sparta in the earthquake (*Alk.* 23. 8). Study of

Alkibiades' movements from Thourioi has suggested that he was at Dekeleia with Agis.[4] The charge remains unsubstantiated even if Alkibiades was in Sparta at that time.

καὶ τὸ γεννηθὲν ἐξ αὐτῆς παιδάριον οὐκ ἔφη γινώσκειν ὁ Ἆγις, ἀλλ' ἐξ Ἀλκιβιάδου γεγονέναι.

Plutarch presents this denial, too, as a fact, but still indicates no link with Agesilaos' affairs. Pausanias indicates doubt by setting Agis' refusal to acknowledge Latychidas alongside Ariston's 'rash' rejection and later acknowledgement of Demaratos (iii. 8. 7; cf. Hdt. vi. 63. 2). His support for Latychidas is clear, for he says that 'malicious providence' brought Agis' attitude to official attention, and that remorse made him acknowledge his son before he died. Pausanias earlier judged that Demaratos was unjustly deposed after his enemies had tampered with the oracle at Delphi (iii. 4. 3–5; cf. Hdt. vi. 65. 3–66. 3).

2 τοῦτο δ' οὐ πάνυ δυσκόλως τὴν Τιμαίαν ἐνεγκεῖν φησι Δοῦρις, ἀλλὰ καὶ ψιθυρίζουσαν οἴκοι πρὸς τὰς εἱλωτίδας Ἀλκιβιάδην τὸ παιδίον, οὐ Λεωτυχίδην, καλεῖν· καὶ μέντοι καὶ τὸν Ἀλκιβιάδην αὐτὸν οὐ πρὸς ὕβριν φάναι τῇ Τιμαίᾳ πλησιάζειν, ἀλλὰ φιλοτιμούμενον βασιλεύεσθαι Σπαρτιάτας ὑπὸ τῶν ἐξ ἑαυτοῦ γεγονότων.

Plutarch here changes to an indirect report, in which Agis' wife seems to have confirmed her husband's suspicion that Alkibiades was the father of this child, who is identified by his name, Latychidas, only at the end of the sentence. Douris of Samos (Introd., F.3(j)–(k)) should not be assumed to be the source for the statements made so far, though his account may have provided much of the detail, despite the delayed mention of his name. There is no known source earlier than Douris linking Alkibiades' visit with Agis' wife, but Plutarch was capable of a rational attitude to his evidence (Per. 28. 1 and 3). However, he may not always have wished to exercise his critical faculty explicitly; moreover, since Douris himself is said to have claimed descent from Alkibiades (Alk. 32. 2), his testimony here is not above suspicion. Douris would, by his claim, wish to enhance both his ancestor's reputation and his own aristocratic descent, to favour his exclusive birthright to the Samian tyranny. Regarding the claim of ancestry, it is thought plausible that Alkibiades, given what is known of him, fathered a child in Samos.[5]

According to Thucydides, Alkibiadas was a Lakonian name currently in use at Sparta;[6] it could have been used as a complimentary term of affection by a mother. Apart from the possibility that Douris made the story up, in which case it proves nothing, if the story he heard really circulated in Sparta at or before Agis' death, the evidence is further suspect, for what took place οἴκοι, 'in the house' of the king, including at the more important time of the liaison, was private and unlikely to be reported outside with any authenticity. Helot women were vulnerable, making the source unreliable. Most helots, the Spartans' collectively owned, unfree, Greek labourers, worked on the land, but some did domestic work, perhaps the most privileged—and loyal—in a royal household, as here (see below on ch. 5. 4).[7] The story reaching Douris may, of course, have been made up by the helot women—perhaps under pressure, or for some advantage to themselves—or by Agesilaos' supporters: the maids themselves would hardly be present at the δίκη of ch. 3. 7. However, if Timaia did use the name Alkibiadas as the women are reported to have said, and it was not a pet-name to be ignored, but a fond remembrance of someone, then it could indicate that Latychidas was this Alkibiades' son: but Timaia was unwise if she risked allowing the connection to be made, supposing the timing was right, and relied on respect for privacy. There is no other evidence for Latychidas' age at the death of Agis: other disputed successions were not limited to young men (see Political Aspects below), but unless the story was a gross anachronism, he was still a youth, born after Agis became king. If only Thucydides were not so austere, and Xenophon so biased, their silence might have been conclusive; but there are other factors to be considered below.

At *Alk.* 23. 7–8 Plutarch mentions only friends and attendants, and does not attribute the story to Douris; but he says that Timaia was greatly enamoured and that Agis had many informants—and believed them and the evidence of the earthquake (cf. below, §9). This strengthens Plutarch's evidence for Alkibiades' wanton character: and he confirms the evidence immediately when he attributes the failure of Latychidas' case to Agis' refusal to acknowledge him. There is selection and exclusion to illustrate a point here in *Alkibiades*, but no invention.[8]

3 διὰ ταῦτα μὲν δὴ τῆς Λακεδαίμονος ὁ Ἀλκιβιάδης ὑπεξῆλθε φοβηθεὶς τὸν Ἆγιν.

Thucydides, who records no scandal at viii. 12, reports that Alkibiades departed from Sparta because of a quarrel with Agis, at the time when the Spartans were divided over a proposed expedition to Asia Minor to be led by Chalkideus. Because of this quarrel he suggested to the ephor Endios, a *xenos*, friend of his family, whose father was also named Alkibiades (Thuc. viii. 6. 3),[9] that Agis should be deprived of the credit for the fruits of the expedition. All the ephors were persuaded, and it was as commander of this expedition, with a reduced fleet, that Alkibiades left Sparta. If the quarrel was about the expedition, it will have concerned both Alkibiades and others. Thucydides does not say, but Plutarch, with his sources, may have taken him to be linking the quarrel to the scandal (Thuc. viii. 11–12).

ὁ δὲ παῖς τὸν μὲν ἄλλον χρόνον ὕποπτος ἦν τῷ Ἄγιδι καὶ γνησίου τιμὴν οὐκ εἶχε παρ᾽ αὐτῷ, νοσοῦντι δὲ προσπεσὼν καὶ δακρύων ἔπεισεν υἱὸν ἀποφῆναι πολλῶν ἐναντίον.

Plutarch introduces his account of Agesilaos' accession ἔξω τοῦ δράματος, as it were, for this reference to the disputed legitimacy is his first explicit link between the succession and the charge that Alkibiades seduced the king's wife. If the dispute over the succession broke out only when the king fell ill, or if its imminence was not suspected until then, Latychidas will naturally have sought this confirmation from the dying king. While Plutarch gives no location for the recantation here, he says at *Lys.* 22. 4 that Agis fell sick at Heraia (in Arkadia), where Latychidas and his friends persuaded him to acknowledge his legitimacy. Clearly Latychidas was not carrying on the contest alone; but that does not authenticate the recantation, for his advisers could, even if they arrived after Agis' death (400), have fabricated his favourable answer and arranged the presence of 'many witnesses'. The recantation is not mentioned in *Alkibiades* and the Spartans evidently disregarded it, though this again proves nothing. Fraud, though massive, seems to be a possibility, or the report of it after the evidence was dissipated. There are other mysteries—here, Phoibidas, Sphodrias, Kinadon; and elsewhere, the terminal illnesses of Soviet presidents in this century, and perhaps El Cid. Lane Fox (1973) discusses the mystery of Alexander's death (pp. 461–72).

The report of Agis' death is withheld here in this context, though at *Lys.* 22. 4 it is given after the recantation. Xenophon records that Agis fell ill at Heraia on his way back from Elis and Delphi, but was still living when he reached home (*Hell.* iii. 3. 1). Pausanias (iii. 8. 7) says that Agis fell ill as he was returning from Arkadia, and that the people of Heraia in Arkadia who had witnessed the recantation came to Sparta to support Latychidas. Agis' denial and recantation are, perhaps unsurprisingly, not recorded by Xenophon.

Plutarch's account stems partly from Douris and partly from Xenophon, though the latter did not name Alkibiades. The reason for Xenophon's omission could be that the scandal was not mentioned openly in the dispute, but other suggestions have been made: that if he knew of it, he did not believe in the connection; that he suppressed it through loyalty to Athens and Alkibiades; that he wished to avoid introducing unsavoury or politically dangerous accusations which might tarnish Agesilaos' accession.[10] Alkibiades' name does not recur in this chapter, which, together with the doubts already manifest about his reported involvement, suggests that the public dispute in Sparta may have been conducted without his being named. Plutarch may have included the episode in order to enliven the start of the narrative, perhaps feeling the need to clarify in advance the precise identity of the supposed father of Timaia's child. He may have felt that the nature of the evidence was obvious to the reader without explicit comment, and sufficiently unreliable to leave in doubt the legitimacy of the means by which Agesilaos secured the succession recorded in what follows. The important historical fact, for Plutarch, is that the Spartans made Agesilaos their king.

4 οὐ μὴν ἀλλὰ τελευτήσαντος τοῦ Ἄγιδος ὁ Λύσανδρος, ἤδη κατα-
νεναυμαχηκὼς Ἀθηναίους καὶ μέγιστον ἐν Σπάρτῃ δυνάμενος, τὸν
Ἀγησίλαον ἐπὶ τὴν βασιλείαν προῆγεν, ὡς οὐ προσήκουσαν ὄντι νόθῳ
τῷ Λεωτυχίδῃ.

Plutarch marks the move forward in time with the genitive absolute which closes the reign of Agis and starts Agesilaos' first action of the *Life*, his struggle for the accession. He punctuates his narrative with significant repetitions of words and phrases, using here for the third time a participial form to refer to one of the kings, as at the beginning both of ch. 1 and of this chapter.

Xenophon and Pausanias put the death of Agis after a journey, which suggests that at the time of his departure the danger of his dying was not thought imminent; though, since he had already reigned for nearly thirty years, if the question of the succession was still open it will inevitably have been in the minds of some of those concerned.

Plutarch established the relationship between Agesilaos and Lysander in ch. 2, and is now able to show the continued importance of the association. Lysander had become powerful as a result of his contribution to the 'naval defeat' of Athens, but had then met opposition over his handling of the victory and his exploits in Asia Minor, northern Greece, and the Hellespont, from where he was recalled by the ephors in 403 (*Lys.* 3–20. 3).[11] His settlement of Athenian affairs was then overruled (Xen. *Hell.* ii. 4. 29–38), and it may be that he now looked to Agesilaos' accession as the means to re-establish his influence by becoming the new king's adviser. Xenophon is restrained in referring to Lysander (see Introd., E.3(*a*); cf. chs. 6. 2, 7. 2), and does not give him credit for suggesting the bid to become king, mentioning only his support.

Plutarch, having introduced Alkibiades outside the action, similarly records Lysander's statement, alleging the illegitimacy of Latychidas, before the public debate and as part of a preliminary private discussion between Lysander and Agesilaos, where it is one of the reasons given for contesting the succession. It seems clear from all the sources that the challenger was Agesilaos and that, in public at any rate, the challenge was made either only after or shortly before Agis died. Plutarch here gives no explicit judgement, but, by another significant repetition, seems to imply a belief that the 'prerogative', expressed, as at ch. 1, in προσήκουσαν, belonged to Latychidas and had been accepted as valid until it was denied in this challenge.

5 πολλοὶ δὲ καὶ τῶν ἄλλων πολιτῶν, διὰ τὴν ἀρετὴν τοῦ Ἀγησιλάου καὶ τὸ συντετράφθαι καὶ μετεσχηκέναι τῆς ἀγωγῆς, ἐφιλοτιμοῦντο καὶ συνέπραττον αὐτῷ προθύμως.

The popular support reported here is for Agesilaos. At *Lys.* 22. 4–5, however, there is support for his rival too: not only do the witnesses of Agis' recantation favour him, but Diopeithes' intervention harms Agesilaos, and many defer to the oracle and incline towards Latychidas. Here the only response to the oracle is

Lysander's argument for rejecting it (see below, §8). Plutarch presents unanimity among the Spartiates, as does Xenophon (*Agesilaos*, 1. 5), but transfers the grounds given there for their concluding vote—birth and character—to explain their support for Agesilaos' initial bid for the throne: 'birth' becomes 'shared upbringing', which, as he stressed in the first chapter, was recognized and appreciated among the Spartans.

The active virtue of ἀρετή may explain why Agesilaos attracted the support of friends, including those of Lysander, whose policies and intentions were adventurous and expansive, especially in Asia Minor (*Lys.* 3, 5, 18). Their plans would be hindered, perhaps, if they had to manage a youthful king, still without authority and experience, but led by supporters of the less active policies of the opposing groups, which were perhaps more in agreement with those followed after the war by the other king, Pausanias.

6 ἦν δὲ Διοπείθης ἀνὴρ χρησμολόγος ἐν Σπάρτῃ μαντειῶν τε παλαιῶν ὑπόπλεως καὶ δοκῶν περὶ τὰ θεῖα σοφὸς εἶναι καὶ περιττός. **7** οὗτος οὐκ ἔφη θεμιτὸν εἶναι χωλὸν γενέσθαι τῆς Λακεδαίμονος βασιλέα καὶ χρησμὸν ἐν τῇ δίκῃ τοιοῦτον ἀνεγίνωσκε·

> Φράζεο δή, Σπάρτη, καίπερ μεγάλαυχος ἐοῦσα,
> μὴ σέθεν ἀρτίποδος βλάστῃ χωλὴ βασιλεία·
> δηρὸν γὰρ νοῦσοί σε κατασχήσουσιν ἄελπτοι
> φθισίβροτόν τ' ἐπὶ κῦμα κυλινδόμενον πολέμοιο.

Whether Diopeithes resided in Sparta permanently or only temporarily—even perhaps brought in for this purpose—is not stated, but he is said to have been highly thought of, and was presumably well known there. His name, perhaps 'Zeus-obeying', seems appropriate, but it was borne by a minor Athenian politician of the 430s (*Per.* 32. 1), referred to as ὁ μέγας for his expertise on oracles (Ar. *Birds*, 988). Whether he is the same man perhaps depends on Plutarch's words here, 'in Sparta', and the literal accuracy of Xenophon's 'said' (εἶπεν and ἀντεῖπεν) at *Hell.* iii. 3. 3: at *Lys.* 22. 5 the oracle was merely 'brought to bear' (προσφέρων). There is no certainty here, but repute rather than presence would determine the authority of the seer and source of his oracle. The public debate begins here, with a suggestion that the Spartans should be guided by divine sanction. Appeals to the approval or disapproval of the gods carry weight on several important occa-

sions (ch. 30. 1; cf. Thuc. vii. 18. 2, Diod. xi. 50. 4).[12] Diopeithes
refers to lameness in the king himself, but Lysander argues
below (§8) that the abstract noun, βασιλεία, refers the lameness to
the 'kingdom' or 'kingship'. Diopeithes' interpretation makes
Lysander's argument less applicable to Latychidas and tells
directly against Agesilaos; but it is vulnerable, since the objection
to taking the lameness impersonally is diminished by the use in
the oracle of the similar metaphor describing Sparta as 'sound of
foot'.

Pausanias, the only other authority who gives the text of the
oracle (iii. 8. 9), draws attention to the failure of the Spartans to
consult the priests at Delphi about the interpretation of the oracle.
He blames Lysander for this, indicating his own expectation that
Delphi would have supported Latychidas (cf. above, §1). Those in
opposition to Agesilaos clearly did not think of it, or, perhaps
remembering the corruption on the previous occasions (Hdt. vi.
66. 3, *Lys.* 25. 3, 26. 2), believed that the god would not give the
answer that suited them.

The procedure for accession

The court was held apparently in an assembly of the people,[13] if
Plutarch's words here indicate the involvement of ordinary
Spartans in formal ratification, and if Xenophon's 'in the judgement of the city' (*Agesilaos*, 1. 5; cf. *Hell.* iii. 3. 4) marks the
formal conclusion of the debate. This may also be suggested by
Xenophon's reference to the procedure for appointing the king's
successor (*Hell.* iii. 3. 1), as if there was a regular ceremonial
pattern: Thucydides' report of the Delphic instruction for the
restoration of King Pleistoanax in 421 suggests some of the
ceremonial that was perhaps still attached to the appointment
(v. 16. 3).

The procedure adopted previously when a king's accession was
the result of disputed legitimacy is described by Herodotos as the
concern of all the Spartiates: to ensure an heir (vi. 63. 3), and to
consult Delphi (vi. 66. 1). The ephors and elders are first concerned (v. 39. 2–40. 1), though the final appointment involves the
whole citizen body (v. 42. 2). However, since Pausanias (iii. 5. 2)
refers to the Spartan court set up for a king's trial as consisting of
the twenty-eight elders, the ephors, and the other king, it is

thought that, while the Assembly may have ratified the decision, the ruling on legitimacy was more probably given in the Gerousia.[14] Xenophon's approved 'by the best', ὑπὸ τῶν ἀρίστων (*Agesilaos*, 1. 5), does not indicate the select group in the Gerousia;[15] the three superlatives there all stress the distinction of being king of Sparta rather than of any other state. Plutarch and Xenophon demonstrate that Agesilaos had the unanimous support and approval of the people: the king would know that after his accession he could rely on the armies he would be leading.

8 πρὸς ταῦτα Λύσανδρος ἔλεγεν ὡς, εἰ πάνυ φοβοῖντο τὸν χρησμὸν οἱ Σπαρτιᾶται, φυλακτέον αὐτοῖς εἴη τὸν Λεωτυχίδην· οὐ γὰρ εἰ προσπταίσας τις τὸν πόδα βασιλεύοι, τῷ θεῷ διαφέρειν, ἀλλ' εἰ μὴ γνήσιος ὢν μηδ' Ἡρακλείδης, τοῦτο τὴν χωλὴν εἶναι βασιλείαν.

Lysander turns Diopeithes' oracle against Latychidas by taking the abstract noun βασιλεία, 'kingship', literally and the adjective χωλός, 'lame', as a metaphor. He separates two issues here, since illegitimacy and direct descent from Herakles are not mutually exclusive. Legitimacy is a constitutional requirement, whereas descent from Herakles is a narrow limit imposed by privileged families who would seek divine or some other sanction for it. Simple illegitimacy is the point made at *Lys.* 22. 6, whereas Xenophon's phrase gives only the Heraklid element (*Hell.* iii. 3. 3). Strictly, the terms of the oracle would present no obstacle if the illegitimate son's father was a Heraklid.

Plutarch (*Agis*, 11. 2–4) reports the use of a law regulating the choice of wife by a Heraklid: he might not have children 'by a wife from elsewhere', ἐκ γυναικὸς ἀλλοδαπῆς, which Plutarch exemplifies immediately with the case of Leonidas, who married abroad. This, then, does not indicate the need for both parents to be of Heraklid families.[16]

This passage, together with Xenophon's similar phrase (*Hell.* iii. 3. 3), seems to be the only evidence that can be adduced to determine whether the lameness was congenital or the result of injury (see above, on ch. 2. 3). If it was not caused by injury, Lysander's argument would be vulnerable to the objection that Agesilaos' lameness was not in the same category as the example he has given.

9 ὁ δ' Ἀγησίλαος ἔφη καὶ τὸν Ποσειδῶνα καταμαρτυρεῖν τοῦ

Λεωτυχίδου τὴν νοθείαν, ἐκβαλόντα σεισμῷ τοῦ θαλάμου τὸν Ἆγιν· ἀπ᾽ ἐκείνου δὲ πλέον ἢ δέκα μηνῶν διελθόντων γενέσθαι τὸν Λεωτυχίδην.

The earthquake did not feature in Plutarch's account of Alkibiades' involvement with Timaia at §§1–2 above. It is not mentioned at *Lys.* 22. 4, in the preliminary narrative (cf. above, §3), where Agis simply counts the months and repudiates Latychidas for no other reason, but it is mentioned at *Alk.* 23. 8. At first sight Plutarch now seems to be about to show, in Agesilaos' words, that Poseidon, using his power as god of earthquakes, indicated an act of seduction. In Xenophon's account (*Hell.* iii. 3. 2) this is indeed what Agesilaos uses the reference to Poseidon to suggest, and he necessarily implies that the identity of the seducer was known at the time; but neither the seducer nor a witness who saw his escape is named. Even if Alkibiades' visit to Sparta was considered relevant at the time of the dispute, from ten to fifteen years had elapsed since then and the testimony would be difficult to authenticate. The witness may be supposed to have reported the incident and even to have identified the man at the time of the earthquake, but to be seen exiting from a house does not prove adultery: its supposed significance would become apparent only later. It is not clear what made the witness suspicious, nor what resulted from the challenge, if the man had no business there. The god's sign was not a direct communication, but required human interpretation, which was subject to query on the very points at issue. It was open to the sceptical to comment that the earthquake was a coincidental occurrence which forced the real or alleged father to flee εἰς τὸ φανερόν, into the open air, to avoid not detection but destruction. Seduction might be confirmed but not established by the birth in the tenth month. Xenophon does not say who made the calculation.

Plutarch escapes a weakness which Xenophon's account contains: Agesilaos does not have to name the witness—there is none—for he names Agis as the man leaving the apartment. However, Plutarch has a weakness, for the earthquake is not now a sign of seduction and it is nowhere explained why Agis should react in this way, whereas in the other version a guilty adulterer, even if not superstitious, might fear exposure if caught in the aftermath of the earthquake, and would hope to escape undetected. Plutarch may have misinterpreted Xenophon, who, once this debate has started, does not mention Agis by name, only the man Latychidas calls his father. Xenophon thus evades the problem of explaining the identity of the fugitive from the earthquake, who though left nameless is clearly not Agis. However, the words 'your father', coming after the reference to Agis as 'the man you call father', could easily be mistaken for another reference to Agis.

Plutarch's identification of the fugitive as Agis necessitated another change. Xenophon makes Agesilaos say to Latychidas, 'You were born in the tenth month after the earthquake' (*Hell*. iii. 3. 2), hinting that the fugitive was the father. In the similar situation which Herodotos reported (§1 above), Ariston's calculation, according to which he disowned Demaratos, of the critical ten lunar months, showed that his marriage had taken place too recently (vi. 63. 1–2). Here, in order to show that the fugitive— Agis—was not the father, the absence has to be longer than this. In Plutarch's version, therefore, Latychidas was born 'more than ten months after'. The announcement of the court's decision is delayed by Plutarch until the start of the next chapter.

The literary evidence: Xenophon, Nepos, Pausanias, and Plutarch

(*a*) The brief account given by Xenophon in *Agesilaos* (1. 5) makes no reference to any debate or why there was a dispute, only to the struggle itself. There is no suggestion that Latychidas was disqualified on grounds of illegitimacy, perhaps to avoid insinuations which might damage Agesilaos' reputation. The two were 'contending for the office' as if it was vacant, without an heir apparent. Xenophon reinforces this impression by making Agesilaos contend, strangely, 'as son of Archidamos' and not as brother of Agis, while Latychidas contends 'as son of Agis'. By bringing only the two fathers, both kings, into consideration in this way, he obscures the issue of legitimacy—both were of royal birth; eligibility was judged only on personal grounds of character.[17] Indeed, the episode proves that Agesilaos' excellence did not depend on the later achievements of his kingship, but was attested by the judgement of the Spartans themselves which also settled the constitutional issue of the succession. Thus it was a matter of political importance—majority support for whatever was known of his plans and intentions. The account may reflect the form of a public notice issued at the time of the accession.

(*b*) Xenophon's fuller account (*Hell.* iii. 3. 1–4) suggests that, even if it was a political issue, it was conducted as a constitutional question of legitimacy. The two men contend, as in *Agesilaos*, without any indication of why the succession was not normal, but now Agesilaos' claim is as brother of Agis. The public discussion is in three distinct parts. Latychidas opens the debate by upholding his prerogative—the king's son has precedence over his brother. Agesilaos' case is made in two parts, legitimacy of birth and eligibility as a descendant of Herakles.

The question of legitimacy is conducted by Agesilaos himself in response to Latychidas' report of his mother's testimony in his favour. The question of eligibility is conducted by Lysander in response to Diopeithes, who, supporting Latychidas, reports only briefly from Apollo's oracle the warning against lameness (*Hell.* iii. 3. 3). There is no positive support for Latychidas here, and if, as Lysander seems to have assumed, Agesilaos has made his case for illegitimacy and Agis has had no heir for the whole or the latter part of his reign, Diopeithes can only disqualify Agesilaos without reinstating Latychidas.

Lysander regards the oracle as stating a special requirement of eligibility by birth, that only a true Heraklid should rule. He invalidates the objection against Agesilaos' physical lameness, though without disposing of any physical disability other than a hypothetical minor accident. However, only if the charge of illegitimacy, alleged by Agesilaos, is upheld, would Lysander's argument carry weight, and then only to duplicate the disqualification of Latychidas; for his claim to be a Heraklid is refuted only along with his status as Agis' son. Lysander gives no support to Agesilaos' allegation, and if it fails to persuade the Spartans, Latychidas is eligible both as Agis' son and as a Heraklid. The episode ends with the Spartans' decision to prefer Agesilaos. There is a ring of braggadocio in the tale, which could have been told to Xenophon by Agesilaos later in explaining how he became king.

(*c*) Nepos presents the two requirements of the Spartan rules for the inheritance of the kingship (*Agesilaus*, 1. 2–5): descent within the Heraklid line and legitimacy as the oldest son of the king, with the nearest relative next in line. He first raises a doubt about Latychidas' birth: Agis 'did not acknowledge him at birth, but as he died said he was his own'. This would leave Sparta without an heir apparent from the time of Agis' accession until his last illness. But in three phrases he implies that Latychidas *was* the true heir of Agis: he calls Latychidas the son of Agesilaos' brother (1. 2), says that Agis left a son Latychidas (1. 4), and names Agesilaos as his uncle (1. 4). He assigns the reason for the Spartans' preference for Agesilaos to the powerful support of Lysander, as Plutarch, too, has done at *Lys.* 22. 6.

What Pausanias says may stem from what Arkadian guides told him, anxious, perhaps, to enhance the part their ancestors had played in history. Their evidence supports Latychidas' argument against Agesilaos but again the influence of Lysander prevails (iii. 8. 10).

(*d*) Plutarch gives new coherent structure to Xenophon's account and removes the imprecision over the alleged seducer's identity. Alkibiades' visit to Sparta leads, however fictitiously, to the illegitimacy charge against Latychidas, but the recantation by Agis, which Xenophon omits, turns the reader's mind at this point towards Latychidas' legitimacy. After Lysander's private allegation, Diopeithes' oracle fits well and if successful will disqualify Agesilaos, though it will not reinstate Latychidas; Lysander's challenge both disqualifies Latychidas and reinstates Agesilaos. When Agesilaos then refers to the earthquake and the time of the birth, he is strengthening, however fictitiously, Lysander's insinuation, with new support for the charge of illegitimacy. Plutarch's order of presentation, then, improves the argumentation and the rhetorical quality of the debate. A priest of Apollo at Delphi, he omits the god's name as the author of the oracle, and so avoids associating him with a cause of Sparta's decline. He leaves the reader with only Agesilaos' case to consider, removes the mystery of the identity of the suspect, and voices no judgement at this stage.

(*e*) The different presentations indicate varying authorial intentions. After the death of Agis, Plutarch allows his reader to approach Agesilaos' reign, like the Spartans, without the complication of doubts about the legality of the succession; the reader, again like the Spartans, will be enlightened later (ch. 30; cf. *Comp.* 1. 2). When Agesilaos died, Xenophon may have wished to defend his reputation (see Introd., E.1, F.2(*a*)) against criticism that Sparta had declined during his reign: in his *Agesilaos* the defence was that his ἀρετή had already proved him fit to rule; later, in

Hellenika, the two signs of divine preference, Apollo's oracle and Poseidon's earthquake, meet the criticism that Sparta had offended divine providence (cf. 6. 11 and 22. 3 below).[18]

Events leading to the choice of Agesilaos

(*a*) *Constitutional aspects.* In 427 Agesilaos, at the age of about 18, may have become the heir presumptive as the younger brother of Agis, who was apparently childless (unless Latychidas was already born, though this is nowhere stated). Thereafter Agesilaos' succession would be straightforward unless and until Agis produced a legitimate heir, for there is nowhere mentioned any trace of another contender. If Latychidas was of an age to have his birth linked with an earthquake which happened during Alkibiades' visit to Sparta, the immediate acknowledgement of the child as heir apparent will have changed Agesilaos' life: he was no longer 'a heartbeat from the throne'. If Agis, at the birth of Latychidas, openly believed the talk about the boy's paternity, he could hardly avoid disowning him. There would be pressure on him to produce an heir, and an arrangement would be made, as in other cases where the royal line was in danger (Hdt. vi. 63; cf. *Lak. Pol.* 1. 7, *Lyk.* 15. 6). If Agis received the information or acted upon it later, perhaps near the time of his death, proof of paternity would be difficult, for Latychidas would then be up to 12 or even 16 years old.

The link with Alkibiades cannot be proved, and 425, marked by another earthquake, has been proposed as Latychidas' date of birth. This would mean that Alkibiades was not Latychidas' father, though leaving it open that he may have seduced Timaia later.[19] Lakonia is subject to frequent earthquakes,[20] and both the choice of the earthquake of 425 and, in consequence, this date of birth have been rejected.[21] If the son was acknowledged at this earlier date, only two years into Agis' reign, Agesilaos' immediate disappointment would be less. If the child's legitimacy was disputed only at Agis' death about twenty-five years later, proof would be even more difficult to find. From whatever time Agis rejected Latychidas, or, as Pausanias explains (iii. 8. 7), comparing Ariston's procedure (Hdt. vi. 63. 2), said in the hearing of the ephors that he was not his son, there would be no recognized direct successor unless the statements were ignored. If Pausanias

intended his parallel to continue, Herodotos goes on to say that
the ephors 'took no action': Pausanias does not mention any
action, though that may be assimilation on his part. If Latychidas
was disinherited, the childless king's younger brother Agesilaos
would be undisputed as next in line.

If Agesilaos was the recognized heir, the challenge on the death
of Agis would be made on behalf of Latychidas; but it is clear that
the challenge came not from Latychidas but from Agesilaos. At
Hellenika, iii. 3. 2 Agesilaos' speech proves that the succession was
only now in question. Xenophon does not say that he was the
undisputed heir presumptive, but that he was 'pronounced worthy
of the highest privilege' even before his reign (*Agesilaos*, 1. 5).
That Agesilaos was the challenger is clear, too, from Plutarch's
statement, if, as seems likely, it is correct, that Agesilaos benefited
from having undergone the Spartan ἀγωγή, which implies that
Latychidas did not have this distinction but had at the time been
exempt as the recognized heir. The evidence suggests that
Latychidas was the legitimate heir of Agis and Agesilaos was a
usurper.

(b) *Political aspects.* One of Agesilaos' ancestors, another
Latychidas, brought the charge of illegitimacy against King
Demaratos, because of disagreements with Kleomenes over policy
(Hdt. v. 75, vi. 50, 64–5). The story of the deposition will have
been familiar in Sparta, and may have guided Agesilaos' procedure: a dubious claim that Demaratos' father had disowned
him, made twenty years after his accession by his second-cousin
and Agesilaos' great-grandfather, Latychidas, who then became
king himself.[22]

The political reasons for replacing Latychidas are not recorded
and nothing is known of any participation by Agesilaos in public
life before his accession; but Lysander's career provides evidence
for the relevant political struggles. Political factions in Sparta have
been identified.[23] There were differences concerning Sparta's
attitudes to mainland Greece and to Asia Minor after the
Peloponnesian war. Conflicting groups of supporters associated
themselves with one or other of the two kings, Agis and Pausanias,
but as a result of his major contribution to victory in the war
Lysander had prestige and influence, for a time invincible. The
alignments of the candidates' supporters in the struggle for the

succession are not specified, but Latychidas was not alone (§3) and Lysander was Agesilaos' main strength.

Lysander was checked by the brief co-operation between Agis and Pausanias over his treatment of Athens after the Peloponnesian war (Xen. *Hell.* ii. 4. 29–38), though Pausanias was then brought to trial and acquitted by a majority which did not include Agis (Paus. iii. 5. 2). Agis was again less aggressive in not pressing Elis in the campaign he was conducting just before he died, having previously withdrawn his army, perhaps prematurely, after an earthquake. Pausanias was later to be condemned in his absence—perhaps wrongly (*Lys.* 28. 2–5)—for failing to keep a rendezvous at Haliartos with Lysander, who was killed (*Hell.* iii. v. 17–25). These are indications of conflict between supporters of limited imperialism or allied autonomy, and supporters of Lysander's expansionist aims in Greece and Asia Minor after the war. If the new king were a minor, influenced by friends of his father, the late king, the supporters of adventurous policies would be frustrated.

Lysander is reported to have taken steps to advance himself by a reform of the kingship (see below, ch. 20). The transfer of the kingship to Agesilaos would perhaps be more popular and serve the same purpose: and fear of that may have inspired the appeal for the deathbed confirmation of Latychidas. If this was the motive for the transfer, it is also true that it was the will of the Spartans that prevailed; and if Agis preferred Latychidas to his brother, his rejection shows that the Spartans preferred Lysander's policies. Again, that it was the city that chose Agesilaos (Xen. *Hell.* iii. 3. 4, *Agesilaos*, 1. 3) indicates that the principle that justice was identical with the interests of Sparta guided the Spartans' choice, here as elsewhere (ch. 23). The Spartans sanctioned strong and active leadership, and this, perhaps, is the most significant aspect of the succession; see Introd., E.1.

The character of Agesilaos and of Sparta: developing a cohesive constituency

Xen. *Agesilaos*, 4. 5, 6. 4–5, 7. 2–3, 8. 1–2.

4. Agesilaos courts favour among powerful Spartans

1 Οὕτω δὲ καὶ διὰ ταῦτα βασιλεὺς ἀποδειχθεὶς ὁ Ἀγησίλαος εὐθὺς εἶχε καὶ τὰ χρήματα τοῦ Ἄγιδος, ὡς νόθον ἀπελάσας τὸν Λεωτυχίδην.

Agesilaos' appointment as king marks the beginning of the main theme, the story of his reign. Plutarch creates suspense by holding Agesilaos' name back to the end of the phrase. He dissociates himself from any judgement about the fairness of the appointment by his use of ὡς, and by omitting legitimation by the city (Xen. *Agesilaos*, 1. 5: κρίνασα ἡ πόλις). Indeed, the first five words draw attention to the 'manner and means' of the procedure without approving them. This perhaps reveals some unease with the procedure, which demonstrated the qualities of φιλοτιμία and φιλονικία ascribed to Agesilaos in ch. 2.

The process which determined Agis' successor as king determined also the inheritance of his estate. Xenophon refers to this only indirectly (*Agesilaos*, 4. 5), using the sharing of his inheritance of Agis' wealth with poor relatives to illustrate Agesilaos' justice in money matters. The exceptional wealth of Sparta's kings is indicated by the large fine imposed by the ephors on Agis (Thuc. v. 63. 2).

Approximately twenty years of Agesilaos' adult life are passed over. Although Xenophon (*Agesilaos*, 1. 5) says, 'There are not wanting signs that even before his reign Agesilaos was deemed worthy to be king', he gives no details there or in *Hellenika*, and Thucydides did not mention him. Plutarch says only that many citizens were convinced of his worth (ch. 3. 5). Agesilaos' training in the ἀγωγή may have led to military service of some sort in the Peloponnesian war, unless the heir was required to remain in

Sparta whenever a king was conducting a campaign, as Agis was in Attica (427–426) and from 413 in occupation of Dekeleia. If, until the birth of Latychidas, he was being prepared for rule, he may have been given experience of at least minor command, though in his twenties peace with Athens removed for a time the opportunities for major campaigns. We cannot make assumptions here, for we do not know how these things were managed, but later his son, Archidamos, then aged over 30, had command in the 'Tearless Battle' (ch. 33. 5), while Agesilaos remained in Sparta. Xenophon does not include military service among the 'signs' of worth.

ὁρῶν δὲ τοὺς ἀπὸ μητρὸς οἰκείους ἐπιεικεῖς μὲν ὄντας ἰσχυρῶς δὲ πενομένους, ἀπένειμεν αὐτοῖς τὰ ἡμίσεα τῶν χρημάτων, εὔνοιαν ἑαυτῷ καὶ δόξαν ἀντὶ φθόνου καὶ δυσμενείας ἐπὶ τῇ κληρονομίᾳ κατασκευαζόμενος.

Agesilaos' first act as king is a personal one of generosity which allows scope for Plutarch's interest in character to move from the active virtues of ch. 3 to the quieter qualities here. He illustrates τὸ φιλάνθρωπον in the first part of this chapter, and in the second part reintroduces τὸ δημοτικόν, both attributed to him in ch. 1. Alliteration of k at the end of the sentence, 'winning him goodwill and credit instead of envy and hatred over the inheritance', perhaps marks deliberate manipulation to win influence: Agesilaos uses the quieter virtues to enhance what he had already achieved using the competitive qualities. The process of building Agesilaos' power-base which starts here is continued in ch. 5.

Plutarch has not made it clear whether these are the maternal relatives of Agesilaos or of Latychidas: 'les parents maternels du jeune homme' (Flacelière and Chambry, Budé); 'his kinsmen on his mother's side', ambiguously (Perrin, Loeb). Xenophon does not mention Latychidas anywhere in this context, and plainly refers to Agesilaos' mother's relatives (Agesilaos, 4. 5). If Plutarch intended to follow Xenophon, the point would be, not that Agesilaos' enrichment was others' deprivation, but that of itself it was ἐπίφθονον, 'odious', until the distribution showed he was not merely out for himself. Here, the proximity of 'mother' to the name Latychidas, itself set in the final position of its sentence, in closer proximity to χρήματα than to βασιλεύς, also closer to the following terms of the financial settlement with relatives, together with the omission of Xenophon's αὐτῷ, and the absence of a 'possessive' definite article (τῆς μητρός), permits interpretation as Latychidas' relatives on his mother's side. Plutarch would then seem to see the generosity as tinged with pragmatism, benefiting Agesilaos. The stress on the avoidance of resentment is more appropriate if Plutarch refers to the relatives of Latychidas' mother as the recipients, for Agesilaos' enrichment had not deprived his own kinsmen. This view is further supported by the recognition of the kinsmen's 'suitability', ἐπιεικεῖς—missing in Xenophon—which determines Agesilaos' decision, suggesting a conciliatory contrast between the discredited Latychidas and his family.

We are not otherwise told anywhere what happened to Latychidas and his mother Timaia. The former, presumably deprived of full citizen qualification, now will have belonged to one of the inferior classes, perhaps the Hypomeiones, if that is what Spartans who were not full citizens were called—again there is little to go on[1]—while the latter, though not herself of royal stock, may, like Kyniska (ch. 20. 1), have had resources of her own, even if her kinsmen did not. Agesilaos' attitude to the extravagant personal use of accumulated wealth is given by Plutarch at ch. 20.

Property ownership at Sparta: the economic causes of decline

This episode indicates the relative poverty that existed in Sparta, and the possibility of accumulation and also of alienation of property, though not by sale here. This is a topic discussed for its own sake and in explanation of the decline of Sparta.[2] The statement that Lykourgos required equal contributions to the *syssitia* (*Lak. Pol.* 7. 3–6) perhaps led later authorities to believe in equal estate ownership, too, but although the seventh-century compromise brought stability for a time, ownership of landed property was never equal and became more unequal over the course of time.[3]

The concentration of wealth, especially in land, in the hands of fewer and fewer families entails some form of transfer, allowing the self-indulgent expenditure in those families responsible, for instance, for almost a score of Spartan victories in Olympic chariot races recorded between c.548 and c.368.[4] The spread of landlessness caused the poverty that explains the declining number of the Spartan citizen population: 'those who were too poor to contribute their *syssitia* dues were excluded from citizenship' (Arist. *Pol.* 1271ª26–37).[5]

Plutarch (*Agis*, 5. 2–3) attributes to Epitadeus a *rhetra*, 'enactment', permitting gift and bequest which caused the inequalities. Suggested dating to the fourth century[6] and even his existence have been questioned: 'Aristotle knew nothing of this near contemporary figure and states it as a Lykourgan regulation . . . The roots of the trouble it is said to have produced lie well behind the fourth century.'[7] Here (*Pol.* 1270ª15), Aristotle, as frequently, does not name 'the legislator', but this could refer to the fourth century only if he were uncharacteristically as inexact as an Attic orator for whom laws currently in force—even the manifestly recent—may be 'Solon's laws'.

A distinction is drawn by ancient writers between an alienable type of ownership and some other equal (Polyb. vi. 45. 3) inalienable 'ancient share': 'It is shameful for the Lakedaimonians to sell land; and it is illegal to sell the ancient portion' (Herakleides Lembos, 12, said to be derived from Aristotle's *Lak. Pol.* in the second century BC).[8] Others make no distinction: 'The legislator made it dishonourable to buy property or sell what one has, but those who wished he permitted to give it away and to bequeath it' (Arist. *Pol.* 1270ª19–21). Transfer of property by gift or bequest may have been a disguised form of sale by secret contracts for mutual benefit,[9] but such transfers would not grow in scale until precious-metal coinage was available.

Plutarch reports from more than one authority state allocation of 9,000 lots in Lakonia to Spartiates which may have been 'the ancient portion' (*Lyk.* 8. 3–4).[10] The alienable land may have been in the territory acquired later, following the annexation of Messenia,[11] although as the citizen population declined unallocated Lakonian plots may have been made available for purchase, too. However, the inequalities which led to Sparta's ultimate decline would develop only in a system of land tenure and inheritance as 'private estates transmitted by partible inheritance and diverging devolution and open to alienation through lifetime gifts, testamentary bequests and betrothal of heiresses', in which 'the ancient portions were either subject to the same rules as the rest' or 'comprised only a small fraction of Spartiate estates'.[12]

All newly admitted young members had to contribute their

syssition dues even if they had not inherited. Plutarch's state allocation of lots at birth (*Lyk.* 16. 1) would ensure to eldest and younger sons the means to contribute the dues without waiting for family inheritance. Lack of means would then explain the decline in citizen numbers only if the value of the produce of the lot had diminished since the first allocations were fixed, and could not now, without supplementation, provide the further resources needed for other everyday living expenses, especially when these increased on marriage, although the dowry, if attracted, may have been adequate for this. Yet whatever its current value, those who had no supporting income from their family's estates would be at a disadvantage (cf. *Lak. Pol.* 5. 3). Like those who failed to pass the initial selection (κάδδιχος) they could join a less élite *syssition*; but some would be too proud to try, or too unpopular to be accepted anywhere. Their failures to join a *syssition* would further reduce the number of Spartiates,[13] including anyone just above the borderline at which Aristotle's 'poor' would be compulsorily refused admittance and so in danger of losing citizen rights. They would forfeit their basic allotment and we do not know how they would find a living in Spartan society. Plutarch records the subservience of the impoverished who 'had no time for any honourable pursuits'—presumably such as attendance at the *syssition*—but 'sat by in the city without rights and resources' (*Agis*, 5. 4).[14] Some Inferiors served in the army and others no doubt set themselves up in farming, without Spartiate status.

   A strong argument against acceptance of Plutarch's evidence is the inconsistency of inheritance intact by a single son of the father's estate, κλῆρος, and allocation by the city at birth (*Agis*, 5. 1, *Lyk.* 16. 1).[15] But if the young man's estate had to be supplied voluntarily by his family, in anticipation of his eventual inheritance, there were problems for the less wealthy, aggravated, of course, if there were more than one son. Resistance to the effects of partible inheritance could in this case partially explain the decline in the Spartiate population; a family might refuse the necessary gift, unless the state used compulsion. Provision could then be made either from the wider family's resources or by adoption procedures, as in the case of *mothakes*. The state may have made some stipulation at birth, even if its implementation were delayed for twenty years. Since informal local knowledge will have circulated orally in Sparta,[16] the record need not have been impossible to maintain in the small social units. There is, however, no evidence for these suggestions—or any other.

2 ὃ δέ φησιν ὁ Ξενοφῶν, ὅτι πάντα τῇ πατρίδι πειθόμενος ἴσχυε πλεῖστον, ὥστε ποιεῖν ὃ βούλοιτο, τοιοῦτόν ἐστι.

Plutarch refers to Agesilaos' obedience again, moving from τὸ φιλάνθρωπον to τὸ δημοτικόν at this point, from private relations to public, and associating these with the acquisition of power. He also moves on from the time of the accession, to give a prospectus of the *Life* against a relevant historical background. Xenophon reports that in return for obedience to his country Agesilaos won important political influence (*Agesilaos*, 6. 4).[17] Plutarch changes the sense here and in the rest of the chapter, for whereas Xenophon eulogizes, he finds cunning. Although Agesilaos does not ever do *freely* 'what he wished', Plutarch shows him exploiting obedience to authority to free himself from constitutional restrictions imposed on the kings.

3 τῶν ἐφόρων ἦν τότε καὶ τῶν γερόντων τὸ μέγιστον ἐν τῇ πολιτείᾳ κράτος, ὧν οἱ μὲν ἐνιαυτὸν ἄρχουσι μόνον, οἱ δὲ γέροντες διὰ βίου ταύτην ἔχουσι τὴν τιμήν, ἐπὶ τῷ μὴ πάντα τοῖς βασιλεῦσιν ἐξεῖναι συνταχθέντες, ὡς ἐν τοῖς περὶ Λυκούργου γέγραπται.

With the kings and the Assembly these two groups, ephors and councillors, make up the four sections of the citizen body in Sparta. These are the ingredients of the 'mixed constitution' attributed to Sparta by some ancient authorities (see below, ch. 5. 4). That the ephors, who held their office for one year, and the councillors, who held theirs for life, together had the greatest power in the state, is an over-simplification—some of their powers extended over the kings, but in command of the army the kings were supreme (Hdt. vi. 56, Arist. *Pol.* 1285ᵃ7–8),[18] their prerogatives being increased 'in direct proportion to their personal ability and willingness to meet' the military needs of the state.[19] In this *Life* the ephors wield judicial, military, and religious powers: they fine the king (ch. 5. 4) and an errant warrior (ch. 34. 11), recall Agesilaos from Asia (ch. 15. 2), order attacks on Boiotia (ch. 17. 1) and Thebes, assembling the allies (ch. 28. 5), control the Gymnopaidiai (ch. 29. 4), and authorize executions (ch. 32. 11). The élite council (Gerousia) at Sparta was elected from among men above 60 years old, in fierce competition for the honour (*Lak.*

Pol. 10. 1–3). One member advises Agesilaos about Lysander's speech (ch. 20. 5). Plutarch omits the assembly here, but at ch. 6 it votes for the expedition to Asia Minor, and at ch. 30, on the advice of Agesilaos, it allows the laws to sleep for a day. Those who praise the Spartan constitution attribute its stability and good order to the competition between these sections, and blame the departure from its principles for the city's decline (see below, ch. 5. 4).

Plutarch attributes the initiation of the office of the ephors to Lykourgos' successors (*Lyk.* 7. 1; cf. Arist. *Pol.* 1313ᵃ25–30, Plato, *Leg.* 692 A). The statement that the office was instituted to restrain the power of the kings refers to a time for which there are no contemporary records.[20] That it was intended to support the kings is suggested by the oaths exchanged by kings and ephors each month, pledging respectively to uphold the law and the kingship (*Lak. Pol.* 15. 7; cf. *Kl.* 10. 2–3).[21] The limitation of the kings' powers, as those of the ephors grew, may be attributed not to one reform but to a series.[22]

Annual election of ephors reflected popular reaction to policies, whether already operating or as yet only proposed, and bestowed powerful support for the moment, while their short tenure and collegiality prevented long-term programmes and growing influence. The competition among elders for selection as councillors favoured men who had maintained leading status for a long time, acquiring experience and prestige over the years, along, perhaps, with cautious, conservative attitudes.[23] The kings retained privileges and duties at home, mainly in religion, the authority of which in Sparta was of great importance in political decision-making, as elsewhere in Greece;[24] and when they were abroad on campaigns, they held supreme power in the conduct of war, though it was not always within their competence to settle the terms of peace. The council and the ephors, however, had retrospective power over the kings and could bring them to trial (see below, §5, ch. 5. 4).

4 διὸ καὶ πατρικήν τινα πρὸς αὐτοὺς ἀπὸ τοῦ παλαιοῦ διετέλουν εὐθὺς οἱ βασιλεῖς φιλονικίαν καὶ διαφορὰν παραλαμβάνοντες.

The competitive elements in the ἀγωγή and elsewhere (*Lak. Pol.* 4. 2) are stressed in chs. 1 and 2, and in ch. 5. 5 their introduction (διαφορὰν καὶ ἄμιλλαν) is associated with the constitutional reformer. Plutarch attributes the same aggressiveness to early

kings, using strong words that force a striking contrast with what
he says next about Agesilaos' manner of handling the ephors and
councillors—earlier kings did not have their Xenophons to eulogize them. There is not the detailed information needed to justify
speaking about continuous disagreement between ephors and
kings,[25] as Plutarch does, but there were occasional differences.
Nor was the ephorate itself always of one mind. King Pausanias
had the support only of the majority in disallowing Lysander's
handling of the terms of peace with Athens in 403 (Xen. *Hell*. ii. 4.
29).[26] There were other offices, too, in Sparta's government, and
the personal influence of a Lysander at his peak, which resulted
from his long-continued success, in and out of office, was a threat
to the establishment.

5 ὁ δ' Ἀγησίλαος ἐπὶ τὴν ἐναντίαν ὁδὸν ἦλθε, καὶ τὸ πολεμεῖν καὶ τὸ
προσκρούειν αὐτοῖς ἐάσας ἐθεράπευε, . . .

Plutarch makes explicit Agesilaos' move away from his predecessors' competitive, inherited virtues as he extends his power-base
beyond his kinsmen; he is criticized for abandoning them in the
next chapter. That the competitive virtues could alternate with the
acquired quality of deference is consistent with Plutarch's earlier
study of character at the end of ch. 1, particularly the final phrase.
Agesilaos may have been unlike other kings (§4 above) in his
'deference' to the ephors and elders, but the verb ἐθεράπευε, which
has connotations of servility, attributes to him the same attitude as
Lysander displayed (*Lys*. 2. 3, 4. 2; *Lak. Pol*. 8. 2; see Introd.,
E.3(a) and (c)), perhaps studied by Agesilaos.

. . . πάσης μὲν ἀπ' ἐκείνων πράξεως ἀρχόμενος, εἰ δὲ κληθείη, θᾶττον ἢ
βάδην ἐπειγόμενος, ὁσάκις δὲ τύχοι καθήμενος ἐν τῷ βασιλικῷ θώκῳ
καὶ χρηματίζων, ἐπιοῦσι τοῖς ἐφόροις ὑπεξανίστατο, τῶν δ' εἰς τὴν
γερουσίαν ἀεὶ καταταττομένων ἑκάστῳ χλαῖναν ἔπεμπε καὶ βοῦν
ἀριστεῖον.

Agesilaos' obedience to the ephors and the elders is first illustrated
at length. Xenophon records his deference to the ephors on his
recall from Asia (*Agesilaos*, 1. 36 and *Hell*. iv. 2. 3; see below, ch.
15. 2), and talks about the courtesies and protocol surrounding the
Spartan kings and magistrates (*Lak. Pol*. 8. 2, 15. 6): Spartiates
hurry when summoned; they rise when the king enters, except the
ephors on their ephoric seats. Plutarch has adapted *Lak. Pol*. and

Hellenika, and the similarity of phrases is striking: for 'hurry', θᾶττον ἢ βάδην (cf. *Hell.* v. 4. 53, but in the context of retreating troops) matches μὴ βαδίζοντες (*Lak. Pol.* 8. 2), and for 'seats', ἐν τῷ βασιλικῷ θώκῳ matches ἀπὸ τῶν ἐφορικῶν δίφρων (*Lak. Pol.* 15. 6). The king's reversal of the compliment in rising from his official seat would be a most impressive and significant mark of respect.[27] Since the ephorate was an annual office such a temporary and perhaps constantly repeated gesture was intended to be as effective as the gifts devised for members of the Gerousia.[28]

Acts of generosity are recognized in *Lak. Pol.* 15. 4: under the Lykourgan constitution the kings, in their Royal Mess, received double portions at meals, 'not that they might eat enough for two, but that they might have the wherewithal to honour anyone whom they chose'. Comparative anthropology provides other evidence for this use of wealth to maintain or win power.[29] Gifts in kind, rather than money, would be appropriate in Sparta, and the generosity displayed at the time of appointment to the Gerousia would perhaps serve long into the future, especially in legal cases tried before it, the most important court at Sparta.[30] Although in general Plutarch seems to have regarded the Gerousia as more important than Thucydides, who never mentions it, or *Lak. Pol.* (the *gerontia*, 10. 1), it perhaps had effective informal influence, and if Agesilaos was the first Spartan king to practise this generosity widely, he was developing a cohesive constituency in a city that already had a strong sense of unanimity in one political aim, to ensure the survival of a relatively small number of citizens in a relatively large geographical and demographical context. But he was weakening the curbing effect of the 'mixed' constitution.

Plutarch is interpreting reported facts independently in order to present, most explicitly in §6, a hostile portrait, following the citation from Xenophon on winning influence (*Agesilaos*, 6. 4; see above, §2).

6 ἐκ δὲ τούτων τιμᾶν δοκῶν καὶ μεγαλύνειν τὸ ἀξίωμα τῆς ἐκείνων ἀρχῆς, ἐλάνθανεν αὔξων τὴν ἑαυτοῦ δύναμιν καὶ τῇ βασιλείᾳ προστιθεὶς μέγεθος ἐκ τῆς πρὸς αὐτὸν εὐνοίας συγχωρούμενον.

Decision-making at Sparta is rarely open to inspection in the literary evidence, and since such evidence is partly of a biographical nature for this period, it is inevitable that Agesilaos often appears to have determined Spartan policy during his reign. The power of Spartan royal patronage to which Plutarch draws attention is generally recognized.[31] He introduces a critical tone in attributing duplicity to Agesilaos, and seems not to intend that the ephors should be blamed for not noticing what he was doing: rather Agesilaos was at fault here as he was later (ch. 5. 4). Analysis of Agesilaos' methods of establishing his power-base is a proper subject for the biographer, involving the impenetrable areas of intention and private affective reaction. He does not just record facts but offers an interpretation which leads to a wider issue: the detrimental effect that Agesilaos' procedure has on the Lykourgan constitution. This is as yet 'unnoticed' (ἐλάνθανεν). It becomes overt when the ephors react publicly to a similar procedure (ch. 5. 4).

5. Agesilaos courts favour among the citizens: the danger of tyranny

Xen. *Agesilaos*, 6. 4–5, 7. 2–3, 8. 1–2.

The chapter is in two parts: a continuation from the previous chapter of the analysis of Agesilaos' character, showing a subversion of popular morality (§§1–4), and an analysis of a putative philosophical parallel with the making of the Spartan constitution from which that subversion diverges (§§5–7). Plutarch reveals doubts about Agesilaos' conduct in political management and links it with the decline in Sparta's fortunes.

1 Ἐν δὲ ταῖς πρὸς τοὺς ἄλλους πολίτας ὁμιλίαις ἐχθρὸς ἦν ἀμεμπτότερος ἢ φίλος. τοὺς μὲν γὰρ ἐχθροὺς ἀδίκως οὐκ ἔβλαπτε, τοῖς δὲ φίλοις καὶ τὰ μὴ δίκαια συνέπραττε.

After describing Agesilaos' private courting of relatives and other Spartans in powerful offices, Plutarch shows how he extended his power-base among ordinary citizens (cf. ch. 20 below). Plutarch adapts and turns against Agesilaos remarks about his attitudes to friends and opponents which are eulogistic in Xenophon's *Agesilaos*: he benefits friends financially (4. 3), wins their prompt service by kindness (6. 4), supports and rescues opponents in trouble (7. 3), joins friends in all their efforts (8. 2), welcomes total devotion (11. 3), is feared by enemies, and is hard to deceive, but is gentle, generous, and compliant to friends (11. 10–13). Elsewhere, Agesilaos' policy regarding enemies was not only to harm them by force but also to win them over by gentleness, πρᾳότης (Xen. *Agesilaos*, 1. 20; cf. Plut. *Marc.* 10. 3–11. 1).[1] Neither Xenophon nor Plutarch names individuals or instances here, but Lysander (ch. 6. 5), Peisander (ch. 10. 11), Nikias (ch. 13. 5), Teleutias (ch. 21. 1), and Phoibidas and Sphodrias (chs. 23–5) were beneficiaries.

The basis for Plutarch's thought in revising Xenophon is the fundamental assumption approved by Greek popular morality, that justice is rendering what is deserved—help to friends and harm to enemies (Plato, *Resp.* 331 E–332D; see Introd., E.4(*a*)).[2] He also adopts its vocabulary: Agesilaos gives unjust friends help they do not deserve and withholds from enemies harm they do deserve. Thus he 'renders good' to both supporters and opponents and harm to neither (cf. Plato, *Resp.* 335 E); he avoids resentment and antagonism, as did Lysander (*Lys.* 5. 4), ensuring their commitment to himself personally, an immoral motive: Agesilaos was not thinking in Plutarch's or Plato's terms. (Socrates would presumably think that *not* to punish Sphodrias and 'make him better' was to harm him.)

To do justice to enemies is to harm them—ἔβλαπτε. With οὐκ ἔβλαπτε, Agesilaos' treatment of enemies is unjust—ἀδίκως, as is his treatment of friends, with συνέπραττε. Plutarch finds the one unjust but less blameworthy, ἀμεμπτότερος, than the other. If ἀδίκως οὐκ ἔβλαπτε means 'did not harm them without just cause', Agesilaos would be free of all blame: Plutarch's point would be less striking, though perhaps adequate.

2 καὶ τοὺς μὲν ἐχθροὺς ᾐσχύνετο μὴ τιμᾶν κατορθοῦντας, τοὺς δὲ φίλους οὐκ ἠδύνατο ψέγειν ἁμαρτάνοντας, ἀλλὰ καὶ βοηθῶν ἠγάλλετο καὶ συνεξαμαρτάνων αὐτοῖς· οὐδὲν γὰρ ᾤετο τῶν φιλικῶν ὑπουργημάτων αἰσχρὸν εἶναι.

Agesilaos was more generous to successful opponents and erring friends. The present participles show that he did not wait for the final outcome. He honoured enemies, 'recognized their worth', on their way to success, and helped friends while they were making their mistake.

The quality of αἰσχύνη (αἰσχρόν), 'shame, restraint', was developed to an unusual degree in Agesilaos' upbringing in the ἀγωγή and the συσσίτιον (*Lyk.* 8. 3, 18. 2–3, 21). In ch. 2 it contributed to the self-control which impressed Lysander, as he carried out the orders and accepted the censure of his seniors. With οὐδὲν ᾤετο αἰσχρόν, it contributes in this chapter to justify the building of his power-base. Like the Spartans' sense of justice, this quality is not the standard virtue, but is pragmatic, reflecting the citizens' 'practice of philosophy' without theoretical study of principles in their education (*Lyk.* 31. 2).

Plutarch's ἠγάλλετο, 'exulted', reflects Xenophon's claim that service to friends and the defeat of enemies is justified because it yields pleasure, ἡδοναί, as well as benefit (*Mem.* iv. 5. 10). But Agesilaos' motive is to win their allegiance (§3); at ch. 23. 7 he defends his practice by defining justice as 'acting in the interest of the state' (cf. ch. 37. 11; Plato, *Resp.* 338 E 6.). The Spartan's bridge from natural instinct to prescriptive norm in this regard is expediency rather than the traditional *talio*, repayment in kind.[3]

3 τοῖς δ᾽ αὖ διαφόροις καὶ πταίσασι πρῶτος συναχθόμενος καὶ δεηθεῖσι συμπράττων προθύμως ἐδημαγώγει καὶ προσήγετο πάντας.

Agesilaos' treatment of defeated opponents corresponds to that of unjust friends (§1), and the same verb is used, συμπράττων, 'joining in'. If Plutarch intended in ch. 4 that Agis' estate was shared with Latychidas' family, Agesilaos' action in avoiding resentment might be put into this category.

The verb ἐδημαγώγει gives a pejorative reference to the quality attributed to Agesilaos in ch. 1, τὸ δημοτικόν, 'a harmonious relationship with the people'. It is strong rhetoric used against an opponent for 'currying favour' in public life 'to maintain himself as leader of the people': Xenophon himself and the soldiers (Xen. *An.* vii. 6. 4); the kings and ephors (Arist. *Pol.* 1270^{b}14–15); Theramenes accused by the Thirty (Xen. *Hell.* ii. 3. 27); Kleomenes, who opposed Theramenes (*Lys.* 14. 5). The demagogue seeks only popular glory (*Agis*, 1. 2), yet Agis and Kleomenes are classed as demagogues; although, like the Gracchi, they attempted to reform their states, they failed because they relied on popular support (*Agis*, 2. 6). The people give power in return for services and the demagogue reciprocates with more and more favours (*Agis*, 2. 4). Kleomenes displays Agesilaos' quality of τὸ δημοτικόν, but is still a demagogue (*Kl.* 13. 1–2).

The second phrase, προσήγετο πάντας, summarizes Agesilaos' success in all these bids for power (cf. ch. 4). 'Winning universal support' approaches tyranny (see below, §4). Plutarch compares Agesilaos' treatment of enemies 'favourably' with that of his friends (ἀμεμπτότερος, §1 above). He follows Plato's Socrates, who would approve the rule of 'Harm no one'—though not the application of 'Help friends' to those who ought to be redefined as enemies or reformed by persuasion (*Resp.* 335 D, *Ap.* 26, 32; cf. *Sert.* 10. 3). Plutarch's purpose here is to reveal Agesilaos' flawed relationships which weaken the Lykourgan constitution—the bond between citizens competing to benefit the whole state (see below, §§4–5). Now their leader is binding them to further his own interests. Agesilaos' relations with his friends and enemies is a theme which runs throughout the *Life*.

4 ὁρῶντες οὖν οἱ ἔφοροι ταῦτα καὶ φοβούμενοι τὴν δύναμιν ἐζημίωσαν αὐτόν, αἰτίαν ὑπειπόντες ὅτι τοὺς κοινοὺς πολίτας ἰδίους κτᾶται.

The ephorate was introduced by the successors of Lykourgos (see above, ch. 4. 3; cf. Arist. *Pol.* 1265^{b}35–9) to provide competing elements that should counterbalance or curb the influence and powers of sectional interests (*Lyk.* 5. 6–7, 7. 1; cf. Plato, *Leg.* 692 B, Polyb. vi. 10).[4] Plutarch's record of the punishment is not a comment on its effectiveness—he reverts to Agesilaos' evasion of these curbs at ch. 20—but exemplifies the strife which is the next topic (§§5–7).

Plutarch's analysis seems to fit a charge of attempted tyranny, not made in ch. 4, though the word δύναμις was used there too (§6). When the ephors received the benefit, they did not detect Agesilaos' motive; here they notice that he is courting others and fine him for it. This fine, and indeed that reported by Theophrastos (ch. 2), may result from 'illegitimate inference'[5] by propagandists in or from anecdotal material about small stature and political donations (cf. *Mor.* 1D); but here there is a more serious case, requiring action by the ephors, who may have regarded Agesilaos as in breach of the oath sworn monthly to rule according to traditional practice (*Lak. Pol.* 15. 7). That Xenophon does not mention it is not unexpected.

The phrase τοὺς κοινοὺς πολίτας, 'the commonalty of citizens', appears to stand for ὅμοιοι, 'political equals',[6] a word first used by Xenophon to distinguish the Spartiates from the conspirators led by Kinadon, drawn from Helots, Freed Helots, Perioikoi, and Lesser Spartans (*Hell.* iii. 3. 4–11; see below, on ch. 6. 1).[7] The influence of the family was weakened by the Spartan constitution, so that all citizens equally owed loyalty and obedience to the state (*Lak. Pol.* 2. 2, 5. 2, 6. 1). Plutarch's expression τοὺς κοινοὺς πολίτας suggests that they 'belonged' to the state: κοινοὺς τῆς πόλεως (*Lyk.* 15. 8). They were free to transfer their political support in response to the essential competitive processes, but that they should have been bound irrevocably to Agesilaos by the ties he was forging, of loyalty to himself as personal possessions, ἰδίους, would inhibit Lykourgan competition among equals and dispossess the state of their loyalty.

5 καθάπερ γὰρ οἱ φυσικοὶ τὸ νεῖκος οἴονται καὶ τὴν ἔριν, εἰ τῶν ὅλων ἐξαιρεθείη, στῆναι μὲν ἂν τὰ οὐράνια, παύσασθαι δὲ πάντων τὴν γένεσιν καὶ κίνησιν ὑπὸ τῆς πρὸς πάντα πάντων ἁρμονίας, . . .

In §4, at the conclusion of the account, begun in ch. 4, of the tenor of the reign, Plutarch uses the ephors' fine imposed on Agesilaos to present criticism indirectly: Agesilaos achieved the power which the ephors feared by the innovatory pursuit of support and favour and by exploiting his own special qualities, τὸ δημοτικὸν καὶ φιλάνθρωπον (ch. 1), not by competition as his predecessors did and as Xenophon gave us to believe the mythical Kyros did (*Kyr.* viii. 2. 26–8).[8] Plutarch now explains (γάρ)—and justifies—the ephors' punishment of Agesilaos by his own indictment that he was weakening the Lykourgan constitution. In a brief analysis of philosophical theories which supposedly underlie the structure of Spartan society, he exposes Agesilaos' threat to the traditional constitution: his development of power through personal relationships was incompatible with the mainspring of Spartan society, the Lykourgan competitive virtues of τὸ φιλότιμον καὶ φιλόνικον. That Plutarch should refer to philosophy to justify his criticisms indicates their prime importance for him.

The start of the second half of the chapter is clearly indicated by καθάπερ, 'precisely as', a formalized expression found in legal documents (papyrological citation in LSJ 848); it conveys the impression of exact similarity (*Pomp.* 46. 4, 50. 3; Xen. *Hell.* iii. 4. 21, *Agesilaos* 1. 29; cf. the definition at ch. 23. 9). Plutarch shows interest in cosmology and theories about the natural world: character change in animals (*Pomp.* 28. 5), bodily symptoms

(*Alex*. 4. 5–6), the sun, musical harmony, divine governance (*Phok*. 2. 4–5), and eclipses (*Aem*. 17. 7–10).

Natural philosophy: a note on οἱ φυσικοί

The origin of the constitution is here set in a context of the theories of the Presocratics.[9] Plutarch's suggestion of a model perhaps records an interesting parallel observed by later theorists, but it is an anachronism. The lawgivers' reforms, those attributed to Lykourgos in Sparta[10] and Solon in Athens, are usually placed in the seventh and sixth centuries. The Presocratics lived in the sixth and fifth centuries,[11] and as they systematized their thoughts on cosmology and politics, they exploited the terms used already in the theories of medicine, dietetics, and metallurgy. Political evolution was a necessary precondition for their sense of awareness of questions about origins, and an important factor in determining their terminology, but Sparta did not take part in this theoretical development.

The name οἱ φυσικοί should indicate the materialist philosophers who concerned themselves with φύσις, nature, moving on from the earlier cosmogony, and it strictly refers to the earliest enquiries of the cosmologists into the nature of things. The name is here made to include later thinkers who discovered more abstract laws or principles such as those concerning the 'opposites within the unity' (Anaximander, Herakleitos)[12] or 'Love and Strife' (Empedokles).[13] The resulting 'harmony', ἁρμονία, combined things into compounds according to the divine, universal λόγος, 'reason', and νόμος, 'law' (Parmenides, Alkmaion, Empedokles).[14] The early theorists who discussed developments in city organization and administration, with associated political conflicts, applied the cosmologists' terminology as analogies in their political models (Anaximander, Alkmaion, and Sophists).[15]

Love and Strife alternate in prevalence (cf. ἄρχειν καὶ ἄρχεσθαι; see above after ch. 1. 5).[16] Plutarch regards Strife as the motive power that makes things happen, the divinity which keeps the 'world-order', τὰ οὐράνια, in place. In an orderly city the outward manifestation of unity is created from the striving citizens. Conflict between various factions and interests, the rich and the poor, creates a balance—ἁρμονία—and there is danger to survival if the balance in households and larger communities is disturbed.

For the theorists, when Love predominates completely the elements form a spherical deity, pure mind that does nothing but think. This corresponds with Plutarch's heavenly standstill 'if Strife and Discord were removed'.

Details of this picture are recognizable in the traditional Lykourgan constitution of Sparta, though this is not to say that it provided the model for the reformer. According to the parallel of the Presocratic systems, what the Spartans did by introducing competition, or 'Strife', was not only to activate and perpetuate the military virtues in the individual but also to create the 'mixed' constitution to ensure the harmonious pursuit under the best leaders of the best interests of all the Spartan peers. In the new friendly relationships that Agesilaos is now forging, by contrast, 'Strife' is put into decline, and Love, in the form of reciprocal favours, tends to eliminate all but the leader's policy and destroys competitive virtue, the means of Sparta's survival.

. . . οὕτως ἔοικεν ὁ Λακωνικὸς νομοθέτης ὑπέκκαυμα τῆς ἀρετῆς ἐμβαλεῖν εἰς τὴν πολιτείαν τὸ φιλότιμον καὶ φιλόνικον, ἀεί τινα τοῖς ἀγαθοῖς διαφορὰν καὶ ἄμιλλαν εἶναι πρὸς ἀλλήλους βουλόμενος·

The similarity of Spartan competition which has been observed by Plutarch (for διαφορά see ch. 4. 4 and here, §§3, 5) is not attributed to deliberate imitation by the lawgiver. As in the first part of the sentence Plutarch brought into consideration only the *removal* of 'Strife' from among the constituent parts, so here he mentions only its *introduction* into the constitution. The competition was to be citizen against citizen, and parallels Kyros' introduction of competition in good actions among citizens to promote commitment to the king or state instead of to each other's welfare (Xen. *Cyr.* viii. 2. 26–8).[17] The Spartan lawgiver's intention was to stimulate courage: the competition which creates the harmonious internal structure of the state also supplies courageous citizens for its defence. It was after the acquisition of Messenia that the elements of competition at Sparta, in the ἀγωγή and in the determination of policies, were recorded as part of the means of ensuring survival.

The metaphor, ὑπέκκαυμα, 'a provocative incentive', derives from combustible matter, fuel and food. It fuels φιλοτιμία at *Pomp.* 30. 8, as here, and in the verb form at *Agis*, 2. 5 and *Kl.* 2. 2; with war below at ch. 31. 4, anger at *Fab.* 7. 2, and people's spirits at

TG 13. 4; in the Lykourgan literature it sparked affection in marriage (*Lyk.* 15. 5).

'Ambition' is a poor rendering of φιλότιμον in this context, as elsewhere in Plutarch's Spartan *Lives*, in which the emphasis is often on the Spartans' 'desire for significant achievement for the benefit of the state', with no implication of personal gain, a striking example being Lysander, on the authority of Theopompos (*Lys.* 30. 2). There can be only positive meaning, 'competitive rivalry', in φιλόνικον here.

τὴν γὰρ ἀνθυπείκουσαν τῷ ἀνελέγκτῳ χάριν ἀργὴν καὶ ἀνανταγώνιστον οὖσαν οὐκ ὀρθῶς ὁμόνοιαν λέγεσθαι.

The descriptions of this undesirable complaisance indicate what was, before Agesilaos, a supposed correspondence between Lykourgos and the philosophers in their view of ἁρμονία. The concord in each case followed not from the removal of one of the conflicting elements, but from the state of equilibrium achieved by the continual struggle for supremacy. This may seem to be at variance with the ἄρχεσθαι element in the ἀγωγή of ch. 1, but, continuing the philosophical metaphor, in the ἀγωγή where both qualities, ἄρχειν καὶ ἄρχεσθαι (see above, §5), were encouraged, the conflict of opposites created the balance, or ὁμόνοια. There is play on the words ἁρμονία and ὁμόνοια (parechesis).

Plutarch records that Lykourgos committed suicide, and by having his ashes scattered in the sea ensured that the Spartans' oath to observe his constitution until he should return would never be cancelled (*Lyk.* 29. 5, 31. 5); the Spartans followed his rules for centuries thereafter. Solon also went abroad, leaving the Athenians to follow his rules in his absence (*Solon*, 25. 5). Plutarch may have seen a further link between natural and political philosophy, for Anaxagoras' Mind (*Nous*), the creative and ordering power, withdrew once the process was under way.[18]

6 τοῦτο δ᾽ ἀμέλει συνεωρακέναι καὶ τὸν Ὅμηρον οἴονταί τινες· οὐ γὰρ ἂν τὸν Ἀγαμέμνονα ποιῆσαι χαίροντα τοῦ Ὀδυσσέως καὶ τοῦ Ἀχιλλέως εἰς λοιδορίαν προαχθέντων 'ἐκπάγλοις ἐπέεσσι', εἰ μὴ μέγα τοῖς κοινοῖς ἀγαθὸν ἐνόμιζεν εἶναι τὸν πρὸς ἀλλήλους ζῆλον καὶ τὴν διαφορὰν τῶν ἀρίστων.

The use of Homeric quotation (*Od.* viii. 77–8) in support of an argument is a rhetorical technique, and demonstrates cultural continuity with the past in Plutarch's thinking. Here τινες, 'some people', support their argument: Plutarch rejects its extreme form. He rounds off the topic in ring composition with the word διαφορά, which recalls §§3 and 5, and the early competition approved for the kings (ch. 4. 4).

Homer can be read for historical evidence, true or false, as Thucydides shows: ὡς Ὅμηρος τοῦτο δεδήλωκεν, εἴ τῳ ἱκανὸς τεκμηριῶσαι (i. 9. 4), as well as for pleasure. Here, more typically of Homeric fundamentalists, he is presented as—for some—composing an effective reaction for his own selected didactic purpose, the revelation of useful, lasting truths (cf. Plato, *Ion*). Heroic competition was to excel, αἰὲν ἀριστεύειν (*Il.* vi. 208), for personal repute, but Plutarch's citation supposes Agamemnon to recognize that rivalry was also a public good, as it was in Sparta, where citizens developed the means to secure Sparta's survival; from boyhood they were warriors, πολεμικώτεροι, 'pretty bellicose' (*Lak. Pol.* 2. 7). In Homer's context Agamemnon is reminded of an unspecified prophecy, in which a scholiast predictably finds a promise of Greek victory following a quarrel. The prophecy is associated with the accomplishment of the designs of Zeus (*Od.* viii. 81–2; cf. *Il.* 1. 5). Plutarch seems to make a causal connection between quarrel and victory.

7 ταῦτα μὲν οὖν οὐκ ἂν οὕτως τις ἁπλῶς συγχωρήσειεν· αἱ γὰρ ὑπερβολαὶ τῶν φιλονικιῶν χαλεπαὶ ταῖς πόλεσι καὶ μεγάλους κινδύνους ἔχουσαι.

Plutarch does not name Lykourgos in this chapter as responsible for introducing the competitive element which was later abused, but speaks only of the Lakonian lawgiver, avoiding, like Aristotle,[19] a direct criticism of him by name, for he greatly admired him (*Lyk.* 28. 6, 29–30). Here, too, he speaks only of αἱ ὑπερβολαὶ τῶν φιλονικιῶν, 'excesses of competitive rivalry', leaving out τὸ φιλότιμον, paired with it above as introduced by the lawgiver. Plutarch's rejection of the extreme argument, then, strictly refers only to Homer's 'rivalry' and does not include τὸ φιλότιμον. This element in the Spartan constitution is reserved for consideration in chs. 7 and 8.

Plutarch's critique of Agesilaos' politics

Plutarch, in this passage of self-revelation, judges by the Delphic maxim μηδὲν ἄγαν, though he does not quote it.[20] Agesilaos is guilty of two excesses. He puts Sparta at risk by destroying Lykourgan competition through excessive friendliness, and although his early competitive traits were acceptable Lykourgan virtues, later his introduction of excessive rivalry and conflict into Spartan life is to be a thoroughly destructive force (chs. 7–8, 22–3, 26, 28, 36). Plutarch himself rejected the complete removal of competition, which was later the doctrine of Epicureanism, because it meant withdrawal from public life.[21] He expresses in this conclusion to the chapter a more moderate lesson relevant to readers of his own time and place. He is more explicit elsewhere, recommending Greeks to serve Rome but not to seek aggrandizement for themselves, that they should be content with local power, and that the aim of Greek statesmen should be only concord (*Mor.* 814 C–F, 470 C, 824 C).[22]

Agesilaos may have been encouraged to assume his lenient attitude (§2 above) by the harshness of Spartan life. Yet the removal of the competitive element in the management of public affairs by manipulating his relations with the citizens destroyed what Plutarch thought best in Sparta, and deprived its policies of true ἁρμονία, substituting an unacceptable form of χάρις, 'partiality'. Agesilaos' acquisition of excessive powers was recognized—and punished—by the ephors, and, because Plutarch relates that to his treatment of friends and enemies, this, too, is to be seen as injurious to the state.

Agesilaos was not alone responsible, of course. In the same— reprehensible—way Lysander manipulated his friends and allies in Asia Minor, winning their allegiance by favours and complicity in injustices and wrongdoing: and with 'to win universal support' (*Lys.* 5. 4) Plutarch indicates the same result there, using a phrase, ὥστε προσέχειν ἅπαντας αὐτῷ, reminiscent of §3 here. In Sparta, too, Lysander's friends and allies won governmental positions as prizes (*Lys.* 19. 1), upsetting both leaders and peers; later he expected to be supported by them in his bid for the throne (*Lys.* 24. 4–5). These two Spartan *Lives* consistently illustrate the philosophical analysis here.

Plutarch's political theory, beginning to be revealed here,

illustrates the dilemma of government, and the conflict between leadership and freedom. The English judiciary in 1986 defined national interest as 'what the government says it is'. This is the form in which Agesilaos wishes to define justice—as the interest of Sparta—and so to justify his own actions. If Agesilaos and Lysander were in a position to impose their leadership in an innovative way, what needs to be considered is *what* national interest they should have used their powers to achieve. Plutarch's answer is given at *Lykourgos*, 30. 2: good order and justice, under the Spartan constitution of Lykourgos. Aristotle saw the need for the state to ensure its survival by strong defence (*Pol.* 1265ᵃ17–25), but he would not approve of Agesilaos' policies designed to control others—in the Peloponnese, in Boiotia, and elsewhere— outside the borders of Lakonia.²³ Agesilaos' suppression of the Lykourgan virtue of 'competitive rivalry', φιλονικία, among the Spartan peers, and the excesses of his own competitive rivalry in accumulating power at home and abroad in disregard of Lykourgan injunctions, are important themes that Plutarch introduces in this chapter and illustrates in the rest of *Agesilaos*.

Agesilaos' campaigns in Asia Minor

Lys. 23. 1–27. 4, *Pel.* 20. 3–22. 2, *Artax.* 23. 1; Xen. *Hell.* iii. 4. 1–29, *Agesilaos*, 1. 6–35, 3. 3, 4. 6; Diod. xiv. 79. 1–3, 80. 1–8; *Hell. Ox.* vi. i–ix. i, xvi. 1 (Bruce (1967), 77–93, 132–5); Nepos, *Agesilaus*, 2. 1–4, 3. 4–6; Paus. iii. 9. 1–7; Polyain. 2. 1. 6, 9; Frontin. *Strat.* 1. 8. 12, 11. 17.

6. Assembling the expedition to Asia Minor; an ill omen at Aulis

1 Τοῦ δ' Ἀγησιλάου τὴν βασιλείαν νεωστὶ παρειληφότος, ἀπήγγελλόν τινες ἐξ Ἀσίας ἥκοντες ὡς ὁ Περσῶν βασιλεὺς παρασκευάζοιτο μεγάλῳ στόλῳ Λακεδαιμονίους ἐκβαλεῖν τῆς θαλάσσης.

Plutarch indicates a vague but short interval of time since the accession, returning to the arrival of the messengers after tracing the development of Agesilaos' power well into his reign (chs. 4–5). Xenophon indicates a similar interval at *Agesilaos*, 1. 6, where he omits the conspiracy of Kinadon. He records it in *Hellenika* as the reign's first event during its first year (iii. 3. 4–11; see above, on ch. 5. 4),[1] and appears to commend both the aspiration of decent 'lesser' Spartans to be equal to the best, and the success of the authorities in suppressing it (*Hell.* iii. 3. 5, 11). Plutarch omits it, perhaps because in Xenophon's account, although Agesilaos has a share in exposing it, it is not directed against him, and the ephors take the countermeasures.[2] He, perhaps, would not wish to hint at signs of Spartan social decline so early in his narrative. Later he reports two conspiracies, which mark discontent with Sparta's decline and are dealt with by Agesilaos himself (ch. 32. 6–11).

Xenophon reports that a Syracusan, Herodas, brought information about the gathering of the Persian fleet, though he could not specify its intended destination (*Hell.* iii. 4. 1). In his *Agesilaos* the fleet, together with a land force, was to attack Greeks (1. 6). It is surprising that the Spartan admiral Pharax, who was operating in the area (Diod. xiv. 79. 4), did not send word of it. Since

Derkylidas, the harmost in command of Spartan land forces there, had undertaken to report his proposed settlement with Tissaphernes to Sparta (*Hell.* iii. 2. 20), the dispatch of Agesilaos may have developed in part from this consultation, rather than only from Herodas' information (cf. *Lys.* 23. 1).

Plutarch's phrase 'drive the Spartans from the sea' targets the waters off Karia to which the ephors had already sent Pharax and Derkylidas (*Hell.* iii. 2. 12)—a more realistic interpretation of Persian concerns with the Greek world.[3] There was no danger of the invasion of Greece to which the startled response of the Spartans points (*Hell.* iii. 4. 2). Preparations for transporting 8,000 men by sea begin in *Hellenika* after the punishment of Kinadon, and will have occupied several months.

2 ὁ δὲ Λύσανδρος ἐπιθυμῶν αὖθις εἰς Ἀσίαν ἀποσταλῆναι καὶ βοηθῆσαι τοῖς φίλοις, οὓς αὐτὸς μὲν ἄρχοντας καὶ κυρίους τῶν πόλεων ἀπέλιπε, κακῶς δὲ χρώμενοι καὶ βιαίως τοῖς πράγμασιν ἐξέπιπτον ὑπὸ τῶν πολιτῶν καὶ ἀπέθνησκον, ἀνέπεισε τὸν Ἀγησίλαον ἐπιθέσθαι τῇ στρατείᾳ καὶ προπολεμῆσαι τῆς Ἑλλάδος ἀπωτάτω διαβάντα καὶ φθάσαντα τὴν τοῦ βαρβάρου παρασκευήν.

Plutarch gives to Lysander the initiative for urging the expedition to Asia Minor. He presents him with two motives: his private wish, the rescue of his friends there from violence, and his proposal, the pre-emptive strike in defence of Greece. The 'friends' are the dekarchs appointed by Lysander (see note below) and, as Xenophon, unlike Plutarch, explains, abandoned by the ephors, who in 403 decreed the restoration of 'ancestral' authority (Xen. *Hell.* iii. 4. 2; see on ch. 14. 4). The phrase is clearly an emotive, propagandist one, for governments, including some tyrannies, seek and claim constitutional validation by advertising continuity with the past. In 403 Pausanias replaced Lysander's extreme oligarchy in Athens with 'ancestral' government, of reconciled moderates and democrats. In Samos the survivors from Lysander's dekarchy probably survived until 401, and, as Agesilaos found elsewhere in Asia Minor, perhaps continued to 394, according to Shipley 1987: it was then that ancestral, more moderate, constitutions prevailed (see §3 below and on ch. 15. 1). Plutarch mentions only the prior cause which led to the decree, the unpopularity of the oppressors of whom he evidently disapproved, and the violence of the citizens to which he refers again:

eventually Agesilaos himself restores order (chs. 7. 2, 14. 4, 15. 1; cf. Xen. *Agesilaos*, 1. 37). Lysander's motive is more aggressive at *Lysander*, 23. 1, where he urges destroying the Persians, although they present no threat.

The initiative in Xenophon's *Agesilaos* is not Lysander's but Agesilaos' own. A defensive panhellenist motive is the first one given: at 1. 6–8 the intention is initially to try to make peace, but if the Persian wishes to make war, to hinder him from attacking the Greeks. The further motive, of revenge for Persia's earlier invasion, is extended to setting up at Persian expense a contest not about Greece but about Asia. The omission here of Lysander's part enables Xenophon to show that Agesilaos' eagerness to undertake the expedition, fight Persia, and protect Greece, won an enthusiastic response. Xenophon's purpose is to summon up over-whelming admiration (1. 36) for the king's concern to promote Greek interests: Plutarch retains only the defensive aspect.

In *Hellenika* (iii. 4. 2) Xenophon assigns the initiative to Lysander.[4] He advises Agesilaos to undertake an expedition to Asia, confident in Greek naval superiority and in the example of those who had safely accompanied Kyros to Kounaxa and returned, an indirect compliment to Xenophon himself (cf. Tissaphernes' respect for them at *Hell.* iii. 2. 18), which Plutarch omits (but cf. ch. 9. 2). Lysander is given prominence by Xenophon here, perhaps, so that he may take responsibility for the false military expectations, and for the failure of the proposed restoration of the dekarchies: he was not a whole-hearted admirer of Lysander (cf. *Hell.* i. 6. 1–11).[5] He adds Lysander's wish to accompany the expedition and to restore his dekarchies. Given the Spartans' divergent political priorities, it is unlikely that Lysander would declare this aim in public, and that would explain why Xenophon merely appended it to his list; or perhaps he con-jectured it from hindsight. The panhellenist gesture of the visit to Aulis will have obscured this aspect of the mission's purpose; Plutarch elevates it to first place. The panhellenist potential of the campaign recurs at ch. 15. 3 (see Introd., E.7(*a–b*)).

Xenophon's divergent accounts of the expedition's objectives are paralleled by his judgements at the end: interruption of a glorious scheme of conquest (*Agesilaos*, 1. 36), or of a more modest plan to detach tribes from the King[6] after the larger ambi-tions had not been fulfilled (*Hell.* iv. 1. 41). At *Agesilaos*, 7. 5–7 he praises Agesilaos as a committed 'philhellene' and 'hater of Persians', ever contemplating a war of revenge; his assessment of the eventual success of the campaign is more restrained in *Hellenika*, where he did not wish—or perhaps did not feel free—to give the original initiative exclusively to Agesilaos.

Plutarch, like Xenophon in *Hellenika* but not in *Agesilaos*, needs Lysander in the quarrel which takes place immediately after the arrival in Ephesos, and his initial influence is needed to decline as Agesilaos' authority is enhanced. That Plutarch does not follow Xenophon's *Agesilaos* and give Agesilaos the initiative for proposing the expedition is consistent with his apparent wish not to present the campaigning in Asia Minor as a glorious military achievement. As the concluding sections of Xenophon's accounts reflect their initial tones, so Plutarch concludes in a significant but different vein at the recall (ch. 15), regretting the shameful outbreak of yet another war of Greek against Greek and the postponement of the humbling of the King, but proving Agesilaos' greatness by his immediate obedience.

Spartan expansionism

The expansionist activity of Sparta has been traced to Lysander.[7] Sparta's special interest in Asia Minor was to control the route to mainland Greece. Lysander was admiral in his own right in 407, and then, in 405 (*Hell.* ii. 1. 7), because a second term in the same office was not allowed, he was sent as ἐπιστολεύς, 'secretary', under a nominal admiral, to take command at Aigospotamoi—illegally.[8] He had a close relationship with the satrap Kyros, who was supporting the Spartans (Xen. *Hell.* i. 4. 3), and built up Spartan naval strength, paid for by Kyros' Persian money, which was vital in winning the Peloponnesian war. Lysander's subsequent settlement of Asia Minor set up regimes in the cities—oligarchs and dekarchs, attested by Diodoros (xiv. 13. 1; cf. *Lys.* 13. 3–4), some moderate, some wealthy and noble, others men of ability, with a harmost sometimes, as in Samos (Xen. *Hell.* ii. 7; Diod. xiv. 3. 5, 13. 1),[9] all owing him personal loyalty.[10]

But there was opposition in Sparta to the expansionist policy, perhaps from those whose first priority was internal security; and the Kinadon episode indicates the dangers that were to be feared. The enterprises undertaken by Lysander were curtailed when in

403 or 402 the ephors proclaimed restoration of 'traditional government' in the Ionian cities, according to Xenophon (*Hell.* iii. 4. 2), for whom the phrase usually indicates some form of aristocracy. They presumably cancelled the policy of installing harmosts, which had become unpopular in the cities, though it is not stated whether the ruling was actively enforced.[11] Xenophon refers to later prolonged disorders (*Hell.* iii. 4. 7), which Plutarch seems to indicate above resulted in their final expulsion (§2: ἐξέπιπτον ὑπὸ τῶν πολιτῶν), though made possible by the ephors (*Hell.* iii. 4. 2: ἐκπεπτωκυίας δὲ διὰ τοὺς ἐφόρους).

After repaying Kyros for his help against Athens by supporting his unsuccessful bid for the throne until his death at Kounaxa, the Spartans were involved again in Asia Minor in response to Ionian appeals for assistance against Tissaphernes, who had been sent by Artaxerxes to recover his former possessions there (Xen. *Hell.* iii. 1. 3, iii. 2. 12). Thibron and Derkylidas, sent out during and after the last years of Agis' reign, in 400 and 399–397 respectively, achieved little of the intended liberation but were not eliminated by the local resources of Tissaphernes (Diod. xiv. 36–8). Despite the ephors' decision in 403/2, the Spartan fleet remained dominant until the battle off Knidos in 394, and Sparta continued to use the Aegean Sea for transporting troops.

The King now agreed to the proposal by Pharnabazos, the Persian satrap (i.e. governor) of Daskylitis, to build a fleet, evidently he was determined to stop Spartan intervention in Asia Minor, and perhaps to punish Sparta for helping Kyros. Pharnabazos' main concern was no doubt for the coastal cities of northern Anatolia where Xenophon and the remnant of the Ten Thousand had ended their march. It would take some time to build and support the fleet, and to hire and train the crews, and it was not ready in time to intercept Agesilaos. Konon, the former Athenian general, who had been with Evagoras in Cyprus since escaping from Aigospotamoi, was appointed admiral of the Persian fleet by Pharnabazos (Diod. xiv. 39). It sailed in 396 and first operated successfully in the east and then in Greek waters after Knidos (394). This threat faced the Spartans after the withdrawal from Asia.

3 ἅμα δὲ τοῖς ἐν Ἀσίᾳ φίλοις ἐπέστελλε πέμπειν εἰς Λακεδαίμονα καὶ στρατηγὸν Ἀγησίλαον αἰτεῖσθαι.

Xenophon presents complex motivation for the expedition: later, on arrival in Asia, when communicating with Tissaphernes, Agesilaos states a more simple requirement, autonomy for the cities (*Agesilaos*, 1. 10, *Hell*. iii. 4. 5). Plutarch may be right to mention their involvement here: at *Lysander*, 23. 1–2, it is not news of the Persian fleet but the envoys sent in response to Lysander's message who provide the opportunity to bring the proposed expedition before the Spartans. Xenophon does not mention any request at this time, but he records the earlier request of the Ionian allies—and Kyros—for the reappointment of Lysander (*Hell*. ii. 1. 6; cf. *Lys*. 7. 1–2). Perhaps Plutarch saw the likelihood of Lysander's intrigue again at this point.[12] The theme of friendship recurs: the friends installed by Lysander shared reciprocal obligations and benefits with him, and the transitivity of these relationships would require him to share their hostility to their opponents.[13] Agesilaos' mission would give him the opportunity.

Politics in Greek Asia Minor

From 404/3, Lysander's friends, who had no doubt been approved by Kyros, may have been among those who co-operated with him against Tissaphernes in their disputes over the control of their satrapal areas (*Hell*. iii. 1. 3), and feared the latter when in 400 Artaxerxes appointed him as satrap of his own and Kyros' provinces. At *Hell*. iii. 4. 7 Xenophon reports confusion in the cities: 'It was not a democracy as in the time of Athenian rule, nor dekarchy as in the time of Lysander.' Plutarch seems to be referring to this situation when he speaks above of the violent reaction of the citizens to the unjust rule of force, which would be a chance for a greater element of democracy—of a kind—to emerge: a moderate form of oligarchy is probably indicated.[14] The leaders would be of the same class as their predecessors, but less extreme. In ch. 7. 3, Plutarch says the petitioners preferred to approach Lysander when they saw that Agesilaos was, in contrast, δημοτικός. It is clear from their petitions that they were not in power in their cities but were the extreme oligarchic elements that Lysander had it in mind to help.

4 παρελθὼν οὖν εἰς τὸ πλῆθος Ἀγησίλαος ἀνεδέξατο τὸν πόλεμον, εἰ δοῖεν αὐτῷ τριάκοντα μὲν ἡγεμόνας καὶ συμβούλους Σπαρτιάτας, νεοδαμώδεις δὲ λογάδας δισχιλίους, τὴν δὲ συμμαχικὴν εἰς ἑξακισχιλίους δύναμιν.

Plutarch used the phrase ἐν τῇ δίκῃ in ch. 3. 7 over the succession. Here he shows a similar procedure in an appeal for the approval of the people before the undertaking of war, a procedure perhaps demonstrating continuity with Agamemnon's invitation to his army to approve a major operation in which the willingness of troops to follow the leader was essential (Hom. *Il.* ii. 73–5). Xenophon records similar proceedings in a meeting of the allies (*Hell.* iii. 4. 2–3).

Kings were customarily accompanied by two ephors on campaign (*Hell.* ii. 4. 36). There were ephors at the battle of Plataia, 479 (Hdt. ix. 76. 3), and 'advisers' for the first time in 418 when Agis was given a commission of ten at the battle of Mantineia. They were not uncommon in the case of other commanders at sea and on land.[15] Plutarch's ἡγεμόνας, 'officers', may misrepresent their position, for in Xenophon the appointment is simply as 'Thirty Spartiates' (*Hell.* iii. 4. 2) and their status is not supervisory (cf. ch. 12. 5 and Xen. *Agesilaos*, 1. 13, where they are easily downcast).

'Spartan' armies, at any rate armies operating outside the Peloponnese in the disturbed period since the 420s, often contained Spartan generals, and mainly non-citizen and non-Spartan troops far outnumbering the Spartiates.[16] Thucydides describes the similar make-up of Brasidas' army in Thrace (iv. 80. 4). The identity and status of νεοδαμώδεις, 'new people', are obscure. Seven hundred helots were enrolled as hoplites in Brasidas' army in 424 (Thuc. iv. 80), and in 421, after they had returned from Chalkidike, the name is used, for the first time, of the people they joined, apparently as a frontier garrison (Thuc. v. 34. 1). The fact that Brasidas' helots, now liberated, were settled together with colonists who already had that status at Lepreon on the Elis border, suggests a similar helot origin for the two groups, but whereas the new men were given freedom *after* hoplite service, νεοδαμώδεις in service were already free.[17] Xenophon includes νεοδαμώδεις in Kinadon's list of the discontented, placed between helots and ὑπομείονες. If the list is in ascending order of status, the reply to the ephors' enquiry about the source of the conspirators' arms may suggest that all but the lowest rank, ὁ ὄχλος, were in the army and fully armed (*Hell*. iii. 3. 6–7). λογάδας may indicate their exclusive training as hoplites.

5 συμπράττοντος δὲ τοῦ Λυσάνδρου, πάντα προθύμως ἐψηφίσαντο, καὶ τὸν Ἀγησίλαον ἐξέπεμπον ἔχοντα τοὺς τριάκοντα Σπαρτιάτας, ὧν ὁ Λύσανδρος ἦν πρῶτος, οὐ διὰ τὴν ἑαυτοῦ δόξαν καὶ δύναμιν μόνον, ἀλλὰ καὶ διὰ τὴν Ἀγησιλάου φιλίαν, ᾧ μεῖζον ἐδόκει τῆς βασιλείας ἀγαθὸν διαπεπρᾶχθαι τὴν στρατηγίαν ἐκείνην.

The vote will have authorized pay for troops until they could live by plundering enemy territory in Asia Minor. In Xenophon (*Hell*. iii. 4. 3) the Lakedaimonians give provisions for six months. Plutarch shows Agesilaos' consistent attitude to friendship, in that Lysander's personal influence reinforced his official status and reputation, to make him the closest and most senior adviser. The debt of gratitude—the reciprocity of friendships—may have been among Agesilaos' feelings, or it may be the conjecture of the author, who perhaps stresses the obligations of friendship in readiness for the coming quarrel (cf. *Comp*. 1. 3). The reality, probably prearranged—like the bid for the kingship—and secret, of course, would be that Lysander, of proven ability and experience, was automatically first choice from the start. Having procured the kingship, Agesilaos would need to have command in a military campaign also 'fixed', διαπεπρᾶχθαι, in order to make something of it. Xenophon uses the same verb in Tissaphernes' speech urging Agesilaos to arrange the armistice with him (*Hell*. iii. 4. 5).

The powers of a Spartan king derived from his duty to lead the Spartan army in war and his competence in doing this.[18] The reputation and experience Agesilaos obtained in Asia would be the foundation on which he built his special influence and authority in other fields, such as policy-making, within the limitations of restrictions operating through the ephorate, council and assembly, unless he could outmanoeuvre them.

6 ἀθροιζομένης δὲ τῆς δυνάμεως εἰς Γεραιστόν, αὐτὸς εἰς Αὐλίδα κατελθὼν μετὰ τῶν φίλων καὶ νυκτερεύσας, ἔδοξε κατὰ τοὺς ὕπνους εἰπεῖν τινα πρὸς αὐτόν·

The harbour at the southern end of Euboia was a convenient departure point for Asia Minor and the regular base at Ephesos, and, being at the extremity of the safe home waters, a suitable assembly point for a naval expedition whose units made their own way there from other parts of Greece. Boiotian Aulis, on the mainland, opposite Chalkis in Euboia, assembly point for Agamemnon's Trojan expedition in Homer, was less exposed, but it was not available to Agesilaos.

Sparta and Thebes

Spartan relations with Thebes began to deteriorate soon after the Peloponnesian war, when controversy arose over the booty at Dekeleia and the treatment of Athens (Xen. *Hell*. ii. 2. 19–20, iii. 5. 5; cf. *Lys*. 27). The Thebans helped the Athenian exiles in 404–403 at Phyle, harboured them in Thebes, and refused to contribute troops for the Elis expedition in 401 and for Agesilaos' present campaign (Xen. *Hell*. iii. 5. 5).

There could be an ancient justificatory ground for antagonism. The grave of Hektor son of Priam, worshipped by the Thebans and shown to Pausanias at Oedipus' Fountain (Paus. ix. 18. 5),[19] may commemorate an early conflict between two Greek communities[20] which was later transferred to Ilion (cf. Pausanias, iii. 19. 9 on the worship of Helen and Menelaos at Therapne). The shrine may not predate 300 BC,[21] but the cult of Hektor has been related to the fourth century and the Theban hegemony or earlier,[22] and would provide material for popular propaganda as well as the charge of medism. The popularity of Herakles on Theban coinage in the fifth century and his cult in holy places as part of the rehabilitation of Thebes[23] offer a parallel.

The sacrifice at Aulis

Xenophon has no reference to Agesilaos' dream in *Hellenika*, and in *Agesilaos* no reference at all to Aulis here; at *Hell*. iii. 4. 3 Agesilaos makes the visit explicitly with Agamemnon in mind, apparently without companions, but with the sacrifice as its purpose. Plutarch records Agesilaos' dream at Aulis[24] and adds the friends—perhaps the 'advisers'—but not the reason for the visit, for it has a purpose only after the dream. Dreams lend themselves as ornaments—for the dreamer in the original propaganda, or for the author of a later record. For the historian their evidence cannot be substantiated: only the dreamer knows what was in the dream, and no one can prove a dream fabricated. Dreams are a recognized vehicle for divine communication, used, like oracles, to reveal or deny support for human action, and it may be Plutarch's intention to portray this here. He could have secured greater verisimilitude by placing the dream at Geraistos, for a planned visit involving sacrifice seems the more likely, and the spread of news of the intention would explain the timely arrival of the Boiotians, as in Xenophon's account.

Agamemnon sacrificed to Artemis to obtain a favourable wind at Aulis, and it would be blameworthy not to do the same, particularly if the wind was later adverse. Agesilaos was not alone in paying respect to heroes by visiting a Homeric place—Alexander visited Troy. It is not possible to read Agesilaos' mind in going to Aulis, whether he wished to announce to the rest of Greece the scale of his ambitions, frighten Persia, stress the panhellenist purpose, or obscure Lysander's aims. He was perhaps making a gesture of Spartan annoyance and strength in view of the Thebans' rejection of his call for contingents from other cities to join the expedition (Xen. *Hell.* iii. 4. 3). Xenophon does not exploit the episode, except with Agesilaos' anger, directed, presumably, against Thebes. Perhaps he realized that there was a bad omen here for the expedition, which is the point for Plutarch, compounded by the suggestion in the dream of divine motivation; see Introd., E.7(*a*).

7 Ὦ βασιλεῦ Λακεδαιμονίων, ὅτι μὲν οὐδεὶς τῆς Ἑλλάδος ὁμοῦ συμπάσης ἀπεδείχθη στρατηγὸς ἢ πρότερον Ἀγαμέμνων καὶ σὺ νῦν μετ' ἐκεῖνον, ἐννοεῖς δήπουθεν· ἐπεὶ δὲ τῶν μὲν αὐτῶν ἄρχεις ἐκείνῳ, τοῖς δ' αὐτοῖς πολεμεῖς, ἀπὸ δὲ τῶν αὐτῶν τόπων ὁρμᾷς ἐπὶ τὸν πόλεμον, εἰκός ἐστι καὶ θῦσαί σε τῇ θεῷ θυσίαν ἣν ἐκεῖνος ἐνταῦθα θύσας ἐξέπλευσεν.

The address begins with the first three-and-a-half feet of a dactylic hexameter, with caesura in the second and fourth feet, lending dignity to the communication and honour to the recipient. A reader may think that Agesilaos, the first narrator of the dream, composed the verse, or suppose that it is a quotation recollected in the dream—or in the telling—from other oracular utterances. Agesilaos is further honoured by being linked more objectively to the literary hero than if it had been his own wish to imitate him.

The triplet, with anaphora, is a formal feature in the expression, alliteration and polyptosis adding to the formality. Plutarch follows Xenophon in referring to the sacrifice as θυσία (*Hell*. iii. 4. 3–4; Paus. ix. 19. 6–7).[25]

8 ἅμα δέ πως ὑπῆλθε τὸν Ἀγησίλαον ὁ τῆς κόρης σφαγιασμός, ἣν ὁ πατὴρ ἔσφαξε πεισθεὶς τοῖς μάντεσιν.

A similar dream occurs before Leuktra, commanding Pelopidas to sacrifice a maiden if he wishes to win victory (*Pel.* 21–2).[26] Euripides' *Iphigeneia at Aulis*, performed first in 405 after his death, indicates contemporary circulation of that story. Plutarch names neither Artemis, the deity, nor the victim, Iphigeneia. Homer has Kalchas as the prophet at Aulis and at Troy, but does not name Iphigeneia, though Aeschylus does (*Ag.* 1527–55). Human sacrifice is thought to explain marks on children's skeletons found at Knossos in 1986, dated to the fifteenth century BC,[27] but the report by the Lesbian philosopher, Phanias, of sacrifices before Salamis, seems not to have convinced Plutarch (*Them.* 13. 2, cf. *Pel.* 21), and is not mentioned by Herodotos. Functional and ritual distinctions in sacrificial offerings for mantic and propitiatory purposes may be indicated in the use of θύειν and σφάζειν. Agamemnon was required to propitiate Artemis before crossing the sea, Pelopidas to honour heroines before battle: Agesilaos may be thought to be avoiding divine wrath for ignoring a precedent, but there were always 'signs' available for divination by the seer and Plutarch mentions the altar.[28] However, he may contrast the 'sacrificial bloodletting' (σφάζειν) in Agamemnon's sacrifice with the humane responses of both Agesilaos and Pelopidas (§9).[29]

οὐ μὴν διετάραξεν αὐτόν, ἀλλ' ἀναστὰς καὶ διηγησάμενος τοῖς φίλοις τὰ φανέντα τὴν μὲν θεὸν ἔφη τιμήσειν οἷς εἰκός ἐστι χαίρειν θεὸν οὖσαν, οὐ μιμήσεσθαι δὲ τὴν ἀπάθειαν τοῦ τότε στρατηγοῦ.

Once Agesilaos tells of his dream, the story can enter the stream of tradition and be passed down as can any other event, such as the communication of his intention to honour the goddess, observed and related by the friends, whose presence at Aulis with Agesilaos was therefore necessary to the narrative.

9 καὶ καταστέψας ἔλαφον ἐκέλευσεν ἀπάρξασθαι τὸν ἑαυτοῦ μάντιν, οὐχ ὥσπερ εἰώθει τοῦτο ποιεῖν ὁ ὑπὸ τῶν Βοιωτῶν τεταγμένος.

Agesilaos performs on his own authority the substitution made by Artemis at Euripides, *IT* 28, being thus more civilized than Agamemnon, as is Pelopidas, who sacrifices a chestnut filly.[30] A king's priestly office gives him the authority to make decisions about sacrifices. His seer is present but rather than consult him, Agesilaos directs him about the procedure he is to follow. One expects the use of a shrine to be regulated by the authorities of the place, such as those who appeared in Sophocles' play (*OC* 117) to protect their shrine, in order to avoid the deity's displeasure by misunderstanding of local ritual. Agesilaos might have employed the official custodian of the site rather than his own man, but relations with Thebes precluded that.

10 ἀκούσαντες οὖν οἱ Βοιωτάρχαι πρὸς ὀργὴν ἔπεμψαν ὑπηρέτας, ἀπαγορεύοντες τῷ Ἀγησιλάῳ μὴ θύειν παρὰ τοὺς νόμους καὶ τὰ πάτρια Βοιωτῶν.

Plutarch's version of the intervention of the Boiotians may have come from local tradition. At this time eleven officers, the Boiotarchs, managed the common interests of the Boiotian Confederacy, four elected by Thebes, the most powerful state in the league, the rest distributed for election among the lesser cities or groups of cities (*Hell. Ox.* XI. 2–4).[31] Anger is not accounted a good guide for action, but here it is righteous anger, and the decisive intervention of the Boiotians reveals a determination to demonstrate their independence. Plutarch, a Boiotian and a priest of Delphi, would be sensitive about the violation of the territory and the sanctity of the shrine, and he stresses the Boiotarchs' concern for local laws and customs, omitted by Xenophon. The Corinthian war was to begin in Agesilaos' absence.

οἱ δὲ καὶ ταῦτ' ἀπήγγειλαν καὶ τὰ μηρία διέρριψαν ἀπὸ τοῦ βωμοῦ.

Xenophon says horsemen were sent, which may indicate that they came from a distance, perhaps from Thebes. They throw the victims from the altar 'already sacrificed' (*Hell.* iii. 4. 4). Plutarch omits the participle, perhaps wishing it to be thought that the interruption came before the completion of the sacrifice, which was therefore invalid.

11 χαλεπῶς οὖν ἔχων ὁ Ἀγησίλαος ἀπέπλει, τοῖς τε Θηβαίοις διωργισμένος καὶ γεγονὼς δύσελπις διὰ τὸν οἰωνόν, ὡς ἀτελῶν αὐτῷ τῶν πράξεων γενησομένων καὶ τῆς στρατείας ἐπὶ τὸ προσῆκον οὐκ ἀφιξομένης.

Agesilaos evidently wished to retaliate in some way but, with only the few friends there, could not enforce his will. He, too, is portrayed as regarding the sacrifice as incomplete. This is a typical situation for 'tragic history',[32] when a religious function cannot for religious reasons be performed properly. The outcome may be expected to be serious, both for the expedition because of the unfulfilled ritual, and for the Spartans because of the sacrilege (cf. *Pel.* 21. 3). Readers are prepared for a lack of success at the end of the expedition, and evaluation of the Asia Minor campaign should take this passage into account. Plutarch voices the presentiment only in the mind of Agesilaos (cf. similar restraint over the legality of the accession in ch. 3). His explanation of the end of the campaign is not the sacrilege but Sparta's need of Agesilaos at home;[33] but omens portend future events which then have their own causes.

7. Agesilaos and Lysander at Ephesos: a question of protocol

Plutarch devotes this chapter and the next to the quarrel between Agesilaos and Lysander.[1] Several features seem to cast doubt on the authenticity of the available accounts of the quarrel. Xenophon describes it at *Hell.* iii. 4. 7–10, but in *Agesilaos* mentions neither the quarrel nor Lysander, doubtless thinking both unsuited to his encomium. Clashes of personality explain events in other *Lives*, notably *Alexander*, but the winning of Spithridates described in ch. 8 may be interpreted more meaningfully as a deliberate diplomatic enterprise, rather than the chance healing of a personal breach of friendship. Agesilaos will initially have tried to install friendly governments made up of Lysander's associates; but he clearly found that impossible. Lysander's departure to the Hellespont, perhaps on a mission which was kept secret, may have given rise to speculation among the 'thirty' about a rift, and Xenophon's account may derive from their jealous talk.

The dishonouring (ἀτιμάζωνται) of men of virtue like Lysander by those with more honourable status like Agesilaos (Arist. *Pol.* 1306^{b}31–3) comes into question, if the evidence is the personal terms used in the record of a political dispute.[2] Xenophon had recently joined this force and as there was some explaining to do about the earlier behaviour of Kyros' former troops (*Hell.* iii. 2. 6–7), he perhaps witnessed the episode only from a distance, before his friendship with Agesilaos began. Detailed comparison of the accounts given in Plutarch and Xenophon indicates that certainty in this instance is far from possible, but further reason for doubt comes from the attempted and apparently successful destruction of Lysander's character after his death reported by Plutarch (see below, ch. 20. 3–4), which suggests that, at that later time, Agesilaos or his friends found or invented evidence of aggrandizement in this earlier episode. It may have been this discrediting of Lysander that determined Xenophon's view of him; see Introd., E.3(*c*). If it is true that character is displayed by actions, these should properly be studied, rather than the personal terms used in the record.

Political issues in Asia Minor

There are signs of political issues in the background, for at this time Lysander was likely to be investigating the restoration of his friends to power in the cities. Xenophon describes the cities while Agesilaos was at Ephesos as 'in a state of confusion' (*Hell.* iii. 4. 7; see above, on ch. 6. 3). The political dimension in the 'quarrel' would be the practicability of restoration in the face of violent opposition. If the military objectives were to be attempted without diverting manpower into protective garrisons, both men would wish to have friendly, stable, governments to rely on, and Lysander's briefing would lead first to installing his friends. It appears that that plan did not succeed, and it was abandoned (§8 below). Later (chs. 14. 4–15. 1) Agesilaos installed rulers grateful to himself, Lysander having left for home.

The current overlords had taken over after, perhaps long after, 403/2 (see above, ch. 6. 3);[3] there is no evidence for active enforcement of the ephors' decree. There were now likely to be claims by Lysander's friends for reinstatement, repossession of confiscated property, and redress of alleged injustices committed in the intervening years. In the light of the reason given by Lysander for his

coming to Asia Minor, the petitioners will mainly have been his
friends, the former extreme oligarchs.[4] Yet at *Agesilaos*, 1. 37
Xenophon records that the cities had suffered from factional strife
since the end of the Athenian empire, and seeks praise for
Agesilaos on the ground that he brought constitutional harmony
and prosperity without banishment and death. This suggests that
there was a settlement of the differences in the cities on Agesilaos'
terms, and a settlement, too, of the differences in Spartan policies,
which had been divided between support for the extreme
oligarchies that Lysander desired to reinstate and support for their
replacement by more moderate regimes.

The account of the 'quarrel' might suggest a serious rift
between Agesilaos and Lysander, but Lysander's surrender indicates that he was now convinced that resistance to the extremists
would prevail. If so, he would wish usefully to employ his experience and influence on other matters before the expiry of his year of
office. At Xen. *Hell.* iii. 4. 13 Agesilaos makes his first military
expedition to the north, reaching Daskyleion, near the Hellespont,
presumably using intelligence provided by Spithridates. Although
Xenophon's account, which Plutarch broadly follows, may yet be
thought largely acceptable, a more coherent design at the highest
level may have been withheld from him at this early stage in
his service with the Spartan expedition, with access only to less
privileged and less reliable informers.

1 Ἐπεὶ δ' ἧκεν εἰς Ἔφεσον, εὐθὺς ἀξίωμα μέγα καὶ δύναμις ἦν ἐπαχθὴς
καὶ βαρεῖα περὶ τὸν Λύσανδρον, ὄχλου φοιτῶντος ἐπὶ τὰς θύρας
ἑκάστοτε καὶ πάντων παρακολουθούντων καὶ θεραπευόντων ἐκεῖνον, ὡς
ὄνομα μὲν καὶ σχῆμα τῆς στρατηγίας τὸν Ἀγησίλαον ὄντα διὰ τὸν
νόμον, ἔργῳ δὲ κύριον ἁπάντων καὶ δυνάμενον καὶ πράττοντα πάντα τὸν
Λύσανδρον.

The area of the three rivers, Maiandros, Kaystros, and Hermos,
the scene of Agesilaos' campaigns, was known to the Spartans
through previous commanders, Thibron and Derkylidas, and in
an area renowned for competent cartographers, travellers were not
entirely dependent on guides.[5] Plutarch describes Ephesos as a
city well disposed to Sparta when Lysander arrived as admiral
towards the end of the Peloponnesian war: it was then poor and,
since it was the Persian headquarters, it was adopting Persian
customs (*Lys.* 3. 2). Lysander made it his base and transformed it

into a busy and prosperous port, with shipbuilding facilities; this will have brought him the popularity referred to in this chapter. Agesilaos' name appears, with erasures, scratched on a column base from the temple of Artemision at Ephesos: [Ἀ]γησίλα[ο]ς.[6]

Plutarch reports that Agesilaos was displeased with the high regard and power enjoyed by Lysander, though at *Lysander*, 23. 5 he refers more pointedly to Lysander's excessive φιλοτιμία. He does not give the reason here for Lysander's prominence, which he explains below (§2) as the result of former contacts (cf. *Lys.* 23. 3). Agesilaos will have been aware at the outset of Lysander's associations with his friends in the cities, and he no doubt knew his purpose in visiting Asia Minor again. Despite Xenophon's use of πάντες, 'everyone' (*Hell.* iii. 4. 7), the people consulting at this level would be largely his oligarchic friends (see above, and ch. 6. 3), and it was only to be expected that they would welcome the opportunity to renew contact with him.

Although Xenophon's attitude to Lysander is often restrained, his account of the episode begins without personal animosity between the two Spartans (*Hell.* iii. 4. 7). He points out that because Lysander was already known, he was asked to obtain *from Agesilaos* what petitioners wanted. He was not asked to grant it in his own right, and there is no suggestion that this exclusive consultation was encouraged by Lysander. It was the crowd regularly attending on him that misrepresented the king's relative status. The other Spartiates, motivated by jealousy of Lysander, complained to Agesilaos about the breach of protocol; they, not Xenophon, assign the guilt to Lysander. Agesilaos reacted to the situation angrily (*Hell.* iii. 4. 8), but only later, and dealt directly with the errant petitioners.

Plutarch reorganizes the narrative.[7] He first refers to the 'throng', ὄχλος, of petitioners, who then all (πάντες) make their petition, while Xenophon suggests that all the citizens, πάντες, approached Lysander, and only then described them as ὄχλος. Plutarch has enlivened the situation with rhetorical *amplificatio*: where Xenophon refers to the reversed 'royal' and 'non-office-holding' status of the men in two words, βασιλεύς and ἰδιώτης, he contrasts the supposed reality of Lysander's power with Agesilaos' nominal and formal status, and adds 'because of the law'—as if the petitioners thought that, if Lysander wanted, he could change that, too—he was 'first' adviser (ch. 6. 5). The phrase ἐπὶ τὰς θύρας, 'to the doors', used by Xenophon (*An.* i. 9. 3) and others for the Persian court, suggests the 'court' of Lysander.

With ὡς, Plutarch allows the petitioners' thoughts to explain why they consulted Lysander; in Xenophon's account the Spartiates compare Lysander's apparent status with their own, and no doubt with Agesilaos', their complaint to the latter. Thus the issue in Xenophon is the subjective feeling of Lysander's opponents that they are being disadvantaged by him, while Plutarch presents the problem objectively in the petitioners' act of consultation. There is a double irony here. Agesilaos, whose capacity to court favour was demonstrated—and punished—above (ch. 5. 4), now suffers humiliation from the 'courting of favour' by the petitioners, θεραπευόντων, and while the same trait, θεραπευτικός, was attributed to Lysander (*Lys.* 2. 3), the petitioners' attentions now discomfort him.[8]

2 οὐδεὶς γὰρ ἐνδοξότερος οὐδὲ φοβερώτερος ἐκείνου τῶν εἰς τὴν Ἀσίαν ἀποσταλέντων ἐγένετο στρατηγῶν, οὐδὲ μείζονα τοὺς φίλους τις ἀνὴρ ἄλλος εὐεργέτησεν οὐδὲ κακὰ τηλικαῦτα τοὺς ἐχθροὺς ἐποίησεν. **3** ὧν ἔτι προσφάτων ὄντων οἱ ἄνθρωποι μνημονεύοντες, . . .

Plutarch interrupts the account of the quarrel to give, in his own words, the reasons for Lysander's prominent position, based on his activity in Ionia, well within the memories of the petitioners, when he set up the dekarchies. He may have had in mind Lysander's promise to help his friends at Miletos (in 405) to overthrow their democratic opponents, and the treacherous manoeuvres which lured the leading democrats to their deaths (*Lys.* 8. 1–3). Lysander's traditional attitude to the popular rule of 'Help Friends, Harm Enemies' (see above, ch. 5), in contrast to that of Agesilaos, who modified the rule, wins approval (cf. ch. 6. 5), not explicitly from Plutarch, and from the oligarchs not (one suspects) from principles of popular philosophy, but because they benefited by it.

. . . ἄλλως δὲ τὸν μὲν Ἀγησίλαον ἀφελῆ καὶ λιτὸν ἐν ταῖς ὁμιλίαις καὶ δημοτικὸν ὁρῶντες, ἐκείνῳ δὲ τὴν αὐτὴν ὁμοίως σφοδρότητα καὶ τραχύτητα καὶ βραχυλογίαν παροῦσαν, ὑπέπιπτον αὐτῷ παντάπασι καὶ μόνῳ προσεῖχον.

The unpretentious attributes here are in keeping with Plutarch's earlier character study of Agesilaos in chs. 1–2, where he, as well as the Spartans, approved of them, but the oligarchs' view of the same qualities is not complimentary. Not only was he not impressive in his bearing: his attitude to ordinary people rendered Lysander's friends less well disposed to him. Their negative reaction to Agesilaos' Spartan standards would be offensive to his supporters, as would be the local response to Lysander's qualities indicated in the scornful vocabulary which follows. The suggestions of Persian customs at Ephesos (§1; cf. *Lys.* 3. 2) are now reinforced with the verbs ὑπέπιπτον, 'fell down', used of cringing suppliants (*Mor.* 540 D) and fawning flatterers, and προσέχω, used by Xenophon in a Persian context (*Cyr.* v. 5. 40) for 'pay court'. Plutarch uses the theme at *Lysander*, 18 where Lysander was said to be the first Greek in whose honour Greek cities erected altars and offered sacrifices as though he were a god.[9] Resentment of Lysander is made to seem more justified in Plutarch's account because of the exaggerated terms used for the petitioners' attentions.

4 ἐκ δὲ τούτου πρῶτον μὲν οἱ λοιποὶ Σπαρτιᾶται χαλεπῶς ἔφερον ὑπηρέται Λυσάνδρου μᾶλλον ἢ σύμβουλοι βασιλέως ὄντες· ἔπειτα δ' αὐτὸς ὁ Ἀγησίλαος, εἰ καὶ μὴ φθονερὸς ἦν μηδ' ἤχθετο τοῖς τιμωμένοις, ἀλλὰ φιλότιμος ὢν σφόδρα καὶ φιλόνικος ἐφοβεῖτο μή, κἂν ἐνέγκωσί τι λαμπρὸν αἱ πράξεις, τοῦτο Λυσάνδρου γένηται διὰ τὴν δόξαν.

In Xenophon's narrative the Spartiates' jealousy follows from the reduced status of their king (*Hell.* iii. 4. 8). Plutarch rewrites: it is their own status *vis-à-vis* Lysander that annoys them, and jealousy enters only to be denied emphatically of Agesilaos. Since Agesilaos knows of their dissatisfaction with Lysander's behaviour, he has no reason for envy, or to be other than confident of their support. His quarrel is a personal one, but it is not the Spartiates' envy of Lysander to which he reacts. Plutarch sees that the breach of protocol by the petitioners presents Agesilaos with a real challenge. The adjectives φιλότιμος and φιλόνικος which characterize Agesilaos (chs. 2. 2–3, with n. 22) are here the ground for his response to the challenge. The first gives the sense 'desiring the achievements to be his own', not 'desiring *recognition* of his achievements'. The second, which Plutarch substitutes for the anger assigned to Agesilaos by Xenophon (*Hell.* iii. 4. 8), indicates his readiness to assert himself 'competitively'.

In the end, while Xenophon's Agesilaos, unlike the Spartiates, reacts to the petitioners' behaviour, Plutarch's Agesilaos reacts to a perceived threat from Lysander, and does so for his own reason, fearing to forfeit the chance of significant achievement. Plutarch's changes not only enliven the narrative but give the impression that the issue here is personal rivalry, an impression he has given even more strongly at *Lysander*, 23, where the Spartiates play no part at all, and Lysander is deprived of opportunities for action. Xenophon now indicates the personal dimension of the quarrel: Lysander's distress and resentment, to which Agesilaos responds sharply (*Hell.* iii. 4. 9).

5 οὕτως οὖν ἐποίει· πρῶτον ἀντέκρουε ταῖς συμβουλίαις αὐτοῦ, καὶ πρὸς ἃς ἐκεῖνος ἐσπουδάκει μάλιστα πράξεις ἐῶν χαίρειν καὶ παραμελῶν, ἕτερα πρὸ ἐκείνων ἔπραττεν· **6** ἔπειτα τῶν ἐντυγχανόντων καὶ δεομένων οὓς αἴσθοιτο Λυσάνδρῳ μάλιστα πεποιθότας, ἀπράκτους ἀπέπεμπε· **7** καὶ περὶ τὰς κρίσεις ὁμοίως οἷς ἐκεῖνος ἐπηρεάζοι, τούτους ἔδει πλέον ἔχοντας ἀπελθεῖν, καὶ τοὐναντίον οὓς φανερὸς γένοιτο προθυμούμενος ὠφελεῖν, χαλεπὸν ἦν μὴ καὶ ζημιωθῆναι.

The metaphor ἀντέκρουε, from boxing, and naval and other warfare, suggests a vigorous response.[10] Xenophon directs the retaliatory action only towards the petitioners brought by Lysander, whereas here Agesilaos reacts against Lysander, and, using *amplificatio* to give details where Xenophon only summarizes, Plutarch mentions the rejection of advice and enterprises, then of petitions, and finally of legal cases. He also exhausts the possibilities by adding approval of cases opposed by Lysander. Here Agesilaos operates 'Help Friends (Lysander's enemies), Harm Enemies (Lysander's friends)' normally but unjustly. These were not vital military decisions while the truce lasted, and in private matters inconsistency and its consequences would be less serious politically. If the issue of who should rule in the cities, which perhaps lies behind the incident (see above, ch. 6 n. following §3), has now been settled, it will be the petitioners' suits for reinstatement that fail.

8 γινομένων δὲ τούτων οὐ κατὰ τύχην, ἀλλ᾽ οἷον ἐκ παρασκευῆς καὶ ὁμαλῶς, αἰσθανόμενος τὴν αἰτίαν ὁ Λύσανδρος οὐκ ἀπεκρύπτετο πρὸς τοὺς φίλους, ἀλλ᾽ ἔλεγεν ὡς δι᾽ αὐτὸν ἀτιμάζοιντο, καὶ παρεκάλει θεραπεύειν ἰόντας τὸν βασιλέα καὶ τοὺς μᾶλλον αὐτοῦ δυναμένους.

For οὐ κατὰ τύχην Perrin has 'not casually'; the Budé translator has 'pas l'effet du hasard'. The required sense is 'not at random', in order to balance the following 'purposely, without exception'. Cases deliberately prepared by Agesilaos with the set plan of thwarting Lysander at all turns would be more likely to succeed than actions decided on the spur of the moment. Consistent treatment was necessary for Plutarch so that Lysander would eventually see what was happening and 'perceive that he was responsible'. Lysander's remarks constitute a full realization of that responsibility and he attempts to restore Agesilaos' position in the regard of the petitioners—the need to secure the loyalty of former friends for the new settlement would be the inevitable consequence of a decision to abandon the dekarchies. This goes beyond what Xenophon records at *Hell.* iii. 4. 8, where Lysander, discontinuing his own audiences, admits only that his support is a handicap. Plutarch gives the impression that Lysander did not take offence but genuinely acknowledged Agesilaos' superior position by his reference to the king's title and the reality of his power. There has been at this stage no aggressive confrontation, but, although there are faults on both sides, the pendulum is swinging away from Agesilaos.

8. Agesilaos' differences with Lysander settled: the arrival of Spithridates

1 Ὡς οὖν ταῦτα πράττειν καὶ λέγειν ἐδόκει φθόνον ἐκείνῳ μηχανώμενος, ἔτι μᾶλλον αὐτοῦ καθάψασθαι βουλόμενος Ἀγησίλαος ἀπέδειξε κρεοδαίτην καὶ προσεῖπεν, ὡς λέγεται, πολλῶν ἀκουόντων· Νῦν οὖν θεραπευέτωσαν οὗτοι ἀπιόντες τὸν ἐμὸν κρεοδαίτην.

The function of the king's carver in real life may have been to protect him against poisoning, and Plutarch himself explains the regular nature of the appointment (*Mor.* 644 B). Here it is an insult as Plutarch builds up a personal rift between the two men. Agesilaos imputes to Lysander deliberate provocation which can be supported only if the confession in ch. 7 was insincere. In his account at *Lysander*, 23. 7 Plutarch records the continuing respect of the people for Lysander, and the attention he still received, which annoyed Agesilaos. Further insulting treatment and new humiliation by Agesilaos followed which served to motivate that work's climax: Lysander's attempted revenge in Sparta. In Xenophon there is no further humiliation by Agesilaos, only Lysander's distress (see above, ch. 7. 4). Plutarch, or his source, may have taken this to refer to another disgrace, implied in Agesilaos' delayed reaction (*Hell*. iii. 4. 8; see above, ch. 7. 1).

Plutarch, indicating an anonymous source, introduces the public dialogue with the insulting remark made by Agesilaos apparently to Lysander. Humour may also be intended, although at *Lysander*, 23 Agesilaos seriously undermines Lysander's relations with his friends. At the start of the dialogue Agesilaos is in a less favourable light than the repentant Lysander at the end of the previous chapter. In Xenophon the dialogue follows Lysander's original distress. His complaint brings to the surface the more personal element already introduced by Plutarch, and begins the direct confrontation in an interview instigated by him, apparently in private (*Hell*. iii. 4. 9).

2 ἀχθόμενος οὖν ὁ Λύσανδρος λέγει πρὸς αὐτόν· Ἥιδεις ἄρα σαφῶς, Ἀγησίλαε, φίλους ἐλαττοῦν. Ἥιδειν, ἔφη, τούς γ᾽ ἐμοῦ μεῖζον δύνασθαι βουλομένους. καὶ ὁ Λύσανδρος, Ἀλλ᾽ ἴσως, ἔφη, ταῦτα σοὶ λέλεκται βέλτιον ἢ ἐμοὶ πέπρακται.

Lysander's criticism of Agesilaos' treatment of friends revives the theme set out by Plutarch in ch. 5 and developed in ch. 7. Agesilaos' short response disposes of Lysander's universal statement. He in turn casts more reasonable doubt on Lysander's friendship, for he diminished his friend first. The source for the dialogue was evidently well disposed to Agesilaos and Xenophon's statement that he reciprocates (see above, ch. 5, and below 12. 9) when friends serve him well puts him in a more favourable light, after his sharp response, and leads to Lysander's offer to make amends (*Hell*. iii. 4. 9). Plutarch included this at *Lysander*, 23. 8 but he omits it here, although the omission weakens the motivation for Lysander's generous response. Lysander admitted his error to himself in ch. 7. 8, and took action with the petitioners to restore Agesilaos' authority. Now he surrenders to him in person.

In all the versions of his speeches Lysander concedes Agesilaos' successful justification of his actions but also accuses him of disloyalty. He has been taken here to be comparing the reasonableness of two acts, his help over the accession and Agesilaos' more discerning humiliation of him.[1] It has been argued rightly that Agesilaos could not have taken Lysander's words to refer to the accession without more precise explanation.[2] Rather, then, Xenophon presents a comparison between two actions; Agesilaos' verbal confrontation which re-established his position, and Lysander's alleged arrogant behaviour in the meetings with the petitioners. Plutarch clarifies this by changing the first verb: 'What you have *said* . . . what I have *done*.'

δὸς δέ μοι τινὰ τάξιν καὶ χώραν, ἔνθα μὴ λυπῶν ἔσομαί σοι χρήσιμος.

Lysander now seems to be magnanimous in defeat—contrary to the character already drawn by Plutarch—and so earns the reader's sympathy, which in the earliest part of the narrative he was presented as not deserving. He acknowledges his subordinate position, and at the same time restores Agesilaos' status as commander.

3 ἐκ τούτου πέμπεται μὲν ἐφ' Ἑλλήσποντον, καὶ Σπιθριδάτην, ἄνδρα Πέρσην, ἀπὸ τῆς Φαρναβάζου χώρας μετὰ χρημάτων συχνῶν καὶ διακοσίων ἱππέων ἤγαγε πρὸς τὸν Ἀγησίλαον.

Three significant aspects remain unexplained here: that an important enterprise develops casually from an argument; that there is now mutual trust for such a mission; that there is no precise briefing. Xenophon, using the active verb πέμπει, 'sent', credits Agesilaos with the initiative more explicitly than Plutarch (*Hell.* iii. 4. 10), again indicating the predilection of his source. Yet Lysander's superior knowledge suggests that he was more likely to originate the plan. Although Xenophon (*Hell.* iii. 4. 7) puts the quarrel after the truce with Tissaphernes was agreed, and makes Lysander's expedition result from the quarrel, the campaign in the north may already have been in their minds; the gathering of intelligence was a necessary preliminary.

By naming Spithridates prominently—Lysander, though continuously engaged, is not named between §§2 and 6—Plutarch highlights the Persian, yet does not indicate how he was won, that he had been treated badly by Pharnabazos (cf. ch. 11. 4), or how pleased Agesilaos was at his arrival. This part of the narrative gives credit to Agesilaos for his actions and leaves him with tangible success. The friendship appears to have been restored, but Agesilaos has not contributed to the traditional reciprocity.

He is pleased at *Hell.* iii. 4. 10, but, despite his earlier claim (§9), does not reward him: Plutarch omitted that claim at §2 above (see on §4 below). Valuable benefits accrued from the excursion: money, needed for the purchase of supplies in friendly territories, and cavalry, a major deficiency in Agesilaos' force. Plutarch, unlike Xenophon, makes no mention of the more important benefit, information about Pharnabazos and his country, and perhaps also about routes and defending forces.

οὐκ ἔληγε δὲ τῆς ὀργῆς, ἀλλὰ βαρέως φέρων ἤδη τὸν λοιπὸν χρόνον ἐβούλευεν ὅπως τῶν δυεῖν οἴκων τὴν βασιλείαν ἀφελόμενος εἰς μέσον ἅπασιν ἀποδοίη Σπαρτιάταις. **4** καὶ ἐδόκει μεγάλην ἂν ἀπεργάσασθαι κίνησιν ἐκ ταύτης τῆς διαφορᾶς, εἰ μὴ πρότερον ἐτελεύτησεν εἰς Βοιωτίαν στρατεύσας.

The rest of the chapter indicates Plutarch's dissatisfaction with the behaviour of both men. Although he makes amends, Lysander is presented in an unfavourable light. Xenophon ends the episode happily with the delight of Agesilaos—ignored by Plutarch—on the arrival of Spithridates (*Hell.* iii. 4. 10), a delight which would be equally relevant after the success of a properly planned mission. Lysander is not mentioned by Xenophon again until §20, when he leaves Asia. Plutarch's account of his continuing anger is abridged from *Lysander*, 23–4 and seems to provide a strange conclusion for an episode which turns out advantageous to both men, an opportunity for Lysander to redeem himself by performing a useful service, and for Agesilaos to establish his commanding position and perhaps to show some gratitude.[3] In life resentment might follow, and here it imposes no incoherence on Lysander's character, but Plutarch did not find it in Xenophon; he has a different line to follow.

The reason for this and other variations between the three versions lies, perhaps, in the literary intentions of the respective authors. Xenophon at the start limits the personal animosity between the two men, particularly before the dialogue, and in the end finds nothing reprehensible in Agesilaos, but evidently wishes to illustrate his sense of fairness and his reward. It could be that the disappointed friends of Lysander had voiced their discontent and Xenophon, or his source, wished to exonerate Agesilaos. In *Lysander* Plutarch was concerned to motivate Lysander's plan to reform the kingship on his return to Greece. Here, since Plutarch presents both men at fault in the conclusion of this chapter, he includes Agesilaos' unnecessary insults, retains Lysander's resentment, but omits the rewarding of loyal friends, which would have brought some mitigation of Agesilaos' conduct. Each author fulfils his apparent literary purpose, but even if personal relations broke down in Asia Minor, and whether or not Agesilaos could use his influence in Sparta for or against him, Lysander was still in favour there, and willing to continue to serve. He received—recalled, perhaps, to take—the command for the campaign in which he died at Haliartos; at his death the Spartans paid him many honours (*Lys.* 30. 5). At *Lysander*, 24. 2 Plutarch records both the end of his term as adviser and his departure from Asia Minor, but here he passes quickly on to the sequel, mentioning neither.

Lysander's alleged constitutional reform

Plutarch's expression of Lysander's resentment, βαρέως φέρων, used also by Xenophon at the start of the dialogue (*Hell.* iii. 4. 9), suggests thoughts of violent revolution, but at ch. 20. 4 ἐν τῷ δήμῳ, 'in the assembly', indicates legitimate methods of constitutional reform. Lysander was killed at Haliartos in the autumn battle, having returned from Asia Minor in the spring. The 'plot', which is not mentioned by Xenophon, lapsed, but was 'discovered' after his death (Diod. xiv. 13. 8). When the late Lysander's house was being searched for some documents, a speech was discovered, written for him by the rhetorician Kleon of Halikarnassos, which Lysander had intended to deliver in the assembly. In the version attributed to Ephoros by Plutarch at *Lysander*, 30. 3, the speech outlined a plan to reform the kingship by removing the exclusive prerogative of the two royal houses so as to make all Spartans eligible.[4] If Lysander intended to attempt his reform by this means, it was hardly a conspiracy. The idea that there was need for reform,[5] whether to ensure that the Spartan system survived under more efficient leadership, or to abandon it for something else, flouts the basic principle of Spartan, and indeed *polis*, morality, that the good citizen upholds the constitution. Socrates, however, advocated changing it by persuasion, or going into voluntary exile (*Crito*, 51–2). If Plutarch thought at ch. 20. 4 that Lysander intended persuasion ἐν τῷ δήμῳ, then the intended reform determines its acceptability: his regret at Sparta's decline suggests a flexible attitude, but Lysander's imperialism would make him, in Plutarch's view, an unacceptable reformer.

5 οὕτως αἱ φιλότιμοι φύσεις ἐν ταῖς πολιτείαις, τὸ ἄγαν μὴ φυλαξάμεναι, τοῦ ἀγαθοῦ μεῖζον τὸ κακὸν ἔχουσι.

The value of φιλοτιμία was stated in ch. 2, but now Plutarch warns of the great harm that comes from excess. This is the moral to be drawn from the quarrel. The two qualities, φιλοτιμία and φιλονικία (attributed to Agesilaos in ch. 2. 2–3), were mentioned together at ch. 5. 5 as the lawgiver's incentives to virtue. Plutarch then warned (ch. 5. 7) that excessive φιλονικία, rivalry, endangers the state, and now warns of excessive φιλοτιμία.[6] An excess of each has now been recognized in Agesilaos' character. He is about to be criticized for ineptitude. Although Plutarch criticizes Agesilaos and Lysander in this way, there is no immediate consequence detrimental to Sparta, but the reader's expectations have been raised.

6 καὶ γὰρ εἰ Λύσανδρος ἦν φορτικός, ὥσπερ ἦν, ὑπερβάλλων τῇ φιλοτιμίᾳ τὸν καιρόν, οὐκ ἠγνόει δήπουθεν Ἀγησίλαος ἑτέραν ἀμεμπτοτέραν ἐπανόρθωσιν οὖσαν ἀνδρὸς ἐνδόξου καὶ φίλου πλημμελοῦντος.

For φορτικός, the Budé translators have 'insupportable' and Perrin 'troublesome'; rather, Lysander is 'overbearing', as Menekrates is (ch. 21. 10); Aristotle criticizes deviant lawmakers as 'coarse' in substituting expediency for principle (*Pol.* 1333ᵇ9–10). Plutarch may intend καιρός in its moral meaning, 'what is proper and right', which develops from its temporal sense, 'the seasonal'. Agesilaos, too, fails to recognize it (chs. 28. 6–7, 35. 6, 36. 4). The metaphor, πλημμελοῦντος, is musical, 'striking a false note'—'erring'; cf. *Arist.* 26. 3, *Lyk.* 18. 3; *Mor.* 800 E, of a politician's peccadillo. Plutarch uses ἐκμελὴς φιλοτιμία at *Lys.* 23. 5. The opposite is ἐμμελής, of civic harmony (*Pel.* 19. 2, *Brut.* 1. 3, *Phok.* 2. 5).

7 ἀλλ᾽ ἔοικε ταὐτῷ πάθει μήτ᾽ ἐκεῖνος ἄρχοντος ἐξουσίαν γνῶναι μήθ᾽ οὗτος ἄγνοιαν ἐνεγκεῖν συνήθους.

Plutarch reflects Aristotle's response (*NE* vii. 2–3) to the Socratic doctrine that knowledge of the good precludes doing anything else—that a man does wrong only through ignorance: 'A man can, from a variety of causes, fail to apply knowledge which he has.'[7] If Lysander had recognized superior authority in Agesilaos' office, he might have restrained his desire for achievement, but πάθος, 'emotion', distorted his perception, just as it distorted Agesilaos' knowledge of a better way of dealing with him, making him intolerant of his friend's 'failure to recognize him'. The πάθος was explained as 'overbearing rivalry' (§6), and now it is attributed to Agesilaos, too. Rivalry was encouraged in the ἀγωγή (ch. 5. 5); the Spartans failed to develop the means to control its excess.

The seeds of Sparta's problem revealed

It may be doubted that these disagreements were discussed only in public, particularly since Xenophon hinted at a private interview, or that they were settled by such repartee. Nevertheless, although Lysander's mission may have been planned independently, any disagreement, perhaps about the administration of the cities, may have taken place as Xenophon has it. The rejection of the oligarchs' petitions supported by Lysander and the approval of those he opposed would follow naturally on a decision that their reinstatement was now impracticable, as also his advice to discontinue petitioning him. Plutarch largely accepts Xenophon's account, but he enlarges parts of the canvas so that readers see for themselves things as they were (ἐνάργεια). He abandons Xenophon's assessment generally favouring Agesilaos, although he does not transfer from the Spartiates to Agesilaos the personal feeling of jealousy which causes the clash at *Hell.* iii. 4. 8. He specifically denies it at ch. 7. 4, and it does not fit the interpretation of Agesilaos' character here, though at *Lysander*, 23. 7 he reacts enviously later to the continued attentions paid to Lysander by the petitioners. In Xenophon's account Agesilaos is slow to take offence, more balanced in his treatment of people, and pleased with the exploit in the end; Lysander is at fault, but he redeems himself by accepting service as a subordinate: a Spartan still, perhaps a willing scapegoat. Xenophon makes no reference to the proposed reform of the kingship, except, perhaps, when he mentions that to those who visited them Lysander appeared as king, Λύσανδρος βασιλεύς (*Hell.* iii. 4. 7): if inadvertently, an idea possibly suggested by the later revelation of what Lysander had attempted, in a function of the subconscious—a 'Freudian slip'; if deliberately,[8] an oblique reference to the plot, perhaps malicious. Plutarch draws his own conclusion from Xenophon's account:

that the two men shared a common fault, πάθος, which limited their powers of perception and self-control. The Spartan ἀγωγή did not include the study of philosophy as such, but Spartans will have known the injunction, μηδὲν ἄγαν, 'nothing to excess' (whether it was correctly attributed to Chilon, the sixth-century Spartan sage[9]) when they saw it displayed when they visited Apollo's temple at Delphi (Paus. x. 24. 1). Plutarch was no doubt guided by the writings of Aristotle in advocating the mean (§5), and by his criticism of the Spartan constitution for its concentration on military virtue (*Pol.* 1333^{b}12–14, 29–31; 1333^{b}38–1334^{a}4; see below, chs. 27. 7 and 35. 5). Plutarch's didactic theme is relevant to his own age (see above, ch. 5. 7 n.), but he presents it in the Spartan context. He makes the quarrel a criticism of φιλοτιμία and φιλονικία, and his emphasis on the dangers of excess in these echoes his view of the potential ills of contemporary Greek city-politics (*Mor.* 801 A, 819 F–20 C) and complements the danger exposed in ch. 5 when Agesilaos abandons them.[10] This episode in Plutarch's interpretation of his source contributes to his analysis of Spartan society and reveals the lack of intellectual training which could have led to greater self-knowledge and insight (ch. 26 n., ch. 36. 4; see Introd., E.3(*d*)).[11]

Plutarch punctuates the whole work by inserting this sort of analysis where it will make a significant impact; here it marks the point at which Agesilaos takes sole control of affairs. He is about to embark on the second of the two objectives of his mission—the military campaign—without Lysander. The failure of the first—the restoration of the oligarchs to power in the cities—is not recorded, nor is it recorded whether it was ever an objective of Agesilaos himself; but if it was not, then the time to disagree was before embarkation, when a younger, inexperienced commander, new to his kingship, could be supported in argument by Lysander's opponents, who would suspect, even if it was not made public, that it would be attempted. Its abandonment may be inferred from the rejection of the petitioners and the later installation of men loyal to himself: the thirty Spartiates were there to advise, and the true origin of the whole episode may lie in their discussions.

9. The first campaign in Asia Minor:
Agesilaos recruits cavalry

Xenophon leaves unexplained Agesilaos' motives in the conduct of this campaign, in particular why he turned north, away from Tissaphernes' base. Although at *Agesilaos*, 1. 9 he offers to reveal the strategy, he refers only to Tissaphernes' perjury. If he had no direct Persian source in *Hellenika*, he was limited in explaining observed enemy actions to what was understood of the Persian 'psychologie' in the Spartan camp.[1] His account of the campaign (iii. 4. 11–15) seems to present only an official report or an eye-witness account at a subordinate level. The distant cavalry engagement ends with the sudden appearance of Agesilaos and the hoplites coming to the rescue (§14), without explanation. When Xenophon reports the concentration of Tissaphernes' forces in Karia, he gives Tissaphernes' supposed strategical analysis, but he reveals no understanding of the larger perspectives.[2]

Plutarch seems to have been puzzled about Agesilaos' intentions. He uses a retrospective mention of deception later in Xenophon (*Agesilaos*, 1. 17) to provide the missing motive for the surprising decision to move the theatre of war to Phrygia. The transferred deception helps, if only to indicate a real difficulty where further interpretation is necessary; perhaps a new policy was formulated involving the northern border tribes.

1 Ἐπεὶ δὲ Τισσαφέρνης ἐν ἀρχῇ μὲν φοβηθεὶς τὸν Ἀγησίλαον ἐποιήσατο σπονδάς, ὡς τὰς πόλεις αὐτῷ τὰς Ἑλληνίδας ἀφήσοντος αὐτονόμους βασιλέως, ὕστερον δὲ πεισθεὶς ἔχειν δύναμιν ἱκανὴν ἐξήνεγκε τὸν πόλεμον, ἄσμενος ὁ Ἀγησίλαος ἐδέξατο.

At Ephesos (ch. 7. 1) Agesilaos faced Tissaphernes, the King's Persian satrap or governor with headquarters at Sardis in Lydia but private estates in Karia, across the river Maiandros to the south. Tissaphernes had been supreme commander in Asia Minor (Xen. *Hell*. iii. 1. 3 and 2. 13), appointed to recover the King's possessions in that area following the end of Kyros' bid for the throne (see above, ch. 6). The King had earlier assigned to him the task of collecting tribute from Athens' Ionian allies (Thuc. viii. 5; Xen. *Hell*. i. 1. 9), but they had revolted from him (Xen. *An*. i. 1) and then in 401 had risen with Kyros against the King. They now remained independent, having called on Sparta, the late Kyros' former ally, for support against Tissaphernes in his new capacity.[3]

Xenophon records the truce immediately on Agesilaos' arrival, when Tissaphernes enquired about his intentions, and agreed to submit Agesilaos' proposed terms to the King: autonomy for the Greek cities. Agesilaos was no doubt playing for time before revealing more adventurous intentions, as was Tissaphernes, who also needed the King's approval and military support: he could be sure of rejection. Plutarch, in giving fear as Tissaphernes' reason for making the treaty with Agesilaos, retails the hostile Greek stereotypical view of the eastern or barbarian character (Hdt. ix. 122, Arist. *Pol.* 1327^{b}23–30, Hippok. *de Aer.* 12, 16, 24, and Isok. 4. 150–1; cf. *Art.* 22. 1–2; see Introd., E.7). Reports of Agesilaos' expedition either had not come in time for Tissaphernes' preparations for defence to be completed, or were not acted upon until after its arrival. That Tissaphernes should immediately concede all that Sparta wanted—and without first consulting the King— seems unlikely. Xenophon says rather that he undertook to obtain independence for the cities from the King, but violated his oath by asking instead for reinforcements (*Hell.* iii. 4. 5–6). He is presented here by Plutarch with enhanced autonomous status, perhaps to benefit that of Agesilaos. If Xenophon's digression on the Eleian war (*Hell.* iii. 2. 21–31) has obscured the timing of the transfer of command from Derkylidas to Agesilaos,[4] Tissaphernes' consultations with the King were already in progress, following his truce with Derkylidas (*Hell.* iii. 2. 20). The new commander was probably not bound by Derkylidas' truce, though he could renew or confirm it, if his present aim was to secure autonomy for the Greek cities.

Plutarch does not mention Tissaphernes' secret request for help from the King, but he connects the declaration of war with the increased strength now available to him. He does not say specifically that Tissaphernes anticipated the ending of the truce, though this may be implied by the omission of any reference to its expiry, but there is a suggestion that the declaration reverses the promise of autonomy for the cities. No doubt when Tissaphernes asked the King for a decision about the cities' autonomy, he requested reinforcements if he was to be required to refuse it. This may not have constituted a breach of the truce.[5] The arrival of reinforcements and the declaration of war indicate that the envoys had now returned, bringing the King's rejection of the proposal, and that would end the truce.

That war should begin with a Persian aggressive initiative is surprising, even if it was only a bluff, for the propaganda of Agesilaos' visit to Aulis entailed Greek aggression. Unless Agesilaos had in mind even then not a full-scale war on the King but only the limited aim of protecting the Greek cities, there is inconsistency. The scale of the operation should be recognized at the start: the full might of Persia was not involved, nor did Agesilaos' force represent the full might of Greece. The King had other affairs to attend to, including his preoccupation with an independent Egypt,[6] which now had an alliance with Sparta (Diod. xiv. 79. 4). A border incident or a piratical raid would be nearer the truth from the Persian point of view: a peripheral problem to be dealt with by local officials and mainly their own resources, just like, perhaps, the incursion of Alexander in 334.[7] The Spartan efforts suffered from inadequate finance under Thibron and Derkylidas,[8] and achieved no permanent results before Agesilaos arrived. Xenophon indicates the reality: stalemate resulting in a truce (*Hell*. iii. 2. 18–20).

Xenophon uses Tissaphernes' announcement to contrast Agesilaos' confidence with the nervousness of the rest of the Spartans; Agesilaos receives the news with joy (see below, §2 on φαιδρῷ) and expresses his gratitude that Tissaphernes has put the gods on the Greek side by violating his oath (*Hell*. iii. 4. 11, *Agesilaos*, 1. 13), evidently in requesting troops (*Hell*. iii. 4. 6, *Agesilaos*, 1. 11). The resourceful general successfully restores the spirits of anxious troops who thought themselves an inferior force, in almost the same way that Xenophon did in a speech to his men (*An*. iii. 2). Plutarch marks Tissaphernes' announcement with Agesilaos' delight as if it now provides an excuse for war. He omits the perjury which in Xenophon explains Agesilaos' joy, and provides his own explanation for it (§2). His present interest is in Agesilaos' mind, not his generalship.

2 προσδοκία γὰρ ἦν μεγάλη τῆς στρατείας· καὶ δεινὸν ἡγεῖτο τοὺς μὲν σὺν Ξενοφῶντι μυρίους ἥκειν ἐπὶ θάλατταν, ὁσάκις ἐβουλήθησαν αὐτοὶ τοσαυτάκις βασιλέα νενικηκότας, αὐτοῦ δὲ Λακεδαιμονίων ἄρχοντος ἡγουμένων γῆς καὶ θαλάσσης μηδὲν ἔργον ἄξιον μνήμης φανῆναι πρὸς τοὺς Ἕλληνας.

Plutarch refers Agesilaos' joy (§1) to the opportunity to fulfil his grand expectations: the pessimism expressed after the interruption of the sacrifice at Aulis (ch. 6) and the fear of being deprived of credit (ch. 7. 4) are gone. Agesilaos is again motivated by φιλοτιμία and αἰσχύνη, with the thought that he could avoid unfavourable comparison with Xenophon and the Ten Thousand. Not long ago he had declined immediate battle and accepted a truce instead. Plutarch is interested in character and motivation, and therefore attempts to penetrate Agesilaos' thoughts; Xenophon, as a more practical man of action, is content to record what is seen and heard, demonstrating the qualities of a good general who repairs limitations and deficiencies in his force.[9] Their interests and approaches diverge at this point.

Their vocabularies and methodologies also diverge, for the internal ἄσμενος, 'delighted', and ἡγεῖτο, 'thought', contrast with the external φαιδρῷ, 'beaming'. Plutarch discards Xenophon's word φαιδρός, surprisingly at this point, for he favours it 'in such emotional scenes, but normally of the encouraging *commanders*'.[10] He records Agesilaos' invisible feelings, and the record is significant, but cannot be proved: Xenophon records what all there could see, but reveals nothing about the real inner feelings of the man, as opposed to the outward, possibly feigned, appearance. Plutarch was aware of the rich subtleties of biographical studies compared with painting (*Kim.* 2. 2–5), and elsewhere records that facial expressions were deliberately composed (*Fab.* 17. 5, *Arat.* 40. 3–4, *Cor.* 21. 1). Here, he prefers psychological portraiture.

Agesilaos' comparison with the Ten Thousand is omitted by Xenophon, although Tissaphernes had 'refused battle' because of their reputation (*Hell.* iii. 2. 18). As a motive for a military commander it is inconsistent with a rational approach and the high value put on the lives of his men by Agesilaos elsewhere (chs. 16. 5, 17. 5), but Plutarch maintains consistency with the theme of Agesilaos' φιλοτιμία. The comparison may have been a commonplace, for these two expeditions are linked by Polybios with the eastern plans of Philip of Makedon (iii. 6. 10). Xenophon, too, links this expedition with his own, albeit vicariously, when Lysander argues for undertaking it (*Hell.* iii. 4. 2). At that point (ch. 6. 2 and at *Lys.* 23. 1) Plutarch excluded the thought from the argument, perhaps reserving it for this moment when it would contribute to the enhancement of Agesilaos' expectations for the future. The transfer illustrates Plutarch's flexible use of sources.

The form is that of a compendious comparison:[11] the reference to the large number of troops available to Xenophon, omitting the quality of the leadership, is contrasted with a reference to his own powerful leadership, omitting the smaller number of his troops; and there is pride in comparing Lakedaimonians, *rerum domini*, with the unspecified nationalities. Perhaps Plutarch has forgotten that Xenophon brought some of Kyros' men with him to Agesilaos. The achievements of the Ten Thousand and the claim in the conventional all-inclusive expression 'of land and sea', like *terra marique*, for the extent of the Spartan hegemony, even following Sparta's defeat of Athens in 404, are exaggerated. The exaggeration shows the light-hearted and cavalier assessments of Greek superiority over Persia at this time, and it gives an encouraging thought to the troops. In mainland Greece, Sparta was soon to be challenged in the Corinthian war, and while Agesilaos had crossed the Aegean unopposed, the Persian fleet being built (ch. 6) was a challenge still threatening for the future (see below, ch. 17. 4).

Xenophon's anecdote about resourcefulness in the face of the Spartiates' depression comes from Agesilaos' repertoire or his diarist's, but the suspicion arises here that he does not penetrate to a true elucidation of the strategy. Agesilaos was in Asia Minor for action, probably briefed about Tissaphernes' Karian base, as Derkylidas was (*Hell.* iii. 2. 12): his avoidance of it needs explanation. Xenophon's account, whatever the source, seems designed to obscure Agesilaos' refusal of an immediate engagement. Plutarch takes up Agesilaos' confident expectations, and the discussion of a grand achievement appropriately explains Agesilaos' inner feelings at the declaration of war. The campaign in Phrygia, as he presents it, demonstrates wise and circumspect generalship in causing damage to the enemy.

In Xenophon, by contrast, the perceived requirement is for action against Tissaphernes, to exploit the support of the gods: yet Agesilaos chooses not to meet him, despite his outward pleasure. This is all the more surprising, since at *Agesilaos*, 1. 10–12 Xenophon claims it as an achievement that Agesilaos has shown Tissaphernes to be a perjurer, not to be trusted, his πρώτη πρᾶξις. The phrase, using a word amply attested as 'action' from Homer onwards, has been taken, as in Polybios, to mean 'a first deliberate stratagem', an early use of the term.[12] But while Xenophon can claim good generalship in the successful outcome of the episode, the perjury was something Agesilaos could not have devised or foreseen, and the initiative for the truce was Tissaphernes' (*Hell.* iii. 4. 5). Plutarch perhaps wisely ignores the ploy here, though he recognizes Agesilaos' generalship.

3 εὐθὺς οὖν ἀμυνόμενος ἀπάτῃ δικαίᾳ τὴν Τισσαφέρνους ἐπιορκίαν, ἐπέδειξεν ὡς ἐπὶ Καρίαν προάξων. ἐκεῖ δὲ τὴν δύναμιν τοῦ βαρβάρου συναθροίσαντος, ἄρας εἰς Φρυγίαν ἐνέβαλε.

Plutarch mentions 'perjury', ἐπιορκία, only now. He evidently refers to the declaration of war (§1), which implies an oath-breaking independent of Tissaphernes' request for troops in Xenophon (see above, on *Hell.* iii. 4. 6, 11; *Agesilaos*, 1. 11, 13). He may have followed *Hellenika*, where Xenophon, on the declaration of war, refers back to the perjury to explain Agesilaos' joy, having inserted the 'quarrel' (chs. 7–8) in the intervening sections, §§7–10. Plutarch may have misread, or deliberately abridged, Xenophon.

There is an oxymoronic element in ἀπάτῃ δικαίᾳ, 'a justifiable deception'. For Xenophon, deception was acceptable as a virtue in a general, once war was being waged (*Agesilaos*, 1. 17, *Mem.* iv. 2. 15; see Introd., E.6(*a*)). Tissaphernes' deception was unacceptable, for it was perpetrated before the war started and, while Agesilaos did not swear to go to Karia, Tissaphernes bound himself by oath. The first mention of deception here in Xenophon's *Hellenika* comes when Agesilaos fears that *he* may be deceived by Tissaphernes (iii. 4. 5), as he immediately is; Agesilaos' deception of Tissaphernes is given prominence only in retrospect (*Agesilaos*, 1. 17).

Xenophon does not mention deception as part of Agesilaos' *plan* (*Hell.* iii. 4. 11–12, *Agesilaos*, 1. 15), which arranges for supplies to be available in the south, and for troops, significantly from the north, to meet him at Ephesos. He does not wait for them there, but meets them in the north, on the march towards Phrygia. Xenophon does not mention that Tissaphernes knows anything of Agesilaos' intentions, when he gives his *rational* grounds for expecting Karia to be invaded: the terrain is unsuited to cavalry and his own residence is there; an invasion of Karia is attractive to an army, like Agesilaos', deficient in cavalry, and offers Agesilaos a chance of revenge for the deception over the truce—information readily available to the Spartans.[13] Xenophon does not stress that Tissaphernes is tricked into responding to a false report of his enemy's plans: Agesilaos seems to change his mind and turns north when he finds that the Persian's forces have been deployed in Karia (*Hell.* iii. 4. 12, *Agesilaos*, 1. 16), and it is clearly cautious generalship to avoid danger. Xenophon's reference to deception by Agesilaos comes only after the reduction of cities in the north, and only in *Agesilaos*, to prove Agesilaos' sound generalship (1. 17; see below).

At the start of the second campaign, Xenophon attributes to Tissaphernes himself the thought (*Hell.* iii. 4. 21) that Agesilaos wants to deceive him again. He realizes that he was deceived before, but not by Agesilaos: he was misled by his own reasoning. These references to deception may have suggested to Plutarch a satisfying dramatic effect, which is important for his analysis of Agesilaos' character as a man able to exploit a situation to his own advantage. The tricking of Tissaphernes illustrates Agesilaos' superior generalship and also supplies the missing explanation of the unexpected course of events. That the deception was deliberate and planned by Agesilaos is open to doubt. Nepos makes Tissaphernes himself responsible for the forecast of Agesilaos' intentions (*Agesilaus*, 3. 1), but credits Agesilaos with the insight that he would suspect the second announcement (*Agesilaus*, 3. 4–5). The stress on Agesilaos' *intention* to deceive seems to be Plutarch's, and he can present it in this way because he transfers Tissaphernes' own grounds for defending Karia to the second campaign, where they reinforce his fear of another deception (see below, ch. 10).

4 καὶ πόλεις μὲν εἷλε συχνὰς καὶ χρημάτων ἀφθόνων ἐκυρίευσεν, ἐπιδεικνύμενος τοῖς φίλοις ὅτι τὸ μὲν σπεισάμενον ἀδικεῖν τῶν θεῶν ἐστι καταφρονεῖν, ἐν δὲ τῷ παραλογίζεσθαι τοὺς πολεμίους οὐ μόνον τὸ δίκαιον, ἀλλὰ καὶ δόξα πολλὴ καὶ τὸ μεθ' ἡδονῆς κερδαίνειν ἔνεστι.

The cities are not named or defined in importance, but they were rich. Plutarch gives fewer details even than Xenophon, but mentions the main achievement of the campaign, the booty. He is more interested in the consequences of the abuse of an oath, a theme found also at ch. 23. 6 when Phoibidas takes the Kadmeia, at ch. 28. 6–7 when Agesilaos excludes Thebes from the peace treaty, and at ch. 35. 3 when he excludes Messene from taking the oath of ratification. Tissaphernes receives his punishment below (ch. 10. 6). Here Plutarch's moralizing conclusion is inspired by Xenophon's *Agesilaos*, 1. 17, where Agesilaos' generalship is praised for his use of deception only when the declaration of war made it just, and for his shrewd enrichment of his friends with the booty. Plutarch lists four achievements: justice, glory, profit, and pleasure.[14] Where Xenophon drifts towards φιλία from τὸ στρατηγικόν in *Agesilaos*, 1. 17–19, Plutarch recasts the complex of ideas to suit the *Leitmotif* of 'Help Friends and Harm Enemies' (ch. 5), as Agesilaos helps his friends by demonstrating the right and wrong ways to harm enemies. Xenophon's eulogizing becomes Plutarch's moralizing. The moralizing is intended chiefly for the reader, but it works on those within the literary context.

The verb παραλογίζεσθαι, in this context, is a more rational expression, 'deceive by exploiting the element of surprise', and he uses the same word when Agesilaos explains to Nektanebo at ch. 38 the secret of the successful stratagem. Here, then, when Tissaphernes indicates by his actions what his calculations have led him to expect, Agesilaos simply does the unexpected; see Introd., E.6(*c*).

5 τοῖς δὲ ἱππεῦσιν ἐλαττωθεὶς καὶ τῶν ἱερῶν ἀλόβων φανέντων, ἀναχωρήσας εἰς Ἔφεσον ἱππικὸν συνῆγε, τοῖς εὐπόροις προειπών, εἰ μὴ βούλονται στρατεύεσθαι, παρασχεῖν ἕκαστον ἵππον ἀνθ' ἑαυτοῦ καὶ ἄνδρα.

Xenophon avoids mentioning this defeat in *Agesilaos* and Plutarch returns to the narrative of events in *Hellenika*, but he enhances its importance by omitting the detail that it involved only Agesilaos' scouts and an equal number of Persians (*Hell.* iii. 4. 13). Like Xenophon (*Hell.* iii. 4. 15) Plutarch records omens and signs. He implies that Agesilaos took note of them here, but he gives no clue to his own attitude, as he did after the episode at Aulis (ch. 6). He continues the demonstration in the previous sentence of Agesilaos' piety, but in a different way. The λοβός is frequently the 'lobe', a projection of the liver, an important part of the sacrificial animal for divination; its absence exposes the portal fissure, from which the gall oozes (cf. Soph. *Ant.* 1010). This is commonly reported in extispicy (*Alex.* 73. 4, Eur. *El.* 827, Xen. *Hell.* iv. 7. 7; cf. Aesch. *PV*, 493–5, Cic. *de Div.* 2. 32).[15]

It was regular practice to call on wealthy men to serve as cavalry. Agesilaos, apparently knowing their reluctance and unsuitability, here uses their wealth and influence to find and equip more efficient substitutes; but most importantly he enforces prompt action by a threat of personal service if the substitute is not provided. The age of these people would be taken into account, but the edict suggests conscription at any age, though in the end Agesilaos seems to want to avoid having men who are not the most physically fit, one of the personal reasons to wish 'to avoid military service'. Unwilling campaigners would not add to the efficiency of Agesilaos' force, but if horses are provided, able riders may be recruited among less wealthy citizens, and finding such recruits is part of the price of exemption.

6 πολλοὶ δ᾽ ἦσαν οὗτοι, καὶ συνέβαινε τῷ Ἀγησιλάῳ ταχὺ πολλοὺς καὶ πολεμικοὺς ἔχειν ἱππεῖς [ἀντὶ δειλῶν ὁπλιτῶν]. ἐμισθοῦντο γὰρ οἱ μὴ βουλόμενοι στρατεύεσθαι [τοὺς βουλομένους στρατεύεσθαι, οἱ δὲ μὴ βουλόμενοι ἱππεύειν] τοὺς βουλομένους ἱππεύειν.

The verb ἐμισθοῦντο is not used of the rich men at this point by Xenophon: Agesilaos exempts those who supply a horse, weapons, and an able man. Plutarch shows that in his opinion they 'were hiring' mercenaries for Agesilaos. Xenophon and Plutarch say that Agesilaos is raising cavalry, but if here he obtains them ἀντὶ δειλῶν ὁπλιτῶν, there is confusion, for Agesilaos was neither recruiting infantry nor transforming existing infantry into cavalry, a process which would be neither quick nor simple—'worthless hoplites' are not likely to become valuable horsemen. The phrase is bracketed as dubious (perhaps adapted from *Mor.* 209 B: ἀντὶ δειλῶν καὶ πλουσίων), a contrived antithesis with πολεμικοὺς ἱππεῖς, 'warlike cavalry'.

Xenophon makes it clear that the rich man eagerly finds a substitute for himself *who will risk his life*, serving presumably as a mercenary with equipment supplied by the beneficiary (*Hell.* iii. 4. 15, *Agesilaos*, 1. 24). Plutarch does not explicitly distinguish between willing and unwilling service, here or in the following sentence. Instead another distinction is made, between μὴ στρατεύεσθαι and ἱππεύειν, between 'to avoid campaigning' and 'to serve as cavalryman', suggested by μὴ στρατεύεσθαι in Xenophon

(*Hell*. iii. 4. 15; *Agesilaos*, 1. 24). Cobet[16] rightly bracketed τοὺς βουλομένους στρατεύεσθαι, οἱ δὲ μὴ βουλόμενοι ἱππεύειν, which on stylistic grounds makes a clumsy sentence and clumsy thinking. The sentence is not found at *Mor*. 209 B, which suggests that it was not Plutarch's. The interpolator was motivated by the idea of a functional distinction between foot and horse; it is rather one of species and genus: cavalry service and campaigning. The point is that the substitutes would improve themselves socially, financially, and in service conditions, while the rich avoided service. The procedure offers the explanation of πολεμικούς.

7 καὶ γὰρ τὸν Ἀγαμέμνονα ποιῆσαι καλῶς, ὅτι θήλειαν ἵππον ἀγαθὴν λαβὼν κακὸν ἄνδρα καὶ πλούσιον ἀπήλλαξε τῆς στρατείας.

This thought is not recorded by Xenophon, who credits Agesilaos only with the efficient means of raising cavalrymen of approved ability. Plutarch draws an example from literature to support his argument. The thought is also in accordance with a plausible reconstruction of Agesilaos' character, since Spartans knew their Homer—the man and his poems—(*Lyk*. 1. 4, 4. 4), and a Peloponnesian leader at war in Asia Minor could hardly fail to think of Agamemnon (cf. ch. 6. 6); and it is consistent with the interpretation of the text offered above that he has the parallel of Agamemnon in mind (*Il*. xxiii. 296), raising good cavalry and freeing the unserviceable rich from the expedition.

8 ἐπεὶ δὲ κελεύσαντος αὐτοῦ τοὺς αἰχμαλώτους ἀποδύοντες ἐπίπρασκον οἱ λαφυροπῶλαι, καὶ τῆς μὲν ἐσθῆτος ἦσαν ὠνηταὶ πολλοί, τῶν δὲ σωμάτων λευκῶν καὶ ἁπαλῶν παντάπασι διὰ τὰς σκιατροφίας γυμνουμένων κατεγέλων ὡς ἀχρήστων καὶ μηδενὸς ἀξίων, ἐπιστὰς ὁ Ἀγησίλαος, Οὗτοι μέν, εἶπεν, οἷς μάχεσθε, ταῦτα δ' ὑπὲρ ὧν μάχεσθε.

Plutarch records another anecdote about separating naked prisoners and their clothes, in which the general offers to his allies the choice of taking the one or the other as their share of the booty: the allies take the more valuable at first sight, the clothing, but the prisoners are ransomed by their relatives more profitably to the Athenians later (*Kim*. 9). Here the sale and the display of effeminate bodies are combined into a single event intended to strengthen the morale of the troops: the low opinion of the men is not, for Agesilaos' purpose, in their saleability, but in their fighting qualities. Agesilaos again displays ἱλαρότης, 'sense of fun' (ch. 2). Plutarch frequently ends an anecdote with direct speech.

At this point (*Agesilaos*, 1. 18–19), Xenophon records that Agesilaos' generalship benefits his friends: he allows them to take captured goods without paying until later, when, in a better market, they receive a higher price. He also makes sure that his friends are told where plunder is available. Plutarch does not use this incident to illustrate how Agesilaos acquired friends: it would, perhaps, conflict with the asceticism ascribed to Agesilaos' own lifestyle and with his attitude to personal extravagance in others. Xenophon approves, but does not place it in the catalogue of virtues (*Agesilaos*, 3–11; see Introd., F.2).

The proposed Karian expedition and the march north

Karia was the natural objective if Agesilaos wished to engage the enemy, for Tissaphernes had assembled his army to the south of the river Maiandros. His purpose may have been to protect his estates, as Xenophon mentions (*Agesilaos*, 1. 15, *Hell*. iii. 4. 12), but he would also be guarding the approaches to the south, where the fleet was based, especially as he probably knew that the expedition had been sent as a response to the building of the fleet, and that its purpose was to prevent a Persian encroachment into the Greek waters of the Aegean (ch. 6. 1). He also knew of the Spartans' interest in Karia from the earlier operations of Derkylidas on the instructions of the ephors (Xen. *Hell*. iii. 2. 12), interrupted by the truce. If that truce had held,[17] a Karian expedition would be a resumption of those operations. Xenophon's chronology is confused: the supply bases and allied contingents are ordered at the time of the departure from Ephesos (*Hell*. iii. 4. 11). Adjustment comes when Agesilaos meets the allies 'on the march' to Phrygia—before they reach the rendezvous: perhaps he intended the northern meeting. The sequence of Agesilaos' decisions and movements regarding Karia need not be disturbed if deliberately planned deception is abandoned, but the change of plan will then be related more meaningfully to the arrival of Spithridates than the sources suggest.

The satrapy of Phrygia, governed by Pharnabazos, whose residence was at Daskyleion, bordered on the Hellespont. Xenophon records suspicion between the two satraps (*Hell*. iii. 1.

9). Pharnabazos had helped the Lakedaimonians in the Peloponnesian war (*Hell*. i. 3. 5 and *passim*) and had also helped the Athenians (*Hell*. i. 3. 8). Then Thibron's successor, Derkylidas, who had earlier been 'insulted' by Pharnabazos, transferred his activities to fight him in the northern satrapy (*Hell*. iii. 1. 9). Plutarch's reference to 'invasion' (§3) is perhaps intended to imply serious hostilities, but there was no major direct engagement. He summarizes events briefly, without naming Pharnabazos, and devotes the rest of the chapter to anecdotal characterizing of Agesilaos.

The importance attached by Xenophon and Plutarch to Agesilaos' aims on his departure from Greece, and to the Aulis affair, is not matched by the military events following his arrival. Despite his joyful reception of the declaration of war, Agesilaos does not take advantage either of the help of the gods, which he was so confident they would give him against the oath-breaker, or of Tissaphernes' lack of preparations and his apparent weakness, or of the element of surprise in an immediate attack. The objective revealed in the treaty-making as autonomy for the Greeks is consistent with the initial requests made by the cities for Spartan intervention on their behalf, but Agesilaos' suspicion of Tissaphernes' promises, and his declaration of war, would have shown him that autonomy was not going to be granted without direct confrontation. Tissaphernes also holds back. He had perhaps arranged possible countermeasures during the truce with Derkylidas, and could do nothing then but wait, but even when he had received reinforcements and declared war, he did not attack Agesilaos at once, and, although Agesilaos was keeping to the agreement and maintaining the peace, seems only to have planned for the defence of Karia.

There was evident reluctance on both sides for direct confrontation. Xenophon reveals the anxiety of the Lakedaimonians when they realized the strength of their enemy (*Hell*. iii. 4. 11); and once Agesilaos, too, had realized, whether on the march (*Agesilaos*, 1. 16) or at an earlier stage, that in Karia he would face Tissaphernes and his strengthened forces, it appears that the strategically sound attack on Karia had become too dangerous to contemplate. Spithridates' advice and topographical guidance instigated or activated the change of plan, and Agesilaos turned north to go just about as far away from Karia as he could, precisely to where

Lysander had spent some time when in Asia Minor before, and close to where he had picked up Spithridates. It seems a logical decision, and it leads to the success of taking cities and booty, but it means that Agesilaos makes no further contact at all with Tissaphernes during this season.

Plutarch perhaps saw the inconsistency here, and reworked the episode to introduce the deception as a deliberate intention to outsmart the enemy. By putting it at the start of the episode, he not only gave it prominence, but made it the sole reason for Tissaphernes' decision to defend Karia. He seems to have adapted Xenophon's reference to deception at *Agesilaos*, 1. 17 for this purpose. That hint of deception may have been invented for propaganda or braggadocio purposes—in retrospect, rather than currently related to military plans, if Agesilaos perhaps later claimed credit for having deceived Tissaphernes in revenge for his treachery, and veiled his decision not to attack Karia.

According to Diodoros (xiv. 79. 3), Agesilaos went straight to the plain of the Kaystros and then on to lay waste Phrygia from a base at Kyme, with no talk of Karia or of deception, here or in the next campaign (xiv. 80). If his source depended on the Oxyrhynchos historian, perhaps the Phrygian campaign was all that he found there. Nepos has no deception by Agesilaos, who 'turned towards Phrygia', although he has Tissaphernes' deception over the treaty and his misjudgement of Agesilaos' movements (*Agesilaus*, 2–3). He puts Tissaphernes' movement of troops to Karia after the truce expired (§3), which does not leave time for more than a short campaign in Phrygia; but since Agesilaos undertook the Phrygian campaign of 395 (Xen. *Hell.* iv. 1. 1) at the beginning of autumn and continued on to Paphlagonia before winter, there was sufficient time for the 396 campaign.

10. Agesilaos defeats Tissaphernes at Sardis and marches on to Phrygia: he is appointed to command by land and sea

Xen. *Hell*. iii. 4. 20–4, *Agesilaos*, 1. 28–34; Diod. xiv. 80. 1–5; *Hell. Ox*. VI. 4–6 (Bruce (1967), 81–4; Breitenbach (1970), 393–6); Nepos, *Agesilaus*, 3. 4–6; Paus. iii. 9. 6; Polyain. 2. 1. 9; Frontin. *Strat*. 1. 8. 12.[1]

The succession of Tithraustes and the execution of Tissaphernes are at the centre of this chapter. On either side are two campaigns, one to Lydia, which includes the battle of Sardis, and one to Phrygia, continued in the following chapters. The first campaign of the new season is given in a straightforward narrative and in respect of deception and plundering activity resembles the campaign of 396. The account of the second campaign begins with the extension of Agesilaos' command.

1 Καιροῦ δ' ὄντος αὖθις ἐμβαλεῖν εἰς τὴν πολεμίαν, προεῖπεν εἰς Λυδίαν ἀνάξειν, οὐκέτι ψευδόμενος ἐνταῦθα τὸν Τισσαφέρνην· ἀλλ' ἐκεῖνος ἑαυτὸν ἐξηπάτησε, διὰ τὴν ἔμπροσθεν ἀπάτην ἀπιστῶν τῷ Ἀγησιλάῳ, καὶ νῦν γοῦν αὐτὸν ἄψεσθαι τῆς Καρίας νομίζων, οὔσης δυσίππου, πολὺ τῷ ἱππικῷ λειπόμενον.

Plutarch implies Agesilaos' earlier deception of Tissaphernes, but presents the second deception as the latter's own misjudgement that Agesilaos' announcement of Lydia as his destination was a trick. In Xenophon's accounts the precise destination is not named, but Tissaphernes himself attributes to Agesilaos the intention to deceive him again, and the denial which follows seems designed to show that Agesilaos is keeping his word (*Hell*. iii. 4. 21 and *Agesilaos*, 1. 29). It is to Karia and the Maiandros that Tissaphernes sends his infantry and cavalry, while Agesilaos again goes to the north. The reason given by Xenophon, 'for the physical and mental preparation of the troops for combat', appears to be more appropriate for the troops newly arrived in the previous year, 396, and is not mentioned here by Plutarch (see below, §2).

The strategic considerations given by Xenophon that in 396 led Tissaphernes to defend Karia and ignored then by Plutarch (ch. 9. 3), are introduced here, where he deceives himself by his reasoning about the terrain and Agesilaos' lack of cavalry. His possession of estates in the area (*Hell*. iii. 4. 12) is of no concern for Agesilaos' biographer, and is omitted. Plutarch's transfer of the reasoning is appropriate to his account, and although the argument was more relevant before Agesilaos had augmented his cavalry, the Persian advantage was not greatly affected in the battle (Xen. *Hell.* iii. 4. 24; see below). It seems that because he considers that Xenophon gives no satisfactory explanation of Agesilaos' two decisions postponing the positive business of the mission, Plutarch again rearranges the material, showing an attitude to the meaning of truth in historiography which is still being explored.[2] He could argue that he does not discard the sources in order to generate a more attractive narrative and one that complements and matches his view of Agesilaos' character; but that where problems of length, complexity, or ambiguity arise in the sources which do not transfer well into his scheme, he creates a new synthesis from the historical details he finds there, without resorting to falsehood. Here there are two known forms of deception, which together provide a more reasonable interpretation of *wie es eigentlich gewesen.*

2 ἐπεὶ δ', ὥσπερ προεῖπεν, ὁ Ἀγησίλαος ἧκεν εἰς τὸ περὶ Σάρδεις πεδίον, ἠναγκάζετο κατὰ σπουδὴν ἐκεῖθεν αὖ βοηθεῖν ὁ Τισσαφέρνης· καὶ τῇ ἵππῳ διεξελαύνων διέφθειρε πολλοὺς τῶν ἀτάκτως τὸ πεδίον πορθούντων.

Plutarch now identifies Agesilaos' destination more closely than Xenophon, who used two imprecise phrases: ἐπὶ τὰ κράτιστα τῆς χώρας (*Hell.* iii. 4. 20, *Agesilaos*, 1. 28), 'the centre of wealth', not of power (he chose the area for the availability of supplies);[3] and εἰς τὸν Σαρδιανὸν τόπον (*Hell.* iii. 4. 21, *Agesilaos*, 1. 29), 'the territory around Sardis': he drove on towards Sardis itself only after the battle (*Agesilaos*, 1. 33). The objectives envisaged at the start (cf. ch. 6) are not indicated.

Xenophon may suggest that Tissaphernes was in Sardis and not on the battlefield (*Hell.* iii. 4. 25). During minor engagements he could be in Sardis taking general charge of the situation, not commanding the army in person. Plutarch assumes that he was with the army in Karia, but now arrives in advance of the infantry, with the cavalry still able to exploit its advantage, even over Agesilaos' enlarged squadrons. The prefix δια- in the compound verb, διεξελαύνων, suggests 'riding out over the plain' before reaching and attacking Agesilaos' scattered plunderers (cf. *Hell.* iii. 4. 22).

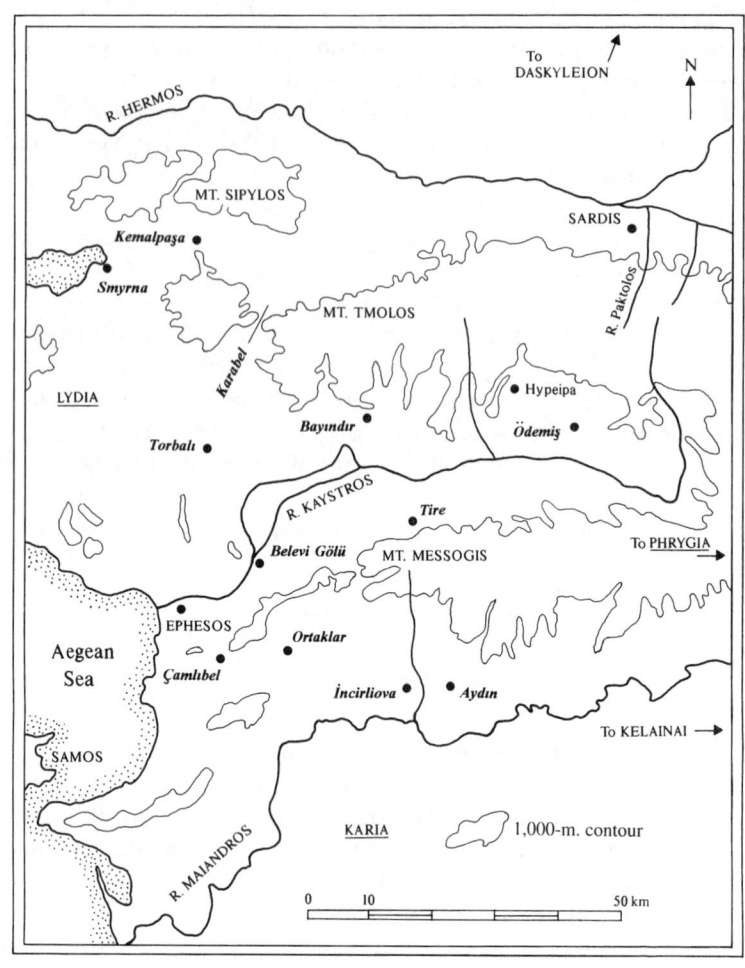

MAP 2. Western Asia Minor

3 ἐννοήσας οὖν ὁ Ἀγησίλαος ὅτι τοῖς πολεμίοις οὔπω πάρεστι τὸ πεζόν, αὐτῷ δὲ τῆς δυνάμεως οὐδὲν ἄπεστιν, ἔσπευσε διαγωνίσασθαι. καὶ τοῖς μὲν ἱππεῦσιν ἀναμίξας τὸ πελταστικόν, ἐλαύνειν ἐκέλευσεν ὡς τάχιστα καὶ προσβάλλειν τοῖς ἐναντίοις, αὐτὸς δ᾽ εὐθὺς τοὺς ὁπλίτας ἐπῆγε.

In Plutarch's brief account the battle of Sardis was fought by Agesilaos when he noticed the unexpected separation of the enemy's cavalry and infantry, as Xenophon also says (*Hell.* iii. 4. 23). Diodoros describes a premeditated engagement involving an ambush (xiv. 80. 2). Plutarch is not concerned with all the details of the fighting, and the episode is therefore treated here separately (see note below). He is concerned with Agesilaos' generalship and the final result of the incident, and concentrates on the successful management of the Greek forces. His previous sentence sufficiently indicates that the whole Persian cavalry was engaged: Xenophon adds that the battle-line was put in formation after the first skirmish.

Plutarch gives his account entirely from Agesilaos' standpoint, highlighting his inspired act of military analysis. The participle ἐννοήσας implies 'observation' from a lookout position rather than receipt of reports as Xenophon's less visual γιγνώσκων suggests. The participle ἀναμίξας, 'mixing together', suffices, with the phrase 'brought up his hoplites', for Xenophon's account of the successive engagement of Agesilaos' four units—young hoplites, peltasts, cavalry, and the whole army (*Hell.* iii. 4. 23). If this represents Plutarch's conflation of Xenophon, it does not indicate innovatory tactics.

A force wholly composed of cavalry is vulnerable to determined infantry opposition: the Thessalian cavalry were turned back by hoplites (Xen. *Hell.* iv. 3. 5; cf. ch. 16. 7); a mixed force such as this would be even more effective.[4] The wish to take advantage of the absence of Persian infantry was sound, but victory could hardly be decisive, and therefore διαγωνίσασθαι, 'decide a contest', is too strong a word.

4 γενομένης δὲ τροπῆς τῶν βαρβάρων, ἐπακολουθήσαντες οἱ Ἕλληνες ἔλαβον τὸ στρατόπεδον καὶ πολλοὺς ἀνεῖλον.

Plutarch again keeps to Agesilaos' standpoint, omits Xenophon's report of Persian resistance and flight to the river, and confines the account of the fighting to the rout. The capture of a camp is a feature in all the accounts of the 'battle of Sardis', but there is no evidence to show where it was, or whether it was a temporary base or a part of the permanent defences of Sardis. It was small enough for Agesilaos to throw a cordon around it, suggesting that it did not include the baggage-train of the whole Persian army.[5] Plutarch, like Xenophon, gives the impression that Agesilaos won a great victory.

5 ἐκ ταύτης τῆς μάχης οὐ μόνον ὑπῆρξεν αὐτοῖς ἄγειν καὶ φέρειν ἀδεῶς τὴν βασιλέως χώραν, ἀλλὰ καὶ δίκην ἐπιδεῖν Τισσαφέρνην διδόντα, μοχθηρὸν ἄνδρα καὶ τῷ γένει τῶν Ἑλλήνων ἀπεχθέστατον. **6** ἔπεμψε γὰρ εὐθέως ὁ βασιλεὺς Τιθραύστην ἐπ᾽ αὐτόν, ὃς ἐκείνου μὲν τὴν κεφαλὴν ἀπέτεμε . . .

The interference experienced up to this point by Agesilaos was from Persian cavalry, and this continues to be the main source of danger to plunderers. Consequently even the modest success achieved in this engagement has significant value for the limited activities that Agesilaos is engaged in now. A direct assault on the city of Sardis would be very different, for the massive hills east and west provide an impregnable base for defenders. The Oxyrhynchos historian (VII. 1)[6] records plundering around Sardis lasting for three days. Xenophon attributes the plundering after the battle to the peltasts (*Hell.* iii. 4. 24, *Agesilaos*, 1. 32), and he shows that Agesilaos established control of the booty by building an encampment round it. At 1. 33–4 there is activity in the outskirts of the town and in the countryside. Xenophon here honours Agesilaos by anticipating the consecration of a hundred talents at Delphi on the return from Asia. In *Hellenika* he refers to camels taken by Agesilaos.

Plutarch and Xenophon attach great importance to the results of the victory at Sardis, linking it with the punishment of Tissaphernes by the King. For Xenophon the victory is enhanced by Tithraustes' offer of autonomy, reversing the King's earlier decision which led Tissaphernes to declare war (ch. 9. 1; Xen. *Hell.* iii. 4. 11). For Plutarch, with strong panhellenist feelings, execution is a proper penalty for his deception of Agesilaos, and the hostility towards the Greeks of Asia Minor which earned his condemnation as 'a man without principles' (μοχθηρὸν ἄνδρα). Tissaphernes' reputation stems from the seizure of the Greek generals (Xen. *An.* ii. 5) and his prolonged efforts to recover the Ionian cities, rather than 'a maliciously prejudiced tradition';[7] and he suffers by contrast with Xenophon's generous portraits of Kyros and Pharnabazos.

The timing of Tissaphernes' execution is confused, for if it was punishment for the apparently minor defeat, it cannot have been carried out immediately, as Xenophon implies (*Hell.* iii. 4. 25). Plutarch also suggests an 'immediate' response after the King heard the news, but the plundering implies an interval, and other activities intervened (Xen. *Agesilaos*, 1. 33–4). The King, Artaxerxes II, may have held Tissaphernes responsible for the larger failure to stop the Spartan intervention in Asia Minor,[8] and according to Diodoros (xiv. 80. 6), his mother Parysatis had now persuaded him to avenge the death of her other son Kyros, for which she blamed Tissaphernes, his long-standing rival. Plans for the replacement may have been made, perhaps at the further instigation of Pharnabazos, to whose satrapy Agesilaos' marauders had earlier been diverted.[9] If the King had approved the reinforcements that Tissaphernes received, such plans would be contingent upon the military outcome. Information about decisions of the King's advisers is not to be thought readily available either to the invaders or to their historians.

. . . τὸν δ' Ἀγησίλαον ἠξίου διαλυσάμενον ἀποπλεῖν οἴκαδε, καὶ χρήματα διδοὺς αὐτῷ προσέπεμψεν. 7 ὁ δὲ τῆς μὲν εἰρήνης ἔφη τὴν πόλιν εἶναι κυρίαν, αὐτὸς δὲ πλουτίζων τοὺς στρατιώτας ἥδεσθαι μᾶλλον ἢ πλουτῶν αὐτός· καὶ ἄλλως γε μέντοι νομίζειν Ἕλληνας καλὸν οὐ δῶρα λαμβάνειν, ἀλλὰ λάφυρα παρὰ τῶν πολεμίων.

In Xenophon's account (*Hell.* iii. 4. 25), money is not offered at this stage; Tithraustes claims credit for the punishment of Tissaphernes (see below, §8) and he delivers the King's demands (βασιλεὺς ἀξιοῖ): Agesilaos to return to Greece and the cities, being autonomous, to pay to the King the ancient tribute. Here it is Tithraustes who 'demanded' this (ἠξίου),[10] with the additional διαλυσάμενον, absent from Xenophon, meaning 'stop the fighting, abandon the expedition'; the offer of money was clearly conditional upon compliance, and departure: Agesilaos refuses and speaks of making war. Tithraustes later suggests that, since he had carried out the punishment himself, Agesilaos should withdraw to Pharnabazos' territory during his consultation with Sparta. Agesilaos agrees to depart (without consulting Sparta), but now demands money for provisions—it is not a spontaneous offer here

(*Hell*. iii. 4. 26). At *Agesilaos*, 4. 6, Xenophon gives no diplomatic details, but illustrates Agesilaos' attitude to money with his honourable refusal on this occasion of the offer of 'huge gifts' if he leaves the country.

Plutarch, perhaps seeing Xenophon's inconsistency, rewrites the moral anecdote into the historical incident, with clear verbal parallels. In §§6–7 he adapts ἀξιοῖ ἀποπλεῖν οἴκαδε (*Hell*. iii. 4. 25), διδόντος πάμπολλα δῶρα (*Agesilaos*, 4. 6; cf. *Mor*. 209 D), (οὐκ) ἄνευ τῶν οἴκοι τελῶν (*Hell*. iii. 4. 26), πλουτίζειν and λάφυρα (*Agesilaos*, 4. 6, the source for the rest of §7, not *Hellenika*). The moral of the rejected offer of money, with its hint of bribery, the Spartans' lack of interest in private wealth, and the preference for booty rather than gifts—presumably they disliked imposed terms—are given in a diplomatic context. Plutarch's adaptations reconcile the moral principle and the practice (§8).

8 ὅμως δὲ τῷ Τιθραύστῃ χαρίζεσθαι βουλόμενος, ὅτι τὸν κοινὸν ἐχθρὸν Ἑλλήνων ἐτετιμώρητο Τισσαφέρνην, μετήγαγεν εἰς Φρυγίαν τὸ στράτευμα, λαβὼν ἐφόδιον παρ' αὐτοῦ τριάκοντα τάλαντα.

Plutarch continues to enhance the consequences of the battle as Agesilaos acknowledges his gratitude to Tithraustes for the punishment of Tissaphernes and picks up the hostility for Tissaphernes felt by Tithraustes (Xen. *Hell*. iii. 4. 25–6). The phrase 'common enemy of the Greeks' assigned here to Agesilaos broadens the base for his gratitude. His departure is not now at anyone's behest: the money is associated not with compliance, but with doing the favour for Tithraustes, and is not demanded here (cf. *Hell*. iii. 4. 26), but simply 'taken' for provisions on the journey. Agesilaos responds with dignity and in accordance with the principle of reciprocity in friendship (chs. 5. 1–3 and 9. 4 above); he departs for Phrygia spontaneously. By combining Xenophon's two divergent moral tales (reported from the talk of the *syssition*, or told to him personally by Agesilaos on different occasions)—a Spartan spurns a bribe (in *Agesilaos*) and imposes his will on a barbarian (in *Hellenika*)—Plutarch writes a moral tale: Agesilaos cannot take a bribe, but returns a favour, for which he will be compensated. Spartans and Persians had known each other long enough to understand the formalities of the occasion: a diplomatic comedy. Similarly, the contrast of simplicity and lifestyle (cf. ch. 12. 2–3) was a convention to be exploited in diplo-

matic gesture; it did not always succeed. Herodotos (ix. 122. 3–4)
implies that Persians retained respect for frugality; but Egyptians
did not (cf. ch. 36. 9–10). Plutarch makes the receipt of money
acceptable on Spartan terms: money and booty were no doubt
now among Agesilaos' prime objectives.[11]

The chronology of these events may be constructed from other
sources. After the battle of Sardis the Oxyrhynchos historian
(VII. 3)[12] records a march through the mountains that divided
Lydia and Phrygia, to the plain of the river Maiandros, the further
march intended being abandoned because of unfavourable
sacrifices. A glance at a map suggests that Agesilaos was possibly
exploring a more easterly route through Karia to the Persian fleet
base in the south, turning back on finding the difficulties too great.
'By conquering Caria, Agesilaos would have deprived the Persian
fleet of a base for the invasion of the Aegean.'[13] The Spartan naval
base at Rhodes was now in the hands of Konon (Diod. xiv. 79.
4–7; *Hell. Ox.* x. 1–2),[14] and the appointment of Agesilaos as naval
commander (see below, §9) suggests a long-term plan for operations south of the Maiandros. Until the new Spartan fleet was
ready, operations would continue in the north. (Cf. Diod. xiv. 79.
3; Xen. *Hell.* iii. 4. 29.) That Xenophon omits this march indicates
his selective method, or that of his source, and the wish to obscure
the lack of positive results from the march.[15] Diodoros reports a
march interrupted by unfavourable sacrifices and goes on to the
death of Tissaphernes arranged by Tithraustes, who then enters
the negotiations with Agesilaos (xiv. 80. 5–8).

9 καὶ καθ' ὁδὸν ὢν σκυτάλην δέχεται παρὰ τῶν οἴκοι τελῶν κελευουσαν
αὐτὸν ἄρχειν ἅμα καὶ τοῦ ναυτικοῦ.

The *skytale* is described as a simple code using a dispatch-roll to
be wound round a staff of standard size so that what was written
across the joins could be read (*Lys.* 19. 5–7; Apollonius Rhodius in
Athenaeus, 451 D). If it is not a reference to the message itself or
the material it was written on, perhaps it was a stick used to
authenticate an oral messenger by matching its broken end to that
of its pair already in the possession of the recipient. Or it may have
been notched as an *aide-mémoire* for the messenger.[16]

The unified command by land and sea suggests that Sparta,
possibly advised by Lysander on his return, had realized that
decisive action in the circumstances could not be expected on land

alone. The instruction in Xenophon is 'to exercise command and appoint an admiral' (*Hell*. iii. 4. 27). It was still necessary to have a separate admiral, but under Agesilaos' supreme command and carrying out his policy.

τοῦτο μόνῳ πάντων ὑπῆρξεν Ἀγησιλάῳ. **10** καὶ μέγιστος μὲν ἦν ὁμολογουμένως καὶ τῶν τότε ζώντων ἐπιφανέστατος, ὡς εἴρηκέ πού καὶ Θεόπομπος, ἑαυτῷ γε μὴν ἐδίδου δι᾽ ἀρετὴν φρονεῖν μεῖζον ἢ διὰ τὴν ἡγεμονίαν.

Theopompos (see Introd., F.3(c)) is quoted for reports of both favourable and unfavourable comments on Agesilaos (chs. 31, 32, 33). In setting his brief encomium of Agesilaos at this point Plutarch is, perhaps, incorporating the idea but not the substance of Xenophon's assessment of him at *Agesilaos*, 1. 36–8. That passage is linked with the expectation of further conquest, prevented only by the order to return home. It presents a eulogistic summary of the campaigns in Asia Minor so far, ending the account of these activities without the events recorded at *Hell*. iii. 4. 27–5. 2 and iv. 1. 1–2. 8, though some appear in *Agesilaos*, 3, 5 and 9. Plutarch's Asiatic section continues to ch. 15.

11 τότε δὲ τοῦ ναυτικοῦ καταστήσας ἄρχοντα Πείσανδρον ἁμαρτεῖν ἔδοξεν, ὅτι πρεσβυτέρων καὶ φρονιμωτέρων παρόντων οὐ σκεψάμενος τὸ τῆς πατρίδος, ἀλλὰ τὴν οἰκειότητα τιμῶν καὶ τῇ γυναικὶ χαριζόμενος, ἧς ἀδελφὸς ἦν ὁ Πείσανδρος, ἐκείνῳ παρέδωκε τὴν ναυαρχίαν.

Xenophon explains that a united command gives strength and efficiency, and reports the building of triremes (*Hell*. iii. 4. 27–8). He records Peisandros' relationship simply, but mixes a compliment to his character with mild criticism of his inexperience (*Hell*. iii. 4. 29). Plutarch adds to Xenophon's criticism by suggesting that more suitable men were available and by interpreting Agesilaos' mind: he honours his kinsman and gratifies his wife. The disregard of Sparta's interests recalls the strong sense of family (ch. 4) and the exploitation of friendship (ch. 5), and anticipates the distortions of justice (chs. 23. 6–26. 1). Peisandros died fighting bravely in the battle of Knidos (Diod. xiv. 83. 7; cf. Xen. *Hell*. iv. 3. 12), but he was defeated. The criticisms of the appointment—not the appointee—are just, with hindsight: it was a Spartan jest that, on being offered a game-cock that would die fighting, one would prefer to wait for one that would kill (*Lyk*. 20.

6, *Mor.* 191 F, 224 C). This is not the only case of the appointment of a relative by Agesilaos. There is another, highly successful, related nominee, Teleutias (ch. 21).

Sardis: the nature and significance of the engagement[17]

The ancient sources give differing accounts of the battle but the evidence is insufficient totally to disprove the credibility of any one. Perhaps more than one engagement occurred, either of which could be selected or omitted by the ancient author for his own reasons.

(*a*) *Topography*. The plain between the river Hermos and the mountain range to the south is flat, broad and rich from Mt Sipylos to well east of Sardis. The heights beside Sardis provide strong defensive positions and a threat to any attackers: the city was not attacked by Agesilaos. The plain offers opportunities both for Xenophon's battle interrupting the plundering and for Diodoros' ambush, which would counter interference with those activities.

Agesilaos is said by Xenophon (*Hell.* iii. 4. 21, *Agesilaos*, 1. 29) to have gone from Ephesos as planned 'straight to the Sardian region'. Tissaphernes' move to Sardis from the Maiandros ended near Paktolos (*Hell.* iii. 4. 22). Possible routes to the north run from Ephesos in the west and from Aydın in the east.[18]

(i) From Ephesos the road across the plain of the Kaystros leads via the Karabel pass to the Hermos plain.[19] The climb over the pass (1,575 feet, 500 m.) presents no problems of gradient. At the northern end of the pass higher mountains in the less penetrable Tmolos range stretch eastwards towards Sardis. To the north is Mt Sipylos,[20] which could be used to place plunderers 'at the western end of the Sardian plain' (Diod. xiv. 80. 1). The Karabel offers 'the shortest route' to rich plunder in the region of Sardis and there is no difficult terrain to delay Agesilaos as he passed west of the enemy on the Maiandros.

(ii) Routes to Sardis from Aydın cross two mountain ranges and the Kaystros valley between. Agesilaos could have joined these routes in the Kaystros plain by a road east from Ephesos through a steep and narrow pass, but he would be under observation as he passed enemy territory. Routes further to the north in the

Kaystros plain would again have taken him some way into the enemy's area and he would still have to cross the Tmolos range to reach Sardis (see below). These do not seem to be obvious choices for him, compared with Karabel.

For Tissaphernes, if his army was near Aydın,[21] the journey to Sardis by an eastern route was not an easy one, although it could be familiar to him if he had recently brought his army to Karia from Sardis. The Messogis ridge between the Maiandros and Kaystros valleys is broken in only two or three places, the most direct route reaching over 3,000 feet (925 m.). The route from the Kaystros over Tmolos climbs steeply to 3,494 feet (1075 m.), passing eventually to the Paktolos valley and to Sardis. Alternative routes are formidable and arrive to the east or west of Sardis. The journey through the lower Paktolos valley presents no problems, but to describe it as 'the normal route to Sardis' from the south hides the difficulties of the climb up from the Kaystros plain.[22] At its northern end the Paktolos valley is too narrow for a 'square formation', but appears viable for unopposed movement by troops familiar with the area, suitable therefore for Tissaphernes' army but not for Agesilaos.

The significant comparison is not between the eastern routes, one of which may have been used by Tissaphernes, but between these and the Karabel, if Agesilaos used it. Their greater difficulty suggests that Tissaphernes would reach the Sardis area after Agesilaos, even allowing for time he spent plundering, since he had a later start, and 'the cavalry's own march will have been delayed by the passage of the hills to a pace which pack-animals (including the famous camels) could follow'.[23]

(iii) Xenophon's description of Agesilaos' destination has been misunderstood since Ch. Dugas (1910), 60:

Agésilas . . . annonce qu'il va envahir la Lydie . . . et marche sur Sardes. Le quatrième jour, il voit apparaître les cavaliers ennemis.

Xenophon's phrases (see above, §2 on *Hell.* iii. 4. 20–1, *Agesilaos* 1. 28–9), are less precise than 'sur Sardes'. Agesilaos set off on the direct route not to Sardis but to 'the Sardian region', the 'centre of wealth'.[24]

The meaning is confirmed by Xenophon's two texts: the rich countryside is to fit the men in body and spirit for the fighting. Agesilaos' aim is not to get to grips with the enemy as quickly as possible. He chose not to fight in Karia, and he would not choose Sardis as an immediate destination preparatory to meeting the enemy, for fighting could be expected there. Xenophon is not saying that Agesilaos reached Sardis from Ephesos in three days.[25] His men had the benefit of a three days' march 'through a country bare of enemies so that he supplied his army with abundance of provisions'; then they were intercepted by cavalry. The text, ἐνέβαλε . . . καὶ πορευόμενος, means that Agesilaos 'invaded—and then marched'.[26] The route from Ephesos to the region of Sipylos indicated by Diodoros (xiv. 80. 1) is likely to be the one indicated by Xenophon, too (cf. *Hell. Ox.* vi. 2–3).[27] That the sources differ on the route taken by Agesilaos is rejected.[28]

(b) *Reports of the engagements.* There are divergences in the ancient accounts of the battle.[29] Xenophon refers to the arrival of the Persian cavalry and records the order for the baggage-train 'to cross the Paktolos and encamp', while the cavalry immediately engaged the Greek foragers. He does not say that the foragers were engaged on the banks of the Paktolos or mention any Persian infantry there.

Diodoros and the Oxyrhynchos historian report that Agesilaos set a successful ambush.[30] Diodoros says that he formed his soldiers into a square when the pillagers were attacked near Mt Sipylos. The distance between Sipylos and the river Paktolos is too great for these to be references to the same site, but the battle in Diodoros' account was not fought immediately. Once the Greeks were in square formation, Tissaphernes hesitated to attack for the rest of that day. Agesilaos overran the countryside as far as Sardis, and midway between Sardis and Thybarnai, on his way back, he sent Xenokles overnight to set an ambush (xiv. 80. 1–2). Diodoros allows time for another engagement.

Mention of the Kaystrian plain in the Oxyrhynchos historian's account (vi. 1–vii. 4)[31] links it with Diodoros' source. As in Diodoros' account, Agesilaos' advance began at daybreak—making clashes on two days—and the Persians followed over the plain in loose formation. Xenokles chose the time to leave the ambush himself, and put the enemy to flight (vi. 4–5).[32] Agesilaos engaged with light-armed troops and cavalry, but the ensuing pursuit failed to contain the enemy, though 600 were killed. The slackness of the guards allowed him to take the camp and seize men and booty.

Diodoros positions the ambush between Sardis and Thybarnai
(xiv. 80. 2), a name preserved nowhere else and unidentified.[33] He
adds that Agesilaos gave the signal to leave the ambush. If his
source was in the main force, he reports the signal of the highest
command, but if that of *Hell. Ox.* was with the ambush, he reports
the signal of the ambush commander. The phrase γενομένης δὲ
καρτερᾶς μάχης (xiv. 80. 3) indicates 'stubborn hand-to-hand
fighting' (cf. Thuc. iv. 96. 2; ch. 18. 5 μάχη γίνεται ἰσχυρὰ), contrasting the earlier 'loose skirmishing'; it does not signify 'important battle' or mark the climax of the action, which, for Diodoros,
is the charge of the ambushers chanting the paean. There is
nothing to suggest that this was a 'full-scale' or 'great' battle or a
'great' victory for Agesilaos,[34] except Diodoros' figure of 6,000
slain, and that is invariably recognized as a mistake for 600.

These engagements were a setback for Tissaphernes, none the
less, and he withdrew to Sardis (Diod. xiv. 80. 5), presumably in
case Agesilaos moved in for what would have been a truly great
military achievement, but neither Sardis itself nor Tissaphernes
was attacked. Agesilaos set up a trophy and allowed the enemy to
collect the dead. The Oxyrhynchos historian (VII. 2)[35] records that
Tissaphernes was not overwhelmed but gathered forces to shadow
Agesilaos on his next march. Xenophon speaks of three days'
plunder of the countryside (*Agesilaos*, 1. 33)—time now for other
engagements.

The two main versions of the battle, those of Xenophon and
Diodoros/*Hell. Ox.*, are said to be irreconcilable, or to have more
significant similarities than differences.[36] The choice of one
account rather than the other entails problems, and some recent
writers accept the possibility of two separate engagements, despite
the suggestion of the unlikelihood that either success would have
been omitted.[37] Each version reveals its author's interests and
limitations: the Oxyrhynchos historian's interest in geographical
detail and stratagems is lacking in Xenophon, who alone records
qualities of generalship and the course of negotiations.[38] Each
could select from the engagements according to his own interests.
A crucial divergence concerns the make-up of the Persian force:
Xenophon specifies cavalry alone, Diodoros (xiv. 80. 1) and the
Oxyrhynchos historian (VI. 5–6)[39] have cavalry and infantry. If the
Persians came from the Maiandros and Karia, their two arms will
not have arrived together. Even if the units were drawn from the

garrison at Sardis, the same separation could occur. The two accounts can be broadly accepted, but not as descriptions of the same battle.

Modern writers assume an exaggerated importance of the event and a duration of no more than four days. Confrontation in a set battle was avoided by both sides, despite announcements of aggressive intentions. Xenophon writes of the affair as an encounter action, and does not suggest that the armies were carefully drawn up for battle.[40] The maximum length of Agesilaos' stay in the area is nowhere given as three days: Xenophon gives a three days' march leading to the meeting of the forces on the fourth, the Oxyrhynchos historian and Diodoros have a night between the two manoeuvres (*Hell. Ox.* VI. 4, xiv. 80. 2),[41] and the former has a wait of three days afterwards (VII. I).[42] A longer time would be needed for the double journey of messengers leading to the execution of Tissaphernes (§5), after which Agesilaos was persuaded by Tithraustes to depart. In a series of actions on the march, pillaging from Ephesos to Sardis, two or more authors or eye-witnesses need not include precisely the same incidents in a limited narrative; the ancient authors had their own reasons for being selective at this point.[43] The Hermos plain is suitable for battles of both kinds. 'It is . . . just possible to argue that the authors are in fact describing two different battles.'[44]

(*c*) *A reconstruction.* Tissaphernes guarded Karia until forced to move to the defence of Sardis by Agesilaos' march to that region. The Persian cavalry, coming from Sardis or from Karia, contacted Agesilaos, who was already plundering in the area, before the infantry arrived. Agesilaos took advantage of this separation and won a success—but against only the Persian cavalry. When the infantry became available, the combined force engaged Agesilaos' plunderers between Sardis and Sipylos or perhaps Thybarnai. Agesilaos formed a square, protected his foragers and booty, but needed the ambush to extricate himself. After his success, the Persians ceased to interfere, and Agesilaos made his way to the Maiandros through the mountains between Lydia and Phrygia.

PART IV (chs. 11–15)

Diplomacy in Asia Minor

Artax. 20. 4, *Dtr.* 42. 3–5, *Alex.* 37. 7, 56. 1; Xen. *Hell.* iv. 1. 1–2. 8, *Agesilaos*, 1. 17–19, 36–8, 3. 3–5, 5. 2, 4–7, 6. 4–8, 8. 1–2, 11. 4–12; Diod. xiv. 83. 1; *Hell. Ox.* XVI. 2–XVII. 4 (Bruce (1967), 135–49); Paus. iii. 9. 12, Nepos, *Agesilaus*, 4. 1–3.

11. Agesilaos and Kotys:[1] personal relationships with non-Greeks

The chapter is one of the longest in this *Life*, which indicates its importance for Plutarch. Agesilaos' plundering and diplomatic activity in Pharnabazos' territory and beyond serve mainly to introduce the character studies which largely occupy the latter part of this chapter, and the concluding account of the campaign in chs. 12–15. Xenophon details little action during the winter of 395–394. He closes *Agesilaos*, 1 with a eulogy which includes brief summaries of the defections from the King and the political settlements in the cities. Spithridates, Kotys, and Pharnabazos are reserved to *Agesilaos*, 3. 2–4, where their confidence in entering Agesilaos' camp illustrates his trustworthiness and its practical benefits in new alliances and additional armed forces; Megabates is reserved to *Agesilaos*, 5. 4. There is the same eulogistic purpose in the fuller account at *Hell.* iv. 1. 1–2. 4.

Xenophon seems to be assembling evidence to disguise the fact that there is little to celebrate, compared with the grand expectations at the start. For him Agesilaos' diplomacy implements a long-standing desire to weaken the King by tampering with his subjects, the king of Paphlagonia, and the satrap of Phrygia, although the outcome is limited (see below, §4 and ch. 12). In the final section before Agesilaos leaves Asia Minor (iv. 1. 41), he creates the impression that Agesilaos is on the brink of completing this policy, that the expedition is a great achievement, promising even more.[2]

1 *Αὐτὸς δὲ τὸν στρατὸν καταστήσας εἰς τὴν ὑπὸ Φαρναβάζῳ*

τεταγμένην χώραν, οὐ μόνον ἐν ἀφθόνοις διῆγε πᾶσιν, ἀλλὰ καὶ χρήματα συνῆγε πολλά·

Plutarch resumes from ch. 10. 8. He names Pharnabazos but not the satrapy, thus featuring the personal elements in the rivalry between the satrapies and in the favour Agesilaos had done Tithraustes. The satrap, older than Agesilaos (Xen. *Hell.* iv. 1. 31), was the son of Pharnakes (Thuc. viii. 6. 1); the satrapy, named Daskylitis by Thucydides (i. 129. 1), is described as rich (Xen. *Hell.* iv. 1. 15–16, 33), with a strong capital (*Hell. Ox.* XVII. 3),[3] and had been given by Xerxes to Artabazos, son of a Pharnakes, c.478/7 (Hdt. vii. 66. 2, ix. 41. 1; Thuc. i. 129. 1). If this Pharnakes was an economic official at the end of the sixth century, the son of Arsames, uncle or grandfather of Dareios I (Hdt. vii. 11. 2; cf. vii. 69. 2 for an Arsames, son of Dareios), he may have belonged to the royal family.[4] The satrapy became more or less hereditary.[5]

One aspect of Agesilaos' activity here is the procuring of money and provisions for the winter season, and for the new fleet. Damage to Pharnabazos' territory is not mentioned.

καὶ προελθὼν ἄχρι Παφλαγονίας προσηγάγετο τὸν βασιλέα τῶν Παφλαγόνων Κότυν, ἐπιθυμήσαντα τῆς φιλίας αὐτοῦ δι' ἀρετὴν καὶ πίστιν.

Plutarch moves quickly on to the affair of Kotys. Paphlagonia, in the north of Asia Minor, was familiar to Xenophon and the veterans of Kyros' expedition still with the Spartans now (*An.* v. 5–vi. 2). It constitutes the hinterland of Greek colonies on the southern shore of the Euxine, and lies between Pharnabazos' Daskyleion and the Greek colonies beyond the Halys. The existence of a power friendly to Sparta here would further the implementation of Spartan hegemony in mainland Greece by establishing control of the lines of communication with Asia Minor.[6] When Xenophon attributes to Spithridates the idea of an alliance with Kotys (*Hell.* iv. 1. 2), Agesilaos' method of detaching people from the King takes a different form: Spithridates was detached from Pharnabazos and remained with Agesilaos on campaign (§2 below); Kotys changes his loyalty but stays in his province (*Hell.* iv. 1. 15). News of these developments in the area would add to the determination of the opponents of Sparta to prosecute the war in Greece, and that would lead to the recall of Agesilaos.

After the conclusion of the alliance with Kotys, Xenophon notes that Agesilaos arranged the marriage of Spithridates' daughter to the Paphlagonian king in gratitude for his having persuaded Kotys also to supply troops. Then in an elaborate structure of dialogue he demonstrates Agesilaos' persuasive talent and his ability to manipulate the wills of others, as he makes Kotys believe that the marriage would be in his own interest.[7] The commendation continues in the account of Agesilaos' attempt to win another of the King's subjects, Pharnabazos (*Hell*. iv. 1. 31–8). The campaign in Asia Minor ends with this lengthy justification.

Plutarch uses both of Xenophon's accounts but does not follow them exclusively. He attributes the initiative for the alliance not to Kotys or to Spithridates but to Agesilaos' political motivation in approaching the King's territory. Whereas Xenophon (*Hell*. iv. 1. 1) gives Kotys as well as Agesilaos a political motive, pointing out that Kotys had refused a summons from the King, Plutarch assigns personal motivation to Kotys, as, by indirect characterization, readers see for themselves the reason why he is inclined towards friendship—Agesilaos' reliability, illustrated in Xenophon's encomiastic passage at *Agesilaos*, 3. 2–4. It is not Plutarch's purpose to create a climax at this point. He reserves the rest of Xenophon's material to provide themes for the remainder of this chapter and the next two.

2 ὁ δὲ Σπιθριδάτης, ὡς ἀποστὰς τοῦ Φαρναβάζου τὸ πρῶτον ἦλθε πρὸς τὸν Ἀγησίλαον, ἀεὶ συναπεδήμει καὶ συνεστράτευεν αὐτῷ, κάλλιστον υἱὸν μὲν ἔχων Μεγαβάτην, οὗ παιδὸς ὄντος ἦρα σφοδρῶς ὁ Ἀγησίλαος, καλὴν δὲ καὶ θυγατέρα παρθένον ἐν ἡλικίᾳ γάμου. **3** ταύτην ἔπεισε γῆμαι τὸν Κότυν ὁ Ἀγησίλαος· καὶ λαβὼν παρ' αὐτοῦ χιλίους ἱππεῖς καὶ δισχιλίους πελταστὰς αὖθις ἀνεχώρησεν εἰς Φρυγίαν . . .

Xenophon gives details of Spithridates' movements and family as they become relevant (*Hell*. iii. 4. 10, iv. 1. 1–28, *Agesilaos*, 3. 2–4). Plutarch does not give these details in ch. 8 or here at §1 with relevance to the diplomacy. He mentions his son and daughter now, where they provide the bridge to the chapter's main purpose, the character study of Agesilaos. The superlative κάλλιστον, 'most handsome', describing the son, indicates where the interest lies for Plutarch (cf. ch. 2. 1). The daughter is mentioned second, and although she is καλή, 'beautiful', this only supports her suitability by age for marriage. Xenophon mentions the two children in the same order (*Hell.* iv. 1. 6), but he mentions the son only for comparison: his concern is with the 'more beautiful' daughter, and the dialogue arranging the marriage. He makes a romance of the affair, although after Agesilaos has ordered a trireme to fetch the girl, he sets off for Daskyleion without waiting for her arrival and the completion of the marriage proceedings. The son has no further part in these events.

Plutarch rewrites Xenophon. He forms a chiastic pattern begun but not continued by him, as the daughter plays her part and then the son. He records the marriage—in seven words—omitted by Xenophon, and reverses the order of events by making the marriage lead to the gift of cavalry and infantry, and to Agesilaos' return to the territory of Pharnabazos. Plutarch may have been influenced by versions of the *Hellenica Oxyrhynchia* in which the troops are sent after the departure of Agesilaos (XVII. 2),[8] although the marriage is not mentioned in the broken text. Agesilaos is not involved in plundering Pharnabazos' camp, but Plutarch adapts Xenophon's narrative so that Spithridates leads to the completion of the chiastic pattern which features his son in an episode as 'romantic' as Xenophon's.

. . . καὶ κακῶς ἐποίει τὴν Φαρναβάζου χώραν, οὐχ ὑπομένοντος οὐδὲ πιστεύοντος τοῖς ἐρύμασιν, ἀλλ' ἔχων ἀεὶ τὰ πλεῖστα σὺν ἑαυτῷ τῶν τιμίων καὶ ἀγαπητῶν ἐξεχώρει καὶ ὑπέφευγεν, ἄλλοτ' ἀλλαχόσε τῆς χώρας μεθιδρυόμενος, μέχρι οὗ παραφυλάξας αὐτὸν ὁ Σπιθριδάτης καὶ παραλαβὼν Ἡριππίδαν τὸν Σπαρτιάτην ἔλαβε τὸ στρατόπεδον καὶ τῶν χρημάτων ἁπάντων ἐκράτησεν.

According to Xenophon, Agesilaos ravaged the surrounding villages (*Hell.* iv. 1. 15–19) and his men enjoyed plentiful supplies during his winter stay at Daskyleion, where Pharnabazos had his palace. The Oxyrhynchos historian records silver and gold stored there and booty dispatched by Agesilaos by sea to the region of Kyzikos, to the west (XVII. 3–4).[9] Xenophon gives Pharnabazos' fear of being besieged as the reason for not staying in a fixed position, but Plutarch's explanation of his movements more simply suggests inadequate defences. He is said to be encamped about 160 stades away (18.5 miles = 29.5 km.) when Spithridates plans his raid (*Hell.* iv. 1. 20). In listing the items seized Xenophon suggests that the camps used in this context did not contain an extraordinary amount of baggage for Pharnabazos to have with him (*Hell.* iv. 1. 24). Plutarch exaggerates the quantity and value of the property involved.

Herippidas,[10] who as harmost at Trachinian Herakleia quelled an uprising in 399 (Diod. xiv. 38. 4), may have been in Asia Minor before Agesilaos' arrival. He was associated with Derkylidas (*Hell.* iii. 4. 6), both appointed after the accession in 400. He was Agesilaos' second chief 'adviser' and was given command of Kyros' former troops (*Hell.* iii. 4. 20). Spithridates tells him of his plan and he obtains troops from Agesilaos (*Hell.* iv. 1. 21–2). Xenophon evidently disliked him (*Hell.* iv. 1. 21–2; cf. iii. 4. 20), perhaps in retrospect after his disgrace as harmost at Thebes and execution by Sparta (*Pel.* 13. 2; Xen. *Hell.* v. 4. 13; Diod. xv. 27. 1–3).[11]

Earlier, Pharnabazos had surprised Agesilaos' marauders 'with two scythe-bearing chariots and about 400 horsemen' (*Hell.* iv. 1. 17). The 700 Greeks were dispersed by a charge and 100 were struck down; the rest fled to the protection of Agesilaos' hoplites nearby. It is relevant to the battle of Sardis to note the scale of the engagement reported here by Xenophon, and that he was willing to record this setback, which Plutarch in his already complex context omits.

4 ἔνθα δὴ πικρὸς ὢν ὁ Ἡριππίδας ἐξεταστὴς τῶν κλαπέντων καὶ τοὺς βαρβάρους ἀναγκάζων ἀποτίθεσθαι, καὶ πάντ' ἐφορῶν καὶ διερευνώμενος παρώξυνε τὸν Σπιθριδάτην, ὥστ' ἀπελθεῖν εὐθὺς εἰς Σάρδεις μετὰ τῶν Παφλαγόνων.

Herippidas 'appointed officers' to ensure careful supervision (*Hell.* iv. 1. 26), whether 'out of greed or out of untimely rectitude',[12] but Plutarch puts him personally in charge. Self-enrichment would be one of Spithridates' objectives in joining Agesilaos, and the discovery that he was likely regularly to be dispossessed, even when he had engineered the enterprise, would be a sufficient reason for his departure. Xenophon says that he went to Ariaios in Sardis because 'he too had revolted from the King', which suggests that Spithridates was looking for the best connection to secure his long-term ambitions and protection against reprisals by Pharnabazos. Plutarch's description of the departure is more brief, and makes it more sudden and dramatic than Xenophon's (*Hell.* iv. 1. 27).

5 τοῦτο λέγεται τῷ Ἀγησιλάῳ γενέσθαι πάντων ἀνιαρότατον. ἤχθετο
μὲν γὰρ ἄνδρα γενναῖον ἀποβεβληκὼς τὸν Σπιθριδάτην καὶ σὺν αὐτῷ
δύναμιν οὐκ ὀλίγην, ᾐσχύνετο δὲ τῇ διαβολῇ τῆς μικρολογίας καὶ
ἀνελευθερίας, ἧς οὐ μόνον αὐτόν, ἀλλὰ καὶ τὴν πατρίδα καθαρεύουσαν
ἀεὶ παρέχειν ἐφιλοτιμεῖτο.

The departure of Spithridates occurred after the close of the
chronological narrative in the first chapter of Xenophon's
Agesilaos and it is omitted. It is omitted also from the tribute to
Agesilaos' control of his affection in the fifth chapter, on which
Plutarch's account is based. With λέγεται Plutarch may indicate a
change not of his source at this point, but of the focus of attention,
from externals to the more difficult analysis of Agesilaos' inner
feelings, a process which is completed immediately in the opening
phrase of the next sentence. Part of Agesilaos' annoyance will be
that denying the Paphlagonians their reward would offend their
king, Kotys, with consequences for his allegiance. Plutarch
stresses the loss of the man and the force, and adds the damage
done to the reputations of Agesilaos and Sparta by the meanness
(ἀνελευθερία; cf. Xen. *Agesilaos*, 4. 1–2, 11. 8). Spartan φιλότιμον, a
key word in this *Life*, is not 'ambition' (ch. 2. 3, with n. 22): ἐφιλοτιμεῖτο: 'he always desired the honour' of upholding his own and
his country's purity; in modern Greek the sense of honour or self-
worth is still called φιλότιμο,[13] and other ancient Greek values have
persisted to the present time. At *Hell*. iv. 1. 28 Xenophon is more
restrained than Plutarch; in his one reference to Agesilaos' regret
for their departure he gives only the three names, Spithridates,
Megabates, the Paphlagonians; and he leaves Sparta out. Plutarch
reserves the departure of the boy for the next sentence (§6).

6 χωρὶς δὲ τῶν ἐμφανῶν τούτων ἔκνιζεν αὐτὸν οὐ μετρίως ὁ τοῦ παιδὸς
ἔρως ἐνεσταγμένος, εἰ καὶ πάνυ παρόντος αὐτοῦ τῷ φιλονίκῳ χρώμενος
ἐπειρᾶτο νεανικῶς ἀπομάχεσθαι πρὸς τὴν ἐπιθυμίαν. 7 καί ποτε τοῦ
Μεγαβάτου προσιόντος ὡς ἀσπασομένου καὶ φιλήσοντος ἐξέκλινεν. ἐπεὶ
δ' ἐκεῖνος αἰσχυνθεὶς ἐπαύσατο καὶ τὸ λοιπὸν ἄπωθεν ἤδη
προσηγόρευεν, ἀχθόμενος αὖ πάλιν καὶ μεταμελόμενος τῇ φυγῇ τοῦ
φιλήματος ὁ Ἀγησίλαος προσεποιεῖτο θαυμάζειν ὅ τι δὴ παθὼν αὐτὸν ὁ
Μεγαβάτης ἀπὸ στόματος οὐ φιλοφρονοῖτο.

Agesilaos employs his 'desire for conquest' (φιλόνικον, another key
word; see ch. 2. 2) to control his emotions, and the military

metaphor is continued in ἀπομάχεσθαι and φυγῇ. This is an area where evidence cannot easily be corroborated, yet biography is legitimately concerned to explore inner thoughts and emotions. Modern biography has the advantage of letters and diaries; psychological novels use a variety of sources. An element of fiction—creative reconstruction—is inevitable in these attempts to show, from a fragmented record, the continuity of the emotional and intellectual conditions of a lifetime in a few pages, and 'to identify the real personality behind the public persona'. Plutarch's viewpoint is generally 'highly evaluative and "character-centred"'.[14] Here he attempts an equally difficult re-creation of Agesilaos' feelings and motivation, constructed from the record of his actions (cf. ch. 2. 3). His venture anticipates, on a small scale, the modern biographer's aims, methods, and achievements. He marks the shift in his interest with a reference to 'the visible pains', as if to persuade the reader that his account of Agesilaos' 'invisible' emotions is on the same level of reality.

Xenophon makes no mention of this topic at *Hell.* iii. 4. 10, where he introduces Megabates as 'the son of Spithridates' without naming him, and at his departure later in *Hellenika* names him, but not as the son of Spithridates and without relating Agesilaos' distress to the affair (iv. 1. 28). He describes the relationship in *Agesilaos* only when he comes to illustrate Agesilaos' control of affections in the list of his virtues (5. 4), and avoids the embarrassing departure. Xenophon there makes it clear that Agesilaos was faced with a form of greeting from Megabates that merely followed the Persian custom and yet 'struggled with all his might' to avoid being kissed. The affront to the young man, which was no doubt potentially a diplomatic affront as well as a personal rejection, though presented only as the latter, was later recognized by Agesilaos. It is as if he was too much personally attracted to the boy to kiss him without feeling excited to what *he* considered to be an unacceptable degree. He tried to make amends by requesting that Megabates should 'show his respect' (τιμᾶν) to him again, but insisted that it should not involve the kiss in future.

Xenophon seems to suggest that for a Spartan even the formal 'diplomatic' kiss demonstrated an unacceptable relationship. Once a kiss had been attempted in public, he was vulnerable to criticism. That there was a risk of the criticism for homosexuality which Agesilaos, or Xenophon on his behalf, wished to avoid, is shown by the Oxyrhynchos historian, who, having described Megabates as 'young and handsome', suggests that Agesilaos accepted the friendship of Spithridates 'mainly because of the boy' (XVI. 4).[15] For Xenophon, Agesilaos' innocence was paramount and even the acceptance of the greeting was too much. A mere disclaimer might not satisfy the critics, and would also miss the important point of self-control. Instead, at *Agesilaos*, 5. 4 Xenophon establishes that there is nothing admirable in restraint where there is no desire, and so, to illustrate Agesilaos' self-control, he admits that there was some affection, but only of the sort acceptable among Spartans, which he expresses in the philosophical form of 'the desire for the greatest good'. Agesilaos was able to resist successfully the physical demonstration of a relationship which would provide an opportunity for improper gratification. The criticism of Agesilaos not only threatened at the time, but could recur later in interpretations of the account Xenophon presents here in fulfilling his encomiastic purpose, and Xenophon will have felt bound to meet it. He does this with the assertion of his convictions about Agesilaos' character, and the claim that he has special knowledge which confirms the absence of any evidence of scandal (*Agesilaos*, 5. 6–7).

Plutarch evidently did not wish to exonerate Agesilaos before he had made his moral point, and therefore there is a difference in his treatment of the episode. He follows Xenophon closely in recording the initial fact, 'he refused unequivocally' (ἐξέκλινεν) the greeting, but uses a more dramatic expression, νεανικῶς ἀπομάχεσθαι, when he 'fought off manfully' the desire. He presents an intense internal struggle in describing the emotional effect on Agesilaos of the boy's negative reaction, leading to his changed attitude, which is not explained by Xenophon; and the expression προσεποιεῖτο θαυμάζειν, 'pretended to wonder', imputing to Agesilaos more knowledge than he displayed of the boy's reason for distress, suggests the wish to portray him as deeply involved emotionally. He replaces Xenophon's τιμᾶν with a more affectionate greeting, φιλοφρονοῖτο (cf. φιλοφροσύνη, used similarly at ch. 13. 2 of Pharnabazos' son; cf. chs. 21. 8, 40. 1). Plutarch's variations and additions indicate a significant element of interpretation on his part, for there can be no further substantiating evidence (cf. *Mor.* 209 D–E).

Xenophon presents what was probably one of Agesilaos' first

meetings with Megabates, but Plutarch mentions it in retrospect at the moment of his departure, suggesting the context of an emotional relationship which developed over a period of time and could have lingering effects after the parting. Indeed, Plutarch suggests that Agesilaos wants the offer of a kiss to be renewed, whereas in Xenophon, although he initiates the negotiation, he asks only for 'respect', τιμᾶν.

8 Σὺ γὰρ αἴτιος, οἱ συνήθεις ἔφασαν, οὐχ ὑποστάς, ἀλλὰ τρέσας τὸ φίλημα τοῦ καλοῦ καὶ φοβηθείς· ἐπεὶ καὶ νῦν ἂν ἔλθοι σοι πεισθεὶς ἐκεῖνος ἐντὸς φιλήματος· ἀλλ' ὅπως αὖθις οὐκ ἀποδειλιάσεις.

The friends in Plutarch apportion blame and urge a more positive response; in Xenophon, the one friend's question, εἰ φιλήσει, implies no urging (*Agesilaos*, 5. 5). Xenophon's version refers to a discussion, not of whether the friend is to try to persuade Megabates, but only of what response to the boy's greeting Agesilaos will commit himself to make.

The use of the technical term, τρέσας,[16] for flight from battle as well as the general words for cowardice, φοβηθείς and ἀποδειλιάσεις, on this light-hearted, jocular, occasion (cf. ch. 2. 3 for the educational and social function of Spartan humour) would, in another context, be a grave insult, and even here it is clearly meant to sting: Agesilaos relieves the survivors of Leuktra of the same stigma, and the city from its consequences (ch. 30. 6).

9 χρόνον οὖν τινα πρὸς ἑαυτῷ γενόμενος ὁ Ἀγησίλαος καὶ διασιωπήσας, Οὐδέν, ἔφη, ⟨δεινὸν⟩ πείθειν ὑμᾶς ἐκεῖνον· ἐγὼ γάρ μοι δοκῶ τήναν τὰν μάχαν τὰν περὶ τοῦ φιλάματος ἄδιον ἂν μάχεσθαι πάλιν ἢ πάνθ' ὅσα τεθέαμαι χρυσία μοι γενέσθαι.

In Xenophon's account Agesilaos proposed that the boy should be persuaded to resume respectful greetings (τιμᾶν), but would not agree to kissing: the 'battle' is in refusing Megabates' form of greeting. In a humorous fantasy Agesilaos rejects the possibility of becoming 'fairest, strongest, and fleetest of men'—a fairy-tale reward for a kiss.[17] He then reflects on the political consequences of the breakdown of relations with Spithridates, appropriately valued in terms of gold (χρυσᾶ), since booty was one of the main aims of the expedition: Agesilaos will forgo the benefits of friendship and gold rather than accept the kiss.

Plutarch maintains the emotional and political tension by

omitting the fairy-tale reward. He removes Xenophon's other fantasy with a change of tense, but improves the financial consequences: instead of 'that everything I see should become golden for me'—or, as he may have taken it, 'that all the golden things I can see should become mine'—he puts 'that all the gold I *have seen* should become mine'. He provides his own narrative enhancement by replacing Xenophon's μᾶλλον βούλεσθαι, 'would rather' fight, with ἅδιον ἂν μάχεσθαι, fight 'with greater pleasure'. This leads to the reading Οὐδέν, ἔφη, δεινόν[18] and gives the sense: '(Persuade him to greet me, but) I shall again enjoy—and win— the fight about the kiss', against his desires (§6). The reading Οὐδέν, ἔφη, δεῖ (Stephanus)—'Do not persuade him'—suggests that Agesilaos has won the battle against wanting the greeting. Plutarch does not necessarily repeat Xenophon's sense. The more positive reading is surely correct, and is consistent with §10, where Agesilaos succeeds in resisting temptation in the boy's presence. Agesilaos will enjoy the bitter-sweet struggle: 'It is not dangerous for you to persuade him: I can handle it.' His moral reputation is untarnished in both authors' accounts, but in Plutarch's version victory is not yet assured and the inner struggle is intense.

10 τοιοῦτος μὲν ἦν τοῦ Μεγαβάτου παρόντος, ἀπελθόντος γε μὴν οὕτω περικαῶς ἔσχεν, ὡς χαλεπὸν εἰπεῖν εἰ πάλιν ⟨ἂν⟩ μεταβαλομένου καὶ φανέντος ἐνεκαρτέρησε μὴ φιληθῆναι.

Plutarch, having digressed to Xenophon's account of a meeting nearer the time of their arrival, now returns to the time of the departure, juxtaposing participles. Xenophon ends with a claim to authenticity, but adds a general rebuttal of conjectured scandalous behaviour (*Agesilaos*, 5. 6). Plutarch, perhaps in response to this, ends with a rhetorical device, a conjecture from known behaviour in one set of circumstances to behaviour in other possible circumstances. As the manuscripts stand, the sense ought to be 'whether, when Megabates changed his mind and appeared, Agesilaos held out against being kissed'; but, as Plutarch's context seems to follow the departure of Spithridates and the boy, the conjecture concerns what might have happened in circumstances not in fact realized: had the boy returned, Agesilaos might not have been able to resist the strong emotions which have been attributed to him. Such counterfactual clauses require ἄν, which Cobet conjectured for αὖ of the MSS (cf. *Ant.* 30. 4). Plutarch is interested in the continuing strength of Agesilaos' affection and his efforts to control it.

Both authors make Agesilaos think hard and long in silence when attempting to rectify his mistake in handling the affair. In Xenophon's account, Agesilaos is working out how to structure a greeting which will allow expression of Megabates' traditional respect while preserving Spartan dignity and integrity, but in Plutarch's account the silence seems to represent Agesilaos' inner struggle against his desire to respond emotionally to the emotional greeting. The outcome is therefore different in the two cases: the security of a greeting without the kiss, in Xenophon: in Plutarch a continuing uncertainty, for Agesilaos may experience uncontrollable emotion if he meets Megabates again.

12. Agesilaos and Pharnabazos; the Greek ideal

Xenophon (*Hell.* iv. 1. 29–38) and Plutarch display two different moral approaches to the meeting of Agesilaos and Pharnabazos, in which the latter complains of Spartan ingratitude in attacking him, and Agesilaos tries to detach Pharnabazos from the Persian King. Another version of the meeting by Theopompos was allegedly plagiaristic, dull, and 'ineffective', ἄπρακτα, when compared by Porphyrios with Xenophon's 'lively' account.[1] This was, perhaps, either an independent contemporary version lacking the Xenophontic features, or an over-elaborated exhibition of declamation.[2] Agesilaos failed to bring Pharnabazos over, as the other versions show: Plutarch's also shows why (§9).

One of Xenophon's purposes[3] is to portray the political wisdom and diplomatic skills of Agesilaos, which he displays in tempting Pharnabazos with the offer to support his independence, if he will come over to serve the interests of the Spartans in their struggle with the King. The words introducing and concluding *Hell.* iv. 1 reveal a more vital purpose that would justify Xenophon's persuasive input: to show how important he regards it that Agesilaos' diplomacy should be seen to have been successful in detaching as many nations as possible from the King. Kotys and Spithridates appear to have been won (iv. 1. 15) but not for long (see above, ch. 11. 4); Pharnabazos does not commit himself (iv. 1. 37). Yet

Xenophon leads the reader to suppose that Sparta has now gained two other valued friends and allies by reporting kept promises; but the promises are only Agesilaos', one immediately to Pharnabazos in leaving his territory, and another to his son in befriending him later. To present these as personal successes was all the more important to Xenophon because they are the climax to the Asian expedition, which is abandoned immediately afterwards (*Hell.* iv. 2. 1–2). Plutarch, apparently not convinced by the supposed diplomatic achievements, creates a different climax, asserting the superiority of Greek culture, and credits Pharnabazos with recognition that this is so, impressed, perhaps, by his rejection of the offer of wealth in Xenophon.

In giving form to the dialogue, the authors have their own focus. Xenophon records Agesilaos' friendly offer of military help to establish Pharnabazos' independence and to build an empire loyal to himself, and so, indirectly, to Sparta, rather than to the King (*Hell.* iv. 1. 36); Agesilaos, by withdrawing his army, concedes his initial principle of treating the King's subjects as enemies. Plutarch makes Agesilaos refuse to repay Pharnabazos' earlier services to Sparta unless he undertakes to abandon the King; relief from Spartan ravaging depends on Pharnabazos' first proving himself friend and ally of the Greeks. He reveals the uncompromising sense of the superiority of Greek freedom over Persian slavery which seems to be uppermost in his mind here.

While Xenophon presents a simplistic pragmatism—the offer of autonomous acquisition of personal wealth and power in exchange for an option to serve the interests of Sparta—Plutarch describes a politically realistic offer of protection, which will be fulfilled if Pharnabazos realizes his newly found potential for honourable friendship with Greece as a free man, and, like a Greek, values nothing more than freedom. This will complete the development of his character, which started with shame for the rich furnishing of the meeting-place, and continues with promised adherence to the 'Help Friends, Harm Enemies' principle (§8).

1 Μετὰ ταῦτα Φαρνάβαζος εἰς λόγους αὐτῷ συνελθεῖν ἠθέλησε, καὶ συνήγαγεν ἀμφοτέροις ὢν ξένος ὁ Κυζικηνὸς Ἀπολλοφάνης.

Agesilaos and Pharnabazos were apparently not themselves in a formal friendship (ξένοι), and the meeting during the current hostilities between the two sides necessitated the services of a

mediator, to secure a truce and guarantee security[4] (Xen. *Hell.* iv.
1. 30: Pharnabazos trusts Agesilaos at *Agesilaos*, 3. 5). He would
be involved also in selecting a place to meet: Pharnabazos was
concealing his encampments (Xen. *Hell.* iv. 1. 25). Plutarch gives
Pharnabazos the initiative in wanting the meeting, evidently to
obtain justice from the Spartans, and he implies that
Apollophanes of Kyzikos was equally the ξένος of both sides. In
Xenophon the link with Agesilaos is the more recent, and
Apollophanes himself makes the offer to bring Pharnabazos to
Agesilaos to discuss friendly relations. He may already have been
in touch with Pharnabazos, since he says that he thinks he can
arrange the meeting with him. The offer is accepted by Agesilaos,
who no doubt sees the opportunity to detach another of the King's
subjects.

That a citizen of Kyzikos should have a Spartan ξένος indicates
the far-ranging contacts of Spartans and of Agesilaos, who had not
had much time as king before leaving Sparta in which to establish
new connections. Sparta's eastern contacts can be traced back to
the 420s,[5] although information will have been accumulating since
Aristagoras met Kleomenes (Hdt. v. 49). Spithridates, with whom
Xenophon had earlier clashed (*An.* vi. 5), was the most recent of
these, and either he[6] or Lysander may have instigated the relationship, for it was from Kyzikos, 64 km. (40 miles) west of
Daskyleion, that Lysander brought him. Kyzikos had been a base
for the combined operations of the Spartan Mindaros and
Pharnabazos (Xen. *Hell.* i. 1. 11–14), who had used the diplomatic
services of Timagoras, an exile from there (Thuc. viii. 6. 1).

2 πρότερος δὲ μετὰ τῶν φίλων ὁ Ἀγησίλαος ἐλθὼν εἰς τὸ χωρίον, ὑπὸ
σκιᾷ τινι πόας οὔσης βαθείας καταβαλὼν ἑαυτόν, ἐνταῦθα περιέμενε τὸν
Φαρνάβαζον.

The 'friends' will be the successors of the Spartiates appointed at
ch. 6, referred to again there when Agesilaos visited Aulis 'with
his friends', and at ch. 7 with the status of 'the king's advisers'.
They were at times, perhaps, not all acting together, but
Xenophon has them all here with Agesilaos (*Hell.* iv. 1. 30), awaiting Pharnabazos.

The outdoor site gives neither side any advantage, is less of a
security risk to the foreigners, and opens the negotiations to the
observation of all those present. It allows Agesilaos' usual lifestyle

to determine the simplicity of the furnishing of the scene, since he was the first to arrive. The simplicity he displayed to Pharnabazos, and later to Tachos in Egypt (ch. 36), seems likely to have been intended to avoid charges on his return home of being corrupted by service overseas (ch. 19. 6) and, more immediately, to discomfort foreigners who were reputed 'to live in luxury' (ἐντρυφῆσαι, Xen. *Hell*. iv. 1. 30; cf. *Art*. 20. 1–2).

3 ὁ δ' ὡς ἐπῆλθεν, ὑποβεβλημένων αὐτῷ κωδίων τε μαλακῶν καὶ ποικίλων δαπίδων, αἰδεσθεὶς τὸν Ἀγησίλαον οὕτω κατακείμενον, κατεκλίνη καὶ αὐτός, ὡς ἔτυχεν, ἐπὶ τῆς πόας χαμᾶζε, καίπερ ἐσθῆτα θαυμαστὴν λεπτότητι καὶ βαφαῖς ἐνδεδυκώς.

It appears from both authors that the Persian attendants arrived before Pharnabazos, which allows them to introduce the Persian style (cf. Xen. *Cyr*. viii. 8. 16). The point is made more vividly here, where their arrangements are completed, than by Xenophon, who has them only beginning to arrange the furnishings when Pharnabazos stops them. Plutarch reflects the elaboration in a chiasmus of nouns and adjectives.

Pharnabazos' inner 'regard', αἰδεσθείς, which Xenophon represents with ᾐσχύνθη, may be interpreted here, not as shame, but as the more positive 'respect' for the superior moral stance of the Greek, adopted by Plutarch above (ch. 9. 1, where φοβηθείς defers to the Greek view). It would have been more difficult to portray that respect if Pharnabazos had arrived before Agesilaos. His cushions and clothing signify effeminacy:[7] his gesture in declining the cushions restores the equality of the two sides, and, in the Greek view, rejects his effeminacy,[8] and this may be sufficient motivation. Plutarch presents the gesture more strikingly than Xenophon, for Pharnabazos sits on the grass along with Agesilaos even though the cushions are in place. He has further enhanced it by describing the Persian clothing, where Xenophon stated only its cost.

4 ἀσπασάμενοι δ' ἀλλήλους, ὁ μὲν Φαρνάβαζος οὐκ ἠπόρει λόγων δικαίων, ἄτε δὴ πολλὰ καὶ μεγάλα Λακεδαιμονίοις χρήσιμος γεγονὼς ἐν τῷ πρὸς Ἀθηναίους πολέμῳ, νῦν δὲ πορθούμενος ὑπ' αὐτῶν·

Xenophon's pair greet one another and, Pharnabazos taking the initiative, extend their right hands (originally demonstrating lack of weapons, following the verbal expression of friendly intention).

Plutarch omits the shaking of hands, shortens the account to a participle and partitive apposition, 'the one' and 'the other', and accelerates the narrative by using indirect speech to summarize the complaints given at length in direct form by Xenophon. It is consistent with Pharnabazos' initiation of the talks about his grievances here that he speaks first, whereas, less convincingly, in Xenophon, who perhaps wished to provide a reason more complimentary to Agesilaos, he speaks first because he is the elder—more complimentary, in that Agesilaos, like a good Spartan, defers to the older man. Pharnabazos claims that by the principles of 'Help Friends' and personal loyalty he merits immunity from hostile action. He had fought for the Spartans near Abydos (Xen. *Hell.* i. 1. 6, 14, 24) and had provided money for the fleet defeated by the Athenians at Arginousai. Relations changed when the Spartans supported Kyros, in revolt from the King, and then the Greeks, resisting the King's attempts to recover lost territories (*Hell.* iii. 1. 1–4). Derkylidas and Agesilaos had both attacked Pharnabazos (*Hell.* iii. 1. 9, iii. 4. 13–15, 26, iv. 1. 15–27).

In Plutarch's account Pharnabazos' forceful description of himself as χρήσιμος, 'rendering valuable service', represents the more formal claim in Xenophon's account that he was their φίλος καὶ σύμμαχος, 'friend and ally' (*Hell.* iv. 1. 32), but in his response Agesilaos acknowledges the friendship by retaining φίλοι (§6). The tension between the two men's attitudes to φιλία arises from their priorities: Pharnabazos stresses the extension of the heroic age's personal bond to inter-state relations, while Agesilaos puts obligations to his own city first.[9] Both attitudes may be justified in simple situations by referring to the transitivity of φιλία,[10] which if perfectly applied would make identical demands in each case. But although the same vocabulary is used in both public and private morality, complex diplomatic situations taking changes in time and policy into account may produce conflicting loyalties.[11]

5 ὁ δ' Ἀγησίλαος, ὁρῶν τοὺς σὺν αὐτῷ Σπαρτιάτας ὑπ' αἰσχύνης κύπτοντας εἰς τὴν γῆν καὶ διαποροῦντας (ἀδικούμενον γὰρ ἑώρων τὸν Φαρνάβαζον), . . .

Xenophon portrays the Spartiates' embarrassment as if they saw that the complaints were just: Plutarch, using the present participle ἀδικούμενον, adds their awareness that the injustice was still going on. This may indicate commendable detachment in recognizing the Persian point of view, but it does not represent the feelings of those in the Greek cities who were in danger of being subjected to Persian rule, who, on the threat from Tissaphernes following the death of Kyros, had appealed for Spartan help (Xen. *Hell.* iii. 1. 3), had sent again asking that Agesilaos should continue the war that Thibron and Derkylidas had been fighting since then (*Lys.* 23. 1), and on whose behalf Agesilaos was engaged in the hostilities. The advisers' 'speechlessness' in Xenophon (ἐσιώπησαν) and their 'paralysis' in Plutarch (διαπορου̂ντας) indicate that the main purpose of both authors here was to highlight Agesilaos' ready justification of the Spartan action, and to enhance his diplomacy in defending Sparta's 'Harm Enemies' position for the moment.

. . . **6** Ἡμεῖς, εἶπεν, ὦ Φαρνάβαζε, καὶ φίλοι πρότερον ὄντες βασιλέως ἐχρώμεθα τοῖς ἐκείνου πράγμασι φιλικῶς, καὶ νῦν πολέμιοι γεγονότες πολεμικῶς. ἐν οὖν καὶ σὲ τῶν βασιλέως κτημάτων ὁρῶντες εἶναι βουλόμενον, εἰκότως διὰ σοῦ βλάπτομεν ἐκεῖνον.

In Xenophon's account Agesilaos explains the attacks as on 'the possessions' of his enemy, the King. Plutarch makes a change in having him say—perhaps tactlessly, unless it was only in his report to Sparta—that Pharnabazos is himself one of the King's possessions. At a later stage Xenophon, too, implies that he is at present ὁμόδουλος, 'a fellow slave' (*Hell.* iv. 1. 36; cf. §7 below, δοῦλος, slave), and refers to the King as Pharnabazos' master (δεσπότης), to whom he does obeisance (προσκυνοῦντα). Both authors represent the Greek view of the barbarian subject's enslaved status under monarchy (Arist. *Pol.* 1285ᵃ17–24), reproduced in Artemisia's alleged pronouncement at Salamis (Hdt. viii. 102. 2; cf. *Alex.* 40. 2). However, with the limited knowledge available of the ancient Persian *mentalité*, it is not possible to say whether Pharnabazos would have been offended (cf. Aesch. *Persae*, 241–2, 584–90, 762–4). Earlier this century, the polite close of a letter was 'I remain your obedient servant.' A letter produced in Greek on behalf of Darius, and preserved in the Gadatas inscription (ML 12), uses δοῦλος of the addressee, perhaps the satrap, or sub-satrap, of Ionia.[12] Xenophon's spokesman in *Oeconomicus* recognizes that the King rewards and punishes the military to keep his subjects under control (4. 5), and that a slave's loyalty is ensured by his having hopes—the free man's can be ignored (5. 16)—or by good feeding, praise and favour, rewards or punishment (13. 9–11, 14. 8–9; cf. *Hell.* iii. 4. 9; *Lys.* 23. 8, and above, ch. 8. 2): and he owes the ideas to the King's code (14. 6); if the same term, δοῦλος, does for all, then it denotes a political, not a social status:[13] a bailiff is unlikely to marry into royalty. Pharnabazos was the King's man, and would serve him so long as the King honoured him (§8 below), aware that a successor could treat him as Tithraustes had treated Tissaphernes: he was, however, to be summoned to marry the King's daughter.

7 ἀφ' ἧς δ' ἂν ἡμέρας σεαυτὸν ἀξιώσῃς Ἑλλήνων φίλον καὶ σύμμαχον μᾶλλον ἢ δοῦλον λέγεσθαι βασιλέως, ταύτην νόμιζε τὴν φάλαγγα καὶ τὰ ὅπλα καὶ τὰς ναῦς καὶ πάντας ἡμᾶς τῶν σῶν κτημάτων φύλακας εἶναι καὶ τῆς ἐλευθερίας, ἧς ἄνευ καλὸν ἀνθρώποις οὐδὲν οὐδὲ ζηλωτόν ἐστιν.

Agesilaos is looking for an inner change that would make Pharnabazos his own judge—ἀξιώσῃς—of his worthiness to be 'friend and ally' (cf. above, on *Hell.* iv. 1. 32), no longer a chattel but free, with reciprocal benefits. This departs significantly from Xenophon's version, where Agesilaos admits the existing state of war, desires 'that we [Spartans] become friends' of Pharnabazos (*Hell.* iv. 1. 34), and offers him the positive and material incentives of *gaining* autonomy, wealth, and power. He envisages that Pharnabazos could 'employ him as ally' (*Hell.* iv. 1. 36), perhaps in mercenary service. Plutarch stresses Agesilaos' uncompromising attitude. Agesilaos rejects any obligation to relieve Pharnabazos of the effects of the war against the King and promises only to *defend* his possessions and freedom in the future. Pharnabazos must himself claim his freedom and rebel. Agesilaos later denies Spartan medizing; it is rather 'Medes Lakonizing' (ch. 23. 4).

8 ἐκ τούτου λέγει πρὸς αὐτὸν ὁ Φαρνάβαζος ἣν εἶχε διάνοιαν· Ἐγὼ γάρ, εἶπεν, ἐὰν μὲν ἄλλον ἐκπέμψῃ βασιλεὺς στρατηγόν, ἔσομαι μεθ' ὑμῶν, ἐὰν δ' ἐμοὶ παραδῷ τὴν ἡγεμονίαν, οὐδὲν ἐλλείψω προθυμίας ἀμυνόμενος ὑμᾶς καὶ κακῶς ποιῶν ὑπὲρ ἐκείνου.

Pharnabazos, as might be expected, does not announce any immediate intention to revolt from the King, but promises adherence to the 'Help Friends, Harm Enemies' principle and establishes his own loyalty to obligations in which he found Agesilaos wanting. He keeps open the chance to accept the offer of friendship if he loses command. Perhaps he has outwitted Agesilaos (see §9 below).

Xenophon's Pharnabazos links doing his 'best' for the King with φιλοτιμία, 'desire for attainment' (*Hell.* iv. 1. 37; cf. Introd., C.1(*c*) iii, ch. 2. 3), for which Plutarch puts οὐδὲν ἐλλείψω προθυμίας:[14] 'I shall not fail in desire'—to harm you, his enemy.

9 ταῦτ' ἀκούσας ὁ Ἀγησίλαος ἥσθη, . . .

In Xenophon's account, where the answer represents rejection of Agesilaos' suggestion, Agesilaos shows his approval for Pharnabazos' demonstration of loyalty only by his wish that he may become the Spartans' friend. Plutarch can add Agesilaos' delight in the answer, because, although he has not solicited his friendship, the qualities of manliness, loyalty, and respect already displayed by Pharnabazos (§3) will make him a valuable friend and ally, if and when he chooses to satisfy the new conditions of freedom and recognition of its worth. In Xenophon's version he will increase his material possessions.

. . . καὶ τῆς δεξιᾶς αὐτοῦ λαβόμενος καὶ συνεξαναστάς, Εἴθ', εἶπεν, ὦ Φαρνάβαζε, τοιοῦτος ὢν φίλος ἡμῖν γένοιο μᾶλλον ἢ πολέμιος.

Both authors report Agesilaos' initiative this time in grasping Pharnabazos' right hand. Plutarch proves consistent in his attitude to Pharnabazos by using only the simple name, abandoning Xenophon's friendly form of address, 'My good sir', ὦ λῷστε σύ (cf. Xen. *Symp.* iv. 1), and alone referring to his real status, 'the enemy'. Agesilaos hopes for friendship but does not abandon the obligation to harm him if he fails to adopt Greek ethical values and become a friend: he can do both only if the King relieves him of his loyal obligations by dispensing with his services. Plutarch perhaps regarded this conclusion as leading more strikingly on to the spontaneous gesture of friendship made by Pharnabazos' son in the next chapter in response to Agesilaos' wish; the young Persian recognizes the superiority of the Greek ideal of freedom which he cannot yet achieve.

Xenophon makes Agesilaos' answer more elaborate, as if premeditated (*Hell.* iv. 1. 38): attempting to detach Pharnabazos from his loyalty to the King, he has urged the setting up of a rival empire, so forming a buffer-state between Persians and Greeks of Asia Minor, a policy of which later traces have been found in

Isokrates (4. 161–6).[15] Agesilaos abandons his initial principle of harming the enemy and his possessions (*Hell.* iv. 1. 34–6). His promise—to leave Pharnabazos' territory as quickly as he can and to refrain from attacking it if there are other lands for him to attack—removes the alleged injustice. In return Pharnabazos only keeps open the possibility of closer co-operation.

Xenophon reports the preparations for Agesilaos' intended march further into the interior, in the hope of detaching other peoples from the King. He claims a diplomatic success in implementing this major policy in Asia Minor, perhaps to compensate for the limited military success he is able to record. Neither Plutarch nor Xenophon comments on Pharnabazos' decision not to join the Spartan side. He was, jointly with the Athenian Konon, admiral of the Persian fleet which defeated the Spartans at the battle near Knidos (ch. 17. 4, Xen. *Hell.* iv. 3. 11, 8. 7–8).

13. Agesilaos and Pharnabazos' son: the obligations of friendship

Plutarch records the end of Agesilaos' contact with Pharnabazos and three further cases of his relations with friends (cf. ch. 5). The first two cases relate to Xenophon's *Hellenika*, as the source (iv. 1. 40) and as a close parallel (v. 4. 31). The last is attributed to the Peripatetic philosopher Hieronymos; see Introd., F.3(*b*). Xenophon provides evidence for Agesilaos' general attitude to friendship, where friends are helped in different ways (*Agesilaos*, 1. 17–19, 6. 4–8, 8. 1–2, and 11. 4–12; cf. ch. 5. 1–4). He eulogizes, approving of Agesilaos' pragmatism—the question, it seems, is whether helping friends is in his interest. Plutarch finds there material for a critical judgement (cf. chs. 19. 5, 20. 7–9), combining statements (11. 6 and 10), reinterpreting them (11. 4), or reassessing the pragmatism (8. 2), for he applies different, more absolute, criteria.

1 Ἀπιόντος δὲ τοῦ Φαρναβάζου μετὰ τῶν φίλων, ὁ υἱὸς ὑπολειφθεὶς προσέδραμε τῷ Ἀγησιλάῳ καὶ μειδιῶν εἶπεν· Ἐγώ σε ξένον, ὦ Ἀγησίλαε, ποιοῦμαι· καὶ παλτὸν ἔχων ἐν τῇ χειρὶ δίδωσιν αὐτῷ.

The incidents that took place during the departure of the son of Pharnabazos allow Plutarch to revert to the theme of Agesilaos' affections introduced on the departure of Megabates (ch. 11). Plutarch recalls Xenophon's words closely (*Hell.* iv. 1. 39), but adds colour to each feature. He concentrates the attention on the personal interactions rather than on objective descriptions of people and things, notably in Agesilaos' need to choose unexpectedly an appropriate gift for the boy. He changes Xenophon's account of the conversation in direct speech to a single statement followed by indirect narrative, changes historic tenses to the vivid present—the imperfect for the longer 'looking round'—and passes over the boy's departure. Whereas Xenophon describes the boy and the two gifts directly as 'handsome' (καλός, καλόν, and πάγκαλα), Plutarch leaves the gifts without epithets and instead enhances the *actions* appropriately—with a 'smile', μειδιῶν, as he speaks; with a moral quality, 'nobility' (καλῷ καὶ γενναίῳ), as the suitable gift is chosen; with 'youth' (τῷ μειρακίῳ) as he receives Agesilaos' attention. The spontaneity of the personal relationship is displayed in Agesilaos' delight and the way he selects and gives the gift. Although Agesilaos' response is improvised, in both authors it starts a formal friendship (ξενία) with the terminology of the ritual initiatory declaration. The Homeric ritual adds an oath, and the option of a shared meal, but this occasion was evidently not suitable for these.[1]

2 δεξάμενος οὖν ὁ Ἀγησίλαος καὶ ἡσθεὶς τῇ τε ὄψει καὶ τῇ φιλοφροσύνῃ τοῦ παιδὸς ἐπεσκόπει τοὺς παρόντας, εἴ τις ἔχοι τι τοιοῦτον οἷον ἀντιδοῦναι καλῷ καὶ γενναίῳ δῶρον. ἰδὼν δ' ἵππον Ἰδαίου τοῦ γραφέως κεκοσμημένον φαλάροις, ταχὺ ταῦτα περισπάσας τῷ μειρακίῳ δίδωσι.

The participial phrase shows Agesilaos delighting in the visual and ethical elements, ὄψις, 'appearance', and φιλοφροσύνη, 'kindliness' (cf. Megabates, Kallippides, and Nektanebo, chs. 11. 7, 21. 8, 40. 1). It gives prominence to Agesilaos and changes direct description of the boy (Xen. *Hell.* iv. 1. 39) to indirect as Agesilaos reacts to him—his inner thoughts provide the motivation. Xenophon has nothing which might authenticate the suggestiveness of this expression; he may, as elsewhere, be responding to accusations made against Agesilaos.[2]

In *Hellenika* Agesilaos simply takes his gift from Idaios' horse, but here he is careful to find something suitable. Plutarch substitutes a noun, τῷ μειρακίῳ, for Xenophon's simple pronoun, stressing the age difference and perhaps externalizing Agesilaos' own thought. Nothing more is known of Idaios, Agesilaos' secretary.³

3 καὶ τὸ λοιπὸν οὐκ ἐπαύετο μεμνημένος, ἀλλὰ καὶ χρόνῳ περιιόντι τὸν οἶκον ἀποστερηθέντος αὐτοῦ καὶ φυγόντος ὑπὸ τῶν ἀδελφῶν εἰς Πελοπόννησον, ἰσχυρῶς ἐπεμελεῖτο·

Agesilaos' treatment of friends develops from his contact with Pharnabazos' son, who institutes the formal relationship which later binds Agesilaos. Plutarch, concentrating on Agesilaos, ignores Xenophon's account of the boy's departure, thus avoiding formal closure of the episode, and omits the injunction, 'Remember' (Μέμνησό νυν): Agesilaos shows himself 'mindful' (μεμνημένος) of his contractual involvement. Plutarch introduces pathos into Xenophon's account of the boy's exile: he puts 'took great care', ἰσχυρῶς ἐπεμελεῖτο, for 'cared', and losing 'his home', τὸν οἶκον, for losing 'his power', τὴν ἀρχήν.

Xenophon twice identifies the boy only by his mother's name, Parapita, and mentions only one brother who is nameless (*Hell.* iv. 1. 39–40). Plutarch, by lapse of memory or from a different source, has 'brothers', and states that they were the boy's brothers; Xenophon's phrase is ambiguous (see after §4).⁴

καί τι καὶ τῶν ἐρωτικῶν αὐτῷ συνέπραξεν. **4** ἠράσθη γὰρ ἀθλητοῦ παιδὸς ἐξ Ἀθηνῶν· ἐπεὶ δὲ μέγας ὢν καὶ σκληρὸς Ὀλυμπίασιν ἐκινδύνευεν ἐκκριθῆναι, καταφεύγει πρὸς τὸν Ἀγησίλαον ὁ Πέρσης δεόμενος ὑπὲρ τοῦ παιδός·

Plutarch enlarges Xenophon's simple statement of intervention in the boy's love-affair so that Agesilaos himself extends his obligation as ξένος to collusion in furthering these friendships (cf. on Agesipolis, ch. 20. 9). He implies below (καὶ τοῦτο) that Agesilaos has given other help in this love-affair, not specified by Xenophon, although he mentions other forms of attention (*Hell.* iv. 1. 40). Agesilaos intervenes in response to the request of the young Persian on behalf of his Athenian friend, matching his alleged intervention in response to the request of his son, Archidamos, on behalf of his friend's father, Sphodrias (ch. 25). Xenophon identifies the Athenian boy as the son of Eualces. Plutarch avoids naming him but explains that he was an athlete. He introduces a more significant athletic factor by referring to the boy's strength, and emphasizes this by using two adjectives where Xenophon has only one, although that is the superlative, 'the biggest of the boys' (μέγιστος ὢν τῶν παίδων). There is a paradox or surprise, in that the 'danger' to the athlete, exclusion (ἐκκριθῆναι) from the Olympic games, leads to the friend's 'seeking refuge' (καταφεύγει).

Xenophon does not speak of exclusion but only of *admittance* (ἐγκριθείη) to the sprint, τὸ στάδιον (*Hell.* iv. 1. 40), though exclusion from it is implied by Agesilaos' intervention. According to Plutarch, who presumably had no other source, the youth was excluded because the Hellanodikai judged in view of his physique that he could not be under the age limit of 18 for the boys' race[5] and, perhaps unfairly, required him to race against men. If Xenophon's participial phrase, μέγιστος ὢν τῶν παίδων, is causal, τὸ στάδιον refers to the men's race, and Agesilaos obtained dispensation for the under-age youth to compete for greater glory at the higher level because he was physically mature.[6] Pythagoras, excluded from the boys' boxing, won the men's event, and later the stadion, perhaps in Ol. 16 (*Numa*, 1. 3, D.H. ii. 58), and a true Spartiate might seek to do the same, but this was an Athenian, under no more compulsion to spurn an easy victory than the trophy-hunters from Theagenes of Thasos onwards who collected and boasted of their many crowns (cf. *Mor.* 811 D–E). If the participial phrase is concessive, τὸ στάδιον refers to the boys' race and both authors are saying the same thing.[7] Xenophon's superlative does not accord with reinstatement to the boys' race, 'although he was physically mature'—'ce qui lui valut sans doute une victoire facile'[8]—as if the tallest youth were debarred automatically, although the disparity may have seemed only too great for his statement of age to be true. Xenophon could have been more explicit, but he was interested in Agesilaos, not in the boy: Plutarch's moderate phrase, μέγας ὤν, avoids ambiguity and his interpretation gives clarification. In each case Agesilaos overturned the disqualification that followed the challenge of irregular entry as a boy over or under the age-limit, from other, smaller, boys, or from men who feared embarrassment.

Size and strength only provided evidence of age, which could be supported by other processes of substantiation possible in societies with no birth certificates and no agreed chronology. However, in this case Agesilaos could himself have had no independent knowledge of the facts; that made his unequal intervention surely irregular.

Chronology

Neither author provides the chronological context of the relevant Olympiad, but Xenophon explains that Pharnabazos was absent when Parapita's son was driven into exile (*Hell.* iv. 1. 39, 40). Pharnabazos was not 'retired' by the King in 394 (cf. ch. 12. 8) but commanded the Persian fleet (394–393) with Konon the Athenian at Knidos and Kythera (Xen. *Hell.* iv. 8. 1–8). In the year of the next Olympiad, 392, Konon and the fleet were still operating and the Spartans sent Antalkidas to arrange peace with Tiribazos. This was no time for the exile to be in the hostile Peloponnese.[9] By the next Olympiad (388) or soon after, Pharnabazos was recalled to the Persian capital to marry the King's daughter and was replaced by Ariobarzanes (Xen. *Hell.* v. 1. 28). This is a possible time for the boy's visit.

Even in normal circumstances, Agesilaos would have difficulty in persuading the Eleians, jealous of their control of the Games, to allow special dispensation—not to mention accusations of unfairness from other competitors—but Sparta had been banned from the Olympic games by Elis from 420 for alleged violation of the truce (Thuc. v. 49–50), Agis had twice entered and ravaged the territory of Elis between 402 and 400 (Xen. *Hell.* iii. 2. 23–7), and he had sacrificed at Olympia just before his death at the end of the war.[10] After Agis' intervention, however, Elis was 'overtly' loyal to Sparta, until its co-operation with Thebes between 370 and 365,[11] and perhaps more accommodating.

If the satrapy was hereditary (see above, ch. 11. 1), Ariobarzanes may have been related to Pharnabazos. Since his name was that of a grandson of Pharnabazos (Arr. *Anab.* iii. 23. 7), he may have been his brother or a son.[12] If he was the Ariobarzanes who was Antalkidas' ξένος—probably before 400— and mentioned in 407 with Pharnabazos by Xenophon (*Hell.* i. 4. 7), he was perhaps one of the sons of Pharnakes (Thuc. viii. 58. 1).[13] Ariobarzanes will then, perhaps, be the brother who deposed his nephew, Pharnabazos' rightful heir.[14] If the absence of Pharnabazos and the exile of his heir are linked with Ariobarzanes, this was Parapita's son (Xen. *Hell.* iv. 1. 40). No reaction of

Pharnabazos is recorded. He was in favour with the King during his absences until, perhaps, his failure in Egypt in 374, but his marriage to the King's daughter may have involved passing over Parapita's son and his exile in favour of Ariobarzanes. The Olympiad was perhaps in the 380s.[15]

A son of the marriage (388–7) of Pharnabazos and Artaxerxes' daughter Apamea (*Artax.* 27. 4) is thought to be an Artabazos (*Alex.* 21. 9; for the family name see above on ch. 11. 1). He was prevented from recovering his satrapy by Ariobarzanes, who was allied with Sparta and helped by Agesilaos (Xen. *Agesilaos*, 2. 26) during his revolt of 366; Artabazos was then of age. Pharnabazos died shortly after his absences between 385 and 374 for the two attempts to recover Egypt for the King (*Artax.* 24; Diod. xv. 29. 3, 41–43; Polyainos, 3. 9. 38, 56, 59).[16] If Xenophon is wrong about the mother, and Apamea's son, Artabazos, was the nephew exiled by Ariobarzanes, he was very young in the 380s, and only much later to be befriended, with his 'lover', by Agesilaos; but by 366 Agesilaos was employed by Ariobarzanes (Xen. *Agesilaos*, 2. 26), and Pharnabazos probably dead.

If the exile was not satrapal deposition, Xenophon and Plutarch may refer to the boy's 'brother' or 'brothers' and his 'home' may indicate a disputed private inheritance; the date then remains unclear.

ὁ δὲ καὶ τοῦτο βουλόμενος αὐτῷ χαρίζεσθαι μάλα μόλις διεπράξατο σὺν πολλῇ πραγματείᾳ.

While χαρίζεσθαι, 'gratification', is used in an erotic sense[17] and the context may bring to mind that sense when it is used as a metaphor, here the sense is 'wishing to do him even *this* service as a favour', as in the almost identical phrase at ch. 25. 10, 'wishing to do his son the service as a favour'. By the use of alliteration, a compound verb, and the prepositional phrase, Plutarch makes more of Agesilaos' intervention than Xenophon does. For διεπράξατο, 'fixed', see ch. 21. 1; cf. 15. 5, 20. 6).

5 τἆλλα μὲν γὰρ ἦν ἀκριβὴς καὶ νόμιμος, ἐν δὲ τοῖς φιλικοῖς πρόφασιν ἐνόμιζεν εἶναι τὸ λίαν δίκαιον.

Plutarch explains (γάρ) the significance of the incidents just described, observing that Agesilaos distinguished the morality of friendship from that of other situations, so that while he was otherwise 'strict' and 'conformed to custom, observed normal standards', in the case of friendship he believed that rules need not be strictly applied. Plutarch now implies that the youth was strictly ineligible, and that the rules were ignored. Xenophon does not require this assumption; Agesilaos was able to convince the judges that the boy was eligible. Plutarch records his criticism of Agesilaos' handling of political friends at ch. 5. 1. He now attributes to him an arbitrary disregard of moral principles in favour of the more pragmatic aim of helping friends (cf. *Mor.* 807 E–F). No doubt, if strict justice did not suit his own interests, Agesilaos ignored it, and expected the same flexibility from others.

ἀναφέρεται γοῦν ἐπιστόλιον αὐτοῦ πρὸς Ἰδριέα τὸν Κᾶρα τοιοῦτο· Νικίας εἰ μὲν μὴ ἀδικεῖ, ἄφες· εἰ δ' ἀδικεῖ, ἀμὶν ἄφες· πάντως δ' ἄφες.

The letter is hardly 'in circulation' (Perrin) but is rather 'mentioned in sources'. Agesilaos' request for special consideration from one friend for another again shows his indifference to strict justice. 'Acquit him', in accordance with strict interpretation of justice and with what Agesilaos desires. 'Acquit him', that is, as a favour, disregarding strict justice. 'Just acquit him.' If Hidrieus refuses this acquittal, Agesilaos will say that he should not use strict justice as a πρόφασις, but gratify his friend.

Plutarch does not reveal Nikias' identity or difficulty here or elsewhere (*Mor.* 191 B, 209 F, 808 A). He is possibly but not certainly Spartan.[18] Hidrieus (Hydrieus at Perrin, v. 538, 'otherwise unknown')[19] is thought unlikely to have been the successor to his sister Artemisia as satrap of Karia in 351 (see Diod. xvi. 36. 2, 45. 7, 69. 2, 74. 2.).[20] The identification is not impossible, since Idrieus was linked in action with Mausolos (Polyainos, vii. 23. 2), whose accession is dated 377/6. Agesilaos, Mausolos' guest-friend, ξένος, was paid for some service in Asia Minor (Xen. *Agesilaos*, 2. 26–7; see below, ch. 36), when he, and perhaps Nikias, may have had relevant dealings with Idrieus long before he was satrap.[21]

Plutarch transfers to this case Archidamos' grounds for his plea to Agesilaos in the case of Sphodrias, recorded by Xenophon.[22] 'I know you would have acquitted Sphodrias if he had done no wrong; if he has done wrong, acquit him for my sake' (*Hell.* v. 4. 31). Plutarch's treatment of that case omits this plea (ch. 25).

6 ἐν μὲν οὖν τοῖς πλείστοις τοιοῦτος ὑπὲρ τῶν φίλων ὁ Ἀγησίλαος· ἔστι δ᾽ ὅπου πρὸς τὸ συμφέρον ἐχρῆτο τῷ καιρῷ μᾶλλον, ὡς ἐδήλωσεν, ἀναζυγῆς αὐτῷ θορυβωδεστέρας γενομένης, ἀσθενοῦντα καταλιπὼν τὸν ἐρώμενον. **7** ἐκείνου γὰρ δεομένου καὶ καλοῦντος αὐτὸν ἀπιόντα, μεταστραφεὶς εἶπεν ὡς χαλεπὸν ἐλεεῖν ἅμα καὶ φρονεῖν.

Plutarch implies confirmation that in the case of Nikias Agesilaos was ignoring the law for the benefit of his *guilty* friend, as usual. The disregard of strict justice had also benefited some of the petitioners at ch. 7, and in all those cases Agesilaos benefited indirectly, too. The example presented now is of another kind, for the wounded friend, who thinks he has a right to be saved under the rule of 'Help Friends', suffers from the disregard of the strict principle, and is denied this right. Plutarch's phrase, πρὸς τὸ συμφέρον, 'for his own advantage' (Perrin), suggests that it was Agesilaos again who benefited, and if so, Plutarch's example will stand as a misuse of justice.

However, this is not a simple case of miscarriage of justice. Plutarch presents Agesilaos with a conflict of obligations, for any effort to save the innocent friend endangers the rest of the army, involving the disregard of a stronger obligation: the general's duty to all his men. Plutarch shows that Agesilaos was aware of the problem of reconciling two virtues, ἐλεεῖν ἅμα καὶ φρονεῖν. The first, 'to pity', is emotional, the virtue of a friend, compassion for the wounded man. The second, 'to be prudent', is rational, the virtue of a general, security for the state. For Agesilaos, justice is 'the interest of the state'. He preserves his reputation as a general but sacrifices his friend.

A general must recognize the καιρός, the proper moment for action,[23] and Plutarch repeatedly comments on this aspect of Agesilaos' character and generalship (chs. 8. 6, 39. 2 and 4). This moment gives him the choice between two obligations, and he chooses 'expediency'. In turning back he recognizes his obligation to the wounded man, and, in the tradition of a Spartan, the man will accept Agesilaos' resolution of the dilemma in the interest of Sparta (cf. *Mor.* 241, 242). Plutarch presents the complexity of the issue.

τουτὶ μὲν οὖν Ἱερώνυμος ὁ φιλόσοφος ἱστόρηκεν.

This anecdote is found at *Mor.* 191 B and 209 E–F but is not attributed to Hieronymos there. The philosopher's context will have been the moral dilemma of conflicting duties.[24]

14. Agesilaos' austerity: Lykourgan principles exemplified

Plutarch's interpretations of Agesilaos' character have previously been unfavourable, but here and in the next chapter he follows Xenophon's *Agesilaos* in approving selected traits. These are the qualities thought especially to have been legislated for by Lykourgos, and developed in the ἀγωγή and in the συσσίτια (*Lak. Pol.* 2, *Lyk.* 10. 1–2, 13. 1–2, 16. 4–6, 19). Plutarch distinguishes what he evidently regards as these true Spartan characteristics from the individual Spartan's deviations from them.

1 Ἤδη δὲ περιϊόντος ἐνιαυτοῦ δευτέρου τῇ στρατηγίᾳ, πολὺς ἄνω λόγος ἐχώρει τοῦ Ἀγησιλάου, καὶ δόξα θαυμαστὴ κατεῖχε τῆς τε σωφροσύνης αὐτοῦ καὶ εὐτελείας καὶ μετριότητος.

Plutarch resumes the chronological narrative from ch. 13. 2, after digressing to the theme of Agesilaos' distorted sense of justice in serving his friends. The temporal connection creates the impression of a narrative moving on in time towards the end of the campaign in Asia Minor, allowing the interval that was needed for these developments to take place. In the absence of a culminating military achievement, Xenophon concludes his account of the campaign with a eulogistic passage at *Agesilaos*, 1. 35–9. Plutarch, in seeking a suitable climax before the order for return arrives, follows Agesilaos' diplomacy (chs. 11–13) with a study of relevant personal characteristics. This so-called 'eidological' (descriptive) passage is integrated into the 'chronographic' (narrative),[1] and the study begins, not as Plutarch's intrusive assessment in his own words, but as indirect characterization—the talk about Agesilaos' reputation currently circulating in the hinterland. Three abstract nouns set out Plutarch's programme for the first part of the chapter. Two are features of Agesilaos' character displayed in previous chapters: from ch. 11 (Megabates), σωφροσύνη, 'self-restraint', which includes πρᾳότης (cf. *Alex.* 4. 8, *Dtr.* 1. 3);[2] from ch. 12 (Pharnabazos), εὐτέλεια, 'frugality', introduced, perhaps from Crete (*Lyk.* 4. 1–2), by Lykourgos, whose public messes, συσσίτια, discouraged the pursuit of wealth (*Lyk.* 10; cf. *Lyk.* 8, *Lak. Pol.* 5. 2, 7. 2–3, Arist. *Pol.* 1294ᵇ25–7);[3] Plutarch adds a third, μετριότης, 'a moderate disposition', which was inculcated in the Spartan ἀγωγή (*Lyk.* 10, 12, 16. 6–7, *Lak. Pol.* 2. 3–5).

2 ἐσκήνου μὲν γὰρ ἀποδημῶν καθ᾽ αὑτὸν ἐν τοῖς ἁγιωτάτοις ἱεροῖς, ἃ
μὴ πολλοὶ καθορῶσιν ἄνθρωποι πράττοντας ἡμᾶς, τούτων τοὺς θεοὺς
ποιούμενος ἐπόπτας καὶ μάρτυρας·

Plutarch identifies features which gave rise in the intervening two
years to the favourable opinion, now prevalent in Asia Minor, of
Agesilaos' way of life. On his control of sensuality, ἀφροδίσια,
Xenophon proved that nothing discreditable took place in the
affair of Megabates by describing how Agesilaos lodged either in a
temple, itself a sufficient prohibition, or in the open, where public
observation is called to witness (*Agesilaos*, 5. 4–7).[4] Guest-houses
provided accommodation for pilgrims and suppliants and other
facilities were available, with inevitable exploitation and dangers,
but temple authorities controlled their precinct and their special
guests' privileges (cf. Hdt. i. 54. 2). Plutarch did not need the
choice of lodgings in discussing Agesilaos' self-control at ch. 11,
and introduces it here.[5] Away from home Agesilaos lodged
(ἐσκήνου) in temples[6] where the deities would punish sacrilege; and
the emphatic ἁγιωτάτοις, 'most holy', provides a double safeguard.
It seems in both versions that Agesilaos slept in full view of the
cult statue in the deity's house, but whereas Xenophon (5. 6)
suggests that the behaviour *suspected* of Agesilaos was 'not
possible' in a temple, Plutarch makes the gods overseers and
witnesses—of Agesilaos' innocence: others have no one to testify
to private behaviour—'what few men see us doing'; Agesilaos'
open lodging (Xen. *Agesilaos*, 5. 7) would provide no safeguard in
this respect, and is omitted.

ἐν δὲ χιλιάσι στρατιωτῶν τοσαύταις οὐ ῥᾳδίως ἄν τις εἶδε φαυλοτέραν
στιβάδα τῆς Ἀγησιλάου.

Plutarch moves away from moral purity with the second quality,
adapting material used by Xenophon in other contexts. He uses
'open lodging' (Xen. *Agesilaos*, 5. 7) to manifest, not purity, but
frugality, in the spareness of his bed, which anyone could
witness.[7] For Xenophon Agesilaos' humble bed proves that his
powers of physical endurance are superior to those of his soldiers
(*Agesilaos*, 5. 2–3). This quality is also contrasted with rulers'
luxury below (§4).

3 πρός τε θάλπος οὕτω καὶ ψῦχος εἶχεν ὥσπερ μόνος ἀεὶ χρῆσθαι ταῖς
ὑπὸ τοῦ θεοῦ κεκραμέναις ὥραις πεφυκώς.

The third term, μετριότης, suggests another physical aspect of Agesilaos' endurance, his ability to face conditions of heat and cold imposed by the deity. Plutarch incorporates here one of Xenophon's proofs of Agesilaos' superiority over the Persian King, who shuns heat and cold while Agesilaos endures climatic conditions, divinely determined (*Agesilaos*, 9. 5).[8] The illustrations of Agesilaos' moderation complete his regulated responses in the three areas, private, public, and divine.

4 ἥδιστον δὲ θέαμα τοῖς κατοικοῦσι τὴν Ἀσίαν Ἕλλησιν ἦσαν οἱ πάλαι βαρεῖς καὶ ἀφόρητοι καὶ διαρρέοντες ὑπὸ πλούτου καὶ τρυφῆς ὕπαρχοι καὶ στρατηγοὶ δεδιότες καὶ θεραπεύοντες ἄνθρωπον ἐν τρίβωνι περιιόντα λιτῷ, καὶ πρὸς ἓν ῥῆμα βραχὺ καὶ Λακωνικὸν ἁρμόζοντες ἑαυτοὺς καὶ μετασχηματίζοντες . . .

In the second part of the chapter Plutarch returns to the Greeks of Asia with whom he began (ring structure). He exploits indirect characterization of Agesilaos: the favourable impact on the Greeks of his restraint is complemented by their favourable reaction to the transformation of their former rulers brought about by Spartan austerity.[9] The metaphor of change, μετασχηματισμός, is a powerful image in the (Heraclitean) processes of 'generation' (Arist. *Cael*. 298 B, 305 A–B, *GC* 335 B). It is mysterious, in the heightened language of Plato's myth dealing with the (physical) transformation of the soul in reincarnation (*Ll*. 903 E; cf. 906 C);[10] in the transformation of each of seven letters in four ways to represent twenty-eight sounds in the language of a distant island (Diod. ii. 57. 4); in changes in the shape of the body's channels as a cause of hunger and thirst (*Mor*. 687 B–C). It signifies disguise (Josephus, *AJ* viii. 11. 1), and the preacher's brief personation of the weakness of his audience (1 *Cor*. 4. 6). The oppressors' changes—in 'form' (appearance), responding to Agesilaos' laconic words—may lack substance. The traditional Spartan brevity advocated by Lykourgos (*Lyk*. 19. 1) is a further element in establishing Agesilaos' superiority and influence.

Plutarch names the residents but does not identify the oppressors. Their titles may refer to Persians.[11] 'Satraps' and their deputies are called ὕπαρχοι by Thucydides (viii. 16. 3, 31. 2, 87. 1, and 108. 4); Tissaphernes, στρατηγός, 'general', was of a higher rank (viii. 5. 4).[12] In Xenophon's phrase at *Agesilaos*, 1. 34, it is non-Greek oppressors who 'avoid eye contact'. Oppression by

Greek governors had also occurred (for Thibron see Xen. *Hell*. iii. 2. 1), and Ephesos was tainted by Persian customs (*Lys*. 3. 2). It was Lysander of whom the petitioners said that 'none of the generals sent to Asia was more powerful and formidable' (ch. 7. 2). When Spartan support for the dekarchies was withdrawn in favour of 'ancestral constitutions' (*Hell*. iii. 4. 2), no doubt it was because the extreme oligarchs, some of whom were friends of Lysander, were unpopular among other leading residents who were not his friends, or not in the class from which the dekarchs came (cf. the Thirty at Athens), but lesser landowners, who traditionally held office—perhaps as democrats, or as oligarchs, but less extreme—and had been most vulnerable to oppression by the dekarchs. It was most probably oligarchs who bestowed divine honours on Lysander at Samos, where the games in honour of Hera were renamed 'Lysandreia', according to Douris, with fourth-century epigraphical attestation from the Samian Heraion.[13] Men appointed by Lysander were not from the traditional leading families, and were therefore more loyal to him personally, capable of the most radical of measures such as the deification at Samos.[14] When the oligarchs at Byzantion were removed by Thrasyboulos later there was similar joy (Xen. *Hell*. iv. 8. 27).

The phrase 'overflowing with wealth and luxury' suggests non-Greeks, but it fits the wealthy Greeks at Ephesos whom Agesilaos did not want as cavalrymen (ch. 9). Xenophon at *Agesilaos*, 1. 37 describes Agesilaos' settlement of the factional unrest in Asia Minor consequent upon the defeat of Athens in terms which suggest that he now favoured a more moderate regime (ch. 6. 2). Plutarch's ἁρμόζοντες ἑαυτούς, suggestive of both 'harmony' (cf. below, ch. 15. 1) and the Spartan 'harmost' (*Lak. Pol*. 14. 2), and μετασχηματίζοντες, 'change of form', are perhaps more easily applicable to Greeks. There was a moral element in Agesilaos' negotiations with Tithraustes (ch. 10. 7–8); and Pharnabazos gave up his comfort, although he could not bring himself entirely to accept the culture (ch. 12). If Pharnabazos is to be included among the Persians who dreaded Agesilaos, it is an exaggeration (cf. φοβηθείς, used of Tissaphernes at ch. 9): he avoided battle, and his son exchanged gifts of friendship with Agesilaos, but there is no mention of fear: he intended to fight hard for the King (ch. 12). The omission of the Persian name may indicate that Plutarch's concern here is to show the superiority of Agesilaos' Spartan character over that of both his countrymen and his opponents.

. . . ὥστε πολλοῖς ἐπήει τὰ τοῦ Τιμοθέου λέγειν, Ἄρης τύραννος· χρυσὸν δ' Ἑλλὰς οὐ δέδοικε.

Literary quotation is used in support of an argument. Plutarch does not directly support his own argument, but presents indirectly, and more objectively within the context, a quotation which occurred to the Greeks of Asia Minor who were so impressed. The first part of the quotation is used differently of Demetrius (*Dtr.* 42. 3), where he rejected his subjects' petitions discourteously, but was moved by an old woman, who shouted, 'Then don't be king.' Plutarch goes on: 'Nothing so fits a king as the work of justice. For Ares is a tyrant, as Timotheos says, but law is the king of all, according to Pindar' (*Fr.* 169a. 1; for Timotheos see Page (1962), fr. 790 = (1968), fr. 424). This sense of τύραννος is strong, making the contrast with 'king', but it is not always pejorative. For Plutarch the quotation, though not directly his own, strengthens his proof of the superiority of the Spartan character as demonstrated by Agesilaos, who established military supremacy and ensured that the Greeks in Asia were no longer ruled by oppressors or their wealth.

15. Agesilaos' obedience: the supreme Lykourgan virtue; Agesilaos' campaign in Asia Minor ends

In his account of the final stage of Agesilaos' campaign in Asia Minor, Plutarch affirms, at his recall to Sparta, the virtues attributed to him in ch. 1, as ruler, general, friend, and companion; notably his obedience. Plutarch regrets the interruption of his achievements, actual and planned, from a panhellenist viewpoint (see Introd., E.7 above).

1 Κινουμένης δὲ τῆς Ἀσίας καὶ πολλαχοῦ πρὸς ἀπόστασιν ὑπεικούσης, ἁρμοσάμενος τὰς αὐτόθι πόλεις, καὶ ταῖς πολιτείαις δίχα φόνου καὶ φυγῆς ἀνθρώπων ἀποδοὺς τὸν προσήκοντα κόσμον, . . .

At *Agesilaos*, 1. 36–8 Xenophon surrounds the order for Agesilaos' recall with eulogies, the first for his military achievements and future hopes, the second for his civic achievements, recording the affection and sorrow shown at his departure. The recent unsettled state of Asia Minor is not a topic for eulogy, and Xenophon refers to the political disturbances (πόλεις στασιαζούσας) and the over-throw of democratic or moderate administrations in Asia Minor by Lysander, following the defeat of Athens, but does not include later developments. Thereafter, as requested by the cities, probably the pro-Spartan elements, Sparta sent out Thibron and Derkylidas, who, with varied success, tried to provide protection against Tissaphernes' efforts to re-establish the King's rule; as the cities changed hands, leading citizens with conflicting allegiances gained or lost power (Xen. *Hell*. iii. i. 6–7). Three paradigmatic elements can be identified in Samos (404): citizens, one-time citizens—here a division resulting from democrats' and oligarchs' conflicts which led to the departure of the latter to Samian terri-tory on the mainland, the *peraia*, now to be reinstated—and the dekarchs set in charge (Xen. *Hell*. ii. 3. 7).[1]

For recent events Plutarch turns to *Hellenika*, where Xenophon gives details of the situation in Asia not found in *Agesilaos*. He reports that the cities needed to be liberated from Persian control (iii. 4. 5), and that, while Agesilaos was at Ephesos, there was confusion in the cities, since there was no longer rule of either democracy or dekarchy (iii. 4. 7). But Plutarch did not find there what Agesilaos did to settle the unrest, for the process of the administrative settlement lies hidden behind his quarrel with Lysander (*Hell*. iii. 4. 7–9; cf. above chs. 7–8).

Plutarch gives these themes a progressive structure, presenting chronological continuity throughout the chapter, and placing the recall in context. At the start of the first sentence two present participles define conditions in Asia Minor, which he had described at ch. 6. 2, not after the fall of Athens but after the accession of Agesilaos. Then two aorist participles summarizing Agesilaos' civic administration form the temporal bridge to the military plans in mind at the time of the recall.

Although the structure is his own, Plutarch's wording reveals his use of his sources. For the phrase 'he restored their proper form', describing what was put in place after the apparent failure of the original plan to reinstate Lysander's friends (ch. 6. 2), he turns to Xenophon's *Hellenika* (iii. 4. 2) and uses 'the ancestral constitutions' of the ephors' edict, suggesting that Agesilaos followed the form prescribed by them. For the manner of the settlement, he returns to Xenophon's retrospect (*Agesilaos*, 1. 37) and echoes the phrase ἄνευ φυγῆς καὶ θανάτου, 'without banishment or death'. Xenophon's reference to the fall of the Athenians is rightly omitted by Plutarch as too remote for his context, since it was not they but Spartans, Persians, and the citizens themselves who were responsible for the present situation.

. . . ἐγνώκει πρόσω χωρεῖν καὶ τὸν πόλεμον διάρας ἀπὸ τῆς Ἑλληνικῆς θαλάττης, περὶ τοῦ σώματος βασιλεῖ καὶ τῆς ἐν Ἐκβατάνοις καὶ Σούσοις εὐδαιμονίας διαμάχεσθαι, καὶ περισπάσαι πρῶτον αὐτοῦ τὴν σχολήν, ὡς μὴ καθέζοιτο τοὺς πολέμους βραβεύων τοῖς Ἕλλησι καὶ διαφθείρων τοὺς δημαγωγούς.

The plans for the future, introduced by the main verb, continue the chronological progression. Plutarch's phrase πρόσω χωρεῖν, 'to march forward', recalls one of the original aims of the expedition, 'to carry the war forward far across the sea' (ch. 6. 2), and Xenophon's reference to the final march 'as far inland as possible' (*Hell*. iv. 1. 41). This plan is more realistic than the claim in the rest of the sentence; but that Agesilaos is about to restrain the King both personally and as a world power repeats the emotionally expressed intention in Xenophon's *Agesilaos* (1. 36) to destroy the empire that marched against Greece.

The proposed attacks on the King's residences at Ekbatana and Susa are not mentioned elsewhere. Plutarch augments *Mor*. 211 A, perhaps in an attempt to stretch the imagination by implying a comparison with Alexander, who is repeatedly said to be marching on King Dareios (*Alex*. 17. 3, 20. 4, 29. 9, 33. 4, 42. 5). The Oxyrhynchos historian speaks only of the less ambitious and more feasible plan to march to Kappadokia (XVII. 4);[2] Diodoros (xiv. 83. 1) mentions the recall and departure without comment. The King himself had not been pressed by Agesilaos yet, only his satraps. Any extension of the activity would suit Plutarch's panhellenist theme.

Plutarch introduces the striking verb, βραβεύων, 'umpiring' (cf. *Artax*. 21. 4). He uses forms of the word frequently in the *Lives* for legal judges and arbiters (*Pomp*. 4. 2, 55. 4, *Cat. Min*. 44. 1, *Cic*. 9. 1, 2, 35. 1), for those holding elections (*Cam*. 42. 5, *Pomp*. 54. 2, *Cat. Min*. 44. 6), bestowing political power (*Dion*. 53. 4), or arranging peace (*Caes*. 12. 2). Ephors arbitrate between Spartan kings (*Agis*, 12. 2), old men between Spartan youth in political disputes (*Mor.* 795 A), birds between Romulus and Remus (*Rom.* 9. 5), and Fortune or god between military opponents (*Pel.* 13. 3, *Brut.* 40. 8). It is otherwise found in connection with athletic games (*Arat.* 27. 2) and in dramatists and fourth-century orators, in the sense of 'arbiter'.

Theopompos, in Photios' epitome, has Artaxerxes 'umpiring' between the Greeks over peace: περὶ τῆς εἰρήνης ἦν αὐτὸς τοῖς Ἕλλησιν ἐβράβευσεν.³ He mentions Antalkidas' Peace of 386 at §8: ἔθεντο εἰρήνην, 'made peace', after the naval battle at Cyprus (§6). His ἐβράβευσεν, 'arbitrated' between Greek equals, Sparta and Athens, similarly implied by Isokrates (ἐπικυδέστερα ἐποίησεν, iv. 139), would be appropriate before then in the choice Artaxerxes made between them in 392, when Strouthas, who favoured Athens, replaced Tiribazos (Xen. *Hell.* iv. 8. 17); also when the Spartans benefited, ἐπικυδέστεροι ἐγένοντο, from the peace negotiations of 387/6 (Xen. *Hell.* v. 1. 36). This may be Plutarch's meaning here, assimilating also the King's later interventions as arbiter with his attitude to Lysander's oligarchies which brought Thibron and Agesilaos to Asia Minor (Xen. *Hell.* iii. 1. 3, 4. 2).

The bribery, explained by Plutarch in the anecdote which closes the chapter, is used by Xenophon to introduce his resumption of the affairs of mainland Greece at the start of the Corinthian war. He records that Tithraustes, driven to desperation by Agesilaos, sent Timokrates of Rhodes with money for the leaders in the cities to finance war against the Lakedaimonians (*Hell.* iii. 5. 1; cf. *Hell. Ox.* 11. 2–5;⁴ Polyainos, i. 48. 3; Paus. iii. 9. 8). Plutarch's phrase, corrupting 'the people's leaders', reflects this, in pejorative terms in keeping with his anti-Persian theme. The final chiasmus, centred on τοῖς Ἕλλησι, highlights his indignation.

2 ἐν τούτῳ δ' ἀφικνεῖται πρὸς αὐτὸν Ἐπικυδίδας ὁ Σπαρτιάτης, ἀπαγγέλλων ὅτι πολὺς περιέστηκε τὴν Σπάρτην πόλεμος Ἑλληνικός, καὶ καλοῦσιν ἐκεῖνον οἱ ἔφοροι καὶ κελεύουσι τοῖς οἴκοι βοηθεῖν.

The arrival of Epikydidas dramatically interrupts the plans for future achievements with which Plutarch has raised expectations. The message begins with a brief statement of the events in Greece that necessitated the order for Agesilaos' recall, the full force of which comes at the very end. Diodoros distinguishes the 'Boiotian' and 'Corinthian' wars (xiv. 81. 3, 86. 6; cf. *Lys.* 27. 1).⁵

That Plutarch speaks of a 'Greek war' is a mark of the indignation he is about to express; the epithet does not identify, but condemns.[6] The order for recall is issued by the ephors only in Plutarch, but he may infer this from Xenophon's observation that Agesilaos obeyed 'just as if he were standing before them in the Ephoreion' (*Agesilaos*, 1. 36).

3 Ὦ βάρβαρ' ἐξευρόντες Ἕλληνες κακά.

The dramatic tension is heightened with Plutarch's own reaction, expressed in a (chiastic) quotation from Euripides, *Tro.* 764, where Andromache has just been told of the impending murder of her son by the Greeks. There the words are poignant, since the barbaric evils are done to barbarians, not by barbarians, but by Greeks. Now Greeks inflict them on Greeks (cf. ch. 26. 1)—on Spartans (§2). There is, perhaps, an unintended irony in the assimilation of the Spartans to the defeated and helpless Trojans, and a reversal of Agesilaos' own self-assimilation with Agamemnon (ch. 6. 7; see below, on ἐφ' ἑαυτούς): Lysander had just lost Haliartos (Xen. *Hell.* iii. 5. 19).

If Agesilaos had been allowed to stay, barbaric evils would again have been done, but by Greeks to barbarians—more rightly, in the ordinary Greek view. The attitude to Thebes and other 'medizers' after the Persian and Peloponnesian wars shows that cultural distinctions gave way to feelings of betrayal and outright hostility, played on by the panhellenic propagandists. Plutarch makes the point as a moralist in a narrowly Hellenic view: an effective attack on the King was clearly beyond Agesilaos' available resources.

τί γὰρ ἄν τις ἄλλο τὸν φθόνον ἐκεῖνον προσείποι καὶ τὴν τότε σύστασιν καὶ σύνταξιν ἐφ' ἑαυτοὺς τῶν Ἑλλήνων, οἳ τῆς τύχης ἄνω φερομένης ἐπελάβοντο, καὶ τὰ ὅπλα πρὸς τοὺς βαρβάρους βλέποντα καὶ τὸν πόλεμον ἤδη τῆς Ἑλλάδος ἐξῳκισμένον αὖθις εἰς ἑαυτοὺς ἔτρεψαν;

The rhetorical question continues the chronological progression by commenting on the diversion of Agesilaos' forces to the Greek homeland. Plutarch is predicating barbarism of the malice, political alignments, and military organization of the Greeks involved in the Corinthian war, and adjusts the reference of Euripides' 'Greeks' by the reciprocal ἐφ' ἑαυτούς, 'upon themselves'. The sentiment applies not only to the anti-Spartan alliance, as if the war was motivated by the wish to deprive the Spartans of the glory of taking revenge on the King. Plutarch is rather making a perceptive comment on the failure of the classical Greeks to achieve the political unity implied in the recognized contrast between their national identity and 'foreigners' which would prevent internecine war. His designation of 'envy', φθόνος, as a cause of the complicated web of defensive alliances that repeatedly led to conflict, suggests the need to find a more just distribution of wealth and power (cf. ch. 27. 7).

Plutarch uses ἐξῴκισε literally of a transfer of people (*Rom.* 24. 3). Agesilaos' wish to 'depopulate' Messenia (*Comp.* 3. 2) substitutes place for people. Lykourgos' 'banishment' of gold and silver from Sparta is a full metaphor (*Arist.–Cato Maj. Comp.* 3. 1). Here the imagery of ἐξῳκισμένον, 'deported', of war, recognizes that it was endemic; Agesilaos had taken war far from Greece (ch. 6. 2).

Plutarch overlooks the potential of the federal solution which the Thebans attempted in the Confederacy of his native Boiotia. He approves the political motive of a unifying crusade against a common enemy in the east advocated at the time; see Introd., E.7(*d*), (*h*). But Persian wealth was divisive: powerful cities sought financial support in return for military services to one or other of the Kings and satraps only to secure their own domination. Plutarch condemns profit intended to finance 'Greek wars' (chs. 36. 2, *Comp.* 5. 1).

No united Greek expedition was undertaken before Philip of Makedon formed the League of Corinth in 337 and declared war on Persia. Apart from Alexander no Greek before or since Agesilaos had won such great fame and power in Asia (*Comp.* 2. 6). In his own day, perhaps, Plutarch would think the Roman achievement a successful fulfilment of the two objectives, world power and peace in Greece (see Introd., E.7(*d*)–(*f*), (*h*)), having observed the failure of Alexander's empire to survive in the form he had described in his *Life*. Mercenary troops found employment in the east, many in Persian service, and Greek traders and settlers in Persian lands, by their presence, did more for the spread of Hellenism than the panhellenists' propaganda, which the leading cities used largely to further their own status. Plutarch had no imperial aims in exploiting these themes. For him they served to enhance the cultural and moral impact of his works. He recognized an acceptable form of internal panhellenism at ch. 27. 7 in the plea for lasting peace for the common benefit of Greece: his wish for the success of the crusade stems from 'the "naturalized" and legitimized' attitudes of Greek to barbarian.[7]

4 οὐ γὰρ ἔγωγε συμφέρομαι τῷ Κορινθίῳ Δημαράτῳ μεγάλης ἡδονῆς ἀπολελεῖφθαι φήσαντι τοὺς μὴ θεασαμένους Ἕλληνας Ἀλέξανδρον ἐν τῷ Δαρείου θρόνῳ καθήμενον, ἀλλ᾽ εἰκότως ἂν οἶμαι δακρῦσαι, συννοήσαντας ὅτι ταῦτ᾽ ἀλλ᾽ Ἀλεξάνδρῳ καὶ Μακεδόσιν ἀπέλιπον οἱ τότε τοὺς τῶν Ἑλλήνων στρατηγοὺς περὶ Λεῦκτρα καὶ Κορώνειαν καὶ Κόρινθον καὶ Ἀρκαδίαν καταναλώσαντες.

For the first time in this *Life* Plutarch intervenes explicitly in the first person. The remark of Demaratos, a 'frank but well-disposed' ancestral guest-friend (ξένος) of Alexander, was made first at the enthronement, and a second time before he died after seeing Alexander again (*Alex.* 9. 12–13, 37. 7, 56. 1). Plutarch seems to regret two things: that Agesilaos did not go on to achieve the triumph that Alexander later did achieve; and that Alexander, who achieved it, was Makedonian, not Greek (cf. *Kim.* 19. 3, *Flam.* 5. 8, *Arat.* 38. 5–6).[8]

In the battles mentioned, the Spartan king, Kleombrotos, died at Leuktra and the Boiotian, Epameinondas, died at Mantineia: but since no generals, στρατηγοί, are named as casualties at Corinth and Koroneia, the conjecture στρατούς, 'armies', has been preferred (Ziegler, following Emperius). However, since καταναλώσαντες need not mean killed, but 'squandered the lives of' (Perrin), 'sacrifié' (Flacelière), and neither whole armies nor all generals were lost in these battles, the meaning must be 'wasted [the potential of]', and the change is unnecessary. The concern below (ch. 16. 6) is that Greeks who lost their lives in internecine wars were not available to conquer the barbarians.

5 Ἀγησιλάῳ μέντοι οὐδὲν κρεῖσσον ἢ μεῖζόν ἐστι τῆς ἀναχωρήσεως ἐκείνης διαπεπραγμένον, οὐδὲ γέγονε παράδειγμα πειθαρχίας καὶ δικαιοσύνης ἕτερον κάλλιον.

After his moralizing intervention, Plutarch continues the progression with a comment on Agesilaos' response to the order he has just received. He hints that we have reached the zenith, having just anticipated what will be the nadir, in Leuktra and Mantineia. It is not a simple *peripeteia*, for the traditional Spartan way of life retains Plutarch's admiration. He shows it at its best in the obedience attributed to Agesilaos' Lykourgan upbringing (ch. 1. 4). At *Hell.* iv. 2. 3 Xenophon makes no favourable comment, but expresses Agesilaos' annoyance at the recall. At *Agesilaos*, 1. 36, where Agesilaos' reaction was immediately to obey, he makes extravagant claims of patriotism, loyalty, self-denial, and justice. Plutarch couples justice with obedience, having referred already to the plans that were to be abandoned. For Agesilaos, justice will be defined later as the best interest of Sparta.

6 ὅπου γὰρ Ἀννίβας ἤδη κακῶς πράττων καὶ περιωθούμενος ἐκ τῆς Ἰταλίας μάλα μόλις ὑπήκουσε τοῖς ἐπὶ τὸν οἴκοι πόλεμον καλοῦσιν, Ἀλέξανδρος δὲ καὶ προσεπέσκωψε πυθόμενος τὴν πρὸς Ἆγιν Ἀντιπάτρου μάχην εἰπών, Ἔοικεν, ὦ ἄνδρες, ὅτε Δαρεῖον ἡμεῖς ἐνικῶμεν ἐνταῦθ', ἐκεῖ τις ἐν Ἀρκαδίᾳ γεγονέναι μυομαχία·

Plutarch employs the comparative method (*synkrisis*) with two counter-examples showing Agesilaos' superiority. The distinguishing features are the lack of any prospect of success to be sacrificed by the defeated Hannibal on his recall in 203, and the failure of Alexander to return in 331. The examples exhaust the possibilities: Agesilaos' obedience with sacrifice, Hannibal's obedience without sacrifice, and Alexander's supposed 'disobedience' without sacrifice; disobedience with sacrifice is irrelevant. The anecdote is not included in *Alexander*; Plutarch records there (chs. 11. 4, 14. 1) that Alexander secured mainland Greece before he began his Persian campaign. Ieturn was unnecessary. To his further discredit, he indicates in his jest a cavalier attitude which contrasts with Plutarch's reaction to the Corinthian war (§3).[9]

πῶς οὐκ ἦν ἄξιον τὴν Σπάρτην μακαρίσαι τῆς Ἀγησιλάου τιμῆς πρός τ' αὐτὴν καὶ πρὸς τοὺς νόμους τῆς εὐλαβείας; **7** ὃς ἅμα τῷ τὴν σκυτάλην ἐλθεῖν εὐτυχίαν τοσαύτην καὶ δύναμιν παροῦσαν καὶ τηλικαύτας ἐλπίδας ὑφηγουμένας ἀφεὶς καὶ προέμενος, εὐθὺς ἀπέπλευσεν "ἀτελευτήτῳ ἐπὶ ἔργῳ", πολὺν ἑαυτοῦ πόθον τοῖς συμμάχοις ἀπολιπών, . . .

Plutarch's first phrase recalls Xenophon's tribute at *Agesilaos*, 1. 36. He enlarges upon the two abstract qualities praised in §5, justice and obedience, and expressed now in practical terms, honour for Sparta and respect for law. He records, in context, the hopes that Agesilaos gives up at his departure, whereas Xenophon at this point gives a retrospective account of his achievements.

Both authors continue by recording the allies' attitude to Agesilaos. Xenophon expresses their 'grief', ἐλυποῦντο (*Agesilaos*, 1. 38), and 'tears', ἐδάκρυσαν (*Hell*. iv. 2. 4). Plutarch expresses only their restrained 'regret', for he leaves 'with task unfinished', a literary quotation from *Il*. iv. 175. He marks the fulfilment of the omen at Aulis (ch. 6) and stresses the critical moment with other literary ornaments: a rhetorical question, which contains a chiastic pattern; a complex pattern of paired nouns and participles; and alliteration of *a* and *p*.

. . . καὶ μάλιστα δὴ τὸν Ἐρασιστράτου τοῦ Φαίακος ἐλέγξας λόγον εἰπόντος ὡς εἰσὶ δημοσίᾳ μὲν Λακεδαιμόνιοι βελτίονες, ἰδίᾳ δ' Ἀθηναῖοι. **8** βασιλέα γὰρ ἑαυτὸν καὶ στρατηγὸν ἄριστον ἐπιδειξάμενος, ἔτι βελτίονα καὶ ἡδίονα τοῖς χρωμένοις ἰδίᾳ φίλον καὶ συνήθη παρέσχε.

Plutarch enlarges on the allies' regret and returns to Agesilaos' obedience with another quotation, a saying of Erasistratos (see Introd., F.3(*i*)). He refutes this attack on the general character of the Spartans by giving his judgement, at this stage, of Agesilaos as king, general, friend, and companion, the four categories presented in the programmatic ch. 1. Agesilaos' success in these functions renders the Spartans superior to the Athenians as individuals in private life, and not only in public life as a community (cf. Plato, *Ap*. 30 B: καὶ ἰδίᾳ καὶ δημοσίᾳ), which Erasistratos concedes.

τοῦ δὲ Περσικοῦ νομίσματος χάραγμα τοξότην ἔχοντος, ἀναζευγνύων ἔφη [τρισ]μυρίοις τοξόταις ὑπὸ βασιλέως ἐξελαύνεσθαι τῆς Ἀσίας· τοσούτων γὰρ εἰς Ἀθήνας καὶ Θήβας κομισθέντων καὶ διαδοθέντων τοῖς δημαγωγοῖς ἐξεπολεμώθησαν οἱ δῆμοι πρὸς τοὺς Σπαρτιάτας.

The anecdote,[10] showing Agesilaos' sense of humour, recalls his jesting at ch. 2. 3 (cf. Xen. *Agesilaos*, 8. 2). His claim regarding Persian money refers to one of the alleged antecedents of the war in Greece—the funds sent to the opponents of Sparta (§1)—which led to the order for his recall. Pausanias (iii. 9. 8, iv. 17. 5) speaks of 'failure' to conquer Persia, and mentions the Persian money as a cause of the war, but the Oxyrhynchos historian allows it only minor importance (II. 2, 5).[11] Xenophon makes this money the explanation of the outbreak of war (*Hell*. iii. 5. 1), listing Thebes, Argos, and Corinth as the recipients, but omitting Athens. Plutarch agrees with the Oxyrhynchos historian (II. 2) in including Athens, and he is thought to be right;[12] but he does not follow him in naming Pharnabazos as the Persian benefactor (*Hell. Ox.* II. 5), no doubt regarding the King as the originator of the policy and the source of the money, as he did earlier in the chapter (§1). According to Polyainos it was Konon who persuaded Pharnabazos to send the money to Greece, perhaps while they were both at Rhodes (i. 48. 3). Finally, Xenophon says it was Tithraustes who sent Timokrates with the money, after having replaced Tissaphernes (*Hell.* iii. 5. 1). Either there is confusion here, which also involves the chronology, or Timokrates was perhaps sent on two missions, a year apart, 396 and 395, the second of which led to the outbreak of war.[13] The variations in the lists of recipients, agents, and sources here, and insinuations of Persian bribery, recall recent parallels in which political developments have been attributed to the secret interventions of the intelligence agencies of great powers, including developments that resulted from exploitation of those powers by local politicians and governments for their own partisan advantages.

There is confusion also over the amount of money. Here the manuscripts have 10,000 archers; *Mor.* 211 B and *Artax.* 20. 4 have τρισμυρίοις τοξόταις, the number of Timokrates' gold pieces, Darics; Xenophon has gold to the value of 50 talents of silver (*Hell.* iii. 5. 1). At *An.* 1. 7. 18 Xenophon equates 3,000 Darics with 10 talents, paid in gold, so that 50 talents would be 15,000 Darics; 30,000 Darics would be 100 talents, and the manuscripts' 10,000 would be 33⅓ talents. At the rate of pay of 1 Daric per month (Xen. *An.* i. 3. 21, vii. 6. 1), 100 talents would pay for 30,000 soldiers for a month for the war against Sparta, 10,000 Darics would pay for 10,000 soldiers.

The Budé and Teubner editors accept ⟨τρισ⟩μυρίοις. It may be more likely that τρισ- was omitted than added; perhaps it was a suitably large figure for an anecdotal story at *Mor.* 211 B, corrected here by comparison with Xenophon's sum. Xenophon's figure of 50 talents could be a rounding up of 33⅓ talents, converted from 10,000 Darics.[14] But his figure probably represents correctly the Persian money delivered to the four cities,[15] which would pay 15,000 men for a month. What Agesilaos may have said in Asia and what money was reported to have reached Greece would come from different sources.

There were other 'causes' of the Corinthian war—enmities between the Greek states and discontent over Spartan expansion.[16] The Oxyrhynchos historian (II. 2)[17] asserts, perhaps perceptively, that the main cause was long-standing hostility to Sparta, rather than the money. The occasion for the outbreak of war, and the Persian financial assistance, may have been the perceived Spartan threat in the Hellespontine area (see above, chs. 6 and 12). Plutarch is mainly concerned to explain not the war but Agesilaos'—and his own—resentment against the King of Persia.

The return from Asia Minor

Xen. *Hell.* iv. 3. 1–iv. 4. 1, *Agesilaos*, 2. 1–16, 7. 5; Diod. xiv. 83. 3–84. 2;
Nepos, *Agesilaus*, 4. 5–6, 5. 1; Paus. iii. 9. 12–13, ix. 6. 4; Polyain. ii. 1.
3–5, 19, 23; Frontin. *Strat.* ii. 6. 6.

16. Agesilaos in northern Greece: verbal stratagems backed by force

Prefatory note: the situation in northern Greece

On his return journey in 394 in the context of the Corinthian war
Agesilaos faced the consequences of Spartan military action in
northern Greece over the past hundred years. After the defeat of
Persia, King Latychidas II in 478 led an expedition into Thessaly
against medizers, perhaps the Aleuadai (Hdt. vi. 72. 1; cf. Plataia:
Hdt. vi. 108. 2, Thuc. iii. 68); Spartans hostile to Athens may, just
before the earthquake of 465, secretly have promised Thasos to
invade Attica (Thuc. i. 101);[1] a Spartan colony was founded at
Herakleia (426), and Brasidas operated against Athenian interests
in Thrace; later Agis raised money for a fleet by plundering in the
area of the Malian Gulf (Thuc. iii. 92; iv. 78, 102; viii. 3. 1). In an
attempt, apparently, to encircle Thebes in Boiotia between 405
and 400, Spartans were in action in Thrace, Chalkidike, Larissa,
Pharsalos, Pherai, Herakleia, and perhaps Thasos (*Lys.* 16. 1, 19.
2, 20. 5; Diod. xiv. 38. 3–4, 82).[2] Early in the fourth century
Derkylidas protected eleven towns from Thracian neighbours
with a wall across the Chersonese (Xen. *Hell.* iii. 2. 2, 11–12).

These activities made few friends for Sparta. Diodoros records
Sparta's loss of influence in many areas (xiv. 81. 2–83. 2):
Lysander's death at Haliartos, the alliance of Boiotians,
Athenians, Corinthians, and Argives, the Council of Corinth in
395, and the recruiting of members—the Chalkidians of Thrace—
from among the allies of the Lakedaimonians. This situation, with
troops gathered in Corinth, leads to the recall of Agesilaos (xiv.
83. 1). Diodoros' readers are not surprised that he met opposition.

Xenophon says only that the largest cities had united against Sparta (*Hell.* iv. 2. 1). Plutarch leaves the hostility unexplained.

1 Ὡς δὲ διαβὰς τὸν Ἑλλήσποντον ἐβάδιζε διὰ τῆς Θρᾴκης, ἐδεήθη μὲν οὐδενὸς τῶν βαρβάρων, πέμπων δὲ πρὸς ἑκάστους ἐπυνθάνετο πότερον ὡς φιλίαν ἢ ὡς πολεμίαν διαπορεύηται τὴν χώραν.³

Xenophon reports the declaration of war at *Hell.* iv. 2. 9 but does not record any hostility in northern Greece. Although according to Plutarch he returned with Agesilaos from the east (ch. 18. 2), he omits detailed reference to his route from the Hellespont through Thrace, perhaps because he considered the journey uneventful. He first reports that at Amphipolis Agesilaos received news from Derkylidas of the Spartans' victory at the River Nemea, and then, passing through Makedon, reached Thessaly (*Hell.* iv. 3. 1–3). Plutarch makes no comment about Greek cities in the northern area, which may suggest that Agesilaos followed a route largely avoiding them, but his reference to 'barbarians' sufficiently prepares the reader to expect a hostile reception here for the Greeks. Perhaps Agesilaos took one of the inland routes to Amphipolis: his question implies confidence that he could cope with both peace and war, again indicating that he expected no major confrontation.

The chapter contains a rhetorical series of six cases, in two sets of three (*Mor.* 211 C–F), illustrating Agesilaos' wit, laconic brevity, confidence, and bluff. His question is asked in the first three cases, where there is no initial state of conflict and peaceful passage is possible, but it is not asked in the second part of the journey, where Agesilaos faces allies of Sparta's enemies already committed, as he would learn from Derkylidas at Amphipolis (Xen. *Hell.* iv. 3. 1). Either a peaceful passage or an enforced passage ensues, resulting from the three possibilities: diplomatic agreement, resistance, aggression.

The first three cases in the order peaceful, enforced, peaceful, and the second three in reverse order, enforced, peaceful, enforced, make two chiastic patterns. In the first, two peaceful passages through Thrace and Makedon represent Agesilaos' diplomatic successes, contrasting his diplomatic failure, which these frame—the violent action against the Tralleis. In the two contested passages of the second pattern, through Thessaly, Agesilaos is at first the aggressor, contrasting the final conflict, started by his opponents, the Pharsalians. These frame the peaceful passage under the truce with the Larissaians. The first case in each series is given without complications, in a general form, setting a standard for the following contrasted pairs of consequences, in which peace can be broken or maintained, violence can be avoided or resumed. Agesilaos takes appropriate action, and achieves his desired passage in all possible situations. Rhetorical arrangement may have played a large part in portraying the complete range of Agesilaos' leadership, celebrated finally with the trophy at Narthakion.

2 οἱ μὲν οὖν ἄλλοι πάντες φιλικῶς ἐδέχοντο καὶ παρέπεμπον, ὡς ἕκαστος δυνάμεως εἶχεν· οἱ δὲ καλούμενοι Τράλλεις, οἷς καὶ Ξέρξης ἔδωκεν, ὡς λέγεται, δῶρα, τῆς διόδου μισθὸν ᾔτουν τὸν Ἀγησίλαον ἑκατὸν ἀργυρίου τάλαντα καὶ τοσαύτας γυναῖκας.

Plutarch briefly records the first of the responses, freely granting a friendly passage but allowing for differences according to the resources of each city. He alone records the Tralleis, their demands, and Xerxes' gifts, detailed circumstantial evidence that is not in Xenophon, but he leaves it incomplete and uncertain. 'As reported' (ὡς λέγεται), used when he does not mention his source, perhaps extends the uncertainty to the name of the people.[4]

Agesilaos is confident in his military superiority, unlike Xerxes, who resorted to bribery. Plutarch may have been reminded of Xerxes by Xenophon's statement that Agesilaos was travelling the same route as the King (*Hell.* iv. 2. 8, *Agesilaos*, 2. 1). He preserves details otherwise unknown, perhaps from northern sources: the women, not mentioned elsewhere, were no doubt part of the collected booty.

3 ὁ δὲ κατειρωνευσάμενος αὐτοὺς καὶ φήσας· Τί οὖν οὐκ εὐθὺς ἦλθον ληψόμενοι; προῆγε, καὶ συμβαλὼν αὐτοῖς παρατεταγμένοις ἐτρέψατο καὶ διέφθειρε πολλούς.

The refusal of unconditional peaceful passage by this tribe elicits from Agesilaos a suitable rhetorical challenge, suggesting that they should have attacked him even before receiving his message, εὐθὺς, 'immediately', and should have taken the payment without even asking for it. Plutarch, here and in two cases following, uses direct speech to allow readers to see for themselves the audacious, quick-witted, and humane Agesilaos in action. His aggression corresponds to the second of the two possibilities anticipated in the list, 'as enemy territory'.

The Thasians of this area are named at *Mor.* 210 B–C, which attributes to them the episode recorded by Plutarch at ch. 36, in which Agesilaos rejects gifts offered by the Egyptians (cf. Nepos, *Agesilaus*, 8. 3). The following anecdote (*Mor.* 210 D) uniquely recounts his rejection also of the Thasians' offer of divine honours. This offer is of doubtful authenticity, but it has also been accepted and placed in 394.[5] As a Greek colony Thasos belongs neither with the 'barbarians' in Thrace nor with their neighbours the Makedonians: Agesilaos was in too much of a hurry to reach home to deal with problems which might have led to the honour.

Neither Xenophon nor Plutarch here mentions the rejection of divine honours, although it would be highly appropriate in the list of his virtues in Xenophon's *Agesilaos*, and in ch. 19 below, where the adverse effect on him of travel abroad is discounted. Omission by Xenophon of an event is not proof of his ignorance of it.[6] The name at *Mor.* 210 B–C is not secure and there may be positive grounds for accepting that it belongs to the Egyptian campaign (see ch. 36). The rejection of deification may echo the rejection of a statue (ch. 2. 4; Xen. *Agesilaos*, 11. 7).

4 τὸ δ' αὐτὸ καὶ τῷ βασιλεῖ τῶν Μακεδόνων ἐρώτημα προσέπεμψε· φήσαντος δὲ βουλεύσεσθαι, Βουλευέσθω τοίνυν ἐκεῖνος, εἶπεν, ἡμεῖς δ' ἤδη πορευώμεθα. θαυμάσας οὖν τὴν τόλμαν αὐτοῦ καὶ δείσας ὁ βασιλεὺς ἐκέλευσεν ὡς φίλον προάγειν.

Makedon at this time (July 394, shortly before the eclipse of 14 August; see below, ch. 17. 4) suffered from internal and external upsets. King Archelaos (d. 400/399) was succeeded by the boy Orestes, whose guardian, Aeropos, murdered him and reigned for six years (Diod. xiv. 37. 5–7; cf. Arist. *Pol.* 1311ᵇ8–20). His successor, Pausanias, was assassinated after a year by Amyntas (III) (Diod. xiv. 84. 6, 89. 2). A summary of Makedonian kings (Eusebios, i. 227)[7] places another Amyntas (II) (μικρός, 'Little', Arist. *Pol.* 1311ᵇ3) between Aeropos and Pausanias. Greek chronologies were not uniform and did not coincide, making it difficult to reconcile Makedonian and other cities' records, and by inclusive counting—taking a period of twelve months—the year 394/3 saw four kings.[8] The biographer leaves the king in this confrontation unnamed but he may be identified if he is the one referred to by Polyainos, who records that Agesilaos obtained an agreed passage through Makedon by bluffing the king, Aeropos, into thinking that he had a large cavalry force by placing it behind his infantry in two lines, mixed with asses, mules and packhorses (ii. 1. 17).

The second country, Makedon, opens a third possible response, neither granting nor refusing passage. Again the failure to offer unconditional passage elicits a rhetorical challenge. Agesilaos' reputation is shown to be formidable. This second peaceful passage corresponds to the first of the possibilities listed, but safe passage is exacted by firmness, not freely granted. The two exacted passages are linked by the repetition of the verb 'lead on' (προῆγε, προάγειν).

5 τῶν δὲ Θετταλῶν τοῖς πολεμίοις συμμαχούντων ἐπόρθει τὴν χώραν.

Plutarch here apparently attributes to Agesilaos knowledge of the alliances of the Council of Corinth, the foundation of which was mentioned by Diodoros but ignored by Xenophon, who, however, shows that Agesilaos had an opportunity of being briefed by Derkylidas at Amphipolis. The already existing state of hostility brings a new approach by Agesilaos, and new responses from the peoples he met, although, since Xenophon does not list Thessalians among the forces at the Nemea, there evidently was not open war in the area. As Thucydides pointed out, 'It was never easy to go through Thessaly unescorted and of course with an army it was harder still' (iv. 78. 2). Here, appropriately, there is no preliminary enquiry, only immediate and aggressive plundering. Xenophon, on the other hand, attributes the first—and repeated—aggression to the four named Thessalian cities, Larissa, Krannon, Skotoussa, and Pharsalos (*Hell.* iv. 3. 3). These 'allies' could only protect their own property: to prevent Agesilaos reaching their enemies would require support from the Council of Corinth, but after the battle of the River Nemea this was not readily available. The existence of several passes through the mountains, which explains the past medizing, would make it difficult to stop Agesilaos completely.

εἰς δὲ Λάρισσαν ἔπεμψε Ξενοκλέα καὶ Σκύθην περὶ φιλίας· συλληφθέντων δὲ τούτων καὶ παραφυλασσομένων, οἱ μὲν ἄλλοι βαρέως φέροντες ᾤοντο δεῖν τὸν Ἀγησίλαον περιστρατοπεδεύσαντα πολιορκεῖν τὴν Λάρισσαν, ὁ δὲ φήσας οὐκ ἂν ἐθελῆσαι Θεσσαλίαν ὅλην λαβεῖν ἀπολέσας τῶν ἀνδρῶν τὸν ἕτερον, ὑποσπόνδους αὐτοὺς ἀπέλαβε.

Agesilaos' second reaction in hostile territory is to negotiate an unopposed way past Larissa. Diodoros records the beginning of the Corinthian—he says Boiotian—war at Haliartos (396) and the withdrawal of Sparta's allies in the north. Medios of Larissa seized Pharsalos, with its garrison of Lakedaimonians. The Boiotians and Argives then took Herakleia in Trachis, killing the Lakedaimonians there, and restoring the Trachinians they had banished. Ismenias the Theban won over the Ainianes and Athamanes further north, and together the allies defeated the Phokians, with their Lakonian commander Alkisthenes, and slew nearly 1,000 (Diod. xiv. 81. 1–2, 83. 2).

Agesilaos' negotiations were unsuccessful, in contrast to his previous belligerence. The seizure of the envoys, Xenokles and Skythes,[9] as hostages indicates the underlying potential for hostilities. Neither Xenophon (*Hell.* iv. 3. 3) nor Diodoros (xiv. 83. 3) mentions this incident, but Xenophon records that Xenokles commanded the cavalry in Asia (*Hell.* iii. 4. 20), and, according to Diodoros (xiv. 80. 2) and the Oxyrhynchos historian (VI. 4–5),[10] a man of that name led the ambushers at Sardis (see above, pp. 167–9). Skythes was commander of the Neodamodeis in Asia (*Hell.* iii. 4. 20). His name may mark a family connection (*xenia*) with Scythia, where Skythes, son of Herakles, founded a Heraklid dynasty (Hdt. iv. 10. 1–3). Other Spartans are named Knidis (d. 420/19: Thuc. v. 51. 2); Boiotios (an envoy to the King, 409/8: *Hell.* i. 4. 2); Samios (two: Hdt. iii. 55. 2; *Hell.* iii. 1. 1–2; 'Samos' at Diod. xiv. 19. 4–5); Libys, Lysander's brother (Diod. xiv. 13. 6); and Thessalos (d. c.510: Hdt. v. 46).[11] Spartan aristocrats had a special relationship with Samos;[12] Archias (d. 525), great-grandfather of Samios, *nauarchos* in 401, was perhaps a self-appointed ἐθελοπρόξενος.[13]

The advisers' suggestion of violent action, juxtaposed with the violence of the Larissaians, is framed by Agesilaos' non-violence before and after, in a chiastic pattern. The capture of the town would have been a blow to the anti-Spartan alliance, but Agesilaos had not been successful in besieging cities in Asia, and delay would be unwelcome. Agesilaos rejects the suggestion, unwilling to risk the envoys' lives, and the truce shows a willingness on the part of the Thessalians, too, to keep a low profile. The agreement may have guaranteed unobstructed passage in return for ending the plundering which marked the early stage. If the envoys were held as hostages for a time, they and the Thessalian escort would ensure freedom from incident.

6 καὶ τοῦτ' ἴσως ἐπ' Ἀγησιλάῳ θαυμαστὸν οὐκ ἦν, ὃς πυθόμενος μάχην μεγάλην γεγονέναι περὶ Κόρινθον καὶ ἄνδρας τῶν πάνυ ἐνδόξων ὡς ἔνι μάλιστ' αἰφνίδιον ἀπολωλέναι καὶ Σπαρτιατῶν μὲν ὀλίγους παντάπασι τεθνηκέναι, παμπόλλους δὲ τῶν πολεμίων, οὐκ ὤφθη περιχαρὴς οὐδ' ἐπηρμένος, ἀλλὰ καὶ πάνυ βαρὺ στενάξας, Φεῦ τῆς Ἑλλάδος, ἔφη, τοσούτους ἄνδρας ἀπολωλεκυίας ὑφ' αὐτῆς, ὅσοι ζῶντες ἐδύναντο νικᾶν ὁμοῦ σύμπαντας τοὺς βαρβάρους μαχόμενοι.

Plutarch takes Agesilaos' respect for life further. The series of encounters is interrupted by his reaction to news of the battle fought near the Nemea, which took place before Agesilaos reached Greece. In Xenophon's account (*Hell.* iv. 3. 1–3) he received the report at Amphipolis and transmitted it to Asia without drawing any moral. Xenophon excludes the battle from the chronological narrative of *Agesilaos*, 2, reserving it for separate mention, without naming Amphipolis, at 7. 5 where he links Agesilaos' humane character with extreme anti-Persian sentiment; there is no joy over the Spartan victory, only sadness at the loss to Greece of men sufficient to defeat all the barbarians. Plutarch, too, takes the story out of its context at Amphipolis, which he also does not name, and uses it to reinforce the humanity displayed by Agesilaos in preserving the envoys' lives (§5).[14] He retains some of the wording in Xenophon's *Agesilaos*, but he also credits Agesilaos with other feelings which he evidently shares with regard to the heavy casualties on the side of Sparta's enemies: where Xenophon gives numbers of dead, Plutarch speaks of their glory, the suddenness of their loss, the internecine war, and Agesilaos' deep groan. He preserves the link with panhellenism and the exclamation which emphasizes the sentiments that follow (cf. ch. 15. 3 above), but he adds 'all together' (ὁμοῦ), as if contemplating victory in a single battle. The episode ends with words spoken by Agesilaos (cf. ch. 9. 8 above).

7 τῶν δὲ Φαρσαλίων προσκειμένων αὐτῷ καὶ κακούντων τὸ στράτευμα, πεντακοσίοις ἱππεῦσιν ἐμβαλεῖν κελεύσας σὺν αὐτῷ καὶ τρεψάμενος ἔστησε τρόπαιον ὑπὸ τῷ Ναρθακίῳ.

Plutarch resumes his account of the march, which at this point seems to be diverging again (§1) from Xerxes' coastal route to Halos (Hdt. vii. 197. 1), to pass over the Achaian mountains and on towards the Boiotian border. He gives the impression that the harassment was a new development, initiated by the Pharsalians: Xenophon says the four Thessalian cities (above, §5) attacked continually, though, even there, the culmination is a confrontation in lines of battle in which only Polycharmos and his Pharsalian cavalry are prominent. It is not clear whether the Pharsalians or Agesilaos intended a last-minute demonstration of strength before he reached the border, but Xenophon indicates a positive Spartan effort in using all reserves of cavalry to force the retreat, after the Thessalians had shown hesitation in engaging in battle with cavalry against hoplites (*Hell*. iv. 3. 5; cf. ch. 10. 3).

In Xenophon's account of Agesilaos' response to the harassment (*Hell*. iv. 3. 4–8), he committed the vanguard of his cavalry alone, and only later also his specialist escort, but there is no suggestion that Agesilaos went with them. Polycharmos, the Pharsalian leader, fell fighting with his troopers. Plutarch seems to suggest that Agesilaos, too, led his horsemen in person, whether creating an illustration of his personal courage, or misinterpreting Xenophon.

8 καὶ τὴν νίκην ὑπερηγάπησεν ἐκείνην, ὅτι συστησάμενος ἱππικὸν αὐτὸς δι᾽ ἑαυτοῦ, τούτῳ μόνῳ τοὺς μέγιστον ἐφ᾽ ἱππικῇ φρονοῦντας ἐκράτησεν.

The incident at the end of the series of events in Thessaly, like the previous one, leads to a comment on an aspect of Agesilaos' character: his reaction to the battle. Xenophon has given a detailed description of this engagement (*Hell*. iv. 3. 4–8), although it was not a significant event and would hardly merit attention for its own sake. The obvious reason for its prominence in *Hellenika* is Agesilaos' use of cavalry, which demonstrates the value of its formation in Asia Minor (*Hell*. iv. 3. 9)—perhaps, it may be conjectured, under the supervision at Ephesos of Xenophon, himself a cavalry expert (*Hell*. iii. 4. 15). Plutarch's description at §7 is compact, using four participles for the whole action, but he involves the cavalry, so that, like Xenophon, he may record Agesilaos' delight in the victory which it achieved. The report of Agesilaos' own words forms the conclusion.

The topography of the march and the battle of Narthakion

At the Hellespont, Xenophon defines Agesilaos' route as that taken by Xerxes (*Hell*. iv. 2. 8, *Agesilaos*, 2. 1; for the crossing see Hdt. vii. 55. 1). He mentions Amphipolis where Derkylidas meets him with the news of the Spartans' victory near the Nemea, and then reports that Agesilaos crossed Makedon into Thessaly (Xen. *Hell*. iv. 3. 3). Entry into Thessaly may have been through Tempe (Hdt. vii. 128).[15] Diodoros devotes three sentences to this part of Agesilaos' journey, mentioning opposition in Thrace and the march through Makedon, Thessaly, and the pass of Thermopylai (xiv. 83. 3–4). Then there is a lacuna in the text.

According to Plutarch, Agesilaos made an arrangement with the Thessalian cities (above, §5) to pass through their lands, while they perhaps held his ambassadors as hostages. This allowed a mainly peaceful passage to Pharsalos, for which both sides were likely to prefer the direct route, and minimum expenditure of supplies and time. The plain of Pharsalos offers ground suitable for the operation of cavalry. Another route to the east of the four towns[16] involves a detour and hilly territory less suitable for the square formation mentioned by Xenophon (*Hell*. iv. 3. 4), and also passes the powerful city of Pherai, which Xenophon does not mention.

Although topographical details are often obscure in literature, accurate information was necessarily available to Spartans like Brasidas (Thuc. iv. 78) operating in these areas and it would be kept up to date by those on duty in the garrisons established there. Xenophon reports briefly that Agesilaos led his army through Thessaly in hollow square formation until lines were drawn up for battle (*Agesilaos*, 2. 2–3; *Hell*. iv. 3. 4–9). He gives it no precise location, but it was fought against a Thessalian force in which the commander of the Pharsalian cavalry, Polycharmos, was alone prominent. The Thessalians, defeated by Agesilaos' cavalry, eventually retreated into Mt Narthakion. Agesilaos set up a trophy of victory between there and Pras, and remained on the site with relish. On the next day he crossed the Achaian mountains of Phthia into friendly territory. The boundary between Thessaly and Achaia Phthiotis was formed by the River Enipeus near Meliteia,[17] and Sparta's friends may be identified as those nearby cities that sent men to Lysander at Haliartos: Oitaians,

Herakleians, Malians, and Ainianes (Xen. *Hell.* iii. 5. 6), though the last two later became allies of the Boiotians (*Hell.* iv. 2. 17, 3. 15).

An appropriate route south for Agesilaos if he passed west of Pharsalos, skirts the plain of Pharsalos close by the foothills on its eastern boundary, passing, for example, Brysia, whose name indicates the available water-supply, on the way to modern Domokos and Lamia. This was on the normal route between the lower Spercheios valley and Thessaly, passing Meliteia, Lake Xynias, Thaumakoi, and Pharsalos,[18] and, while certainty is impossible, may best be assumed for Agesilaos. It passes west of Mt Narthakion, which has been put immediately south of Pharsalos.[19] The slopes of the foothills near Pharsalos on the south-west side of the town present no obvious difficulties to hinder the initial stages of the Thessalians' flight, in which they did not stop until they reached Mt Narthakion (Xen. *Hell.* iv. 3. 8). The hills soon give what should be adequate protection from further pursuit, without the need for deep penetration. There seems to be no topographical objection to this site.

However, an inscription referring to archons of Narthakion was reported in 1882 to have been found incorporated in the chapel of St John at a short distance from Limogardi.[20] The towns of Narthakion and Pras were accordingly resited much further south than the foothills near Pharsalos, and slightly to the east, at Limogardi and Divri, on the south side of the mountain range named Othrys which forms the northern border of the plain of Lamia.[21] This position of Narthakion, the town and the mountain, seems to have been adopted ever since—except in the maps of ESYE (1963/1972) and Koder and Hild (1976).

Even if the inscription proves the site of a town of Narthakion, it cannot determine the position of Xenophon's mountain and battle, which should be inside the territorial interests that the men of Pharsalos would be concerned to defend: they would not wish to cross mountains before the battle, exposing themselves to a long and difficult march home and an insecure line of retreat, just when the enemy they were shadowing was leaving their territory.

On the day after the battle and the erection of the trophy, Agesilaos crossed the Achaian mountains of Phthia and marched through friendly territory to Boiotia (Xen. *Hell.* iv. 3. 9).[22] Yet, in the atlases that show the Narthakion of the battle and the Pras of the trophy near Limogardi and Divri on the southern slopes of the range, the Achaian mountains are shown to the north and would have to be crossed *before* the battle. There can be no doubt that Xenophon, who mentions the area several times in *Hellenika* (i. 2. 18, vi. 4. 28, 33), puts the battle to the north of the Achaian mountains, not to the south.

The march across these mountains on the day after the battle, starting nearer Pharsalos at the southern end of the plain—a straight line of about 20 to 25 km. (about 15 miles)—seems to be well within Agesilaos' capabilities.[23]

17. To the Boiotian border

1 Ἐνταῦθα Διφρίδας οἴκοθεν ἔφορος ὢν ἀπήντησεν αὐτῷ, κελεύων εὐθὺς ἐμβαλεῖν εἰς τὴν Βοιωτίαν.

In ch. 15 the ephors sent Epikydidas, described simply as 'the Spartiate', with their instructions for the recall of Agesilaos from Asia Minor (Xen. *Hell.* iv. 2. 2, cf. iii. 2. 12). Apart from the greater distance, Asia Minor would involve travel outside mainland Greece, taking an ephor beyond the sphere of his duties. Here the ephor Diphridas (cf. Xen. *Hell.* iv. 8. 21) made the shorter journey from Sparta. If he met Agesilaos at the southern border of Thessaly, he will have avoided enemy territory in Boiotia by crossing the Gulf of Corinth and using the pass via Amphissa to Gravia. The order to invade Boiotia does not come as a surprise, for Plutarch explained the outbreak of the war at ch. 15, and in ch. 16, after leaving Larissa, Agesilaos spoke of the casualties in the battle at the River Nemea ('fought near Corinth'). Xenophon does not say that Agesilaos was ordered to invade Boiotia: he was given information, when Derkylidas met him at Amphipolis (Xen. *Hell.* iv. 3. 1), but Diphridas and his instructions are not mentioned. His narrative suggests that it was the normal route for Agesilaos to be following that brought him to the Boiotian border (*Hell.* iv. 3. 9–10, 15). Xenophon (*Hell.* iii. 5. 3–4) and the Oxyrhynchos historian (XIII. 2–5)[1] give adequate notice of hostilities in Boiotia, and describe in detail how the anti-Spartan Thebans engineered a dispute between Lokris and Phokis in which the Lokrians appealed to Thebes for help and the Phokians to Sparta (cf. Diod. xiv. 81. 1, 82. 6–10).

2 ὁ δέ, καίπερ ἀπὸ μείζονος παρασκευῆς ὕστερον τοῦτο ποιῆσαι διανοούμενος, οὐδὲν ᾤετο δεῖν ἀπειθεῖν τοῖς ἄρχουσιν, ἀλλὰ τοῖς τε μεθ᾽ ἑαυτοῦ προεῖπεν ἐγγὺς εἶναι τὴν ἡμέραν ἐφ᾽ ἣν ἐξ Ἀσίας ἥκουσι, καὶ δύο μόρας μετεπέμψατο τῶν περὶ Κόρινθον στρατευομένων.

We do not hear of this prior intention to invade Boiotia anywhere else, but it is a reasonable assumption, considering the route Agesilaos was taking and the advantage of opening a second front in the north to relieve pressure on the Spartans at the Isthmus. Any reinforcements from Corinth that Agesilaos had intended to wait for would have been sent across the Gulf, as would those he now requested. The obedience of Agesilaos to the commands of the ephors is illustrated for the second time. 'Those with him' are probably the advisers, not the whole army: it is too early for the pre-battle exhortation, but not for a high-level briefing in preparation for the important engagement in view. At *Agesilaos*, 2. 6 Xenophon claims that Agesilaos drew up his army for battle without delay, but Plutarch turns to *Hellenika*, iv. 3. 15, where the Spartans transferred to Agesilaos one unit (μόρα) from Corinth, and half a unit from the garrison at Orchomenos, which had been there perhaps since Lysander had caused the city to revolt from Thebes before Haliartos. Plutarch's report of two μόραι seems to be a mistake.

3 οἱ δ᾽ ἐν τῇ πόλει Λακεδαιμόνιοι τιμῶντες αὐτὸν ἐκήρυξαν τῶν νέων ἀπογράφεσθαι τὸν βουλόμενον τῷ βασιλεῖ βοηθεῖν. ἀπογραψαμένων δὲ πάντων προθύμως, οἱ ἄρχοντες πεντήκοντα τοὺς ἀκμαιοτάτους καὶ ῥωμαλεωτάτους ἐκλέξαντες ἀπέστειλαν.

Voluntary enlistment or participation in a campaign 'in the ranks' is not the same as the voluntary service of a mercenary, or of the officers who had served with Kyros. The call for volunteers is strange, and would not fit in with the normal call-up procedure with which the war had begun (Xen. *Hell.* iii. 5. 6), even if there had been a partial stand-down after the River Nemea, though none is mentioned by Xenophon (*Hell.* iv. 2. 23). The size of the contingent is significant. Spartiates were usually sent out in small numbers: a commander—Gylippos to Syracuse; or an advisory board—with Agesilaos to Asia. Most of the troops were usually

Peloponnesians or emancipated Helots (Xen. *Hell*. iii. 1. 4, iii. 4. 2, iv. 3. 15).[2] Plutarch assigns these fifty volunteers to Agesilaos' bodyguard (ch. 18. 5). They could be a detachment of the unmounted knights, the Hippeis (*Lak. Pol*. 4. 4).[3] Their presence would honour Agesilaos and would also, perhaps, be a practical recognition of the need to increase the proportion of Spartiates in the force, which was now about to face formidable opponents. A call for volunteers from the 300 young Hippeis followed by selection of the fifty most suitable (for ῥωμαλεώτατος, 'full of vigour', cf. *C. Gracch*. 4. 1, Hdt. iii. 22. 2), keeping the rest at home, makes more sense than selection by 'age-classes' for this purpose.

4 ὁ δ' Ἀγησίλαος εἴσω Πυλῶν παρελθὼν καὶ διοδεύσας τὴν Φωκίδα φίλην οὖσαν, . . .

Since the Lokrian tribes are among the listed allies of Thebes, the route followed may not have taken Agesilaos through Thermopylai into Lokris.[4] After Koroneia, Gylis withdrew the army into Phokis and from there invaded Lokris (Xen. *Hell*. iv. 3. 21), which was no place for casual entry, for Gylis was killed in the fighting there. After the crossing of the Hellespont, Xenophon says that Agesilaos was following the same route as Xerxes, but this need not include Thermopylai, which he does not mention, for he is only contrasting the two armies' rates of progress (*Agesilaos*, 2. 1; cf. *Hell*. iv. 2. 8). Although in Diodoros, as in Plutarch, the route passes through Thermopylai, they do not mention Xerxes at the point when Agesilaos crossed the Hellespont, but only later as he crosses Makedon and Thessaly (xiv. 83. 4). Xenophon's reference to Xerxes' route might suggest including Thermopylai, and if mention of Xerxes is postponed until later, as in Diodoros' version, then Thermopylai will be in mind; it would be natural for a later writer to mention another famous name, just as Xenophon mentions Xerxes. But Xenophon, without naming Phokis, says that Agesilaos' route was through friendly territory until he reached Boiotia (*Hell*. iv. 3. 9), where the allies were drawn up, and it may be that he avoided Lokris.

Plutarch presumably knew the area well, living at Chaironeia, and may have added the famous site independently of Xenophon, or from another source. Spartans, too, would accumulate topographical knowledge of the area when on garrison duty in the colony they had established at Herakleia in 426 (Thuc. iii. 92. 1), and subsequently when Herippidas was sent there in 400 (Diod. xiv. 38. 4).[5] From Narthakion the direct route to Boiotia goes south, using the Asopos valley where the pass rises to less than 600 m. In Herodotos, after the battle of Thermopylai, Xerxes' main army marched through Trachis, Doris, and Phokis:[6] Doris was regarded as the early home of the Dorians (viii. 31). Even if Agesilaos turned east for Thermopylai, he would still, of course, avoid most of Lokris by using a south-westerly route from Thermopylai through one of several passes over the mountains. Either way he would have a mountain range to cross before reaching the Kephisos valley.

. . . ἐπεὶ τῆς Βοιωτίας πρῶτον ἐπέβη καὶ περὶ τὴν Χαιρώνειαν κατεστρατοπέδευσεν, ἅμα μὲν τὸν ἥλιον ἐκλείποντα καὶ γινόμενον μηνοειδῆ κατεῖδεν, ἅμα δ᾽ ἤκουσε τεθνάναι Πείσανδρον ἡττημένον ναυμαχίᾳ περὶ Κνίδον ὑπὸ Φαρναβάζου καὶ Κόνωνος.

Plutarch takes the opportunity to mention his home town, not named elsewhere at this point; perhaps it was a piece of history locally preserved. While Xenophon briefly reports the sun's crescent-shaped appearance (*Hell.* iv. 3. 10), Plutarch makes more of it: he creates a chiastic pattern of nouns and participles by adding the technical 'eclipsed', ἐκλείποντα; and by saying that Agesilaos himself both saw the eclipse and heard about Peisandros' death and the defeat of the fleet—Xenophon puts the defeat first—implies that the eclipse (of 14 August 394) was an omen for him. He emphasizes the coincidence with the repeated ἅμα, 'at the same time', and, omitting with laconic brevity Peisandros' rank, places the effective word, the infinitive, first, and withholds the full impact and significance until the name. The gods apparently timed the sign in heaven to suit the announcement on earth. The announcement of the disaster to the *mora* from Lechaion is similarly coincident (ch. 22. 3).

Diodoros, who reports the battle at xiv. 83. 4–7, shows that Peisandros battled in a way worthy of Sparta, though when Plutarch and Xenophon reported Agesilaos' appointment of his young and inexperienced brother-in-law as admiral in Asia Minor, both seemed, with hindsight, to doubt his wisdom (ch. 10. 11; *Hell.* iii. 4. 29, iv. 3. 11–12; cf. iv. 8. 1).[7]

Pharnabazos was pro-Lakonian (Xen. *Hell.* i. 4. 5–7), but lost nine cities in Aiolis to Derkylidas in eight days (*Hell.* iii. 2. 1): he was not so dissatisfied with his appointment as admiral that he left the King's service after meeting Agesilaos (cf. ch. 12. 8; *Hell.* iv. 1. 37).

5 ἠχθέσθη μὲν οὖν, ὡς εἰκός, ἐπὶ τούτοις καὶ διὰ τὸν ἄνδρα καὶ διὰ τὴν πόλιν, ὅπως δὲ μὴ τοῖς στρατιώταις ἐπὶ μάχην βαδίζουσιν ἀθυμία καὶ φόβος ἐμπέσῃ, τἀναντία λέγειν ἐκέλευσε τοὺς ἀπὸ θαλάττης ἥκοντας, ὅτι νικῶσι τῇ ναυμαχίᾳ.

Agesilaos' personal distress, not mentioned by Xenophon, is prominently stated first here, both as private grief for his wife's brother, and as concern for the city for which it meant the loss of a valuable young admiral of aristocratic rank. Plutarch is thus establishing Agesilaos' humane character before he goes on to what might otherwise be the unfeeling concealment of the news.

Xenophon has Agesilaos himself make the 'false announcement', ψευδαγγελία, which in Plutarch the messengers are ordered to do. He exploits a regular stratagem, a *salubre mendacium*, 'a beneficial lie', to deceive his own men, as Eteonikos had done after the Spartan defeat at Arginousai (Xen. *Hell.* i. 6. 36).[8] Neither Plutarch nor Xenophon comments on the morality or ingenuity of this action, or even on the risk of divine displeasure incurred in offering thanks to the gods as if for good news, despite the Spartans' strong sense of religious guilt[9] (see below, ch. 30. 1). At *Hipparchikos*, 5. 8 Xenophon recommends the commander to deceive the enemy with false announcements, though he does not say he should deceive his own men, and warns him to work 'with the god' (5. 14). He seems to approve the suggestion of Socrates that a general's falsification of reports of defeat is just (*Mem.* iv. 2. 17). On this occasion, too, he seems to approve, for he attributes success in a skirmish to the ploy. There are no reports of displeasure shown by the gods, and this may have satisfied Plutarch.

It was now impossible for Agesilaos to entertain, or profess to his friends from Asia Minor, any hope of resuming his campaign there.[10] One might expect the truth perhaps to have been withheld temporarily until after the battle, so that the troops would not be depressed, and also to avoid a mass desertion of the contingent that had accompanied Agesilaos from Asia Minor on the wave of enthusiasm following the promise of his return (*Hell.* iv. 2. 3–4): this may have included some of the Ten Thousand (Xen. *An.* vii. 8, Diod. xiv. 37. 4). The deception of his troops in this way was dangerous, but the arrival of the messengers by sea, perhaps difficult to hide, may have raised expectations of a statement. Agesilaos took a risk, and no doubt the troops from mainland Greece would see the justification in the light of the outcome.

καὶ προελθὼν αὐτὸς ἐστεφανωμένος ἔθυσεν εὐαγγέλια καὶ διέπεμπε μερίδας τοῖς φίλοις ἀπὸ τῶν τεθυμένων.

The irony of offering sacrifice for 'good news' (εὐαγγέλια) after perpetrating ψευδαγγελία must be very close to the surface, though not explicit, and the friends who received portions of the meat may have felt uncomfortable at having participated in this way, in case the gods were offended by being made accomplices in the deception. Agesilaos' involvement of the gods, comparable with Tissaphernes' perjury, goes without comment and the criticism made of Agesilaos' attitude to strict justice in ch. 13. 5 (cf. ch. 23. 9) is not repeated.

18. Koroneia: a disputed victory

Xen. *Hell.* iv. 3. 15–19, *Agesilaos*, 2. 9–12;[1] Diod. xiv. 84. 1–2; Paus. iii. 9. 13, ix. 6. 4; Polyain. ii. 1. 19; Nepos, *Agesilaus*, 4. 5–6; Just. vi. 4. 13; Frontin. *Strat.* ii. 6. 6.

Ancient Koroneia, near which the Thebans made their base, was at the south-eastern end of Mt Helikon, on a low hill overlooking to the east and north the south-western part of the Kopaic basin.[2] The shore of the then Lake Kopais was close to a spur of the Helikon range, creating a narrow gap suitable for the Boiotian attempt to block Agesilaos' progress towards Thebes. Beyond it there is no serious natural obstacle to the invader wishing to threaten Thebes. The Thebans, therefore, were involved in the vital defence of their homeland, and no doubt were at full strength, although, despite the silence of the authorities on this point, some troops may well have been stationed in the gap to offer a further barrier, for the gap was not attacked.

1 Ἐπεὶ δὲ προϊὼν καὶ γενόμενος ἐν Κορωνείᾳ κατεῖδε τοὺς πολεμίους καὶ κατώφθη, παρετάξατο, δοὺς Ὀρχομενίοις τὸ εὐώνυμον κέρας, αὐτὸς δὲ τὸ δεξιὸν ἐπῆγεν.

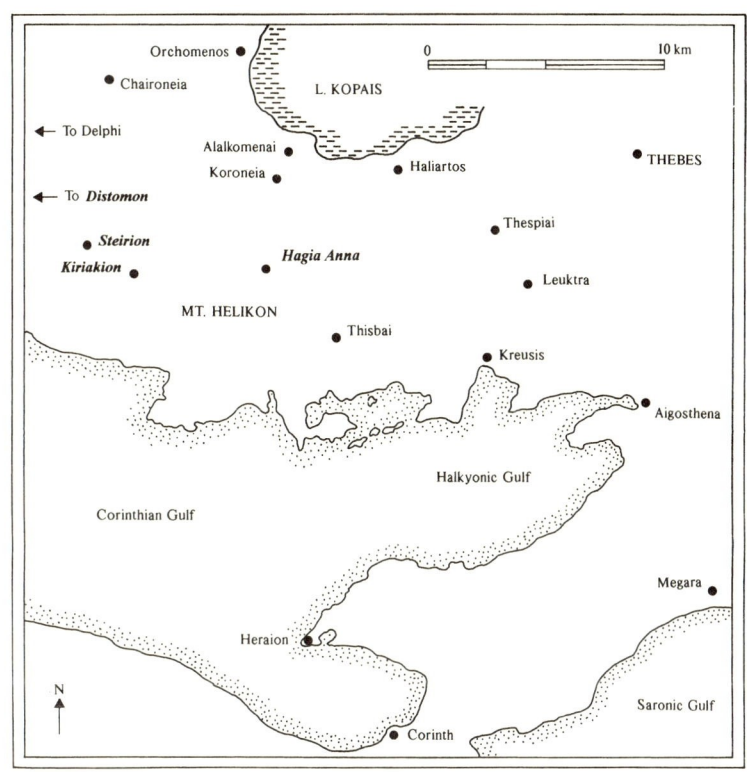

MAP 3. Boiotia and Corinthian Gulf

Xenophon gives details of Agesilaos' forces and of the allies whom he found already in position opposing him (*Hell.* iv. 3. 15, *Agesilaos*, 2. 6), for they will have had reports of his progress from the north. The Orchomenians are given prominence, not only by Agesilaos in stationing them on the wing, but by Plutarch, who mentions them alone among the Spartan allies, omitting the Phokians and the other contingents recorded by Xenophon. Plutarch may have been stirred by patriotism to show which side they were fighting on, for they had controlled Chaironeia, Plutarch's home, before 424 (Thuc. iv. 76. 3; *Hell. Ox.* XI. 3).[3] They were ancient rivals of Thebes for the leadership of the Boiotian League,[4] and encouraged by Lysander had revolted from Thebes (Xen. *Hell.* iii. 5. 17). Their estrangement may explain their absence from the allies' force at the River Nemea (Xen. *Hell.* iv. 2. 17). Xenophon calls them Sparta's 'local' allies, and they may have seized the site for the Spartan camp here before Agesilaos arrived.

οἱ δὲ Θηβαῖοι τὸ μὲν δεξιὸν εἶχον αὐτοί, τὸ δ' εὐώνυμον Ἀργεῖοι.

Of the Boiotians, Plutarch names only the Thebans, and although Xenophon names Boiotians at *Hell.* iv. 3. 15, he then refers to 'the Thebans' (*Hell.* iv. 3. 16, *Agesilaos*, 2. 9), giving them prominence. Of their allies, Plutarch mentions only the Argives, and thus highlights the forces on the wings, where the main actions took place. The choice of wings was significant, for while the Spartans held the place of honour on the right, the Thebans, on their own right, were covering the vital route behind them into Boiotia; they would be anxious to prevent Agesilaos' army from reaching the Peloponnese intact, to be an important reinforcement for the Lakedaimonians. The allocation of stations also meant that the Thebans and the Argives were each facing their traditional rivals in the Orchomenians and Spartans respectively. Plutarch's artistic arrangement completes a chiastic pattern, begun in the previous sentence; he juxtaposes the Spartans and the Thebans on the right wings, and frames them with their Orchomenian and Argive allies; the Spartans and Orchomenians preceded their wing placings, but the Thebans, Argives, and their wings form a second chiasmus, by *variatio*. Xenophon presents the formation of both lines of battle logically, putting the honoured right wings first. (See §3 below, for another chiastic pattern.)

2 λέγει δὲ τὴν μάχην ὁ Ξενοφῶν ἐκείνην οἵαν οὐκ ἄλλην τῶν τότε γενέσθαι· καὶ παρῆν αὐτὸς τῷ Ἀγησιλάῳ συναγωνιζόμενος, ἐξ Ἀσίας διαβεβηκώς.

Plutarch and Xenophon mark this as a unique battle; Xenophon because it was somehow different from others 'in *our* time' (*Hell.* iv. 3. 16), Plutarch, of necessity adjusting Xenophon's pronominal expression, because it was somehow different from others 'at that time', the simple substitute, τῶν τότε (a conjecture of Solanus adopted by editors, for the manuscripts' more colourful 'at any time', τῶν πώποτε, perhaps exaggerated because of the local interest and the importance of the event for Boiotia). No details are given explicitly to identify the special nature of this battle, but there are features that distinguish it. There were two distinct engagements. In the first, both the Spartan and the Theban wings were successful. In the second, the directions from which the two sides approached and faced each other were reversed. Most importantly, perhaps, the Spartans, who failed in the end to achieve either their immediate objective of invading Boiotia, or their main aim of destroying the enemy, nevertheless remained in possession of the battleground and did manage to return home eventually, while the Thebans were undefeated, successful in defending their territory, yet unable to avoid asking permission to recover their dead.

Xenophon was mentioned at ch. 9. 2, but his presence at the time in Asia was not then noticed. He records his return with Agesilaos, at least as far as Boiotia (*An.* v. 3. 5), and his offering to Apollo at Delphi, also mentioned there, may have been made at this time. Plutarch notes Xenophon's presence only to validate the description of the battle as unique, not to substantiate his own account. Xenophon exploits his advantage as eyewitness, as he did earlier at Ephesos (*Hell.* iii. 4. 16–19), with ἐνάργεια, 'vivid description' of the sounds and sights of battle. He contrasts the silence of the approaching forces with the sudden battle-cry of the Thebans (*Hell.* iv. 3. 17, *Agesilaos*, 2. 10), and reports a peculiar noise (*Agesilaos*, 2. 12) produced in furious battle, 'neither shouting nor silence'. Plutarch avoids imitating Xenophon's vivid description (see below, §6), and analyses actions and feelings, with prominence given both to Agesilaos himself and to his opponents.

3 ἡ μὲν οὖν πρώτη σύρραξις οὐκ ἔσχεν ὠθισμὸν οὐδ' ἀγῶνα πολύν, ἀλλ' οἵ τε Θηβαῖοι ταχὺ τοὺς Ὀρχομενίους ἐτρέψαντο καὶ τοὺς Ἀργείους ὁ Ἀγησίλαος·

Plutarch limits the action in the first engagement to the wings. Xenophon records in more detail that the initial advance was made by the Thebans, but that Herippidas[5] advanced from Agesilaos' phalanx three plethra away (30 m.), after which the whole force of Asian allies joined in the charge 'to within spearthrust' (*Hell.* iv. 3. 17). This charge routed 'the enemy in their sector', that is the Thebans' allies excluding the Argives, who, facing Agesilaos himself, and so alone named by Xenophon, fled to Mt Helikon without a fight. Xenophon next mentions the Thebans only later, and in a different context, when news was brought to Agesilaos that they were at the Spartan base, and when, as the Thebans noticed, their allies were on Helikon (*Hell.* iv. 3. 18). Plutarch, on the other hand, records the Theban success in routing the Orchomenians before he mentions the Argives' route by the Spartans, and puts it in its proper battle context and in a chiastic pattern around the verb. He was not misled by Xenophon's failure specifically to exclude the Thebans from the defeat.

4 ἐπεὶ δ᾽ ἀκούσαντες ἀμφότεροι τὰ εὐώνυμα πιέζεσθαι καὶ φεύγειν ἀνέστρεψαν, ἐνταῦθα τῆς νίκης ἀκινδύνου παρούσης, εἰ τῆς κατὰ στόμα μάχης ὑφέσθαι τοῖς Θηβαίοις ἠθέλησε καὶ παίειν ἑπόμενος παραλλάξαντας, ὑπὸ θυμοῦ καὶ φιλονικίας ἐναντίος ἐχώρει τοῖς ἀνδράσιν, ὤσασθαι κατὰ κράτος βουλόμενος.

The superiority of the right wing was frequently planned by deliberate strengthening, by the Thebans at Delion and by the Boiotians at the River Nemea (Thuc. iv. 93. 4; Xen. *Hell.* iv. 2. 18),[6] but the confusion here is unusual, for the inequality occurred on both wings simultaneously. Plutarch's arrangement allows him to stress the strikingly balanced situation in a way that Xenophon was unable to do because he failed to reveal the Theban success in its battle context: he reported it later, during Agesilaos' premature rejoicing. He relates the battle as Agesilaos viewed it, or perhaps from the viewpoint of a participant, not knowing the whole result until the messenger arrived from the baggage-train; but then it is he who gives the measure of the Thebans' success. Plutarch inevitably adopts the synoptic view of the external observer, but hastens to reach the features of the second engagement that interested him, without locating the Thebans among the baggage-train.

In Xenophon's account, while the Argives fled at once to Mt Helikon, the Thebans' success against the Orchomenians carried them into the Spartan baggage area (*Hell.* iv. 3. 17–18), which perhaps still contained the booty brought from Asia Minor. Plutarch has both sides now simply countermarching against the enemy, but, while this may have been easy for Agesilaos, for the Thebans, already engaged in plunder, the reorganizing of their phalanx was a considerable achievement. They were cut off from their base and would have to penetrate, unaided, the main Spartan force.

Plutarch does not at this point enlarge on the Theban success, but concentrates on Agesilaos' generalship. With Xenophon (*Hell.* iv. 3. 19, *Agesilaos*, 2. 12), he suggests that the safest plan was to allow the Thebans to pass through his lines and then attack them. He then uses characteristics already attributed, 'because of strong feelings and desire for victory', ὑπὸ θυμοῦ καὶ φιλονικίας, to explain the alternative direct attack (for ὤσασθαι, see below, §§6–7) which Xenophon found inexplicable. Excessive 'desire for victory' was attributed to Agesilaos at ch. 7. 4, and 'feelings' are found in other *Lives* as a cause of downturn in a general's fortunes (*Pel.* 32. 6–7, cf. below, ch. 28. 7). Plutarch reveals here a clue to Agesilaos' later decline, hatred of Thebes, an emotion which Xenophon shared with him. He might have attributed Agesilaos' decision to his φιλοτιμία, in the sense of significant achievement, for with sound logic he was aiming for 'annihilating victory', as has rightly been recognized.[7] However, he is not seeking to eulogize here, following Xenophon, who marks Agesilaos' next move as a courageous one, but, with a preference for the prudent, judges that it was not the most secure, ἀσφαλέστατα (*Hell.* iv. 3. 19, *Agesilaos*, 2. 12), a phrase reflected here by Plutarch in 'victory being secure', ἀκινδύνου. Xenophon also represents the Thebans unfavourably, as 'wishing to slip away' to the safety of their base—they moved 'vigorously', ἐρρωμένως, before the Spartans were drawn up. His verb διαπίπτω—used three times—is not complimentary: Plato uses it (*Phd.* 80 c) of what happens to corpses; it occurs with deliberate holding back by the opposing forces (ἀμελησάντων) at *Hell.* iii. 2. 4, and here (παρέντι) at iv. 3. 19, to let troops pass.

5 οἱ δ' οὐχ ἧττον ἐρρωμένως ἐδέξαντο, καὶ μάχη γίνεται δι' ὅλου μὲν ἰσχυρὰ τοῦ στρατεύματος, ἰσχυροτάτη δὲ κατ' ἐκεῖνον αὐτὸν ἐν τοῖς πεντήκοντα τεταγμένον, ὧν εἰς καιρὸν ἔοικεν ἡ φιλοτιμία τῷ βασιλεῖ γενέσθαι σωτήριος.

Agesilaos' choice of tactics allows Plutarch to present greater honour for the Thebans, for he seems to imply that, just as Agesilaos prefers to attempt to win outright victory, so the Thebans welcome the challenge, and would feel that they had lost by trickery, if Agesilaos had succeeded with the other tactic. Plutarch uses Xenophon's expression, ἐρρωμένως, 'vigorously', not to describe the Thebans' later efforts to reach their base on Helikon (*Hell.* iv. 3. 18) but in a complimentary context, to show how they 'received Agesilaos' attack'.

Plutarch's narrative is not taken directly from Xenophon's account. The fifty who save the king may be the volunteers chosen at ch. 17. 3, but not mentioned by Xenophon either then or now. Their φιλοτιμία seems to supply the more rational 'desire for achievement' not displayed here by Agesilaos, and they make good his deficiency with 'a timely measure of deliverance' (εἰς καιρόν and σωτήριος) which it is usually the general's duty to ensure (καιρός: cf. chs. 8. 6, 28. 6 and 7, 34. 6, 35. 6, 36. 4, 37. 2, 39. 2 and 4; σωτήριος: 39. 4 and cf. 16. 5).

6 ἀγωνιζόμενοι γὰρ ἐκθύμως καὶ προκινδυνεύοντες, ἄτρωτον μὲν αὐτὸν οὐκ ἐδυνήθησαν φυλάξαι, πολλὰς δὲ διὰ τῶν ὅπλων δεξάμενον εἰς τὸ σῶμα πληγὰς δόρασι καὶ ξίφεσι μόλις ἀνήρπασαν ζῶντα, καὶ συμφράξαντες πρὸ αὐτοῦ πολλοὺς μὲν ἀνῄρουν, πολλοὶ δ' ἔπιπτον.

The volunteers compensate for the destructive motivation of Agesilaos, so mitigating the excess which might otherwise be fatal, as in other *Lives*. Xenophon does not record Agesilaos' wound until he assigns the victory to him (ch. 20). By placing it here, Plutarch properly gives it a context on the battlefield which indicates the intensity of the fighting and shows that the Thebans were taking the Spartans' ground. The chiastic pattern, framing δεξάμενον with accusatives and prepositional phrases, leaves δόρασι καὶ ξίφεσι unattached, suggesting that in their defence of Agesilaos the volunteers, like the enemy, fought hand to hand with spears and swords; and they killed and were killed, just as in Xenophon's account the Spartans and the Thebans fought 'face to face with clashing shields: they shoved, fought, killed, died' (*Hell.* iv. 3. 19).

Plutarch matches Xenophon's vivid description, ἐνάργεια, in an independent way, not by repeating or imitating his striking groups of words: his phrase δόρασι καὶ ξίφεσι enhances Xenophon's παντοίοις ὅπλοις (*Agesilaos*, 2. 13; cf. πολλὰ τραύματα at *Hell.* iv. 3. 20).[8]

7 ὡς δὲ μέγα ἔργον ἦν ὤσασθαι προτροπάδην τοὺς Θηβαίους, ἠναγκάσθησαν ὅπερ ἐξ ἀρχῆς οὐκ ἐβούλοντο ποιῆσαι. **8** διέστησαν γὰρ αὐτοῖς τὴν φάλαγγα καὶ διέσχον, εἶτ᾽ ἀτακτότερον ἤδη πορευομένους, ὡς διεξέπεσον, ἀκολουθοῦντες καὶ παραθέοντες ἐκ πλαγίων ἔπαιον.

Plutarch repeats the infinitive, ὤσασθαι,[9] used above (§4) to express the aim Agesilaos originally preferred, and so highlights his present inability to achieve his wish, before describing how he has to let the Thebans through. Xenophon, who also says at the start that Agesilaos 'might have let them through and overcome them from behind' (*Hell.* iv. 3. 19), reported that, in the battle at the River Nemea, the Spartans deliberately marched to their right (*Hell.* iv. 2. 19–20) to create an overlap before turning into line to attack the Athenians from the flank.[10] There is no overlap at Koroneia, but an attack from the flanks on the enemy rear is involved in the suggestions of Xenophon and Plutarch. Neither author attributes the manoeuvre to the initial thinking of Agesilaos himself, but perhaps its successful use at the Nemea had been reported to him through Derkylidas. The manoeuvre, difficult even for the highly trained Spartans[11]—Agesilaos chose not to attempt it initially—would be more complicated once the two sides were locked in the second engagement. The Thebans, some of whom were at the Nemea and witnessed the successful move by Agesipolis' regent, now avoided being in a disorganized and straggling line a second time (Xen. *Hell.* iv. 2. 22–3), having formed up in close order (Xen. *Hell.* iv. 3. 18) for the return encounter.

The Theban breakthrough

Xenophon uses the verb διαπίπτω three times to refer to the Thebans' efforts to reach Mt Helikon (*Hell.* iv. 3. 18–19), and since, in the opening stages, he envisages the possibility that, after the Thebans were committed to the charge, the Spartans could open a gap in their line to let them pass through (διαπίπτω), he evidently did not think Spartan drill incapable of the manoeuvre during the engagement.[12] He perhaps mentions the possibility of the initial manoeuvre at the beginning only to highlight by contrast the difficulty of what Agesilaos eventually does.

Plutarch, on the other hand, exploits the rhetorical effect of having him do in the end what he rejected at the start, but shows, too, that the Thebans forced it upon him. He also enhances the Theban success by making the purpose of their struggle the positive one of resisting the Spartan onslaught, rather than a desperate attempt (see on ἐρρωμένως, 'vigorously', §4 above) to escape to base. Xenophon's account is not more impartial, however. Although he allows the Spartan line to be pierced, he obscures the Theban success, and stresses their losses. He uses the verb διαπίπτω for the third time, surely with the same nuance, reinforced by ἀποχωροῦντες, usually of withdrawal following defeat (cf. *Hell.* iv. 4. 11), and with the repeated reference to fatalities, as the Thebans 'slipped through' to reach their base (*Hell.* iv. 3. 19). Plutarch uses the same verb, but in the more purposeful form διεκπίπτω, 'break out through', reminiscent of the successful naval attacking manoeuvre, διέκπλους (Thuc. ii. 83. 5, 89. 8).

The gap, sufficient for several thousand men to pour through, would, as Lazenby points out, need to be a wide one, and, if forced by the Thebans, could involve more Spartan casualties than are mentioned by Diodoros (xiv. 84. 2): 350 of the Lakedaimonians and their allies dead, compared with over 600 Boiotians and their allies. Deliberate or feigned retreats, intended to cause disorder in the enemy ranks,[13] are recorded, and in a long-drawn-out engagement any temporary lull might allow trained men to change formation and tactics before the next attack.

The divergences between the accounts of Plutarch and Xenophon suggest that Plutarch is following a patriotic local tradition as well as his own source analysis. His phrases often relate to Xenophon's, his incidents and his interpretations develop from Xenophon's narrative, but he rearranges the context—Agesilaos' wounding; makes realistic assumptions—he was personally and hotly engaged; and reasonably infers fierce defence by Spartiate bodyguards. He helps to make better sense on the Theban side of the clearly described but nevertheless ambiguous final situation of the two armies (ch. 19. 1–4 below). Frontinus (*Strat.* ii. 6. 6) and Polyainos (ii. 1. 19) do not wholly accord with Xenophon's account, but suggest, like Plutarch, that the Spartans deliberately opened ranks to let the Thebans through:[14] Frontinus, however, explains that Agesilaos' plan was to avoid making the Thebans fight in a more desperate situation, and with Polyainos assigns success to Agesilaos, restricting the dead to the fleeing Thebans.

9 οὐ μὴν ἐτρέψαντό γ', ἀλλ' ἀπεχώρησαν οἱ Θηβαῖοι πρὸς τὸν Ἑλικῶνα μέγα τῇ μάχῃ φρονοῦντες, ὡς ἀήττητοι καθ' αὑτοὺς γεγονότες.

By expressing his strong denial with ἐτρέψαντο, the verb used to denote the earlier rout (§3), Plutarch shows that the Thebans were far from defeated in their sector and limits the Spartan success suggested by Xenophon. Xenophon records that in reaching Helikon the Thebans lost many men and gives the victory to Agesilaos (*Hell.* iv. 3. 19–20); the Thebans are not mentioned again until they send heralds to arrange a truce (*Hell.* iv. 3. 21). He appears to record only what could be observed from the Spartan camp, without access to a Theban informant.[15] Plutarch either had a supplementary source or was not convinced that Xenophon's narrative justified his conclusion. The positions on the battlefield at the start of the second engagement were the result of the chance course of the first action, the two sides having won each on its own right wing: the Thebans were cut off from base, and the Spartans were in possession of the battlefield, though not of their camp. After the second engagement, the Spartans were still in possession of the battlefield, but the Thebans had successfully regained their base. That Plutarch believed this to be a Theban success, if not a total victory, becomes even more clear in ch. 19 (cf. Paus. iii. 9. 13).[16]

19. 1–4. The aftermath of the battle

Xen. *Hell.* iv. 3. 20–1, *Agesilaos*, 2. 13, 16; Diod. xiv. 84. 2; Nepos, *Agesilaus*, 4. 6; Paus. iii. 9. 13; Polyain. ii. 1. 5.

1 Ἀγησίλαος δέ, καίπερ ὑπὸ τραυμάτων πολλῶν κακῶς τὸ σῶμα διακείμενος, οὐ πρότερον ἐπὶ σκηνὴν ἀπῆλθεν ἢ φοράδην ἐνεχθῆναι πρὸς τὴν φάλαγγα καὶ τοὺς νεκροὺς ἰδεῖν ἐντὸς τῶν ὅπλων συγκεκομισμένους.

Xenophon reports that Agesilaos was wounded only at the point where he attributes victory to him, and links wounds and victory with his return to camp (*Hell.* iv. 3. 20). A second reference to the wounds is linked with the release of the enemy from the sanctuary of the temple of Athena: despite the wounds Agesilaos still remembers his piety. Plutarch, who reported the wounds and the Thebans' claim to have been undefeated at ch. 18, ignores Xenophon's statement giving victory to Agesilaos. He does not link that report with Agesilaos' retirement, and reserves the release of the refugees for the next episode. He delays Agesilaos' departure to his tent until he has shown courage, endurance, and self-denial in his concern for the troops and collecting the dead. Agesilaos, then, still remembers his piety, but in a different way, and at the same time enhances his standing as a humane general.

Plutarch presents a different version of the reference to the phalanx made by Xenophon, who appears to signify only that Agesilaos' wounds caused him temporarily to leave the battle-line, and to use πρὸς τὴν φάλαγγα here, unusually, to refer to 'the Spartan camp'. Plutarch, either reinterpreting or misunderstanding him, uses it as the 'battle-line', and suggests that before the king goes to his tent he is paraded in front of the phalanx, perhaps to show that he is still alive. The collection of the dead εἴσω φάλαγγος in Xenophon's *Agesilaos* (2. 15) may be interpreted as 'behind the Spartan line', but Plutarch's phrase ἐντὸς τῶν ὅπλων identifies the Spartan 'camp'. This expedient is unusual, but perhaps it provides another reason why Xenophon regards the battle as unlike others, for Agesilaos is not confident that he can maintain possession of the bodies in another battle unless they are temporarily moved to safety and guarded. That battle would otherwise have to be fought on the field where the corpses still lay, since he could have neither time nor opportunity beforehand to bury them properly. Polyainos explains, perhaps from another source, that Agesilaos hid Spartan corpses with dust, not wishing the number of dead to be known: victory was undecided, but the Thebans were despondent as if defeated (ii. 1. 23).

2 ὅσοι μέντοι τῶν πολεμίων εἰς τὸ ἱερὸν κατέφυγον, πάντας ἐκέλευσεν ἀφεθῆναι. πλησίον γὰρ ὁ νεώς ἐστιν ὁ τῆς Ἰτωνίας Ἀθηνᾶς, καὶ πρὸ αὐτοῦ τρόπαιον ἔστηκεν, ὃ πάλαι Βοιωτοὶ Σπάρτωνος στρατηγοῦντος ἐνταῦθα νικήσαντες Ἀθηναίους καὶ Τολμίδην ἀποκτείναντες ἔστησαν·

Plutarch often praises Agesilaos' piety, but does not follow Xenophon here, making only a statement of the pious act with no comment. Xenophon alone mentions the presence of cavalry at this point, when horsemen ride up to report that about eighty of the enemy, still armed, are in the sanctuary. They could be the last few Thebans trying to pass through the Spartan lines, who, finding themselves outnumbered and unable to follow the rest to Helikon, took refuge there, pursued by the cavalry. At *Agesilaos*, 2. 13 they were given a cavalry escort to take them to safety.

The flight of the refugees into the temple leads Plutarch to recall the nearby monument. He diverts attention from Agesilaos, and adds another celebration to be savoured by his fellow-countrymen. This seems to be the reason for delaying the reference to Agesilaos' pious act, which Xenophon recorded earlier. Plutarch, with evident pride, introduces an ornamental style into the passage, making chiastic patterns of the three participles and their associated nouns.

When Plutarch refers to battles at Koroneia, Haliartos, and Tegyra (*Per.* 18. 2–3, *Lys.* 28–9, *Pel.* 16) it is without significant resort to his own local topographical observations for military matters. Rather, he takes the opportunity to record local history, legends, heroes, deities, and oracles.[1] The temple of Athena Itonia, between Alalkomenai and Koroneia (Paus. ix. 34. 1), remains unlocated. Stones of an ancient temple are retained at a site around the chapel of Metamorphosis, now Soteia, in the modern village of Mamoura, near Hagia Paraskevi.[2]

In his context of a Boiotian success, Plutarch takes the opportunity for a patriotic reference to another success at Koroneia, one which was undisputed, won by Boiotians but over the Athenians, in 447 (*Per.* 18, Thuc. i. 113. 2, Diod. xii. 6. 2; Xen. *Mem.* iii. 5. 4, an unusual acknowledgement of Thebes and Theban leadership). The commander's name Sparton was connected with the legendary Spartoi, 'sprung from the dragon's teeth'. Five Spartoi were reputed ancestors of the Theban aristocracy, including Epameinondas (Pindar, i. 1. 30, Paus. viii. 11. 8, ix. 5. 3, *Suda* s.v. Ἐπαμεινώνδας).[3]

3 ἅμα δ' ἡμέρᾳ βουλόμενος ἐξελέγξαι τοὺς Θηβαίους ὁ Ἀγησίλαος εἰ διαμαχοῦνται, στεφανοῦσθαι μὲν ἐκέλευσε τοὺς στρατιώτας, αὐλεῖν δὲ τοὺς αὐλητάς, ἱστάναι δὲ καὶ κοσμεῖν τρόπαιον ὡς νενικηκότας.

The Thebans' success (ch. 18) in fighting a way through the Spartan line leaves the Spartans in command of the battlefield and of the dead. In order to recover what, in normal circumstances, the victory they claimed would immediately have given them, the Thebans would now have to fight another full-scale engagement, with the initial disadvantage of having to meet the Spartans already occupying what was before the neutral ground. But, perhaps most importantly, they are still in their original positions for the defence of their territory against the Spartan invaders.

Neither the Boiotians nor the Spartans were routed in the fighting, and the final issue was still undecided. The technicalities of deciding the victory were still to be settled. In his two accounts (*Agesilaos*, 2. 15–16, *Hell.* iv. 3. 21) Xenophon, despite claiming that victory belonged to Agesilaos, indicates that the Spartans could not assume that the Thebans accepted this decision, and shows Agesilaos' own need for confirmation by having him stage the parade in battle formation ready for further action. Plutarch makes it Agesilaos' explicit purpose to challenge the Thebans, and further suggests, with ὡς νενικηκότας, 'believing themselves victorious', that even in Agesilaos' mind his victory was not wholly certain (LSJ s.v. ὡς C. I. 2; cf. Thuc. iv. 5. 1, Pl. *Resp.* 338 E; Polyain. ii. 1. 23).

Xenophon, whose words may represent the form in which Agesilaos gave his instructions to Gylis, starts with the main business of the formation of the battle-line and the erection of the trophy, and then specifies minor matters of dress and ceremonial. Plutarch arranges the activities in a temporal sequence, as if viewed by a privileged onlooker. Agesilaos' elaborate display of troops and trophy was intended, no doubt, to encourage his own men, as much as to intimidate the Thebans.

4 ὡς δ᾽ ἔπεμψαν οἱ πολέμιοι νεκρῶν ἀναίρεσιν αἰτοῦντες, ἐσπείσατο, καὶ τὴν νίκην οὕτως ἐκβεβαιωσάμενος, εἰς Δελφοὺς ἀπεκομίσθη, Πυθίων ἀγομένων, καὶ τήν τε πομπὴν ἐπετέλει τῷ θεῷ καὶ τὴν δεκάτην ἀπέθυσε τῶν ἐκ τῆς Ἀσίας λαφύρων, ἑκατὸν ταλάντων γενομένην.

The Thebans realized that they would have to fight again if they were to recover their dead, and, like Agesilaos at Larissa, they showed discretion, and did not accept the Spartan challenge when it came. Both Plutarch and Xenophon record that the Thebans waited until then before sending heralds. The request for the recovery of the dead seems to be interpreted by Plutarch more as an acceptance by the Thebans of the difficulties of the chance situation they were in than an inevitable admission of defeat. If Polyainos (ii. 1. 23; see above, §1) judged the battle undecided, so, too, might the Thebans. Plutarch now shows that Agesilaos' explicit challenge assured formal recognition of victory: the next Spartan moves reveal its limitations.

For Agesilaos, the campaigning ends with the journey to Delphi to deposit the tithe (a tenth) of the booty he had brought from Asia, amounting to not less than 100 talents (cf. Xen. *Hell.* iv. 3. 21, *Agesilaos*, 1. 34). He arrived during the Pythian festival, when offerings were brought to Apollo. The Pythia were held in Boukatios, the August–September lunation, two years after the Olympics—hence in 394. The ceremonial procession, πομπή, 'the sending, escorting', was conducted along the traditional Sacred Way, controlled by the authorities of the sanctuary, with rituals performed at points on the route to the temple. Plutarch describes two parts of the ceremonial, the procession (πομπὴν ἐπετέλει, 'completed the escort'), and the act of offering, ἀπέθυσε, the verb used also by Xenophon.

An assessment of Agesilaos' campaign

If Diodoros' figures are correct (xiv. 84. 2),[4] and more than 600 Boiotians and 350 Lakedaimonians died, they can be expressed as a ratio of 1.7 : 1, or 12 : 7 in lives; 9 : 7 in strength. At the battle of the River Nemea, the figures given (xiv. 83. 2) are 2,800 and 1,100 respectively, 2.5 : 1, and when the Boiotians fought against the Phokians (xiv. 82. 9), they killed 1,000 and lost 500, 2 : 1. If the Boiotians had 20,000 men and the Spartans 15,000, their casualties represent 3 per cent and 2.3 per cent respectively.[5] The figures show the relative importance in this respect of these battles, and the differing costs of victory: for the Thebans the value of the battle of Koroneia lay in preventing the invasion of their territory; and Plutarch, with Boiotian pride, perhaps following local tradition, honours their achievement in remaining undefeated against the Spartans.

Xenophon perhaps disguised some of the truth about the indecisive nature of the battle and the larger strategic outcome, but he also retained an indication of the shortfall in Agesilaos' achievement—his return by sea (*Hell.* iv. 4. 1). Victory at Koroneia would have opened the way to Thebes, and helped to secure the Isthmus route for Sparta, which might have been significant for the future conduct of the war. It may have been the original intention to return across the Corinthian Gulf, and the order to invade Boiotia may have been connected with opening the land route.

At the end of the campaign in Asia Minor, the tangible results, it seems, were trophies near Narthakion and Koroneia, and booty, which, without the tithe, amounted to almost 1,000 talents. Agesilaos did not choose to drive home his advantage by making an outright attack on the Theban camp, or by attempting to enter Boiotia; which marks the real success of the Thebans at Koroneia. In *Hellenika* Xenophon brings Agesilaos home to Sparta in the rather sombre circumstances of Gylis' defeat and death in Lokris, after what he had presented as a glorious campaign in Asia Minor (iv. 3. 21–3), and in *Agesilaos* he records the moral climax, that Agesilaos went home choosing, instead of pre-eminence in Asia, 'to rule and be ruled' (2. 16). Plutarch, despite recognizing the Theban achievement, says nothing here that might detract from Agesilaos' own satisfaction at this point. He even mentions that Agesilaos arrived in Delphi during the Pythian Games and took part in the procession in honour of the god, which Xenophon has omitted. But at *Comp.* 3. 1 he judges that Agesilaos' military achievement in general was limited. The omen of the interrupted sacrifice at Aulis seems to have been fulfilled.

PART VI (chs. 19. 5–20. 9)

The returning general

Xen. *Hell.* v. 3. 20, *Agesilaos*, 8. 2, 6–8, 9. 6–7; Nepos, *Agesilaus*, 7. 3–4;
Lys. 3. 1–5; Plut. *Lys.* 25–6, 30. 3–4; Diod. xiv. 13. 1–8.

19. 5–11 Agesilaos at home

5 ἐπεὶ δ' ἀπενόστησεν οἴκαδε, προσφιλὴς μὲν ἦν εὐθὺς τοῖς πολίταις
καὶ περίβλεπτος ἀπὸ τοῦ βίου καὶ τῆς διαίτης· **6** οὐ γάρ, ὥσπερ οἱ
πλεῖστοι τῶν στρατηγῶν, καινὸς ἐπανῆλθεν ἀπὸ τῆς ξένης,
κατακεκηλημένος ὑπ' ἀλλοτρίων ἐθῶν, καὶ δυσκολαίνων πρὸς τὰ οἴκοι
καὶ ζυγομαχῶν.

After the return Xenophon says nothing more about Agesilaos in
Hellenika until at iv. 4. 19 he describes the attack on the territory
of the Argives, who had by then taken control of Corinth (*Hell.* iv.
4. 6). In *Agesilaos* he goes straight on to record this invasion as
Agesilaos' next action (2. 17), without indicating the passage of
time. Plutarch deals with it in ch. 21, and, perhaps to denote an
interval, takes the opportunity of Agesilaos' return to Sparta to
comment on qualities of character relevant to the resumed domestic context, which are omitted by Xenophon the historian. He now
turns to Xenophon's *Agesilaos* and selects and develops references
found in several places there. The first topic is Agesilaos' conduct
at home as a private individual enjoying affection (προσφιλής),
which occupies the rest of this chapter, and the second, which
occupies the next chapter, presents him as a public figure, enjoying admiration (περίβλεπτος). The nouns referring to these two
topics in the prepositional phrase are in reverse (chiastic) order,
βίος, the 'Life' to be written, δίαιτα, the 'style of living', and the
order is again reversed in the following narrative. Whereas
Plutarch concentrates on domestic themes, Xenophon sees
military significance in some of the traits, so that, for example, the
affection in which Agesilaos was held won for him the loyalty of
his troops (*Agesilaos*, 6. 4).

Plutarch at this point appropriately praises Agesilaos as

unaffected by service away from Sparta, the theme of the 'return-
ing general'; see Introd., C.1(*b*). The Athenian envoys at
Thucydides, i. 77 voiced the cultural dangers that Spartans faced
in going abroad. They appear to refer to the lavish behaviour of
Pausanias at Byzantion, anticipating the description in
Thucydides' retrospective digression (i. 95); other instances of
Spartans abroad involve harsh and incompetent administration
(Thuc. i. 130. 1, iii. 93. 3, v. 52. 1). Plutarch is concerned with
Agesilaos' rejection of self-aggrandizement such as Pausanias',
and he could draw on Xenophon (*Agesilaos*, 1. 37, 2. 16). There,
Xenophon points out that Agesilaos resisted the temptation to
disobey the command to return to Sparta, where his ambition
would be curtailed, and to add to his powers in Asia instead.
Plutarch develops the theme of his adherence to the simple
domestic standards of his Spartan upbringing.[6]

ἀλλ' ὁμοίως τοῖς μηδεπώποτε τὸν Εὐρώταν διαβεβηκόσι τὰ παρόντα
τιμῶν καὶ στέργων, οὐ δεῖπνον ἤλλαξεν, οὐ λουτρόν, οὐ θεραπείαν
γυναικός, οὐχ ὅπλων κόσμον, οὐκ οἰκίας κατασκευήν, ἀλλὰ καὶ τὰς
θύρας ἀφῆκεν οὕτως οὔσας σφόδρα παλαιὰς ὡς δοκεῖν εἶναι ταύτας
ἐκείνας ἃς ἐπέθηκεν Ἀριστόδημος. 7 καὶ τὸ κάνναθρόν φησιν ὁ
Ξενοφῶν οὐδέν τι σεμνότερον εἶναι τῆς ἐκείνου θυγατρὸς ἢ τῶν ἄλλων.

Much of Plutarch's material comes from Xenophon's *Agesilaos*,
where he commends the simple lifestyle which Agesilaos substituted for the Great King's pretentiousness (9. 1), and treats his
attitude to the pleasures of food and drink as part of a contrast
with the King's expensive taste (9. 3): Agesilaos is above such
excessive pleasures (5. 1). Xenophon lists the simplicity of his
house, the doors and other furnishings, his furniture, his sacrificial
meals, the carriage used by his daughter; the stress is on matching
expenditure to income, on which Agesilaos and the King differ, as
if the carriage might have been more elaborate (8. 7–8). Plutarch
again shows by the context that he links the simplicity with
Agesilaos' contentment with Spartan standards in his personal
and family ways of living. It is for the sake of conformity to
Spartan tradition that Agesilaos does not renew the old doors.
There is no suggestion of pride in their antiquity, but an assumed
'uncultured primitivism' in the carpentry. Plutarch gives only
Aristodemos' name, unlike Xenophon, who refers to his 'return'
as a descendant of Herakles. Herodotos assigns that version to

Lakedaimonian tradition: others record Aristodemos' death before the arrival of his sons (vi. 52. 1–2; Apollodoros, ii. 8. 2, Paus. iii. 1. 5–6).

8 κάνναθρα δὲ καλοῦσιν εἴδωλα γρυπῶν ξύλινα καὶ τραγελάφων, ἐν οἷς κομίζουσι τὰς παῖδας ἐν ταῖς πομπαῖς.

Here Plutarch does show antiquarian interest in adding to Xenophon the adornments of the carriage for the reader's benefit, but he then confirms that Agesilaos was only keeping to the vehicle in general ceremonial use for the girls conveying offerings to the sanctuary (cf. §4 above). Athenaios seems to contrast expensively furnished carriages, καννάθρων πολυτελῶς κατασκευασμένων, with yoked chariots contesting in a public spectacle (139 F). The festival is not mentioned at Xenophon's *Agesilaos*, 8. 6–7, where the public carriage takes the girl to Amyklai, about 5 km. south from Sparta. At *Hell.* iv. 5. 11–12 the Amyklaians, as usual, return from Corinth for the Hyakinthia, a possibly pre-Hellenic festival, later associated with Apollo (cf. Xenophon, *Agesilaos*, 2. 17, where Agesilaos joins in the hymn to the god). Across the river is the Menelaion, the supposed burial-place of Helen and Menelaos (Paus. iii. 19. 9), possibly the maidens' destination (cf. Hesych. 483 on κάνναθρα taking girls to the shrine of Helen), who would leave Sparta on the Amyklai road and cross the Eurotas by the bridge mentioned by Xenophon (*Hell.* vi. 5. 27).[7]

9 ὁ μὲν οὖν Ξενοφῶν ὄνομα τῆς Ἀγησιλάου θυγατρὸς οὐ γέγραφε, καὶ ὁ Δικαίαρχος ἐπηγανάκτησεν ὡς μήτε τὴν Ἀγησιλάου θυγατέρα μήτε τὴν Ἐπαμεινώνδου μητέρα γινωσκόντων ἡμῶν, **10** ἡμεῖς δ' εὕρομεν ἐν ταῖς Λακωνικαῖς ἀναγραφαῖς ὀνομαζομένην γυναῖκα μὲν Ἀγησιλάου Κλεόραν, θυγατέρας δ' Εὐπωλίαν καὶ Προαύγαν.

Antiquarian interest in names may be less significant here for Plutarch than the importance he attaches to recording details about members of Agesilaos' family, and especially the female members (see Introd., B.2), brought to mind by the reference to the daughter's carriage. Eupolia (cf. ch. 1. 1), from πῶλος, 'foal', and Proauga, 'Flash' (Αὐγώ, the name of a hound at Xen. *Kyn.* 7. 5, cf. αὐγή, 'light'), like Kyniska, 'puppy' (ch. 20. 1), indicate a family interest in breeding (Xen. *Agesilaos*, 9. 6). The prosopographical information is potentially significant for hints of Agesilaos' political associates: Kleora's brother was Peisandros

(ch. 10. 11); her father (Pausanias, iii. 9. 3 says Agesilaos' maternal
grandfather), Aristomelidas;[8] he was friendly with Thebans, no
doubt aristocratic collaborators of Phoibidas and victims of
Pelopidas, like Leontiadas (chs. 23. 11, 24. 2), suggesting aggrava-
tion of Agesilaos' hatred of Thebes under Leontiadas' opponent
Ismenias. The daughters' names are not given at Xen. *Agesilaos*,
8. 7.

Plutarch indicates that he had access to archives of some kind at
Sparta, but Xenophon says nothing about them. The inclusion of
these names in archives suggests a domestic collection of documents, like that in Lysander's house (*Lys.* 30. 3; cf. ch. 20. 3), but
nothing more is known of them. The digression on the absence
from the tradition of the names of Agesilaos' close relatives brings
out a contrast with the monumental inscriptions in other cities,
whether private or public, from which such information could be
obtained for males and citizens, less often for women, reflecting
the comparatively small stock of epigraphical, as of numismatic,
evidence for Sparta under the unusual ideological constraints of
its constitution: it required personal research to find these names
at Sparta, which confirms Plutarch's special interest in the family,
matching that of Agesilaos himself. Xenophon's lack of interest
matches that of Attic orators in court, who seem to have been
least reluctant to name a woman when she was related to their
opponents or of low reputation; the role of respectable women in
the family restricted their public identity,[9] but others were
identifiable, perhaps because of their notoriety. But Xenophon
was writing for a panhellenic audience, restricted rather by
general Greek sensibilities. For Plutarch, writing centuries later,
there was no such constraint.

11 ἔστι δὲ καὶ λόγχην ἰδεῖν αὐτοῦ κειμένην ἄχρι νῦν ἐν Λακεδαίμονι,
μηδὲν τῶν ἄλλων διαφέρουσαν.

Again the point is not to show the unique antiquarian value of the
spear, but explicitly that people could see for themselves what is
exemplified by Agesilaos' very ordinary spear—how ordinary
their king was. Plutarch uses a visual image to round off the
subject of Agesilaos' popular appeal through moderation in
private self-advertisement. Xenophon brings out its military
significance, for he contrasts Agesilaos' personal simplicity with
his public concern to ensure the high quality of the army's equip-

ment (*Agesilaos*, 11. 11). Plutarch, however, maintains the continuity of his domestic theme by drawing attention to the social significance even of Agesilaos' military equipment.[10] The spear was evidently on public display in Plutarch's time and no doubt contributed to the Spartan image which so impressed him. Public display of arms captured from the enemy may have been felt in other cities to be beneficial in preparing the coming generations of warriors, but not at Sparta.[11] Perhaps, instead, the warrior culture was encouraged there by the domestic display of real weapons of war, available for use.

20. Agesilaos' influence at Sparta: Lykourgan principles upheld and abandoned

On Kyniska, Paus. iii. 8. 1–2, iii. 15. 1, v. 12. 5, vi. 1. 6; on Skillous, Paus. v. 6. 5–6; on Agesipolis, Diod. xv. 19. 4.

Plutarch moves on from Agesilaos' domestic life to his influence in a public context (cf. ch. 15. 7–8), interweaving the biographical narrative, the portrayal of Agesilaos' character, and the practice of the moral values of Lykourgan Sparta. Five illustrations of Agesilaos' political influence focus on four named individuals and one anonymous group.[1]

In the first, Agesilaos aims to divert the Spartans' competitive efforts away from extravagant display and expenditure of wealth towards a politically more serviceable end, the development of ἀρετή, Spartan 'excellence'. Next Agesilaos advocates the familiar aim of Spartan education, ἄρχεσθαι καὶ ἄρχειν, obedience and leadership. Then the two parts of this phrase are separated, presenting a negative and a positive example, in reverse (chiastic) order. The last two revive the topic dealt with in ch. 5, the elimination of political opponents, who were placed in public offices where their conduct was exposed to accountability, or were brought under his influence through the development of the personal relationship of an older with a younger man which was typical in Spartan society, as it is presented in the tradition.

Agesilaos' influence is given positive definition by ring composition as Plutarch returns in the last sentence to a word used in the first, ἀρετή. At the end of the chapter the reference to Lykourgos suggests a legitimacy which extends to the whole series, as if Agesilaos was in all this practising and encouraging the competitive principles underlying the Spartan way of life. The thematic links between the several illustrations of Agesilaos' influence show rhetorical skills of selection, presentation and arrangement. Plutarch places this study of Spartan character at the halfway point, in the twentieth chapter of the forty. There is no hint that it is flawed, but the removal of opposition—or competition (cf. ch. 5)—eventually proves to be a turning-point.

1 Οὐ μὴν ἀλλ᾽ ὁρῶν ἐνίους τῶν πολιτῶν ἀφ᾽ ἱπποτροφίας δοκοῦντας εἶναί τινας καὶ μέγα φρονοῦντας, ἔπεισε τὴν ἀδελφὴν Κυνίσκαν ἅρμα καθεῖσαν Ὀλυμπίασιν ἀγωνίσασθαι, βουλόμενος ἐνδείξασθαι τοῖς Ἕλλησιν ὡς οὐδεμιᾶς ἐστιν ἀρετῆς, ἀλλὰ πλούτου καὶ δαπάνης ἡ νίκη.

Xenophon uses his sister Kyniska's victory in the chariot races as part of a proof that Agesilaos, a man of action not of wealth, who keeps hounds and war-horses, is superior to the Persian King, who breeds chariot-horses (*Agesilaos*, 9. 6). The glory of winning at chariot-racing is dismissed by Xenophon in defining a ruler's true service to the state (*Hiero*, 11. 5–9). The horse-breeding citizens are not identified by name, but their existence indicated the unequal distribution of wealth in Sparta, recognized by Aristotle (*Pol.* 1270^{a}15–22, 1307^{a}26–36; see above, ch. 4 n.). Agesilaos' suggestion that by the use of great wealth to acquire and train a chariot team a woman might win at Olympia, where a woman was not allowed even to be a spectator (Paus. v. 6. 7),[2] is presented here as a protest against the non-participating racehorse breeder. Efforts directed towards display of wealth, without any contribution to the perceived interest of the city, damaged the harmony of Sparta's society of 'Equals'. A demonstration of ἀρετή, on the other hand, could be encouraged by the right sort of competition, though again it had to be in the right field, for Agesilaos supported only Sparta's own competitive games, and, in particular, those for the young (ch. 21. 7). In the competitions which he held in Asia and in the Chersonese, the only prizes awarded to individuals were for excellence in weapon-training; the others were awarded collectively to the best large contingents of soldiers (Xen. *Hell.* iii. 4. 16, iv. 2. 6; cf. *Hipp.* 1. 26).

Kyniska

An inscription (*IG* v (1). 213), formerly dated to the 440s or 430s, more recently to after 403, records a dedication of the Spartan Damonon to the guardian deity, Ἀθαναα[ι] Πολιάχοι, claiming more victories than his contemporaries in chariot races and boys' (vs. 35–49) events by himself and his son Enymakratidas at other Games. Pausanias does not mention him but lists several Spartan Olympic victors at vi. 1. 6–2. 3, where he mentions the prominence of Spartan breeders after 480. Other inscriptional evidence, *IG* v (1). 235, from the pedestal marking Kyniska's Olympic victory (Paus. vi. 1. 6), dated early fourth century by its lettering, may indicate that this passage refers to a time after Agesilaos' accession.[3] She seems to have won more than once, for Pausanias speaks of her 'victories' (vi. 1. 6). At iii. 8. 1 he suggests that although she was the first woman competitor, she was not the last Lakonian woman to win Olympic victories. Agesilaos' action may have had the reverse effect, if, as Plutarch suggests, he intended discouragement—politically naïve, perhaps, but surely Lykourgan—and led the way to an increase in this form of the display of wealth. Her posthumous honour with heroization and a shrine in Sparta (Paus. iii. 15. 1) would demonstrate the prestige to be won in this way, despite Agesilaos' efforts. Her inscription and the statue, described by Pausanias as a less than life-size group of bronze horses (Paus. v. 12. 5), chariot and driver as well as Kyniska, said to have been created by Apelles, are also inconsistent with her brother's dislike of such manifestations of wealth rather than virtue (ch. 2. 4; Xen. *Agesilaos*, 11. 7).[4] Kyniska's entries in the Olympic Games in the 390s coincide, perhaps significantly, with Agesilaos' most active panhellenist period,[5] and the claim in the inscription that she, a member of the Spartan royal family, was the first woman in all Greece to have won the crown, draws attention to Sparta's leading position at the time—without engaging the men. Pausanias makes it clear that she was not the charioteer, though a few owners drove their chariots in person, such as Herodotos of Thebes (Pindar, *Isthm.* i. 61).[6]

This evidence suggests that Agesilaos' moral task was great, if Plutarch's claim is correct. At ch. 21. 5–7 he points to Agesilaos' view of trivial successes in Games; here the stress is on wealth. The wealthy Spartiate would not willingly provide a suitable model for Agesilaos, and he, also ineligible (cf. *Hiero* above), might choose Kyniska, who would be the first woman victor, for greater impact in a man's field at Olympia: female gymnastic exercise at Sparta was a useful precedent, but if Plutarch was mistaken, the panhellenist prestige would provide the motive.

2 Ξενοφῶντα δὲ τὸν σοφὸν ἔχων μεθ᾽ ἑαυτοῦ σπουδαζόμενον ἐκέλευε τοὺς παῖδας ἐν Λακεδαίμονι τρέφειν μεταπεμψάμενον, ὡς μαθησομένους τῶν μαθημάτων τὸ κάλλιστον, ἄρχεσθαι καὶ ἄρχειν.

Xenophon was in exile after offending the Athenians by joining Kyros and then the Spartans in Asia Minor; he became a friend of Agesilaos and for his services was rewarded with an estate at Skillous (Xen. *Hell.* iii. 2. 6–7, *An.* iii. 1. 4, v. 3. 7, vii. 7. 57, D.L. ii. 51–2, 58),[7] in territory annexed from the Pisatai by Elis early in the fifth century and then from Elis by the Spartan king Agis. He may have continued in Spartan service for a time even while living at Skillous, which was possibly a frontier outpost.[8] The estate was not far from Olympia on the road from Sparta, and is described as in good hunting country, with all kinds of game and good fishing in the river. We do not know how long Xenophon had to wait for the estate. It was still being developed when Megabyzos visited him for the Olympic games in 392 or later, bringing the proceeds of his share of the booty dedicated to Artemis (*An.* v. 3. 6): Xenophon built a temple and altar to the goddess whose produce was available to visitors to the festival (Xen. *An.* v. 3. 7–13, Paus. v. 6. 4–6). In the ancient world Xenophon was regarded highly as a philosopher,[9] but he has been overshadowed by the more powerful minds of his contemporaries and successors.

Xenophon had no children in Asia Minor before 399 and probably was unmarried at that time (*An.* vii. 6. 34), but he may have married Philesia (D.L. quoting Demetrios of Magnesia) and set up home there between then and his return (394). No home is known in Greece from which to bring his family to live in Skillous[10] and to provide a reference for μεταπεμψάμενον, 'sent for them to come'. Xenophon does not mention the education of his sons, but Diogenes Laertius (third century AD) records that Grylos and Diodoros were twins, and, according to Diokles' (b. *c*.75 BC) *Lives of the Philosophers*, were educated at Sparta (ii. 52, 54).[11] Whether they completed the full ἀγωγή is not known

but they were qualified to be Athenian citizens, and Grylos died
serving with his brother in the Athenian cavalry before the battle
of Mantineia in 362 (ch. 35, Paus. i. 3. 4, viii. 11. 6).[12]

The privilege of admittance to Spartan education, no doubt
highly valued by some, equipped non-Spartans to serve as
cavalrymen and hoplites, perhaps with the Spartan army, thus
easing to some extent the shortage of citizens (ὀλιγανθρωπία).
There were Spartan-trained 'adopted aliens' (ξένοι τῶν τροφίμων
καλουμένων) with the young king Agesipolis at Olynthos after
the death of Teleutias there (Xen. *Hell*. v. 3. 6, 9). Plutarch
encourages Spartan ideals, particularly the familiar one of
'obedience and leadership', ἄρχεσθαι καὶ ἄρχειν (see above after
ch. 1. 5. for other references; cf. *Lyk*. 30. 4). The priority he gives
to obedience suggests 'obedience as well as command'. This is the
theme in what follows.

3 τοῦ δὲ Λυσάνδρου τετελευτηκότος, εὑρὼν ἑταιρίαν πολλὴν συνεστῶ-
σαν, ἣν ἐκεῖνος εὐθὺς ἐπανελθὼν ἀπὸ τῆς Ἀσίας συνέστησεν ἐπὶ τὸν
Ἀγησίλαον, ὥρμησεν αὐτὸν ἐξελέγχειν οἷος ἦν ζῶν πολίτης·

Plutarch refers here to the discovery of the formation by Lysander
of a political club directed against Agesilaos, but does not say how
the discovery of the club was made. He referred separately at ch. 8
to Lysander's plan to change the Spartan hereditary kingship
(see Introd., E.3(*c*)), without revealing the way it was discovered.
At *Lysander*, 25. 1, 30. 3 he, like Diodoros, links it with the speech
of Kleon of Halikarnassos advocating the reform (§4; see above,
ch. 8. 3–4) found during a search for documents at the late
Lysander's home. Plutarch, but not Diodoros, makes Agesilaos
responsible for conducting the search. Lysander was to memorize
and deliver the speech, but how this was known is not stated, nor
if it was constitutionally possible for Lysander to deliver it;[13] he
realized that support needed to be engineered among the citizens
to ensure the success of the reform (*Lys*. 25. 2).[14] He may have
been responding to King Pausanias, who is said to have written on
the Spartan constitution after his exile,[15] unless Pausanias was
responding to Lysander's initiative.

It is difficult for historians to penetrate secret institutions, and
to authenticate their existence or aims; secrecy means that little of
the available information is reliable and most comes from the
winning side. Xenophon omits the episode, no doubt unwilling to

refer directly to any threat to Agesilaos' position as king, but recorded expressions of social unrest, though none that threatened the kingship: Kinadon led a protest against inferior status (*Hell.* iii. 3. 11), and the Perioikoi defected (vi. 5. 25, 32, vii. 2. 2). Plutarch adds mutiny and conspiracy (ch. 32. 6–9, 10–12).[16]

Lysander's alleged intrigues

Lys. 20. 5–6, 24. 2–26. 4, 30. 3–4, *Mor.* 212 C–D, 229 F, Nep. *Lys.* 3. 5, Diod. xiv. 13. 2–8.

By the end of the Peloponnesian war (Diod. xiv. 13. 1, Nep. *Lys.* 3. 1), Lysander's part in Sparta's victory had enhanced his reputation, suggesting the support he might have relied upon for his plan to deprive the royal houses of their exclusive right to the kingship. Plutarch (*Lys.* 18) records the self-advertisement at this time. At this time, too, Lysander may have been hoping in due course that he would succeed the ageing Agis, rather than the minor Latychidas, if he really was the heir apparent (see chs. 2–4). Diodoros here gives only ambition as the motive, whereas stronger reasons for a bid to take power are to be found in the political disagreement with Pausanias over the Athenian settlement (xiv. 33. 6), and in the decree of the ephors, which at least withdrew support from Lysander's system of rule by dekarchies (Xen. *Hell.* iii. 4. 2). A date before Agesilaos' reign began would be appropriate for a change in the kingship (see above, ch. 3).

Lysander's intentions may be indicated by the arrangement of Agesilaos' campaign in Asia Minor soon after his accession, suggesting that, if Lysander had become king, he would have resumed aggressive imperial expansion, which would be popular with his friends. That there was resistance to the so-called Lykourgan restraints on the accumulation and expenditure of wealth is manifested by the unparalleled succession of seven Spartan victories in the Olympic four-horse chariot races, starting in 448 and ending in 420, when Lichas[17] entered his team as Boiotian in order to avoid the Eleian ban on Spartan participation (Thuc. v. 50. 4, Xen. *Hell.* iii. 2. 21). His reputation for entertaining foreign visitors to the Spartan Gymnopaidiai festivals (*Kim.* 10. 5–6, Xen. *Mem.* i. 2. 61) shows that wealth was used to secure social and political prominence. The continuing problem is revealed by Agesilaos' opposition to wealthy breeders of racehorses; the disappointing withdrawal from Asia Minor would trigger the unrest to which Plutarch here shows him responding.

In deference to Spartan religious scruples (Diod. xiv. 13. 3–7, Nep. *Lys.* 3. 1–4), Lysander is reported to have sought oracular favour for his plan from Delphi, Dodona, and Ammon in 403, though without success, but the facts were unknown until the speech with which he hoped to persuade the Spartans was found at his home after his death (*Lys.* 30. 3–4, Diod. xiv. 13. 8, Nep. *Lys.* 3. 5). Plutarch acknowledges this early date if only for the plan, for when he describes Lysander's visit to Ammon to perform a promised sacrifice (*Lys.* 20. 4), he foreshadows the alternative suggestion of Ephoros (see Introd., F.1)—that it was to win the oracle's support (*Lys.* 25. 3). This subversive reason for Lysander's visit to the oracle of Ammon (Diod. xiv. 13. 5) may be doubted. The details would be known only from what the parties directly concerned were prepared to say in public. It has been suggested that he was engaged in diplomacy concerning Egypt rather than in purely religious matters. The later hostile tradition perhaps originated with King Pausanias,[18] who, unpopular and in exile since Lysander's death (Xen. *Hell.* iii. 5. 25), had been strongly backed against him at Athens in 403, and in his acquittal on subsequent trial, but there were still friends of the late Lysander in Sparta.

Plutarch assigns the proposed implementation of the plan to the time of his return from Asia (*Lys.* 24. 2), with the delivery of the speech of Kleon of Halikarnassos and the impersonation of Apollo's son by an accomplice, Silenus, to obtain and announce oracles from Delphi. The plot was abandoned when a helper failed to play his part (*Lys.* 25, 26). Plutarch omits this in *Agesilaos*, since it was planned before the accession of Agesilaos and failed before his return from Asia.

Plutarch's account (*Lys.* 26. 4, 30. 3) preserves Diodoros' separation in time of the plot and the discovery of the speech, but there is no reference to public disclosure, to later intrigues, or to any subsequent exploitation by Agesilaos. Here in *Agesilaos* Plutarch links the club with Lysander's discontent over his departure from Asia, and he inserts the account of the discovery of the conspiracy at this point, which is clearly later than Lysander's death at Haliartos; but the quarrel provides only a petty motive for constitutional reform. Lysander did not have very long in which to set up his 'society' between his return from Asia Minor and his death at Haliartos. He had taken command of an army in Boiotia: subversive activity is doubtful.

Plutarch suggests that on his return Agesilaos faced a crisis, and related it to supporters of Lysander's former policies. In the battle of Haliartos, they lost their most powerful leader, but their remaining strength is indicated by Pausanias' flight into exile, rather than face trial. Not only they, however, but also those Spartans who had welcomed his policies, will have continued to cherish their hopes and to wish to expand Agesilaos' restricted 'imperialist' policies. The presentation of the expedition to Asia Minor, after Agesilaos' accession, as intended to prevent war coming to the mainland, indicates the range of slogans created to attract wider support for the military command which Lysander obtained for the king. Imperialism was, for some, the best means to secure Sparta's survival and influence in the Peloponnese and beyond; for others an opportunity for positions of responsibility and residence abroad, to win and to use wealth for their conspicuous consumption. These clearly had continued to wish to enjoy their wealth in Agesilaos' reign as before.

The intended disclosure of Lysander's supposed plot is not aimed simply to discredit the memory of the man himself at this time. Plutarch, or his source, sees it as part of the machinery of Agesilaos' current attempts to establish control of the Spartan citizens who were opposing him, and who evidently could be identified as seeking to return to policies advocated in the preceding decade, which they had then presumably supported. Agesilaos is shown to have sought to discredit them by linking them with the reformist plans of Lysander which he had discovered—revolutionary, and even sacrilegious, without the approval of Delphi (*Lyk.* 29. 4), which Lysander had failed to obtain.

The Spartans paid Lysander many honours at his death (*Lys.* 30. 5), and if, by claiming to be acting in his name, his associates were gaining support for unacceptable policies, Agesilaos and the authorities may have resorted to blackening Lysander's record by presenting him as having aimed to take over from Agesilaos. The aftermath of the quarrel in Asia (chs. 7–8) could provide the pretext. The 'discovery' of the plot after Lysander's death provided a possible recent date for what may really have been proposed earlier, after the war, as legitimate reform. In Aristotle's view

(*Pol.* 1301ᵇ20), Lysander intended the overthrow (καταλῦσαι) of a particular office. The name could be retained, for the personal influence to be won by a king would replace the power lost to Lysander when his oligarchic policies were suspended. What he might use it for is unknown, but the moment for vision came with the realization of Sparta's opportunity—duty, even—in victory. Without religious sanction, and the support that would bring, the moment passed. After Agesilaos' 'discovery' it was not a question of current reform of the kingship, but of the use Agesilaos made of the evidence.

4 καὶ λόγον ἀναγνοὺς ἐν βιβλίῳ ἀπολελειμμένον, ὃν ἔγραψε μὲν Κλέων ὁ Ἁλικαρνασσεύς, ἔμελλε δὲ λέγειν ἀναλαβὼν ὁ Λύσανδρος ἐν τῷ δήμῳ περὶ πραγμάτων καινῶν καὶ μεταστάσεως τοῦ πολιτεύματος, ἠθέλησεν εἰς μέσον ἐξενεγκεῖν.

Grote[19] suggested that the speech may have been one—perhaps unsolicited—of the many manifestations of enthusiastic support for Lysander at the time of the renaming in Samos of Hera's festival as Lysandreia (*Lys.* 18. 4).[20] Its preservation in a private house provides a parallel to the archival records found in Sparta by Plutarch (ch. 19. 10) and evidence for literacy at Sparta at this level of society, perhaps with technical assistance.[21] Such documents may also have contained the information relevant to the dispute among the allies, for which Agesilaos was conducting the search (*Lys.* 30. 3). In retailing Diodoros (xiv. 13. 8) or Ephoros Plutarch gives no more evidence for Lysander's intentions and motives, which could be known only from a special informant. If Lysander did intend to make his proposal before the people, this was evidently constitutional reform rather than revolution; the process would not be completed thereafter without a struggle with the reigning kings, and the Gerusia, empowered by the famous amendment to the Great Rhetra to overrule the assembly, unless all agreed: Agesilaos needed to ensure their loyalty to him (ch. 4. 5). As Grote argues,[22] though from a different starting-point, the change in selecting the kings might have been validated in full legal form with no appeal to violence, if the kings' families and supporters formed the minority and were outvoted.

5 ἐπεὶ δέ τις τῶν γερόντων τὸν λόγον ἀναγνοὺς καὶ φοβηθεὶς τὴν δεινότητα, συνεβούλευσε μὴ τὸν Λύσανδρον ἀνορύττειν, ἀλλὰ τὸν λόγον μᾶλλον αὐτῷ συγκατορύττειν, ἐπείσθη καὶ καθησύχαζε.

The fear gives a hint of the possible strength of the opposition and of the determination of the establishment to avoid weakening the state in open confrontation by publishing the speech and possibly also evidence of others involved. The advice of 'one of the Elders' avoids making formal accusations of any kind. Suspicions may be aroused by the secrecy and by the obscurity of the adviser. He is not named in Diod. xiv. 13, and, although he was said, on the authority of Ephoros (*Lys.* 30. 3), to be the senior ephor, Lakratidas (*Mor.* 229 F: Kratidas),[23] he is otherwise unknown in the sources. That the intention to publicize details of the plot was unfulfilled may raise further speculation that what took place at this time was all invented for the purpose of propaganda. Suppression of publication is a convenient cover to put accusations of conspiracy beyond challenge. It would not preclude mention of the discovery of the plot itself and the ἑταιρία (§3), or its use as a veiled threat to any who were known to have had links with Lysander; Agesilaos' opponents (§6) were first made aware that they were marked men, and then sent off with the chance to behave properly on public service, subjected to further manipulation if need be.

Lysander's desire for rule, ἄρχειν, to be won by reforming the kingship, here demonstrates his failure to learn its necessary counterpart, ἄρχεσθαι, obedience to law (§2 above), whereas Agesilaos, having learnt both, obeys his adviser and continues to exercise his kingly function. The discovery, if not the details, will have been published at the time or it would not have come into the record: it will have rallied the king's loyal supporters to a show of strength.

6 τοὺς δ' ὑπεναντιουμένους αὐτῷ φανερῶς μὲν οὐκ ἔβλαπτε, διαπραττόμενος δὲ πέμπεσθαί τινας ἀεὶ στρατηγοὺς καὶ ἄρχοντας ἐξ αὐτῶν, ἐπεδείκνυε γινομένους ἐν ταῖς ἐξουσίαις πονηροὺς καὶ πλεονέκτας, . . .

Plutarch may be continuing from ch. 5 the topic of converting opponents into friends, but he could be starting an account of Agesilaos' efforts to rebuild his power-base on his return from Asia Minor, in particular to win over his young colleague Agesipolis (§§7–8). His use of deception is well documented in the

Life. Plutarch seems to be enlarging on Xenophon's references to similar paternalistic treatment of opponents, designed to avoid their alienation or destruction (*Agesilaos*, 7. 3). If this device may be compared with the Athenians' resort to the courts in political conflicts, what was going on would be less obvious to Agesilaos' victims, but in the end charges will have been threatened for malpractices in the positions of responsibility held later. There were risks in making these appointments: διαπραττόμενος, 'by intrigue', implies that they were not made easily or unopposed (cf. ch. 21. 1).

. . . εἶτα κρινομένοις πάλιν αὖ βοηθῶν καὶ συναγωνιζόμενος, οἰκείους ἐκ διαφόρων ἐποιεῖτο καὶ μεθίστη πρὸς αὐτόν, ὥστε μηδέν' ἀντίπαλον εἶναι.

This constitutes the second of a double use of deception in Agesilaos' scheming, his response after their misuse of authority in office; the first lay in apparently making no response to their opposition. They had erred twice and would be doubly indebted to him when they realized what he had done for them.

7 ὁ γὰρ ἕτερος βασιλεὺς Ἀγησίπολις, ἅτε δὴ πατρὸς μὲν ὢν φυγάδος, ἡλικίᾳ δὲ παντάπασι μειράκιον, φύσει δὲ πρᾶος καὶ κόσμιος, οὐ πολλὰ τῶν πολιτικῶν ἔπραττεν.

Agesipolis and Agesilaos share the innate qualities of gentleness and orderliness, φύσει δὲ πρᾶος καὶ κόσμιος, yet their characters and actions diverge (cf. *Mor.* 2 A–B, 3 A–B). Plutarch attributes Agesipolis' limited political activity to externally imposed restraints connected with his father's banishment, to his youth, and to the internal restraints imposed by these qualities. His situation was not likely to give him the confidence and positive motivation which Agesilaos enjoyed (ch. 2. 1–2) and he would not easily resist Agesilaos' manipulative powers, whose πρᾳότης, at least, could be deliberately assumed (ch. 2. 2).

8 οὐ μὴν ἀλλὰ καὶ τοῦτον ἐποιεῖτο χειροήθη. συσσιτοῦσι γὰρ οἱ βασιλεῖς εἰς τὸ αὐτὸ φοιτῶντες φιδίτιον, ὅταν ἐπιδημῶσιν.

Plutarch emphasizes Agesilaos' desire for influence even in the case of his newly appointed colleague, and he implies that the part Agesipolis, guided by his family and advisers, had played in public affairs since his accession was sometimes in opposition to the absent Agesilaos. Xenophon, too, gives a hint of political disagreement when he describes, perhaps in defensive terms, Agesilaos' response to news of his colleague's death in Chalkidike (*Hell*. v. 3. 19–20; see below, §9).

Plutarch discusses the names of the Spartan messes at *Lyk*. 12. 1: Xenophon uses συσκηνία and related words at *Hell*. v. 3. 19–20, where he also reports the kings' public mess (cf. *Lak. Pol*. 5. 2, 15. 4). The similarity of the two kings' names was perhaps deliberately created in the naming of the younger man: the suffix -λαος, 'of the people', by then associated with Agesilaos' alleged δημοτικὸν καὶ φιλάνθρωπον (ch. 1; cf. Archidamos, Doric -δαμος (δῆμος), the name of his father and his son), to be countered with -πολις, 'of the city', leading the whole community. There was little chance of success for Agesipolis; in view of his father's record at Athens, Haliartos and Mantineia (Xen. *Hell*. v. 2. 5–6), he was not likely to be aligned with Lysander's men, and his own gentle nature suggests a less aggressive tendency and perhaps a more peaceful policy than Agesilaos' (Diod. xv. 19. 4).[24] The metaphor χειρόηθης, tame, was used of Agesilaos (ch. 1. 3).

9 εἰδὼς οὖν ἔνοχον ὄντα τοῖς ἐρωτικοῖς τὸν Ἀγησίπολιν, ὥσπερ ἦν αὐτός, ἀεί τινος ὑπῆρχε λόγου περὶ τῶν ἐν ὥρᾳ· καὶ προῆγε τὸν νεανίσκον εἰς ταὐτὸ καὶ συνήρα καὶ συνέπραττε, τῶν Λακωνικῶν ἐρώτων οὐδὲν αἰσχρόν, αἰδῶ δὲ πολλὴν καὶ φιλοτιμίαν καὶ ζῆλον ἀρετῆς ἐχόντων, ὡς ἐν τοῖς περὶ Λυκούργου γέγραπται.

Plutarch seems to have taken the situations and conversations described here from Xenophon (*Hell*. v. 3. 20, *Agesilaos*, 8. 2), where the two men are similarly well-matched (ἱκανός) and discuss shared interests. He interprets Xenophon's παιδικοὶ λόγοι as 'talk of love' (τοῖς ἐρωτικοῖς), reverting to the topic of chs. 11 and 13. This meaning may not be what Xenophon intended, though his readers may have so taken it. It does not suit his context, where Agesilaos hears the report of the death of Agesipolis 'with tears, not, as might be expected, with joy, as of an opponent' (*Hell*. v. 3. 20; his word ἀντιπάλῳ, 'opponent', was used by Plutarch above, §6). Xenophon goes on to list four interests they talked of, in a chiastic pattern: hunting and horsemanship, the inner pair, are active pursuits; the two outer words, ἡβητικοί, παιδικοί, both meaning 'youthful', suggest 'playful, light-hearted', perhaps 'educative' pastimes, considering that associated words occur as terms for Spartan age-groups (Xen. *Hell.* v. 4. 32, *Lak. Pol.* 3–4). Furthermore, at *Agesilaos*, 5. 4, dealing with control of affections, Xenophon compares Agesilaos' love for Megabates with the love that a most earnest nature feels for the κάλλιστον, which in the abstract context for Xenophon the philosopher means 'that which is most honourable'.[25] Plutarch's version stretches Xenophon's meaning, but he, like Xenophon, presents only the conversations of the two men, and the relevant passages in *Lykourgos* are educational (17. 1 and 18. 4). The emphasis there is on the friends' mutual dedication to honour that results from these relationships. While at chs. 11 and 13 Plutarch shows Agesilaos simply enjoying the company of young men, the language in these contexts is ambiguous, and others, like Cicero (*Tusc.* iv. 70), will take a more hard-headed view.

PART VII (chs. 21–2)

The Corinthian war

Artax. 20. 3–4; Xen. *Hell.* iii. 5. 1–25, iv. 2. 9–23, 3. 10–12, 4. 1–7, 19, 5. 5–18, 6. 1–7. 1; *Agesilaos*, 2. 17–21; Diod. xiv. 81. 1–86. 6, 91. 2–92. 2, 97. 5; *Hell. Ox.* II. 2, XI. 1, XIII. 1–5 (Bruce (1967), 58–61, 102, 116–22); Nepos, *Iphicr.* 2. 3; Paus. iii. 9. 8–12, iv. 17. 5; Polyain. ii. 1. 1, 10.

21. Games at Corinth, and Spartan attitudes to games

Lyk. 20. 5; Xen. *Hell.* iv. 5. 1–2; Diod. xiv. 86. 5; Paus. iii. 10. 1.[1]

1 Μέγιστον οὖν δυνάμενος ἐν τῇ πόλει, διαπράττεται Τελευτίαν τὸν ὁμομήτριον ἀδελφὸν ἐπὶ τοῦ ναυτικοῦ γενέσθαι.

When Xenophon describes the joint expedition to Argos and Corinth (*Hell.* iv. 4. 19), he does not record Teleutias' appointment by his brother Agesilaos but he stresses their relationship. It will have been harder to justify this appointment of a relative in Sparta than the earlier one of Peisandros (ch. 10. 11) in Asia Minor where fewer eligible Spartans were available. Teleutias and Peisandros were given charge of a fleet while the king himself commanded the army, but the defeat sustained by the first appointment will not have made the second any easier. Plutarch, who was interested in the family, surprisingly does not comment on the significance of the relationship of the two successful commanders for their mother, whose delight is pointed out by Xenophon (*Hell.* iv. 4. 19), though there is a lacuna in the text here. The appointment follows Agesilaos' achievement of the position of power in Sparta which was engaging him in ch. 20 above. That difficult negotiations, even devious methods, were required behind the scenes to repeat the appointment of a kinsman is implied by Plutarch's choice of verb, διαπράττεται, 'arranged', used already of Agesilaos (chs. 13. 4, 20. 6). The prominent placing of this verb, alongside the claim that Agesilaos' power was supreme in the city, points to influential opposition, which it would take all Agesilaos' political skills and subtle pressure to overcome.

The Spartiates

Even in Sparta at this time, and not only in Asia Minor, strong candidates were presumably in short supply. In any one generation or year group, there can have been only a limited and small number of talented Spartans, if the total citizenship was little over 1,000. Aristotle's claim that after Leuktra the number dropped below 1,000 (*Pol.* 1270ᵃ29–34) suggests a figure of about 1,350 before then, following the already significant decline of the previous decades.[2] In numbers, the Spartan Assembly is comparable with a senior school of 1,000 pupils at the present day. Leaders are required each year as prefects, captains of sports teams, principals, and administrators of other activities. The school's 'year group' is about 120, the annual intake, and the age range is about eight years. Sparta's hoplite age range is perhaps roughly (since some did not live to retiring age) four times as much, so that Sparta's 'year group' would be in the order of 30.

This is a small pool from which to take men of excellence to be responsible for state activities that called for qualities of leadership, but the hierarchical organization of the ἀγωγή enabled selection at each stage to be based on practical experience, however fallible that might be, and leaders did emerge. Thucydides' presentation of the principal Spartan leaders distinguishes between those in the majority who 'exhibited typically Spartan qualities: slow, cautious, conventional, lacking in inspiration and imagination', and Brasidas, 'the antithesis of the typical Spartan leader', 'an un-Spartan Spartan'.[3] Despite the presentation of him by Xenophon, Lysander was a successful Spartan leader (see Introd., E.3),[4] and Teleutias was an able admiral and general (Xen. *Hell.* v. 1. 2–4, 13–24, 2. 37–3. 6).

2 καὶ στρατευσάμενος εἰς Κόρινθον, αὐτὸς μὲν ᾔρει κατὰ γῆν τὰ μακρὰ τείχη, ταῖς δὲ ναυσὶν ὁ Τελευτίας ⟨καὶ τὰ νεώρια⟩. **3** Ἀργείων δὲ τὴν Κόρινθον ἐχόντων τότε καὶ τὰ Ἴσθμια συντελούντων, . . .

The lacuna may be filled from Xenophon (*Hell.* iv. 4. 19), who associates Teleutias' seizure of the dockyards with the first of Agesilaos' two expeditions, in which he ravaged Argive territory and captured the walls of Corinth. He records a second expedition during the games at the Isthmus, after which Agesilaos took Peiraion (iv. 5. 1). Plutarch does not separate the two campaigns, perhaps because Xenophon seems to indicate only a temporary absence for the festival of Hyakinthos (*Agesilaos*, 2. 17). However, the essential military details are given in two parts, the second continuing in ch. 22, after the development in this chapter of the theme of competition in athletic contests.

Union of Argos and Corinth

The two cities, Argos and Corinth, had united by now to become one, in some way (Xen. *Hell*. iv. 4. 2–6), following a violent uprising against the supporters of peace who wanted to reintroduce co-operation with Sparta. Since Agesilaos was not involved, Plutarch mentions it only now. 'An experiment with considerable potential',[5] it might, despite its origin, have been extended with benefit to other cities in time, although the evidence does not make it possible to accept as certain a full merger of Corinth into the Argive polity. Xenophon retails the hostile propaganda of his Corinthian friends (cf. *Hell*. iv. 5. 1, 8. 15, 34), who saw in the union the 'disappearance' of their city.[6] There were Corinthians still in power (Xen. *Hell*. iv. 4. 5), no doubt democrats who wanted Argive support just as the aristocrats enjoyed Spartan support.[7] But with an Argive presence they gained the greater security which a Spartan garrison gave later to the Theban oligarchs (Xen. *Hell*. v. 2. 26). Diodoros (xiv. 92. 1) describes massive Argive intervention when allied control of Corinth was under threat. The situation of Corinth at the time suggests a military arrangement, made with Sparta's traditional enemy by the faction opposed to Sparta, for mutual defence, backed by political act of formalization recognizing that the interests of the two cities were as one, as Winston Churchill once proposed between Britain and endangered France: internal political dispute in Corinth created new external relationships.

Plutarch turns to the celebration of the Isthmian Games by the Argives, whose presidency is implied by Xenophon: 'as though Argos were Corinth' (*Hell*. iv. 5. 1; cf. iv. 4. 6, Andocides, iii, Diod. xiv. 86. 1, 92. 1). The isopolity allowed participation in religious matters, although sole Argive presidency is disputed.[8] Even joint celebration would be a powerful declaration of the solidarity of the opposition to Sparta (cf. Paus. iii. 10. 1). The cities were separated again by the insistence of Agesilaos on the terms of the Peace of Antalkidas, as Sparta could not accept

the legalizing of Corinth's transformation from a former ally into a
new enemy, the enhancement of Argos, her old rival for leadership
in the Peloponnese, and the combined strength of the new unit
able to control the Isthmus.

. . . ἐπιφανεὶς ἐκείνους μὲν ἐξήλασεν ἄρτι τῷ θεῷ τεθυκότας, τὴν
παρασκευὴν ἅπασαν ἀπολιπόντας· 4 ἐπεὶ δὲ τῶν Κορινθίων ὅσοι
φυγάδες ἔτυχον παρόντες ἐδεήθησαν αὐτοῦ τὸν ἀγῶνα διαθεῖναι, τοῦτο
μὲν οὐκ ἐποίησεν, αὐτῶν δ' ἐκείνων διατιθέντων καὶ συντελούντων,
παρέμεινε καὶ παρέσχεν ἀσφάλειαν. 5 ὕστερον δ' ἀπελθόντος αὐτοῦ,
πάλιν ὑπ' Ἀργείων ἤχθη τὰ Ἴσθμια, . . .

When the Argives abandoned their sacrifices, Agesilaos encamped
in the sacred enclosure, offered sacrifices to the god Poseidon, and
waited while the Corinthian exiles conducted the games (*Hell.* iv.
5. 2). Plutarch does not mention the sacrilege of interfering with
the sacrifices, which his version more strongly implies, but he
credits Agesilaos with refusing the invitation, which does not
occur in Xenophon, to manage the games: he does not even
sacrifice here, as he does in Xenophon, and will not preside but
only gives protection to others who are politically acceptable. He
is contrasted with both of the parties who celebrate the games, the
members of the *isopoliteia* and the exiled Corinthians. Plutarch
takes this to indicate Agesilaos' dispraise of these and other games;
it is more explicit at §§6–7 below.

Plutarch follows Xenophon in using the 'Argive' name, which
the aristocrats found it impossible to live with (Xen. *Hell.* iv. 4. 3,
6), to distinguish the *isopoliteia* from the exiles he still calls
Corinthians. He perhaps shared Xenophon's disapproval of
democracy in Corinth.

. . . καί τινες μὲν ἐνίκησαν πάλιν, εἰσὶ δ' οἳ νενικηκότες πρότερον,
ἡττημένοι δ' ὕστερον, ἀνεγράφησαν. 6 ἐπὶ τούτῳ δὲ πολλὴν ἀπέφηνε
δειλίαν κατηγορεῖν ἑαυτῶν τοὺς Ἀργείους ὁ Ἀγησίλαος, εἰ σεμνὸν οὕτω
καὶ μέγα τὴν ἀγωνοθεσίαν ἡγούμενοι, μάχεσθαι περὶ αὐτῆς οὐκ
ἐτόλμησαν.

Plutarch's observation is not quite the same as Xenophon's who
notes simply that some results were repeated (*Hell.* iv. 5. 2). It is
more subtle, slightly humorous: the second official list revealed
that some winners did not win again. Plutarch's change casts
doubt on these results as marks of prowess, just as the Argives'

refusal to fight for the games devalues success in their competition, and allows Agesilaos to question the sincerity of their respect for the festival.

7 αὐτὸς δὲ πρὸς ταῦτα πάντα μετρίως ᾤετο δεῖν ἔχειν· καὶ τοὺς μὲν οἴκοι χοροὺς καὶ ἀγῶνας ἐπεκόσμει, καὶ συμπαρῆν ἀεὶ φιλοτιμίας καὶ σπουδῆς μεστὸς ὤν, καὶ οὔτε παίδων οὔτε παρθένων ἁμίλλης ἀπολειπόμενος, ἃ δὲ τοὺς ἄλλους ἑώρα θαυμάζοντας ἐδόκει μηδὲ γινώσκειν.

For Plutarch Agesilaos regards participation in competitive games as a complex issue: 'restraint' forbids competing at international games, but not at Sparta's. The basis for distinction is not made clear until §8. The Spartan record at Olympia reveals a decline from about half the victors in running down to 600 BC, to barely 20 per cent in all events in the fifth century, the majority in equestrian events.[9] This indicates that the Spartan attitude to athletic contests changed. Increasing professionalism in other cities produced specialists with narrow physical development, and the Spartans perhaps recognized that specialized training for speed was incompatible with their own emphasis on toughness and general fitness, with a view to military service. While competition in international sprinting was sacrificed, the Spartans did not neglect speed in military training: their young hoplites once overtook enemy peltasts (Xen. *Hell.* iv. 4. 16).

Spartan games at home, οἴκοι, receive different consideration. Contests in the ἀγωγή, including the organized battles between the boys' units (*Lyk.* 16. 5–17. 1), and civic choral functions, which may have been suggested to Plutarch by the Hyakinthia and the Gymnopaidiai mentioned in connection with Agesilaos (Xen. *Agesilaos*, 2. 17, *Hell.* vi. 4. 16), were an essential formative part of Spartan life. Girls exercised, too, in athletics, performed in festivals of music and dance, and inspired young men by mockery and praise, composing their own songs (*Lyk.* 14. 2–15. 1; *Lak. Pol.* 1. 4). That these were to be enhanced, and attended by Agesilaos, reflects his own participation in the ἀγωγή and his desire to encourage particularly the young participants he was watching. An illuminating parallel for Agesilaos' interest in contests for the young comes from Roman Sparta, when a wealthy Spartan contemporary of Plutarch with possibly royal claims, C. Iulius Agesilaus, funds prizes in the Leonidean Games for a new age-class of *paides*, the κρίσις Ἀγησιλάου, 'Agesilaos' event': perhaps he is deliberately echoing his famous namesake's interests.[10]

Spartan youths, if not in real life, at least in the traditional view, which Plutarch seems to have admired, often fought each other when they met. The combatants were separated, not by competitive rules, but by watching adults (*Lak. Pol.* 4. 6), or even by the death of one fighter. Perhaps it was in such a fight that the exiled Drakontios, one of the few Spartiates with Xenophon in Asia, had accidentally killed a boy with a dagger (*An.* iv. 8. 25–6): 'No real Spartan ever surrendered.'[11]

For Plutarch's purpose of revealing Agesilaos' attitude, the emphasis is on courage. The Argives' refusal to fight for control of the Games, though the victories were subsequently celebrated by the competitors, is contrasted with Agesilaos' moderate attitude to his own recent victories: as if to show that he had fought and won the battle that gave him control of the Games, if he had wanted it, but had rejected it as worthless display. Spartan real achievement is contrasted with the empty glory of competitive games, forming a bridge to the next section, Agesilaos' view of empty glories that have impressed others.

8 καί ποτε Καλλιππίδης ὁ τῶν τραγῳδιῶν ὑποκριτὴς ὄνομα καὶ δόξαν ἔχων ἐν τοῖς Ἕλλησι καὶ σπουδαζόμενος ὑπὸ πάντων, πρῶτον μὲν ἀπήντησεν αὐτῷ καὶ προσεῖπεν, ἔπειτα σοβαρῶς εἰς τοὺς συμπεριπατοῦντας ἐμβαλὼν ἑαυτὸν ἐπεδείκνυτο, νομίζων ἐκεῖνον ἄρξειν τινὸς φιλοφροσύνης, τέλος δ' εἶπεν, Οὐκ ἐπιγινώσκεις με, ὦ βασιλεῦ; κἀκεῖνος ἀποβλέψας πρὸς αὐτὸν εἶπεν, Ἀλλ' οὐ τύγ' ἐσσὶ Καλλιππίδας ὁ δεικηλίκτας; οὕτω δὲ Λακεδαιμόνιοι τοὺς μίμους καλοῦσι. **9** παρακαλούμενος δὲ πάλιν ἀκοῦσαι τοῦ τὴν ἀηδόνα μιμουμένου, παρῃτήσατο φήσας, Αὐτᾶς ἄκουκα. **10** τοῦ δ' ἰατροῦ Μενεκράτους, ἐπεὶ κατατυχὼν ἔν τισιν ἀπεγνωσμέναις θεραπείαις Ζεὺς ἐπεκλήθη, φορτικῶς ταύτῃ χρωμένου τῇ προσωνυμίᾳ καὶ δὴ καὶ πρὸς ἐκεῖνον ἐπιστεῖλαι τολμήσαντος οὕτως· Μενεκράτης Ζεὺς βασιλεῖ Ἀγησιλάῳ χαίρειν, ἀντέγραψε· Βασιλεὺς Ἀγησίλαος Μενεκράτει ὑγιαίνειν.

Plutarch presents three anecdotes, found also in *Apophth. Lak.* (*Mor.* 191 A–B, 212 F, 213 A; cf. 348 E) and elsewhere. They do not directly disparage competitive games—perhaps he found no one suitable except Kyniska (ch. 20)—but refer to the lack of restraint (§7) associated with performers and their admirers. Two are men already criticized (see below); the other trivializes imitation:

indirect characterization avoids any insult. The first is Kallippides, a tragic actor known for his pride (Xen. *Smp.* iii. 11); the second (§9) an anonymous imitator of the nightingale (*Lyk.* 20. 5). They earn the admiration they enjoy here as theatrical entertainers who please their audiences, and they relish the fame of their successes.

Douris of Samos recorded that Kallippides gave the rhythm of the stroke to the crew of the ship that brought Alkibiades into the harbour of Mounychia on his triumphant return from Samos, and, although Plutarch prefers a different account, the fame, and perhaps the flamboyance of Kallippides, is proved by Douris' use of his name (*Alk.* 32. 2). Kallippides won prizes in the Lenaian competitions five times, including that of 419, and may have been the eponym of a comedy of Strattis (*c.*409–375). Aristotle quotes criticism of him as an 'ape' by the actor Mynniskos for 'exceeding the bounds' (*Poet.* 1461^{b}34–62^a; cf. Aristophanes, fr. 490 K–A). The contemptuous label 'the showman', δεικηλίκτας, which Athenaios associates with κωμικὴ παιδιά, 'the childish amusement of comic drama', σκευοποιοί, 'makers of masks', μιμηταί, 'impersonators' (621 D–E), must have been a grave insult to the tragic actor in sharp contrast with his reputation elsewhere, illustrating the fierce humour with which the Spartans strengthened their sense of superiority.[12] This sense of humour shows in many of the anecdotes in *Apophth. Lak.* For Spartan contempt for other entertainments, see *Kl.* 12. 3.

The third anecdote (§10) introduces Menekrates, an unusually successful medical doctor whose grateful patients called him Zeus, still known to Aelian (*VH* xii. 51). Athenaios (289 A–90 B), quoting Hegesander of Delphi (anecdotist, 2nd cent.) and the play *Minos* by Alexis of Thourioi (comic poet, *c.*372–270), tells of his letter similarly addressed to Archidamos, and the letter of the anecdote addressed to Philip of Makedon; Menekrates accused Philip of murdering ὑγιαίνοντες, 'the healthy'; Philip's ὑγιαίνειν suggests that he might be a victim.

The three have in common not only their fame, but also their presumptuous demands to be acknowledged by Agesilaos, in insisting respectively on recognition at sight, on the acceptance of an invitation to witness a performance, and on the return use of a flattering form of address (for φορτικῶς cf. ch. 8. 6; Arist. *Pol.* 1333^{h}9). Although their eminent achievements, two of them highly valued, cannot be in doubt, Agesilaos refuses each demand.

The less worthy case of the bird imitator, however, suggests that Agesilaos' objections to international games were directed against both the quest for immoderate fame and participation in trivial activities.

Praise for success even in war was restrained at Sparta, though there is to be an exception (ch. 33. 6): only men who died in battle and women who died in childbirth were normally allowed gravestones.[13] International games were thus—for Agesilaos and Plutarch—unworthy activities, and victory in them should not earn the competitor an entitlement at Sparta to public acclaim for proven ἀρετή. A distinction is drawn between specialist sprinting events and tests of strength (§7 above): the appropriate Spartan reward for the latter was the privilege of fighting 'before' the king (*Lyk.* 22. 4).

Plutarch continues the character study of ch. 20, and completes the Olympic reference by extending it here to the non-equestrian events in the games at the Isthmus. The Spartan view must be distinguished from the disdain for popular entertainment of the Roman aristocrat who turned to political or literary pursuits. In Plutarch's Sparta the preference is for activity which benefits the state in respect of its survival against its enemies, but he adds the moral dimension of moderation and self-control, which Kallippides and Menekrates lacked.

22. Retribution at Corinth: rehabilitation in Akarnania

Plutarch continues Agesilaos' second campaign, from before the digression (ch. 21. 8). He selects three military actions complimentary to Agesilaos, the successes at Corinth, at the Corinthian Heraion, and in Akarnania, and separates these with two longer passages in which moral failures are associated with the humiliation of Sparta. In this way he illustrates and judges both competence and character.

1 Διατρίβοντος δὲ περὶ τὴν Κορινθίαν αὐτοῦ καὶ τὸ Ἡραῖον εἰληφότος καὶ τὰ αἰχμάλωτα τοὺς στρατιώτας ἄγοντας καὶ φέροντας ἐπιβλέποντος, . . .

Agesilaos approached the site of the Isthmian Games, near the shore of the Saronic Gulf, from Corinth to the west (Xen. *Hell.* iv. 5. 1). He then moved north to reach Peiraion, 'the land beyond' still in Corinthian territory, where the citizens had evacuated their stock. The remains of the temple of Hera are in a beautiful setting on the sea-shore near the tip of the Perachora peninsula, facing the city of Corinth across the Corinthian Gulf.[1] The adjacent tiny harbour was probably used by the pilgrims coming here from Corinth at festival times, but now, following the seizure of Lechaion to the north of the city (Xen. *Agesilaos*, 2. 18), it provided for communications between Corinth and the allies in central Greece, for there is also convenient access to the Boiotian coast through the port of Kreusis, which lies to the north-east across the Halkyonic Gulf. Another port, Aigosthena, further to the east in Megarian territory, provides for communication with Athens.

Agesilaos found Peiraion strongly guarded by the Athenian general Iphikrates and his peltasts and withdrew to Corinth, to where the defenders also hastened overnight. Agesilaos returned next morning to capture Peiraion and its fort, Oinoe, and the refugees in the Heraion surrendered with all their possessions (Xen. *Hell.* iv. 5. 3–6, *Agesilaos*, 2. 18–19). Agesilaos now handed over to his friends, the Corinthian exiles, those who had been ejected in the violent uprising and massacre in Corinth (*Hell.* iv. 4. 2). Xenophon omits this at *Agesilaos*, 2. 19, where it would be unsuitable for the encomium. He also omits Agesilaos' error of judgement, when in the attack on Peiraion his men spent a night on the mountain without suitable clothing (*Hell.* iv. 5. 4). These topics would contribute nothing to the military and moral themes of the chapter. Plutarch, too, omits all this, and conveys the full measure of Agesilaos' success with a pattern of five participles.

. . . ἀφίκοντο πρέσβεις ἐκ Θηβῶν περὶ φιλίας. **2** ὁ δὲ μισῶν μὲν ἀεὶ τὴν πόλιν, οἰόμενος δὲ τότε καὶ συμφέρειν ἐνυβρίσαι, προσεποιεῖτο μήθ᾽ ὁρᾶν αὐτοὺς μήτ᾽ ἀκούειν ἐντυγχανόντων.

Plutarch continues with the events in chronological order, and Agesilaos is already supervising the booty when the envoys approach. He substitutes Thebes for Xenophon's Boiotians, and so can add Agesilaos' regular attitude to the city (chs. 6. 11, 26. 6, 28. 2–3) as the cause of his moral lapse in ignoring them; and he sharpens the contrast by putting περὶ φιλίας, 'about friendship', for περὶ εἰρήνης, 'about peace'. The desire to negotiate indicates that the allies' situation was serious, although Plutarch does not mention this. Such important negotiations may have needed higher authorization, although the envoys' sudden change of heart seems to have been locally motivated. The presence of the Spartan forces at the Isthmus already imperilled allied land communications, and Agesilaos' capture of the harbour here now deprives the northern allies in Corinth of their remaining access by sea both to supplies from Boiotia and Athens, and to their line of retreat.

The oxymoron in the juxtaposition συμφέρειν ἐνυβρίσαι, 'to be well to insult', and the all-inclusive 'neither to see nor to hear', intensify Agesilaos' aberration against the Thebans. The impact of the aberration will be sharpened by the immediate arrival of messengers with news of disaster 'while the Thebans are still there' (§3). A sense of outrage is clearly in Plutarch's mind: there can, in the religious view, be no lasting advantage to be won from such insolence (*Mor.* 548–68).

Xenophon does not refer to this discreditable episode in *Agesilaos*. In *Hellenika*, too, he seems reluctant to expose Agesilaos' insulting treatment of the Thebans to divine anger, portraying his arrogance instead. The surrender of the refugees is followed by the arrival of several embassies in addition to the Boiotian peace mission, but neither the purpose of the other envoys nor Agesilaos' response to them is stated; and when Xenophon remarks on Agesilaos' 'great arrogance' in ignoring the envoys, the focus is on the Thebans because their agent Pharax was trying to attract his attention. Xenophon then presents Agesilaos seated in a circular building and, in a further act of arrogance, watching in exultation as the booty is brought from the Heraion (*Hell.* iv. 5. 6).[2]

This is the moment when the messenger of disaster arrives. Xenophon does not refer to retribution but the catalogue of errors culminates in the juxtaposition of Agesilaos' exultation and the gloomy face of the messenger, σκυθρωπὸς ὤν (*Hell.* iv. 5. 7); and although Agesilaos takes prompt action to go to the rescue, the gloom continues with the news that only bodies are recovered.

3 ἔπαθε δὲ πρᾶγμα νεμεσητόν· οὔπω γὰρ ἀπηλλαγμένων τῶν Θηβαίων ἧκόν τινες ἀπαγγέλλοντες αὐτῷ τὴν μόραν ὑπ' Ἰφικράτους κατακεκόφθαι.

Religious retribution[3] is explicit here, although Plutarch does not exploit the air of mystery introduced by Xenophon earlier, regarding the unknown cause of a fire in the temple of Poseidon, after Agesilaos had sent braziers to the troops on the mountain (*Hell.* iv. 5. 4). The 'world view'[4] of the two writers is similar in this respect: actions on the human plane have a causal influence on, or are a response to, other actions on the same or a higher plane.[5] The Spartans were conscious of being punished by the gods for contravening 'natural law': over the restoration of Pleistoanax, at least if they believed his enemies, and over the start of the Peloponnesian war (Thuc. v. 16–17, vii. 18. 2; cf. ch. 30. 1–2). Plutarch, too, was conscious of the intervention of the gods at Aulis, most explicitly at *Pelopidas*, 21. 4.

The engagement[6] is identified here only by the name of the Athenian commander, Iphikrates. Agesilaos followed custom by allowing the Spartiates from Amyklai, one of Sparta's five villages, to return home for the festival of the Hyakinthia, escorted past Corinth by cavalry and a unit, μόρα, of hoplites stationed at Lechaion (Xen. *Hell.* iv. 5. 10–18). As the escort returned from Sikyon, Iphikrates and the allies attacked them and killed 250, nearly half their number.[7] Xenophon's first brief mention of the disaster, at *Hell.* iv. 5. 7[8] follows immediately upon Agesilaos' excessive exultation, suggesting a link between the two. His full account is postponed while he first re-establishes the Spartans' reputation and self-confidence by recording Agesilaos' demonstration at Corinth of his continuing power to ravage the territory unopposed.

4 καὶ πάθος τοῦτο μέγα διὰ πολλοῦ χρόνου συνέπεσεν αὐτοῖς· πολλοὺς γὰρ ἄνδρας ἀγαθοὺς ἀπέβαλον κρατηθέντας ὑπό τε πελταστῶν ὁπλίτας καὶ μισθοφόρων Λακεδαιμονίους.

The noun, πάθος, recalls the verb, ἔπαθε (§3). The 'disaster' at Lechaion, and not the report, was the 'act of retribution', despite the delay, just as the eclipse before Koroneia coincided with the report of Knidos, not with the battle itself (ch. 17. 4). Plutarch's view of the omniscience and absolute competence of the gods is shared with Xenophon; the Spartans are favoured and deterred (*Hell.* iv. 4. 12, vi. 4. 3; cf. *Mor.* 316–26, esp. 324 B).[9] Agesilaos' moral lapse marks the start of the downturn in Spartan affairs, soon after the half-way stage in the *Life*. It is not a continuous

slide from this point on. Plutarch presents, in both Sparta and
Agesilaos, a complex character, neither perfect nor wholly bad. He
perhaps has in mind a comparison with the Spartan disaster at
Koryphasion (Thuc. iv. 3–20).

Xenophon records distress throughout the army, but describes
the disaster less colourfully as 'unusual' for the Spartans (*Hell.* iv.
5. 10), and records the Spartan commander's mistaken confidence
that his hoplites would not be attacked by peltasts (*Hell.* iv. 5. 12),
whom they despised (*Hell.* iv. 4. 17). Plutarch's pattern of words,
juxtaposing light and heavy armed troops, mercenaries and
Lakedaimonians, highlights the paradoxical aspect of the engagement which impressed Xenophon. He holds the Spartan name
back to the emphatic position at the end of the sentence, heightening the sense of the shock to the hoplites hitherto considered
invincible, prefiguring, perhaps, the decline in Spartan power in
the rest of Agesilaos' reign. He keeps the focus on Agesilaos
himself, omitting weaknesses recorded by Xenophon—the failure
to press the retreating peltasts, the faint-heartedness under attack,
and the flight as the Athenian hoplites approach (*Hell.* iv. 5.
16–17).

5 ἀνεπήδησε μὲν οὖν εὐθὺς ὁ Ἀγησίλαος ὡς βοηθήσων· ἐπεὶ δ᾽ ἔγνω
διαπεπραγμένους, αὖθις εἰς τὸ Ἡραῖον ἧκε, καὶ τοὺς Βοιωτοὺς τότε
πρυσελθεῖν κελεύσας ἐχρημάτιζεν.

Both authors show Agesilaos' immediate response to the crisis,
but while Plutarch preserves chronological order and indicates the
immediacy by placing the verb first, Xenophon describes the
reaction before he describes the disaster (*Hell.* iv. 5. 7–10, 11–18).
The downturn, for Plutarch, is not in Agesilaos' generalship: his
show of readiness to do business with the envoys is an ineffectual
attempt to recover from the lapse in moral character. It is a
military loss that Sparta has suffered, but Agesilaos' generalship
cannot retrieve it.

6 ὡς δ᾽ ἀνθυβρίζοντες ἐκεῖνοι τῆς μὲν εἰρήνης οὐκέτ᾽ ἐμέμνηντο,
παρεθῆναι δ᾽ ἠξίουν εἰς Κόρινθον, ὀργισθεὶς ὁ Ἀγησίλαος εἶπεν·

The retribution continues in the envoys' change of heart, adequately motivated by their knowledge of the serious loss of
Spartiates. The number of Spartans still in the area had also
been reduced by the departure of all the Amyklaians in the army,

deliberately left behind at Lechaion (Xen. *Hell.* iv. 5. 11). On the other hand, Iphikrates' success had revived the confidence of the allies at Corinth. The envoys' request was unlikely to be granted by Agesilaos, who would not wish it to be reported to the allies that he had suffered such losses, and the Spartan habit of secrecy still prevailed (cf. Thuc. v. 68. 2). Xenophon's report of Agesilaos' rejection of the request describes the external display of humour that accompanied his words (*Hell.* iv. 5. 9), an example of ἐνάργεια allowing the readers to observe the scene for themselves. He does not make explicit what lies behind that display, but presents Agesilaos as if still in control of the situation. Plutarch prefers to present Agesilaos' frustration on the reversal of his progress in the war. His account suggests that the envoys' revived confidence leads Agesilaos into further moral decline in succumbing to anger, which is often taken by Plutarch to precede downfall (*Pel.* 32. 6–7, *Alex.* 62. 3, 74. 3).

Εἴγε βούλεσθε τοὺς φίλους ὑμῶν ἰδεῖν μέγα φρονοῦντας ἐφ' οἷς εὐτυχοῦσιν, αὔριον ἀσφαλῶς ὑμῖν τοῦθ' ὑπάρξει.

Agesilaos' irony is perhaps matched by the irony of Plutarch, whose phrase μέγα φρονοῦντας, 'arrogant', closely resembles the words used by Xenophon in criticizing Agesilaos for keeping the envoys waiting (*Hell.* iv. 5. 6). His display of force may have made a deeper impression on his own troops, perhaps as he intended.

7 καὶ παραλαβὼν αὐτοὺς τῇ ὑστεραίᾳ τήν τε χώραν τῶν Κορινθίων ἔκοπτε καὶ πρὸς τὴν πόλιν αὐτὴν προσῆλθεν. οὕτω δὲ τοὺς Κορινθίους ἐξελέγξας ἀμύνεσθαι μὴ τολμῶντας, ἀφῆκε τὴν πρεσβείαν.

Agesilaos demonstrates his continuing strength, characteristically by devastation of the countryside (cf. §9). The Corinthians—the democratic 'Argives'—were not likely to accept his challenge. The moderate effect of the disaster on the strength of the whole Lakedaimonian army was not commensurate with its greater impact on the resources of the Spartiates themselves, and their enemy's morale.

8 αὐτὸς δὲ τοὺς περιλελειμμένους ἄνδρας ἐκ τῆς μόρας ἀναλαβὼν ἀπῆγεν εἰς Λακεδαίμονα, πρὸ ἡμέρας ποιούμενος τὰς ἀναζεύξεις καὶ πάλιν σκοταίους τὰς καταλύσεις, ὅπως οἱ μισοῦντες καὶ βασκαίνοντες τῶν Ἀρκάδων μὴ ἐπιχαίρωσιν.

This perhaps is a more valid indication of the real state of the conflict than Agesilaos' freedom of movement around Corinth. Plutarch presents it more clearly than Xenophon, who postpones the account of the disaster, and uses it to separate the Spartan challenge at Corinth (*Hell.* iv. 5. 10) from the departure of the army for home (*Hell.* iv. 5. 18): it was unsafe for Agesilaos to stay in the Corinthia. The Lakedaimonians held on to Lechaion, but Iphikrates recovered all other places taken by Agesilaos (Xen. *Hell.* iv. 5. 10, Diod. xiv. 91. 3). The secrecy observed on the march home is explained by Plutarch, following Xenophon, as Agesilaos' wish to avoid exposing the troops to humiliation. He would also wish to avoid being attacked at critical stages, and, by lengthening the day's march, to expedite his arrival in Sparta. Since he had with him only the remnant of the defeated μόρα (*Hell.* iv. 5. 18), it was important for the Spartans not to allow its reduced strength to be observed by an enemy that had recovered some of its high spirits.

The route through the more friendly eastern Arkadia, which avoided the powerful enemy Argos, passed through the territory of Orchomenos, Mantineia, and either Tegea or Asea, before reaching Sparta.[10] Arkadia had been invaded and ravaged by Iphikrates (Xen. *Hell.* iv. 4. 15–16), but the Mantineians had been mocked by the Spartans for their flight before an onslaught of peltasts outside the Lechaion wall (Xen. *Hell.* iv. 4. 16–17; cf. §4).

9 ἐκ τούτου χαριζόμενος τοῖς Ἀχαιοῖς διέβαινεν εἰς Ἀκαρνανίαν στρατιᾷ μετ' αὐτῶν καὶ πολλὴν μὲν ἠλάσατο λείαν, μάχῃ δὲ τοὺς Ἀκαρνᾶνας ἐνίκησε.

Agesilaos needed to respond in order to keep the route open through Arkadia and its northern neighbour, Achaia, to give access to the Isthmus and across the gulf to central Greece. The Achaians in possession of Kalydon, earlier an Aitolian town near the border with Akarnania, had been attacked by the Akarnanians and their Athenian and Boiotian allies, for the Akarnanians had deserted Sparta and joined the allies of the Council of Corinth (Diod. xiv. 82. 2); they were on the Athenian side in the battle at the Nemea (Xen. *Hell.* iv. 2. 17). The Achaians had called on the Spartans, under threat of abandoning them, to repay them for their support (Xen. *Hell.* iv. 6. 1–3).

Plutarch ends the chapter with a brief but exaggerated account of the successes won against the Akarnanians, omitting the historical background given by Xenophon, and portraying Agesilaos still as a formidable general. Yet Xenophon did not describe Agesilaos' campaign as an unqualified success, except in the capture of cattle, horses, and slaves, and in the devastation of the countryside (*Hell.* iv. 6. 1–14). The Akarnanian peltasts were superior in guerrilla actions, but the Lakedaimonian hoplites won an engagement for which Agesilaos set up a trophy. Xenophon stresses his failure to capture any of the towns he assaulted,[11] and further implies his inability to recover Naupaktos for the Aitolians. This important base, where Messenians from Ithome had been settled by Athens, was retaken after the end of the Peloponnesian war (Paus. iv. 26. 1–2, x. 38. 9–10; Diod. xiv. 34. 2–3) and then occupied by the Lokrians (cf. ch. 34. 1). Its recovery for friends of Sparta would have been a major achievement. Plutarch's selections from Xenophon (*Hell.* iv. 6. 6, 13; 7. 1) give a favourable picture of Agesilaos' generalship.

10 δεομένων δὲ τῶν Ἀχαιῶν ὅπως τὸν χειμῶνα παραμείνας ἀφέληται τὸν σπόρον τῶν πολεμίων, τοὐναντίον ἔφη ποιήσειν· μᾶλλον γὰρ φοβήσεσθαι τὸν πόλεμον αὐτούς, ἐὰν ἐσπαρμένην τὴν γῆν εἰς ὥρας ἔχωσιν· ὃ καὶ συνέβη. **11** παραγγελλομένης γὰρ αὖθις ἐπ᾽ αὐτοὺς στρατείας, διηλλάγησαν τοῖς Ἀχαιοῖς.

Agesilaos' generalship is further enhanced by his decision at the end of the campaign, presenting him as a skilled strategist: the crops would be vulnerable and the invaders would have supplies at hand. The seasons, winter and spring, are relevant to techniques of ravaging crops. Before winter Agesilaos drove off cattle (§9) and cut and burned crops, ἔκοπτε καὶ ἔκαε (Xen. *Hell.* iv. 6. 12, cf. iv. 5. 10), when they would be dry. In spring new growth, even vines and young trees, could be trampled and cut.[12]

Plutarch concludes that Agesilaos' military judgement was correct: the decline suffered by Sparta was not due to any deficiency in his competence as commander. He does not record the historical significance of the strategy: the Akarnanians transferred their allegiance and joined the Spartan alliance (Xen. *Hell.* iv. 7. 1).

Failures of Spartan justice

23. The Peace of Antalkidas and the Kadmeia episode

Art. 21. 4–5, 22. 2, *Pel.* 5. 1–6. 1, 6. 4–13. 4, 14. 1–3, *Mor.* 213 B 1–13; Xen. *Hell.* iv. 8. 1–v. 1. 36, v. 2. 24–32, 4. 1–13, 15, 20–34, *Agesilaos,* 2. 21, 8. 3–4; Diod. iv. 110. 2–4, xv. 1. 1–5, 5. 1, 20. 1–3, 23. 3–4, 25. 1–28. 5, 29. 5–7; Isok. 4. 126–7, 175–80; Polyb. i. 6. 1–2; Nepos, *Pel.* 1. 2–4. 1.

Plutarch's ideal, panhellenism, occupies him here, and the responsibility for Sparta's policies on Persia and Thebes, which are the reverse of panhellenist. He deals favourably with Agesilaos during the making of the Peace of Antalkidas, but is critical of his part in Phoibidas' seizure of the Kadmeia. He gives a favourable analysis of Agesilaos' theoretical attitude to justice, but is critical of his judgement of Phoibidas.

Chronological arrangement and responsibility

After describing activity on land during the Corinthian war (chs. 21, 22), Plutarch now summarizes Konon's exploits with the Persian fleet which force Sparta to make peace with the King. The temporal conjunction 'when' (ἐπεί) at the start of this chapter introduces events in which Agesilaos has no part; he preludes the peace with Spartan problems.

Xenophon records Antalkidas' unsuccessful attempt to end Konon's activities and make peace (*Hell.* iv. 8. 12, 15); he preludes the Peace of Antalkidas (387/6; v. 1. 32) with Athenian problems at Aigina and Abydos: Athens is ready for peace, while the Lakedaimonians merely find the war 'irksome' (v. 1. 24, 27–31). Diodoros omits the first peace move, describes the war at sea (xiv. 83. 5–85. 4), and summarizes the intervening war on land (xiv. 91. 2–3). Spartan weakness preludes their request for peace, for the Lakedaimonians are suffering from their double war (xiv. 110. 2).

1 Ἐπεὶ δὲ Κόνων καὶ Φαρνάβαζος τῷ βασιλέως ναυτικῷ θαλαττοκρα-

τοῦντες ἐπόρθουν τὰ παράλια τῆς Λακωνικῆς, ἐτειχίσθη δὲ καὶ τὸ ἄστυ τῶν Ἀθηναίων, Φαρναβάζου χρήματα δόντος, ἔδοξε τοῖς Λακεδαιμονίοις εἰρήνην ποιεῖσθαι πρὸς βασιλέα·

Whereas Xenophon gives precedence to Pharnabazos in this episode (*Hell.* iv. 8. 1), Plutarch puts the Greek commander first, as if he, like Diodoros (xiv. 81. 4), considers Konon to be the initiator of the enterprise. He resents this Greek treachery, the attack on Lakonia resourced by the King and the abandonment of Sparta's fight. The two thrusts of panhellenism clash: the end of a Greek war against Greeks ends a crusade against Persia. The Athenians had already started to rebuild their walls, with the help of volunteers from Boiotia and other cities (*Hell.* iv. 8. 10).[1]

Konon, the Athenian, was given command of the fleet which Pharnabazos had persuaded the King to build (Diod. xiv. 39. 1–2), but he was later made joint commander with Pharnabazos (Diod. xiv. 81. 6). The fleet was intended to deal with the trouble in Cyprus and Egypt and with the Spartan interventions in Asia Minor (Diod. xiv. 35. 3–4, 39. 1, 98. 2); it was one reason given for Agesilaos' expedition (ch. 6). The defeat of the Spartan fleet under Peisandros off Knidos (ch. 17. 4) led to Konon's activity in the Aegean, and at this time it was clear that the King was concentrating his efforts against Greece on Sparta. Xenophon passes lightly over the raids on Lakonia, saying only that Kythera receives an Athenian garrison (*Hell.* iv. 8. 8), yet the sense of insecurity created for Sparta by the hostile forces threatening Lakonia itself may be judged by the consternation caused by the Athenian occupations of Koryphasion and Kythera in 425–424 (Thuc. iv. 1–41, 53–5); it brought the threat of a helot uprising closer. Kythera was the port for ships bringing grain from Egypt and Libya (cf. Hdt. vii. 235; Thuc. iv. 53. 4, 55, vii. 26; Diod. xiv. 79. 4; Paus. i. 27. 6).[2]

2 καὶ πέμπουσιν Ἀνταλκίδαν πρὸς Τιρίβαζον, αἴσχιστα καὶ παρανομώτατα τοὺς τὴν Ἀσίαν κατοικοῦντας Ἕλληνας, ὑπὲρ ὧν ἐπολέμησεν Ἀγησίλαος, βασιλεῖ παραδιδόντες.

Antalkidas got on well with Tiribazos and was ξένος of Ariobarzanes (Xen. *Hell.* v. 1. 6, 28), who replaced Pharnabazos as satrap at Daskyleion. He may be the son of the Leon (*Art.* 21. 5) who was, among other things,[3] the Olympic victor in 440, a colonist of Herakleia (Thuc. iii. 92. 5), and ephor of 419/18 (Xen.

Hell. ii. 3. 10). Leon was a common name[4] but if Antalkidas' father was the Leon known to Thucydides and father also of Pedaritos, Antalkidas was likely to be related to Teleutias and his half-brother Agesilaos through their mother Teleutia (*Mor.* 241 D–E).[5] This relationship would not disprove, but might tell against, the notion of Agesilaos' hostility to Antalkidas and his Peace: whatever the truth, he might prefer to be free subsequently to denounce disadvantageous terms, or deplore them.

Movement towards peace

When the Athenians learned of Antalkidas' mission, they, the Boiotians, the Corinthians, and the Argives sent envoys to prevent agreement because they did not want to be deprived of their various dependencies (Xen. *Hell.* iv. 8. 13–14). About five years later, by Xenophon's account, Antalkidas was navarch, and, sailing from Aigina to Ephesos, made his way from there to the King, with whom he agreed a Spartan alliance and the conditions of the peace named after him (*Hell.* v. 1. 6, 25, 35; Diod. xiv. 110. 3–4; *Art.* 21. 4–5, *Mor.* 213 B). Plutarch apparently attaches the second, successful, mission to the preliminaries of the first, which was inconclusive. He omits the new motivations for peace— Artaxerxes' transfer of support to Sparta with the arrest of Konon, the reverses at sea inflicted on Athens by Teleutias, the concession that Athens was to retain Lemnos, Imbros, and Skyros, Sparta's weariness of the situation at the Isthmus, and its anxiety over the revival of the Athenian hegemony under Thrasyboulos, Iphikrates, and Chabrias (Xen. *Hell.* iv. 8. 25–31, 34–9, v. 1. 10; Diod. xiv. 92. 1).[6]

Possession of Abydos appears to have been a crucial factor on both sides, giving control of ships sailing from the Pontos to Athens (Xen. *Hell.* v. 1. 27–8). Iphikrates had besieged the city for Athens, taking it when its Spartan governor Anaxibios had been killed (*Hell.* iv. 8. 39). Antalkidas sent Nikolochos to reoccupy it, but he was blockaded by the Athenians. Antalkidas relieved him and the Spartan ships under siege there, forcing the Athenians to seek peace. He then negotiated with Persia, and agreed that the cities in Asia should, as before 479, belong to Artaxerxes (*Hell.* v. 1. 7, 25–8, 31).

The betrayal of Ionia

Plutarch strengthens the criticism from which at §3 he excludes
Agesilaos, recording as his judgement (cf. *Mor.* 213 B) that the
surrender to the King of the Greeks living in Asia Minor (*Art.* 21.
5) was 'shameful and unparalleled', αἴσχιστα καὶ παρανομώτατα. He
shows more concern and moral outrage over this betrayal than was
immediately evident (Xen. *Hell.* v. 1. 25, 32, 36).[7] Ionia had
frequently endured domination since the reign of the Lydian,
Gyges, in the seventh century. Some Greek cities preserved independent status by paying tribute to the King, just as non-Greeks
in the area did.[8] Greeks in the cities were at times willing to
co-operate with Persians in return for political power (Xen. *Hell.*
iii. 1. 6). A proposal to seek a Persian alliance was discussed at
Sparta before the Peloponnesian war (Thuc. i. 82), and during it
both sides competed for Persian favour (Thuc. ii. 67. 1, iv. 50).
Then the panhellenist war against Persia was urged in order to
end war between Greeks, without success; see Introd., E.7(*c–d*).
The peace initiative, identified by the motivations stated above
and dated to 392, failed,[9] although Plutarch does not mention
this.

3 ὅθεν ἥκιστα συνέβη τῆς κακοδοξίας ταύτης Ἀγησιλάῳ μετασχεῖν·

There is no trace of 'discredit' in Xenophon's accounts of the two
occasions when Antalkidas took his proposals to Asia Minor. The
allies' immediate responses were fears that the autonomy clause
would deprive them of possessions (*Hell.* iv. 8. 15, v. 1. 6, 25).[10]
There is in this no personal attack on anyone, except that the King
is said to have specified the terms,[11] though Xenophon suggests
that he rather accepted Sparta's initiative (Xen. *Hell.* v. 1. 25).[12]
Later Diodoros claims that the abandonment of the cities distressed the Athenians, the Thebans, and other Greeks who agreed
only of necessity (xiv. 110. 4), and 'discredited' Sparta (xv. 9. 5,
19. 4; cf. Philochoros (fl. 306–260), *FGrH* 328 F 149a).[13] Lysias
blamed Sparta in 384 'because much of Greece was subject to the
foreigner' (xxxiii. 4–7, cf. ii. 57–9).[14] According to Isokrates *c.*380
(4. 129–31, 12. 103, 106), the shame of the Peace should inspire
Greece to mount a war against Persia and end internal rivalries
and hostilities; cf. Introd., E.7(*d*).

Plutarch's 'incident of serious and mournful import'[15] presents

Sparta in an unfavourable light over the issue of the Greek cities in Asia Minor. But 'practical politicians, dealing with the everyday needs and ambitions of their states, saw no danger in medizing'.[16] Many sought Persian support when it suited them to do so, disregarding the danger; Persian expansion and diplomacy forced them into war. Yet after the peace the cities enjoyed increased prosperity;[17] affairs in Cyprus and Egypt now occupied the King (Diod. xiv. 110, xv. 2).

ὁ γὰρ Ἀνταλκίδας ἐχθρὸς ἦν αὐτῷ, καὶ τὴν εἰρήνην ἐξ ἅπαντος ἔπραττεν ὡς τοῦ πολέμου τὸν Ἀγησίλαον αὔξοντος καὶ ποιοῦντος ἐνδοξότατον καὶ μέγιστον.

Agesilaos is not mentioned by Xenophon as concerned directly in the diplomacy that led to the peace—it was a Lakedaimonian initiative—and it appears that Plutarch took his absence from the record to mean that he was opposed to it. This could be a reasonable interpretation for him to make, in view of Agesilaos' earlier campaigns against the Persians, and given the tendency to personalize policy-making. He may have recalled that at *Agesilaos*, 2. 21 Xenophon mentions his opposition, but this was only to force the restoration of his exiled friends.

Plutarch needs to explain the political difference between the two men. In ch. 26. 3 Antalkidas claims that Agesilaos' wound was a tuition fee for teaching the Thebans in many battles how to fight (*Mor.* 213 F), but this does not prove that the two were enemies, and rivalry with Agesilaos is not the only possible explanation of Antalkidas' prominent part. Agesilaos' record of hostility to Persia presumably required him to be excluded personally—or given no part by Xenophon—from the negotiation of the peace: he would share Teleutias' proud independence (Xen. *Hell.* v. 1. 17). That Xenophon associates the peace with Antalkidas (*Hell.* v. 1. 36) does not prove political disagreement.

In giving personal rivalry as the reason for the political differences—at *Art.* 21. 4 Antalkidas made peace independently through his friendship with the King—Plutarch is largely following *Mor.* 213 B, and portraying character indirectly, for Antalkidas' thought expresses an implied criticism of Agesilaos as 'fond of war', φιλοπόλεμος, also found in Diodoros (xv. 19. 4). Two military reasons for the Spartans' decision to make peace are already given (§1); mention of the personal differences diverts the expression of the strong feelings about the betrayal of the cities away from Agesilaos.

The criticism of Agesilaos is inappropriate in this context, for his reputation had not been enhanced by Sparta's plight, his humiliating return with his army from Corinth, and his limited success in Akarnania. Some later actions had been more successful, but the credit for them did not belong to Agesilaos, the most decisive, which forced Athens to accept the peace, being won at sea, by Teleutias in the Saronic Gulf, and by Antalkidas himself— apparently no pacifist—at Abydos. The statement could have been made more truly about the campaigns in Asia Minor, though still only with some qualification, as has been seen above; Diodoros' remark above (xv. 19. 4) follows Agesilaos' aggressive policies after the Peace. This anecdote, without a context, may conflate two originally detached; the negotiations of 372–371 may be more appropriate (cf. ch. 27. 7, Xen. *Hell.* vi. 3. 12).

4 οὐ μὴν ἀλλὰ καὶ πρὸς τὸν εἰπόντα τοὺς Λακεδαιμονίους μηδίζειν ὁ Ἀγησίλαος ἀπεκρίνατο μᾶλλον τοὺς Μήδους λακωνίζειν.

Plutarch continues with a saying which reveals Agesilaos' attitude to the peace: the Persians do not 'Hellenize' but 'Lakonize', λακωνίζειν. The word highlights Sparta's position as leader of Greece, and favours and compliments Sparta: the peace is in Sparta's interest. The statement will be closer to the truth, if the terms of the peace are attributable to the Spartan side originally.

Agesilaos' remark is in chiastic order of word stems, Λακ- μηδ- Μηδ- λακ-. It occurs in a different form (*Art.* 22. 2) with chiastic order of the parts of speech: verb, noun, noun, verb, as again in reported speech (*Mor.* 213 B). Plutarch is not tied to any one of the three different versions which he can claim as Agesilaos' original, and he uses different names, Lakedaimonians and Lakonians. The anecdote reinforces the presentation of Agesilaos' contempt for the Persians, while he benefits from the peace.[18]

5 τοῖς δὲ μὴ βουλομένοις δέχεσθαι τὴν εἰρήνην ἀπειλῶν καὶ καταγγέλλων πόλεμον, ἠνάγκασεν ἐμμένειν ἅπαντας οἷς ὁ Πέρσης ἐδικαίωσε, μάλιστα διὰ τοὺς Θηβαίους, ὅπως αὐτόνομον τὴν Βοιωτίαν ἀφέντες ἀσθενέστεροι γένωνται.

The Corinthians refused to dismiss the Argive garrison; the Thebans refused to disband the Boiotian Confederacy (Xen. *Hell.*

v. 1. 34–6) and to send troops on campaign against Olynthos (Xen. *Hell*. v. 2. 27). Both were required to comply by Agesilaos' threat of war to enforce his interpretation of the autonomy clause in the Peace.[19] This now becomes a powerful weapon in mainland Greece; equally it is the main factor in forming hostile attitudes to Sparta. Its enforcement in Sparta's interest offended many allies, and spurred Thebes to resume the leadership of a revived and revised Boiotian Confederacy.[20] Plutarch implies that the opportunity to harm Thebes changed Agesilaos' attitude.

δῆλον δὲ τοῦτο τοῖς ὕστερον ἐποίησεν. 6 ἐπεὶ γὰρ Φοιβίδας ἔργον εἰργάσατο δεινὸν ἐν σπονδαῖς καὶ εἰρήνῃ τὴν Καδμείαν καταλαβών, καὶ πάντες μὲν ἠγανάκτουν οἱ Ἕλληνες, χαλεπῶς δ' ἔφερον οἱ Σπαρτιᾶται,

A bridge from Antalkidas' peace at §1 to the rest of the chapter is provided first by his clash with Agesilaos, then by Agesilaos' treatment of Thebes. Thebes, like Sparta, had no unassailable citadel.[21] The Kadmeia is a striking feature, but not a formidable stronghold.[22] Its importance for the Spartan occupation was its use for meetings of the Council of the Confederacy.

Plutarch condemns the action of Phoibidas in taking the Kadmeia in 382 as a violation of the Peace. He overlooks Xenophon's unattributed report, perhaps intended as uncomplimentary to Thebes by its author, whoever that was, of a conversation between Phoibidas and one of the polemarchs, Leontiadas— 'intimate' friends (*Hell*. v. 2. 26–7, cf *Pel*. 5. 2)—arranging the betrayal of the Kadmeia. Such secret arrangements cannot be checked, but other features of the event render this aspect less important: what matters is why and how the seizure was accomplished. Sparta's interest in the northern region, Thrace and the cities of Chalkidike (Xen. *Hell*. v. 2. 11–36), can be understood as designed to frustrate Theban attempts to secure friends who might counteract the encirclement of Boiotia by Spartan garrisons.

Xenophon records that the assembly of the allies allowed the Lakedaimonians to fine states that failed to supply troops when required; that according to Leontiadas a proclamation had been made forbidding Thebans to serve in the force which Phoibidas was collecting for the Thracian expedition; and that Phoibidas, who had been sent to help Apollonia and Akanthos against the encroachments of Olynthos, had encamped near the *gymnasion* outside Thebes (*Hell.* v. 2. 22, 25, 27). He gives no reason why Phoibidas should have delayed his march north, but the three recorded facts may be connected: Phoibidas was there to collect either the troops or the fine. Collusion with Leontiadas, who was friendly to Sparta and may have used Phoibidas to score over his opponent, Ismenias, made the task easier. When Leontiadas later came to Sparta to address the Lakedaimonians, he promised that Thebes would fulfil all demands that were made. The Lakedaimonians were now in better spirits for the expedition (*Hell.* v. 2. 34, 37), having ensured that a friendly Thebes would not hinder their communications, or block any retreat of the allies. Plutarch's complaint is still justified, for occupation exceeded what was allowed, the collection of the fine. Xenophon admitted that it caused annoyance to the Spartiates and ephors and aroused the indignation of the gods (*Hell.* v. 2. 32, 4. 1).

καὶ μάλισθ' οἱ διαφερόμενοι τῷ Ἀγησιλάῳ μετ' ὀργῆς ἐπυνθάνοντο τοῦ Φοιβίδου τίνος ταῦτα κελεύσαντος ἔπραξεν, εἰς ἐκεῖνον τὴν ὑπόνοιαν τρέποντες,

If the above interpretation is correct, Phoibidas was empowered to deal with the question of the Theban contribution to the expeditionary force, and that may explain Diodoros' statement (xv. 20. 2) that Spartan commanders were given secret instructions to take any opportunity to seize the Kadmeia, although according to the ephors and the majority of the citizens the occupation of the Kadmeia was not so authorized (Xen. *Hell.* v. 2. 32). Xenophon, at this point, ignores the question of the fine, and instead stresses the personal elements: Leontiadas' flattery of Phoibidas, the criticism of Phoibidas' character (*Hell.* v. 2. 27–8), and Agesilaos' suggestion that, if Sparta benefited, Phoibidas was right to have acted on his own initiative (*Hell.* v. 2. 32). The seizure of the Kadmeia is separated by Xenophon from the decision to keep a guard there, which is taken only after Leontiadas advises it (v. 2. 33–5), removing the guilt from the Spartans. Plutarch appears dissatisfied with Xenophon's failure to confront the issue, and implies the existence at Sparta of suspicion that there were secret instructions.

7 οὐκ ὤκνησε τῷ Φοιβίδᾳ βοηθῶν λέγειν ἀναφανδὸν ὅτι δεῖ τὴν πρᾶξιν αὐτὴν εἴ τι χρήσιμον ἔχει σκοπεῖν· τὰ γὰρ συμφέροντα τῇ Λακεδαίμονι καλῶς ἔχειν αὐτοματίζεσθαι, κἂν μηδεὶς κελεύσῃ.

In ch. 20 Plutarch described how Agesilaos made friends by helping men in trouble; he soon appoints Phoibidas as harmost at Thespiai (Xen. *Hell.* v. 4. 41–4). In practical politics, the interest of the state—ultimately its survival—is paramount. Plutarch records Agesilaos' equation of honourable action with national interest, an equation found also in the Melian Dialogue (Thuc. v. 105. 4); according to Thucydides' Athenians, the Spartans more than others believe that what suits their interest is just (quoted by the Byzantine Anaxilaos in his defence at *Alk.* 31. 6; cf. Plato, *Resp.* 338 E 6; ch. 37. 9 below).[23]

Xenophon reports Agesilaos' view, avoiding further enquiry, that, 'based on ancient practice', authorization is not required for service to the state. The question, whether the deed was good or bad, is related not to ethical principle but to state interest (*Hell.* v. 2. 32). Thus Spartan justice defines crime as injury to the state, while service to the state is a matter not for the laws of morality but for individual decision and endeavour. Agesilaos absolves Sparta from responsibility and Phoibidas from guilt. Xenophon records no punishment of Phoibidas, and it is Leontiadas the Theban who convinces the Spartans that it is in their interest to continue the occupation; but Plutarch does not use Leontiadas to absolve Agesilaos from this responsibility (see below, §11). Here he introduces the moral element, preferring 'is good', καλῶς ἔχειν, to Xenophon's 'is customary, lawful', νόμιμον, and so can take the discussion further into the theory of ethics in the rest of the chapter. The 'world view' has changed.[24]

8 καίτοι τῷ λόγῳ πανταχοῦ τὴν δικαιοσύνην ἀπέφαινε πρωτεύειν τῶν ἀρετῶν· ἀνδρίας μὲν γὰρ οὐδὲν ὄφελος εἶναι, μὴ παρούσης δικαιοσύνης, εἰ δὲ δίκαιοι πάντες γένοιντο, μηδὲν ἀνδρίας δεήσεσθαι.

Plutarch attributes to Agesilaos a contradiction between his policy and his belief in the primacy of the principle of justice. Since he gives it priority over other virtues, Phoibidas' 'unjust action' is not to be defended successfully by expediency. To facilitate Plutarch's *a fortiori* argument, the expedient action of Phoibidas is replaced by the example of the chief active virtue, courage (ἀνδρία). 'Courage is useless if it lacks justice; courage is not required if there is already justice.' The instability of the competitive virtue, courage, contrasts with the stability of the co-operative virtue, justice. Courage is desirable in order to effect change *to*, not *in* or *from*, a just situation.

9 πρὸς δὲ τοὺς λέγοντας ὅτι ταῦτα δοκεῖ τῷ μεγάλῳ βασιλεῖ, Τί δ᾽ ἐκεῖνος ἐμοῦ, εἶπε, μείζων, εἰ μὴ καὶ δικαιότερος; ὀρθῶς καὶ καλῶς οἰόμενος δεῖν τῷ δικαίῳ καθάπερ μέτρῳ βασιλικῷ μετρεῖσθαι τὴν ὑπεροχὴν τοῦ μείζονος.

The argument that this confirms the King's greatness is questioned by a suggestion of an invalid counter-example, which concedes the supposed Persian lack of courage: 'the King is not disadvantaged without it'. He could prove his greatness—'that he is more entitled to be called Great King'—by being more just; but justice is an even clearer supposed Persian deficiency. Agesilaos' superior belief in the primacy of justice is thus confirmed. In suggesting that 'justice must be the standard by which precisely to measure the greatness of a king', he departs from the Homeric standard of ἀρετή, 'ever to be bravest' (*Il.* vi. 208). The phrase, καθάπερ μέτρῳ βασιλικῷ, is perhaps a play on βασίλειος πῆχυς, the royal cubit, which, Herodotos reports, was greater than the standard one by three fingers' width (i. 178. 3).

10 ἦν δὲ τῆς εἰρήνης γενομένης ἔπεμψεν αὐτῷ περὶ ξενίας καὶ φιλίας ἐπιστολὴν ὁ βασιλεὺς οὐκ ἔλαβεν, εἰπὼν ἐξαρκεῖν τὴν κοινὴν φιλίαν καὶ μηδὲν ἰδίας δεήσεσθαι μενούσης ἐκείνης.

Having disposed of the chief rival contender for primacy, ἀνδρία, Plutarch now returns the argument to the absolute value of the co-operative virtues, for, in Agesilaos' reply to the King, the security of the friendly relationship implies the primacy of honour.

Agesilaos persistently exploited ξενία.[25] Here—*Mor.* 213 D–E gives the context 'after the peace'—he may be keeping doors open.[26] When Ariobarzanes in revolt was gathering Greek mercenaries (366–365), including Agesilaos,[27] this may have been his response to a letter from the King attempting to divert his favour. Later, at the height of the Satraps' revolt (362), the King's request for mercenaries was rejected by both Agesilaos and the exhausted cities of Greece. Friendship with Sparta at either time would require the reversal of the King's recognition in 367–366 of the autonomy of Messene as a necessary preliminary.[28] When Xenophon refers to this letter (*Agesilaos*, 8. 3; cf. *Hell.* iv. 1. 15, Aelian, *VH* x. 20) he suggests that Agesilaos' negative reply demonstrates 'high-mindedness', μεγαλογνωμοσύνη, in putting the requirements of the state before personal considerations.

11 ἐν δὲ τοῖς ἔργοις οὐκέτι ταύτην διαφυλάττων τὴν δόξαν, ἀλλὰ τῇ φιλοτιμίᾳ καὶ τῇ φιλονικίᾳ πολλαχοῦ συνεκφερόμενος, καὶ μάλιστα τῇ πρὸς Θηβαίους,

Plutarch now resumes the case of Phoibidas and the theme of the decline of Agesilaos. He believed that a man's character was displayed in his actions. In Thucydides' sense, words and actions are equivalents (i. 23), but if a man's actions and words are not consistent, it is his actions that count. What Agesilaos does is more revealing than what he says; the two competitive virtues attributed to him, φιλοτιμία and φιλονικία (ch. 2), determine his actions, rather than the abstract professions just assigned to him. At ch. 5 Plutarch warned that, although these virtues were encouraged by the Spartan lawgiver, there were reservations, and the quarrel between Agesilaos and Lysander at chs. 7–8 illustrated the dangers caused by pursuing them to excess. Here Agesilaos takes his competition with Thebes to 'excessive lengths', συνεκφερόμενος. Plutarch approves the Lykourgan ideal, but finds fault with Agesilaos' deviation from it: he lacks the philosopher's restraint.

οὐ μόνον ἔσωσε τὸν Φοιβίδαν, ἀλλὰ καὶ τὴν πόλιν ἔπεισεν εἰς ἑαυτὴν ἀναδέξασθαι τὸ ἀδίκημα καὶ κατέχειν τὴν Καδμείαν δι' ἑαυτῆς, τῶν δὲ πραγμάτων καὶ τῆς πολιτείας Ἀρχίαν καὶ Λεοντιάδαν ἀποδεῖξαι κυρίους, δι' ὧν ὁ Φοιβίδας εἰσῆλθε καὶ κατέλαβε τὴν ἀκρόπολιν.

With the saving of Phoibidas, Plutarch returns to the beginning of the argument, when Agesilaos helped him by defending him. There is a continuity in the argument, in that the competitive virtues activate the principle of the interest of Sparta, overpowering other virtues, and this leads to the unjust acquittal of Phoibidas. Plutarch shows that Agesilaos persuades Sparta to share the responsibility for the seizure, and, omitting Leontiadas' intervention (cf. §7), to authorize the continued occupation of the Kadmeia. The city is guilty of 'injustice', explicitly, giving definition to the original ἔργον δεινόν (§6), and may now share in the eventual decline, having compounded the crime by handing Thebes over to the traitors Archias and Leontiadas. Xenophon names only Leontiadas as the conspirator and leader of the government set up by the Spartans, but (at *Hell.* v. 4. 2) Archias is polemarch, and both are killed by the liberators. It is only at this point that Plutarch mentions Theban collaborators, having focused attention on the moral argument, and the parts played by Phoibidas, Agesilaos, and Sparta.

24. Spartan interventions in Thebes and Attica

1 Ἦν μὲν οὖν εὐθὺς ἐκ τούτων ὑπόνοια Φοιβίδου μὲν ἔργον εἶναι, βούλευμα δ᾽ Ἀγησιλάου τὸ πεπραγμένον· αἱ δ᾽ ὕστερον πράξεις ὁμολογουμένην ἐποίησαν τὴν αἰτίαν.

Agesilaos was suspected when the seizure of the Kadmeia (382) was first known (ch. 23). Now his rescue of Phoibidas and the retention of the Kadmeia arouse suspicion that he planned the seizure, and his subsequent actions produce general agreement to the charge. Plutarch evidently accepts that Agesilaos was involved in the affair.

2 ὡς γὰρ ἐξέβαλον οἱ Θηβαῖοι τὴν φρουρὰν καὶ τὴν πόλιν ἠλευθέρωσαν, ἐγκαλῶν αὐτοῖς ὅτι τὸν Ἀρχίαν καὶ τὸν Λεοντιάδαν ἀπεκτόνεσαν, ἔργῳ μὲν τυράννους, λόγῳ δὲ πολεμάρχους ὄντας, ἐξήνεγκε πόλεμον πρὸς αὐτούς.

Plutarch omits much of Xenophon's narrative for the next three years, but reflects his admission of the despotic rule of Thebes under Lakedaimonian control (*Hell.* v. 4. 1) in referring to Archias and Leontiadas as tyrants. He gives full accounts of the liberation in 379 at *Mor.* 594 B–598 and *Pelopidas*, 7–13, but he avoids duplication here as Agesilaos took no part.[1]

Neither Xenophon nor Diodoros mentions Agesilaos' accusation against the Thebans. Both record the punishment of the one or more in command of the Spartan garrison. Xenophon gives the alleged motive of the Lakedaimonians in going to war as to help the tyrants (*Hell.* v. 4. 13), not to punish anyone. Plutarch assigns the accusation to Agesilaos, no doubt in order to advertise that the tyrants were installed by him, and to imply that his motive for declaring war was to replace them.

3 καὶ Κλεόμβροτος ἤδη βασιλεύων Ἀγησιπόλιδος τεθνηκότος εἰς Βοιωτίαν ἐπέμφθη μετὰ δυνάμεως·

Agesipolis died of fever in 380 on the campaign against Olynthos (Xen. *Hell.* v. 3. 18–19). He took command after first Phoibidas and his brother Eudamidas[2] had been sent, and then Teleutias (*Hell.* v. 2. 24, 37). Since Agesilaos was not involved, Plutarch omits the episode, but now explains why Kleombrotos was sent to Thebes and not Agesipolis (*Hell.* v. 4. 13–14).

ὁ γὰρ Ἀγησίλαος, ὡς ἔτη τεσσαράκοντα γεγονὼς ἀφ' ἥβης καὶ στρατείας ἔχων ἄφεσιν ὑπὸ τῶν νόμων, ἔφυγε τὴν στρατηγίαν ἐκείνην, αἰσχυνόμενος εἰ Φλιασίοις ὀλίγον ἔμπροσθεν ὑπὲρ φυγάδων πεπολεμηκὼς αὖθις ὀφθήσεται Θηβαίους κακῶς ποιῶν διὰ τοὺς τυράννους.

Xenophon records Agesilaos' duplicitous refusal of the command to avoid political damage in helping the tyrants at Thebes, originally installed with Spartan support (*Hell.* v. 4. 1, 13); he said it was because of his age. Plutarch's rewriting is intricate. He abandons duplicity and politics; he presents the exemption as legally available to Agesilaos, and internalizes his real reason for taking the option: the 'shame' of being seen to be helping tyrants in Thebes after having helped the exiles at Phleious.[3] Here Plutarch presumes the exiles to be tyrants; for when Xenophon records it he mentions the Lakedaimonians' criticism that they were making themselves unpopular 'for the sake of a few' (*Hell.* v. 3. 10–25, esp. 16): the majority, making a dramatic statement, had held their democratic assemblies in the open, outside the city. The indirect form—as being Agesilaos' thought—of the criticisms in the two cases provides the link, which, Plutarch implies, further proves Agesilaos' original involvement. The residual moral element in Agesilaos' phrase 'doing a wrong to the Thebans' indicates Plutarch's attitude.

Phleious, long a member of the Peloponnesian League, was made a democracy by Iphikrates in 394, its loyalty to Sparta already in question (Xen. *Hell.* iv. 2. 16, 4. 15); but, in further fear of Corinth, it took in a Lakedaimonian garrison, supplied by Sparta despite the banished pro-Spartan former rulers, the oligarchs, who were not restored (390). In 384, responding to their appeal, the ephors obtained the agreement of the people—afraid of internal strife if they refused—for their return (*Hell.* v. 2. 1, 8–10); but, following their later request for Spartan support (381), the ephors declared war, and Agesilaos, after a long siege, imposed his oligarchy (*c.*379; *Hell.* v. 3. 10–13, 21).

4 ἦν δέ τις Λάκων Σφοδρίας ἐκ τῆς ὑπεναντίας στάσεως τῷ Ἀγησιλάῳ τεταγμένος ἐν Θεσπιαῖς ἁρμοστής, οὐκ ἄτολμος μὲν οὐδ' ἀφιλότιμος ἀνήρ, ἀεὶ δ' ἐλπίδων μᾶλλον ἢ φρενῶν ἀγαθῶν μεστός.

This opening formula, like 'Once upon a time', gives Plutarch the opportunity to present background information, and to introduce key words denoting the characteristics which determine the progress of the episode: Sphodrias' daring, enterprise, optimism, and intellectual weakness. Xenophon gives no character study here (*Hell.* v. 4. 20–1), but Phoibidas was 'without judgement', οὐ μέντοι λογιστικός γε οὐδὲ πάνυ φρόνιμος, and desired some 'brilliant' achievement (*Hell.* v. 2. 28). Plutarch may adapt these phrases in describing Sphodrias and analysing his performance. We are told he was 'rash and unstable', φύσει ὄντος μετεώρου καὶ προπετοῦς (Diod. xv. 29. 5); 'too lightweight and precipitate', εὐήθη τε εἶναι λίαν καὶ κοῦφον πρὸς τὰς ἐλπίδας (Kallisthenes).[4]

Although in *Hellenika* Xenophon records both the raid into Attica in 378 and the reactions to it, he omits the episode in *Agesilaos*: it would be inappropriate in the encomium to suggest Agesilaos' personal involvement in what, as Xenophon himself says, many judged the most unjust decision ever made in Lakedaimon (*Hell.* v. 4. 24), perhaps forgetting Helen's decision to elope with Paris. Plutarch is not bound by the restrictions of the eulogistic genre and is aware that even in *Hellenika* Xenophon fails to penetrate to the central issues.

5 οὗτος ἐπιθυμῶν ὀνόματος μεγάλου καὶ τὸν Φοιβίδαν νομίζων ἔνδοξον γεγονέναι καὶ περιβόητον ἀπὸ τοῦ περὶ Θήβας τολμήματος, ἐπείσθη πολὺ κάλλιον εἶναι καὶ λαμπρότερον εἰ τὸν Πειραιᾶ καταλάβοι δι' ἑαυτοῦ καὶ τῶν Ἀθηναίων ἀφέλοιτο τὴν θάλασσαν, ἐκ γῆς ἀπροσδοκήτως ἐπελθών.

Plutarch reinforces the idea of Sphodrias' hopeful character with the wish, which Xenophon does not mention, to rival the 'brilliant' achievement of Phoibidas. The approach to Peiraieus from the west across the Thriasian Plain,[5] out of sight of Athens, was not impossible topographically and the port will certainly have seemed vulnerable; Konon's repaired walls may have been breached again after the Peace (*Hell.* v. 1. 20). Brasidas and Knemos in 429 planned but did not complete an attack by sea (Thuc. ii. 93–4; cf. viii. 76. 5, 96. 3–4), and in 387 Teleutias made a successful naval attack (Xen. *Hell.* v. 1. 19–24), finding the

Athenians totally unprepared. The significance of the port is Athens' vital need of imported grain (sc. wheat).

6 λέγουσι δὲ τοῦτο μηχάνημα γενέσθαι τῶν περὶ Πελοπίδαν καὶ Μέλωνα βοιωταρχῶν. ὑπέπεμψαν γὰρ ἀνθρώπους λακωνίζειν προσποιουμένους, οἳ τὸν Σφοδρίαν ἐπαινοῦντες καὶ μεγαλύνοντες ὡς ἔργου τηλικούτου μόνον ἄξιον, ἐπῆραν καὶ παρώρμησαν ἀνελέσθαι πρᾶξιν ἄδικον μὲν ὁμοίως ἐκείνῃ καὶ παράνομον, τόλμης δὲ καὶ τύχης ἐνδεᾶ γενομένην.

Plutarch shows Theban exploitation of Sphodrias' weakness in persuading him to undertake the mission. He retains the Theban intrigue from Xenophon's account (*Hell.* v. 4. 20), but only to reinforce by flattery the existing temptation, and he discards Xenophon's suggestion that bribery was suspected; he almost does explicitly after he mentions the offer at *Pelopidas*, 14. 2, but suggests that Sphodrias was 'persuaded', words, in his judgement, weighing more heavily with him than money. Plutarch there names only two Thebans, Pelopidas and Gorgidas, and they use a single merchant as intermediary. At the start he indicates the unjust nature of the expedition, and adds that the essential requirements, good luck and daring, failed.

7 ἡμέρα γὰρ αὐτὸν ἐν τῷ Θριασίῳ πεδίῳ κατέλαβε καὶ κατέλαμψεν ἐλπίσαντα νυκτὸς προσμίξειν τῷ Πειραιεῖ· καὶ φῶς ἀφ' ἱερῶν τινων Ἐλευσινόθεν ἰδόντας λέγουσι φρῖξαι καὶ περιφόβους γενέσθαι τοὺς στρατιώτας. **8** αὐτὸς δὲ τοῦ θράσους ἐξέπεσεν, ὡς οὐκέτι λαθεῖν ἦν, καί τινα βραχεῖαν ἁρπαγὴν θέμενος, αἰσχρῶς ἀνεχώρησε καὶ ἀδόξως εἰς τὰς Θεσπιάς.

Plutarch's verb suggests that Sphodrias was unlucky to be 'caught, overtaken' by daylight, and the consequence—that his hope of reaching Peiraieus in darkness was unfulfilled—immediately warns of the ultimate failure of the mission, forming a turning-point in the story. The soldiers may fear that the light that appears is a divine warning; Sphodrias' failure of nerve is more rational—he was not without daring at §4. But the elaborate composition marks Plutarch's emphasis on the moral aspect of the failure: in describing the nervousness of the soldiers, he places their fears first and them last; in describing Sphodrias' fear, he places him first and his fear last, in chiasmus, contrasting the commander with his men by juxtaposition. Plutarch extends the pattern by framing the chiasmus with the reasons for their nervousness and the commander's fear at lack of concealment; this latter provides Plutarch's explanation for his next course of action. And that is condemned by Plutarch's adverbs, returning in ring composition to the adverse tone of his initial description.

9 ἐκ δὲ τούτου κατήγοροι μὲν ἐπέμφθησαν εἰς Σπάρτην ἐξ Ἀθηνῶν, εὗρον δὲ κατηγόρων μηδὲν ἐπὶ τὸν Σφοδρίαν δεομένους τοὺς ἄρχοντας, ἀλλὰ θανάτου κρίσιν αὐτῷ προειρηκότας, ἣν ἐκεῖνος ὑπομένειν ἀπέγνω, φοβούμενος τὴν ὀργὴν τῶν πολιτῶν, αἰσχυνομένων τοὺς Ἀθηναίους καὶ βουλομένων συναδικεῖσθαι δοκεῖν, ἵνα μὴ συναδικεῖν δοκῶσιν.

Plutarch omits Xenophon's report that three Lakedaimonian envoys were in Athens at this time. Athenian accusers may have gone to Sparta to reinforce the envoys' complaint, and the two versions could be complementary rather than contradictory. The capital charge brought by the magistrates also fits with the envoys' expectations. Sphodrias' assessment of the expected reaction of the citizens again corresponds in function, though not in content, to that of the envoys in Athens, suggesting that the enterprise was not authorized by the city. The episode closes with the two verbs whose stems relate to the first description of the action as ἄδικον (§6).

The aims of the invasion of Attica by Sphodrias

The nature of Theban involvement is a problem in this secret operation. Xenophon records it explicitly, and adds that bribery was suspected (*Hell.* v. 4. 20). Plutarch, indicating some uncertainty (λέγουσι), ignores the bribe here (cf. on §6 above). He and Xenophon make no further reference to Theban responsibility. The Athenians were in no doubt, for they at once denounced Sphodrias to the Spartans, and it is difficult to see that they could so readily have joined the Thebans at v. 4. 34, if they suspected them of complicity. It is difficult to explain how the Thebans would expect to bring Athens into war with Sparta in this way, since they could not be sure that Sparta would not disown Sphodrias' action, especially if it was a striking success; their involvement may be discounted. Plutarch's suggestion, that Sphodrias acted on his own initiative, is not mentioned in his defence, although Agesilaos' defence of Phoibidas' initiative was successful (Xen. *Hell.* v. 2. 32).

Plutarch does not distinguish between an invasion of Attica and the capture of Peiraieus as the objective, mentioning only the latter, which Xenophon attributes only to the mind of Sphodrias (*Hell.* v. 4. 20), evidence circulating from careless or hostile talk. The distance involved, approximately 75 km. (46 miles), makes Peiraieus an unlikely destination for an overnight march, one which an experienced Spartan harmost is unlikely to have attempted, and since it was not attained, the expedition may be considered as completed. Plutarch follows Xenophon in recording the final plundering of the land, but while he says it was no longer possible to escape observation, Xenophon says that even at Thria Sphodrias did nothing to avoid it. This suggests, if it was not a private initiative, that he may have been ordered to demonstrate the vulnerability of the unguarded frontier of Attica, and the night march will then have been timed to ensure reaching Athenian territory in darkness; or he may have been sent out to establish Spartan control of the pass by the garrison of Thespiai, which Agesilaos later made secure apparently without opposition (cf. *Hell.* v. 4. 37–8). Once in Attica, according to Xenophon, Sphodrias' presence was noticed and reported to the Athenians, who arranged to intercept him. There is no criticism of Sphodrias at this stage in Xenophon's account, and he makes no comment at the start of the march back to Thespiai. Plutarch ends the action with the Spartans' loss of nerve, absent from Xenophon's account. He is explaining what he sees as the failure of the expedition, and again blames weakness of character (§4).

The King's Peace was still observed at this time, but the situation was becoming tense, for in consequence of the episode the Athenians prepared for war; the outrage was the occasion for breaking the Peace and caused the resumption of hostilities .(ch. 26. 1–2; Xen. *Hell.* v. 4. 34–5). It was believed also to have led Athens to found the Second Confederacy, until Diodoros' account (xv. 25–35) was largely reinstated. He shows it to have been founded early in 378, before Sphodrias' raid, for which it was therefore responsible.[6]

The affairs of Athens and Thebes, from the seizure of the Kadmeia down to 379/8, even disregarding the foundation of the Confederacy, reveal that Athenian relations with Sparta had been tense. Further embroilment in Theban politics at the liberation (379/8) meant that Athens' position regarding possible reprisals was far from secure. There had been a strong Spartan garrison in Thebes and another at Thespiai, and Plataia still supplied help to the Spartans in response to the harmost's appeal (Xen. *Hell.* v. 4. 10). The Athenians were already alert to danger at the frontier when they sent Chabrias out to guard the pass at Eleutherai (Xen. *Hell.* v. 4. 14–16), and the guard was retained, conceivably in case Kleombrotos returned that way from Thespiai. It may also have been keeping the Athenians' line of retreat open, for according to Diodoros their help in the liberation of Thebes included the dispatch of an expedition by formal decree (xv. 25. 4–26. 1). Some Athenians were at Thebes attacking the Acropolis soon after the city was recovered (Xen. *Hell.* v. 4. 9, 10), and Athenians still there saved endangered citizens after the garrison's withdrawal from the Acropolis (Xen. *Hell.* v. 4. 12). If the decree mentioned by the orator Dinarchos (i. 39) about help to be sent for the Theban exiles refers to the recovery of the Kadmeia,[7] it is evidence that the Athenian presence was officially sanctioned.

Whether or not Athens had authorized the troops, Kleombrotos, who was sent to Boiotia, may not have wished to break the Peace by engaging them. It was after his return that the two Athenian generals were brought to trial: again, perhaps, to preserve the Peace. Xenophon gives no evidence to show whether the Athenian assistance was official or unofficial, but he indicates that the condemnation of the generals was not because of their guilt; they were made the scapegoats for fear of war with Sparta (*Hell.* v. 4. 19). He claimed that Sparta had secured the isolation of Athens (*Hell.* v. 3. 27); and the troops left by Kleombrotos at Thespiai would not have reduced tension at Athens (Xen. *Hell.* v. 4. 15).

The isolation, however, refers only to Sparta's hold on Olynthos and Central Greece. Sparta also had reason to be anxious, for Athens had begun to make ostensibly defensive, anti-Spartan treaties soon after the King's Peace; an inscription[8] shows Chios in alliance by 384/3. This Athenian diplomatic activity, the shelter provided for the exiles—always a threat to the puppet government in Thebes—and the support given to the liberators, could appear to the Spartans as signs of an approaching crisis, and if the new Theban regime continued to enjoy this support, it would be indebted to the Athenians and friendly to them, an intolerable prospect for Sparta, requiring firm action. The raid and the embassy, which Xenophon records at Athens without specifying its purpose, may be perceived as a Spartan reaction to the same event, the foundation of the Second Athenian Confederacy.[9] Even if this Confederacy was not yet fully in existence, it still presented a potential threat to Sparta while it was evolving, before Sphodrias' raid. The embassy was perhaps intended to put pressure on Athens to remain neutral, and to discourage the new League, if, as is probable, it was one of those mentioned by Diodoros (xv. 28. 4).[10] Sphodrias' expedition would increase the pressure by making a demonstration of force, in impatience with Athenian resistance to Sparta's diplomacy. If this was so, the plan failed; the Athenians may have been divided (Xen. *Hell.* v. 4. 34), but were not likely to waver; they were alerted and defended themselves and their port (v. 4. 21).

25. Negotiating the acquittal of Sphodrias

The trial of Sphodrias was announced by Plutarch at ch. 24. 9 and by Xenophon at *Hell.* v. 4. 24, where he also reported his acquittal, and judged it most unjust. Plutarch recorded Sphodrias' anxiety that the city's judgement would make him a scapegoat. He does not give the result until ch. 26.

1 Εἶχεν οὖν υἱὸν ὁ Σφοδρίας Κλεώνυμον, οὗ παιδὸς ὄντος ἔτι καὶ καλοῦ τὴν ὄψιν Ἀρχίδαμος ὁ Ἀγησιλάου τοῦ βασιλέως υἱὸς ἤρα.

Kleonymos' age-group

Xenophon describes Kleonymos not as a 'boy', παῖς, but as 'just beyond boyhood', ἄρτι ἐκ παίδων (*Hell.* v. 4. 25; cf. *Lak. Pol.* 3. 1). Two late glosses—on Herodotos (ix. 85. 1) and Strabo—suggest that παῖς designated one of the 18-year-old group and that boyhood ended at 20.[1] But according to Xenophon, while Spartans were supervised until they reached 20, boyhood ceased by the end of the eighteenth year (*Lak. Pol.* 2. 11, 4. 1; cf. *Lyk.* 17. 2).[2] He also designates Kleonymos' father successively as παῖς, παιδίσκος, ἡβῶν (*Hell.* v. 4. 32; see below, §5), and is the more likely to know the technical Spartan terminology here.

Xenophon and Plutarch

Xenophon introduces Kleonymos in the same narrative style that Plutarch used to introduce Sphodrias (ch. 24). Plutarch retains the story-teller's stance but uses a variation of the formula, and creates patterns: the sons (υἱόν, υἱός) and their names frame their fathers' names, reversing the order (in chiasmus) so that the sons' names are central.

Both authors use the terminology of a legal trial, but they record only the development of attitudes in advance of the hearing of the case by a court, Plutarch with sympathy, Xenophon with a pervasive sense of Sphodrias' guilt. Of the trial only the verdict is known (cf. Arist. *Pol.* 1275^{b}5–11).[3] The political and social alignments are resolved in the context of the sort of friendship that was important for both Xenophon and Plutarch. It occurs at chs. 2, 11, 13, and now involves Agesilaos' son Archidamos and his friend Kleonymos, the son of Sphodrias, whom Xenophon describes as 'the most handsome and respected of his peers' (*Hell.* v. 4. 25). Plutarch ignores the social advantage in the friendship in favour of the personal attraction.

2 καὶ τότε συνηγωνία μὲν ὡς εἰκὸς αὐτῷ κινδυνεύοντι περὶ τοῦ πατρός, συμπράττειν δὲ φανερῶς καὶ βοηθεῖν οὐκ εἶχεν· ἦν γὰρ ὁ Σφοδρίας ἐκ τῶν διαφόρων τοῦ Ἀγησιλάου.

Archidamos' involvement is introduced by Xenophon only in response to Kleonymos' request for help, but Plutarch portrays his spontaneous desire to help, and records its frustration by the opposing political alignments of their fathers (cf. ch. 23. 6). Xenophon comments initially only that the friends of the other king, Kleombrotos, were associates of Sphodrias, and wished to acquit him. He does not speak of opposition directly, though they 'feared' Agesilaos and his friends because of Sphodrias' 'dreadful deed' (*Hell.* v. 4. 25, 32). That one king's son associates with the son of a friend of the other king indicates a degree of social mobility, which may, perhaps, have been reflected in their attendance earlier at the same mess (Xen. *Hell.* v. 4. 28; *Lyk.* 12. 4,

cf. *Lak. Pol.* 3. 5).[4] Agesilaos may have exploited his son's relationships, either by planning this connection from its inception or
by manipulating it now, in order to infiltrate his colleague's
circle.[5]

3 τοῦ δὲ Κλεωνύμου προσελθόντος αὐτῷ καὶ μετὰ δεήσεως καὶ
δακρύων ἐντυχόντος, ὅπως τὸν Ἀγησίλαον εὔνουν παράσχῃ, μάλιστα
γὰρ ἐκεῖνον αὐτοῖς φοβερὸν εἶναι, τρεῖς μὲν ἢ τέσσαρας ἡμέρας
αἰδούμενος τὸν πατέρα καὶ δεδιὼς σιωπῇ παρηκολούθει· **4** τέλος δὲ τῆς
κρίσεως ἐγγὺς οὔσης, ἐτόλμησεν εἰπεῖν πρὸς τὸν Ἀγησίλαον ὅτι
Κλεώνυμος αὐτοῦ δεηθείη περὶ τοῦ πατρός.

In recording Kleonymos' approach to Archidamos, Plutarch again
presents a spontaneous action which enhances the relationship,
whereas Xenophon makes it Sphodrias' suggestion that his son
should seek his friend's help. Here Agesilaos is feared already by
Sphodrias and Kleonymos, and soon by Archidamos, too. The
tension is matched in Xenophon's account by the courage of
Kleonymos in approaching Archidamos, and by the anxiety of
Kleombrotos and his friends who wish to acquit Sphodrias. In
neither version does Agesilaos declare himself at this point but
he is in both, for him, untypically unapproachable (cf. ch. 1).
Xenophon generates suspense with Archidamos' repeated delays
and avoidance of contact with his friend (*Hell.* v. 4. 29). Plutarch
quantifies the interval to three or four days, and moves on to the
impending trial. He postpones the suspension of contact until
after Agesilaos' disappointing response (§7), and ends the chapter
with his love of children, reversing the impression of inaccessi-
bility. Xenophon makes more of it, repeating Archidamos' hesita-
tions (*Hell.* v. 4. 27–31).

5 ὁ δ' Ἀγησίλαος εἰδὼς ἐρῶντα τὸν Ἀρχίδαμον οὐκ ἔπαυσεν· ἦν γὰρ ὁ
Κλεώνυμος εὐθὺς ἐκ παίδων ἐπίδοξος, εἴ τις καὶ ἄλλος, ἀνὴρ ἔσεσθαι
σπουδαῖος. **6** οὐ μὴν ἐνέδωκέ τι τότε χρηστὸν ἢ φιλάνθρωπον ἐλπίσαι
δεομένῳ τῷ παιδί, σκέψεσθαι δὲ φήσας ὅ τι καλῶς ἔχοι καὶ πρεπόντως,
ἀπῆλθεν.

That Agesilaos had noticed but not stopped the friendship, may
have been suggested to Plutarch by Xenophon's reference to his
disregard of his suspicions of Archidamos' movements (*Hell.* v. 4.
29). Plutarch perhaps inferred Agesilaos' approval of his son's
friendship from his commendation in his final judgement of

Sphodrias' behaviour as a youth (Xen. *Hell.* v. 4. 32). He curtails Xenophon's narrative by allowing the request to be made on only one occasion, instead of Xenophon's two: he had used Archidamos' second plea for pardon—'for our sake'—at ch. 13 in Agesilaos' request for the acquittal of Nikias.[6] Xenophon makes Archidamos acknowledge Sphodrias' guilt, in agreeing with Agesilaos' condemnation without making a reply, and in pleading for a pardon (*Hell.* v. 4. 27, 31); and Agesilaos asserts Sphodrias' guilt on two occasions (*Hell.* v. 4. 30, 32). Plutarch makes him only resolve to consider what is right and proper.

7 αἰδούμενος οὖν ὁ Ἀρχίδαμος ἐξέλειπε τὸ προσιέναι τῷ Κλεωνύμῳ, καίπερ εἰωθὼς τοῦτο πολλάκις τῆς ἡμέρας ποιεῖν πρότερον. 8 ἐκ δὲ τούτου κἀκεῖνοι τὰ κατὰ τὸν Σφοδρίαν μᾶλλον ἀπέγνωσαν, ἄχρι οὗ τῶν Ἀγησιλάου φίλων Ἐτυμοκλῆς ἔν τινι κοινολογίᾳ πρὸς αὐτοὺς ἀπεγύμνωσε τὴν γνώμην τοῦ Ἀγησιλάου· 9 τὸ μὲν γὰρ ἔργον ὡς ἔνι μάλιστα ψέγειν αὐτόν, ἄλλως γε μὴν ἄνδρα τὸν Σφοδρίαν ἀγαθὸν ἡγεῖσθαι καὶ τὴν πόλιν ὁρᾶν τοιούτων στρατιωτῶν δεομένην.

The anxious wait in Xenophon's account preceded Archidamos' first approach to his father, and the second approach was quickly followed by Etymokles' announcement to Sphodrias' friend (*Hell.* v. 4. 29–32). With only one request here (§5), Archidamos' abstention from visiting his friend is exploited for the creation of suspense while Agesilaos is coming to his decision. Plutarch does not reveal any reason why Etymokles was chosen to carry the news. Xenophon names him as one of the three envoys at Athens at the time of the raid, suspected there of involvement in the plot (*Hell.* v. 4. 22). Their sense of outrage is consistent with that of the ephors in recalling Sphodrias to face the death penalty, and with Agesilaos' apparent reluctance to respond positively to his son's pleas for help.

Sphodrias' friend, in Xenophon's account, questions Etymokles as one of the friends of Agesilaos who (he thought) favoured executing Sphodrias, and so his changed view is significant for the outcome. In Plutarch, Etymokles conveys his news unasked, suggesting, perhaps, that he had come from Agesilaos to do so, and again curtailing Xenophon's account. It is at this point that Agesilaos' criticism of Sphodrias is revealed by Plutarch, and it is followed immediately by the mitigating factor—Sparta's need of soldiers. The prospect of war and the effect of casualties on the

small Spartiate community (see above, ch. 22. 4) will explain
Agesilaos' reluctance to lose Sphodrias, but the emphasis, here
and in Xenophon, is on the shortage of men of his quality.

10 τούτους γὰρ ὁ Ἀγησίλαος ἑκάστοτε τοὺς λόγους ἐποιεῖτο περὶ τῆς
δίκης, τῷ παιδὶ χαρίζεσθαι βουλόμενος, ὥστε καὶ τὸν Κλεώνυμον εὐθὺς
αἰσθάνεσθαι τὴν σπουδὴν τοῦ Ἀρχιδάμου καὶ τοὺς φίλους τοὺς τοῦ
Σφοδρίου θαρροῦντας ἤδη βοηθεῖν.

The wish to gratify his son is Plutarch's interpretation of
Agesilaos' thoughts, though Xenophon suggested it by making
him respond directly to Archidamos' personal plea for pardon
(Hell. v. 4. 31–2). Xenophon offers no other considerations which
might have led Agesilaos to acquit Sphodrias, despite his persistent condemnation of the raid. Plutarch avoids this violent
reversal, since he does not commit Agesilaos to clear statements of
Sphodrias' guilt. He ends the account of the working of the
friendship with only the encouraging effect of Agesilaos' pro-
nouncements on the friends of Sphodrias who can now help to
save him. He does not report Kleonymos' promise to repay
Archidamos by loyal service or its fulfilment with his death at
Leuktra (Hell. v. 4. 33, vi. 4. 14; ch. 28. 8), which conclude
Xenophon's account. Xenophon's final reference to loyalty seems
intended to turn attention away from Agesilaos' decision towards
the more pleasing aspects of traditional Spartan friendships—and
so of all good friendships.

11 ἦν δὲ καὶ φιλότεκνος ὁ Ἀγησίλαος διαφερόντως· καὶ περὶ ἐκείνου τὸ
τῆς παιδιᾶς λέγουσιν, ὅτι μικροῖς τοῖς παιδίοις οὖσι κάλαμον
περιβεβηκὼς ὥσπερ ἵππον οἴκοι συνέπαιζεν, ὀφθεὶς δ' ὑπό τινος τῶν
φίλων παρεκάλει μηδενὶ φράσαι, πρὶν ἂν καὶ αὐτὸς πατὴρ παίδων
γένηται.

At the end of the chapter Plutarch returns the focus to Agesilaos
with the anecdote about his playfulness when his children were
young. He reverts in ring composition to the personal ties
established in §1 on which the narrative has concentrated, suggesting that they were so strong in Agesilaos' nature as to justify the
part they are said earlier to have played. Plutarch reveals his own
interest in domestic life, here and in the references in this Life to
the female members of the family. The result of the trial is not
given until the next chapter.

The trial of Sphodrias

Plutarch's account of Sphodrias' trial is adapted from Xenophon's *Hellenika*; it is not mentioned in his *Agesilaos*. Xenophon gives only an incomplete and superficial version of the treatment of the case at Sparta. He says (*Hell.* v. 4. 24) that in his account he is responding to the widespread opinion that 'the decision in this case was the most unjust ever known in Lakedaimon', the view of the Athenians (*Hell.* v. 4. 34); but Sphodrias is guilty of disregarding Spartan interests (*Hell.* v. 4. 30–1), rather than the offence against the Athenians denounced by the embassy. Despite this there is praise for Sphodrias in the end, and the friendship of the two young men is made the basis for settlement: it represents the *rapprochement* between the larger factions. Perhaps the most useful hint of the procedure is the political realignment that leads to a vote in which the king's influence was most powerful: but it is doubtful that he decided only on the grounds stated by Xenophon. It cannot be supposed that there were no discussions of wider political implications.

Xenophon does not say on what grounds Sphodrias was charged. The embassy claimed that he acted without the knowledge of the city, but it was established in the case of Phoibidas that the use of initiative was not prohibited, if it benefited the state. Agesilaos' first pronouncement was to condemn a man who harmed the state for his own profit, for which Xenophon had already prepared the way by recording the suspicion that the Thebans had bribed him—a suspicion which the Athenians seem not to have shared (v. 4. 34). Agesilaos' final thought, reported by Etymokles, was that Sphodrias had done wrong (v. 4. 32), which, on the basis of Phoibidas' case, means that his action, as it turned out, had not been in the best interest of the city.

It is also not stated on what grounds Sphodrias sought Agesilaos' help: he seems to have felt that he was being made a scapegoat, and his guilt was evidently maintained publicly to the end. Sphodrias did not go to Sparta, despite his recall by the ephors to face the charge. This does not prove his guilt, but it may show that he did not expect justice—or that he was not free to go. It served the Spartans' need for secrecy that he was absent during the proceedings, for his answer to the charge might have been embarrassing if he had acted on orders; but it would have been expedient that he should not stand trial, or that he should be blamed: the trial may have been set up to calm Athens, and the acquittal required long consideration. His request for Agesilaos' support indicates that he had some grounds for expecting help, and he continued to act honourably until he fell at Leuktra (Xen. *Hell.* v. 4. 33). His confidence would be more secure if he was obeying higher authority than if he had taken a bribe or had acted without authorization (see ch. 24. 4–6). In his position as harmost at Thespiai, Sphodrias could pass confidential information to Agesilaos through their sons, and this might concern the orders he was obeying and include intelligence about the situations in Athens and Thebes. This would have to be considered in Sparta in secret, and there would be no record for Xenophon to see.

That some authority sanctioned the raid is equally open to conjecture. A secret mission is inevitably difficult to penetrate. Although Xenophon gives no hint that Sphodrias was acting under orders and the illegality has been accepted,[7] Kleombrotos had left him as harmost at Thespiai with a third of all his allied troops and all the money he had brought from home, bidding him hire a mercenary force (*Hell.* v. 4. 15). Diodoros (xv. 29. 5) claims that it was Kleombrotos who persuaded Sphodriades, no doubt the same Sphodrias, without the knowledge of the ephors, to seize Peiraieus (specified by Xenophon too), which he attempted with more than 10,000 soldiers. His view has been accepted.[8] None of the ancient traditions can be proved,[9] but the account given by Xenophon and largely followed by Plutarch may not be realistic.

The veil is not lifted by either Plutarch or Xenophon to reveal what negotiations were going on with Athens, what divided the Spartan factions, what bargains were made among them, or what considerations of foreign policy regarding Athens and Thebes were taken into account. Xenophon indicates two political groupings led by the kings. Their alignments at Sparta are known. Sphodrias was appointed harmost at Thespiai by Kleombrotos, whose friends, as associates also of Sphodrias, wanted to acquit him but feared Agesilaos and his friends, who were all thought to be going to condemn him (Xen. *Hell.* v. 4. 32). Kleombrotos may have been opposed to Agesilaos' hostile attitude to Thebes (cf. *Hell.* v. 4. 15–16, vi. 4. 5). The mission of Agesilaos' friend Etymokles is not disclosed, but may be assumed to have concerned Athens' alignment with Thebes. The identity of other uncommitted Spartiates, οἱ διὰ μέσου, without royal leadership (*Hell.* v. 4. 25), is not known, but they at first aligned themselves individually with Agesilaos (Xen. *Hell.* v. 4. 25). The realignment of all these determined the final decision (v. 4. 32).

At the time there had been no violation of the Peace, and Athens was not expected to be involved in hostilities against the Lakedaimonians (Xen. *Hell.* v. 4. 20), although the Athenians had taken part in the attack on the Theban acropolis which led to the withdrawal of the Spartan garrison (Xen. *Hell.* v. 4. 10–12), and there was growing tension (see above, ch. 24. 3). Differences between Athens and Sparta would be, following Thucydides' distinction, the real cause of crisis, and the deed of Sphodrias or his acquittal was only the spark, or was symbolic. Xenophon (*Hell.* v. 4. 34) indicates that the preparations for war were begun only when the Athenians who favoured the Boiotian alliance pointed out that the plot against them had been commended by Sparta: until then it was not the case that 'the *rapprochement* between Athens and Thebes could not now be prevented'.[10] If the Spartans had been willing to accept the Athenians' ambitions, they could ensure that after their liberation the Thebans did not gain a powerful ally whose sympathy with the liberators had long been evident; and they could have turned the blame on to Thebes by exploiting the suggestion of bribery, or, as a first gesture, they could have condemned Sphodrias. The decision to acquit him was taken in the knowledge that Athens would join Thebes and go to war. Just as the raid implied an intention to do something to injure Athens, and a disregard of the consequences of direct provocation of Athens,[11] so the Spartans did not avoid the consequences of the offence which the acquittal would give. A new alignment of the three cities was no doubt the issue behind the veil, and its resolution in favour of the alliance of Thebes and Athens will have followed the resolution of political differences in Sparta. If Sphodrias' raid was intended not to take Peiraieus, but to influence the Athenians towards Sparta, it failed to do so; the enemies of Sparta used it in anti-Spartan propaganda, and benefited even further by exploiting his unjust acquittal.

Agesilaos' condemnation of Sphodrias' 'wrongdoing' is then a recognition of the failure of the military mission, but it failed because Athens was not intimidated. The decision to acquit him seems to follow the failure of the Spartan diplomatic attempt to disengage Athens from Thebes, and is a recognition that war was Sparta's best option. Sparta's 'need for such soldiers' is a form of words to which all Spartan parties could subscribe. The Athenians were not satisfied with the Spartan condemnation of the wrongdoing without the symbolic punishment of the local commander, but they also had other, more vital, interests to consider in determining their ambitious foreign policy. They took immediate defensive action, and perhaps rejected the diplomatic initiative while the Spartan involvement in the raid was being dealt with. In Sparta, the time before the acquittal would be spent in assessing the prospects for a new military solution to the underlying issues. What is significant, then, is not the verdict on Sphodrias, but its effect on the balance of power in Greece.

Perhaps Xenophon puts the emphasis, in the coda, on the loyalty of Spartan friendships in an attempt to save Spartan self-respect. There is no blame here for anyone: Kleombrotos need have no remorse concerning Sphodrias, if he did give him the order for the raid; Kleonymos is now pledged to serve Archidamos and Sparta, and Xenophon can look ahead to record that he died for them at Leuktra; Sphodrias, having been acquitted, has something to be grateful for if he was really guilty of acting without orders. He would also have reason to be grateful if he was relieved of having to pay the penalty as the scapegoat for a policy which had gone wrong. But the pronouncement by Agesilaos is the decisive influence, which Plutarch exploits in ch. 26.

The emergence of Thebes

Lyk. 13. 6, *Pel.* 15. 1–3, 16. 1–3, 17, 20–23; Xen. *Hell.* v. 4. 34–41, 45, 47–55, 58–60, vi. 3. 7–9, 18–20, 4. 2, 4–5, 8–15, *Agesilaos*, 2. 23; Diod. xv. 32. 1, 33. 2–3, 34. 2, 37, 39, 50. 4, 51. 3–53. 4, 55–6; Nepos, *Ep.* 6. 3–4; Paus. ix. 13. 2, 3–12.

26. Agesilaos takes command against Boiotia; his growing unpopularity

Plutarch's criticism of Agesilaos' conduct, character, and judgement becomes more explicit and pointed than the hints already given, though much of the *Life* is complimentary; cf. Introd., E. He faulted Agesilaos' excesses (chs. 5, 7), his sense of justice (ch. 5), his abuse of friendship (chs. 5, 13, 24–5), and recorded signs of divine displeasure (chs. 6, 17, 22); but the persistent theme from ch. 22 is Agesilaos' attitude to Thebes. Plutarch as a Boiotian may be thought prejudiced against Agesilaos in favour of Thebes, but one of the main thrusts of *Agesilaos* is to extol Lykourgos' rule to avoid imperialism. Agesilaos' wars against Thebes (378–371) are criticized by Plutarch, by his colleague Kleombrotos, and by Antalkidas; the futility of such wars is expressed in the opposition of other Greeks to Sparta's domination, which will be ended at Leuktra (chs. 27–8).

1 Ἀπολυθέντος δὲ τοῦ Σφοδρίου, καὶ τῶν Ἀθηναίων, ὡς ἐπύθοντο, πρὸς πόλεμον τραπομένων, σφόδρα κακῶς ὁ Ἀγησίλαος ἤκουσε δι᾽ ἐπιθυμίαν ἄτοπον καὶ παιδαριώδη δοκῶν ἐμποδὼν γεγονέναι κρίσει δικαίᾳ καὶ τὴν πόλιν παραίτιον ἀπειργάσθαι παρανομημάτων τηλικούτων εἰς τοὺς Ἕλληνας.

Plutarch creates suspense by delaying the announcement of Sphodrias' acquittal, which leads the Athenians to turn to war and introduces the next topic, the harsh criticism of Agesilaos. Two participial phrases, arranged in a chiastic pattern, give an ominous start (cf. the similarly patterned phrases at the beginning of ch. 15, just before the order for Agesilaos' recall from the east arrives). In the encomium Xenophon says that the purpose of Agesilaos' campaign against Thebes was to help his friends (*Agesilaos*, 2. 22), but in *Hellenika*, having admitted the injustice of the acquittal, he blames the Athenian friends of Boiotia for urging preparations for war because Sphodrias remained unpunished by the Spartans (v. 4. 34). Plutarch disregards this further reference to his guilt, and concentrates on the shameful reasons for Agesilaos' verdict. The critics are, no doubt, his former friends who favoured execution, and who now, introducing panhellenist thinking, regret inflicting war on Greece. Plutarch ignores the Athenian interpretation, found in Xenophon, that the Spartans as a whole were responsible. The attitude of Agesilaos' fellow-citizens shows, by indirect characterization,[1] the decline in his reputation and Plutarch says nothing to make the reader dissent from their judgement. The frequent *p* sounds suggest emphasis, contempt, and indignation.

2 ἐπεὶ δὲ τὸν Κλεόμβροτον οὐχ ἑώρα πρόθυμον ὄντα πολεμεῖν τοῖς Θηβαίοις, οὕτω δὴ χαίρειν τὸν νόμον ἐάσας ᾧ πρόσθεν ἐχρῆτο περὶ τῆς στρατείας, αὐτὸς εἰς Βοιωτίαν ἐνέβαλλεν ἤδη καὶ κακῶς ἐποίει τοὺς Θηβαίους καὶ πάλιν ἀντέπασχεν, **3** ὥστε καὶ τρωθέντος αὐτοῦ τότε τὸν Ἀνταλκίδαν εἰπεῖν·

Agesilaos disregarded strict justice, which he approved in other cases, in order to help friends (ch. 13). He repeats the inconsistency now in waiving the retirement rule (cf. ch. 24. 3), in order to harm enemies. Plutarch gives him the initiative for invading Boiotia and does not eulogize his readiness to comply with the city's needs. In contrast, Xenophon, moving away from criticism, makes two complimentary points: the ephors ask Agesilaos to take command and he willingly agrees (*Hell.* v. 4. 35); his changed attitude to military service in Boiotia is not explained (cf. *Hell.* v. 4. 13). Plutarch continues the critical theme, juxtaposing the damage Agesilaos inflicts and the damage he suffers. He implies an element of retribution, for his disregard of the rule and his conduct of the campaigns (cf. ch. 27. 1–4). The phrase κακῶς ἐποίει retains a moral element (cf. ch. 24. 3), for the invasion is another of the destructive internal conflicts regretted in ch. 15. 3.

Although Plutarch's summary is brief, giving only one campaign, it is otherwise accurate, for Xenophon, too, describes reverses, including the death of Phoibidas, as well as successes (*Hell.* v. 4. 35–55). He records two campaigns in Theban territory, which was protected with Athenian help, and also, to some extent, by the innovatory strategy of ditch and stockade.[2] Agesilaos twice ravages the countryside, but does not blockade the city. On his departure the Theban situation is gradually eased, especially at Thespiai as a result of a citizen uprising against the Spartan garrison (*Hell.* v. 4. 46, 55, 63). Xenophon does not record that Agesilaos was wounded here: Plutarch's next anecdote is perhaps not in its chronological context.

Ἦ καλὰ τὰ διδασκάλια παρὰ Θηβαίων ἀπολαμβάνεις, μὴ βουλομένους αὐτοὺς μηδ᾽ ἐπισταμένους μάχεσθαι διδάξας. 4 τῷ γὰρ ὄντι Θηβαίους αὐτοὺς ἑαυτῶν πολεμικωτάτους τότε γενέσθαι φασί, ταῖς πολλαῖς στρατείαις τῶν Λακεδαιμονίων ἐπ᾽ αὐτοὺς ὥσπερ ἐγγυμνασαμένους. 5 διὸ καὶ Λυκοῦργος ὁ παλαιὸς ἐν ταῖς καλουμέναις τρισὶ ῥήτραις ἀπεῖπε μὴ πολλάκις ἐπὶ τοὺς αὐτοὺς στρατεύειν, ὅπως μὴ πολεμεῖν μανθάνωσιν.

Agesilaos' reputation is now, Plutarch asserts, being attacked on other grounds by an opponent exploiting one of the occasions when he was wounded (see also ch. 36. 3). This passage is an indictment of Agesilaos as the aberrant king who, by fighting the same enemy repeatedly, departed from the principle set out in one of three *rhetrai*, 'enactments', attributed to Lykourgos, the highest judge of Sparta's best interest (*Lyk.* 13. 5). Another *rhetra*, controversial but important evidence for the constitution of Sparta, designated in modern works 'the Great Rhetra', is attributed to the oracle at Delphi (*Lyk.* 6. 1).[3]

The anecdote occurs at *Mor.* 213 F, at *Pelopidas*, 15. 2, and at *Lykourgos*, 13. 6, where it is also recorded that the *rhetra* was quoted in criticism of Agesilaos. There is, no doubt, some truth in the charge, but the source of the anecdote is perhaps in the Spartans' own tradition, since it enhances their reputation for military prowess (cf. Tacitus, *Agricola*, 8, 16–17, 29. 3–4), though it lends itself to the interpretation that they brought on their own defeat. The improvement in the Theban fighting qualities more probably came from the confidence of having at least survived several conflicts with Spartan and other armies. The Thebans also recognized the value of training and organization, as Plutarch says (*Pel.* 17–18) and Xenophon acknowledges (*Hell.* vii. 5. 19). The

successes of the Theban army began before they met the Spartans
as enemies, with Delion, the battle fought in 424 against the
Athenians, where they introduced the concentration of the
phalanx (Thuc. iv. 93. 4). This tactic might not have been
developed, if what Plutarch suggests were true, and if the
Thebans had followed only Spartan practice; it required creative
observation and imagination, which were not inculcated at Sparta
by Lykourgan education.[4] Plutarch, however, who takes the
opportunity to charge Agesilaos with disregarding the Lykourgan
rhetra, prepares for his further decline on grounds other than
military.

6 ἦν δὲ καὶ τοῖς συμμάχοις τῶν Λακεδαιμονίων ἐπαχθὴς ὁ Ἀγησίλαος,
ὡς δι' οὐδὲν ἔγκλημα δημόσιον, ἀλλὰ θυμῷ τινι καὶ φιλονικίᾳ τοὺς
Θηβαίους ἀπολέσαι ζητῶν. οὐδὲν οὖν ἔλεγον δεόμενοι φθείρεσθαι δεῦρο
κἀκεῖσε καθ' ἕκαστον ἐνιαυτὸν ὀλίγοις τοσοῦτοι συνακολουθοῦντες.

Plutarch now traces Agesilaos' declining reputation further afield.
The criticism has progressed from the natural hostility of external
enemies, the Athenians, to that of his opponents in Sparta, and
now to the allies. It is given again indirectly, as the observation by
people involved that Agesilaos had compounded his aberration for
a private prejudice against Thebes. The allies had a valid point,
even discounting the personal issue, for the alliance was not
designed to be exploited only for the Spartan interests in view
here. That the unrest was significant enough to affect Sparta's
claim to the leadership of Greece was revealed at a meeting in the
Peloponnese, following Kleombrotos' failure to penetrate beyond
Kithairon: the allies decided that naval action against Athens
should replace the exhausting land campaigns against Thebes
(Xen. *Hell.* v. 4. 60). Xenophon shows that Agesilaos could starve
the Thebans, but he could not take their city (*Hell.* v. 4. 56–7).

Plutarch uses θυμός, 'rage', in a blemished character as an
irrational factor leading to catastrophe: Pelopidas brought about
his own death in battle when his feelings overcame reason (*Pel.* 32.
6–7). Xenophon makes the point, when Teleutias, in rage,
pursued the enemy too close to the wall of Olynthos and was killed
(*Hell.* v. 3. 5–6). Plutarch adds the trait, un-Spartan by
Lykourgan standards and detrimental to the Spartan interest, to
the excessive 'competitiveness' attributed to Agesilaos in the
quarrel with Lysander (ch. 7).

7 ἔνθα δὲ δὴ λέγεται τὸν Ἀγησίλαον ἐξελέγξαι βουλόμενον αὐτῶν τὸ πλῆθος τόδε μηχανήσασθαι. πάντας ἐκέλευσε καθίσαι τοὺς συμμάχους μετ᾽ ἀλλήλων ἀναμεμιγμένους, ἰδίᾳ δὲ τοὺς Λακεδαιμονίους ἐφ᾽ ἑαυτῶν. 8 εἶτ᾽ ἐκήρυττε τοὺς κεραμεῖς ἀνίστασθαι πρῶτον· ὡς δὲ ἀνέστησαν οὗτοι, δεύτερον ἐκήρυττε τοὺς χαλκεῖς, εἶτα τέκτονας ἐφεξῆς καὶ οἰκοδόμους καὶ τῶν ἄλλων τεχνῶν ἑκάστην.

Plutarch may be right to have illustrated at this point the inadequacy and arrogance of the Spartans' perception of their ability to provide or to secure the resources necessary for the maintenance of their hegemony. There are two aspects of the numerical problem: the proportion of Spartans in an army was inevitably a small one, because Sparta demanded that each of the allies should contribute the same fraction of their total manpower; and the size of the eligible citizen body at Sparta was small and diminishing. Yet it is hard to believe that Agesilaos devised this performance now, for the insult would not increase morale, but would aggravate the present allied mood, and the isolation of the Spartan contingent, sitting apart, would reveal to all the other contingents their own numerical superiority.

9 πάντες οὖν ὀλίγου δεῖν ἀνέστησαν οἱ σύμμαχοι, τῶν δὲ Λακεδαιμονίων οὐδείς· ἀπείρητο γὰρ αὐτοῖς τέχνην ἐργάζεσθαι καὶ μανθάνειν βάναυσον.

Some at least of the allied hoplite so-called 'potters', and so on, no doubt possessed the property qualification required for citizens of hoplite status not as manual craftsmen but as factory-owners. Not everyone would be deceived or convinced by the trick. The story resembles the searches among craftsmen attributed in Plato's early dialogues to Socrates, who found none with the political wisdom required to justify government by a democratic assembly (e.g. *Ap.* 21 A–22 E).

Plutarch attributes the ban on craft to Lykourgos' attack on luxury (*Lyk.* 9. 3). It is rather the need from the seventh or sixth century onwards for total devotion to military preparedness that meant the progressive curtailment of other activities and produced the legal prohibition of banausic occupations for citizens, as concentration of landed property ownership reduced their numbers (Arist. *Pol.* 1270ᵃ29–34; Xen. *Oik.* 4. 3; and see ch. 4 n. following §1).[5] Agesilaos' device may be used as a further illustration of the tradition of the Spartans' exclusive need to be 'expert craftsmen of war' (*Pel.* 23. 3; *Lak. Pol.* 13. 5).⁶ British excavations reported as early as 1905–7 (*BSA* 12, 13) show Sparta as not so austere as Thucydides (1. 10) is taken to suggest: he was concerned with evidence for power. 'Spartans kept abreast of developments in (sculpture in bronze) during the fifth and sixth centuries', and in figure supports (cf. caryatids), and pottery; the sanctuary of Artemis Orthia contained striking votive offerings.⁷ By the time of Epameinondas' invasions there were again houses to be plundered that contained many valuables (Xen. *Hell.* vi. 5. 27).

οὕτω δὴ γελάσας ὁ Ἀγησίλαος, Ὁρᾶτ', εἶπεν, ὦ ἄνδρες, ὅσῳ πλείονας ὑμῶν στρατιώτας ἐκπέμπομεν ἡμεῖς.

It is not clear whether by laughing Agesilaos is further mocking the allies or making light of their discomfiture. Quotation of speech, which again closes the anecdote, suggests that it originated in the private braggadocio of the Spartan *syssitia*.

27. The weakness of Agesilaos and Sparta; the peace conference at Sparta

1 Ἐν δὲ Μεγάροις, ὅτε τὴν στρατιὰν ἀπῆγεν ἐκ Θηβῶν, ἀναβαίνοντος αὐτοῦ πρὸς τὸ ἀρχεῖον εἰς τὴν ἀκρόπολιν, σπάσμα καὶ πόνος ἰσχυρὸς ἔλαβε τὸ ὑγιὲς σκέλος· ἐκ δὲ τούτου διογκωθὲν αἵματος ἔδοξε μεστὸν γεγονέναι καὶ φλεγμονὴν ὑπερβάλλουσαν παρεῖχεν.

Megara: topography and history

Like Thebes, Megara was the victim of a hostile tradition in the surviving literary sources: 'the widespread anti-Megarian attitude . . . projects the stereotype of an ignorant, brutish and vulgar folk'.¹ Routes through the Megarid were vital for Sparta's activities in central and northern Greece,² and Megara suffered a long history of being alternately courted and threatened for the privilege of unhindered military passage through the Isthmus, while proximity to Corinth's superior facilities for trade at times denied Megara access to compensatory wealth.³ In the fourth century the Megarians favoured a policy of friendly relations with all, a neutral attitude permitting passage without promoting retaliatory hostilities,⁴ though a hostile Corinth, in the Corinthian war, forced Sparta to use the sea-crossings of the Corinthian Gulf to Phokis (Krisa), or to Kreusis in Boiotia (Xen. *Hell*. iv. 3. 15, 4. 1, v. 4. 46, 60, vi. 1. 1; cf. Thuc. i. 103. 3–4).

Agesilaos' visit to the ἀρχεῖον, 'Government Building', at Megara may have had a diplomatic purpose concerning the use of the land route. There are two small hills, close together, about 300 m. in height, the eastern Karia, according to Pausanias, with a sanctuary of Aphrodite Epistrophia (i. 40. 5), and the western Citadel of Alkathous (i. 42. 1), with a βουλευτήριον, 'Council House' (i. 42. 4), and the πρυτανεῖον, 'City Hall' (i. 42. 7), for religious and secular use. Pausanias reports another βουλευτήριον in the city, perhaps on lower ground (i. 43. 2). Xenophon indicates that Agesilaos made his ascent from the temple of Aphrodite (*Hell*. v. 4. 58; Paus. i. 43. 6).

Medical theory

Plutarch's attempt to detail Agesilaos' symptoms, to follow the development of the crisis, and to account for the cure, is reminiscent of observations described in the Hippocratic writings, and illustrates the interest of historians in recording and circulating medical information. There was a twofold affinity in methodology and purpose between history and medicine: a concern to recognize early signs of developing conditions (diagnosis) and a wish to observe and record the course of those developments for future use (prognosis).[5] The nature of Agesilaos' injury cannot now be diagnosed with certainty on the evidence available. Muscular strain may have caused swelling and internal haemorrhage. Thrombophlebitis[6] and 'deep venous thrombosis'[7] have been suggested. The Syracusan doctor's blood-letting would cause the fainting. The flow of blood would cease only when the clot formed—Xenophon's τότε μέντοι ἐπαύσατο (τὸ ῥεῦμα), 'but then (the flow) ceased' (*Hell*. v. 4. 58), gives no explanation.

The ancient world's lack of knowledge of the circulation of the blood means that ancient writers' descriptions cannot be related to modern practice, and the attempt to do so is not very helpful. The texts may be used to indicate some of the theory on which the treatment was based. For Homer, mortals were distinguished from gods by blood (*Il*. v. 340), αἱματικὴ τροφή, 'nourishment', which came from food and drink in the diet (Arist. *GA* 726^{b}10, *HA*

511ᵇ30 ff., quoting Diogenes of Apollonia).[8] It was distributed to the parts of the body as in an irrigation system.[9] The theory of the four elements of Empedokles of Akragas suggested the analogue of the four cardinal body humours or fluids recorded in later medical literature, of which one was blood.[10] This allows a connection with Agesilaos' Sicilian doctor, who would have the benefit only of the earliest ideas. He may have followed the thinking of the Sicilian Empedokles, with which the theory of disease became linked, as it appears in the Hippocratic treatise *Nature of Man*.[11] The loss of harmony among the body's fluids, which disturbed its well-being, could be caused by excessive exercise or eating.[12] The doctor would attempt to restore the balance by reducing the excess.

Xenophon and Plutarch record that Agesilaos, now approaching the age of 70, was climbing up to the acropolis, indicating physical strain as the immediate cause of the malady. Plutarch omits the bursting vein, mentioned by Xenophon as allowing the blood from the body to flow into the leg, which became swollen between the knee and the ankle, but he retains the swelling, and adds inflammation, perhaps from his own experience, or from later medical writers such as Erasistratos.[13] The swelling, attributed by Xenophon to excess of blood in the leg, indicated that there was internal blockage or piercing of a vein, which allowed blood to collect there. Purging and control of diet could be tried to induce a reduction in the supply of blood, but a speedier remedy might be desired. The body was thought to have channels running through it and out of it, carrying the various fluids.[14] Other excess fluids could be encouraged by the doctor to escape through the body's existing open-ended channels, so as to restore the harmony: excess blood needed an artificial channel.

2 ἰατροῦ δέ τινος Συρακοσίου τὴν ὑπὸ τῷ σφυρῷ φλέβα σχάσαντος, αἱ μὲν ἀλγηδόνες ἔληξαν, αἵματος δὲ πολλοῦ φερομένου καὶ ῥέοντος ἀνεπισχέτως, λιποψυχία πολλὴ καὶ κίνδυνος ὀξὺς ἀπ᾽ αὐτῆς περιέστη τὸν Ἀγησίλαον. **3** οὐ μὴν ἀλλὰ τοῦτό γε τὴν φορὰν τοῦ αἵματος ἔπαυσε· καὶ κομισθεὶς εἰς Λακεδαίμονα, πολὺν χρόνον ἔσχεν ἀρρώστως καὶ πρὸς τὰς στρατείας ἀδυνάτως.

Phlebotomy

Two later cases of the natural discharge of blood through the nose, which are described at *Aphorisms*, v. 33, *Epidemics*, vii. 123,[15]

provide a helpful illustration here. Blood, normally held within
the body unseen, conveying its nourishment, 'flowed' visibly only
when it was passing out through the body's channels, as in the
reported cases of nose-bleeding,[16] or when the outer skin was
accidentally pierced. Otherwise, the channel must be provided by
opening a vein. The danger was that an artery might be severed, as
may have been the case with Agesilaos, since the loss of blood was
great. Phlebotomy became popular, perhaps, because of the link
with Empedokles and the influential theories of the four humours.
That there was controversy between its advocates and those who
preferred starving the patient, is shown by Galen's revision of his
attitude to the theories of Erasistratos.[17] The modern reaction is
one of horror, for it is judged that Agesilaos' 'serious injury . . .
had been aggravated by incompetent medical attention',[18] but
modern standards are not relevant to our understanding of
medical data in ancient literature. The author's intention may
have been quite different, for Agesilaos recovered. His case
perhaps enhanced the reputations of the Syracusan doctor, and of
venesection; purging and phlebotomy were still practised in the
eighteenth century, and in some places even later.

Plutarch seems to describe a causal connection between the loss
of consciousness and the check to the flow of blood which released
Agesilaos from danger, though τοῦτο does not express 'because of
the fainting' clearly; the two may have only coincided in time
(Xen. *Hell.* v. 4. 58; see above, §1). His conclusion is a specific
reference to Agesilaos' inability to go on campaign, but gives only
a vague indication of its duration. Xenophon places the injury in
the spring (377) and says that Agesilaos was ill during the summer
and winter (*Hell.* v. 4. 58). He was still incapacitated in 371 (vi. 4.
18), and, in a period of Spartan decline, he is not mentioned by
Xenophon, except at the Peace Conference of that year (vi. 3. 19).
In 370 he is sent to Mantineia as an envoy (vi. 5. 4), and takes
command later that year (vi. 5. 11).

4 ἐν δὲ τῷ χρόνῳ τούτῳ πολλὰ συνέβη πταίσματα τοῖς Σπαρτιάταις
καὶ κατὰ γῆν καὶ κατὰ θάλατταν·

In this summary, Plutarch expresses the full purport of the
several campaigns in which Agesilaos was not engaged. At
Agesilaus, 2. 23 Xenophon passes from the campaign in Boiotia
(377) to the events at Tegea (370), in the year following Leuktra.

He bridges the gap by denying that Agesilaos' generalship was responsible for the intervening 'failures', σφάλματα—with no mention of the injury at Megara. The events to 373 detailed in *Hellenika* (v. 4. 59–vi. 2. 39) embrace the two fruitless efforts to contain the Thebans' recovery of the neighbouring cities of Boiotia, the discontent among the allies, and the naval operations. The Spartan fleet had had little success in the Saronic and Corinthian Gulfs, and in the Ionian and Aegean Seas, against Timotheos, Chabrias, Iphikrates, and the fleet of an Athens still angered by Sphodrias' raid. In *Hellenika* Agesilaos re-emerged after six years' absence as the key figure in Spartan affairs, a month before Leuktra, at the oath-taking ceremony (vi. 3. 19), when the Athenians had dissociated themselves from the ever more powerful Thebans, and had initiated another peace conference in Sparta.

ὧν ἦν τὸ περὶ Τεγύρας μέγιστον, ὅπου πρῶτον ἐκ παρατάξεως κρατηθέντες ὑπὸ Θηβαίων ἡττήθησαν.

The Theban victory at Tegyra in 375 continues for Plutarch the theme of the Spartans' weakness, adding substance to the reference to their reverses. Xenophon does not mention the battle—which it will not have helped Spartan morale to remember—and so fails to indicate the growth of the Thebans' military strength before Leuktra: indeed, at vi. 3. 20 he draws attention to their despondency.[19] Plutarch (*Pel.* 16 17) claims Tegyra as the preliminary to Leuktra and, as he does here, as the first victory against Sparta won in a pitched battle. He also describes the failure of the Spartan manoeuvre creating a gap, in expectation of letting the Thebans pass through the lines, as they had done at Koroneia (see ch. 18. 8; cf. Frontin. *Strat.* ii. 6. 6; Polyain. ii. 1. 19; Xen. *Hell.* iv. 3. 19). Pelopidas is said to have ignored the temptation to escape through the gap, and instead attacked the cramped Spartan formation that resulted from the manoeuvre and caused the rout. Diodoros seems to have used the same source; he also records this victory as the first against Sparta to be celebrated by a Theban trophy (xv. 81. 2). Since only two *morai* were present, the importance of the defeat for the Spartans has no doubt been exaggerated in the Boiotian tradition, but this does not detract from its importance for the Thebans' spirits and reputation, and for the move for peace.

5 ἔδοξεν οὖν πᾶσι θέσθαι πρὸς πάντας εἰρήνην· καὶ συνῆλθον ἀπὸ τῆς
Ἑλλάδος πρέσβεις εἰς Λακεδαίμονα, ποιησόμενοι τὰς διαλύσεις.

Xenophon (*Hell.* vi. 3. 1–2) suggests that the initiative for peace
came from the Athenians, because they no longer approved of
Theban actions against Plataia, Thespiai, and Phokis. At vi. 2. 38
he reports that Iphikrates was about to ravage Lakonian territory,
and although a commendation of the Athenian intervenes to
obscure the link, at vi. 3. 18 he reveals that the Spartans voted to
accept peace. There is also a hint of Persian pressure at *Hell.* vi. 3.
12, when, in denying Athenian fear of the King's money, he indicates that Antalkidas' arrival from Persia is imminent.[20]

6 ὧν εἷς ἦν Ἐπαμεινώνδας, ἀνὴρ ἔνδοξος ἐπὶ παιδείᾳ καὶ φιλοσοφίᾳ,
στρατηγίας δὲ πεῖραν οὔπω δεδωκώς.

Thebes became the home of the exiled Pythagorean philosopher
Lysis of Taras, who may then have become Epameinondas' tutor.
Plutarch seems to present a contrast with the Spartan system of
education, as he described it in chs. 1–2. In ch. 33. 4 he, like
Aristotle (*Pol.* 1271b1–19), notes the intellectual deficiency in the
system. The usual picture of Thebes is not a valid one. This
'peripheral' city, charged with Medism at Thermopylai, barely
restored its image, damaged in the prevailing literary sources
and more central cultured societies—Pindar complained of the
'Boiotian pig' slur (*Olympian*, 6. 90; cf. *Mor.* 993 A): perhaps to be
seen rather as a sign of good eating in good farmland; another
source of wealth, the reeds grown by Lake Kopais, brought
Thebans recognition as the best *auletes*—but Alkibiades
consigned his instrument to the Thebans (*Alk.* 2. 4–5), because
they could ignore harm done to good looks. Alliance with Sparta
in the Peloponnesian war eventually brought temporary relief.[21]
The museum at Thebes reveals material and cultural riches, and
signs of the acceptance of innovatory techniques, including the
contemporary and possibly unique etched black stones honouring
warriors, who perhaps fell at Delion;[22] the portraits are
reminiscent of etchings from Egypt and on Etruscan hand-
mirrors.

7 οὗτος ὁρῶν τοὺς ἄλλους ἅπαντας ὑποκατακλινομένους τῷ Ἀγησιλάῳ,
μόνος ἐχρήσατο φρονήματι παρρησίαν ἔχοντι, καὶ διεξῆλθε λόγον οὐχ
ὑπὲρ Θηβαίων, ἀλλ' ὑπὲρ τῆς Ἑλλάδος ὁμοῦ κοινόν, τὸν μὲν πόλεμον

ἀποδεικνύων αὔξοντα τὴν Σπάρτην ἐξ ὧν ἅπαντες οἱ λοιποὶ κακῶς πάσχουσι, . . .

Plutarch, recording Epameinondas' view, suggests indirectly that Agesilaos owed his predominance to the moral, rather than the military, weakness of the other Greeks. The striking double compound word, ὑποκατακλινομένους, is a very strong metaphor, expressing, perhaps, a deeply felt judgement; it may highlight one of the morals of this work, the danger of 'submissiveness', which the Theban envoys understood at Perachora (ch. 22) and, by ch. 30. 1, the Spartans too. Plutarch then, a Boiotian, attributes to Epameinondas alone the courage to speak frankly, exploring the spring of the action in the mind, 'pride and confidence', φρονήματι. He commends his panhellenic patriotism (see Introd., E.7(h) and ch. 27. 7) in speaking for all Greece, evaluating in anticipation the words about to be reported. The words used by Antalkidas against Agesilaos (ch. 23. 3) are now employed by Epameinondas: τὸν πόλεμον αὔξοντα, 'war will bring Sparta greatness'.

Xenophon, although he records the Athenian invitation to the Thebans to join the conference, does not record their dispatch, but he acknowledges a Theban presence for the signature. He does not name Epameinondas, and mentions only the speeches made by three of the Athenian envoys.[23] At *Hell*. vi. 3. 7–9 he has Autokles, one of the Athenians, express an identical criticism of Sparta, in a speech showing sympathy with Thebes. Plutarch may be right to assign this statement to Epameinondas instead of an Athenian. The suggestion of Athenian sympathy is not consistent with the changed Athenian attitude to Thebes, which was given by Xenophon as the reason why Athens desired peace (*Hell*. vi. 3. 1). That attitude is expressed by the third speaker, Kallistratos, who objects to the Thebans' recovery of control over the formerly independent cities (*Hell*. vi. 3. 11, 13). The Athenians hoped the Thebans would be 'decimated' (vi. 3. 20 and 5. 35). This translation of Xenophon's δεκατευθῆναι suggests the modern sense of 'almost exterminated' rather than the Roman military punishment of killing one man in ten. His Athenian speakers identify it as a recognized expression, τὸ λεγόμενον, presumably fitting the context—and their emotions. It is understood by LSJ of a tithe or tax, of a tenth, but in the first context the Thebans are not signatories to the treaty, and war soon follows, as on the second occasion.

These speakers present arguments for peace: the friendship between Athens and Sparta from legendary times, the ending of Sparta's 'despotism' (*Hell.* vi. 3. 8), and the renewal of the dual leadership. There is consistency between the first speech and the third, not shared with the second. Diodoros agrees with Plutarch in giving the case against Sparta to Epameinondas (xv. 38. 3), and Nepos attributes to him the condemnation of Spartan tyranny which helped eventually to end it (*Epaminondas*, 6. 4). Xenophon seems to have substituted an Athenian speaker, avoiding mention of the Theban. His account of the conflicting ambassadorial views has been explained as an ingenious strategy designed 'to make Athenian neutrality acceptable'.[24] Autokles' speech is judged too frank and offensive for the Athenian cause (cf. *Hell.* vi. 3. 20) but perhaps credible as evidence of 'Greek individualism and amateurism'.[25] Its positive reception by discontented allies suggests a committed advocate; the tone better suits the Theban view of Agesilaos' demands (v. 1. 32, vi. 4. 3).

. . . τὴν δ' εἰρήνην ἰσότητι καὶ τῷ δικαίῳ κτᾶσθαι κελεύων· οὕτω γὰρ αὐτὴν διαμενεῖν, ἴσων ἁπάντων γενομένων.

Epameinondas' rhetoric gives way to his implied criticism of the selfish use of the autonomy clause in the Peace of Antalkidas by Sparta, in the interest of—and only of—imperialist Sparta.[26] Plutarch gives in a prominent concluding phrase Epameinondas' proposal of a new panhellenism, one based not on the usual anti-Persian crusade, but on equality and justice for all Greeks. This is in line with the idealist interpretation of the principles of federation in the earlier Boiotian League (*Hell. Ox.* XI),[27] in the democratic elements of later Theban leadership of Boiotia, and again in the attempted Theban settlement of the Peloponnese.[28] The promise of an enduring peace here rests on an ideal balance, stressed by repetition of 'equality'. The one-sided settlements that Sparta imposed and the dual control by Athens and Sparta proposed by Kallistratos (vi. 3. 14) were flawed, for both had had the military strength needed to enforce peace, yet failed.

The Thebans, especially Epameinondas, studied philosophy and advocated higher principles. It is less true to say that the Thebans had no ideology to offer than that other states could not respond to the Theban proposal of federalism because their aim was to preserve the autonomy of the *polis* and its potential for wider hegemony. In practical politics, however, the need was for a combination of powerful enforcement with enlightened states-manship, whether federalist or, as Aristotle advised, benevolent hegemony (*Pol.* 1327^{b}31–3, 1333^{b}35–1334^{a}10; cf. 1294^{b}14–18; see above, ch. 8 n.).[29] Neither Sparta nor Thebes could now supply both these needs. If Plutarch was thinking of his own times in these terms, perhaps Rome, instead of Sparta, supplies the ele-ment of power, while other parts of Greece offer philosophical enlightenment. Diodoros' obituary notice places Epameinondas first for wise statesmanship (xv. 88).

28. Confrontation with the Thebans in conference and in the battle of Leuktra

1 Ὀρῶν οὖν ὁ Ἀγησίλαος ὑπερφυῶς ἀγαμένους καὶ προσέχοντας αὐτῷ τοὺς Ἕλληνας, ἠρώτησεν εἰ νομίζει δίκαιον εἶναι καὶ ἴσον αὐτονομεῖσθαι τὴν Βοιωτίαν.

The metaphor from natural growth, ὑπερφυῶς, put into Agesilaos' mind, may suggest 'overgrown, unnatural' admiration, but as Plutarch's thought it suggests that the Greeks were responding 'marvellously well', encouraged by the example of Epameinondas. Agesilaos' δίκαιον καὶ ἴσον, 'just and equal', repeat the sense of 'equality and justice' in Epameinondas' speech (ch. 27. 7), in reverse (chiastic) order. Epameinondas' concern was for 'all other Greeks': Agesilaos refers to 'Theban rule over some, the Boiotians'.

Plutarch recorded the Peace of Antalkidas at ch. 23 without referring to Agesilaos' refusal to allow the Thebans to take the oath as Boiotians (Xen. *Hell.* v. 1. 32), apparently reserving the argument for Epameinondas, and avoiding some of Xenophon's repetition. In Xenophon's account of that first conference the Thebans voiced their claim to Boiotian hegemony before signing, but signed under threat. At this conference of summer 371 (*Hell.* vi. 3. 19–20), the confrontation arises on the day after the treaty has been made, when the Thebans ask that 'Boiotians' be substi-tuted for 'Thebans' in the text, and Agesilaos, who is not named until now, refuses their request, and threatens that if they do not wish to be in the treaty, he will erase their name. It is possible that in taking the oath as Thebans they believed it to stand for Boiotians, especially if, as it seems, there was no other Boiotian presence and no Boiotian protest, and they returned next day on finding out that this was not understood by others. The Thebans continued the controversy and Kleombrotos was instructed to march on Thebes (vi. 4. 3). These accounts of the confrontations are consolidated by Plutarch.[1] He continues the discussion started by Epameinondas in ch. 27, not as the retrospective protest, but in the dialogue here and at §§2–3 in advance of the signing, displaying the contrasted characters of the two opponents. Xenophon's attitude is, perhaps, expressed indirectly in the Athenians' hope that there would now be massive Theban casualties (*Hell.* vi. 3. 20, 5. 35; see above, ch. 27. 7 on 'decimated').

The Greeks' attitude to the peace settlement which Epameinondas proposes perhaps represents, indirectly, Plutarch's own judgement. It suggests that the relationship of the voting members of the Boiotian Confederacy with Thebes was no less autonomous than that of the voting members of the Peloponnesian League with Sparta. In Lakonia and Messenia, the *Perioikoi*, who were autonomous only locally in their own communities, and the Helots, who were not autonomous at all, did not vote.[2] No members of the Boiotian League were in this position. The issue is complicated, perhaps deliberately, by Xenophon's choice of words: the 'Lakedaimonians', that is the Spartans, take the oath 'for themselves and their allies' (cf. *Hell.* vi. 3. 7–9, 19). This phrase excludes the Perioikic cities of Lakonia and Messenia, for they were not allies in the Peloponnesian League. The Athenians and their allies take the oath 'city by city'. For Thebes and the Boiotian Confederacy, the equivalent is 'Thebans and their allies' or 'Boiotians'. Boiotians in their federal organization are not exactly parallel with Spartans and their allies but in no way parallel with Helots and *Perioikoi*.

2 ἀντερωτήσαντος δὲ τοῦ Ἐπαμεινώνδου ταχὺ καὶ τεθαρρηκότως εἰ κἀκεῖνος οἴεται δίκαιον αὐτονομεῖσθαι τὴν Λακωνικήν, . . .

As Agesilaos had countered Epameinondas' demand by turning on Thebes, so Epameinondas attacks Sparta, exploiting the weakness to which Agesilaos had exposed himself by confusing alliance, confederation and autonomy.[3] The concern so strongly voiced here still motivated Epameinondas to secure the autonomy of Messenia after Leuktra.

. . . ἀναπηδήσας ὁ Ἀγησίλαος μετ᾽ ὀργῆς ἐκέλευσε λέγειν σαφῶς αὐτὸν εἰ τὴν Βοιωτίαν ἀφίησιν αὐτόνομον. 3 τὸ δ᾽ αὐτὸ τοῦτο πάλιν τοῦ Ἐπαμεινώνδου φήσαντος, εἰ τὴν Λακωνικὴν ἀφίησιν αὐτόνομον, . . .

Plutarch's 'leaping up' vividly describes (ἐνάργεια) Agesilaos' characteristic action (ch. 22. 5). There is no 'anger' in Xenophon's account, where Agesilaos' words indicate irritation, but Plutarch's μετ᾽ ὀργῆς perhaps interprets the hatred of *Hell.* v. 1. 33. Agesilaos resorts in rage to autocratic domination; Epameinondas' argument is reasoned.

. . . οὕτω τραχέως ἔσχεν ὁ Ἀγησίλαος καὶ τὴν πρόφασιν ἠγάπησεν, ὡς εὐθὺς ἐξαλεῖψαι τὸ τῶν Θηβαίων ὄνομα τῆς εἰρήνης καὶ προειπεῖν πόλεμον αὐτοῖς· 4 τοὺς δ᾽ ἄλλους Ἕλληνας διαλλαγέντας ἐκέλευσεν ἀπιέναι, τὰ μὲν ἀκεστὰ τῆς εἰρήνης, τὰ δ᾽ ἀνήκεστα τοῦ πολέμου ποιοῦντας. ἔργον γὰρ ἦν πάσας ἐκκαθῆραι καὶ διαλῦσαι τὰς ἀμφιλογίας.

The rage is so violent that action takes the place of words. Agesilaos' 'delight' recalls his joy at ch. 9. 1 when Tissaphernes broke the truce. The 'bellicose' characterization of Agesilaos by Antalkidas and Epameinondas is continued (chs. 23. 3, 27. 7; cf. Diod. xv. 19. 4). Xenophon does not record the deletion of the name or the declaration of war, but has the Spartan assembly alert Kleombrotos in Phokis, and when the Thebans do not disband their army, as the treaty would require, he duly enters Boiotia (*Hell.* vi. 4. 3). Xenophon comments ominously on the assembly's decision that it seemed to be 'led on by a divine power' (*Hell.* vi. 4. 3), as if the Thebans were not bound by the peace which 'the others had made' (*Hell.* vi. 3. 20).

5 ἔτυχε δὲ κατ᾽ ἐκεῖνον τὸν χρόνον ἐν Φωκεῦσιν ὢν ὁ Κλεόμβροτος μετὰ δυνάμεως.

Xenophon recorded Kleombrotos' mission to Phokis (375), with four *morai* and corresponding contingents of allies, at *Hell.* vi. 1. 1. Phokis was said there to be under attack from Thebes, but when Polydamas of Pharsalos reported in Sparta that Jason was expanding his influence in this area, the Spartans took no further action. It appears that they had been trying to separate the Thebans from Jason, their ally still in 371 (vi. 1. 2–17, 4. 20). Thebes thereafter defended the passes into Boiotia. Xenophon makes no further reference to Kleombrotos until vi. 4. 2, when the Lakedaimonians decide not to withdraw him along with their garrisons in other cities. It is unlikely that he was kept with such a large part of the army in this area for so long once the Athenians had withdrawn from the war and concluded peace (375/4) with Sparta (*Hell.* vi. 2. 1). However, at *Pelopidas*, 16. 1, 17. 4, Plutarch speaks of two *morai* at Orchomenos replaced from Sparta in rotation (διαδοχήν). Pelopidas had attacked Orchomenos, left without defenders while these *morai* were away in Lokris, but he was deterred by the arrival of their replacement, and it was on their return from Lokris that they met Pelopidas at Tegyra (ch. 27. 4). Perhaps Kleombrotos had brought the replacements now in Orchomenos. This is not reported by Xenophon, who does not refer to Tegyra; but he does admit that the Theban cavalry had good practice in the war with the Orchomenians (*Hell.* vi. 4. 10).

εὐθὺς οὖν ἔπεμπον οἱ ἔφοροι κελεύοντες αὐτὸν ἐπὶ Θηβαίους ἄγειν τὸ στράτευμα· καὶ τοὺς συμμάχους περιπέμποντες ἤθροιζον, ἀπροθύμους μὲν ὄντας καὶ βαρυνομένους τὸν πόλεμον, οὔπω δὲ θαρροῦντας ἀντιλέγειν οὐδ' ἀπειθεῖν τοῖς Λακεδαιμονίοις.

Plutarch gives an account of Leuktra at *Pelopidas*, 20–3. Agesilaos was not engaged, and here only the preliminaries and the result of the battle are recorded. The interpretation of the allies' morale before the battle seems to be adapted from Xenophon, though he records their discontent only after the battle (*Hell.* vi. 4. 15). Xenophon tends to obscure the Theban achievement, highlighting rather Kleombrotos' early successes and Spartan bravery in the battle.

Topography

Plutarch says nothing about the topography of Kleombrotos' approach to Leuktra here and in *Pelopidas*, perhaps because this appeared in the lost *Epameinondas* (see below, on §6). Xenophon reports that Kleombrotos approached Boiotia by a mountainous and unexpected route from Phokis to Thisbai and Kreusis, where he captured twelve Theban triremes (*Hell.* vi. 4. 4, Diod. xv. 53. 1). He massacred a Theban outpost under Chaireas (Paus. ix. 13. 3). This route runs along the Helikon range, through the valleys

below the main ridge on the side towards the sea, from Distomon
to Steirion, Kyriakion and Hagia Anna, described as the 'High
Road'.[4] A country track now leads through a series of narrow
passes which open on to high plateaux, enclosed on either side by
the upper slopes of the mountain. The final approach of the
Spartans to the plain of Leuktra, after their detour to Kreusis, was
up the valley of the River Libadostras and over the low ridge, the
eastern spur of Mount Korombili. Recent studies show that
Kleombrotos reached the plain just to the west of the modern
town.[5]

Xenophon reveals, not from a Theban source but as
Kleombrotos' observation, that the Thebans were guarding a
narrow pass (*Hell.* vi. 4. 4). This was identified as Koroneia by
Diodoros (xv. 52. 7; cf. ch. 18. 1), who reports (xv. 52. 1) that the
Spartans were awaiting their allies at Chaironeia.[6] When
Kleombrotos turned to the mountain route, the Thebans would
return to Thebes by the direct route past Lake Kopais and across
the plain. A road to Thespiai would take them on to Leuktra, but
the risk that Kleombrotos might slip through in front of them,
gaining a commanding position between themselves and Thebes,
suggests that they would prefer the longer march in order to
protect the western approaches to the city.

6 πολλῶν δὲ σημείων μοχθηρῶν γενομένων, ὡς ἐν τῷ περὶ
Ἐπαμεινώνδου γέγραπται, καὶ Προθόου τοῦ Λάκωνος ἐναντιουμένου
πρὸς τὴν στρατείαν, οὐκ ἀνῆκεν ὁ Ἀγησίλαος, ἀλλ᾽ ἐξέπραξε τὸν
πόλεμον,

Plutarch's Epameinondas

The survival of *Agesilaos* and *Pelopidas* provides material for an
attempt to analyse Plutarch's treatment of historical material and
its deployment in historically interrelated *Lives*, but the loss of
Plutarch's *Epameinondas* is a major disadvantage. Pausanias (ix.
13–15) has been thought to epitomize the lost *Life*[7] but analysis
shows that this hypothesis cannot be sustained.[8] Some few items
may be paralleled in Plutarch's texts but three times as many are
un-Plutarchan or contaminated from other sources.[9] In devoting
almost half its space to the battle of Leuktra Pausanias fails to preserve biographical balance, and he does not maintain a consistent
biographical focus throughout the section (cf. 13. 4–5 on

Kleombrotos and Skedasos, 14. 2–3 on Thespians):[10] he not only erroneously associates Antalkidas with the peace of 371 (13. 2; cf. ch. 23. 2–3)[11] but omits what Plutarch would surely stress in *Epameinondas*, as he does at ch. 27, his character's most significant and enlightened desire for a just peace for all Greece.

The independent or contradictory nature of some un-Plutarchan material is a reminder of the selective use by Pausanias and Plutarch of biographical and antiquarian sources available to them.[12] Pausanias' description of the battle (ix. 13. 3–12) provides valuable additional information: Kleombrotos' mountain route through Ambrossos in Phokis (13. 3; cf. Xen. *Hell.* vi. 4. 3); the Boiotarchs' disagreement about joining battle (13. 6–7; cf. *Pel.* 20. 2, Diod. xv. 53. 3); the separate collection of the dead—more than a thousand Lakedaimonians (13. 11–12; cf. *Mor.* 193 B); Plutarch gives precisely 1,000 (§8).

The gods' signs reflect the human unease and do not favour the Spartan enterprise. Xenophon mentions that it was opposed by Prothoos,[13] both on legal grounds and to avoid offending the gods; he says that the advice was rejected, not by Agesilaos, but by the assembly (*Hell.* vi. 4. 2). Prothoos is given no introduction by Xenophon, though the preceding phrase 'the authorities' may include him. If Plutarch's description precludes his being an Elder or an ephor, Prothoos will be an example of an ordinary Spartiate addressing the assembly, which had the right to decide but not to debate (Arist. *Pol.* 1273ᵃ11–12).[14] Xenophon introduces the influence of the gods again, albeit with some hesitation: an oracle warning of a Lakedaimonian defeat, and signs of encouragement reportedly given to the Thebans. He records a belief that these were engineered by the generals (*Hell.* vi. 4. 7); Diodoros attributes them to Epameinondas' ingenuity (xv. 53. 4–54. 4). At *Pelopidas*, 20. 3, 21. 1 Pelopidas has a dream which includes the instruction to sacrifice to the daughters of Skedasos, a resident of Leuktra, who were violated by two Spartans.[15] In Pausanias Epameinondas performs the sacrifice, linking the battle with avenging the violation.

ἐλπίζων αὐτοῖς μὲν ὁμοῦ τι τῆς Ἑλλάδος ὅλης ὑπαρχούσης, ἐκσπόνδων δὲ τῶν Θηβαίων γεγονότων, καιρὸν εἶναι δίκην λαβεῖν παρ᾽ αὐτῶν. **7** δηλοῖ δὲ τὸ σὺν ὀργῇ μᾶλλον ἢ λογισμῷ γενέσθαι τὴν στρατείαν ἐκείνην ὁ καιρός.

Agesilaos believes that the isolation of Thebes in the peace conference (Xen. *Hell.* vi. 3. 19) puts Sparta in a position, after
victory in the coming conflict, to settle accounts, since at this
moment he had ensured by his diplomacy that none of the signatories would come to Thebes' assistance. Considering how coldly
the Theban victory was received, he was quite right; but that it
was reasonable to expect military victory is less clear, judged with
the benefit of hindsight: the Thebans had grown in confidence and
strength over the years. Yet it has been suggested that Agesilaos
was justified, and that victory at Leuktra would also have vindi-
cated his policy for Sparta.[16] For Plutarch, however, that assessment of the opportunity, framed strikingly by the repetition of
καιρός, was not rational (cf. chs. 8. 6, 36. 4–5). Agesilaos was motivated by anger, and that marks one of the successive stages in the
decline of Agesilaos' character. The same combination of words
describes the fall of Pelopidas when he fails 'to control his rage by
judgement' (*Pel.* 32. 6). The 'tragic flaw' (ἁμαρτία), for which
Pelopidas himself pays, there wins glory, but Agesilaos' ἁμαρτία is
paid for by the deaths of others. Plutarch is, perhaps, interpreting
the pejorative terms in which Xenophon records the rejection of
the advice of Prothoos that Sparta should abide by the terms of
the peace just agreed: 'the assembly considered he was talking like
a fool' (*Hell.* vi. 4. 3). This striking phrase indicates strongly the
irrational nature of the Spartan reaction to what seems to be an
orthodox and rational proposal. If Xenophon composed it to
describe the atmosphere of the meeting, or to represent the views
expressed and voted upon, Plutarch may have sensed a veiled
criticism of the leadership for tolerating this reaction.
Responsibility for the defeat at Leuktra does not appear to rest
only with the general on the battlefield. Agesilaos' misreading of
the καιρός, a rare occurrence in a military situation, compounds his
responsibility, for the word denotes everything which it was his
duty as the king to take into account before committing the city to
action (cf. chs. 37. 2, 39. 2): here anger renders his judgement
defective.[17] Xenophon regrets the effect of anger when he
describes the death of Teleutias at Olynthos (*Hell.* v. 3. 5–7).

τῇ γὰρ τετράδι ἐπὶ δέκα τοῦ Σκιροφοριῶνος μηνὸς ἐποιήσαντο τὰς
σπονδὰς ἐν Λακεδαίμονι, τῇ δὲ πέμπτῃ τοῦ Ἑκατομβαιῶνος ἡττήθησαν
ἐν Λεύκτροις ἡμερῶν εἴκοσι διαγενομένων. **8** ἀπέθανον δὲ χίλιοι

Λακεδαιμονίων καὶ Κλεόμβροτος ὁ βασιλεὺς καὶ περὶ αὐτὸν οἱ κράτιστοι τῶν Σπαρτιατῶν.

The precise Julian date of the battle seems to be incalculable, though mid-August has been proposed, but the twenty days between it and the Peace are suspect.[18] Calculations of the date consider the reported movements of Kleombrotos and the (unspecified) time taken; the discrepancies between the different calendars in use; and Plutarch's own statements, here and at *Cam.* 19. 2; but without reaching conclusions of any certainty. A serious complication is the need in years of 13 new moons (such as 371 BC) for intercalation, which might extend the interval here to 49 days or thereabouts. There seems to be no obvious significance in the precise number of days: the gods' anger would have to wait while the order reached Kleombrotos and while he then reached the battlefield, delayed by the diversion from Koroneia to Kreusis. Other victims of divine retribution have waited longer, and Plutarch may simply wish to provide a brief temporal link in order to clarify the retributive element. For Plutarch the Spartans' defeat and heavy casualties prove the error of Agesilaos' decision for war.

The battle of Leuktra (371)[19]

The two armies were drawn up in positions resulting from their respective lines of approach. The plain of Leuktra is not wide at this point, and lies between roughly parallel low ridges to the north and south. Behind the Theban line, the road to Thebes offered little chance of further organized resistance once the Spartans had broken through. The Theban strength was concentrated on the left, to face the Spartans. The reason for this was surely the lesson learnt at the battle of Koroneia, where the Thebans did not themselves face the Spartans, and, despite their own victory, found the Spartans behind them. If this happened at Leuktra, Thebes could have been taken, whether the Thebans themselves won or lost. Their only hope of saving Thebes was to defeat the Spartans, and, after victory, remain in position between them and the city.

The Thebans were the main strength of their fighting force, massed in unprecedented depth of phalanx. They were also fighting with the desperation of defending their homes and

families from certain destruction. Their strategy, tactical formation, and motivation will have contributed most to their victory,
adding to sound training, confidence, and past battle experience.
The supposed innovatory tactics of the Thebans at Leuktra are
disputed,[20] but the combination of the deepened phalanx and the
oblique advance (Xen. *Hell*. vi. 4. 12, 14, Diod. xv. 55. 2) meant
that 'the Spartans were confronted by a wholly novel tactical
situation'.[21] On their side, the Spartans' failure to learn the value
of the deep phalanx rendered their courage and reputation
ineffectual, in addition to the confusion of the initial cavalry clash
and of possible last-minute corrective manoeuvring.

Xenophon gives nearly 1,000 Lakedaimonian dead, but adds
that of 700 Spartiates present, more than 400 fell. Kleombrotos
and then Kleonymos died. The sources do not identify the
Lakedaimonian casualties. They cannot have been allies and
mercenaries, for they were evidently on the Spartan left (*Hell*. vi.
4. 14) and, if Diodoros is correct (xv. 55. 2), were not engaged by
Epameinondas' right wing. References in Xenophon to Perioikoi
and the difficulties resulting from exclusive training of Spartans in
the army suggest that they were not integrated into the Spartiate
units,[22] unless there were arrangements for recruiting and training
unknown to us. Not all scholars agree, however, but suggest that
Spartans and Perioikoi were brigaded together, though the statement: 'The non-Spartiates in the army needed to be well practised
[in the drills], if confusion was to be avoided' leaves the training
unexplained.[23]

The decline in the number of Spartiates available for military
service may partly have been made good by recruiting those fully
trained but disqualified.[24] The Perioikoi will have been with the
allies and the mercenaries on the left wing, and may have had few
casualties. The Spartan cavalry were the first to be engaged by the
Thebans and were quickly routed (*Hell*. vi. 4. 13), so that they
suffered casualties. The cavalry were not all full citizens.[25] At *Hell*.
vi. 4. 11 the richest men rear the horses, and the riders are
assigned only at the call-up and have to be given horse and arms; it
seems that at Sparta these recruits did not have hoplite status. The
cavalry will have contributed to the 600 casualties who were not
Spartiates, and, of the hoplites, the ὑπομείονες, who had been
through the ἀγωγή, trained and served alongside the Spartiates in
the phalanx, but were now without Spartiate status.[26]

Spartiate status, that is membership of *syssitia*, was part of Spartan social and religious life, and probably not part of the military organization,[27] so that the Spartiate casualties will indicate decline in the citizen body, not in Lakedaimonian military resources (cf. ch. 30. 5). The emphasis placed on casualties among Spartiates represents their importance for the survival of the essential fabric of Spartan society, for they were in a minority as regards not only Perioikoi and Helots, but also those Inferiors. Their small number was already visible to Kinadon's conspirators.[28]

Leuktra was decisive, not so much because the Spartan army had been destroyed . . . but because it put an end to the myth of Spartan invincibility.[29]

ἐν οἷς καὶ Κλεώνυμόν φασι τὸν Σφοδρίου τὸν καλὸν τρὶς πεσόντα πρὸ τοῦ βασιλέως καὶ τοσαυτάκις ἐξαναστάντα καὶ μαχόμενον τοῖς Θηβαίοις ἀποθανεῖν.

Like Xenophon, who describes the Spartans' heroism in defeat by recording the wish of some to fight again (*Hell.* vi. 4. 14–15), Plutarch ends his account of the battle with praise, but he does it by adding to Xenophon's brief notice of Kleonymos' death an anonymous report—φασι—that he stood up after falling three times, fighting in front of the king. He was fulfilling his promise to Archidamos not to shame him. Plutarch did not mention it at ch. 25, and Xenophon does not refer to it directly here, but makes the link by adding Sphodrias, now one of the king's council, to the list of dead (*Hell.* vi. 4. 14).

Sparta after the battle

Cam. 19. 2; Xen. *Hell.* vi. 4. 18, 5. 4–5, 6, 10–12, 15–21, *Agesilaos*, 2. 23–4; Diod. xv. 58–9, 62.

29. Spartan greatness in adversity

In chs. 29–30 Plutarch reveals critical assessments of Agesilaos and Sparta just before he describes in the next five chapters the eclipse of the city as leader even in the limited area of the Peloponnese. His rhetorical techniques are powerfully deployed in a highly sensitive account of the Spartans' response to their crisis.

1 Συμβάντος δὲ τοῖς τε Λακεδαιμονίοις πταίσματος ἀπροσδοκήτου καὶ τοῖς Θηβαίοις παρὰ δόξαν εὐτυχήματος, οἷον οὐ γέγονεν ἄλλοις Ἕλλησι πρὸς Ἕλληνας ἀγωνισαμένοις, . . .

The Lakedaimonian disaster is correspondingly a Theban success. Xenophon (*Hell.* vi. 4. 15) praised the Spartans' desire to fight again, but the mood changed to depression; the dead had to be recovered under truce and the news taken to Sparta. The Thebans set up a trophy, but at *Hell.* vi. 4. 19–25 their failure to secure the support of the Athenians and Jason of Pherai neutralizes their success. Plutarch, ignoring this, presents his comments on each side in a single rhetorical expression, exploiting the element of surprise, which is common to both, in a chiastic pattern of contrasted nouns and their synonymous attributes. He suggests that the Spartans were not expecting disaster and the Thebans were not expecting success: both were unable to foresee that the reverse of their expectations would be the result. The event is described as surpassing others of its kind, in another rhetorical expression reminiscent of passages at *Nikias*, 27. 6 (Ἕλληνες πρὸς Ἕλληνας) and Thucydides, vii. 87. 5 (τοῖς τε κρατήσασι λαμπρότατον καὶ τοῖς διαφθαρεῖσι δυστυχέστατον). Here rhetoric does not impede a correct assessment of political significance, for the unique circumstance of Leuktra was that the supposed invincibility of the

Spartan army ended, unexpectedly and, with hindsight, unambiguously. It was left for Xenophon's successors to make this explicit. In Aristotle's view (*Pol.* 1270ᵃ33), a single blow was too much for Sparta.

. . . οὐδὲν ἄν τις ἧττον ἐζήλωσε τῆς ἀρετῆς καὶ ἠγάσθη τὴν ἡττημένην πόλιν ἢ τὴν νικῶσαν.

Plutarch commends the Spartans' behaviour, with a paradoxical comparison generous to both cities. The events show that the character of a people, like that of an individual, is constant, and that the Spartans behaved as courageously in their difficult situation, true to their traditions, as the victorious Thebans behaved. The judgement is presented not as Plutarch's alone, but as one beyond challenge. The commendation of the Spartans' courage is in strong contrast to the increasingly widespread criticism of Agesilaos on other grounds which began in ch. 22. 2–3. Plutarch draws a distinction for the moment between the Spartans and the behaviour of their king, and is establishing at this stage his approval of the traditional character of Lykourgan Spartan society. Equally, he is establishing a standard of community behaviour in the Sparta that he admired, against which he will set the later, very different, reactions of Spartans to another national crisis, to be described almost immediately, in ch. 31 and again in ch. 33.

2 ὁ μὲν γὰρ Ξενοφῶν φησι τῶν ἀγαθῶν ἀνδρῶν ἔχειν τι καὶ τὰς ἐν οἴνῳ καὶ παιδιᾷ φωνὰς καὶ διατριβὰς ἀξιομνημόνευτον, ὀρθῶς λέγων·

For Plutarch as a biographer trivial events manifest the virtues and vices of a character as illustrious deeds often do not (*Alex.* 1. 1–2). He regarded Xenophon as important for his philosophical works and appealed to him as 'the philosopher' (ch. 20. 2). Having in the previous sentence compared the cities in defeat and victory, he quotes him for support in his new comparison; for Xenophon too recorded both the serious actions and the trivialities of good men (*Symp.* 1. 1). But Plutarch modifies the quotation. He narrows the references, omitting his 'serious' element, and retains only his 'light-hearted amusements', adding 'while drinking wine'. He also broadens the references, adding forms of 'speech' to Xenophon's forms of 'action'. He is creating a chiastic pattern: (§1 above) defeat and victory, (§2) enjoyment and misfortune (παρὰ τὰς τύχας, below). The modification is necessary for the presentation of the argument: the women's reaction to disaster is a form of speech—its absence—as well as joyful pride (§7). With the illustrious—heroism at war—he contrasts deeds which are 'trivial' but still heroism: heroism at home, in the agora, and in the shrines.

ἔστι δ᾽ οὐχ ἧττον, ἀλλὰ καὶ μᾶλλον ἄξιον κατανοεῖν καὶ θεᾶσθαι τῶν ἀγαθῶν ἃ παρὰ τὰς τύχας πράττουσι καὶ λέγουσι διευσχημονοῦντες.

Having established the paradox, Plutarch improves on his valuation of symposiastic trivial circumstances. He uses a refined form of simile, so that what he compares does not match but surpasses the given standard. He claims that a stronger proof of character is 'preserving dignified forms', διευσχημονοῦντες, of action and speech when fortune militates against them (cf. πρᾳότης, ch. 2. 2). Plato also uses this metaphor (cf. *Smp.* 196 A for the physical 'grace' of Eros) in testing the reactions to panic and pleasure, joy and grief, of future 'guardians' and others (*Resp.* 413 E, *Ll.* 732 C): it may be only assumed (Eur. *Med.* 584); cf. ch. 14. 4, on μετασχηματίζοντες. The rhetorical 'improvement' made to Xenophon's *Symp.* 1. 1 enables Plutarch to discuss Spartan courageous behaviour 'in a serious situation', and to consider speech—and its absence (§7)—and action. Plutarch's sentiments are consistent with his approval of Spartan heroism and with Stoic *apatheia*, 'freedom from emotion' (cf. *Lyk.* 18. 1, *Mor.* 82 F);[1] Spartan models were vital to Stoic inspiration.[2] Elsewhere (chs. 1 and 2), he approves Agesilaos' kindness and humanity, as a Stoic would not, without strict adherence to virtue.

3 ἔτυχε μὲν γὰρ ἡ πόλις ἑορτὴν ἄγουσα καὶ ξένων οὖσα μεστή· γυμνοπαιδίαι γὰρ ἦσαν, ἀγωνιζομένων χορῶν ἐν τῷ θεάτρῳ· παρῆσαν δ᾽ ἀπὸ Λεύκτρων οἱ τὴν συμφορὰν ἀπαγγέλλοντες.

After digressing to establish his principle, Plutarch reintroduces the conduct of the city on receipt of the news of the disaster at Leuktra. The arrival of the messengers during the festival makes sadly ironical the reference to enjoyment at §2. Apparently in planning Kleombrotos' expedition to Boiotia, the ephors disregarded the approaching festival. Plutarch realizes that the presence of the foreign spectators (§2, θεᾶσθαι)—not mentioned by Xenophon—increases the embarrassment, for it was important for

Spartans not to allow their enemies and potential enemies to be encouraged by witnessing their internal problems. Better news would have been a different matter.

The city at festival receiving news of disaster begins a chiastic pattern which is completed in §4 with the ephors' refusal to allow the disaster to interrupt the festival.

4 οἱ δ' ἔφοροι, καίπερ εὐθὺς ὄντος καταφανοῦς ὅτι διέφθαρται τὰ πράγματα καὶ τὴν ἀρχὴν ἀπολωλέκασιν, οὔτε χορὸν ἐξελθεῖν εἴασαν οὔτε τὸ σχῆμα τῆς ἑορτῆς μεταβαλεῖν τὴν πόλιν, ἀλλὰ κατ' οἰκίαν τῶν τεθνεώτων τοῖς προσήκουσι τὰ ὀνόματα πέμψαντες, αὐτοὶ τὰ περὶ τὴν θέαν καὶ τὸν ἀγῶνα τῶν χορῶν ἔπραττον.

At *Hell.* vi. 4. 16 Xenophon concentrates on the self-control of the ephors, reporting that they were distressed but allowed the chorus to be concluded. In communicating the names of the dead to the relatives, they imposed silence on the women, so that the subsequent behaviour of the relatives is in obedience to their command. Plutarch gives less recognition of the ephors' self-control: their sense of shock here instead of grief portrays the impact of Leuktra on the whole of Greece, and on Sparta, too, in this wider context. This is not advertised in Xenophon's account. Plutarch adds that the ephors—no doubt in their desire for secrecy—circulated the news of casualties only to the relatives in their homes, and continued with the rest of the festival, without giving any order for silence. In his reference to the unchanged 'programme of the festival', σχῆμα—the spectacle seen by visitors—Plutarch denotes, in ring composition, the outer 'form' or manifestation of the Spartans' inner sense of 'dignified forms' posited above in διευσχημονοῦντες.

5 ἅμα δ' ἡμέρᾳ φανερῶν ἤδη γεγονότων πᾶσι τῶν τε σῳζομένων καὶ τῶν τεθνεώτων, οἱ μὲν τῶν τεθνεώτων πατέρες καὶ κηδεσταὶ καὶ οἰκεῖοι καταβαίνοντες εἰς ἀγορὰν ἀλλήλους ἐδεξιοῦντο λιπαροὶ τὰ πρόσωπα, φρονήματος μεστοὶ καὶ γήθους, **6** οἱ δὲ τῶν σῳζομένων, ὥσπερ ἐπὶ πένθει, μετὰ τῶν γυναικῶν οἴκοι διέτριβον, εἰ δέ τις ὑπ' ἀνάγκης προέλθοι, καὶ σχήματι καὶ φωνῇ καὶ βλέμματι ταπεινὸς ἐφαίνετο καὶ συνεσταλμένος.

Xenophon says that it was on the last day of the festival that the messengers arrived; visitors would soon be departing from Sparta, and the news of the disaster was not made fully public until the following day (*Hell*. vi. 4. 16), when foreigners were perhaps going home. After the announcement the situation in Sparta is similar to the situation in the Spartan army after the announcement of the disaster at Lechaion. Xenophon records general mourning there, except among the relatives of the fallen, who followed Spartan patriotic tradition and rejoiced (*Hell*. iv. 5. 10). On this occasion, too, Xenophon, followed in the remainder of the chapter by Plutarch, records the reversal of usual human reactions to such news. But Plutarch presents the behaviour of the Spartans as a spontaneous response, a commendation for the relatives' own self-control as they themselves reacted with Spartan courage and composure; Xenophon commended their obedience to the ephors' command.

Plutarch restructures the passage, making four parts of Xenophon's two. He divides the relatives of the dead and those of the survivors into two further categories, the male and the female, again showing his interest in all members of the family. He also introduces expressions which are more concrete and specific. The male 'relatives of the dead' are expanded into 'fathers, kinsmen, friends'; and 'public' becomes 'the *agora*'. Xenophon's wholly physical description, λιπαροὺς καὶ φαιδρούς, 'bright and radiant', is represented by 'bright of countenance', an external description, but enlarged by the explanatory 'full of pride and joy' (cf. the similar internalizing change concerning Agesilaos at ch. 9. 1 above). The male relatives of the survivors are either out of sight at home, or, if constrained to go out of the house, described in concrete detail, of 'mien, voice, and look'. For the condition of these relatives Xenophon has used only two adjectives, 'sullen and dejected', but his main point is that few were seen. Plutarch refers this not to their number but to their reluctance to be seen, stressing their mood, which perhaps reflects their expectation that the men returning will receive the treatment described in ch. 30. 3–4.

7 ἔτι δὲ μᾶλλον τῶν γυναικῶν ἰδεῖν ἦν καὶ πυθέσθαι τὴν μὲν ζῶντα προσδεξομένην υἱὸν ἀπὸ τῆς μάχης κατηφῆ καὶ σιωπηλήν, τὰς δὲ τῶν πεπτωκέναι λεγομένων ἔν τε τοῖς ἱεροῖς εὐθὺς ἀναστρεφομένας, καὶ πρὸς ἀλλήλας ἱλαρῶς καὶ φιλοτίμως βαδιζούσας.

Further expansion and heightening are achieved by Plutarch's treatment of the women separately from the male relatives. He is careful to explain that verbal reports were available, so that he can describe the women who were said not to be seen abroad. The patterns of situation and response are similar for men and women, but the vocabulary for women is changed, becoming more striking and also more appropriate. For the female relatives of the survivors, Xenophon's 'sullen and dejected' becomes 'downcast and silent'. Their silence—explicit and spontaneous here, but in Xenophon imposed by the ephors and not mentioned again—is significant as the negative of the category 'speech' added in the modified quotation from *Symposion* (§2). For the female relatives of the dead, 'public' is interpreted in two specific and highly relevant contexts, one religious, 'the shrines', and one domestic, 'each other's homes'; and inner feelings, 'with joy and a sense of achievement', replace Xenophon's external appearances. Plutarch also arranges the order of survivors and slain in a chiastic pattern, beginning and ending with the examples which correspond most closely to his starting-point—behaviour in adversity; for it is the way the bereaved carry their grief that displays the unique Spartan character.

The effect of these changes is to introduce a strong element of ἐνάργεια[3] into the narrative, which, with the expanded length of the passage, gives due prominence to Plutarch's main concern, the Spartan character. Rhetoric has been criticized as destroying the historical truth of an author's work.[4] It is the function of rhetorical training to develop skills in presentation and sharpen insight into human character and situation. The comparison between Plutarch's version and the probable source passage in Xenophon indicates that there is no distortion of the less rhetorical account, which itself appears to be that of an eyewitness, though not necessarily the author himself. The problem for the historian in this case is to represent truthfully the impact of the event on the human emotional level as well as on the political, and it is only this impact which benefits from the use of evocative creativity to paint the picture. Plutarch brings extra life and depth to an already vivid description by visualizing and internalizing the details. He amplifies beyond Xenophon's evidence, certainly concerning the details of the women's activities, but does not falsify.

30. A failure of nerve: Agesilaos suspends the law; he invades Arkadia

Plutarch develops three themes on reactions at Sparta to Leuktra: guilt for the disregard of the oracle at Agesilaos' accession, the plight of the disgraced survivors, and the depressed spirits of the young. These themes gradually re-establish the worth of Spartan values despite the further decline that follows. Plutarch draws from several references in Xenophon, but, unless he had another source, he adds reasonable inferences—'creative reconstruction'[1] —from a wider knowledge of Spartan thinking, especially in the middle section.

1 Οὐ μὴν ἀλλὰ τοῖς πολλοῖς, ὡς ἀφίσταντο μὲν οἱ σύμμαχοι, προσεδοκᾶτο δὲ νενικηκὼς Ἐπαμεινώνδας καὶ μεγαλοφρονῶν ἐμβαλεῖν εἰς Πελοπόννησον, ἔννοια τῶν χρησμῶν ἐνέπεσε τότε πρὸς τὴν χωλότητα τοῦ Ἀγησιλάου . . .

In the aftermath of Leuktra Diodoros notes Theban generous and humane feelings, φιλανθρωπία, in the treatment of Orchomenos (xv. 57. 1), a Lakedaimonian reverse in Arkadia (62. 1–3; Xen. *Hell.* vi. 5. 14), invasion of the Peloponnese by Epameinondas (62. 4–5), and a mood of helplessness at Sparta on the secession of the allies (63. 1). Xenophon says less of Spartan difficulties, but records that some of the allies were pleased (vi. 4. 15), which Plutarch takes to mean they defected. A renewed attack on the Lakedaimonians at Leuktra threatened by the Thebans was abandoned only when Jason of Pherai advised against it (*Hell.* vi. 4. 22); Plutarch suggests anxiety in the Peloponnese.

Before Leuktra Xenophon recognized the daemonic influence leading the Spartans to neglect the advice of Prothoos on the importance of divine favour (ch. 28. 6–7; Xen. *Hell.* vi. 4. 2). Plutarch's concern for the reputation of the god required that disregard of the advice should have been punished.[2] He will have assumed recriminations after the battle and the recall by the Spartans of Diopeithes' warning (ch. 3; cf. *Comp.* 1. 2). Agesilaos' disability was always available for any opposition to exploit, though the terms of the oracle (ch. 3) limited its relevance to effects of lasting duration.

. . . καὶ δυσθυμία πολλὴ καὶ πτοία πρὸς τὸ θεῖον, ὡς διὰ τοῦτο

πραττούσης κακῶς τῆς πόλεως, ὅτι τὸν ἀρτίποδα τῆς βασιλείας
ἐκβαλόντες εἵλοντο χωλὸν καὶ πεπηρωμένον· ὃ παντὸς μᾶλλον αὐτοὺς
ἐδίδασκε φράζεσθαι καὶ φυλάττεσθαι τὸ δαιμόνιον·

This interpretation of the oracle means that Diopeithes was right
in thinking that the lameness intended was in the king, not in the
kingdom, and the consequence of the 'man-destroying war' was
one which would affect the kingdom (ch. 3), as Leuktra did. In
his defence, Agesilaos could claim that Lysander, not he, was
responsible for the erroneous interpretation, but this would not
relieve the city of its responsibility for having chosen him. The
Spartans' tendency to see a disaster as the consequence of guilt is
exemplified by Thucydides (vii. 18. 2); contrary to sworn agreement (the truce of 445: i. 115. 1), they had refused arbitration in
their dispute with Athens (i. 78. 4). The indirect and often
ambiguous expressions used in oracles, as here, necessitated
human intervention to interpret their meaning, and the quality of
the interpretation was something to be ascertained. Diotima
explains to Socrates (Plato, *Smp.* 203 A) that communication
between gods and mortals requires a superior human with skill in
divination. In this case, the authority of Lysander was accepted by
the Spartans, in defiance of the authority of a recognized diviner.[3]
Plutarch's orthodox view makes them collectively responsible for
their misfortunes.

2 διὰ δὲ τὴν ἄλλην δύναμιν αὐτοῦ καὶ ἀρετὴν καὶ δόξαν οὐ μόνον
ἐχρῶντο βασιλεῖ καὶ στρατηγῷ τῶν κατὰ πόλεμον, ἀλλὰ καὶ τῶν
πολιτικῶν ἀποριῶν ἰατρῷ καὶ διαιτητῇ, τοῖς ἐν τῇ μάχῃ κατα-
δειλιάσασιν, οὓς αὐτοὶ τρέσαντας ὀνομάζουσιν, ὀκνοῦντες τὰς ἐκ τῶν
νόμων ἀτιμίας προσάγειν, πολλοῖς οὖσι καὶ δυνατοῖς, φοβούμενοι νεωτερισμὸν ἀπ' αὐτῶν.

Throughout the *Life*, Plutarch commends Agesilaos as king and
general, but although his next employment makes other demands,
his authority would lead the citizens to accept his judgement, just
as they had accepted Lysander's interpretation of the oracle.
However, 'judgement' is not only missing from the list of his
qualifications; it is being questioned by the critics, including
Plutarch, over his handling of Sparta's relations with Thebes. At
the same time, the citizens have been questioning their own
judgement in making Agesilaos their king.

For the new appointment Plutarch uses two medical metaphors: 'a man with a remedy', ἰατρός, and 'a mediator' or arbitrator, διαιτητής, for the health of their institutions (διαιτήματα). For the statesman as doctor for an unhealthy state see *Mor.* 823 F–825 D. The metaphors are frequently used for political and constitutional reforms and settlements (ch. 33. 3; *Lyk.* 4. 3, *Sol.* 15. 1, *Cam.* 9. 2, *Per.* 15. 3, 34. 3, *Pomp.* 55. 4, *Caes.* 28. 6, *Dion.* 11. 3, 37. 7, *Kl.* 10. 4; cf. Thuc. vi. 14), for military measures (*Pomp.* 67. 8–9, *Marc.* 24. 2), and in a love-affair (*Dtr.* 38. 7). Agesilaos is not disqualified because he himself needed a doctor at Megara (ch. 27. 2); yet his disability is now in the citizens' minds (§1).

The 'cowardice' explains why the men are named τρέσαντες, runaways, 'tremblers' (cf. *Il.* xiv. 522: Ζεὺς ἐν φόβον ὄρσῃ). The title (*Lyk.* 21. 1) was given to a Spartan whose companion died without him at Thermopylai (Hdt. vii. 231).[4] The information about the present crisis comes only from Plutarch; the ephors were perhaps the first to express concern (*Mor.* 191 C, 214 B). Xenophon omits this episode, and no other contemporary source for it is extant, but Plutarch may have had one. If not, he responds 'creatively', some would say unreasonably, to the expectation that the Spartans would do something about the survivors: he had a precedent in the similar occasion when the Spartans, fearing revolt, removed the rights of citizenship from the prisoners from Pylos sent home by the Athenians. Thucydides reports that some important men were debarred from holding any office or command; they were restored later (v. 34. 2).

3 οὐ γὰρ μόνον ἀρχῆς ἀπείργονται πάσης, ἀλλὰ καὶ δοῦναί τινι τούτων γυναῖκα καὶ λαβεῖν ἄδοξόν ἐστι· παίει δ᾽ ὁ βουλόμενος αὐτοὺς τῶν ἐντυγχανόντων. **4** οἱ δὲ καρτεροῦσι περιϊόντες αὐχμηροὶ καὶ ταπεινοί, τρίβωνάς τε προσερραμμένους χρώματος βαπτοῦ φοροῦσι καὶ ξυρῶνται μέρος τῆς ὑπήνης, μέρος δὲ τρέφουσι.

Other marks of degradation are recorded by Herodotos (vii. 231), and at *Lak. Pol.* 9 Lykourgos is said to have introduced them to encourage men to prefer death to disgrace.[5] They withhold all opportunities to compete for honour, respect, and status. The victims were exposed to public derision amounting to the most humiliating forms of institutionalized jesting, with the aim of con-solidating the Lykourgan system.[6] Known cases are rare, perhaps a mark of the effectiveness of these sanctions, but possibly a sign that they belonged largely to the Spartans' self-created image. On this occasion, no men suffering the punishments would be in sight on the day when visitors were still in Sparta, so that only the 'evidence' given by the Spartans themselves would reach the rest of Greece, to contribute to the transmitted myth.

5 δεινὸν οὖν ἦν τοιούτους ἐν τῇ πόλει περιορᾶν πολλούς, οὐκ ὀλίγων δεομένῃ στρατιωτῶν. καὶ νομοθέτην αἱροῦνται τὸν Ἀγησίλαον.

The link with the numbers available to serve in the army seems to be false (see above, ch. 28. 8 n.). Service as hoplites was not excluded by Plutarch's ἀτιμία, 'loss of status' (§2; cf. *Lak. Pol.* 9. 6, Thuc. v. 34. 2), for soldiers were not recruited only from the Spartiate class.[7] Deprivation of Spartiate status was not significant for Sparta's total military numerical strength, but the decrease in their numbers threatened the survival of the social system which ensured their privileged position as the ruling oligarchy. That became vulnerable if they were seen to be too few to defend it, or if they could not fill posts of responsibility from their own ranks (cf. the reinstatement recorded at Thuc. v. 34. 2). A *perioikos* held command at sea in 412, and occasionally harmosts may have been non-Spartiate and perhaps *perioikoi* (Thuc. viii. 22. 1, Xen. *Hell.* i. 1. 32, ii. 2. 2, iii. 5. 12), if the term Λάκων, Lakonian, suggests that.[8] Agesilaos exploited Sparta's need for soldiers of quality in defending Sphodrias (ch. 25), preferring, no doubt, not to reveal other reasons. But Plutarch was right to refer above to social unrest. Fear of a revolt of helots arose while the men from Pylos were held by the Athenians (Thuc. iv. 80. 2), and Kinadon plotted soon after Agesilaos' accession (Xen. *Hell.* iii. 3. 4–11). The large proportion of discontented men that would now be created presented an even greater threat to the state.

6 ὁ δὲ μήτε προσθείς τι μήτε ἀφελὼν μήτε μεταγράψας, εἰσῆλθεν εἰς τὸ πλῆθος τῶν Λακεδαιμονίων· καὶ φήσας ὅτι τοὺς νόμους δεῖ σήμερον ἐᾶν καθεύδειν, ἐκ δὲ τῆς αὔριον ἡμέρας κυρίους εἶναι πρὸς τὸ λοιπόν, ἅμα τούς τε νόμους τῇ πόλει καὶ τοὺς ἄνδρας ἐπιτίμους ἐφύλαξε.

Plutarch's other versions of Agesilaos' appointment as νομοθέτης, lawmaker, show that the ephors wished to annul the punishment but to guard the laws (*Mor.* 191 C, 214 B). He enacts that the present laws should be in force 'from tomorrow'; that they should sleep 'for today' is an embellishment. The remedy, which avoids discontent rather than adding to it, is equivalent in outcome to the earlier reinstatement (Thuc. v. 34. 2), but has the advantage that it takes effect immediately, escaping the risk of an uprising and also the embarrassment of reversing the decision which the earlier solution necessitated.

The large number of men involved seems to make the charge of cowardice less appropriate than in an individual case, but this was not to be made the point at issue, nor was the opportunity taken to propose reform. Plutarch would probably not have seen such a change as desirable (*Lyk.* 21). Sparta, for him, was admired for the laws which were derived from Lykourgos, and in departing from strict observance the Spartans were now abandoning the very system that had made them what they were, and so, like Agesilaos, they were in moral decline.

This sharing of the responsibility for decline is a new theme for Plutarch. Their respective positions go through several changes. In chs. 19–20 Agesilaos was holding the Spartans to the traditional way of life, but was thereafter at fault over Phoibidas, Sphodrias, and Thebes. In the crisis of ch. 29 the citizens maintained their high moral standard, and at §1 above realized Agesilaos' vulnerable moral position in the kingship. Plutarch perhaps regarded their present decline as starting in their continued reliance on him, especially as 'lawmaker', despite their new interpretation of the oracle.

It is not clear if the question of Spartiate status involved 'Lakedaimonians'. Apparently the rest of the population of Lakonia, the non-Spartiate, thought highly enough of their superiors, the Spartiates, to sympathize with their plight,[9] and recognized the city's need to avoid imposing the regular penalties. If, however, Agesilaos made his proposal in a meeting of the assembly only of the Spartiates, they would perhaps be sympathetic to the plight of the survivors, but would certainly be conscious of their own insecurity: the day 'the laws slept' would be that of the meeting, not the battle. The number of survivors was perhaps half that of the two *morai* and the men beyond the 35 age-class who had remained in Sparta, creating a serious problem for the enforcement of the punishment. Whatever the considerations, the announcement would remove doubts about Spartan security. Plutarch makes no favourable comment on the proposal here, but at *Comparatio*, 2. 3 he says that it was an exceptional political device, σόφισμα, and by attributing it to Agesilaos' 'political virtue' (cf. *Lak. Pol.* 10. 7)[10] shows the word to be commendatory, as σοφία generally is (cf. Introd., D.1(e)), but, like σοφιστής, pragmatic.[11] That the opportunity was not taken for more sweeping change is said to be symptomatic of the failure of Sparta to engage in radical reform, in keeping with the needs of the times, here in the social sphere, as earlier in the military, and after the Peace of Antalkidas.[12] Plutarch seems to approve the retention of the laws attributed to 'Lykourgos'—a convenient fiction, always regarded with reverence, like the Romans' *mos maiorum*[13]—and accepts the means of preserving them in this case.

7 βουλόμενος δὲ τὴν παροῦσαν ἀθυμίαν καὶ κατήφειαν ἀφελεῖν τῶν νέων, ἐνέβαλεν εἰς Ἀρκαδίαν, καὶ μάχην μὲν ἰσχυρῶς ἐφυλάξατο συνάψαι τοῖς ἐναντίοις, ἑλὼν δὲ πολίχνην τινὰ τῶν Μαντινέων καὶ τὴν χώραν ἐπιδραμών, ἐλαφροτέρον ἐποίησε ταῖς ἐλπίσι καὶ ἡδίω τὴν πόλιν, ὡς οὐ παντάπασιν ἀπεγνωσμένην.

The signatories to the King's Peace reaffirmed at Athens in 371 the autonomy of the cities of Greece, including the Peloponnese. Mantineia re-established democracy (Xen. *Hell.* vi. 5. 3, 4–5; cf. v. 2. 7), and rejected Agesilaos' attempt to retain Spartan influence; Sparta was isolated, and Xenophon uses the autonomy clause to excuse his inability to reassert Spartan influence (*Hell.* vi. 5. 5). Democratic Tegeans urged all the Arkadian peoples to unite: their opponents took to arms but fled to Sparta when the Mantineians brought support to the democrats.[14] Agesilaos was put in command of an expedition against them to avenge the Tegean exiles (Xen. *Hell.* vi. 5. 10–11, Diod. xv. 59. 1–4, 62. 1–2).

That any risk of further depletion of numbers was removed by avoiding a pitched battle is indicated by Xenophon's account of this campaign (*Hell.* vi. 5. 11–21).[15] There was no major confrontation: Agesilaos captured Eutaia, a border town, but supplies were purchased, not plundered; he plundered farms near Mantineia, but refused to be persuaded to attack the Arkadians and Argives; and, after the panic of a false alarm at the approach of his allies, the Orchomenians, he managed, by a complex marching manoeuvre, to extricate his army from a valley near Mantineia, which, as Xenophon says, he had entered by mistake at dusk. When Agesilaos withdrew rapidly to Eutaia, very late, Xenophon reports that he wanted to avoid contact, so that he would not be seen to be in flight, and so that it would seem that no one had been willing to engage in battle with him.

Just as the announcement to the Lakedaimonians of the retention of the laws covered any Spartan embarrassment, so the expedition to Arkadia was a valuable psychological rehabilitation of the Spartan military machine, especially for the survivors of Leuktra. Their escape from the indignity of the customary punishments for cowardice would not wholly remove either the public stigma or the personal sense of shame. Some military achievement to offset the shock of a Spartan defeat could also do something to restore the Spartan reputation among the allies, who did not expect the Lakedaimonians to undertake any expedition for a long time (Xen. *Agesilaos*, 2. 23). Plutarch seems to have been influenced by Xenophon's comment that the city was relieved of its despondency (*Hell*. vi. 5. 21), and Agesilaos' honour in the military field was restored. But at the end of the chapter Sparta's position is in some doubt: ὡς οὐ παντάπασιν ἀπεγνωσμένην, 'not entirely desperate', or so it was thought. Xenophon almost suppresses the threat of major trouble which Diodoros reveals in full: Sparta's enemies had secured the help of the Thebans (xv. 62. 3–4, *Hell*. vi. 5. 19; cf. §1 above).[16]

PART XI (chs. 31-5)

In the final dekad, chs. 31-40, Plutarch reaches the climax of the work. In the earlier chapters, he developed and expounded the characters of Agesilaos and Sparta: strengths and weaknesses were exposed, but the fate of Sparta was not decided. Gradually the hostile analysis unfolded, and now Plutarch's judgement is explicit as the decline becomes irreversible. Social insecurity, fragile communal cohesion, the forsaking of traditional Lykourgan values; a powerful external threat and isolation from former allies; the public humiliation of reliance on bought friendships and betrayal: the tragedy is relieved only by the persistence of Agesilaos' private Spartan values and personal military competence. The early complexities contrast with the thematically more straightforward narratives from here to the end.

Epameinondas and Lakonia

Pel. 24. 1–5; Xen. *Hell.* vi. 5. 22–52, vii. 1. 28–32, 4. 9, 4. 32–5. 14, 5. 14–27, *Agesilaos*, 2. 24, 25–7; Diod. xv. 65. 1–67. 1, 72. 3, 82. 1–84. 1, 84–9; Nepos, *Pel.* 4. 3, *Ep.* 8–10, *Agesilaus*, 6. 1–7. 2; Polyain. ii. 1. 14, 15, 27, Paus. viii. 8. 10, 11. 5–9, 27. 2, 49. 3, ix. 14–15.

31. Crisis in Sparta: Epameinondas invades Lakonia[1]

1 Ἐκ δὲ τούτου παρῆν εἰς τὴν Λακωνικὴν ὁ Ἐπαμεινώνδας μετὰ τῶν συμμάχων, οὐκ ἐλάττονας ἔχων τετρακισμυρίων ὁπλιτῶν. 2 πολλοὶ δὲ καὶ ψιλοὶ καὶ ἄνοπλοι πρὸς ἁρπαγὴν συνηκολούθουν, ὥστε μυριάδας ἑπτὰ τοῦ σύμπαντος ὄχλου συνεισβάλλειν καὶ καταβαίνειν εἰς τὴν Λακωνικήν.

The Theban allies with Epameinondas were members of the Arkadian League engaged in a struggle with dissident exiles supported by Sparta (ch. 30. 7; Xen. *Hell.* vi. 5. 11, Diod. xv. 59. 4). Diodoros explains that the Arkadians, with the Argives and Eleians, obtained help from the Thebans, Lokrians, and Phokians, after Athens had refused to help (xv. 62. 3). The decision to invade Lakonia was then taken jointly (370/69).[2] As usual, since

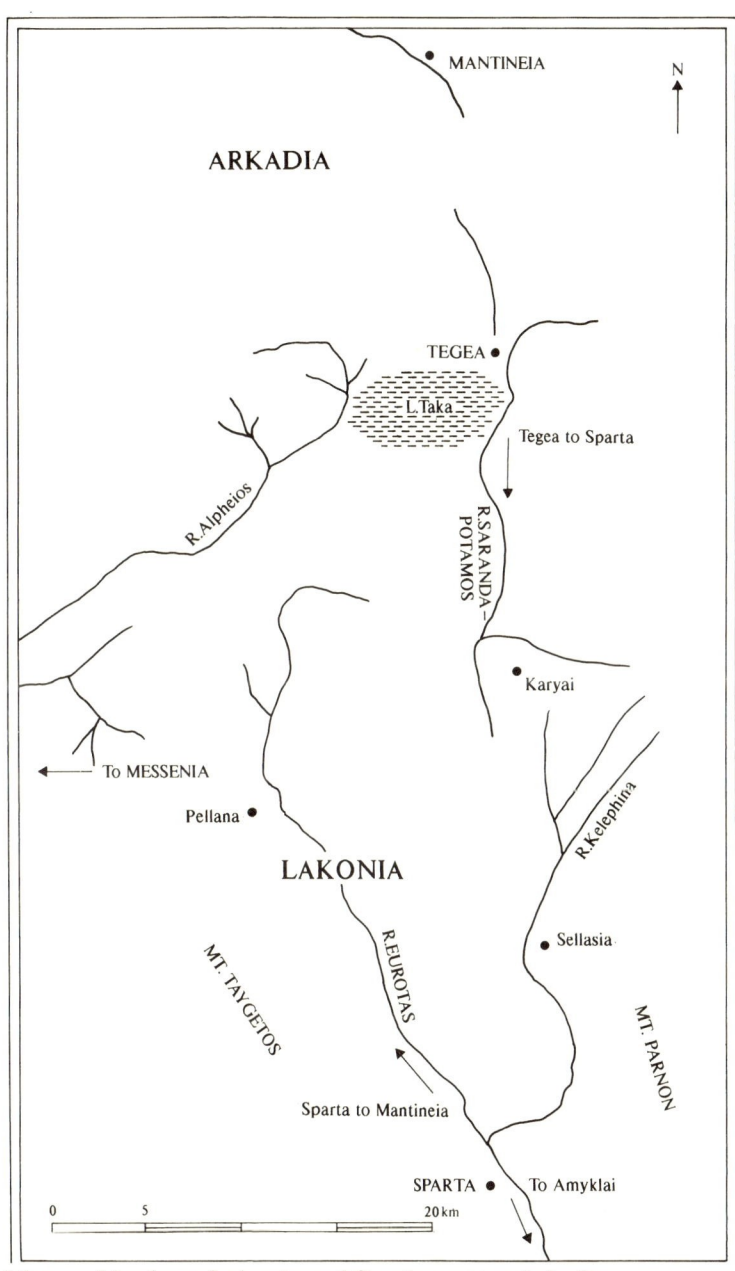

MANTINEIA

N

ARKADIA

TEGEA

L.Taka

Tegea to Sparta

R.Alpheios

R.SARANDA-
POTAMOS

Karyai

To MESSENIA

Pellana

R.Kelephina

LAKONIA

Sellasia

MT. TAYGETOS

R.EUROTAS

MT. PARNON

Sparta to Mantineia

SPARTA   To Amyklai

0   5   20 km

Map 4. Northern Lakonia and South-eastern Arkadia

Agesilaos took no part at this stage, Plutarch omits the preliminary details of the expedition. According to Xenophon, although the Eleians were expecting the Thebans to come, having sent ten talents for their expenses, Agesilaos had disbanded his army (*Hell.* vi. 5. 19, 21). The Thebans, now well trained but 'hesitating' to invade Lakonia, overcame a border guard-post and met no further opposition (*Hell.* vi. 5. 22–9).

The Boiotian Plutarch would be disappointed that Xenophon makes no mention of Epameinondas and he turns to another source, perhaps Ephoros, followed also by Diodoros at xv. 62–6. Although, like Xenophon, he does not explain his arrival in the Peloponnese—it was, no doubt, more fully treated in the lost *Life*—he now highlights the Theban national hero. The abrupt introduction of the new situation exploits the element of shock which the Spartans themselves must have felt and sharpens the contrast with their brief elation in the last chapter.

Plutarch distinguishes the 40,000 hoplites from the total of 70,000, including auxiliaries, given here (Xenophon gives no figures).[3] He gives this figure also at *Pelopidas*, 24. 2, and says that the Thebans formed a twelfth part. The same total figure is given by Diodoros at xv. 81. 2, in the obituary notice of Pelopidas, but in the account of the invasion the figure is 'more than 50,000' (xv. 62. 5). Plutarch's consistency indicates that he used the one source in both places; either Diodoros follows two sources, or there is a textual error.

3 ἦν μὲν δὴ χρόνος οὐκ ἐλάττων ἐτῶν ἑξακοσίων, ἀφ᾽ οὗ κατῴκουν τὴν Λακεδαίμονα Δωριεῖς· ἐν δὲ τούτῳ παντὶ τότε πρῶτον ὤφθησαν ἐν τῇ χώρᾳ πολέμιοι, πρότερον δ᾽ οὐδεὶς ἐτόλμησεν· ἀλλὰ ἀδήωτον καὶ ἄθικτον οὖσαν ἐμβαλόντες ἐπυρπόλουν καὶ διήρπαζον ἄχρι τοῦ ποταμοῦ, τῆς πόλεως μηδενὸς ἐπεξιόντος.

Plutarch shows the low level to which the condition of the Spartans has declined, compared with the immunity from invasion enjoyed in the past. Diodoros refers to Sparta's decline in strength explicitly after five centuries of freedom from devastation by enemies (xv. 63. 1, 65. 1). Xenophon mentions that the women had never seen an enemy (*Hell.* vi. 5. 28). He reveals the report to the Thebans by messengers from Karyai that the Spartans were now isolated (*Hell.* vi. 5. 25). The defections of the *perioikoi* referred to here may explain Agesilaos' anxiety when

Epameinondas challenged him to recognize their autonomy (ch. 28. 3). Plutarch ends the sentence with summary references to immunity, invasion, devastation, and enforced inactivity. That the invaders did not yet cross the river is confirmed by Xenophon (*Hell.* vi. 5. 27): perhaps the bridge was of light construction, designed for ceremonial access to the Menelaion.[4]

4 ὁ γὰρ Ἀγησίλαος οὐκ εἴα πρὸς τοσοῦτον, ὥς φησι Θεόπομπος, ῥεῦμα καὶ κλύδωνα πολέμου μάχεσθαι τοὺς Λακεδαιμονίους, ἀλλὰ τῆς πόλεως τὰ μέσα καὶ κυριώτατα τοῖς ὁπλίταις περιεσπειραμένος, ἐκαρτέρει τὰς ἀπειλὰς καὶ τὰς μεγαλαυχίας τῶν Θηβαίων, προκαλουμένων ἐκεῖνον ὀνομαστὶ καὶ διαμάχεσθαι περὶ τῆς χώρας κελευόντων, ὃς τῶν κακῶν αἴτιός ἐστιν ἐκκαύσας τὸν πόλεμον.

By placing Agesilaos' name immediately after mentioning Spartan inactivity (§3), Plutarch suggests his responsibility for Sparta's weakness; and the metaphor of the waves recalls the 'billows of war' in Diopeithes' oracle (ch. 3. 7). The important point is that against such overwhelming enemy forces the Spartans, now without allies, had not been able successfully to take the action beyond their frontiers that had protected their territory in the past. Agesilaos' generalship is not criticized by Plutarch, who approves of his restraint, mentioned by Xenophon (*Agesilaos*, 2. 24), in not fighting in the open (*Mor.* 214 C; cf. Polyain. ii. 1. 29). Diodoros also mentions the restraint imposed on the Lakedaimonians, but the order there came from the elders (xv. 65. 1).

Plutarch's description of the positions occupied by Agesilaos as 'central and most important'—there was no city wall—will refer to the broken line of high spots west of the Eurotas from Moundouna and the Acropolis south-eastwards,[5] and corresponds more closely to the topography of Sparta than Diodoros' implied single stronghold (xv. 65. 4). Diodoros records Theban taunts challenging Agesilaos to battle; Plutarch refers to these only in the king's stubborn response, but he adds the invaders' charge that Agesilaos caused the war. Xenophon's account of Agesilaos' angry diplomacy in Arkadia (*Hell.* vi. 5. 4) also implies his responsibility.

5 οὐχ ἧττον δὲ τούτων ἐλύπουν τὸν Ἀγησίλαον οἱ κατὰ τὴν πόλιν θόρυβοι καὶ κραυγαὶ καὶ διαδρομαὶ τῶν τε πρεσβυτέρων δυσανασχετούντων τὰ γινόμενα καὶ τῶν γυναικῶν οὐ δυναμένων ἡσυχάζειν, ἀλλὰ παντάπασιν ἐκφρόνων οὐσῶν πρός τε τὴν κραυγὴν καὶ τὸ πῦρ τῶν πολεμίων.

The reactions of the men and women are expressed in the same three nouns, but the participles show a contrast: among the elders, a sense of outrage, no doubt over the military situation, which Plutarch makes explicit later in the chapter, and among the women, their loss of rational control on perceiving the enemy's shouts and fires. The one word, κραυγαί, 'shouts', is used, not only of the enemy, but also of the Spartan men and women; the sound is the same, but what it means is different. The confusion contrasts the disciplined and orderly response to tragedy after Leuktra (ch. 29; Xen. *Hell.* vi. 4. 16) and the quite different picture of courageous Spartan women often presented in *Sayings of Spartan Women (Mor.* 241–2).[6] The danger was closer to Sparta now. Diodoros reports that women as well as old men and children were left to guard Sparta (xv. 65. 2).[7]

Xenophon provides indirect confirmation of Plutarch's description of the scene, in recording the anxiety of the women who saw the smoke of the burning houses. Aristotle's remark, that about (σχεδόν) two-fifths of the property was owned by women (*Pol.* 1270ª23–4), may suggest that some of their initial concern in seeing the smoke was for their property, and at that point, he was noting the intemperate and luxurious lifestyle allowed them, which rendered them of no use in the crisis (*Pol.* 1269ᵇ20–39). That could account for a minority of them, but Xenophon makes it a general point. The approach of the invaders also portended an assault on Sparta itself, and the danger of the familiar fate of women in a captured city. They had reason to fear for their safety, never having envisaged the possibility, and in the knowledge that their security depended on a Spartan army no longer invincible. The anxiety of the men is shown more practically by the action of the authorities, who, in recognition of the isolation of the Spartiates, called for the immediate aid of 6,000 helot volunteers (*Hell.* vi. 5. 28–9). Both authors portray the crisis of confidence by exploiting the transformation of the usual, predominantly domestic environment of the women into the unfamiliar male world of war. That the women's confusion was shared by the Spartan men suggests an exceptional response to an exceptional situation: Sparta was unwalled (Xen. *Hell.* vi. 5. 28). Plutarch recorded examples of the bravery of women of other cities (*Mor.* 242 E–263 C): as well as individual acts of courage their collective exploits concern the defence of Phokis (244 D), Chios (245 B), Argos (245 E), and Melos (246 F).

6 ἠνία δὲ καὶ τὸ τῆς δόξης αὐτόν, ὅτι τὴν πόλιν μεγίστην παραλαβὼν καὶ δυνατωτάτην, ἑώρα συνεσταλμένον αὐτῆς τὸ ἀξίωμα, . . .

Plutarch moves from the effect on Agesilaos' emotions of the Spartans' public actions to a judgement of the effects of his policies on the city. He uses the indirect method to suggest responsibility for Sparta's decline, as Agesilaos realizes the situation damages his reputation. Indirect method usually gives independent validation to judgements, but the validity of the charge is not increased by attributing it to the private thought of Agesilaos, which is not capable of independent authentication—as proof that he admitted, even to himself, the error of his policies; rather he goes on to save his reputation only by taking firm action against others who were also disillusioned. Plutarch's assumption that the comparison, if not the causal connection, was in his mind, is a reasonable one. It would be prosaic—and no longer impartial—for Plutarch to list the charges, and say that Agesilaos grieved, unless there were some consequence to record. The point is left in Agesilaos' mind while he carries on, according to Plutarch, aggravating the problem, except momentarily at ch. 33. 1–2: a psychological drama.

καὶ τὸ αὔχημα κεκολουμένον, ᾧ καὶ αὐτὸς ἐχρήσατο πολλάκις εἰπὼν ὅτι γυνὴ Λάκαινα καπνὸν οὐχ ἑώρακε πολέμιον. **7** λέγεται δὲ καὶ Ἀνταλκίδας, Ἀθηναίου τινὸς ἀμφισβητοῦντος ὑπὲρ ἀνδρείας πρὸς αὐτὸν καὶ εἰπόντος, Ἡμεῖς μέντοι πολλάκις ὑμᾶς ἀπὸ τοῦ Κηφισοῦ ἐδιώξαμεν, ὑποτυχεῖν· Ἀλλ' ἡμεῖς γε οὐδέποτε ὑμᾶς ἀπὸ τοῦ Εὐρώτα. **8** παραπλησίως δὲ καὶ πρὸς τὸν Ἀργεῖον ἀπεκρίνατο τῶν ἀσημοτέρων τις Σπαρτιατῶν· ὁ μὲν γὰρ εἶπε Πολλοὶ ὑμῶν ἐν τῇ Ἀργολίδι κεῖνται, ὁ δ' ἀπήντησεν, Ὑμῶν δέ γ' οὐδεὶς ἐν τῇ Λακωνικῇ.

It is not easy to find suitable historical contexts for Agesilaos' boasts about Lakonia's immunity from invasion, but it is likely that the anecdote is developed from Xenophon's account (*Hell.* vi. 5. 28). Plutarch avoids repetition, having referred to the sight of the enemy already at §3 above. Each of the three anecdotes proves that Spartan territory had never been violated before, but the last two, which are included in *Apophth. Lak.* (*Mor.* 192 C = 217 D, 233 C), carry more conviction as part of the tradition than Agesilaos' boast, for it was only now that enemy fires first signalled a hostile presence in the vicinity of Sparta: Xenophon more correctly said the sight was unbearable. These may all be patriotic witticisms circulating in the Spartan messes, or among visitors to Sparta. In a collection of sayings, no context need be provided, but Plutarch has incorporated them in this narrative, giving them relevance and topicality—which they may or may not have had. His purpose is not stated, but the effect may legitimately be assessed: they come after an apparent admission of grief, and show the height from which Sparta had fallen, with grim humour rather than with criticism, and skilful arrangement. There is a rising tricolon in the anecdotes: the distant vision of fires, the brief approach to the Eurotas, the permanence of burial in Lakonia. All show how the defence of Sparta had previously been undertaken beyond its borders: the Kephisos flowed through Athens (Soph. *OC* 687–9); the battles of Hysiai (669: Paus. ii. 24. 7, viii. 6. 4), Thyreatis (546: Hdt. i. 82. 3–6), and Sepeia (*c.*494: Hdt. vi. 80–3) were in the Argolid.

Here Plutarch reaches the lowest point in Agesilaos' reign.

32. Epameinondas threatens Sparta

Xenophon does not mention Agesilaos from *Hell.* vi. 5. 22 until his brief appearance after the 'Tearless Battle' (vii. 1. 32; ch. 33. 8). He describes Epameinondas' first invasion (vi. 5. 22–52) as if he took no part, and devotes vii. 1–vii. 5. 9 largely to the two invasions of the north Peloponnese by Epameinondas, whom he names for the first time at vii. 1. 41. In *Agesilaos* Xenophon mentions only one invasion, in which Agesilaos kept the city safe, and describes his services in Asia Minor in Sparta's financial interests (2. 24–7). Plutarch, perhaps enlarging on Xenophon's statement that Sparta had troubles for which Agesilaos was not responsible (*Agesilaos*, 2. 23), fills the interval before the fourth invasion (ch. 34. 3; *Hell.* vii. 5. 4) with his account of Sparta's weakness.

1 Τότε μέντοι τὸν Ἀνταλκίδαν φασὶν ἔφορον ὄντα τοὺς παῖδας εἰς Κύθηρα ὑπεκθέσθαι περίφοβον γενόμενον.

The contrast with the earlier confidence of Antalkidas (chs. 26. 3, 31. 7) is perhaps intended to indicate the depth of despair to which even such a prominent Spartan had sunk. Kythera had been depopulated by Konon and Pharnabazos and occupied by a garrison under an Athenian commander (Xen. *Hell.* iv. 8. 8, Diod. xiv. 84. 5), but Sparta will have recovered it under the terms of the Peace. Perhaps Antalkidas was concerned with the reoccupation. That Plutarch uses unnamed authorities here and later in the chapter may indicate that he draws from irregular sources.

2 ὁ δ' Ἀγησίλαος, ἐπιχειρούντων διαβαίνειν τὸν ποταμὸν τῶν πολεμίων καὶ βιάζεσθαι πρὸς τὴν πόλιν, ἐκλιπὼν τὰ λοιπὰ παρετάξατο πρὸ τῶν μέσων καὶ ὑψηλῶν.

At this time Sparta was unwalled (Xen. *Hell.* vi. 5. 28) and, apart from the River Eurotas to the east, the natural defences of the city were extremely limited. Xenophon refers to the occupation of narrow spaces and high ground (*Agesilaos*, 2. 24), which indicates outlying defences, and he mentions inner defence positions, west of the Eurotas, such as the sanctuary of Athena Alea (*Hell.* vi. 5. 27), where the hoplites were drawn up facing the enemy near the bridge.[1] Later, the cavalry stood on the race-course at the sanctuary of Poseidon, and an ambush was set in the sanctuary of the Tyndaridai (*Hell.* vi. 5. 30–1).[2] Plutarch does not name the sanctuaries, but gives general locations.

3 ἐρρύη δὲ πλεῖστος ἑαυτοῦ καὶ μέγιστος τόθ' ὁ Εὐρώτας, χιόνων γενομένων, καὶ τὸ ῥεῦμα μᾶλλον ὑπὸ ψυχρότητος ἢ τραχύτητος ἐγένετο σκληρὸν καὶ χαλεπὸν τοῖς Θηβαίοις.

To the east and north-east of Sparta, the Eurotas has not in summer enough water to fill the stony bed (personal observation), except when in spate after a storm (reported in June 1986). To the north it can be fast-flowing and formidable in a wet winter, and still a considerable obstacle even where it widens a little, below the present road bridge.[3] Plutarch mentions the wintry conditions here to explain why the Thebans did not immediately cross the river; Xenophon says they did not cross because of the hoplites in the sanctuary of Athena Alea (*Hell.* vi. 5. 27); his reference to the winter before the invasion (*Hell.* vi. 5. 20) is not repeated until the departure of the invaders (*Hell.* vi. 5. 50). Both river and hoplites are given by Diodoros (xv. 65. 2).

4 πορευόμενον δὲ πρῶτον τῆς φάλαγγος τὸν Ἐπαμεινώνδαν ἐδείκνυσάν τινες τῷ Ἀγησιλάῳ· κἀκεῖνος, ὡς λέγεται, πολὺν χρόνον ἐμβλέψας αὐτῷ καὶ συμπαραπέμψας τὴν ὄψιν, οὐδὲν ἢ τοσοῦτον μόνον εἶπεν· Ὦ τοῦ μεγαλοπράγμονος ἀνθρώπου.

This piece of ἐνάργεια is reminiscent of the Homeric miniatures, picturing the Greek warriors at the walls of Troy and the confrontation of Achilles and Priam (*Il.* iii. 160–242, xxiv. 482–4). Epameinondas heads his phalanx and is acknowledged by Agesilaos in a guarded statement, 'What a man of great deeds'. This may express disbelief that Epameinondas had dared to attack Sparta; but Plutarch enhances the reputation of the general by giving him a worthy opponent. Xenophon commends his forethought and daring (*Hell.* vii. 5. 8).

5 ἐπεὶ δὲ φιλοτιμούμενος ὁ Ἐπαμεινώνδας ἐν τῇ πόλει μάχην συνάψαι καὶ στῆσαι τρόπαιον οὐκ ἴσχυσεν ἐξαγαγεῖν οὐδὲ προκαλέσασθαι τὸν Ἀγησίλαον, ἐκεῖνος μὲν ἀναζεύξας πάλιν ἐπόρθει τὴν χώραν, . . .

Plutarch reverses Xenophon's judgement that an attack on the city was abandoned for lack of courage (*Hell.* vi. 5. 50), suggesting that Agesilaos refused the challenge. It is unlikely that Epameinondas intended to occupy Sparta or wished to destroy it;[4] elsewhere his restraint saved Orchomenos from destruction (Diod. xv. 57. 1; cf. Paus. ix. 15. 3). Later events showed that Thebes had not the resources with which to garrison Sparta permanently or to maintain permanent control of the Peloponnese. Epameinondas perhaps wished to leave Sparta as a counter-balance to Athens and to powerful rivals in the Peloponnese, as Philip did in 338/7.[5] The destruction of Sparta's reputation for territorial inviolability and military invincibility was a sufficient achievement and a demonstration to the Spartans themselves of the change in the balance of power; and he had founded Messene, with independence, and Megalopolis in strategic positions, and given Thebes a period of hegemony.

Before Xenophon breaks off to describe Sparta's negotiations to bring in Athenian help, he records that the burning of unwalled towns extended to the south coast at Perioikic Gytheion (*Hell.* vi.

5. 27, 32, 33, 49; see below on Isadas, ch. 34. 8–11). Plutarch indicates damage to countryside (τὴν χώραν); Agesilaos on occasions
demonstrated the reality of his military superiority in the same
terms, in Asia Minor and in Greece—Phrygia and Akarnania
(Hell. iv. 1. 1, 6. 5). Epameinondas' demonstration was no less
effective, and will have impressed not only the Spartans, Perioikoi
and Helots, but also the rest of the Greeks, without the risk of
casualties in another battle. These demonstrations, and the social
suspicion and disunity they caused, rather than difficult lasting
material damage in the fields, will explain the strategy.[6]

. . . 6 ἐν δὲ Λακεδαίμονι τῶν πάλαι τινὲς ὑπούλων καὶ πονηρῶν ὡς
διακόσιοι συστραφέντες κατέλαβον τὸ Ἰσσώριον, οὗ τὸ τῆς Ἀρτέμιδος
ἱερόν ἐστιν, εὐερκῆ καὶ δυσεκβίαστον τόπον.

From here to §13, Plutarch speaks of unrest at Sparta, which
demonstrates, as Kinadon had done thirty years earlier, the fragile
social harmony of the Spartan community.[7] Xenophon does not
report this mutiny, but records that some Perioikoi were already
collaborating with the Thebans (Hell. vi. 5. 25; cf. §12 below). In
that crisis the Spartans recruited, probably from Lakonia, 6,000
helots, which further increased the Spartans' anxiety when they
were assembled together (Hell. vi. 5. 29);[8] no doubt, some of the
helots were beginning to realize their capability.

Nepos, in his version of this episode (Agesilaus, 6. 2), speaks of
'young men', as does Polyainos, who also identifies the men in the
Issorion as hoplites and Lakonians (ii. 1. 14). Plutarch's medical
and political metaphors for 'disloyal' suggest men who have lost
their full status, to be distinguished from Perioikoi and Helots and
from the Spartiates specified later.[9] The rebels may therefore have
included Hypomeiones and degraded Spartiates.[10] Since age and
status in both descriptions correspond to those of Kinadon and his
colleagues (Xen. Hell. iii. 3. 5), which perhaps suggested
Plutarch's phrase here, the motive may also correspond: the desire
to be equal with the Spartiates (Xen. Hell. iii. 3. 11). The recruiting of helots may also have stimulated the rebels: they would wish
to benefit from fighting for Sparta, as the helots had done.

Perhaps the timing of the threatened defection was determined
by the expectation of an immediate link-up with the enemy
(Nepos, Agesilaus, 6. 2); the ready surrender would follow the
arrival of allied contingents and the Theban withdrawal, when

Agesilaos could make his unarmed approach without danger to himself from the enemy.

The temple of Artemis was in the territory of the Pitanatai (Paus. iii. 14. 2) which extends to the west from the Spartan acropolis. The Issorion is put to the north of the acropolis, on one of the hills marked Moundouna collectively,[11] hence not far from the enemy across the Eurotas to the east.

7 ἐφ' οὓς βουλομένων εὐθὺς ὠθεῖσθαι τῶν Λακεδαιμονίων, φοβηθεὶς τὸν νεωτερισμὸν ὁ Ἀγησίλαος ἐκέλευσε τοὺς μὲν ἄλλους ἡσυχίαν ἄγειν, αὐτὸς δ' ἐν ἱματίῳ καὶ μεθ' ἑνὸς οἰκέτου προσῄει, βοῶν ἄλλως ἀκηκοέναι τοῦ προστάγματος αὐτούς· οὐ γὰρ ἐνταῦθα κελεῦσαι συνελθεῖν οὐδὲ πάντας, ἀλλὰ τοὺς μὲν ἐκεῖ (δείξας ἕτερον τόπον), τοὺς δ' ἀλλαχόσε τῆς πόλεως.

Agesilaos treats the rebels as soldiers. He characteristically avoids precipitate action and prefers to operate by deception, thus displaying, for Plutarch, two admirable traits of his generalship.

8 οἱ δ' ἀκούσαντες ἥσθησαν οἰόμενοι λανθάνειν, καὶ διαστάντες ἐπὶ τοὺς τόπους οὓς ἐκεῖνος ἐκέλευσεν ἀπεχώρουν. 9 ὁ δὲ τὸ μὲν Ἰσσώριον εὐθὺς μεταπεμψάμενος ἑτέρους κατέσχε, τῶν δὲ συστάντων ἐκείνων περὶ πεντεκαίδεκά τινας συλλαβὼν νυκτὸς ἀπέκτεινεν.

Apparently the deserters found their position hopeless when Epameinondas was seen to have withdrawn, calling off any further attack on the city for the support of which, no doubt, they had seized a vantage-point. Summary execution, particularly without trial, indicates the gravity of the Spartan citizens' regard for their position. Xenophon's account of the punishment of Kinadon and his accomplices (*Hell.* iii. 3. 11), if trustworthy, suggests that it was exceptional. Spartan executions always took place at night (Hdt. iv. 146. 2).

10 ἄλλη δὲ μείζων ἐμηνύθη συνωμοσία καὶ σύνοδος ἀνδρῶν Σπαρτιατῶν ἐπὶ πράγμασι νεωτέροις εἰς οἰκίαν κρύφα συνερχομένων, οὓς καὶ κρίνειν ἄπορον ἦν ἐν ταραχῇ τοσαύτῃ καὶ περιορᾶν ἐπιβουλεύοντας. 11 ἀπέκτεινεν οὖν καὶ τούτους μετὰ τῶν ἐφόρων βουλευσάμενος ὁ Ἀγησίλαος ἀκρίτους, οὐδενὸς δίχα δίκης τεθανατωμένου πρότερον Σπαρτιατῶν.

There is no other report of this second conspiracy, μείζων, 'more serious' (perhaps because it was secret) or 'of a greater number of

Spartiates' (than the 200 mentioned above); the interest in the first, for Polyainos and Nepos, was not Spartan unrest but Agesilaos' handling of the rebels (ii. 1. 14; *Agesilaus*, 6. 2–3). At *Hell.* vi. 5. 25 Xenophon speaks of people coming to the Thebans from Karyai to report the shortage of defenders at Sparta and to offer their services as guides. That he then mentions *perioikoi* separately raises the question of their identity, and the possibility that Plutarch took them to be Spartiates. The secret nature of the proceedings conveniently exposes the tradition to such enlargement. The survivors of the first revolt could, of course, provide their evidence with more reliability than is to be attributed to reporters of the second, which was unlikely to be widely acknowledged at the time; and if there were no survivors, it may be compared with the disappearance of helots (Thuc. iv. 80. 3): 'about exactly how they died no one really knew'.[12]

Plutarch's account of the second conspiracy is accepted by David.[13] It consistently stresses Sparta's difficulties again and explains that the ephors were consulted over the handling of the Spartiates, whereas about fifteen of the first conspirators were executed on Agesilaos' orders. There were possible sources of malcontents, including the *tresantes*, still perhaps in informal disgrace, as well as former supporters of the late Kleombrotos, and any poor Spartiates who felt themselves in danger of losing citizen rights.[14] There is no obvious reason for the invention of the conspiracy. Nevertheless, the execution without trial of Spartiates is extremely doubtful,[15] and the damage to Sparta of such depletion of military strength in the circumstances following the heavy losses at Leuktra, even allowing for possible exaggeration, would have been very serious. Perhaps the unlikely number of executions is a less reliable enhancement of an otherwise credible minor incident.

12 ἐπεὶ δὲ πολλοὶ τῶν συντεταγμένων εἰς τὰ ὅπλα περιοίκων καὶ εἱλώτων ἀπεδίδρασκον ἐκ τῆς πόλεως πρὸς τοὺς πολεμίους, καὶ τοῦτο πλείστην ἀθυμίαν παρεῖχεν, ἐδίδαξε τοὺς ὑπηρέτας περὶ ὄρθρον ἐπιφοιτᾶν ταῖς στιβάσι καὶ τὰ ὅπλα τῶν ἀποκεχωρηκότων λαμβάνειν καὶ ἀποκρύπτειν, ὅπως ἀγνοῆται τὸ πλῆθος.

Revolts and desertions of *perioikoi* are mentioned in the north and south of Lakonia (Xen. *Hell.* vi. 5. 25 and 32), and with Helots and allies at vii. 2. 2. These may have come into the tradition along with details not found in Xenophon's account, such as the two revolts mentioned by Plutarch, but allowance must be made for the hostile nature of such a source. There seems to be some inconsistency if the deserters whose arms were seized are those reported as taking part in the attack on Gytheion (*Hell.* vi. 5. 32); they would need to retain their arms. Perhaps these deserters are simply refusing to fight for Sparta.

13 ἀναχωρῆσαι δὲ τοὺς Θηβαίους ἐκ τῆς Λακωνικῆς οἱ μὲν ἄλλοι λέγουσι χειμώνων γενομένων καὶ τῶν Ἀρκάδων ἀρξαμένων ἀπιέναι καὶ διαρρεῖν ἀτάκτως, τρεῖς μῆνας ἐμμεμενηκότας ὅλους καὶ τὰ πλεῖστα τῆς χώρας διαπεπορθηκότας· **14** Θεόπομπος δέ φησιν, ἤδη τῶν βοιωταρχῶν ἐγνωκότων ἀπαίρειν, ἀφικέσθαι πρὸς αὐτοὺς Φρίξον, ἄνδρα Σπαρτιάτην, παρ' Ἀγησιλάου δέκα τάλαντα κομίζοντα τῆς ἀναχωρήσεως μισθόν, ὥστε τὰ πάλαι δεδογμένα πράττουσιν αὐτοῖς ἐφόδιον παρὰ τῶν πολεμίων προσπεριγενέσθαι.

Xenophon first reports that the Peloponnesian allies went home and then uses the reduction in the size of the army, the lack of provisions now available, and winter, to explain the desire of the Thebans to withdraw (*Hell.* vi. 5. 50). Plutarch uses the winter here to explain only the Theban departure, and confines the premature movements to the Arkadians. Theopompos' further suggestion of bribery also refers only to the Boiotians. Diodoros says that Theopompos ended his *Hellenika* with Knidos (xiv. 84. 7) in 394 and started his history of Philip after the Thasians settled Krenides (xvi. 3. 8) in 360, so that this passage may not be part of either of his main narratives. Bribery is a frequent accusation (cf. Sphodrias at Xen. *Hell.* v. 4. 20) which understandably enters a hostile tradition, but is not likely to be authenticated easily. The additional suggestion that the decision had already been made before the bribe was accepted enlivens the narrative, but is not wholly convincing. It is noticeable that the first explanations of the withdrawal (§13) reveal the difficulties of the Thebans' situation, whereas §14 suggests a fruitless act of desperation on the part of Agesilaos. Diodoros now records the foundation of the town of Messene by Epameinondas and the gathering of its new citizens (xv. 66. 6), which Xenophon overlooks and Plutarch delays until ch. 34.

Chronology

Plutarch's statements that Epameinondas' first invasion took place in winter (§3, cf. *Hell.* vi. 5. 50) and lasted for three months (τρεῖς μῆνας ἐμμεμενηκότας; cf. Diod. xv. 67. 1, 'eighty-five days') assist with the dating of the event. Since the battle of Leuktra (371) was followed by the confirmation of the King's Peace, the independence of Mantineia, and the formation of the Arkadian League, the first invasion could not have begun before 370/69, the third year of Olympiad 102 given by Pausanias for the foundation of Messene (iv. 27. 9), which Diodoros puts at the end of the invasion (xv. 66. 1). Plutarch says that the march to Sparta and Gytheion began near the winter solstice (*Pel.* 24. 1). The invasion therefore lasted from November/December to March/April, 370–369.[16]

33. The eclipse of Lykourgan standards: the Tearless Battle

1 Τοῦτο μὲν οὖν οὐκ οἶδ' ὅπως ἠγνόησαν οἱ ἄλλοι, μόνος δὲ Θεόπομπος ᾔσθετο.

Plutarch casts doubt on Theopompos' report that Agesilaos bribed the Thebans to depart from Lakonia (ch. 32. 14), claiming that it was uncorroborated: Plutarch's wide knowledge of the literature favours his claim, and he judges (*Lys.* 30. 2) that Theopompos was more reliable when he praises than when, as here, he finds fault; the malice in the anecdote would fit that author's reputation—a virtuous, frugal Spartan stooping to bribery, and doing so when the Thebans were going away (cf. ch. 32. 14). He doubts Douris' accusation of brutality against Perikles and the Athenians (*Per.* 28. 2–3), but not his testimony about Timaia (above, ch. 3). He hesitates here over a hostile account, but he quoted without qualification Theopompos' favourable reference to Agesilaos (ch. 10. 10). Corroboration is not to be expected from Xenophon, who would be reluctant to attribute bribery to Agesilaos, both on moral grounds and as indicating military failure. The quotation, though rejected, is perhaps indirect proof that the plight of Sparta was considered serious enough to warrant such drastic measures.

2 τοῦ δὲ σωθῆναι τὴν Σπάρτην τότε πάντες αἴτιον ὁμολογοῦσι γενέσθαι τὸν Ἀγησίλαον, ὅτι τῶν ἐμφύτων αὐτῷ παθῶν, φιλονικίας καὶ φιλοτιμίας, ἀποστὰς ἐχρήσατο τοῖς πράγμασιν ἀσφαλῶς.

Plutarch commends Agesilaos, as usual, for service in the military interests of Sparta (cf. *Comp.* 3. 5). Although at *Agesilaos*, 2. 24 Xenophon judges that Agesilaos saved the city, in *Hellenika* he has no active role in the defence of Sparta from vi. 5. 22 to vii. 5. 9. He appears there only once, at vii. 1. 32, to welcome his son back from war. Xenophon confines himself at *Agesilaos*, 2. 24 to an analysis of the military requirements and approves of Agesilaos' caution in not engaging the enemy. Plutarch relates this caution to a change in Agesilaos' way of thinking, which determines the new policy. The caution Agesilaos exercises here is uncharacteristic, for he has 'abandoned' (ἀποστάς) his interpretation of the 'inherited' (ἐμφύτων) traits displayed in earlier chapters, the competitive virtues of φιλονικία and φιλοτιμία. Fostered by the Lykourgan system, they were approved by Plutarch except when taken to excess. The strong word ἀποστάς indicates that now, in the uncharacteristic circumstances that had been brought about in Sparta, Agesilaos was forced to realize that he could not save the city by the characteristic exercise of those qualities: φιλονικία is 'keenness to win victory' rather than 'contentiousness for its own sake'. Agesilaos' personal interest—his adherence to Lykourgan principles as he would see them—must be sacrificed, if he is to act in the interest of Sparta, again emphasizing the desperate situation brought about—in Plutarch's analysis—by the earlier 'imperialist' departure from those principles.

3 οὐ μέντοι τήν γε δύναμιν καὶ τὴν δόξαν ἐδυνήθη τῆς πόλεως ἀναλαβεῖν ἐκ τοῦ πταίσματος, ἀλλ᾽ ὥσπερ σώματος ὑγιεινοῦ, λίαν δ᾽ ἀκριβεῖ καὶ κατησκημένῃ κεχρημένου διαίτῃ παρὰ πάντα τὸν χρόνον, ἁμαρτία μία καὶ ῥοπὴ τὴν πᾶσαν ἔκλινεν εὐτυχίαν τῆς πόλεως·

Agesilaos ensured the survival of the city, but Sparta's 'power and glory' were lost. They depended on a practice of Lykourgan characteristics which was now abandoned. Plutarch introduces a medical simile to contrast two conditions (cf. ch. 30. 2). The body at the start is healthy, but is harmed by misguided subjection to inflexible rules of health. Lykourgos gave Sparta a healthy regimen by comparing others, like a doctor (*Lyk.* 4. 3). The present difficulties are attributed to the failures of individuals to understand and maintain the Lykourgan rules of Spartan prosperity. The 'too strictly disciplined way of life' which rendered the prosperity vulnerable is defined in §4 below.

Plutarch's phrase, 'a single failure and the (consequent) critical turning-point', recalls the statement of Aristotle: 'The city sank under a single blow', but he does not continue with Aristotle's train of thought about the cause, that it was inequality under its property laws that led to a reduction in the number of citizens (*Pol.* 1270ᵃ29–ᵇ5; see n. following §4). Aristotle's emphasis on the concentration of property ownership is perhaps the source for Plutarch's analysis of Sparta's decline in the *Life of Agis*. He opens the narrative (*Agis*, 3. 1, 5; cf. *Lyk.* 30. 1) with the statement that the Spartans were corrupted by lust for gold and silver. The acquisition of personal wealth brought luxury, greed, and meanness, and decline in traditional toughness. The process is dated to the defeat of the Athenian hegemony and the concentration of landed property made possible by the *rhetra*, 'enactment', of Epitadeus (*Agis*, 5. 2–3).[1] The existence of this *rhetra* has been denied; but the figure of only 100 owners of land in addition to their inherited lot in 244 at the time of Agis has found more favour.[2] There can be no doubt of the importance of Spartan inheritance law and its effect on the well-being of the state for the problem of Sparta's ultimate decline.[3] That Plutarch should recognize this in one *Life*, and in another offer the narrowness of Spartan education and outlook as his theme, perhaps indicates his wish to avoid repetition, but may also remind us that we should not look for only a single factor to explain a complex problem. The theme of the destruction of greatness by wealth and decadence appears also in Roman contexts, as in the picture of Pompey's camp (*Pomp.* 72. 5–6). Livy's stated theme (*Praefatio*, 4, 9, 12) is destruction, failing discipline, avarice, and luxury. The same theme is found in other historians (Sallust and Tacitus), in the Verrine orations of Cicero, and in the satirists; it was the inspiration for the singers of praises for Augustus' new vision.

οὐκ ἀλόγως. **4** πρὸς γὰρ εἰρήνην καὶ ἀρετὴν καὶ ὁμόνοιαν ἄριστα συντεταγμένῳ πολιτεύματι προσαγαγόντες ἀρχὰς καὶ δυναστείας βιαίους, ὧν οὐδενὸς ἡγεῖτο δεῖσθαι πόλιν εὐδαιμόνως βιωσομένην ὁ Λυκοῦργος, ἐσφάλησαν.

Plutarch implies, by his interjected comment (cf. ὀρθῶς λέγων at ch. 29. 2), that with sound reasoning the Spartans would have recognized the mistaken course they were steering, and would have corrected their over-concentration on a limited objective. The Spartans' responsibility for the 'hegemonies and overlordships imposed by violence', ἀρχὰς καὶ δυναστείας βιαίους, is shared by Lysander, for his δυναστεῖαι καὶ τυραννίδες (ch. 6. 2–3, *Lys.* 19. 1) and Agesilaos, for his τύραννοι (ch. 24. 2; Xen. *Hell.* v. 4. 1, 46, 49).

Narrowness of education, which prevented the true understanding of the lawgiver's aims, is a major theme in the *Life.* Aristotle (*Pol.* 1271[b]1–10) also criticizes this narrowness, for because they had regard for one virtue only, they did not know how to live a peaceful life, and concentrated only on the art of war. Spartans were also wrong in their practice even of this single virtue (*Pol.* 1334[a]40–[b]3), for while training in war rightly provides against enslavement, they used their military power to create an empire and to rule over their neighbours despotically, instead of for the good of those they governed (*Pol.* 1333[b]37–1334[a]2).

Plutarch presents two views of the constitution. He favours the earlier condition of Sparta, in which 'prosperity' is defined in Lykourgan terms (cf. *Lyk.*, esp. 30. 1–2, 31. 1–2): obedience of citizens and enjoyment of the city's self-sufficiency, without hegemony. He contrasts this with 'prosperity' in material terms, as the Spartans had come to understand it, depending on empire and power (cf. *Lak. Pol.* 1–2).

Plutarch and Aristotle differ in their interpretations of the intentions of the lawgiver, and hence of his responsibility for the present situation. Aristotle interpreted the Spartan constitution as designed by the lawgiver for military excellence only: for Plutarch, 'empire and power' were added later by the Spartans themselves. The admired objectives, summarized as 'prosperity', dissociate Lykourgos from the criticism implied in the adjective βιαίους, 'violent', and present him, consistently with *Lykourgos*, 23, as a man of peace. While Plutarch's praise for Agesilaos centres on his military activity, it is given strictly for his defence of the city and for panhellenist enterprises: it was hostility towards Thebes

(*Comp.* 3. 2) that made him guilty of the misinterpretation of Lykourgos' intentions.

Ornamentation here and at §8 below (alliteration of *ph*, *d*, *k*, *p*; groups of two and three words) indicates the importance Plutarch attaches to this passage. At this point he completes the development of Xenophon's injunction to consider the behaviour of those in adversity (ch. 29. 2), the first courageous response to disaster contrasting with the later loss of nerve and the decline (chs. 30–2). In the rest of this chapter he considers further decline in Spartan behaviour in other circumstances.

Sparta's decline

It is clear from modern discussions of the 'decline' of Sparta that several factors were involved: social, concerning the fall in numbers of the Spartiates, though not of the Lakedaimonian population as a whole; military, as regards the Spartans' limited innovation in organization and tactical developments; political, as in Plutarch's review of Spartan hegemony. The aggressive policy has been defended,[4] but the position of Sparta in the years following Leuktra[5] shows that this policy failed.[6] A major factor was finance, as suggested by Xenophon when he refers to Agesilaos' service abroad at the end of his career (*Agesilaos*, 2. 25; cf. chs. 35. 6, 36. 2, 40. 2). Sparta, even more than Thebes and Athens, never had resources, either of manpower or of money, sufficient to maintain hegemony of Greece for long,[7] and Xenophon could have made his remark as early as the expedition to Asia Minor; for Sparta's frequent resort to war throughout Agesilaos' reign was required, and in part designed, to provide money by plunder.

An equally valid question is how the Spartiates lasted so long. They were a closely bound society, with a clear commitment to survival at a generally lower standard of comfort and material culture than others. Military professionalism established a reputation for invincibility against others who did not emulate it, and enabled them to choose their conflicts in favourable contexts rather than under attack in their own territory—which was protected at a distance from their city by formidable mountain ranges. Above all, perhaps, their lifestyle attracted admiration and requests for leadership which increased their recognized supremacy—until Agesilaos, misreading the καιρός, sent a less efficiently led force to meet a well-trained, innovatively led, confident enemy fighting to protect its homeland. Leuktra may not have revealed the whole truth, but the invasions of the Spartans' homeland removed their power to re-establish their former hegemony.

5 αὐτὸς μὲν οὖν ὁ Ἀγησίλαος ἤδη πρὸς τὰς στρατείας ἀπειρήκει διὰ τὸ γῆρας, Ἀρχίδαμος δ' ὁ υἱὸς αὐτοῦ τὴν ἐκ Σικελίας ἥκουσαν παρὰ τοῦ τυράννου βοήθειαν ἔχων ἐνίκησεν Ἀρκάδας τὴν λεγομένην ἄδακρυν μάχην· οὐδεὶς γὰρ ἔπεσε τῶν μετ' αὐτοῦ, συχνοὺς δὲ τῶν ἐναντίων ἀνεῖλεν.

After the first invasion, Xenophon records that the Athenians, who had sent Iphikrates to help against the Thebans, formed an alliance with Sparta designed to give them joint hegemony by land and sea (*Hell.* vii. 1. 1; cf. vi. 5. 49), and then, again without explanation, has the Thebans and their allies begin the second invasion of the Peloponnese, which draws help for Sparta from Dionysios of Syracuse (*Hell.* vii. 1. 15–22). Diodoros explains that Lykomedes of Mantineia was continuing the war against Sparta, and the Arkadians with their allies invited Epameinondas to participate again (xv. 67. 2, 68. 1).[8] The second invasion, which Xenophon ends at *Hell.* vii. 1. 23, deprived Sparta of most of its allies in the north of the Peloponnese,[9] and a year later Megalopolis was founded to isolate it further. Meantime, it was the arrival of a second force from Syracuse that encouraged the Spartan expedition of Archidamos (Xen. *Hell.* vii. 1. 28–32).

Neither the second nor the third invasion concerns the biography of Agesilaos directly. His retirement at the age of about 74, not announced by Xenophon but to be assumed from his long absence from the action, allows Plutarch to return to his narrative of events, but does not provide the historical context for the next campaign. It leads to the opportunity for Archidamos, the heir to the kingship, to experience military command in his absence before becoming king, unlike Agesilaos as far as is known. Plutarch usually passes over events in which Agesilaos played no part, and this campaign appears to transfer the focus from Agesilaos to his son, which would be inappropriate in his biography. However, the absence of the name of Dionysios, and the lack of details, about the assistance sent by him and about the action itself (Xen. *Hell.* vii. 1. 28), indicate that Plutarch is not recounting the episode for its own sake (see below, §8).

The need for Sicilian help in the face of Arkadian ambitions (Xen. *Hell.* vii. 1. 28) continues Plutarch's theme of decline, highlighting Sparta's lack of access to sources of manpower in the Peloponnese, which required money and willing allies. Agesilaos' influence and personal responsibility will be further revealed in the sequel to the Arkadian expedition under the command of Archidamos. Xenophon, too, by reporting that the Arkadians defeated the Spartan garrison at Asine in Lakonia, indicates the reality of the military decline of Sparta; and the shortage of citizens is revealed by the enrolment of Geranor as Spartiate, if the manuscript reading is correct (*Hell.* vii. 1. 25), though it has been conjectured that 'the Spartiate Geranor became polemarch'.[10]

In 368, Archidamos recovered Perioikic Karyai and marched, perhaps round the north of Skiritis and down the upper Alpheios valley, to Parrhasia in Arkadia, until the Arkadians threatened to cut off his retreat to Sparta (the direct route would take him to the Eurotas valley); he drew up his battle line 'where the road to Eutresia meets the road to Melea' (Xen. *Hell.* vii. 1. 29), against a force of Arkadians, Messenians, and Argives, at or near where Megalopolis[11] was later founded to block access to this area (Diod. xv. 72. 4).

The ability to mount a Spartan attack on Arkadia shows a separate use of manpower distinct from the defence of Lakonia itself against sudden attack. The expedition perhaps marks an attempt to return to the Spartans' economical policy of securing their defence against potential enemies by mounting attacks beyond their borders. In the past, by establishing a reputation for invincibility in battles fought in favourable circumstances of their own choosing, they had been able to deter invasion. Even Leuktra would have been in this category, for, by his attitude to Thebes over the taking of the oaths at the peace conference, Agesilaos had engineered the opportunity for a victory which would have removed the last threat to Spartan hegemony. A hostile Megalopolis, however, survived (Xen. *Hell.* vii. 5. 5).

Diodoros (xv. 72. 3) quotes the prophecy of the priestesses of Dodona naming the war (*sic*—πόλεμος) as 'tearless' and judges this a notable but unexpected victory after Leuktra. Xenophon (vii. 1. 28–32) presents the campaign as a glorious achievement for Archidamos, starting with his inspiring exhortation and closing with the tears of joy in Sparta. The designation 'tearless' gives all the information about the battle that Plutarch will require when he explains the sequel: the normal Spartan reaction to casualties did not involve tears.

6 αὕτη μάλιστα τὴν ἀσθένειαν ἤλεγξεν ἡ νίκη τῆς πόλεως.

Xenophon's injunction (above, ch. 29. 2) is extended to an examination of behaviour in favourable circumstances. There is no hint in Xenophon or Diodoros of the paradox that this victory could show up Sparta's weakness, but that is to be its purpose here. For Plutarch, the weakness is a matter of the city's unique character—in his account, a weakness that is moral, not military.

πρότερον μὲν γὰρ οὕτω σύνηθες ἡγοῦντο καὶ προσῆκον ἔργον αὐτοῖς εἶναι τὸ νικᾶν τοὺς πολεμίους ὥστε μήτε θύειν τοῖς θεοῖς πλὴν ἀλεκτρυόνα νικητήριον ἐν τῇ πόλει μήτε μεγαληγορεῖν τοὺς ἀγωνισαμένους μήθ᾽ ὑπερχαίρειν τοὺς πυνθανομένους, . . .

Plutarch sets out the earlier characteristics to provide a standard by which to judge the Spartans' current behaviour. Their long-continued successes gave rise to the belief that victory was 'customary and natural', requiring no elaborate acknowledgement or thanksgiving. The material value of the cockerel as a gift may have been high,[12] but as the offering for a victory in battle it is less than that of an ox for victory by cunning (*Marc.* 22. 5), representing, perhaps, Sparta's concern to avoid casualties.[13] No doubt, this was another piece of mythology inspired by the Spartans, designed to impress and discourage opponents, but that belief was shattered at Leuktra. It was now, they hoped, to be revived.

The anaphora of μήτε, 'not', enhances the triple phrasing of the adjacent infinitives.

. . . **7** ἀλλὰ καὶ τῆς ἐν Μαντινείᾳ μάχης γενομένης, ἣν ὁ Θουκυδίδης γέγραφε, τῷ πρώτῳ φράσαντι τὴν νίκην οἱ ἄρχοντες ἐκ φιδιτίου κρέας ἔπεμψαν εὐαγγέλιον, ἄλλο δ᾽ οὐδέν·

Thucydides reports the battle at Mantineia (418 BC) without reference to any reward given to the messenger bringing news of that much more important victory (v. 64–75). This anecdote, which provides evidence that the ephors and other magistrates of any year messed together,[14] indicates the Spartans' earlier unemotional attitude to the achievement of military successes which they always assumed would be theirs. Plutarch contrasts that restraint not with an extravagant reward but with the Spartans' present extravagant behaviour. Agesilaos distributed portions of victims extravagantly at Chaironeia, apparently to good effect (ch. 17. 5; Xen. *Hell.* iv. 3. 14).

8 τότε δὲ τῆς μάχης ἀγγελθείσης καὶ τοῦ Ἀρχιδάμου προσιόντος, οὐδεὶς ἐκαρτέρησεν, ἀλλὰ πρῶτός θ' ὁ πατὴρ ἀπήντα δακρύων ὑπὸ χαρᾶς καὶ μετ' ἐκεῖνον τὰ ἀρχεῖα, τῶν δὲ πρεσβυτέρων καὶ τῶν γυναικῶν τὸ πλῆθος ἐπὶ τὸν ποταμὸν κατῄει, τάς τε χεῖρας ὀρεγόντων καὶ θεοκλυτούντων, . . .

Xenophon reports that after the battle Archidamos set up a trophy and sent a herald home with news of the victory. Agesilaos, the elders, and the ephors, wept for joy; Xenophon does not mention the gods and the people (*Hell.* vii. 1. 32). Plutarch develops an all-inclusive list, involving gods and mortals, the latter including a representative of the warriors and all adult levels of Spartan society in the city—the king, the magistrates, the elders, and the women. Agesilaos is not named here, allowing the alliteration of *p* and *t/th*, especially concentrated in πρῶτός θ' ὁ πατὴρ ἀπήντα, framed by the alliteration and stressing the family nature of the greeting by the one who, of all people, had previously upheld the best traditions of Spartan life. This is the point of the episode (see above, §5): Agesilaos, a spectator here, not a participant, now holds the stage in responding—uncharacteristically (see above, §7)—to his son's success; a sign of Sparta's changed circumstances and values.

Another paradox, that the so-called Tearless Battle now causes tears, is perhaps intended; and whereas in other cities both kinds of tears, expressions of joy and sorrow, would not be exceptional, the tears of Agesilaos (δακρύων)[15] in Sparta now reveal, not strength, as they did by their absence in sorrow after Leuktra, but weakness, by their presence in joy. The abnormality of Spartans thanking the gods for victory, which they had earlier regarded as naturally theirs, betokens both their great sense of relief and the loss of their former composure.

The topography of the Spartan residential area is imperfectly known. Four of the five villages were enclosed within walls in Hellenistic times, but there is no significant descent to the river, unless the procession assembled on the low hill to the north which served as the acropolis. If Archidamos was returning by the direct route from the battle-site (see above, §5), he would already be on the right-hand bank of the Eurotas.[16] That the people go out to meet Archidamos itself signals loss of detachment.

... ὥσπερ ἀπεωσμένης τὰ παρ' ἀξίαν ὀνείδη τῆς Σπάρτης καὶ λαμπρὸν αὖθις ἐξ ἀρχῆς τὸ φῶς ὁρώσης· ἐπεὶ πρότερόν γέ φασιν οὐδὲ ταῖς γυναιξὶν ἀντιβλέπειν τοὺς ἄνδρας, αἰσχυνομένους ἐφ' οἷς ἔπταισαν.

Xenophon records Archidamos' address to the troops before the battle, exhorting the men to be brave, look people in the eye, and be free of shame, as of old (*Hell.* vii. i. 30). Plutarch adapts these ideas and sets them in the later context. He does not, like Xenophon, illustrate Archidamos' generalship, but describes the position after the battle in terms of what the troops had before-hand been urged to achieve. The use of φασιν, with its subject not expressed, is a fiction, no doubt, though Plutarch could assume that someone would comment on the fulfilment of the general's exhortation. It conveniently allows Plutarch to change the context 'creatively'.

The Spartans display self-deception in supposing that the city will now avoid the consequences of Leuktra, which Plutarch has them refer to as an unmerited disgrace, ignoring the political and military consequences of defeat. Mention of τοὺς ἄνδρας, 'the warriors' who had been in Arkadia with Archidamos, completes, in ring composition, the list of the adult citizen population, with the only remaining members. Both the arriving warriors and the people in the city enjoy new vision, the latter seeing something which does not exist, and the former presumably able to look their wives in the face.[17] The start of the next chapter shows the true position, and reveals that the relief was an illusion.

The chapter ends in ring composition with a reference to Leuktra, using the verb ἔπταισαν and its cognate noun πταίσματος, 'disaster' (§3). Another reference to disaster, ἐσφάλησαν, occurring in a significant position at the end of that section, marked the end of Plutarch's analysis of the citizens' collective responsibility for Sparta's decline, resulting from their departure from strict Lykourgan principles.

Plutarch's analysis is reminiscent of Diodoros' censure of the Spartans (xv. i. i–5), attributing the downfall to their own folly in treating their allies harshly. Diodoros comes closest to Plutarch when he says that they deserved the contempt they experienced

for doing away with their ancestral virtues—an unmistakable
reference to the Lykourgan values which Plutarch, too, claims
were abandoned. Agesilaos is held responsible at xv. 19. 4: 'by
nature a man of action, fond of war, aiming to dominate Greece'.

Plutarch began the chapter with the commendation of Agesilaos
for saving Sparta by renouncing the qualities which had earlier led
to the success of the aggressive policies but had also brought about
the disaster of Leuktra. The second half of the chapter exposes the
city's moral weakness, following on its military weakness. By
beginning this section with his name, Plutarch seems to assign
individual responsibility to Agesilaos' leadership. He marks this
with Agesilaos' leadership of the emotional procession, in which
he again renounces characteristic Spartan restraint.

At the end Plutarch returns to the military disaster suffered by
the Spartans, ἔπταισαν, linking it, too, into the chain of Agesilaos'
responsibility.

34. Epameinondas again threatens Sparta

1 Οἰκιζομένης δὲ Μεσσήνης ὑπὸ τῶν περὶ τὸν Ἐπαμεινώνδαν καὶ τῶν
ἀρχαίων πολιτῶν πανταχόθεν εἰς αὐτὴν συμπορευομένων, . . .

Plutarch makes this reference to the foundation of Messene
(370/69) after his account of the Tearless Battle (368). At that time
Diodoros records the founding of Megalopolis (xv. 72. 4), having
indicated that Messene was founded at the end of Epameinondas'
first campaign in Lakonia (xv. 66. 1; cf. Pel. 24. 5; Nepos, Ep. 8.
3–5). Xenophon does not mention the foundation of the city at
that point (Hell. vi. 5. 32), but, by his references to the Theban
and Persian demands for its autonomy and Sparta's refusal to
accept it, indirectly confirms its existence and Diodoros' chronology (Hell. vii. 1. 27).

The Messenians, banished by the Spartans after the fall of
Ithome in 456/5, were settled by the Athenians at Naupaktos
(Thuc. 1. 103. 1–3); Diodoros adds Kephallenia and Messana in
Sicily, said to be named after them (Diod. xv. 66. 5). The new
name, Messana, given to Zankle, is taken from the homeland of
Anaxilas, tyrant of Rhegion, who invited Samian exiles to settle

there and later banished them, 494–489 (Hdt. vi. 22–4, vii. 164. 1; Thuc. vi. 4. 5–6; cf. Strabo, 268 and Paus. iv. 23. 6–9, whose earlier date makes his account less relevant).[1] The Kranioi in Kephallenia received Messenians from Koryphasion in 421 (Thuc. v. 35. 7), and Diodoros reports others settled there after the war (xiv. 34. 3; cf. Xen. *Hell.* i. 2. 18). Diodoros may be right to say that Epameinondas gathered Messenians from these places (xv. 66. 6), for the exiles would be welcomed by their fellow-countrymen wherever they lived, as were the Samians exiled in 365.[2]

Plutarch indicates no firm relative dating for the foundation, and delayed its mention, perhaps, to mark the long period of Agesilaos' failure to recover Messenia leading to Epameinondas' last invasion of Lakonia in 362 (§3), when the attack on Sparta causes the Spartans' deepest resentment of Agesilaos. During this period, Xenophon records Agesilaos' active concern only over Sparta's finances (*Agesilaos*, 2. 25), and assigns no active role to him in *Hellenika*.

Arkadia (369/8–362)[3]

After the second invasion, the Thebans were occupied in northern Greece (*Pel.* 26–9). Relations with the Arkadians worsened as Lykomedes consolidated the Arkadian League (Xen. *Hell.* vii. 1. 23, 38–40), but after defeat in the Tearless Battle and the recognition of Messene won by Pelopidas at Sousa (vii. 1. 37), Epameinondas in 366 decided to invade the Peloponnese for the third time and win the Achaians over from Sparta; they had marched with Archidamos to meet the survivors of the battle of Leuktra (vi. 4. 18). The Achaians came to terms and the Thebans withdrew (vii. 1. 42), but the long-standing rivalries between democrats and aristocrats and between city and city in the area continued; the Thebans maintained some influence by sending harmosts (vii. 1. 43). Corinth, isolated from Sparta by an alliance of the Arkadians and the Athenians, negotiated peace with Thebes in 366/5, with Sparta's permission (vii. 4. 6–10). In 365 Archidamos joined the Eleians in their territorial dispute with the Arkadians; he was wounded and one hundred Spartiates and Perioikoi were captured (vii. 4. 20–7). The Arkadian League finally split when Mantineians accused the Arkadians of using the

sacred treasures of Olympia which they still controlled after their
defeat by the Eleians in the Battle of the Altis in 364 (vii. 4.
28–34).[4] After the settlement there, the Theban commander of a
detachment of 300 Boiotians at Tegea found himself involved in
the dispute over Mantineian aristocrats detained by Arkadians
accused of the sacrilege, and envoys were sent to Thebes to
demand his execution. Since Epameinondas refused the charges, it
was thought by 'those concerned for the Peloponnese' that he
would invade for the fourth time (vii. 4. 35–vii. 5. 3; see §8);
envoys were also sent to obtain help from Sparta (vii. 5. 3; §3
below).

. . . διαμάχεσθαι μὲν οὐκ ἐτόλμων οὐδὲ κωλύειν ἐδύναντο, . . .

Plutarch follows the analysis of the Spartans' moral decline in the
preceding chapter with the effect on their military situation: loss
of courage for battle, loss of power to control events, deprived of
allies in the north of the Peloponnese and isolated by Megalopolis:
the revival under Archidamos was only imagined in Spartan
minds.

A balanced view of the military strength of the Spartans
suggests that their courage remained intact, and, although they
were contained within their boundaries and could no longer be a
great power, they were still a formidable force.[5]

The maintenance of their spirit casts an interesting light on
Plutarch's moral approach to the Spartans' decline and the efficacy
of the Lykourgan values he admired. Other authorities recognize
the early benefits of the system, but do not record unswerving
adherence to its standards in the times they describe. For
Herodotos (i. 65. 2–6. 1), Lykourgos' reforms of Sparta's army,
laws, officers, and society introduced good order and government
(εὐνομία), but his stories tell of activities and influence abroad
when tyrannies are overthrown (v. 63–5, 90); of cruelty, cheating,
and treachery in the affair of the Minyans, though Sparta's
daughters display bravery (iv. 145–6). Thucydides also hails
Sparta's early change from disunity to 400 years of good order and
government (i. 18), but records, too, interference in others' affairs,
especially their reactions to tyranny (vi. 53–9); Spartan standards,
the Athenians claim, are good at home, but not in foreign
relations, where, 'whatever Spartans do' is, in their own view,
'what is honourable', and 'Sparta's interest' is how they define

'justice' (v. 105). Plutarch omits the practicalities of Sparta's early imperialism, and justifiably sets the decline against the perceived original standard. The isolation of Sparta by the foundation of Messene and Megalopolis was one of the main restraints upon its imperial recovery.

. . . χαλεπῶς δὲ καὶ βαρέως πρὸς τὸν Ἀγησίλαον εἶχον, ὅτι χώραν οὔτε πλήθει τῆς Λακωνικῆς ἐλάττονα καὶ πρωτεύουσαν ἀρετῇ τῆς Ἑλληνικῆς ἔχοντες καὶ καρπούμενοι χρόνον τοσοῦτον, ἐπὶ τῆς ἐκείνου βασιλείας ἀπολωλέκασι.

Plutarch makes explicit the criticism of Agesilaos that was merely implied in the last chapter, and assigns to him, not directly, but as the judgement of the Spartans themselves, the responsibility for their weakness and decline. Plutarch's judgement of Agesilaos is not an unreasonable one (cf. Diod. xv. 1. 1–5). His description of the land of Messenia adequately suggests the economic significance of the loss to Sparta of much rich agricultural production which supplemented that of Lakonia. How far this loss contributed to the financial difficulties, which Agesilaos later tried to relieve by undertaking mercenary service overseas (chs. 36–40), cannot be assessed. The loss is described as 'a serious blow that condemned Sparta to take a second place',[6] though no direct connection can be made since 'Sparta' did not own land anywhere, only Spartans, and the working of its treasury is unknown. The effect will have been felt most acutely by owners of estates on the western side of Mt Taygetos (see below), and by the state only if some could not keep up their contributions to their mess. The political and psychological damage is stressed in Isokrates' *Archidamos* (6. 8).

Plutarch's elaborate structure reveals careful composition, and that indicates the importance he attaches to the passage. This is, then, his considered judgement of Agesilaos at this point in his narrative.

2 διὸ καὶ προτεινομένην ὑπὸ τῶν Θηβαίων τὴν εἰρήνην ὁ Ἀγησίλαος οὐκ ἐδέξατο.

Xenophon refers to three peace initiatives (*Hell.* vii. 1. 27, 33–40, 4. 8–12), by Ariobarzanes, Pelopidas, and Corinth (369–8, 367, and 365). The Thebans consistently demanded acceptance by Sparta of the autonomy of the new city of Messene, recollecting

Agesilaos' insistence on the independence from Thebes of the rest of Boiotia in similar circumstances. Ariobarzanes' support for Sparta did not deter them; he was Antalkidas' guest-friend (*Hell.* v. 1. 28). Pelopidas had negotiated peace terms with Artaxerxes, but failed to obtain ratification by any of the other cities of Greece. Plutarch's remark most clearly fits the third initiative, which marked the end of the Peloponnesian League, with only Sparta abstaining in the hope of regaining Messenia (*Hell.* vii. 4. 9).

μὴ βουλόμενος δὲ τῷ λόγῳ προέσθαι τοῖς ἔργῳ κρατοῦσι τὴν χώραν, ἀλλὰ φιλονικῶν, ἐκείνην μὲν οὐκ ἀπέλαβε, μικροῦ δὲ τὴν Σπάρτην προσαπέβαλε καταστρατηγηθείς.

Though the contrasted datives are not parallel grammatically, the usual opposition between word, λόγῳ, and deed, ἔργῳ, still stands, and is here very strong. Plutarch adds word play in the verbs of opposite meaning, ἀπέλαβε and (προσ)απέβαλε, not only did not 'regain' but 'lost as well': four rhyming vowels, transposition of two consonants; the last five letters are palindromic, and read backwards as the other verb.

The Spartans, traditionally regarded as men of action rather than of words, are required to give their verbal acceptance of the actions of others, the Thebans, and the verbs, προέσθαι, 'to give up, abandon', of the Spartans, and κρατεῖν, 'to master', of the Thebans, reverse the traditional norms assumed of the previous era. Similar thoughts are attributed to Archidamos by Isokrates (6. 8, 47, 57): abhorrence of submitting to the Thebans and the reversal of their role, ἡ τύχη τὰ πράγματ' αὐτῶν περιέστησεν, with the same conflict of words and actions.

The loss of Messenia will have cut off the income of those Spartans, whether Spartiates or inferiors, who still had land there, but compared with the time when the population was most numerous, the land required to supply the domestic needs of individual Spartiates, now numbering perhaps only one-tenth as many, will not have been as extensive as before, and the nature and distribution of the financial benefit of private possessions in Messenia will presumably have changed before now.[7] Perhaps the essential needs of most could be met in Lakonia, and the large accumulators of estates (Arist. *Pol.* 1270[a]15–25) may have been hardest hit. Isokrates, in recording the social and political breakdown after Leuktra and the invasions in 366/5, specifically reflects the acrimonious attitude of possessive property-owners to the needy poor who may have lost land (6. 67), and the strength of their desire for the recovery of Messenia (6. 9–13, 16–32, 47, 59, 70).[8]

Of more immediate importance was the proximity of enemy territory on the boundaries of Lakonia, prohibiting assistance from friendly states. Agesilaos' attitude towards Thebes is, as usual, attributed to personal hatred and hostility. Plutarch perhaps implies a retributive connection between the excessive pursuit of Thebes and the penalty for Sparta: Agesilaos had only two options, to accept the independence of Messenia, or to hope to recover it in war. Once Epameinondas had established the autonomous state, its independence was not negotiable: he had to ensure that Sparta remained a minor power. Agesilaos is said not only almost to have lost Sparta in addition to Messenia, but to have done so through being outdone in his main field of competence, generalship. Plutarch goes on (§3 below) to refer this to the defenceless state of the city, when Epameinondas unexpectedly marched south overnight from Tegea, while Agesilaos was marching north to help the Mantineians in response to their request. Xenophon's description of Sparta as 'like a nest without defenders' (*Hell.* vii. 5. 10) provides support for Plutarch's judgement. The verb καταστρατηγεῖν has in Diodoros a technical sense: 'outgeneral by stratagem' (xv. 16. 1; cf. xvi. 11. 4).[9]

3 ἐπεὶ γὰρ οἱ Μαντινεῖς αὖθις ἀπέστησαν τῶν Θηβαίων καὶ μετε-πέμποντο τοὺς Λακεδαιμονίους, αἰσθόμενος ὁ Ἐπαμεινώνδας τὸν Ἀγησίλαον ἐξεστρατευμένον μετὰ δυνάμεως καὶ προσιόντα, λαθὼν τοὺς Μαντινεῖς ἀνέζευξε νυκτὸς ἐκ Τεγέας ἄγων ἐπ' αὐτὴν τὴν Λακεδαίμονα τὸ στράτευμα, καὶ μικρὸν ἐδέησε παραλλάξας τὸν Ἀγησίλαον ἔρημον ἐξαίφνης καταλαβεῖν τὴν πόλιν.

Plutarch describes the fourth invasion of the Peloponnese, and Epameinondas' second attack on Sparta (362), having omitted the invasions which did not involve Agesilaos. Xenophon, who recognized that the Arkadians and others had instigated the first incursion into Lakonia (*Hell.* vi. 5. 23), now gives prominence to the Arkadians' charge that the Thebans aimed to dominate them. He indicates his partiality by referring to them as 'caring for the Peloponnese' (*Hell.* vii. 5. 1). The Thebans were frustrated in their reliance on the unanimity of their Arkadian allies. They had not the resources to do anything but trust their loyalty to the federation. The Mantineian Lykomedes, Xenophon suggests (*Hell*. vii. 1. 23), had encouraged some Arkadians to become hostile to Thebes, though there was also long-standing conflict between those with oligarchic, often pro-Spartan, sympathies and the commonly democratic opposition to Sparta, in addition to old antagonisms, Mantineia against Tegea, Arkadia against Elis.

The events of 364 at Olympia (above, p. 361) reveal the complicated political divisions between aristocrats and others in Arkadia and neighbouring states, and the resort to charges of sacrilege, possibly for political advantage. Xenophon links concern for the gods with aristocrats (τοὺς βελτίστους) and 'those concerned for the Peloponnese', including the Mantineians detained at Tegea (*Hell*. vii. 4. 34–7; vii. 5. 1), with whom he sympathized. The Theban commander at Tegea suffers in the narrative from his association with the opponents of the Mantineians and their sacrilege, yet Xenophon fairly reports that he responded to information and released all the men immediately, claiming in his defence that some Arkadians were communicating with the Lakedaimonians— as they did later (*Hell*. vii. 4. 39, vii. 5. 3). Xenophon quotes Epameinondas' claim that it was because of Arkadians that Thebans were in the war (*Hell*. vii. 4. 40), and the semantic difficulty emerges: the accusers and the accused were Arkadians, some Arkadians were Mantineians. Sparta had friends and enemies in all these cities, Elis, Mantineia, and Tegea, capable of appealing to Thebes, Sparta, and Athens. Xenophon and Sparta are on the side of aristocrats with religious sensibilities, where their interests lie; Plutarch's personal sympathies would coincide with theirs, but he does not try to exploit the religious aspect of the Spartan intervention.

The Athenians, after the Thebans occupied Oropos, had accepted the Arkadian offer of alliance, and the Thebans' inexperience had led their representatives into diplomatic errors, in Achaia and at Tegea (*Hell*. vii. 1. 43, 4. 1, 36–40). Perhaps these tensions inevitably condemned the incipient federation in the Peloponnese to failure from the start, but more general resistance to the idea of federation has also been observed.[10] The dominant tradition attributed only the worst of motives to the Boiotians, who should be judged no more harshly than others if they acted in their own perceived best interests.

Plutarch sets the scene briefly. Epameinondas leaves Tegea before any Lakedaimonians have reached the area, and are still on their way in response to the Mantineian request for help, as also mentioned by Xenophon (*Hell.* vii. 5. 9).[11] In Diodoros' account, on the other hand, Epameinondas sets out to Sparta on learning that they are already plundering in the vicinity of Tegea (xv. 82. 5–6), a danger not mentioned when Xenophon praised Epameinondas for making his base there (*Hell.* vii. 5. 8–9). There are thus two differing versions of these events.

4 Εὐθύνου δὲ Θεσπιέως, ὡς Καλλισθένης φησίν, ὡς δὲ Ξενοφῶν, Κρητός τινος, ἐξαγγείλαντος τῷ Ἀγησιλάῳ, . . .

Xenophon reports that as Agesilaos was marching to Mantineia by way of Pellana in the Eurotas valley (*Hell.* vii. 5. 9),[12] he received warning from a Cretan and turned back in time to defend Sparta. Diodoros mentions Cretan messengers, in the plural (xv. 82. 6), but their function is different, and he gives the name of the Spartan commander as King Agis. The name has been emended to Agesilaos.[13] This 'Agesilaos' is not informed about Epameinondas' march, but only 'guesses' what he will do. The Cretans are then sent to Sparta to alert those left behind. This is a dubious piece of generalship, perhaps substituted to match Epameinondas' stratagem with one of Agesilaos.[14] Diodoros' later statement that Agesilaos had been left behind to defend Sparta (xv. 83. 2) contradicts the earlier suggestion of his whereabouts, and further emendation substitutes the name Archidamos. But Diodoros' source here may have been distinguishing Agesilaos from the cavalry and mercenaries, who seem to have continued on their way to Arkadia after the arrival of the Cretan message, while leaving Agesilaos behind to return to Sparta (Xen. *Hell.* vii. 5. 10).

Plutarch's other source here, Kallisthenes, was from Olynthos and may have provided information from a northern record. Thespiai had a pro-Spartan party, and Spartan garrisons had been there before Leuktra, including one under Sphodrias. This may explain the desertion of the Thespian Euthynos from Epameinondas to Agesilaos, perhaps even by arrangement beforehand as a Spartan sympathizer. The passing of this intelligence was crucial for Sparta's defence, and Xenophon even suggests possible divine responsibility for the Cretan's message to Agesilaos (*Hell.* vii. 5. 10).

There are two other factors which help to clarify the situation.
(1) Confusion over the Cretan participation may be removed.
Plutarch records the dispatch of a mounted messenger sent on
ahead to Sparta by Agesilaos. Xenophon omits this, and perhaps
Diodoros has transferred to the Cretans the function of conveying
to Sparta the information which had been brought by Euthynos or
Xenophon's Cretan but which for him contained the commander's
inspired 'guess'. (2) Topography presents problems for the
movements of the two armies in Diodoros, who does not
explain whether they used the same route or not. In Xenophon's
version, however, while Agesilaos was travelling via Pellana,
Epameinondas will have marched from his camp at Tegea by a
more direct route along the valley of the river Sarandapotamos to
reach Sellasia, on the northern side of Sparta and to the east of the
Eurotas.[15] His intention may have been, partly at least, to force the
Spartans to limit their aid to Mantineia by retaining troops to
defend their own territory, but he may also have tried to reach
Sparta before Agesilaos by exploiting his need to use the western
route because of the Theban presence at Tegea.

. . . ταχὺ προπέμψας ἱππέα τοῖς ἐν τῇ πόλει φράσοντα, μετ' οὐ πολὺ καὶ
αὐτὸς παρῆλθεν εἰς τὴν Σπάρτην. 5 ὀλίγῳ δ' ὕστερον οἱ Θηβαῖοι
διέβαινον τὸν Εὐρώταν καὶ προσέβαλλον τῇ πόλει, μάλ' ἐρρωμένως τοῦ
Ἀγησιλάου καὶ παρ' ἡλικίαν ἐπαμύνοντος.

Plutarch maintains high praise for Agesilaos' military judgement
and activities, again consistently distinguishing his generalship
from other aspects of character. Agesilaos is judged by Diodoros,
on several occasions and in several situations, and his judgements
are perhaps similar to Plutarch's. He praises his generalship in the
defence of Sparta against Epameinondas (xv. 83. 1–3), but condemns his fondness for war (xv. 19. 4) and the abandonment of the
early Spartan virtues (xv. 1. 1–5). Diodoros' judgement at xv. 31.
3–4 also praises his generalship, and it is thought to be inconsistent with that at xv. 19. 4, and only to be explained by a change of
source.[16] However, the key word, δραστικός, 'a man of action',
occurs in both Diodoros' passages, indicating the same consistent
character assessment; commendation of achievement should not
be mistaken for approval of the man.

6 οὐ γάρ, ὡς πρότερον, ἀσφαλείας ἑώρα τὸν καιρὸν ὄντα καὶ φυλακῆς,

ἀλλὰ μᾶλλον ἀπονοίας καὶ τόλμης, οἷς τὸν ἄλλον χρόνον οὐδέποτε
πιστεύσας οὐδὲ χρησάμενος, τότε μόνοις ἀπεώσατο τὸν κίνδυνον, ἐκ
τῶν χειρῶν τοῦ Ἐπαμεινώνδου τὴν πόλιν ἐξαρπάσας, . . .

Agesilaos' previous policy in defence of Sparta, ἀσφαλῶς, 'without
risk', was described as uncharacteristic (ch. 33. 2). Now, abandoning that ἀσφάλεια, he acts again out of character, with 'indiscretion
and audacity', ἀπόνοια καὶ τόλμα. Plutarch's ἀπόνοια comes from
Xenophon's τοῖς ἀπονενοημένοις, denoting the desperate efforts of
all the Spartans, individualized only in Archidamos (*Hell.* vii. 5.
12). In each of his successful defences of Sparta, Agesilaos is said
to have resorted to extremes, the over-cautious and the over-
daring, as if the exercise of his natural moderate characteristics
could not sustain the policies which he was pursuing. Agesilaos'
ability to recognize the καιρός, as here, is usually, for Plutarch, one
of his strengths as a general, except only before Leuktra (ch. 28. 6;
cf. ch. 39. 2, 4). The successful defence of Sparta, in the reduced
circumstances of the time, restores the limited position of internal
security which Plutarch supposes the Lykourgan constitution to
have been designed to maintain. The rest of the chapter reveals
that, in the new circumstances, the traditional Spartan characteristics of fitness, courage, selflessness, and discipline still
flourished. 'Rumours of the death of Sparta . . . are in fact
seriously exaggerated.'[17]

. . . καὶ στήσας τρόπαιον, 7 καὶ τοῖς παισὶ καὶ ταῖς γυναιξὶν ἐπιδείξας
τὰ κάλλιστα τροφεῖα τῇ πατρίδι τοὺς Λακεδαιμονίους ἀποδιδόντας, ἐν
δὲ πρώτοις τὸν Ἀρχίδαμον ἀγωνιζόμενον ὑπερηφάνως τῇ τε ῥώμῃ τῆς
ψυχῆς καὶ τῇ κουφότητι τοῦ σώματος, ὀξέως ἐπὶ τὰ θλιβόμενα τῆς
μάχης διαθέοντα διὰ τῶν στενωπῶν καὶ πανταχοῦ μετ' ὀλίγων
ἀντερείδοντα τοῖς πολεμίοις· 8 Ἰσάδαν δὲ δοκῶ, τὸν Φοιβίδου υἱόν, οὐ
τοῖς πολίταις μόνον, ἀλλὰ καὶ τοῖς πολεμίοις θέαμα φανῆναι καλὸν καὶ
ἀγαστόν. 9 ἦν μὲν γὰρ ἐκπρεπὴς τὸ εἶδος καὶ τὸ μέγεθος τοῦ σώματος,
ὥραν δ' ἐν ᾗ τὸ ἥδιστον ἀνθοῦσιν ἄνθρωποι παριόντες εἰς ἄνδρας ἐκ
παίδων εἶχε, γυμνὸς δὲ καὶ ὅπλων τῶν σκεπόντων καὶ ἱματίων, λίπα
χρισάμενος τὸ σῶμα καὶ τῇ μὲν ἔχων χειρὶ λόγχην, τῇ δὲ ξίφος,
ἐξήλατο τῆς οἰκίας, καὶ διὰ μέσων τῶν μαχομένων ὠσάμενος ἐν τοῖς
πολεμίοις ἀνεστρέφετο, παίων τὸν προστυχόντα καὶ καταβάλλων.

Xenophon does not mention Agesilaos as taking part in the
defence of Sparta, after the Spartiates had posted themselves on
guard following his return from Pellana. He describes

Archidamos' vigorous leadership of a small band of one hundred
men, and gives him the honour of the trophy (*Hell.* vii. 5. 12–13;
cf. Isok. *Epist.* 9. 4). In Plutarch's 'euphuistic' passage reminiscent of the style of the orator Gorgias, Archidamos and Isadas[18]
carry on the fight as substitutes for Agesilaos, who could not be
imagined as taking so active a part at his age; Homer substituted
Diomedes for the absent Achilles (*Il.* v.).[19] These episodes do not
involve Agesilaos directly, but allow Plutarch to portray some of
the traditional Spartan characteristics that he continued to admire.
In particular he carries the attention back to young citizens trained
in the service of the city.

10 ἐτρώθη δ' ὑπ' οὐδενός, εἴτε θεοῦ δι' ἀρετὴν φυλάττοντος αὐτόν, εἴτε
μεῖζόν τι καὶ κρεῖττον ἀνθρώπου φανεὶς τοῖς ἐναντίοις. **11** ἐπὶ τούτῳ δὲ
λέγεται τοὺς ἐφόρους στεφανώσαντας αὐτόν, εἶτα χιλίων δραχμῶν
ἐπιβαλεῖν ζημίαν, ὅτι χωρὶς ὅπλων διακινδυνεύειν ἐτόλμησεν.

Plutarch suggests the possibility either of divine protection or of
divine assimilation. The gods intervene at four different stages in
Xenophon's account (*Hell.* vii. 5. 10, 12, 13, and 26): at one stage
(§12) they favour Archidamos, just as they favour Isadas here, but
there is no assumption of divine appearance.

The paradox of reward and punishment for Isadas' action
reflects a paradox in Agesilaos' leadership. He inspires in Isadas
an action which he might welcome but which he should not
approve, since he made it a principle not to risk soldiers' lives; he
had disapproved of the action of Phoibidas, father of Isadas,[20] but
welcomed it (ch. 23. 7). The series of three incidents ends with
one in which the ephors reassert the traditional Spartan virtue of
strict discipline. Isadas' action may re-enact a practice—perhaps
homosexual—in a 'rite of passage', or a primitive self-immolation,
or similar act of desperation, in the belief that there were special
powers in nudity:[21] Agesilaos impressed the rebels by walking out
almost alone and unarmed (ch. 32. 7). In other versions of this
exploit a young man—essentially Greek—rushes out from the
gymnasium (Aelian, *VH* vi. 3), or, more rationally, carries out an
organized *ruse de guerre* (Polyain. ii. 9).

The successful defence of the unwalled Sparta is impressive.
Epameinondas, who already knew the topography, undertook the
attack in the expectation of finding few vigorous defenders. His
taskforce was not his full strength, and had a long overnight

march, with the disappointment of failing to achieve the full
surprise it needed. The attackers had a difficult task in the narrow
streets of the four villages, against a desperate defence (Xen. *Hell.*
vii. 5. 11, Diod. xv. 83), in the knowledge that the main enemy
army remained intact at Mantineia. There was little to gain in
winning an indefensible base at great cost, and its capture may not
have been Epameinondas' aim (cf. ch. 32. 5). The psychological
effect of his penetration into Lakonia, and the victory hoped for in
the north, would leave Sparta powerless for the future. The main
requirement would be for Epameinondas to return to Mantineia
without further casualties or waste of time, and take advantage of
the absence of at least some of the force sent for its relief.

35. The battle of Mantineia: death of Epameinondas; Sparta isolated

Mor. 214 c–d; Xen. *Hell.* vii. 5. 20–5; Diod. xv. 79. 2, 84. 1–88. 4; Nepos,
Ep. 9. 1–4; Paus. viii. 11. 5–9.[1]

1 Ὀλίγαις δ' ὕστερον ἡμέραις περὶ τὴν Μαντίνειαν ἐμαχέσαντο, καὶ τὸν
Ἐπαμεινώνδαν ἤδη κρατοῦντα τῶν πρώτων, ἔτι δ' ἐγκείμενον καὶ
κατασπεύδοντα τὴν δίωξιν, Ἀντικράτης Λάκων ὑποστὰς ἔπαισε δόρατι
μέν, ὡς Διοσκουρίδης ἱστόρηκε, Λακεδαιμόνιοι δὲ Μαχαιρίωνας ἔτι νῦν
τοὺς ἀπογόνους τοῦ Ἀντικράτους καλοῦσιν, ὡς μαχαίρᾳ πατάξαντος.

Since Agesilaos was not involved in the fighting,[2] Plutarch does
not give an extended account of the battle of Mantineia (362). He
has selected from Xenophon's account of the action the few facts
of the final engagement essential for his purpose, omitting only the
preliminary details and the subsequent movements of the two
sides. The three brief participial phrases correspond almost
exactly to the three stages in Xenophon's account leading to
Epameinondas' death (*Hell.* vii. 5. 25), but Plutarch gives prominent placing to the Boiotian hero's name.

Xenophon names no weapon. A spear is named by Nepos (*Ep.*
9. 3), Diodoros (xv. 87. 1, 5–6), as well as Dioskourides (see
Introd., Γ.3(*l*)).[3] Pausanias, who implies a sword but does not
name it, gives versions which deprive the Spartans of the honour:

a Mantineian story assigns the name Machairion to a Mantineian. Athenian and Theban accounts name Xenophon's son Grylos (viii. 9. 5, 11. 6; cf. i. 3. 4). The variants enable Plutarch to establish the importance for the Spartans of the removal of the much-feared Epameinondas. His evidence is in the family name, Μαχαιρίωνες, Swordsmen, bestowed in honour of Antikrates, the man responsible for his death. Plutarch's generous treatment of the Spartan hero contrasts with the disparagement of the Boiotians by Xenophon, who mocks the victors of Leuktra and their confusion after losing their general (*Hell.* vii. 5. 12, 25).

This is a notable example of the use of indirect description, here family tradition, to give independent authority to an evaluation or judgement. Genealogies, both epigraphical and oral, were preserved partly to establish the political and social status and prestige of public figures, particularly but not exclusively aristocratic. Among the Spartans oral traditions were more important than monumental and other inscriptions typical of more open societies, and they survived through Sparta's Roman period and into Plutarch's time, a potential source of information, as here, relevant to his work, though not therefore infallible, for they could be forged and enhanced.[4]

2 οὕτω γὰρ ἐθαύμασαν καὶ ὑπερηγάπησαν αὐτὸν φόβῳ τοῦ Ἐπα-μεινώνδου ζῶντος, ὥστε τιμὰς μὲν ἐκείνῳ καὶ δωρεὰς ψηφίσασθαι, γένει δ' ἀτέλειαν, ἣν ἔτι καὶ καθ' ἡμᾶς ἔχει Καλλικράτης, εἷς τῶν Ἀντικράτους ἀπογόνων.

The strong wording further highlights the passage dealing with Epameinondas and the relief of the Spartans to be free from him after the troubles he had caused—over a period of at least the nine years from the peace conference before Leuktra (ch. 28) until his death at Mantineia (cf. their relief after the 'Tearless Battle' at ch. 33. 8). The Spartans rewarded Antikrates personally with further honours and gifts and perpetuated his memory by bestowing immunity from taxation on his family.[5] This was a tangible privilege to be preserved and used, evidently at Sparta, suggesting that such verification was still acceptable there and would suffice to authenticate the tradition for Plutarch. He illustrated both the sort of access to oral tradition that was available, and one of the means by which it was transmitted, when he recorded that he heard about the honours still paid in his own day in Magnesia to

Themistokles from a fellow student in the school of Ammonios, one of his descendants (*Them.* 32. 5; see Introd., A, F.3(*o*)). Here the excessive relief felt by the Spartans honours Epameinondas by indirect characterization and the contemporary source shows that the glory of the Boiotian achievement was still remembered.

3 μετὰ δὲ τὴν μάχην καὶ τὸν θάνατον τοῦ Ἐπαμεινώνδου γενομένης εἰρήνης τοῖς Ἕλλησι πρὸς αὐτούς, ἀπήλαυνον οἱ περὶ τὸν Ἀγησίλαον τοῦ ὅρκου τοὺς Μεσσηνίους, ὡς πόλιν οὐκ ἔχοντας.

Diodoros records this attempt to deprive Messene of its recently acquired independence (xv. 89. 2), but he attributes it to the Lakedaimonian representatives at the peace conference, without naming Agesilaos, and perhaps Plutarch assigns to him only an indirect, though influential, role. Since Epameinondas had established the independence of Messenia in his first invasion of the Peloponnese, one year after Leuktra, the grounds for exclusion must be a piece of Spartan rhetoric. The Spartans no doubt wished to avoid universal recognition of Messene, as they had before (*Hell.* vii. 1. 27), in the hope that they would more legitimately be able to claim the right to recover the area by military reconquest, even, perhaps, to call on the other signatories to help in the recovery, that is, without violating the terms of the Peace.

4 ἐπεὶ δ' οἱ λοιποὶ πάντες ἐδέχοντο καὶ τοὺς ὅρκους ἐλάμβανον παρ' αὐτῶν, ἀπέστησαν οἱ Λακεδαιμόνιοι, καὶ μόνοις αὐτοῖς πόλεμος ἦν ἐλπίζουσιν ἀναλήψεσθαι τὴν Μεσσηνίαν.

As a further consequence of Leuktra, the Spartan domination even of peace conferences was ended, but whereas the failure of the earliest attempts to agree peace terms resulted in continuation of wars, the present peace was not aborted by the withdrawal of Sparta (Diod. xv. 89. 1–2). Sparta remained in a state of war, but never recovered Messenia, and did not intervene in 361 when, in response to the request of Megalopolis, Thebes sent Pammenes with cavalry and infantry to suppress conflict with Mantineia and its allies (Diod. xv. 94. 1–3).

5 βίαιος οὖν ἐδόκει καὶ ἀπηνὴς καὶ πολέμων ἄπληστος ὁ Ἀγησίλαος εἶναι, τὰς μὲν κοινὰς διαλύσεις πάντα τρόπον ὑπορύττων καὶ διαβάλλων,
. . .

Agesilaos is once more being judged adversely by Plutarch as aggressive (cf. φιλοπόλεμος (Diod. xv. 19. 4); see chs. 23. 3, 28. 3). From here to the end of the chapter, Plutarch reviews the problems created by this aspect of Agesilaos' character. His policy of isolating Thebes had led to costly hostilities, for which the finance at first, no doubt, came from the tribute paid by the former subjects of Athens, and the plunder captured in Asia Minor. This was no longer available. Plutarch seems to have seen that the opportunity to end these difficulties had come with this latest peace conference. The empire had been lost and there was no possibility that the Spartans could easily recover Messenia: to contemplate this was, for Plutarch, fruitless militarism. Perhaps his admiration for the Lykourgan constitution led him to wish that the Spartans had rather embraced the universal peace and revived their early principles, to become the moral leaders of Greece once more.

His judgement here of Agesilaos may be compared in part with Aristotle's criticism of Sparta's legislator, that 'the whole constitution has regard to one part of virtue only—the virtue of the soldier, which gives victory in war' (*Pol.* 1271^{b}1–6). Elsewhere he advises the military training of citizens for defence, not for conquest of the free for the benefit of the conqueror (*Pol.* 1333^{b}37–42; see ch. 8 n. following §7; chs. 9. 2, 33. 4, 37. 11).[6] Plutarch denies that the main aim of the lawgiver was 'to leave his city as the leader of so many other cities' (*Lyk.* 31. 1). The measures he attributed to Lykourgos concerned happiness and good order, in the city and in the individual (*Lyk.* 5–10). The reason for Sparta's decline was, for Plutarch, not embedded in the constitution. He complained that the proceeds of Lysander's wars undermined the laws of Lykourgos (*Lyk.* 30). Here he defends the provisions of Lykourgos, and regards Agesilaos as responsible for the decline.

. . . **6** πάλιν δ' ὑπὸ χρημάτων ἀπορίας ἀναγκαζόμενος ἐνοχλεῖν τοῖς κατὰ πόλιν φίλοις καὶ δανείζεσθαι καὶ συνερανίζεσθαι.

Xenophon notes that Agesilaos' retirement from campaigning made him realize Sparta's need of money in order 'to win allies'. While he was at home he devised what measures he could and then undertook service abroad (*Agesilaos*, 2. 25–7).[7] Plutarch refers only to the lack of money, omitting the motive for replenishment, and adding normal sources of revenue, loans and levies. He adapts Aristotle's generalization that the Spartans were reluctant to pay taxes (*Pol.* 1271ᵇ10–17), showing that Agesilaos' policies were an unpopular burden for his friends. Thucydides refers to the inconvenience (οὔτε ἐτοίμως) of cash contributions for Spartans (i. 80. 4), but after the war individuals benefited from the coinage made available in Sparta by Lysander (*Lys.* 17. 1, 6; cf. above, on ch. 20. 1).[8]

δέον ἀπηλλάχθαι κακῶν εἰς τοῦτο περιήκοντι τῶν καιρῶν, καὶ μὴ τὴν ἅπασαν ἀρχὴν τοσαύτην γενομένην ἀφεικότα καὶ πόλεις καὶ γῆν καὶ θάλατταν ὑπὲρ τῶν ἐν Μεσσήνῃ κτημάτων καὶ προσόδων σφαδάζειν.

Plutarch gives his interpretation of the καιρός and prepares the way for his criticism of Agesilaos' interpretation in the next chapter (ch. 36. 4). The attempt to recover the resources of Messenia led to the debilitation and isolation of Sparta, which provided the opportunity for ending Greece's internecine wars. Plutarch indicates the crippling financial requirement of Sparta's policies, which relied on mercenaries (Xen. *Hell.* vii. 5. 10); there remained only Agesilaos' own military and diplomatic mercenary services (*Agesilaos*, 2. 26–7).

The chapter ends on a pessimistic note, and with a striking infinitive, σφαδάζειν, strongly metaphorical and derogatory, prominently placed; it marks Sparta's dying struggle to retain hegemony. The word is used in a suggestive parallel of Antony's agony in death (*Ant.* 76. 5), and, by Aeschylus, of the vain 'struggles' of unbroken horses (*Persae*, 194). No further Spartan military activities are recorded for this time. Diodoros gives no Spartan involvement until almost ten years later, when Archidamos promised money and mercenaries secretly to the Phokian, Philomelos, and gave him 15 talents. In Xenophon's *Agesilaos*, after the defence of the city (2. 24), Agesilaos undertook no more campaigns in Greece because of his age, although he was active in some way in Asia Minor (*Agesilaos*, 2. 26–7; see ch. 36. 1). Xenophon's *Hellenika* ends in a mood of doubt with the battle of Mantineia, which the deity had so managed that 'neither side gained anything: Greece was only more confused and unsettled'. Mantineia was not the end of his *Agesilaos*.

Egyptian campaign: the death of Agesilaos

Mor. 191 C–D, 210 B–C, 214 D–215 A, *Artax.* 22. 3; Xen. *Agesilaos*, 2.
26–31; Diod. xv. 90. 1–3, 92. 2–93. 6; Nepos, *Agesilaus*, 8. 1–7, *Chabr.* 2.
1–3; Polyain. ii. 1 22; Paus. iii. 10. 2.

36. The humiliations of Agesilaos' mercenary service

Egypt and Persia in the early fourth century[1]

Under the rebel Pharaoh Amyrtaeus, Egypt became independent
of the Achaemenid empire soon after the end of the Peloponnesian
war (*c*.404). His dynasty was deposed in 381 by Nektanebo I, who
was content to follow a defensive policy, but his successor Tachos
(363), whether son or usurper, attempted to invade the King's
territory of Phoenicia in 362. With him were Greek mercenary
forces led by Agesilaos and Chabrias, the Athenian admiral, while
Orontes,[2] the leader of the satraps already in revolt from the King,
invaded Syria, though he soon returned to his former allegiance.
Tachos, whose harsh taxes had alienated the priests, lost power to
the usurper Nektanebo II. Nektanebo, though under repeated
Persian attacks, instituted a programme of building temples and,
supported by the priests and their efficient tax collection, continued to reign until the 340s, when Egypt returned to Persian
rule. A little more than a decade later it fell to Alexander: a local
legend made him the son of Nektanebo.

The subject of chs. 36–40 is Agesilaos' mercenary service
in Egypt to Tachos and Nektanebo II until his departure and
death. Xenophon praises Agesilaos for intending in his retirement
to punish Persia, and to obtain a reliable friend and a large sum
of money for Sparta. Diodoros is the chief source for the
Satraps' Revolt, but he creates difficulty by replacing Nektanebo
with Tachos. Nepos records only the Egyptian contempt for
the lifestyle of Agesilaos when he arrives to help Tachos, and
the money given by the king, Nektanebo, on his departure. A

summary of the three main sources will show further divergences in detail. In view of these and other differences from the accounts of Xenophon and Diodoros, the preference for Plutarch's version may be attributed to his undoubtedly shrewd analysis and resolution of discrepancies; he may also have had the use of another source, perhaps his teacher, Ammonios the Egyptian philosopher (*Mor.* 385 B).[3]

Plutarch

Agesilaos offers his services to Tachos the Egyptian (36) but on arrival is disappointed not to be given full command. He of necessity accompanies his employer to Phoenicia (37. 2). The emergence of a rival contender, Nektanebo, to the throne forces Agesilaos to choose between the two, and after advice from Chabrias and Sparta he decides to join Nektanebo. A new rival necessitates another choice (38. 1), with suspicions of disloyalty and military incompetence. Military action involving two successful stratagems dispels the suspicion (39). Agesilaos establishes Nektanebo in power and leaves with gifts and honours (40).

Xenophon (Agesilaos, 2. 28–31)

Agesilaos is pleased to be summoned by the Egyptian king, but when the king keeps the whole command, he feels he has been cheated. A revolt of the Egyptian troops causes the flight of the king to Sidon in Phoenicia. In his absence the Egyptians are divided by internal strife, and Agesilaos must choose to serve one or other of two nameless kings in order to obtain pay for the Greek troops. He considers which of the two seems more truly to be 'friendly to the Greeks'. By choosing the stronger friend, Agesilaos secures the apparent interest of Sparta, and he takes the field with him. Xenophon represents the rival contender established with Agesilaos' help as Sparta's friend, and the defeated enemy as μισέλλην, 'hater of Greeks'. Agesilaos sails for home with money to help fight Sparta's enemies.

Diodoros (xv. 92. 2–93. 6)

Agesilaos is sent to Tachos, king of Egypt, by Sparta and is appointed to the command of the mercenary force from Greece of 10,000, including 1,000 Lakedaimonians dispatched with Agesilaos; Tachos' army is of 80,000 Egyptian troops. Tachos leads an expedition to Phoenicia, against Agesilaos' advice that he should remain in Egypt, and in his absence the general left in charge of Egypt revolts. The general persuades Nektanebos (*sic*), his son, who has been sent on from Phoenicia to campaign in Syria, to seize the kingship in Egypt. Tachos then flees to the King to beg forgiveness for his former hostility. After winning Artaxerxes' support, Tachos returns to Agesilaos. They are attacked by Nektanebos. Agesilaos proves his generalship and is rewarded as the one who helped Tachos to recover the kingdom.

1 Ἔτι δὲ μᾶλλον ἠδόξησε Ταχῷ τῷ Αἰγυπτίῳ στρατηγὸν ἐπιδοὺς ἑαυτόν.

Authorities treat this episode in different ways. Plutarch continues the criticism of Agesilaos, the comparative adverb, μᾶλλον, indicating 'further' damage to his reputation among the Spartans. He suggests that Agesilaos' surrender of independence and autonomy in undertaking mercenary service even as commander was thought unworthy. Xenophon ends *Hellenika* without this episode, but at *Agesilaos*, 2. 26–7 he records that after saving Sparta Agesilaos was paid for non-military services to local dynasts in Asia Minor (365),[4] having rescued Ariobarzanes three times from siege. On the last occasion even the besieger, Mausolos, a 'guest-friend', contributed money to Sparta, perhaps in return for some provision of mercenaries.[5]

Xenophon (2. 28–31) records Agesilaos' expedition in the service of the king of Egypt without naming Tachos or any other Egyptians, though where the manuscripts give ταχέως (2. 27), editors have changed this to Ταχώς, creating historical problems of chronology, for the king at the time was Nektanebo I.[6] Grammatically, ταχέως cannot stand, leaving 'Mausolos', with its participle, as subject of a plural verb with its plural participle: another name is needed. The continuation, service in Egypt with an unnamed king, taken to be Tachos (if the change is accepted), should not be the service for which Agesilaos' reward has been mentioned; but Tachos may have been already known to the King to whom he later fled (Diod. xv. 92. 5). The reward he paid to Agesilaos may have been earned in the same area as that of Mausolos, or in Phoenicia (Xen. *Agesilaos*, 2. 30), before he came to Egypt to take the throne; that connection explains how the new service came about.

At 2. 25 Xenophon commends Agesilaos for attending to the financial need of the state; and at §29, with an unrealistic argument, which may be Xenophon's supposition, tinted with panhellenism (cf. chs. 26. 6, 27. 7),[7] he suggests that the offer of command was the opportunity for Agesilaos to liberate the Greeks of Asia Minor, and to punish the Persians for their former hostility and especially for their support of Messenian autonomy: a panhellenist affair only in the sense that Sparta did not recognize Messene as an independent Greek city. Later, at 2. 31, he again refers to money, in reporting Agesilaos' urgent need to obtain pay for the troops, which forced him to choose to serve one or other of the two sides.

Since Agesilaos did not survive the expedition, Xenophon cannot now have had the privileged, direct communications he seems to have drawn on earlier. Nepos (*Agesilaus*, 8. 2–7) treats only the arrival and departure of Agesilaos, omitting all details of the campaigns, but Diodoros, recording the Satraps' Revolt against Artaxerxes (xv. 90. 1),[8] provides the context for Tachos' decision to plan aggression against the King at the same time, using Greek mercenaries. He mentions only the Spartans' resentment of Artaxerxes' wish for Messenian autonomy as the reason for their willingness to join Tachos (xv. 90. 2). His account of the campaign (xv. 92–3) is complimentary to Agesilaos, and ends, unlike the others, with the restoration of Tachos to his kingdom.

2 οὐ γὰρ ἠξίουν ἄνδρα τῆς Ἑλλάδος ἄριστον κεκριμένον καὶ δόξης ἐμπεπληκότα τὴν οἰκουμένην, ἀποστάτῃ βασιλέως, ἀνθρώπῳ βαρβάρῳ, χρῆσθαι τὸ σῶμα καὶ τοὔνομα καὶ τὴν δόξαν ἀποδόσθαι χρημάτων, ἔργα μισθοφόρου καὶ ξεναγοῦ διαπραττόμενον.

The reputation Agesilaos was now jeopardizing recalls the assessment attributed to Theopompos that he was 'the greatest and most illustrious of his time' (ch. 10. 10). The assessment recorded here is that of the Lakedaimonians, so that Plutarch again gives the adverse judgement indirectly (οὐ γὰρ ἠξίουν—'they were indignant'), and reports their current thoughts. The Greeks' contempt for non-Greeks stems in part from the belief that long subjection to the despotic rule of eastern monarchs had made them naturally servile, while a luxurious style of living weakened the spirits of their rulers, too (*Artax.* 20. 1; Hdt. viii. 102. 2; Lys. 33. 3; Isok. 4, 146–51, 162, 184; Arist. *Pol.* 1255ᵃ28; see Introd., E.7). Agesilaos had urged Pharnabazos to regard servility to the King as undesirable (ch. 12. 7), and Plutarch sees this proposed service in the same light. Tachos' predecessors had themselves been subjects of the Persian King before their revolt. Contempt for him is compounded by their treachery, though Agesilaos had previously encouraged such desertions (ch. 12). Service to foreign kings by Greek mercenaries was not unprecedented, however: Alcaeus told of the distinguished mercenary service of his brother, Antimenidas, to the king of Babylon (Strabo, xiii. 617), and Ionian and Karian sailors out plundering were employed by the Egyptian Psammetichos to help him to seize the throne; they became the bodyguard of the next king, Amasis, and there was a Greek presence in Egypt from that time on (Hdt. ii. 152–4. 4).

3 κεἰ γὰρ ὑπὲρ ὀγδοήκοντα γεγονὼς ἔτη καὶ πᾶν ὑπὸ τραυμάτων τὸ σῶμα κατακεκομμένος, ἐκείνην αὖθις ἀνεδέξατο τὴν καλὴν καὶ περίβλεπτον ἡγεμονίαν ὑπὲρ τῆς τῶν Ἑλλήνων ἐλευθερίας, οὐ πάμπαν ἄμεμπτον εἶναι τὴν φιλοτιμίαν·

Plutarch modifies Xenophon's phrasing at 2. 28–9. He puts 'over' for 'about' eighty, gives prominence to the numeral, adds Agesilaos' wounds,[9] and presents Xenophon's suggested panhellenist motive, the achievement of the freedom of the Greeks, only as a supposition to prove the incompatibility of his condition. The only motives attributed to Agesilaos here are the references to money and to mercenary service. Xenophon's commendation becomes Plutarch's criticism. The reader might have expected the panhellenist objective to meet with approval in all circumstances, and the unexpected criticism gains in intensity.

4 τοῦ γὰρ καλοῦ καιρὸν οἰκεῖον εἶναι καὶ ὥραν, μᾶλλον δ' ὅλως τὰ καλὰ τῶν αἰσχρῶν τῷ μετρίῳ διαφέρειν.

The practical rule, that 'the good and honourable course has its own appropriate circumstances and proper time'—requiring, that is, a sounder body and a younger age—is followed by the principle that rational consideration should distinguish the honourable from the shameful by the exercise of moderation (Arist. *NE* 1098ᵃ16, 1166ᵃ12, *Pol.* 1295ᵃ36–ᵇ6, 1333ᵇ1–5), an exercise that would have encouraged self-awareness (see Introd., E.3(*d*), and pp. 140–1, 352, 358–9). The mission was not without some success in practical achievement, but Plutarch explains above (ch. 35. 6) that in his opinion the καιρός at this time was the need to release Greece from internal wars. He earlier faulted Agesilaos for his similar failure truly to appreciate the καιρός in choosing to go to war with Thebes (ch. 28. 7). There anger overpowered reason, and he now explains in what respect Agesilaos failed to meet this requirement here. Lysander, too, and by association Agesilaos, had failed to understand the καιρός in the quarrel; there, however, the context was political (above, ch. 8. 6). Although Plutarch does not enlarge on the subject, here or at chs. 28, 37. 2, 39. 2, the καιρός was a fundamental part of his thinking (see C.1(*c*) vi). Agesilaos begins to understand its requirements again only when he comes into his own in the military field, in Egypt (ch. 39. 4).

5 οὐ μὴν ἐφρόντιζε τούτων ὁ Ἀγησίλαος, οὐδ᾽ ᾤετο παρ᾽ ἀξίαν εἶναι λειτούργημα δημόσιον οὐδέν, ἀλλὰ μᾶλλον ἀνάξιον ἑαυτοῦ τὸ ζῆν ἄπρακτον ἐν τῇ πόλει καὶ καθῆσθαι περιμένοντα τὸν θάνατον.

Plutarch implies that Agesilaos was aware of what people thought of him, perhaps as early as the criticism made at ch. 35. 5; he should have accepted it, but was incapable of making a rational assessment. Plutarch directly refutes Xenophon's claim of universal praise of Agesilaos specifically for his judicious selection of the services he should perform after Sparta had been saved (2. 25). Xenophon then records Agesilaos' delight in accepting the Egyptian offer (2. 28), despite having immediately before this suggested that Agesilaos was beyond the age for active military campaigning. Plutarch evidently saw Xenophon's logical inconsistency. Agesilaos disregarded what came to be known as the Aristotelian mean in judging that there was no service too undignified for him to undertake. Plutarch reinterprets Agesilaos' own thoughts on lifelong public service expressed in Xenophon's final encomium on his character in old age (11. 14–16; cf. *Mor.* 793 A, 797 E, 811 B).

6 ὅθεν ἤθροισε μισθοφόρους ἀφ᾽ ὧν ὁ Τάχως αὐτῷ χρημάτων ἔπεμψε, καὶ πλοῖα πληρώσας ἀνήχθη, τριάκοντα συμβούλους ἔχων μεθ᾽ ἑαυτοῦ Σπαρτιάτας, ὡς πρότερον. **7** ἐπεὶ δὲ κατέπλευσεν εἰς τὴν Αἴγυπτον, εὐθὺς οἱ·πρῶτοι τῶν βασιλικῶν ἡγεμόνων καὶ διοικητῶν ἐβάδιζον ἐπὶ ναῦν θεραπεύοντες αὐτόν. **8** ἦν δὲ καὶ τῶν ἄλλων Αἰγυπτίων σπουδή τε μεγάλη καὶ προσδοκία διὰ τοὔνομα καὶ τὴν δόξαν τοῦ Ἀγησιλάου, καὶ συνετρόχαζον ἅπαντες ἐπὶ τὴν θέαν.

Xenophon gives none of these details, only the offer of the chief command, subsequently revoked. The Egyptian campaign resembles in some ways the campaign in Asia Minor, and Plutarch may have assumed that advisers accompanied Agesilaos as in ch. 6. 4. Here he represents the honorific reception that Agesilaos was entitled to, in preparation for the contrast with the eventual Egyptian reaction (cf. ch. 7. 3).

9 ὡς δ᾽ ἑώρων λαμπρότητα μὲν καὶ κατασκευὴν οὐδεμίαν, ἄνθρωπον δὲ πρεσβύτην κατακείμενον ἔν τινι πόᾳ παρὰ τὴν θάλασσαν, εὐτελῆ καὶ μικρὸν τὸ σῶμα, τραχὺ καὶ φαῦλον ἱμάτιον ἀμπεχόμενον, σκώπτειν αὐτοῖς καὶ γελωτοποιεῖν ἐπῄει . . .

Nepos describes Agesilaos' appearance, furnishings, and dress, in almost the same terms as Plutarch (*Agesilaus*, 8. 2–3), recording the Egyptians' contempt (cf. *Mor.* 214 D–E). They expected regal grandeur, but what they saw was the deliberate Spartan simplicity of lifestyle for which Plutarch so firmly commended Agesilaos at ch. 12 when he met Pharnabazos, and again at chs. 14 and 19. 5–6 after his return to Sparta. Indirect characterization allows Plutarch to preserve his detachment. While Nepos includes Agesilaos' lameness as a cause of contempt, Plutarch, having recorded this at ch. 2. 3, concentrates on inoffensive features here. He uses the respectful word πρεσβύτην, 'elder', instead of 'king', to point to the incongruity.

Yet Plutarch does not approve of Alkibiades, who adopted the standards of the company he was in, for they could be good or bad (*Alk.* 23. 4). Disapproval of these extremes suggests that, for Plutarch, there was again an acceptable mean, in Aristotelian terms. Agesilaos has now lost the approval or admiration of friends, enemies, Spartans, and allies—a comprehensive list. However, in the following chapters he ultimately wins recognition even from the suspicious Egyptians for his military ability, as at *Mor.* 214 E–F, and shows that success in the military field is not inconsistent with the simplicity of the Lykourgan system.

. . . καὶ λέγειν ὅτι τοῦτ' ἦν τὸ μυθολογούμενον· ὠδίνειν ὄρος, εἶτα μῦν ἀποτεκεῖν.

The proverb is given in *Corpus Paroemiographorum Graecorum* (ὤδινεν ὄρος, εἶτα μῦν ἀπέτεκεν, i. 378. 4, ii. 733. 4), and is used by Horace ('parturient montes, nascetur ridiculus mus', *Ars P.* 139). Athenaios attributes it to Tachos (ὤδινεν ὄρος, Ζεὺς δ' ἐφοβεῖτο, τὸ δ' ἔτεκεν μῦν, xiv. 616 D); the metre is the mocking sotadean, which suggests a Greek source, or a Greek translator whose god must be Greek. Zeus feared a reprise of the Giants' War. Cf. μυομαχία at ch. 15. 6, Alexander's scathing reference to the fighting in Arkadia. In the Greek forms it has a chiastic pattern, missing in Horace's version. (See also Phaedrus, iv. 23; Lucian, *Hist. Conscr.* 23; Quintilian, viii. 3. 20.) A Hellenistic source has been suggested.[10] This anecdote presupposes an Egyptian proverb, and perhaps it was brought for the first time into Greek literature in connection with Agesilaos, though, alternatively, a Greek proverb may have been introduced into this Egyptian context. Since Plutarch goes on to present a highly ornamented and expanded account, it may be that he introduced it. Horace's version is the earliest of those listed above.

10 ἔτι δὲ μᾶλλον αὐτοῦ τὴν ἀτοπίαν ἐθαύμασαν, ὅτε ξενίων προσκομισθέντων καὶ προσαχθέντων ἄλευρα μὲν καὶ μόσχους καὶ χῆνας ἔλαβε, τραγήματα δὲ καὶ πέμματα καὶ μύρα διωθεῖτο, καὶ βιαζομένων λαβεῖν καὶ λιπαρούντων, ἐκέλευσε τοῖς εἵλωσι δοῦναι κομίζοντας. 11 τῇ μέντοι στεφανωτρίδι βύβλῳ φησὶν αὐτὸν ἡσθέντα Θεόφραστος διὰ τὴν λιτότητα καὶ καθαριότητα τῶν στεφάνων αἰτήσασθαι καὶ λαβεῖν, ὅτ' ἀπέπλει, παρὰ τοῦ βασιλέως.

An almost identical list of gifts is given at *Mor.* 210 C (cf. Athenaios, 657 B, Aelian, *VH* iii. 20). There Agesilaos accepts only the cereal, the rest, being delicacies, suitable only for the Helots. The gifts are arranged by Plutarch in two lists of three, using the two verbs, ἔλαβε and διωθεῖτο, to portray the regular simplicity of the Spartans, by the 'acceptance' of the wholesome natural foodstuffs and the 'rejection' of the elaborate luxuries. Nepos tells of similar gifts offered, and the renewed contempt for boorishness (*Agesilaus*, 8. 4). Plutarch omits the criticism of Agesilaos' simple taste. Nepos' *coronae*, 'crowns', are more correctly the flowering heads of the papyrus plant (LSJ s.v. βύβλος, citing Theopompos, *FGrHist.* 115 F 106 b), which Plutarch also describes as accepted by Agesilaos for their simplicity and neatness, though only later, as a parting present.

Theophrastos, also cited at ch. 2. 6, is not named at *Mor.* 210 C or by Nepos. Theopompos is the correct authority,[11] but the error may be Plutarch's. This fuller version of the anecdote, containing the attribution to the source and the reference to papyrus crowns, suggests that it belongs here in Egypt rather than at Thasos (cf. above, ch. 16. 3).[12]

37. Spartan self-interest conflicts with friendship: Plutarch accuses Agesilaos of betrayal

1 Τότε δὲ συμμίξας τῷ Ταχῷ παρασκευαζομένῳ πρὸς τὴν στρατείαν, οὐχ, ὥσπερ ἤλπιζεν, ἁπάσης στρατηγὸς ἀπεδείχθη τῆς δυνάμεως, ἀλλὰ τῶν μισθοφόρων μόνων, τοῦ δὲ ναυτικοῦ Χαβρίας ὁ Ἀθηναῖος· ἡγεμὼν δὲ συμπάντων αὐτὸς ἦν ὁ Ταχώς.

Plutarch continues to record the indignities suffered by Agesilaos in being given less responsibility than he expected, command of the mercenary force but not of the fleet. That prestige of command was important is shown by the speech of Kephisodotos, who points out to the Athenians that their command of the helots and mercenaries, in the combined fleet of the allies, would not match the Spartan command of the citizens in their combined land forces (Xen. *Hell.* vii. 1. 12). For Agesilaos the loss of the navy is also part of the indignity, since he had command of both land and sea forces in Asia Minor (ch. 10. 9). Xenophon does not mention that Agesilaos took Spartans or mercenaries with him, or that he retained any part of the command that he had been deceived into thinking was offered to him (*Agesilaos*, 2. 28–30). Diodoros speaks only of the appointment to the command of the mercenaries, and does not mention any deception (Diod. xv. 92. 2).

Xenophon does not mention Chabrias, perhaps because Athenian participation is not relevant, and he had fought with Spartans in the past. A kinsman of Plato and a member of the Academy (*Mor.* 1126 C–D), Chabrias replaced Iphikrates as commander of Athenian troops at Corinth in 389 (Diod. xiv. 92. 1–2).

He was involved, officially or not, from 378 on the Theban side against the Spartans in Boiotia, and went on to defeat the Spartan fleet at Naxos (Xen. *Hell.* v. 4. 14, 54, 61). His career in the eastern Mediterranean proved the value of Greek mercenary peltasts, if not of hoplites.[1] From about 392, Evagoras, king of Salamis in Cyprus, who was allied with Acoris, king of Egypt (392/1–379/8), was under threat from Artaxerxes, from whom he had rebelled (Diod. xiv. 98. 3–4, 110. 5; xv. 2. 2–4). The ten ships sent to him by Athens, perhaps in 391, were captured on the way by Teleutias (Xen. *Hell.* iv. 8. 24),[2] but in 388/7 Chabrias, hired by Evagoras, sailed to Cyprus with ten ships, 800 peltasts, and some hoplites; calling at Aigina he defeated and killed the Spartan general (Xen. *Hell.* v. 1. 10, 12). He was recalled from Cyprus in 386, for the alliance of Athens with Acoris in 388 led Persia to make the Peace of Antalkidas.

In 385–383 Chabrias was brought to Egypt by Acoris (Isok. iv. 141), but Pharnabazos objected and he was recalled by Athens in 379 (Diod. xv. 29. 1–4).[3] When in 362 Tachos hired Chabrias privately for his fleet (Diod. xv. 92. 3),[4] his reputation and experience in the area were well established. Nepos reports his claim that he was not inferior to Agesilaos; he volunteered to command the Egyptian fleet (*Chabr.* 2. 3).[5]

2 καὶ τοῦτο πρῶτον ἠνίασε τὸν Ἀγησίλαον· ἔπειτα τὴν ἄλλην ἀλαζονείαν καὶ κενοφροσύνην τοῦ Αἰγυπτίου βαρυνόμενος ἠναγκάζετο φέρειν· καὶ συνεξέπλευσεν ἐπὶ τοὺς Φοίνικας αὐτῷ, παρὰ τὴν ἀξίαν τὴν ἑαυτοῦ καὶ τὴν φύσιν ὑπείκων καὶ καρτερῶν, ἄχρι οὗ καιρὸν ἔλαβε. **3** Νεκτάνεβις γὰρ ἀνεψιὸς ὢν τοῦ Ταχῶ καὶ μέρος ἔχων ὑφ᾽ ἑαυτῷ τῆς δυνάμεως, ἀπέστη· καὶ βασιλεὺς ὑπὸ τῶν Αἰγυπτίων ἀναγορευθεὶς διεπέμπετο πρὸς τὸν Ἀγησίλαον, ἀξιῶν αὐτῷ βοηθεῖν· τὰ δ᾽ αὐτὰ καὶ τὸν Χαβρίαν παρεκάλει, μεγάλας ὑπισχνούμενος ἀμφοτέροις δωρεάς.

To follow another leader was a new experience for Agesilaos, having previously enjoyed sole military responsibility, full recognition of the successes of his leadership, and respect for the value of his ascetic way of life, as shown by Pharnabazos (ch. 12. 3). Plutarch illustrates the decline of Spartan influence, and of the myth of Spartan invincibility. The Spartans have to earn afresh their place in the changed world, and Plutarch sees that on this occasion the situation made for himself by Agesilaos was unsatisfactory, involving, for the third time, acting out of character (chs.

33. 2, 34. 6). Like Xenophon (2. 31), he shows that Agesilaos and his mercenaries must accompany their paymaster regardless of their own wishes, unless thcy have, or can obtain, the resources needed for survival, and that their standards of loyalty have to be less rigid, if more attractive terms of employment are available.

Xenophon in some confusion records no campaign but a revolt of Egyptian troops which causes the king—supposedly Tachos—to flee to Sidon in Phoenicia, without indicating that it is to the King that he flees. In his absence the Egyptians are divided by internal strife, and there are then two kings, who are not named. Agesilaos is committed to neither, unless Xenophon has deliberately withheld that one was Tachos, and is not presented with an invitation to change sides (2. 30–1).

Plutarch agrees with Diodoros that Agesilaos went to Phoenicia with Tachos, and his διεπέμπετο, 'sent to' (§3), implies that he knew that Nektanebo was either still in the north—in Syria, as Diodoros reports—or now in Egypt. But he omits both the reason for Agesilaos' annoyance—he had advised Tachos himself to stay in Egypt—and the intrigue leading to Nektanebo's usurpation, which does not involve Agesilaos. That Nektanebo was the son of Tachos' general (Diod. xv. 92. 3) may not be inconsistent with Plutarch's claim that he was the cousin of Tachos, for it would not be strange for the dynasty to appoint a relative as the temporary regent. He alone records Agesilaos' dilemma.

4 αἰσθομένου δὲ ταῦτα τοῦ Ταχῶ καὶ τραπομένου πρὸς δέησιν αὐτῶν, ὁ μὲν Χαβρίας ἐπειρᾶτο καὶ τὸν Ἀγησίλαον ἐν τῇ φιλίᾳ τοῦ Ταχῶ πείθων καὶ παραμυθούμενος κατέχειν, **5** ὁ δ' Ἀγησίλαος εἶπεν ὅτι Σοὶ μέν, ὦ Χαβρία, κατὰ σεαυτὸν ἀφιγμένῳ χρῆσθαι τοῖς ἑαυτοῦ λογισμοῖς ἔξεστιν, ἐγὼ δ' ὑπὸ τῆς πατρίδος ἐδόθην Αἰγυπτίοις στρατηγός. **6** οὔκουν ἂν ἔχοι μοι καλῶς οἷς ἐπέμφθην σύμμαχος πολεμεῖν, ἐὰν μὴ πάλιν ἡ πατρὶς κελεύσῃ.

Plutarch diverges from Diodoros in reporting Nektanebo's approach to Agesilaos at §3 and Tachos' pressure here on Agesilaos to stay loyal to him. The mercenary admiral Chabrias has no other identifiable place in the action recorded. Unlike Agesilaos, he went to Egypt in a private capacity, because Athens, with the other Greeks, obstructed the satraps' request for mercenaries: 'They are not aware', thcy said, 'of the existence of any state of war between the King and themselves.'[6] Chabrias retains what is, for a mercenary, obsolete but complimentary terminology in urging that ties of friendship should determine choice of service. Agesilaos also uses loose moral expressions in order to justify his attitude, and to avoid revealing his true intentions. Morality has not in the past been an argument weighing heavily with Agesilaos, and it is not the ground reported later in the chapter, either for his action, or for the ephors' explicit instructions. His phrases imply a Spartan state initiative involving the Egyptian people directly, although at ch. 36. 1 the arrangement was made with Tachos, and apparently at Agesilaos' own suggestion, 'offering himself'. However, it was endorsed by the state with the appointment of the thirty counsellors. Agesilaos' previous deceptions have been approved by Plutarch, and have succeeded, but his manoeuvres are now presented in a bad light, and in an unconvincing form: in the past Agesilaos deceived enemies, but since, in Chabrias' phrase, Tachos was a friend, this case is different.

7 ταῦτα δ' εἰπὼν ἔπεμψεν εἰς Σπάρτην ἄνδρας, οἳ τοῦ μὲν Ταχῶ κατηγορήσειν, ἐπαινέσεσθαι δὲ τὸν Νεκτάνεβιν ἔμελλον. **8** ἔπεμψαν δὲ κἀκεῖνοι δεόμενοι τῶν Λακεδαιμονίων, ὁ μὲν ὡς πάλαι σύμμαχος γεγονὼς καὶ φίλος, ὁ δ' ὡς εὐνούστερος καὶ προθυμότερος περὶ τὴν πόλιν ἐσόμενος.

With this hostile message, Agesilaos prepares the Spartan authorities for his eventual decision to abandon Tachos. Neither Xenophon nor Diodoros report any consultation with Sparta. In Xenophon, Agesilaos must choose to serve one or other of the nameless kings in order to obtain pay for the Greek troops, and he is said to have considered which of the two seemed more truly to be 'friendly to the Greeks' (2. 31). Since Xenophon linked Agesilaos' willingness to undertake the expedition with Spartan hostility towards the King (2. 29), the Egyptian 'friend' should also be required to be no friend of the Persians. In that respect Diodoros' account is flawed, since he records the reconciliation of Tachos with the King: Xenophon gives no guidance on which of the two contenders meets this criterion.

For Plutarch, Tachos was at the start a friend of Sparta, and since his flight comes later as the consequence of the desertion of his mercenaries (ch. 38. 1), he retains a formal claim on Agesilaos' loyalty until then; but meanwhile (§3) the Egyptians themselves force a choice on him by transferring their allegiance to Nektanebo. Both contenders for Agesilaos' services are still available here. Plutarch presents an analysis of the choice facing the Spartans in the form of the contrasting appeals of the envoys of Tachos and Nektanebo in Sparta. He expands Xenophon's simple criterion of friendship by setting the record of past alliance against a promise of goodwill in the future.

The secret message to Sparta and the Spartans' reply indicate a coincidence of views, that the interest of Sparta is best served by future prospect rather than respect for past services, though this conflicts with the principle of 'Help Friends and Harm Enemies' (ch. 5). For Agesilaos the insult caused by the failure to appoint him as supreme commander apparently tells against Tachos, and is the only recorded issue relevant to the principle mentioned here. The Spartan definition of justice as 'the interest of Sparta' predisposes the reader to expect the eventual decision, for the choice is between loyalty to the 'discredited' original agreement and the dictates of practical diplomacy.

9 ἀκούσαντες οὖν οἱ Λακεδαιμόνιοι τοῖς μὲν Αἰγυπτίοις ἀπεκρίναντο φανερῶς Ἀγησιλάῳ περὶ τούτων μελήσειν, ἐκείνῳ δ' ἐπέστειλαν ὁρᾶν κελεύοντες ὅπως πράξει τὸ τῇ Σπάρτῃ συμφέρον.

Plutarch may have used as a model a similar response from the home government to a suggestion made by Agesilaos, not mentioned at the time by Plutarch, but described by Xenophon (*Hell.* v. 3. 25), authorizing him to settle affairs at Phleious. The Spartans now authorize a possible change of loyalty, specifying self-interest as the criterion for the determination of policy, and accepting the definition of this by the commander on the spot. The expression τὸ τῇ Σπάρτῃ συμφέρον, 'the interest of Sparta', is repeated below, first in the form τῷ συμφέροντι τῆς πατρίδος, and then as τῷ τῆς πατρίδος συμφέροντι. This accumulation of references to the concept shows Plutarch's desire to stress his criticism of the Spartan principle of self-interest, which operated earlier in the Phoibidas and Sphodrias affairs: at ch. 23. 7 Agesilaos equates the *honestum* with the *utile*, but here the Lakedaimonians authorize him to give the 'expedient' precedence over the 'honourable', a moral conflict which began at §6. Deference to the polis, Agesilaos declares at §6, can turn desertion into honourable fidelity; but that deference conceals (§7) the guidance on the orders desired in the government's reply. In Spartan terms (Thuc. v. 105) his first duty is to Sparta, and he must choose accordingly. A political judgement might condemn him for the shameful betrayal of ch. 38. 6, which has no basis for a rational calculation of Spartan good.

10 οὕτω δὴ λαβὼν τοὺς μισθοφόρους ὁ Ἀγησίλαος ἀπὸ τοῦ Ταχῶ μετέστη πρὸς τὸν Νεκτάνεβιν, ἀτόπου καὶ ἀλλοκότου πράγματος παρακαλύμματι τῷ συμφέροντι τῆς πατρίδος χρησάμενος· ἐπεὶ ταύτης γε τῆς προφάσεως ἀφαιρεθείσης, τὸ δικαιότατον ὄνομα τῆς πράξεως ἦν προδοσία.

Agesilaos deserts to Nektanebo and so Tachos is robbed of the mercenaries who at ch. 36. 6 Plutarch said were obtained by Agesilaos, using money he had sent him. If Diodoros was correct in saying that Nektanebo had now recovered Egypt (xv. 92. 4), Agesilaos was choosing the easier option, to join the man in possession, Nektanebo, rather than to have to recover for Tachos the territory lost to him. Xenophon (2. 30–1) removes Agesilaos' moral difficulty: his original paymaster deceived him and made him doubt what he should do, but now that he has fled, the only consideration he has in mind is the need to impose an obligation on a new employer and ensure the desired financial rewards. The need to choose the one more likely to be a friend of Greece seems to be an afterthought. By his choice Agesilaos secures the apparent interest of Sparta in having friends, but he has not fulfilled one objective of the mission, to punish Persia, although Xenophon represents his defeated enemy as μισέλλην, 'hater of Greeks' (2. 31).

Plutarch expresses his own unfavourable moral judgement of Agesilaos' conduct in the strongest terms, with some justification for seeing in Xenophon's presentation evidence for the accusation of treachery. There is also justification for thinking that Xenophon may not have penetrated to Agesilaos' real grounds for his choice, for the revolt of the Egyptian army, the flight of Tachos, and the attractiveness of service with Nektanebo, may all have to do, in reality, with their respective attitudes to the King. Although Diodoros records the restoration of Egypt to Tachos, he later shows Nektanebo as king, and as, more importantly, hostile to Persia and in alliance with the King's enemies until his defeat a decade later (xvi. 41. 3, 47. 5, 51. 1). Agesilaos' eventual departure without engaging the King will perhaps be associated with Nektanebo II's return to the defensive policy of Nektanebo I (ch. 36. 1 above; Diod. xv. 42–3. 1; but cf. ch. 40. 1 below).

11 Λακεδαιμόνιοι δὲ τὴν πρώτην τοῦ καλοῦ μερίδα τῷ τῆς πατρίδος συμφέροντι διδόντες, οὔτε μανθάνουσιν οὔτ᾽ ἐπίστανται δίκαιον ἄλλο πλὴν ὃ τὴν Σπάρτην αὔξειν νομίζουσιν.

Plutarch identifies a deficiency both in the education and natural intellectual ability of the Spartans and in their character development. The Spartan view of justice as Sparta's 'interest' is now expressed as Sparta's 'expansion'. The claim is given more extreme expression than before: 'nothing else is just'. This is Plutarch's powerful condemnation of Spartan imperial policies. Their power in war was, as Aristotle said, used for wrong purposes (*Pol.* 1324ᵇ2–9, 1333ᵃ35, ᵇ11–31; see chs. 33. 4, 35. 5). But for Plutarch the lawgiver was not responsible.

38. Agesilaos' generalship is not recognized by his Egyptian employers

1 Ὁ μὲν οὖν Ταχὼς ἐρημωθεὶς τῶν μισθοφόρων ἔφυγεν, ἐκ δὲ Μένδητος ἕτερος ἐπανίσταται τῷ Νεκτανέβιδι βασιλεὺς ἀναγορευθείς· καὶ συναγαγὼν δέκα μυριάδας ἀνθρώπων ἐπῄει.

In juxtaposing the words Ταχὼς ἐρημωθεὶς τῶν μισθοφόρων ἔφυγεν, Plutarch expresses the fact that Agesilaos and the mercenaries hired by Tachos now desert their initial benefactor and bring about his flight. The chronological sequence of the desertion of troops and the flight of the king is identical in all three authors at this point (*Agesilaos,* 2. 30, Diod. xv. 92. 5), if Agesilaos is to be included in Xenophon's 'all the rest of his forces', but here the rivals for the kingship, nameless in Xenophon, are specified as Nektanebo and the Mendesian. Both Xenophon and Plutarch omit the reconciliation of Tachos with Artaxerxes reported by Diodoros (xv. 92. 5), which would no doubt have offended Agesilaos and aided his choice of Nektanebo. Diodoros records neither the third contender nor the desertion of Agesilaos to Nektanebo, but Agesilaos' continued service with Tachos is even less likely—inconceivable rather—in view of Diodoros' report of his appointment as Artaxerxes' commander in Egypt (xv. 92. 5).

2 θαρρύνοντος δὲ τοῦ Νεκτανέβιδος τὸν Ἀγησίλαον, καὶ λέγοντος ὅτι πολλοὶ μέν εἰσιν οἱ πολέμιοι, μιγάδες δὲ καὶ βάναυσοι καὶ δι' ἀπειρίαν εὐκαταφρόνητοι, **3** Καὶ μὴν οὐ τὸ πλῆθος αὐτῶν, ὁ Ἀγησίλαος εἶπεν, ἀλλὰ τὴν ἀπειρίαν φοβοῦμαι καὶ τὴν ἀμαθίαν ὡς δυσεξαπάτητον.

Plutarch continues to present Agesilaos as deprived of the chance to take the initiative, but attention is directed away from questions of morality as military strategy comes into the centre of focus again. Nektanebo becomes a foil to Agesilaos. His observation on the enemy troops' artisan status is reminiscent of Agesilaos' comment on the non-Spartan troops (ch. 26. 7–9). In his reply, Agesilaos begins to reassert his superiority in military wisdom, with the emphasis on deception; he selects as a reason for fear the very quality which Nektanebo thinks encouraging. Diodoros, too, shows Agesilaos instructing his employer, who is still Tachos, not to fear numerical superiority: in that anecdote he advises fear only of outstanding bravery (xv. 93. 2).

4 αἱ γὰρ ἀπάται τὸ παράδοξον ἐπάγουσι τοῖς πρὸς ἄμυναν ὧν ὑπονοοῦσι καὶ προσδοκῶσι τρεπομένοις, ὁ δὲ μὴ προσδοκῶν μηδ' ὑπονοῶν μηδὲν οὐ δίδωσι τῷ παραλογιζομένῳ λαβήν, ὥσπερ οὐδὲ τῷ παλαίοντι ῥοπὴν ὁ μὴ κινούμενος.

Deception of the enemy in war is exempt from the moral standards of peacetime, according to Agesilaos' view reported at ch. 9. 4, and by Xenophon at *Agesilaos*, 1. 17, and so is acceptable here (see Introd., E.6(*a–b*)): 'Nothing is more profitable in war than deception' (*Hipp*. 5. 9). At *Agesilaos*, 6. 5–6 he notes Agesilaos' ideas on deception, anticipation, concealment, and night action (chs. 38. 4, 39. 8–9). ἀπάτη is one of the main terms for stratagem, denoting 'the creative activity of changing an object or situation into something else'.[1] It was an important feature of many victories on the battlefield, at a time when communication between commander and troops over long distances was difficult, and the mobility of armies was so much restricted. Deception played an important part also in many successful assaults on fortified cities.

Agesilaos gives Nektanebo, who commented only on numerical advantage and lack of experience, a superior account of the complexity of strategic considerations, using several technical terms and metaphors from wrestling. His theory supposes that a skilled enemy's rational measures to counter the indications given by an equally rational and skilled commander can be predicted. The commander then renders those measures ineffective by acting other than as he had indicated. But the unskilled enemy lacks the power to make any predictable interpretation of the perceived signals of intentions (see also on ch. 9. 4). The beginner has not learnt the regular counter-moves.

The rationalism of surprise is reflected in the complex arrangement of the words 'suspecting' and 'expecting', repeated in reverse order to form a chiastic pattern: ὑπονοοῦσι καὶ προσδοκῶσι ~ μὴ προσδοκῶν μηδ᾽ ὑπονοῶν. This is also framed by the similar pair, τὸ παράδοξον and τῷ παραλογιζομένῳ, denoting 'false expectation' and 'false inference'. Metaphor and simile provide vivid illumination.

5 ἐκ τούτου καὶ ὁ Μενδήσιος ἔπεμπε πειρῶν τὸν Ἀγησίλαον. ἔδεισεν οὖν ὁ Νεκτάνεβις,

That there is now a third contender for Agesilaos' services corresponds with Xenophon's report of the appointment of the two kings, if these are additional to the existing Tachos, but Diodoros retains Tachos as the only reigning king. Nektanebo's anxiety is understandable, since Agesilaos had already deserted one employer.

. . . καὶ κελεύοντος αὐτοῦ διαμάχεσθαι τὴν ταχίστην καὶ μὴ χρόνῳ πολεμεῖν πρὸς ἀνθρώπους ἀπείρους ἀγῶνος, πολυχειρίᾳ δὲ περιελθεῖν καὶ περιταφρεῦσαι καὶ φθάσαι πολλὰ καὶ προλαβεῖν δυναμένους, ἔτι μᾶλλον ἐν ὑποψίᾳ καὶ φόβῳ γενόμενος πρὸς αὐτὸν ἀπεχώρησεν εἰς πόλιν εὐερκῆ καὶ μέγαν ἔχουσαν περίβολον. **6** ὁ δ᾽ Ἀγησίλαος ἠγανάκτει μὲν ἀπιστούμενος καὶ βαρέως ἔφερεν, αἰσχυνόμενος δὲ καὶ πάλιν μεταστῆναι πρὸς τὸν ἕτερον καὶ τελέως ἀπελθεῖν ἄπρακτος, ἠκολούθησε καὶ συνεισῆλθεν εἰς τὸ τεῖχος.

Agesilaos is still powerless to influence his employer, since his allegiance is now in doubt. He seems to be tempting him to a course of action that conflicts with his own previous caution, if διαμάχεσθαι τὴν ταχίστην means an early, vigorous engagement (such as had been to his advantage at Sardis; ch. 10. 3) rather than χρόνῳ πολεμεῖν. But circumstances have changed, though the later use of stratagem is not ruled out. Agesilaos rejects Nektanebo's reasoning by recalling his statement of the enemy's numbers (§2); he shows that the enemy, with the advantage of 'many hands', πολυχειρία, is threatening circumvallation. Agesilaos' prediction will be relevant to the enemy's next actions (ch. 39. 9).

All three authorities record disagreement at this stage between Agesilaos and his employer. In the accounts of Plutarch and Xenophon, Agesilaos must consider which of the two contenders for the throne he should serve, while in Plutarch and Diodoros he must decide whether to accompany his nervous employer into a large city, against his better judgement, or to change sides, for either the first or the second time.

Plutarch continues to portray the difficulties that Agesilaos has created for himself, and the hostile attitudes to his leadership. He again reveals judgements indirectly through the characters themselves, and continues his account of Agesilaos' situation now made uncomfortable because of the distrust—another new experience for him. Since Agesilaos was too ashamed to change sides again, evidently he was aware of the 'shame' of having done it once. Again αἰσχύνη is an important trait restraining Agesilaos in the face of possible criticism (cf. chs. 2. 2, 5. 2, 11. 5, 24. 3).

When the sacrifice at Aulis was interrupted (ch. 6. 10–11), Plutarch suggested that Agesilaos feared he would fail to complete the Asia Minor campaign. In the event, completion was forestalled by his recall. Now Agesilaos is made to realize for himself the possibility that nothing may be gained for Sparta even from this expedition. Agesilaos has to suffer humiliation, and accept an unwelcome move. The position differs from that of Pompey, who followed an inferior plan against his better judgement (*Pomp.* 67. 7–8); for Agesilaos is in mercenary service and not even in full command. The unfavourable account continues to the end of the chapter, giving the impression that, once the first unworthy decision had been taken, the downward spiral was relentless.

39. Agesilaos declines still further but reasserts his military superiority

1 Ἐπελθόντων δὲ τῶν πολεμίων καὶ περιταφρευόντων τὴν πόλιν, αὖθις αὖ δείσας τὴν πολιορκίαν ὁ Αἰγύπτιος ἐβούλετο μάχεσθαι, καὶ τοὺς Ἕλληνας μάλα συμπροθυμουμένους εἶχεν· οὐ γὰρ ἦν ἐν τῷ χωρίῳ σῖτος.

In the first part of the chapter Plutarch refers to Nektanebo only as the Egyptian, perhaps bringing Agesilaos into greater prominence, now that the clash with the enemy is imminent. Nektanebo's loss of nerve, brought on by his fear this time (αὖθις αὖ) of siege, leads him to wish to break out, although it was his earlier fear of fighting it out that decided him to enter the city (ch. 38. 5). This reversal of policy discredits Nektanebo's military wisdom, but the anxiety infects the Greeks, who are worried by the shortage of provisions, and now support Nektanebo. Plutarch and Diodoros (xv. 93. 2–5) both record these events, but Diodoros has them after Tachos has rejoined Agesilaos and as part of Nektanebo's failed attempt to become king.

2 ὁ δ᾽ Ἀγησίλαος οὐκ ἐῶν, ἀλλὰ κωλύων, ἤκουε μὲν ἔτι μᾶλλον κακῶς ἢ πρότερον ὑπὸ τῶν Αἰγυπτίων καὶ προδότης ἀπεκαλεῖτο τοῦ βασιλέως, ἔφερε δὲ πρᾳότερον ἤδη τὰς διαβολὰς καὶ προσεῖχε τῷ καιρῷ τοῦ στρατηγήματος.

Agesilaos' nadir has now been reached in preparation for a change of fortune—a dramatic peripeteia. He is now isolated, and in opposition to the Greeks, to Nektanebo, and to the Egyptians. However, the reason for the bitterness is the misunderstanding of Agesilaos' military skill and the value of his advice. Generalship is his main strength and he shows firmness and confidence in the correctness of his judgement, and while his influence is negative it ensures that nothing happens until he wants it to. Nevertheless, even at the point where he will prove his supremacy, Plutarch intensifies the theme of Agesilaos' declining popularity, and, while he recognizes that Agesilaos' strategy is that of a wise general, he does not retract his judgement that his action was a betrayal (ch. 37. 10), and he now attributes this judgement also to the Egyptians; but they are Nektanebo's Egyptians, complaining that Agesilaos has betrayed their king, Nektanebo, by keeping them trapped in the city, where they are starving, as are the Greeks.

The reversal of the downward momentum in Agesilaos' reputation and fortunes is signalled by a difference in his responses to the opposition. Whereas previously his reaction was described in βαρυνόμενος and βαρέως ἔφερεν, perhaps denoting 'disgruntlement', (chs. 37. 2, 38. 6; cf. the use of the phrase of Lysander at ch. 8. 3), he now displays three important qualities once more: he endures the criticism 'more patiently', πρᾳότερον, a characteristic attributed to him at ch. 2. 2; deception serves him well in his handling of his employer, as he bides his time; and, in contrast to the other occasions, he is intellectually alert to the requirements of the καιρός. The phrase τῷ καιρῷ τοῦ στρατηγήματος denotes the two qualities most required, 'creative activity' and 'knowledge of exact timing'.[1] It is here that the contrast between Agesilaos and Pompey, his pair in Plutarch's *Lives*, is perhaps most noteworthy. The two concepts, πραότης and καιρός, play important parts in the culminating stages of both men's final battles. In *Pompey* Caesar's troops were calm (68. 7) while awaiting the right moment (69. 6), and Pompey was defeated. Here Agesilaos trusts his own judgement, stays calm until the right moment comes, and so wins the victory.

ἦν δὲ τοιόνδε. **3** τάφρον ἔξωθεν ἦγον οἱ πολέμιοι περὶ τὸ τεῖχος βαθεῖαν, ὡς παντάπασιν ἀποκλείσοντες αὐτούς.

Diodoros reports (xv. 93. 3; cf. *Mor.* 191 D, 214 F–215 A, Polyain. ii. 1. 22) that the enemy's attempt to take the fortified city by storm was costly, but that the large resources of manpower available made circumvallation feasible. His word, πολυχειρία, was used by Agesilaos (ch. 38. 5): the enemy now prove his military foresight. The stratagem will prove Agesilaos right regarding the ineffectiveness of the enemy's numerical superiority (ch. 38. 2–3).

4 ὡς οὖν ἐγγὺς ἦσαν αἱ τελευταὶ τοῦ ὀρύγματος, ἀπαντῶντος αὐτῷ καὶ περιϊόντος ἐν κύκλῳ τὴν πόλιν, ἑσπέραν ἀναμείνας γενέσθαι καὶ κελεύσας ἐξοπλίζεσθαι τοὺς Ἕλληνας, . . .

All circumvallations must reach this point, and offer the same opportunity to the besieged. Like Plutarch, Diodoros records a night enterprise as the work was being completed, but the timing seems to have been determined by Tachos' desperation because provisions were exhausted (xv. 93. 3). Here Agesilaos deliberately chooses the moment.

. . . ἔλεγεν ἐλθὼν πρὸς τὸν Αἰγύπτιον· Ὁ μὲν τῆς σωτηρίας, ὦ νεανία, καιρὸς οὗτός ἐστιν, ὃν ἐγὼ διαφθεῖραι φοβούμενος οὐκ ἔφραζον πρὶν ἐλθεῖν. **5** ἐπεὶ δ' ἡμῖν οἱ πολέμιοι τὴν ἀσφάλειαν αὐτοὶ διὰ τῶν χειρῶν παρεσκευάκασι, τοσαύτην ὀρυξάμενοι τάφρον, ἧς τὸ μὲν ἐξειργασμένον ἐκείνοις ἐμποδών ἐστι τοῦ πλήθους, τὸ δὲ διαλεῖπον ἡμῖν δίδωσιν ἴσῳ καὶ δικαίῳ μέτρῳ διαμάχεσθαι πρὸς αὐτούς, φέρε νῦν, προθυμηθεὶς ἀνὴρ ἀγαθὸς γενέσθαι καὶ μεθ' ἡμῶν ἐπισπόμενος δρόμῳ σῷζε σεαυτὸν

ἅμα καὶ τὴν στρατιάν. **6** ἡμᾶς γὰρ οἱ μὲν κατὰ στόμα τῶν πολεμίων
οὐχ ὑπομενοῦσιν, οἱ δ' ἄλλοι διὰ τὴν τάφρον οὐ βλάψουσιν.

Agesilaos takes advantage even of the situation that was forced
upon him despite his superior generalship, proving that his
inexperienced enemy has trapped himself, as he foresaw. His
speech displays the quality of his generalship in analysing the
military situation, concealing plans even from his colleague, and
encouraging the faint-hearted. His admission of having used his
characteristic skill in deception even on the young man, still not
named, whom he was serving, and the reason given for doing so,
establish his superiority, and he teaches the lesson that a general
must look out for the καιρός. Diodoros briefly credits Agesilaos
with the rescue of a hopeless situation, but in recording Agesilaos'
speech Plutarch also explains in detail the working of the stratagem.

7 ἐθαύμασεν ὁ Νεκτάνεβις τοῦ Ἀγησιλάου τὴν δεινότητα, καὶ δοὺς
ἑαυτὸν εἰς μέσα τὰ τῶν Ἑλλήνων ὅπλα καὶ προσπεσὼν ἐτρέψατο ῥᾳδίως
τοὺς ἀντιστάντας.

The Egyptian is now named, juxtaposed with the Spartan for
effective contrast, and the two names are framed by the verb and
its accusative. At this point the difference of opinion between the
two is resolved in Agesilaos' favour and his skill is generously
acknowledged. Plutarch again expresses the judgement indirectly
by recording the admiration of Nektanebo. Agesilaos' part was to
plan the enterprise, leaving the younger Nektanebo to carry it out.
He responds to the exhortation, and no action by Agesilaos is
required. The description of the action is accordingly brief, as it is
in Xenophon's version (2. 31).

8 ὡς δ' ἅπαξ ἔλαβε πειθόμενον αὐτῷ τὸν Νεκτάνεβιν ὁ Ἀγησίλαος,
αὖθις ἐπῆγε τὸ αὐτὸ στρατήγημα καθάπερ πάλαισμα τοῖς πολεμίοις.

The Egyptian is again named, and juxtaposed with the Spartan,
but the grammatical relations are reversed in favour of Agesilaos.
Thus Plutarch confirms the rehabilitation of Agesilaos, who
enhances his reputation by repeating the successful stratagem.
Plutarch again uses the technical vocabulary and repeats the
wrestling simile (ch. 38. 4). Having won his employer's confidence
with successful generalship, Agesilaos resumes an active part in
devising the next manoeuvres.

9 τὰ μὲν γὰρ ὑποφεύγων καὶ ὑπάγων, τὰ δ᾽ ἀντιπεριχωρῶν ἐμβάλλει τὸ πλῆθος αὐτῶν εἰς τόπον ἔχοντα διώρυχα βαθεῖαν ἐξ ἑκατέρας πλευρᾶς παραρρέουσαν, ὧν τὸ μέσον ἐμφράξας καὶ καταλαβὼν τῷ μετώπῳ τῆς φάλαγγος, ἐξίσωσε πρὸς τοὺς μαχομένους τῶν πολεμίων τὸ πλῆθος, οὐκ ἔχοντας περιδρομὴν καὶ κύκλωσιν. **10** ὅθεν οὐ πολὺν χρόνον ἀντιστάντες ἐτράποντο· καὶ πολλοὶ μὲν ἀνῃρέθησαν, οἱ δὲ φεύγοντες ἐσκεδάσθησαν καὶ διερρύησαν.

In Diodoros' account, after escaping from the city, Agesilaos is being pursued closely on level ground, and is in danger of being surrounded. He himself then seizes a position between the two canals and awaits the attack (xv. 93. 4), so creating for himself a dangerous situation similar to the one from which he has already extricated his army. However, since this restricts the length of the enemy line to equal Agesilaos', the superior courage of the Greeks gains the victory.

Plutarch omits the Egyptian pursuit of the Greeks, but then gives a more detailed account than Diodoros of the manoeuvres in the space between the canals. Instead of facing outwards, as Diodoros implies, Agesilaos 'drives the enemy force into the position' (ἐμβάλλει), by alternate flank attacks and withdrawals. If the canals were fed from a river, there was evidently water on three sides, making escape difficult for the enemy. This plan runs counter to advice attributed to Lykourgos not to force enemies to fight with desperation for survival (*Lyk.* 13, 22; cf. ch. 26. 5), though Plutarch allows them to disperse at the end. It is also difficult to understand how the enemy could allow themselves to be 'drawn' or 'forced into' this irretrievable position, but Nektanebo has mentioned their great inexperience (ch. 38. 2).

Plutarch's version as a whole has been considered the more acceptable,[2] but if Diodoros' description of this manoeuvre is correct, Plutarch's ἐμβάλλει, 'drove', may be a mistaken attempt to 'improve' it. The version of the stratagem recorded twice with minor variations (*Mor.* 191 C–D, 214 F–215 A) does not mention a second engagement, and neither does Xenophon; in Diodoros' account it is only in the second engagement that the enemy's superior numbers are countered. It may appear that the second use of the stratagem, reversing the situations of escape and capture, is a fictional embellishment.

Plutarch marks the final military success of Agesilaos in this chapter with ornamentation, particularly alliteration of *d*, *p*, *s*, often in clusters, clusters too of words containing the consonants *ph*, *ch*, *m*, *p*, *s*, and rhyme, especially in Agesilaos' speech, and in the exciting account of the second stratagem, which closes with rapid short sentences.

40. The final honours for Agesilaos

1 Ἐκ δὲ τούτου καλῶς μὲν εἶχε τὰ πράγματα καὶ βεβαίως τῷ Αἰγυπτίῳ πρὸς ἀσφάλειαν· ἀγαπῶν δὲ καὶ φιλοφρονούμενος ἐδεῖτο μεῖναι καὶ συνδιαχειμάσαι μετ' αὐτοῦ τὸν Ἀγησίλαον.

Plutarch at last adjudges military success to Agesilaos' mission, as at *Comp.* 4. 7–9, 11; cf. Introd., D.1(*k*). He does not name Nektanebo, perhaps to avoid drawing attention at this point to the abandonment of the original employer Tachos. Just as the Greeks of Asia Minor showed appreciation of Agesilaos' services at ch. 15. 7–8 (cf. Xen. *Agesilaos*, 1. 38), so here he wins 'affection and friendship' (cf. ch. 13. 2–3).

2 ὁ δ' ὥρμητο πρὸς τὸν οἴκοι πόλεμον, εἰδὼς χρημάτων δεομένην τὴν πόλιν καὶ ξενοτροφοῦσαν. προὔπεμψεν οὖν αὐτὸν ἐντίμως καὶ μεγαλοπρεπῶς, ἄλλας τε λαβόντα τιμὰς καὶ δωρεὰς καὶ πρὸς τὸν πόλεμον ἀργυρίου διακόσια καὶ τριάκοντα τάλαντα.

Plutarch, like Xenophon (2. 31), presumably refers to projected campaigns for the recovery of Messenia, but they came to nothing, and Sparta played no major role in Greek affairs for the next few decades. The true purpose of Agesilaos' undertaking, the financing of Sparta's wars, is stated clearly (cf. ch. 36. 1–3), so that the panhellenic and anti-Persian claims are confirmed as empty propaganda. Even if Agesilaos had shown by his choice of service with Nektanebo that he was willing to proceed against the King, it had by then, perhaps, become only a face-saving gesture, now that the divided loyalties of the Egyptian forces and their commanders had made the mounting of any immediate effective aggression unrealistic: and the rebel satraps had also made their peace or had been assassinated (Diod. xv. 91).

Diodoros (xv. 94) recalls the foundation earlier of Megalopolis

(368), which hemmed the Spartans in, and shows how the Megalopolitans attracted a further Theban invasion under Pammenes (*c.*361). He records the attempt, in the Amphiktyonic Council, to fine the Lakedaimonians 500 talents for their seizure of the Kadmeia; the gift of 15 talents made by Archidamos to the Phokians to help them seize control of Delphi; more active co-operation with them, after the fine had been doubled, to have it annulled; and a campaign under Archidamos against Megalopolis (xvi. 23. 3, 24. 2, 29. 2, 39. 1).

Agesilaos receives only a small sum compared with what he had brought back from Asia Minor (ch. 19. 4), and with the 1,500 talents brought by Lysander (Diod. xiii. 106. 8).[1] Nepos records the sum of 220 talents, but Xenophon and Diodoros give no figures. Agesilaos wanted money for war and hiring mercenaries (*Mor.* 214D). One quoted rate of a soldier's pay, perhaps a special case, is 1 drachma per day (Thuc. vii. 27. 2); for a sailor 3 obols (½ dr.) per day, with 30 talents per month for 55 ships (Thuc. viii. 29. 1)—a little over 3 obols per day for each man; and later 1 dr., reduced to 3 obols (Thuc. viii. 45. 2).[2] Xenophon quotes 1 daric per month, becoming 1½ (*An.* i. 3. 21, vii. 6. 1); since at *An.* i. 7. 18 he equates 3,000 darics with 10 talents, 1 daric = 20 dr. [A talent, outside Sicily, was regularly 6,000 dr.; the use of the Attic–Euboic standard may be assumed.] Isokrates says that many men were unemployed (v. 120–2) and negotiations show variation of rates over time and for different ranks: even prospective employers would not be certain of the going rate: 1 drachma per day is a useful base for calculation. Then ½ talent (3,000 dr.) pays 100 men 30 dr. each per month; 60 talents will hire 1,000 men for 12 months; 180 talents will hire an army of 3,000 men for a year, and leave 50 out of 230 talents for higher ranks and supplies. If the rate is halved, 6,000 will be hired.

3 χειμῶνος δ' ὄντος ἤδη, τῆς γῆς ἐχόμενος ταῖς ναυσὶ καὶ παρὰ τὴν Λιβύην εἰς χωρίον ἔρημον κομισθείς, ὃ καλοῦσι Μενελάου λιμένα, θνῄσκει, βιώσας μὲν ὀγδοήκοντα καὶ τέσσαρα ἔτη, βασιλεύσας δὲ τῆς Σπάρτης ἑνὶ τῶν τεσσαράκοντα πλέον, καὶ τούτων ὑπὲρ τριάκοντα πάντων μέγιστος καὶ δυνατώτατος γενόμενος, καὶ σχεδὸν ὅλης τῆς Ἑλλάδος ἡγεμὼν καὶ βασιλεὺς νομισθείς, ἄχρι τῆς ἐν Λεύκτροις μάχης.

The ending of Agesilaos' last foreign campaigning at Menelaos'

Harbour, which Nepos also names, balances the Homeric reference to Agamemnon, at Aulis, on his departure for the first (ch. 6).
Plutarch's assessment of Agesilaos' reign here is a generous one,
and should be compared with that in the *Comparatio* (5. 1–2; see
Introd., D.1(*l*)). The death of Agesilaos is described simply, without mention of his name.

Chronology of the life and reign

The figures for his age, and for the length of his reign, do not
allow certainty in the calculation of relevant dates. The most
secure event is the battle of Leuktra, 371, yet Plutarch's 'more
than thirty years' gives a very early date for his accession (402/1).
The Olympic year in which Agis was insulted would then be 404,
followed by his Eleian wars (Xen. *Hell*. iii. 2. 21–31, Paus. iii. 8.
3–5; cf. Diod. xiv. 17. 4–12, 34. 1) and his death (Xen. *Hell*. iii. 3.
1, Paus. iii. 8. 8). If Agesilaos died exactly forty-one years later,
which seems to be a more clearly documented figure,[3] there would
be insufficient time after Mantineia, 362, for the Egyptian expedition.

The accounts of the Eleian wars are not in agreement: the two
invasions led by Agis (Xenophon) and the one led by Pausanias
(Diodoros) may or may not have been synchronous.[4] Unz adduces
the synchronism of the Eleian wars and the campaigns of
Derkylidas in Asia, 399–397 (Xen. *Hell*. iii. 2. 21), and suggests
three successive campaigns, the third following the death of Agis
early in 400, led by Pausanias in 399. But since the sources do not
refer to an Olympic festival held during the hostilities, Pausanias'
campaign may be placed in the year of Agis' second.[5]

A different chronological argument follows from the report of
Artaxerxes' death (Diod. xv. 93. 1) at about the time of Tachos'
flight and the accession of Nektanebo II, which is placed at about
361/0,[6] providing a date for Agesilaos' Egyptian campaign. The
death of Agis will then be related to the Olympic Games of 400,
allowing time for the Elis campaigns after Pausanias' settlement of
Athens in 403.[7] Agesilaos then lived from 445/4 until 360/59 and
reigned forty-one years from 400/399.[8]

4 ἔθους δ' ὄντος Λακωνικοῦ τῶν μὲν ἄλλων ἐπὶ ξένης ἀποθανόντων
αὐτοῦ τὰ σώματα κηδεύειν καὶ ἀπολείπειν, τὰ δὲ τῶν βασιλέων οἴκαδε

κομίζειν, οἱ παρόντες Σπαρτιᾶται κηρὸν ἐπιτήξαντες τῷ νεκρῷ, μέλιτος οὐ παρόντος, ἀπήγαγον εἰς Λακεδαίμονα.

What happened to the body is biographically a part of the full story of the life. Plutarch records Spartan custom regarding disposal of the dead abroad, giving a clue to the attitude of contemporaries to Agesilaos, in that they did not neglect their normal practice, even in circumstances of unusual difficulty (cf. Xen. *Hell.* v. 3. 19). Although Diodoros says that the body was conveyed home in honey, Nepos mentions that wax was substituted.[9]

5 τὴν δὲ βασιλείαν Ἀρχίδαμος ὁ υἱὸς αὐτοῦ παρέλαβε, καὶ διέμεινε τῷ γένει μέχρις Ἄγιδος, ὃν ἐπιχειροῦντα τὴν πάτριον ἀναλαβεῖν πολιτείαν ἀπέκτεινε Λεωνίδας, πέμπτον ἀπ᾽ Ἀγησιλάου γεγονότα.

The glory of Agesilaos lived on in his descendants and for Plutarch this, too, is part of the full story of his character, reported indirectly. Agis (IV) was of the fifth generation but the sixth king after Agesilaos (*Agis*, 3. 2).[10] Sparta ceased to embody the Lykourgan ideal: it was left for Plutarch to revive it.

EPILOGUE

The final chapter draws the *Life* to a quiet close in Agesilaos' death. Biography, like tragedy, has the advantage over history of clearly defined limits,[1] but, in responding to his reading in the sources for the limited biographical lifespan of Agesilaos, Plutarch also sees it as part of the wider historical landscape. Although he nowhere sets out to link the 'parallel' *Lives* together as a systematic account of the different forms of government,[2] the range of the series of biographies encourages an attempt to discover how he evaluated the constitutions of Sparta, Athens, and Rome, as they developed over time, and how he judged the different leaders' roles in the control of affairs.

Plutarch's *Agesilaos* not only describes the reign of Agesilaos but presents it in larger perspectives, of the extended family, his ancestry (ch. 1), and his descendants (ch. 40), and of Sparta's historical fortunes. His interest was equally in the condition of the Spartan character and constitution during Agesilaos' reign, against the background of Lykourgos' intentions. He admired Sparta's mixed constitution, designed to provide most importantly for political moderation and stability (*Lyk.* 5. 6–8, 7. 1) at a time when its survival depended on a cohesive citizenry, long before the Spartan imperial expansion; and he admired Agesilaos for upholding its standards and defending Sparta. He also saw that in Agesilaos' reign the country was invaded for the first time since the Dorians arrived six hundred years earlier; and he was distressed that Sparta abandoned Lykourgan guidance and declined so far from the great city it was at his accession (ch. 31. 3, 6). As a Boiotian, he also judged that existing historical accounts, too readily favouring the Spartan side, left other cities, judgementally and thematically, disadvantaged. His is a critical response to the main sources, combining favourable and unfavourable judgements.

Of the twenty-three Greek *Lives*, the five Spartan *Lives*, of Lykourgos, Lysander, Agesilaos, Agis, and Kleomenes (counted separately), together contribute to a theme extending from the making of the constitution to the end of its wider influence, the city's βίος; see Introd., B.1(*b*), D.3. The themes of the first two *Lives*—in *Lykourgos*, standards introduced, in *Lysander*, changing attitudes—contributed to the themes of *Agesilaos*. *Lysander* and *Agesilaos* together trace declining standards. The theme of restoration, in *Agis* and *Kleomenes*, completes the cycle: both Agis and Kleomenes attempted reform (*Agis*, 2. 6, 6. 1, 8. 1–2, *Kleom.* 3. 2–4, 10. 6–11. 3) but failed, and suffered violent deaths.

Plutarch offers familiar political and military explanations of historical events, the intellectual decisions of leaders and citizens, but for him, when good things go wrong, there is a prior cause, and so he looks for personal moral excesses to explain the sadness of Sparta's decline. Lysander was ambitious; Agesilaos strained Sparta's resources, largely through his hatred of Thebes; Agis displayed 'mildness' (πρᾳότης) in the superlative degree, πρᾳότατος (*Agis*, 21. 3), Kleomenes did not possess it at all: τὸ πρᾷον οὐκ εἶχεν (*Kleom.* 1. 3), and in the face of opposition the one surrendered, the other was overwhelmed (*Agis–Kleom.* 4. 1). The Spartan decline is blamed on later neglect of Lykourgos' ordinances; but prior flaws were present in his treatment of women and helots, his concentration on military training, and his resort to violence (*Lyk.–Num.* 1. 4, 2. 3, 3. 2–4, 4. 8). Plutarch may not have conceived the full programme from the first, but he presents a consistent and cumulative explanation of this arc of Spartan history.

The Spartan *Lives* may be compared with other Greek and Roman *Lives*. Ten of the Greek *Lives* are Athenian, and similarly present ideological analyses, from the origins of the city (*Thes.* 2. 1, 24–5) to its capitulation to Makedon (*Phok.* 32. 4–5, 33. 3, 36. 4)—its βίος. Plutarch gives no systematic account of Athenian democracy, but these *Lives* offer a view which traces the development of the polarity of Athenian politics which is important for him.[3] Perikles exercised aristocratic control for the best interests of all, and instilled his own wisdom in the *demos* (*Per.* 15. 1–2, 17. 1–4).[4] Alkibiades' luxury and extravagance seduced the *demos* but he betrayed Athens (*Alk.* 16. 1–3, 23. 1–2). Phokion was praised for his virtue: hardy, educated by Plato, gentle (πρᾷος), a successful commander (*Phok.* 1. 2, 4. 1, 6. 2–3, 25. 2, 29. 4). Among the Romans, Numa was praised, as king and philosopher (*Num.* 20.

6–7; cf. Plato, *Resp.* 487 E 2–3). But successes were often marred by circumstances: Numa provided no system of character training (*Lyk.–Num.* 4. 4); *Pompey*, paired with *Agesilaos*, identifies selfish personal ambition and corrupt political life as Rome's self-destructive flaws, despite recognizing military achievement (see Introd., C.3, D.2); and although Perikles and Phokion were personally not flawed, sadly 'the fortunes of Greece' were adverse (*Phok.* 1. 2; cf. *Per.* 39. 5).

The constitutional arrangements in the cities are part of the heroes' fortunes. That Agesilaos failed to respect the Lykourgan constitution completely, while others provided good government under less favoured regimes, indicates that the form of government was for Plutarch less important than individual character in ruler and ruled. The historian of the Greek cities traces decline in their fortunes. The biographer further enables his readers to learn those moral lessons of history which are important for the development of their own individual characters: the improvement of individual character was exactly the elevated practical, moral, and intellectual aim of the biographer (*Aem.* 1. 4–5) as of the essayist.[5] He advocates political concord, not reform or resistance (*Mor.* 824 C), and provides examples of virtue and action, which, for statesman and citizen, are in the context of existing political institutions. Plutarch sets out in prefaces (*Per.* 2. 3, *Aem.* 1. 4–5) that he expects, in the course of a single *Life*, to implant the impulse to a general moral improvement by individual emulation of the better examples or avoidance of the worse (*Dtr.* 1. 6). The focus of his response to his sources is consistently on fulfilment of that expectation.

NOTES

PREFACE

1. Russell (1973), 116.
2. Babut (1969a), (1969b); Russell (1973), 160–3; den Boer (1985); Moles (1988), 35, 40; Hershbell (1992); Momigliano (1971a), (1971b); Nikolaides (1982–4); Podlecki (1987), 6–9; Swain (1989b); Stadter (1992a); Yaginuma (1992); Duff (1994) and (forthcoming).
3. Woodman (1988), 5, 45; cf. Berlin (1980), 103–45; Finley (1985), 51–61.
4. Woodman (1988), 197; Finley (1985), 1–6; cf. Becker (1959); Momigliano (1977); Eadie and Ober (1985).
5. M. Grant (1990); R. M. Cook (1962).
6. MacKendrick (1960), (1962); Elton (1967).
7. Tosh (1991), 112; cf. Carr (1986), 107–8; Oakeshott (1962); Plumb (1988); Walsh (1967); T. P. Wiseman (1979).
8. Cameron (1989).
9. Ibid. 10; cf. Tagliasacchi (1960); Xanthakis-Karamanos (1979), 68–9.
10. Brock (1991), 98, 101.
11. Henderson (1989), 68, 76–8.
12. Plutarch allows himself a degree of flexibility (see Introd., B.2(*b*), E.3(*c*) below).
13. Cf. Gill (1993), 42–3 on the two stages of education in Plato leading finally to 'ethical truth'; cf. *Resp.* 377A, 504 D–E.
14. Cameron (1989), 10.
15. See Introd., n. 62.

INTRODUCTION

1. For the evidence see Ziegler (1951), 636–92 = (1964), 4–60; Jones (1971), 1–64. See also Tzannetatos (1960); Barrow (1967); Tsimpoukides (1987).
2. Jones (1966a); Whittaker (1969), 192; Glucker (1978), 124–5, 256–80; Puech (1992), 4835; Malkin (1994), 158–62 and n. 65.
3. Leo (1901); Ziegler (1951), 692 = (1964), 60; Jones (1966b).
4. Geiger (1974); Swain (1990); cf. Desideri (1992).
5. Jones (1971), 99; Pelling (1986b) = (1995), 319–56.

6. Flacelière (1979); Aalders (1982); Ingenkamp (1992).
7. Bowersock (1969), 57, 112; Jones (1971), 1–64, esp. 34; Russell (1973), 8. The evidence of Eusebios and the *Suda* is discussed critically by Nutton (1971), 271.
8. Brink (1940), 919; Dihle (1956); Stadter (1965), (1992*a*); Russell (1966*a*), (1966*b*), (1967); Dorey (1967); Wardman (1971); Frost (1980), ch. 2, esp. pp. 46–59, with Stadter (1984); van der Valk (1982).
9. Den Boer (1974); Pelling (1980), 135–7 = (1995), 142–6; Frazier (1992), 4530–5; for the fluidity of historiographic genres, Duff (1994), 6–10.
10. Pelling (1988*b*), 40.
11. Cf. Homer, *Il*. iii. 154–8: Helen's impact on the Trojan elders; Thuc. vii. 71. 3: the confusion of the sailors participating in the great battle at Syracuse.
12. Pelling (1988*b*), 40 n. 122.
13. Wardman (1971), 256–8; Schneeweiss (1985), 151–3; Valgliglio (1987), 50–60, (1992), 4051; Woodman (1988), 197–215; on *Pompey*, Moreno (1992), 136–41.
14. Momigliano (1971*a*), 13, 69, 71; Cox (1983).
15. Oliva (1966), (1967); Cozzoli (1978*a*); Schneeweiss (1979); David (1982–3); Piccirilli (1980); Manfredini and Piccirilli (1980).
16. *Arist*. 2. 1–2, *Arist*.–*C.M. Comp*. 3. 1–2, *Agis*, 10. 2–3, *AKl*.–*Gr. Comp*. 2. 3, 5. 3, *Pho*. 20. 2–3, *Phi*. 16. 5, *Kl*. 16. 4–6; cf. *Sol*. 16. 1, 22. 2. Renoirte (1951); Larsen (1954), (1973); Moore (1975); den Boer (1979); Dover (1982); J.-P. Martin (1986); de Blois (1992).
17. Tigerstedt (1965–74), ii. 226–60; Aalders (1982), 33–5, 37–8.
18. Frazier (1992), 4535; Valgliglio (1992), 3992.
19. Valgliglio (1992), 3965–92.
20. Wheeldon (1989), 59–62; T. P. Wiseman (1993) 141; Purcell (1994).
21. Pelling (1990*a*), 35–43, cf. (1980), 129–30 = (1995), 129–32.
22. Duff (1994), xii, 19–23; Pelling (1980), 139 = (1995), 150–1; cf. Gomme (1945), 80.
23. Pearson (1968); Bucher-Isler (1972); Edelmann (1974); Halliwell (1990); Pelling (1990*b*); Frazier (1992), 4511.
24. Geiger (1981); van der Valk (1982); Frazier (1987); Desideri (1992); Georgiadou (1992*a*); Larmour (1992).
25. Constanza (1955); Erbse (1956); Stadter (1975); Pelling (1986*a*), (1988*b*), 18–26; Swain (1988), 343–7, (1992); Luppino Manes (1989).
26. For heroes as moral agents in historical action see Frazier (1992), especially her concluding remarks at 4535.
27. Swain (1992), 102.
28. Hirsch (1985), 45.

29. Russell (1973), 110.
30. Stadter (1988), 276, 283–94.
31. Duff (1994), 21–2.
32. Cf. Stadter (1988), 276 and n. 6.
33. Bremmer (1981); Le Corsu (1981); Salvioni (1982).
34. 'auffällige Ähnlichkeiten im Charakter und im Lebenslauf': Erbse (1956), 399 = (1979), 479.
35. Ibid. 406–14 = 487–95; see also Moles (1988), 20–6.
36. Cf. Pérez Jiménez (1973); Pavis d'Escurac (1981); Vernière (1983); Swain (1989*b*).
37. Plutarch himself illustrates the point in the *Comparatio* (see D. below).
38. Van Vriesland (1961); De Wet (1981); Bengtson (1983), 199–227; Cartledge (1987), with Cawkwell (1987), Lazenby (1989); García Valdés (1990); C. D. Hamilton (1992), 4202–3; Dreizehnter (1975); Heftner (1995).
39. For the theme of the returning general (*Pomp.* 21. 3–4, ch. 19. 5) see Wardman (1974), 93–7; Pelling (1986*b*), 180 = (1995), 344–5.
40. Arist. *EN* 1125^{b}26; H. Martin (1960), 66, 68; Stadter (1975), 81; Romilly (1979), 275–92, (1988*a*).
41. Romilly (1979), 291; cf. 277, 281.
42. Romilly (1979), 279, 292.
43. Williams (1978); Romilly (1979), 282.
44. Frazier (1988).
45. Romilly (1979), 281 n. 4.
46. H. Martin (1960), 72.
47. Plutarch apparently used Theophrastos' lost work, Πολιτικὰ πρὸς τοὺς καιρούς, in his *Praecepta gerendae reipublicae*: see Aalders (1982), 49, 64.
48. Pelling (1986*a*), 83–4.
49. Recent biographies of Pompey in English: Leach (1978); Seager (1979); Greenhalgh (1980), (1981). Titchener (1992), 4147 lists specialist articles.
50. Cf. Cic. *Ad Att.* 10. 4. 3 'exitiabile, nisi vicerit, calamitosum etiam si vicerit': 10. 7. 4 'nisi vincit, nomen populi Romani deleatur necesse est, sin autem vincit, Sullano more exemploque vincet'. For Pompey's early career and treatment of the pirates see Keaveney (1982); Strasburger (1965) = (1982). For his acme at *Pomp.* 46. 1 and his decline from *Pomp.* 67. 4 and after Pharsalos see De Wet (1981), 119, 124–8. Cf. Moreno (1992), 135–41.
51. For 'demonic forces' see Brenk (1977); Halliwell (1990), 55–9.
52. Pelling (1980), 134 = (1995), 140.
53. Ibid. 134–5 = (1995), 140–2.

54. Erbse (1956), 403–6 = (1979), 484–7.

55. Stadter (1975); Pelling (1986a), (1988b), 18–26; Luppino Manes (1989); Valgiglio (1992), 4004, 4022–6; Duff (1994), 148–86.

56. Cf. Valgiglio (1992), 4030.

57. Babut (1969a), 354, 359–62.

58. Vernière (1983).

59. Plato, *Protagoras* 312, Cicero, *Brutus* 30; Romilly (1988b), 26–9, 132–3; contrast chs 5 and 7. See also Babut (1969a), 360–4 on πολιτικὴ ἀρετή; Bowersock (1969), 89–100; Bowie (1970), 4–7 = (1974), 168–71; Guthrie (1971); Russell (1973), 3 n. 6, 6, 12, 144; Stanton (1973), 352–3 nn. 9, 10; Kerferd (1981a), (1981b); Glucker (1988), 488; Wheeler (1988), 5, 16 and ch. 2, esp. 27–8; G. Anderson (1990), 92–4, 106–9, (1993); on moral ambiguity, Duff (1994), ch. 3 (esp. pp. 50, 59) and below, Themes, §3.

60. On Epameinondas see Pausanias, ix. 13. 1–15. 6, thought to be an epitome of the lost *Epameinondas*; Peper (1912), 15 ff.; cf. Shrimpton (1971a); Cawkwell (1972), 254–5; Tuplin (1984).

61. See Pelling (1980), 134 = (1995), 140–2.

62. Pelling (1986a), 88–91, (1992), 30; Duff (1994), ch. 3 (esp. pp. 80–2), ch. 7. 4 (esp. 178–9, 184–6).

63. Swain (1992), 102.

64. De Lacy (1952); Stinton (1975); Pelling (1980), 131–5 = (1995), 133–42; Mossman (1988), 84–5.

65. Stadter (1992b), 48.

66. Cf. Cartledge and Spawforth (1989), 38–58; Campagnano di Segni (1978).

67. Bockisch (1974); C. D. Hamilton (1982a), (1991); Bengtson (1983), 184–98; Cartledge (1987), ch. 21; Valgiglio (1992), 4039–40.

68. C. D. Hamilton (1982a), 68 n. 2, 70, (1991), 10; Tuplin (1993), 53 n. 32.

69. Delebecque (1957), 470; Henry (1967), 107–33; Bringmann (1971); D. H. Kelly (1975), 46–60; Hirsch (1985), 53–5; Tuplin (1993), 53 n. 32.

70. Cf. Hirsch (1985), 51–5.

71. De Laix (1974), 23–5; Perlman (1976), 29–30; Huxley (1979), 51–2; David (1982–3); Sandbach (1982); Schütrumpf (1994). On ὀλιγανθρωπία see Figueira (1986); Cozzoli (1978b); Cartledge (1987), 37–43, 232–4.

72. Ollier (1933–43), i, pp. vii–xi; Delebecque (1957), 194–9, 329–31; Bordes (1982), 165–203.

73. Grube (1935); C. H. Kahn (1963), (1976); Dillon (1988); Coventry (1989).

74. G. Shipley (1993), 18–23; cf. Delbrück (1975); Finley (1968), 154–6,

159–60 = (1981), 34–6, 39–40 = (1986), 171–3, 176–7; Cartledge (1977); Holladay and Goodman (1986); Ceadel (1987), 4–5, 12.

75. Cf. Cartledge (1987), 403.

76. Moretti (1957), 53–198; de Ste. Croix (1972), 355.

77. Westlake (1968), 148–65.

78. Cf. Prentice (1934); Bucher-Isler (1972), 1–68; Stadter (1992*b*).

79. Pelling (1988*a*), 268–74.

80. Lotze (1964); Andrewes (1971), (1978), 99–101; Funke (1980), 33–45; Due (1987); see Bommelaer (1981), 25–53 for a discussion of sources.

81. Bommelaer (1981); Valgiglio (1992), 4003–4.

82. Pelling (1988*a*), 272.

83. Cf. ibid. 269 n. 27.

84. Underhill and Marchant, (1906), pp. xxiv f.; Bommelaer (1981), 24–45, 234–41; Proietti (1987), 12; cf. Westlake (1966), 246–69 = (1969), 203–25, who, reviewing Lengauer (1979), deems only Agesilaos, Epameinondas, and Pelopidas ideal commanders (1981*b*).

85. Bielefeld (1964); Zinserling (1965); Flacelière (1970).

86. Cf. Smith (1948). On harmosts see Bockisch (1965).

87. Ronnet (1981); Proietti (1987), 11–25; cf. Gray (1989), 22–4; Krenz (1989), 145–6; Moles (1994).

88. Westlake (1985*b*); Moles (1994), 74–6, 82–4.

89. Bommelaer (1981), 52–3, cf. 193–7; Westlake (1986*b*).

90. David (1979–80); Bernini (1985). For Sparta's tendency to observe oracles and vulnerability to manipulation see Robinson (1992).

91. Bernini (1985), 233–5.

92. Russell (1966*b*), 151–4; Stadter (1992*b*), 42.

93. Lysander as *mothax*: Phylarchos (*FGrHist* 81 ғ 43); Athenaios, vi. 271e–f; Aelian, *VH* xii. 43; cf. *Kl.* 8. 1. See Lotze (1962) 428–9, 433–5; Oliva (1971), 174–7; Bommelaer (1981), 33, 36–8; Cartledge (1987), 28–9.

94. Pelling (1988*a*), 273–4.

95. Cartledge (1987), 411.

96. Cartledge and Spawforth (1989), 38–42.

97. Demand (1980); Cartledge (1987) on the ἀγωγή (24–33), on patronage (139–59); cf. Williams (1978). The evidence and recent literature on age-groups are discussed by Kukofka (1993); Kennell (1995).

98. Blundell (1989), 26–59; Mitchell and Rhodes (1996).

99. Mosley (1971), 323; Blundell (1989), 47–8, 44–7.

100. Cross and Woozley (1964), 20–2; *Crito*, 49b–c; Xen. *Mem.* iv. 8. 10–11; cf. Blundell (1989), 50–2.

101. Cf. Blundell loc. cit., 50; cf. Woozley (1971).

102. Thuc. iii. 82. 6, viii. 54. 4, 65. 2, analysed in Gomme *et al.* (1945–81), ad locc.

103. Cartledge (1981), 27–9 = (1988), 409–11, (1987), 158–9.

104. Finley (1983), 52–3.

105. Tritle (1992).

106. Cf. Cawkwell (1994).

107. Pelling (1979), 78–9, n. 29 = (1995), 273–4, n. 29, (1980), 136–7 = (1995), 145–6.

108. Aalders (1982), 34.

109. Wheeler (1988), ch. 2, esp. 25–49; Bradford (1994), 59, 76–8, and n. 107.

110. Wheeler (1988), 31.

111. Terms used to distinguish the exceptionally able (ξύνεσις, τὸ ξυνετόν) are listed by Gomme (1956) at Thuc. ii. 15. 2.

112. The verb is taken to mean 'cheat' or 'reckon fraudulently' in the keeping of business accounts (LSJ s.v.).

113. Hirsch (1985), 35.

114. Andrewes (1971), 206–16; Adcock and Mosley (1975), 148–51; Lévy (1976), 204–22; Perlman (1976), 18–19; Walser (1984); Nikolaides (1986); Sancisi-Weerdenburg (1987); Tuplin (1993), 56–60; Austin (1993), 203–12; H. A. Kahn (ed.) (1994).

115. J. M. Cook (1962), 139–40; Momigliano (1979), 141.

116. Jüthner (1923); Walser (1967), (1975); Asheri (1983); on hellenocentricity see Cartledge (1987), 184–5, 194; Hornblower (1990a).

117. Briant suggests the true aim of the two men's expeditions was 'une gigantesque entreprise de pillage' rather than reprisals and liberation (1977), 30–5. Philip, Alexander's father, had planned an eastern campaign: he had experienced Persian intervention in 340 in Byzantium and Perinthos, and had been urged by Isokrates (*Philip.* 5) to unite Greece and avenge Persian wrongs. The security of his kingdom, against neighbours in Greece and on the eastern frontier, was served by his plan, the starting-point of Alexander's own action. Cf. J. R. Hamilton (1973), 27, 35, 38–40. The emotional appeal might serve to win some support.

118. Hall (1989), 37.

119. Ibid. 68.

120. Ibid. 2.

121. Ibid.

122. Ibid. 80; Cartledge (1995).

123. Perlman (1976), 12–14.

124. Or Persians: Brommer (1967), 191–5.

125. Boardman (1977), 40–7, (1993), 108, 113–14; Barron (1981), 95–6; Boardman and Finn (1985), 250.

126. Hall (1989), 2, 16. I am grateful to Dr L. A. Holford-Strevens, who in a personal communication made helpful and constructive comments on panhellenism at several points here.
127. Jüthner (1923), 13–28. For references in Plato see Vourveris (1966).
128. Hirsch (1985), ch. 6 and *passim*, reviewed by Hornblower (1988).
129. Coventry (1989), 4–14.
130. *Menexenos*, an enigmatic work, is interpreted differently: Jüthner (1923), 22–5; C. H. Kahn (1963); Vourveris (1966); Hirsch (1985), 142–7.
131. Cawkwell (1979), 39–41; Tuplin (1993), 67, 76; Moles (1994), 76.
132. Sakellariou (1980), 129–34.
133. Austin (1993), 203, 211–12.
134. Perlman (1976), 5, 19–23; Sakellariou (1980), 129–34.
135. Cf. Payrau (1971); Hirsch (1985), 3–4; Cartledge and Spawforth (1989), 19.
136. Plutarch exaggerates in suggesting 70 at *Mor.* 328 E; J. R. Hamilton (1973), 160. See now Fraser (1996).
137. See now Cawkwell (1994).
138. For the importance of the tradition in Roman times see Spawforth (1994).
139. Cauer (1847); Gomme (1945), 54–61; Bos (1947), vi–xx; C. D. Hamilton (1992), 4208–9.
140. Hertzberg (1856); Hatzfeld (1930), (1933); Breitenbach (1966), (1967); Ríos Fernández (1979), (1984), 43–9, 66–7; Sorum (1984), (with bibliographies); Cartledge (1987), 55–6, Appendix; Tuplin (1993), 193–7, 199–200.
141. Barber (1935); Drews (1963), (1976).
142. Delebecque (1957); Drews (1962); Breitenbach (1967); Rice (1974), (1975); Gray (1980), (1987); Westlake (1985*a*), (1986*a*), (1986*b*).
143. Geiger (1985), (1988); Ríos Fernández (1984), 49, 66–7.
144. Walker (1908); Gomme (1954); Botha (1980), (1988); Bruce (1967), 77–96, 118–27, 132–56; Jacoby (1950), 1–11; Bartoletti (1959); Breitenbach (1970); McKechnie and Kern (1988); Tuplin (1993). Chapters are numbered I–XVII, as in Grenfell and Hunt's edition (1908) of the London papyrus; Bartoletti (1959), McKechnie and Kern (1988), and Chambers (1993) add this numeration in parenthesis.
145. Tuplin (1984).
146. Hirsch (1985), 51–2; Cartledge (1987), 55, 66–71.
147. Delebecque (1957), 462–70; Hirsch (1985), 45–9; cf. Ríos Fernández (1984), 70.
148. Ríos Fernández (1984), 45–6.
149. Hart (1982), 94. Riedinger (1993), 527–33, argues that Xenophon

used no direct Theban source, but only hostile intermediaries.
150. Cawkwell (1979), 35; Ríos Fernández (1984), 47–8 and *passim*.
151. Ríos Fernández (1984), 46–8.
152. Delebecque (1957), 171–3.
153. For Timotheos see Page (1962), fr. 791 = (1968), fr. 425.
154. Connor (1968); Shrimpton (1991); Flower (1994).
155. Kebric (1977).
156. Ollier (1933–43), ii. 589.
157. See Andrewes (1981), on Thuc. viii. 73. 3.
158. Donini (1986); Puech (1992).
159. Buckler (1992).
160. Westlake (1977); Pauw (1980).
161. On the historians see further Hornblower (1994*b*), 7–54.

CHAPTER 1

1. Stadter (1988), 275.
2. Momigliano (1971*a*), 11; Jenkinson (1967), 3–6; Gossage (1967), 47–8.
3. Halliwell (1990), 47.
4. Hornblower (1982*a*), 174–5; Kienitz (1953), 95, 156–7, 175.
5. For further discussion see Cartledge (1987), 21.
6. The Eurypontid and Agiad royal families repeat these three names, beginning with Archidamos I (c.660–645), and add the similar Archelaos (c.785–760) and the later Agesipolis. For possible political significance see Cartledge (1987), 23, with Sergent (1976); Forrest (1968), 21–2; and see below, ch. 20. 7.
7. For Zeuxidamos see Hdt. vi. 71. 1–2.
8. Lampito (Hdt. vi. 71. 1–2), daughter of King Leotychidas and step-aunt of Archidamos, 'Shiner': λαμπάς, Λαμπετίη, Λάμπος (Aurora's horse); cf. ch. 19. 10, Cartledge (1987), 149. Aristophanes named a Spartan lady Lampito in *Lysistrata*.
9. See ch. 21 n. 13.
10. Redfield (1977/8); Le Corsu (1981); Demand (1994), ch. 7.
11. Cartledge (1987), 22.
12. Page (1953), fr. 5*a* = (1962), fr. 664*a* = (1968), fr. 400*a*; Demand (1982), 104–5.
13. Demand (1982), 98–102.
14. Campbell (1988), 263, 268–9, 360–9, 434–7 (fr. 59).
15. Demand (1982), 110, 113–14; cf. 127–30 and Appendix, especially on Pythagorean influence in Thebes.
16. Salvioni (1982).

17. Bremmer (1981).
18. Cartledge (1987), 100–2, 336–8.
19. Bordes (1982), 181–4.
20. Ollier (1934), vii–xi; Tazelaar (1967); Forrest (1968), 51; Bordes (1982), 168–71, 171–6; Hodkinson (1983), 241–3, 245–51; Figueira (1984); Cartledge (1987), 56, ch. 3; Kukofka (1993). For a new diachronic approach to the ἀγωγή see Kennell (1995), who shows (pp. 113–14, 115–16) that the name is owed to the Hellenistic period, having never been used in the 5th and 4th cc. to denote the traditional Spartan education system (cf. *Mor.* 235 B), and attempts (pp. 29–30, 31, 107–9, 116–32; cf. 32–9) to clarify the age-groups.
21. Hodkinson (1983), 251–4. The technical term was probably the Doric συσκανία (Xen. *Hell.* 5. 3. 20), but φιδίτιον and φιγίτιον are found (*Lyk.* 12. 1; cf. Xen. *Lak. Pol.* 5. 2, 3–4, 6, *Hell.* 5. 4. 28; Arist. *Pol.* 1271ª27).
22. Russell (1973), 42–62.
23. Cf. Vermeule (1979), 101, 235 n. 22; Cartledge (1987), 23.
24. Stadter (1988), 290.
25. Andrewes (1938), 89–91, 102; Gomme (1945), ad loc.; Piccirilli (1984).
26. H. Martin (1961), 167, 174 and bibliography; Romilly (1988a), 223.
27. See Bucher-Isler (1972), 67–8; Gill (1983), 469–70, 474; Pelling (1988a), 257 and n. 3.
28. Schwartz (1951), 83–6; Lévy (1976), 92–107, 164–90; Romilly (1988b), 45–52, 113–16, 148–52.
29. Bateman (1958), 283.
30. Cf. Sandbach (1975), 14, 31–7, 53–4; Rawson (1969), 90.
31. See H. Martin (1960), 72–3.
32. Halliwell (1990), 46–9.
33. Cf. Aalders (1982), 45–6.
34. Bordes (1982), 179–81.
35. Gill (1983), 473–4.
36. Lazenby (1985), 7–10, 20–5.
37. Ibid. 3–5.
38. Aalders (1973), 6, (1982), 10–11.
39. De Ste. Croix (1972), 359–62, 371–6, (1981), 285, sect. E; Hornblower (1991), 37, 119–20.
40. Finley (1983), 1–2, 102, 106–10, and esp. ch. 6.
41. Todd (1993). It was fear of Sparta that brought the two Athenian generals to trial after the liberation of Thebes (Xen. *Hell.* v. 4. 19), and Diodotos insisted that state interest should override justice (Thuc. iii. 44. 1–3, 46. 4, 47. 5).
42. Finley (1983), 12–14.

CHAPTER 2

1. Bucher-Isler (1972); Gill (1983, 1984, 1990); Pelling (1988*a*), (1990*c*); Swain (1989*a*); Halliwell (1990); Ingenkamp (1992).
2. Pelling (1990*c*), 218–20.
3. Cf. Pelling (1988*a*), 257–63; (1990*c*), 235–40.
4. Valgiglio (1992), 3992–6.
5. Cf. Gill (1983), 469–72.
6. Ibid. 477; Swain (1989*a*).
7. For the ἀγελαι, boys' troops, see on ch. 1. 2.
8. *FGrHist* 81 F 43.
9. Cf. Lotze (1962), 428–9; Bommelaer (1981), 33, 36–8.
10. For the terminology see Adkins (1960), 6–7.
11. Buffière (1980); Cartledge (1981); Dover (1978, 1980, 1988); Hodkinson (1983), 245–6; H. Martin (1984).
12. See Dover (1988), 117, 118.
13. Buffière (1980), 605–17; Cartledge (1981), 22 = (1988), 395–6.
14. Hodkinson (1983), 246.
15. Cartledge (1981), 36 n. 78 = (1988), 410 n. 78.
16. Hodkinson (1983), 252–3, citing Xen. *Lak. Pol.* 3. 5; *Lyk.* 12. 6.
17. Cartledge (1981), 28–9 = (1988), 410–11.
18. Dover (1980), 4.
19. Dover (1978), 191, 202.
20. Cartledge (1981), 24, 29 = (1988), 399, 410–12.
21. Dover (1988), 118.
22. φιλόνικος: see LSJ; Pelling (forthcoming), nn. 78–9.
23. H. Martin (1960). For the wider context and Plutarch's rich related vocabulary see Romilly (1979), (1988*a*).
24. Halliwell (1990), 44–9.
25. For further evidence see below, ch. 3. 8.
26. Gill (1983), 470–1, (1990), 1–5.
27. Cf. C. D. Hamilton (1991), 7–39.
28. Georgiadou (1992*b*), 4617–19.
29. Ducat (1974); David (1989), (1992).
30. Cf. Georgiadou (1992*b*), 4618–20.
31. Frazier (1988).
32. Cartledge (1981), 26, 28 = (1988), 404–5, 410–12; Hodkinson (1983), 248.
33. Wardman (1967), 414–20; Cartledge (1987), 86; Georgiadou (1988), (1992*b*), 4616, 4619–23.
34. Wardman (1967), 417; Cartledge (1987), 418; Mossman (1991).
35. Pelling (1990*a*), 42–3.

CHAPTER 3

1. See Luria (1927); Smits (1939) on *Lys.* 22. 6; Hatzfeld (1951);
   Littman (1969), (1970); Bengtson (1983), 186; Zoepffel (1985); C. D.
   Hamilton (1991), 26–9. For Latychidas, Poralla (1985), no. 489.
2. See on 'Literary evidence', §9.
3. Hatzfeld (1951), 217–18.
4. Westlake (1938), 33–5; but cf. Hatzfeld (1951), 214 n. 1; Andrewes
   (1981) on Thuc. viii. 12. 2.
5. Kebric (1977); G. Shipley (1987), 124 n. 56, including epigraphic
   evidence that other Samians claimed similar descent.
6. Andrewes (1981) on Thuc. viii. 6. 3; Wallace (1970), 197 n. 12. The
   Spartan use of the suffix appears in the names Eurybiades and
   Polybiades (Poralla (1985), nos. 60, 317–18, 624–5; cf. Hdt. viii. 2. 2,
   Xen. *Hell.* v. 3. 20).
7. Ducat (1974), (1990), with Whitby (1992); Oliva (1961), (1971),
   (1975), (1981); Cozzoli (1978*b*); Garlan (1982); Cartledge (1993),
   129–32, and 140 citing this passage.
8. Pelling (1990*a*), 41–3, 50–2; Larmour (1992), 4165–7.
9. Poralla (1985), nos. 60, 264, 743; Kebric (1976).
10. Bos (1947), 38; Littman (1969) 270, (1970), 269–70.
11. Bommelaer (1981), 151–60; see 154 n. 225 for the reading Thasos at
    Lys. 19. 2.
12. Tuplin (1993), 53, adding *Kim.* 16. For Spartan resort to oracles see
    Robinson (1992), 131–2; cf. Brenk (1977); Holladay and Goodman
    (1986); Babut (1988).
13. Plutarch records that Alexander was proclaimed King of Asia,
    perhaps by the Army Assembly of Makedon (*Alex.* 34. 1); Granier
    (1931); J. R. Hamilton (1969), ad loc., (1973), 84–5; Lévy (1978),
    218–21; Cartledge (1987), 111–12.
14. Cartledge (1987), 111, cf. Kahrstedt (1922), 134; de Ste. Croix
    (1972), 350–3 lists the evidence.
15. *Pace* D. H. Kelly (1975), 42–3.
16. *Pace* Cartledge (1987), 96.
17. Cf. Tuplin (1993), 53.
18. D. H. Kelly (1975), 46–60; Tuplin (1993), 53 n. 32.
19. Littman (1969), 273–7, (1970), 269, 275–6.
20. Cartledge (1976*a*). Pausanias reports an earthquake in 401 in which
    Agis was also involved, perhaps still in people's minds (iii. 8. 3).
21. D. H. Kelly (1975), 46–9.
22. Parke (1945).
23. C. D. Hamilton (1970), 294–314, (1979), 79–88; Forrest (1981).

CHAPTER 4

1. Lazenby (1985), 16–19.
2. See Hodkinson (1983, 1986a, 1989, and 1994) for clear expositions; Asheri (1963); Bringmann (1980); Ducat (1983).
3. Hodkinson (1983), 243, (1989), 79, 80, 114.
4. Moretti (1957), 53–198; de Ste. Croix (1972), 332, 354–5; Desideri (1985), (1986).
5. On Aristotle and Sparta see Ollier (1933–43), i. 294–326; Tigerstedt (1965–74), i. 289–304; de Laix (1974); Huxley (1979), 51–2; David (1982–3).
6. Asheri (1961); Butler (1962); Christien (1974); Lévy (1977); Marasco (1980); Poralla (1985), no. 276; Schütrumpf (1987).
7. Forrest (1968), 135–7; Schütrumpf (1987), (1994), 339; Hodkinson (1994), 184–214.
8. Bloch (1940).
9. MacDowell (1986), 93, 106.
10. But see den Boer (1954); Oliva (1966), (1967); Cozzoli (1978a), 89–93; Marasco (1978).
11. MacDowell (1986), 98–9.
12. Hodkinson (1986a), 404–5.
13. Lazenby (1985), 19.
14. Cf. Christien (1974); Marasco (1980); Schütrumpf (1987).
15. Hodkinson (1986a), 378–86, esp. 384–5.
16. Ibid. 400 and n. 103; but cf. 384.
17. A lacuna in the text there has been filled with Plutarch's ἴσχυε πλεῖστον.
18. Cloché (1949).
19. Thomas (1974), 263; Andrewes (1966), 9–10.
20. Forrest (1968), 77; Cartledge (1987), 103, 125.
21. Cartledge (1987), 106, 125.
22. Finley (1968), 144–5 = (1981), 25–6 = (1986), 162–3.
23. Hodkinson (1983), 264, 267–8, 281.
24. Ibid. 273–6.
25. Forrest (1968), 76.
26. Bommelaer (1981), 160–2.
27. Cartledge (1987), 109.
28. More precise details of such gifts are given at *Mor.* 482 C; Cartledge (1987), 154.
29. Sahlins (1974), 133, 149–83.
30. De Ste. Croix (1972), 132, 349–54.
31. Hodkinson (1983), 263–4; Cartledge (1987), ch. 9.

CHAPTER 5

1. Romilly (1979), 282.
2. Blundell (1989), 26–59 gives other references.
3. Ibid. 28.
4. Cf. Arist. *Pol.* 1265^{b}31–66^{a}2, who elsewhere (*Pol.* 1270^{b}17–18, 1293^{b}20, 1294^{b}20–35) records the predominance of oligarchic or democratic elements in Sparta. Aalders (1982), 36; Bordes (1982), 190–8, 280–95; Cartledge (1987), 116–19.
5. Cartledge (1987), 154.
6. Hodkinson (1983), 242–6.
7. Finley (1968), 152–3 = (1981), 32–3 = (1986), 169–70; Cartledge (1979), 97–8, (1992), 52; Lazenby (1985), 16–21; Ducat (1990); G. Shipley (1992).
8. Lewis (1977), 32; Finley (1968), 152 = (1981), 32 = (1986), 169.
9. So astronomers illuminate the moderate constitution: ὥσπερ οὖν τὸν ἥλιον οἱ μαθηματικοὶ λέγουσι (*Phok.* 2. 4–6).
10. Forrest (1967), (1968), 59–60.
11. Hussey (1972), 1; Kerferd (1981*a*); Kirk *et al.* (1957–83).
12. Hussey (1972), 20–3, 41, 48–50.
13. Ibid. 130–3.
14. Ibid. 73–5, cf. 38–40.
15. Ibid. 123–5. See *Vors.* 31 B 14, 81–90, 131, 210–16, 217–46 DK; *PPF* 48–74.
16. Hussey (1972), 131.
17. Lewis (1977), 32.
18. Hussey (1972), 134–40.
19. De Laix (1974), 27.
20. It is attributed by some to Chilon of Sparta, the 6th-c. sage and later one of the Seven Sages (Plato, *Prt.* 343 B; Arist. *Rh.* 1389^{b}4; Cartledge (1987), 107; cf. Hodkinson (1994), 190).
21. Russell (1973), 67–8, quoting *Mor.* 1086 C, 1107 D, and 1128.
22. Ibid. 8; Aalders (1982), 54–5.
23. Cawkwell (1976*a*), 71, 75–7, 80–4.

CHAPTER 6

1. David (1979*a*), (1981); Gómez Espelosín (1990); Cartledge (1993), 130–1.
2. For Plutarch's practice of selection see *Nik.* 1. 4–5, *Alex.* 1. 1–3.
3. Judeich (1892); J. M. Cook (1962), 137, 140, (1983); Lewis (1958),

397, (1977), 141–2 and nn.; Robert (1966); J. K. Anderson (1974*b*), 146–62; Seager (1977); Hornblower (1994*a*).

4. See Bommelaer (1981), 181–2 for a discussion of his motives.
5. Westlake (1966), 260–9 = (1969), 216–25; Moles (1994), 72–3, 77, 83; see Introd., E. 3(*a*–*b*).
6. In this form the word hereinafter refers to the King of Persia.
7. Hornblower (1991), 181–90.
8. Forrest (1968), 120.
9. G. Shipley (1987), 131–2.
10. Cartledge (1987), 90–3.
11. Bommelaer (1981), 124–6; cf. Andrewes (1971), 206–16.
12. See Pelling (1990*a*), 38–41, on 'rearrangement'.
13. Blundell (1989), 44–8.
14. Thompson (1973), 50.
15. Gomme *et al.* (1945–81), on Thuc. ii. 85. 1 in 429, iii. 69. 1 in 427, and v. 63. 4 in 418, viii. 39. 2 in 412–411.
16. Andrewes (1978), 99.
17. Oliva (1971), 165–71; Alfieri Tonini (1975); Lazenby (1985), 14, 42, 47.
18. Cloché (1949), 133; Forrest (1968), 76–7 and *passim*; de Ste. Croix (1972), 138–48; Thomas (1974), 258–62; Cartledge (1987), 99–159.
19. Cf. Finley (1977), 51.
20. Hall (1989), 23.
21. Demand (1982), 12, 62–3.
22. Crusius (1905), 760–88.
23. Demand (1982), 2–3, 48–52, 126.
24. Brenk (1977), 16, 20 with n. 9, 55 with nn. 7–8, and ch. 10; Bommelaer (1983).
25. Jameson (1991), 200–3.
26. Brenk (1975), (1977), 20, 55 with nn. 7–8.
27. Wall *et al.* (1986).
28. Jameson (1991), 200, 204.
29. Brenk (1977), 55–7.
30. Ibid., ch. 4.
31. Cloché (1918), (1952); Larsen (1955*a*), (1968), 178–9; *Hell. Ox.* XI. 2–4 (Bruce (1967), 102–5 with 157–64); Buck (1972), (1979), 154; Buckler (1980*a*), 23; P. Salmon (1981); Stanton (1982); M. L. Cook (1988). For Boiotia see Bintliff (1985); Bintliff and Snodgrass (1985); Schachter (1986).
32. De Lacy (1952); Walbank (1955), (1960); Tagliasacchi (1960); Stinton (1975); Hornblower (1994*b*), 44–5.
33. Brenk (1977), 55 n. 7.

CHAPTER 7

1. Bommelaer (1981), 182–4.
2. Cf. Finley (1968), 151 = (1981), 32 = (1986), 169.
3. D. H. Kelly (1975), 71ff.
4. 'Oligarchs' in a political rather than aristocratic sense; definition of their class is difficult to establish (Lewis (1977), 116 with n. 57).
5. For the earliest preserved Greek map see Johnston (1967), esp. pl. IX; *CAH*, vol. of plates 2. 6.
6. Börker (1980), 72; Wesenberg (1981), 178–9; Cartledge (1987), 5; Tuplin (1993), 56; cf. ch. 14. 2.
7. See Pelling (1990*a*), 35–43.
8. Pelling (1988*a*), 272.
9. The Samians decreed that their festival in honour of Hera should be called the Lysandreia: Homann-Wedeking (1965), 440; G. Shipley (1987), 133–4.
10. Fuhrmann (1964).

CHAPTER 8

1. Smits (1939), 221–2, referring to the parallel passage in Xenophon (*Hell.* iii. 4. 9).
2. Bos (1947), 64–5.
3. Proietti (1987), 96–101. Plutarch describes Lysander's honourable death and burial: *Lys.* 28. 5, 29. 3; Westlake (1985*b*), 121–3.
4. For the royal lines of Sparta see Forrest (1968), 19–22; Thomas (1974); Lazenby (1985), 64–8. For full Spartan citizens (Σπαρτιᾶται, Spartiates) see Hodkinson (1983), 241: at *Lak. Pol.* 5. 3 they existed before the Lykourgan constitution. Lysander's 'plot': C. D. Hamilton (1979), 92–6; Bommelaer (1981), 223–5.
5. Cawkwell (1983), 397–400; Cartledge (1987), 407, and see below, on ch. 20.
6. The order is reversed, in a chiastic pattern.
7. Cross and Woozley (1964), 54–5.
8. Krentz (1995), 185 n. 7; Keen (1996), 290 and n. 43.
9. *Vors.* 88 B 7 DK. Cf. ch. 5 n. 20 above.
10. See also Dover (1974).
11. Cf. Hodkinson (1994), esp. 188–95; Courcelle (1974), i. 83–95; cf. *Mor.* 1107 D–1127 (17, 20).

CHAPTER 9

1. Riedinger (1993), 518–23.
2. Ibid. 521.
3. Hornblower (1991), 185 n. 3, 192–3.
4. D. H. Kelly (1975), 25, 80.
5. Westlake (1981a), 265 and nn. 27–8.
6. J. M. Cook (1962), 137, 140, (1983), 217; Lewis (1958), 397, (1977), 141; Burn (1985); Cartledge (1987), 181, 185–6; Ray (1987), (1992), 39; Hornblower (1994a). See below, ch. 36.
7. Briant (1977), 51–2; Lane Fox (1973), 118–20.
8. Westlake (1981a), 259.
9. Gray (1979), 188–9.
10. Pelling (1988b), 232 on *Ant.* 43. 2; on ἄσμενος see Frazier (1992), 451 n: 'la coloration psychologique'.
11. Hofmann–Szantyr (1965), 826.
12. Arist. *NE* i. 1. 4; Wheeler (1988), 2 n. 4, 41–2.
13. Riedinger (1993), 519, 522.
14. Cf. Blundell (1989), 28.
15. See Denniston (1939), 151.
16. Cobet (1878), defended by Bos (1947), 71.
17. D. H. Kelly (1975), 25, 80; see also Grote (1869), ix. 81.

CHAPTER 10

1. The texts do not contain evidence leading to conclusive arguments on the battle. For modern controversies over the facts of the battle of Sardis and their interpretation, see note following ch. 10. 11.
2. Pelling (1990a), 35, 42–3; Gill and Wiseman (1993).
3. Rühl (1913), 176.
4. J. K. Anderson (1974a), 51. The tombstone of Flavinus, standard-bearer in the *ala Petriana* (Richmond (1951), 72) shows an infantry-man apparently attacking a cavalryman from below. Cf. the memorial of Dexileos son of Lysanias, of Thorikos, in the Kerameikos Cemetery at Athens, and National Archaeological Museum, Exhibit 3708, the base of an early 4th-c. grave-stele found near Plato's Academy. See Spence (1993), 111–13 and pls. 2, 13.
5. J. K. Anderson (1974a), 50.
6. Bruce (1967), 84.
7. Lewis (1977), 151; Westlake (1981a), 277.
8. Westlake (1981a), 270.
9. Ibid. 272.

10. The phrase supports taking διαλυσάμενον here as 'abandon' the expedition, not 'conclure un accord', 'make terms' (Flacelière and Chambry (1973); Perrin (1917), Scott-Kilvert (1973), ad loc.).

11. Subventions of money from the Persians had been acceptable in principle to 5th-c. Spartans, both in peacetime and as allies in war (Thuc. i. 82. 6, ii. 7. 1, 67. 1, iv. 50. 1–2).

12. Bruce (1967), 86.

13. J. K. Anderson (1974a), 28, cf. 53.

14. Bruce (1967), 97–102.

15. J. K. Anderson (1974a), 53.

16. West (1988), 42–7; T. Kelly (1985).

17. For discussions of the topography and the battle see: Dugas (1910); Rühl (1913); Kaupert (1924–31), (1926a); Cornelius (1933); Bruce (1967); Breitenbach (1970); Nellen (1972); J. K. Anderson (1974a); Cawkwell (1976a); Foss (1979); Gray (1979); Botha (1980), (1988); Tuplin (1986); Cartledge (1987); De Voto (1988).

18. Kaupert (1924–31), 275–80, (1926a); cf. Foss (1979), 27–49; Botha (1980), 56–60, (1988), 72–7; personal visit, 1987.

19. Xenophon indicates that plains here were cultivated (Hell. iii. 2. 17).

20. Kaupert (1926a), map 8; J. K. Anderson (1974a), 29.

21. J. K. Anderson (1974a), 38.

22. Dugas (1910), 62, 64; Breitenbach (1970), 393–6; J. K. Anderson (1974a), 38, 40–1 n. 54; Foss (1979), 22. Cf. Botha (1988), 77.

23. J. K. Anderson (1974a), 49.

24. Rühl (1913), 176.

25. Dugas (1910), 60, 62.

26. Rühl (1913), 161.

27. Bruce (1967), 77–8.

28. Gray (1979), 193; cf. Nellen (1972), 47–52; Botha (1988), 77.

29. Tuplin (1986), 56.

30. Hornblower (1994a), 70–1 suggests that Xenophon suppressed the ambush as representing a 'stolen victory'.

31. Bruce (1967), 77–84, 150–6.

32. Ibid. 82–3, 150.

33. But see Botha (1988), 74–5.

34. Bruce (1967), 152; Cawkwell (1976a), 66–7.

35. Bruce (1967), 86.

36. Cornelius (1933), 1; Nellen (1972), 52.

37. Bruce (1967), 152.

38. Nellen (1972), 45–54; J. K. Anderson (1974a), 51–3; Gray (1979), 186, 195–6.

39. Bruce (1967), 83–4, 150.

40. J. K. Anderson (1974a), 47–8.

41. Bruce (1967), 82.
42. Ibid. 82–4.
43. Gray (1979), 186, 197.
44. Cartledge (1987), 215.

CHAPTER 11

1. For Agesilaos' strategy see Seager (1977); D. H. Kelly (1978); West-lake (1986*b*). Xenophon has the name Kotys at *Agesilaos*, 3. 4, but Otys at *Hell.* iv. 1. 3–15. The Oxyrhynchos historian has Gyes (XVII. 1–3; Bruce (1967), 142–5). Theopompos (*FGrHist* 115 F 179) and Aelian (*VH* i. 27) name a Paphlagonian king Thys, and Nepos (*Datames*, 2–3) has Thuys, descended from the Homeric Paphlagonian Pylaimenes (*Il.* 2. 851), though in different contexts. The spellings are discussed by Eduard Meyer (1877), 26; Grenfell and Hunt (1908), 241; McKechnie and Kern (1988), 181. Robert (1963), 449–57, adds epigraphical evidence for Thys, including the form Tys (454–5), demonstrating that it was a name used by Paphlagonians, but that people took names across borders. The spelling Kotys perhaps arose from confusion with Kotys, the king of Thrace, 384–59 (*Mor.* 174 D; Dem. *Aristokrates*, 129, 163; Nepos, *Iphicrates*, 3. 4; Beloch (1912–27), iii/2. 87–91; Herzfeld (1948–9), ii. 7), but no transliteration of the name into Greek can be certain (Bruce (1967), 143). The variant Tys transmitted orally as Otys might become Kotys by literary analogy. If Otys and Kotys are identical with the man represented by Thuys and Θῦς, the satrap was the large, fierce-looking great eater of Nepos and Theopompos.
2. Polybios (iii. 7) minimizes the scale of the military operation.
3. Eduard Meyer (1898–1956), iii. 150; Beloch (1912–27), iii/2. 145–6; Bruce (1967), 146.
4. Burn (1985), 327, 333, 338–9; Hallock (1985), 588–90, 591–2.
5. Lewis (1977), 8, 52; Andrewes (1981), 18; Hornblower (1982*a*), 173 n. 20.
6. Perlman (1964), 76–7, 81; Hornblower (1991), 185.
7. Gray (1981), 321–24, (1989), 49–52.
8. Bruce (1967), 144.
9. Ibid. 146–8.
10. Poralla (1985), no. 349.
11. Cartledge (1987), 375.
12. Lewis (1977), 151 n. 107.
13. I owe this observation to Dr L. A. Holford-Strevens. For other survivals see Walcot (1996).

14. Gill (1983), 471–3 (1990).
15. Bruce (1967), 138–9.
16. I owe this observation to Dr L. A. Holford-Strevens.
17. 'A miraculous cure for his lameness': Hindley (1994), 362.
18. Conj. Reiske (1774–82).

CHAPTER 12

1. *FGrHist* 115 F 21.
2. McKechnie and Kern (1988), 10, 178; Gray (1989), 56.
3. Gray (1981), 324–6.
4. Adcock and Mosley (1975), 62–9; Herman (1987), 44–7.
5. Lewis (1977), 30.
6. Bos (1947), 86.
7. Hall (1993), 130: 'Asia's feminine configurations were thus fundamental to the Athenians' conceptualization of their historic enemy.'
8. Ibid. 116, 119–20.
9. Herman (1987), 1–3.
10. Blundell (1989), 48.
11. Ibid. 50.
12. Hornblower (1982), 19 n. 109.
13. Cf. de Ste. Croix (1972), 63–5; Pomeroy (1994), 241 n. 72.
14. Cf. Aesch. *PV* 341.
15. Lewis (1977), 154 with n. 123.

CHAPTER 13

1. Perlman (1958); Herman (1987), 58–60.
2. Hirsch (1985), 53–5; Krömer (1971), 70–1.
3. Poralla (1985), no. 383; on μειρακίῳ see Ollier (1933–43), i. 32; cf. below, ch. 20. 7.
4. Hatzfeld (1948), ii. 219: 'la construction de la phrase de Xénophon ne permet pas de décider si ἀδελφός désigne un frère ou un autre fils de Pharnabaze'.
5. Ibid. 14 n. 1; Finley and Pleket (1976), 62 (for 'Spartan named Eualces' read 'son of an Athenian named Eualces').
6. Cf. Underhill and Marchant (1906), 121–2.
7. Assumed by Hatzfeld (1948), ii. 14 n. 1.
8. Ibid.; Krentz (1995), 208.
9. Bos (1947), 89–90; but see Xen. *Hell.* iv. 1. 34.
10. Unz (1986); Tuplin (1993), 52–6, 201–5.

11. Cartledge (1987), 353 (cf. 252), 389 (*bis*).
12. Xen. *Hell*. iv. 1. 39–40; Beloch (1912–27), iii/2. 146; Hatzfeld (1948), ii. 219.
13. Beloch (1912–27), iii/2. 147.
14. Hornblower (1982*a*), 173, (1994*a*), 85; cf. Beloch (1912–27), iii/2. 145–9, (1921).
15. There was another uncle, Bagaios, a son of Pharnakes (Thuc. viii. 58. 1, *Alk*. 39. 1 (MSS Magaios), Xen. *Hell*. iii. 4. 13 (a *nothos*), Nepos, *Alc*. 10. 3): the dispute may have been domestic.
16. Beloch (1912–27), iii/1. 213; Hornblower (1982*a*), 171 n. 7, 173 n. 20, (1991), 202; cf. Brunt (1975), 24.
17. Ar. *Ec*. 629, Pl. *Phdr*. 231 c, Xen. *Mem*. 3. 11. 12; see Dover (1978), 91 and *passim* (1980), 3.
18. Poralla (1985), no. 557.
19. Bos (1947), 90 ad loc.
20. For the consanguineous and childless marriages of the Hekatomnid dynasty, Mausolos and Artemisia, Idrieus and Ada, see Hornblower (1982*a*), 358–63: only the third brother, Pixodaros, had issue, from a non-sibling marriage.
21. Hornblower (1982*a*), 35 n. 3, 41; cf. 202.
22. On recasting: see Pelling (1990*a*), 35–43.
23. Wheeler (1988), 26, 48.
24. Cf. Blundell (1989), 50.

CHAPTER 14

1. For the terminology see Weizsäcker (1931); Russell (1973), 115.
2. Schwartz (1951), 51–8, 208–14; H. Martin (1960), 66–8, and n. 10; Romilly (1988*a*).
3. Holladay (1977); Hodkinson (1983), 251–4; Desideri (1985), (1986).
4. At Ephesos, Lysander had his own residence (ch. 7. 1, *Lys*. 23. 3).
5. Pelling (1980), 127–31 = (1995), 125–33, (1990*a*), 35–43.
6. For the Artemision: Börker (1980); Wesenberg (1981); Cartledge (1987), 5; Tuplin (1993), 56.
7. Pelling (1990*a*), 35–43.
8. Ibid.
9. For the concept of 'Asiatic Greeks' see ch. 9. Cf. Seager and Tuplin (1980), esp. 144.
10. Saunders (1973).
11. Cf. Perrin (1917), ad loc.: 'Persian viceroys'.
12. Eduard Meyer (1913–56), iv² (1) 69–70; Andrewes (1981), 12–16, 38, 356–7.

13. *FGrHist* 76 F 26, F 71; Plut. *Lys.* 18; Homann-Wedeking (1965), 440; Habicht (1970), 3–6, 243–4; Bommelaer (1981), 7–23, esp. nos. 16–17; G. Shipley (1987), 133–4.

14. For implied tyrannical and Oriental associations of named dedications, see Hornblower (1982*a*), 283–4.

CHAPTER 15

1. For dekarchy recorded at Samos (Xen. *Hell.* ii. 3. 7) see G. Shipley (1987), 131–3. The demise of the dekarchies started in 403/2 and continued perhaps as late as 397, but there is no record of any steps taken by Sparta to enforce the decree (Andrewes (1971); D. H. Kelly (1975), 71 ff.). See above, ch. 7.

2. Bruce (1967), 148–9.

3. *FGrHist* 115 F 103, §5 (pp. 372–4).

4. Bruce (1967), 58–63.

5. J. B. Salmon (1984), 344. Names like the 'Peloponnesian war' are not contemporary titles (G. Shipley (1993), 3–6).

6. For the causes and course of the Corinthian war see Accame (1951); Barbieri (1955), 90–100; Bruce (1960), (1961), (1967), 12–14, 116–22; Kagan (1961), (1962); Perlman (1964); C. D. Hamilton (1972); Tuplin (1982); Westlake (1983*a*); J. B. Salmon (1984), ch. 24; Unz (1986); Lendon (1989); Buck (1994), ch. 4.

7. Hall (1993), 110.

8. Babut (1969*a*), 357–8, esp. 358 n. 4.

9. In 331 Agis III led a rising against Makedon. The regent Antipatros won the battle at Megalopolis, further reducing Sparta's status and Spartiate numbers: Cartledge (1987), 212; Cartledge and Spawforth (1989), 22–4.

10. Cf. *Artax.* 20. 4, *Mor.* 211 B. On arrows: J. K. Anderson (1991), 21–2, 25, 28.

11. Bruce (1967), 58–60, 62.

12. Cartledge (1987), 290–1.

13. Bruce (1967), 5, 58–60; C. D. Hamilton (1979), 179, 207, and n. 76.

14. Bos (1947), 100.

15. Thebes, Corinth, Argos, Athens (Bruce (1967), 58).

16. Hornblower (1991), 183–95.

17. Bruce (1967), 60–1.

CHAPTER 16

1. Forrest (1968), 85, 90, 100, 102.
2. Andrewes (1978), 95–9; Hornblower (1991), 186–7.
3. Herodotos mentions points on Xerxes' march, from the crossing of the Hellespont at Abydos (vii. 55. 1) to the arrival at Thermopylai (201. 1), with the division of the army into three parts at 121. 2–3, using the coastal route and two inland routes from Doriskos to Akanthos. Xenophon (*Hell.* iv. 2. 8, 3. 1–3, *Agesilaos*, 2. 1) gives no place-names from the Hellespont to Makedon, and in the latter mentions Xerxes' route only to praise Agesilaos' speedy march. In the far north Diodoros (xiv. 83. 3) mentions only a battle won against certain Thracians, and thence refers to Xerxes' route. Plutarch mentions only the one people who refused Agesilaos free passage (§2). Agesilaos may have used one of the inland routes, avoiding coastal towns as far as Amphipolis.
4. There is no certain European identification of the people named variously in MSS here Τρωχαλεῖς (S, the best MS), Τράλλεις (GLN), and at *Mor.* 211 C–D Τρωαδεῖς, which favours the reading of S (Robert (1935), 426–7). Theopompos mentions the, or some, Tralleis in Illyria (*FGrHist* 115 F 377); they do not reappear in a specific context until the time of Alexander (Diod. 17. 65). Perhaps a tribe that moved to Asia, to the town Tralles in the Maiandros plain, left a remnant on the Upper Nestos in Thrace (Lenk (1936), 407), where it has been located on the basis of this passage (Launey (1987), 399); but the support of two late 3rd-c. inscriptions from Samothrace is questionable (ibid. 400), though they show a warlike tribe. *ATL* indicates an assessed but unlocated Trailos in the Thraceward District, which Leake (1835), iii. 228–9, places 7 miles west of Amphipolis.
5. Habicht (1970), 179–84; Flower (1988).
6. Flower (1988), 127; Cawkwell (1979), 33–7.
7. Beloch (1912–27), iii/2. 49; McQueen (1978); Hammond and Griffith (1979); Anson (1985); Errington (1986).
8. Beloch (1912–27), iii/2. 55–6; Hammond and Griffith (1979), 168–9.
9. Poralla (1985), nos. 569, 668.
10. Bruce (1967), 82–3.
11. Poralla (1985), nos. 175, 367, 658–9; Samios: see Hdt. iii. 55 (not, as Poralla, iii. 25).
12. Cartledge (1982), 250–1; G. Shipley (1987), 97.
13. How and Wells (1912), i. 270; Poralla (1985), no. 150; cf. Thuc. iii. 70.
14. For chronological compression and displacement, and manipulation of narrative, see Pelling (1980), 127–8 = (1995), 125–8, (1990a),

35–43; on στενάξας see Frazier (1992), 4511: 'la coloration psychologique'.

15. Other more difficult routes are discussed by How and Wells (1912), ii. 174–5.

16. Philippson (1897), 57–75; Stählin (1924*b*), 81–3, 150–70, 228; Westlake (1935); Béquignon (1937), 36–7. See Stählin (1924*a*), esp. 851–2 for Larissa: (1924*b*) 186–91, (1935), for Narthakion.

17. Béquignon (1937), 36; Gomme (1956), iii. 543–4 on τῷ 'Ενιπεῖ ποταμῷ (Thuc. iv. 78. 3).

18. Ibid. 540–6.

19. Leake (1835); Kiepert (1844).

20. Laticheff (1882); Béquignon (1937), 290–2.

21. Kiepert (1898); Stählin (1924*b*), 186–91, (1935); Ernst Meyer (1965).

22. The manuscripts of *Hellenika* and *Agesilaos*, 2. 5, have ὑπερβάλλων, for which Hirschig proposed the aorist ὑπερβαλών, adopted here. Agesilaos will have reached 'friendly territory' as he passed the summit of the mountain ridge which formed its northern territory.

23. Brasidas had a day's hard march to Pharsalos from Meliteia, but he was leading a newly assembled force of allies (Thuc. iv. 78). See Gomme (1956), iii. 541.

CHAPTER 17

1. Bruce (1967), 118–22.
2. Hodkinson (1993), 152–3.
3. Lazenby (1985), 10–12, 53, cf. (1993), 135, 204.
4. Buck (1994), 46.
5. Béquignon (1937), 346, 352–3; Hornblower (1991), 186.
6. How and Wells (1912), ii. 243–4; *CAH*² vol. iv, maps 7 and 8.
7. Hodkinson (1993), 157–61.
8. Wheeler (1988), 39–40.
9. Brenk (1977), 208 n. 20.
10. Bos (1947), 110.

CHAPTER 18

1. Herman (1987), 14–15 and n. 14 discusses views on Xenophon's presence and participation.
2. Kaupert (1926*b*); Lazenby (1985), 143–8, fig. 11, pl. 12; Pritchett (1965–92), ii. 85–95.
3. Bruce (1967), 107–8, 161; Buck (1979), 97–8, 155–6, (1994), 46–7; at

Riedinger (1993), 524 'face aux Achéens', see rather iv. 3. 15.

4. Larsen (1955*a*), (1960), (1968); Roesch (1965), 42 n. 1; Sordi (1968), 66–75; Amit (1971), 55; Hennig (1974), 346–7; Dull (1977), 305; Buck (1994), 35–7, 39–40.

5. Herippidas crossed the Hellespont with Agesilaos (*Hell*. iv. 2. 8).

6. Lazenby (1985), 156.

7. Ibid. 146.

8. Cf. ch. 36. 3. For the 'culture' of wounds see Leigh (1995); as proof of piety and courage Xen. *Agesilaos*, 2. 13, 6. 2, of cowardice *Caes*. 45. 3–4; at Sparta Tyrtaios, 12. 25–6, cf. Lazenby (1991), 93; here too perhaps the bonding implied in τὸ δημοτικόν (cf. ch. 19. 1). If Xenophon represents the stages in the battle by the order of his verbs, the thrust came before the decisive use of weaponry and lasted for some time. Prolonged shoving by rear ranks of deep phalanxes would build up crushing pressure on men in the front ranks (Lazenby (1991), 99). The Spartans could fight in relays (Diod. xi. 8. 2; Sinclair (1966), 251 and n. 8).

9. For ὤσασθαι (ὠθισμός, the 'shove'), see Holladay (1982), 94–7; Cawkwell (1989), 376–8; Lazenby (1991), 97–100.

10. J. K. Anderson (1970), 153; Lazenby (1985), 135.

11. Lazenby (1985), 146.

12. Similarly complex manoeuvres were performed at the River Nemea even without proper commands (Xen. *Hell*. iv. 2. 22).

13. Wheeler (1988), 44–5.

14. Lazenby (1985), 146.

15. Riedinger (1993), 523–5.

16. Buck (1994), 47.

CHAPTER 19

1. Buckler (1992), 4804.

2. See Leake (1835); Papagiannopoulos-Palaios (1956–7); Pritchett (1965–92), ii. 85–9, 93–4; Papahatzis (1969); Dull (1977), 308; Roesch (1982), 222–4.

3. Dull (1977), 312–13; Buck (1979), 150–3; Demand (1982), 34–6, ch. 4.

4. See Vaughn (1991), 38–40.

5. Lazenby (1985), 143–8, (1991), 101, 109 n. 10.

6. Chrimes (1949); Stubbs (1950); R. M. Cook (1962); Holladay (1977); Clauss (1983).

7. Armstrong *et al.* (1992), 295–6.

8. The text of Pausanias, iii. 9. 3, styling Aristomelidas 'the father of the

mother of Agesilaos', contradicts the greater authority of Plutarch (ch. 1. 1), who makes Eupolia the daughter of Melesippidas. The change to γυναικός, suggested by Hertzberg (1856, 235 n. 19a; cf. Poralla (1983), no. 134), makes Pausanias' text a reference to 'the father of Agesilaos' wife' Kleora. There is no manuscript evidence in the Teubner Pausanias (2nd rev. edn., 1989) for the new reading, but the link with the judges who condemned the surrendered Plataian garrison in 427 (cf. Thuc. iii. 52. 3), and with the embassy to Thebes in 396, would give his Aristomelidas an age of up to 90 years at that time. The relationship with Kleora's father gives a more suitable age and provides useful evidence for Agesilaos' contact with Leontidas (ch. 23. 11). See Cartledge (1987), 144–50, who also suggests that one daughter's husband, Chilon (Xen. *Hell.* vii. 4. 23), may be the descendant of the ancient Spartan sage Chilon (Hodkinson (1994), 190), and possibly the harmost of Aigina in 395, mentioned by Aischines (2. 78; cf. Milon at *Hell. Ox.* I. 3, III. 1–2). Other relatives are Teleutias (ch. 21) and perhaps Antalkidas (ch. 23. 2).

9. Schaps (1977), 326, 330.
10. Wheeler (1991), 165 n. 98.
11. Jackson (1991), 231–6.

CHAPTER 20

1. Versions of four of these five items are found among the 'Sayings of Spartans' (*Mor.* 212 A–D). Other sources are: (1) Xenophon (*Agesilaos*, 9); (2) Diokles (*Lives of the Philosophers*, as reported by Diogenes Laërtius, ii. 54); (3) Diodoros, xiv. 13. 2–8; (4) perhaps Xenophon (*Agesilaos*, 7). The last is found only in Xenophon, *Hell.* v. 3. 20 and *Agesilaos*, 8. These 'Sayings' clearly go back to a source before Plutarch, whether or not he was the collector (Flower (1988), 123 n. 2).
2. Finley and Pleket (1976), 45–6; Swaddling (1980), 41–2.
3. Moretti (1953), 40–4, (1957), 114, no. 373; de Ste. Croix (1972), 354–5; Ebert (1972), no. 33, trans. Cartledge (1987), 150; Jeffery (1990), 196–7, 448; *IG* V (1). 1564a; *Anth. Pal.* xiii. 16.
4. Hodkinson (1989), 95–100; Flower (1991), 89–90.
5. Cartledge (1987), 150.
6. Swaddling (1980), 70.
7. Delebecque (1957), 117–23.
8. J. K. Anderson (1974*b*), 165; Krentz (1995), 168.
9. For his studies at Skillous see Delebecque (1957), 206–11, 239–42.
10. Ibid. 124–7, 239–42.

11. Ibid. 171–3.

12. Ibid. 359–63.

13. Prothoos addressed the Spartans, perhaps without holding office (see below, ch. 28).

14. Bommelaer (1981), 180; Cartledge (1987), 95–7. For the constitutional problems see Andrewes (1966), 20 n. 24; Bommelaer (1981), 191–2, 223–5; Flower (1991), 81–3 n. 33; de Ste. Croix (1972), 127–8.

15. Arist. *Pol.* 1301^b, 1333^b; David (1979*b*), 101–5, 106–9; Cartledge (1987), 163; Hodkinson (1994), 200–1, 211–12.

16. David (1980), 301–2, 303–7, 308.

17. Moretti (1957), no. 110; Poralla (1985), no. 492; Cartledge (1987), 188; Hodkinson (1989), 97.

18. Forrest (1968), 126; Malkin (1990); Hornblower (1991), 190.

19. Grote (1869), ix. 59.

20. G. Shipley (1987), 131–4, 144–5.

21. Cartledge (1978), 28–9.

22. Grote (1869), ix. 60–1.

23. Poralla (1985), no. 470.

24. Cawkwell (1976*a*), 77–82; Hodkinson (1983), 279).

25. Cartledge (1981), 22; Gray (1989), 63; cf. Hindley (1994), 361, 366, and nn. 63–4, 67.

CHAPTER 21

1. Accame (1951); Bruce (1960); Kagan (1961), (1962); Aucello (1964); Perlman (1964); J. K. Anderson (1974*b*), 162–71; Lehmann (1978); J. B. Salmon (1984), 342–70; Lendon (1989); Buck (1994), 30–59.

2. Cartledge (1987), 38.

3. Westlake (1968), 122, 156.

4. Id. (1966), 260–9 = (1969), 216–25.

5. Griffith (1950); Kagan (1962); C. D. Hamilton (1972), (1979), 255–6, 260, 267–78; J. B. Salmon (1984), 362, 411.

6. Bordes (1982), 71–7.

7. Ibid. 72.

8. Griffith (1950), 242–50; Tuplin (1982); C. D. Hamilton (1979), 270–1; J. B. Salmon (1984), 357–62, 411.

9. Finley and Pleket (1976), 70.

10. *IG* V (1). 18–19; Cartledge and Spawforth (1989), 192, 264 n. 4. Dr Spawforth brought this to my attention.

11. Finley and Pleket (1976), 71; Poralla (1985), no. 250.

12. David (1989), 7–8 and 21 nn. 43–6. A noun derived from a verb, denoting a *nomen agentis*, is usually accented on the final syllable

(oxytone), like σοφιστής, and this accentuation survives into modern Greek, in καθηγητής, μαθητής; but some, like δεικηλίκτας, are exceptional (paroxytone): δείκτης, δράτης, δραπέτης.

13. *Lyk.* 27. 2, if the reading is correctly interpreted; Cartledge (1979), 309, citing *IG* V (1). 713; Schaps (1977), 326, 330.

CHAPTER 22

1. Payne (1940), 10–18; Blackman (1966); J. B. Salmon (1984), 26–8, 364–6; cf. Heurtley (1923).
2. Two circular buildings have been identified at Perachora, the more likely one higher up the peninsula from the sanctuary area (Tomlinson (1985), 261). The other, partly or mostly submerged, can be observed on the seashore, near the lake, now a lagoon. The purpose of the buildings cannot be determined, but in the vicinity of the upper circle are several elaborate constructions concerned with a water-supply. Following the loss of control of this area, the early surrender of those in the Heraion would be inevitable, since there would be no water for men or for animals.
3. Brenk (1977), 26, ch. 12, esp. 272–4.
4. Murray (1972), 202.
5. Brenk (1977), 209 with n. 21.
6. Xen. *Hell.* iv. 5. 11–18, Diod. xiv. 91. 2, Nepos, *Iphicr.* 2. 3, Paus. iii. 10. 1. On Amyklai see Kennell (1995), 162–9.
7. Lazenby (1985), 148–50.
8. Other brief reports: Diod. xiv. 91. 2, Nepos, *Iphic.* 2. 3, Paus. iii. 10. 1.
9. Brenk (1977), 83, 151.
10. Armstrong *et al.* (1992), 296, Route 1.
11. Westlake (1983*b*).
12. Foxhall (1993), 138–9, 140.

CHAPTER 23

1. Barbieri (1955); Seager (1967); Perlman (1968); Costa (1974); Cawkwell (1976*b*), (1984); Lévy (1983); De Voto (1986); Jehne (1994). For inscriptional evidence see Tod (1948), no. 107.
2. Lewis (1977), 144–5 and n. 60; Hornblower (1991), 196–7, cf. 133.
3. Poralla (1985), nos. 97, 482.
4. Andrewes (1981), 69, on Thuc. viii. 28. 5.
5. Poralla (1985), nos. 97, 482, 599, 688–9; Cartledge (1987), 145–6.

6. Ryder (1965); Seager (1967), 105, (1974); Cawkwell (1976*b*), 276–7, (1981*b*); Buckler (1977); Griffith (1978), 127–35; Lanzillotta (1980); Thompson (1983).

7. For the concept of 'the Greeks in Asia' see Seager and Tuplin (1980).

8. Lewis (1977), 122; J. M. Cook (1983), 178–82; Jehne (1991).

9. Bruce (1966), 277–8; Lewis (1977), 145–6.

10. Seager (1967), 104–5; Seager and Tuplin (1980), 145 and n. 51.

11. V. Martin (1944), 14–24; Cartledge (1987), 196, citing Tod (1948), no. 133. 23–4 for the name 'King's Peace'; cf. Xen. *Hell.* v. 1. 30–1, 35.

12. For 'Peace of Antalkidas' see Diod. xv. 5. 1, 19. 1; cf. xiv. 110. 3, Xen. *Hell.* v. 1. 36.

13. On the evidence of Didymos (c.80–10) and Aelius Aristeides (*c.*AD 129–89) see Bruce (1966), 273, 276; C. D. Hamilton (1979), 318–22.

14. For this date rather than the previous Olympiad (Diod. xiv. 109. 3), see Lewis (1994), 139 n. 82.

15. Grote (1869), ix. 215.

16. Hammond (1986), 467.

17. Hornblower (1991), 175.

18. Lewis (1977), 145 n. 61.

19. Ryder (1963*a*); Seager (1974); Cawkwell (1981*b*); Athenian historiography created a tradition unfavourable to peripheral cities such as Thebes, overshadowed by Athens and Sparta: cf. Demand (1982), 3, 10, 42, 80, with *Mor.* 583 and ch. 27 n. 1 below.

20. For Thebes and the Boiotian Confederacy see *Hell. Ox.* XI. 1–XII. 2 (Bruce (1967), 102–14); Larsen (1955*a*), (1955*b*), (1968); Beister (1970); Fuscagni (1972); Buck (1979), (1994); Buckler (1979), (1980*a*); Stanton (1982).

21. For topography, see Symeonoglou (1985), with Huxley (1987). For Phoibidas, see Poralla (1985), no. 734; but refer to this chapter and to ch. 24; Hack (1978).

22. The stone wall round it has been identified as of late 4th-c. construction.

23. Cf. Todd (1993): Athenian justice was not so different, but issues were discussed as well as voted in the Assembly.

24. Murray (1972), 200, 213.

25. See Herman (1987), App. A, 170.

26. Ibid. 159 n. 118.

27. Hatzfeld (1946); Cartledge (1987), 325–6; Hornblower (1991), 231–2.

28. Cartledge (1987), 201.

CHAPTER 24

1. Sordi (1973); Rice (1974), (1975); Riley (1977). For a full account of the relevant events at Phleious see Cartledge (1987), 226–9, 262–6.
2. Poralla (1985), nos. 734, 295.
3. The classical form is Φλειοῦς, Φλειάσιος; Plutarch's Φλι- is a later spelling.
4. *FGrHist* 124 F 9. Kallisthenes' *Hellenika* acknowledged by Diodoros (xiv. 117. 8, xvi. 14. 4). See Introd., F. 3 (*f*). MacDonald (1972) defends Diodoros' account (xv. 29. 5–6). On manipulation of sources see Pelling (1990*a*), 35–42.
5. For topography see Vanderpool (1978); Ober (1985), 105–6, 118–20.
6. Cawkwell (1973), (1984), cf. (1981*a*); Kallet-Marx (1985), 133–47, further modifies the chronology, so that the events of Diod. xv. 28. 2 precede even those of xv. 27. 3; cf. Burnett (1962); Bruce (1963), (1966); Perlman (1968); Buckler (1971); Cargill (1981), with Hornblower (1982*b*), and Sherwin-White (1982); Plezia (1982); Strauss (1986).
7. Cawkwell (1973), 57.
8. Tod (1948), no. 118; Kallet-Marx (1985), 131.
9. Cawkwell (1973), 55.
10. Ibid. 55.

CHAPTER 25

1. MacDowell (1986), 161–4.
2. Hodkinson (1983), 242, 245–51, (1986*b*), 232; Kukofka (1993).
3. De Ste. Croix (1972), 349–50.
4. Hodkinson (1983), 252–3.
5. Cartledge (1987), 147.
6. Pelling (1990*a*), 35–40.
7. Cawkwell (1973), 55.
8. MacDonald (1972), 40–4; Rice (1975), 109–10.
9. Kallet-Marx (1985), 150–1.
10. *Pace* Cartledge (1987), 137.
11. Forrest (1968), 129.

CHAPTER 26

1. Pelling (1988*b*), 40.
2. Munn (1987), (1993).

3. Butler (1962); Bringmann (1975); Lévy (1977); Schütrumpf (1987); cf. ch. 33 n. 1
4. Cawkwell (1983), 395–400; Hodkinson (1983), 267–73.
5. Finley (1968), 143–9 = (1981), 24–9 = (1986), 161–6; Lavery (1973–4); Cartledge (1976b), 119, (1987), 14–17, 37–44; Hodkinson (1989).
6. Aristotle makes the similar point, that the Spartans trained but others did not (*Pol.* 1338^b28–9).
7. Farrell (1907–8), Lane (1933–4); Holladay (1977); Tomlinson (1992), 254; for a survey see Waterhouse (1986), 18–20, 105–7.

CHAPTER 27

1. Legon (1981), 11, 33–4, 266–85. In Fable 15 (Perry (1965) 24–6) of the poet Babrius (2nd c. AD) an uncultured Theban cannot match a sophisticated Athenian as a speaker, though intelligent enough finally to outwit him. I owe this reference to Dr I. G. Spence.
2. Hammond (1954); Ober (1985), 208–22; Van de Maele (1987), 191, 204.
3. On Megara see Legon (1981).
4. Legon (1981), 264–5.
5. Longrigg (1980), 212, to whom I owe some of the references, (1988b), (1993); López Férez (1990).
6. Michler (1963); Legon (1981), 272.
7. Tuplin (1993), 130 n. 14.
8. Longrigg (1985), 278–82.
9. Id. (1988b), 477–9.
10. Id. (1989), 14–22.
11. Id. (1988a), 21.
12. Id. (1988b), 477–9.
13. Ibid.
14. King (1989), 22–3.
15. Ibid. 14–15.
16. Ibid. 14.
17. Brain (1986), with Longrigg (1988a), 20–1.
18. Cartledge (1987), 232.
19. Cf. Riedinger (1993), 543.
20. Cawkwell (1963); Hornblower (1991), 217.
21. Demand (1982), chs. 1, 5. See Fossey (1979) for L. Kopais as a source of wealth in Boiotia.
22. Ninou (1981), 74–5 and pl. 39.
23. Mosley (1962), (1972); Ryder (1963b), 240–1, (1965), 64–5; Westlake (1966), 257–9 = (1969), 214–6; C. D. Hamilton (1991), 200–1; Tuplin

(1977), (1993), 101–10.
24. Ryder (1963*b*), 241.
25. J. R. Grant (1965), 264 n. 2.
26. Larsen (1962); Ryder (1965), 67–9, 127–30.
27. Larsen (1925), (1955*b*), (1960), (1968); Bruce (1967), 102–9, 157–64; Stanton (1982).
28. Larsen (1954), (1973); Beister (1970); Dull (1975); Demand (1982), 34; Buckler (1980*a*), 23–6, 36–7, 220–2, (1982); Pascual González (1990); Buck (1994), 106–10, 117–20.
29. Huxley (1979), 52.

CHAPTER 28

1. Ryder (1963*b*); Mosley (1971), (1972); Cawkwell (1972), 264–5; Bengtson (1975); Buckler (1980*a*), 49–54; Lonis (1980); Missiou-Ladi (1987); Buck (1994), 111–13. On manipulation of sources see Pelling (1990*a*), 35–42.
2. Cartledge (1987), 15–16, 40–1.
3. Cf. Ryder (1965), 69; C. D. Hamilton (1991), 201–2.
4. Heurtley (1923); Burn (1949); Tomlinson and Fossey (1970); Buckler (1980*a*), 57–9; personal observation.
5. Tuplin (1987), 72–7.
6. So MSS, defended by Tuplin (1979), 351–6 against Koroneia, the emendation of Wesseling (1746).
7. Wilamowitz (1874), 439 n. 2 = (1935–72), V (1). 253 n. 2, (1879), 11–12 = (1935–72), iv. 595–6; Peper (1912); cf. Shrimpton (1971*a*); Brunt (1980); Buckler (1980*a*), 272–4, 292 n. 5.
8. Tuplin (1984).
9. Ibid. 357.
10. Ibid. 350–1.
11. Ibid. 354.
12. Ibid. 354–7.
13. Poralla (1985), no. 643; Smith (1953–4).
14. Cf. de Ste. Croix (1972), 127–9, 147.
15. Cf. *Mor.* 773 C–774 D; Pausanias (ix. 13. 3). Diodoros implies an early date, for Leuktros, whose daughters were also violated, gave his name to the area (xv. 54. 2). Skedasos' daughters were called Leuktrides after the place (*Pel.* 20. 3).
16. Cawkwell (1976*a*), 78–9, 80–4, (1983), 397–400.
17. Pompey also corrupted his judgement, but by surrendering to unwise counsels (*Pomp.* 67. 7).
18. Tuplin (1987), 77–8, 83.

19. *Pel.* 20–3; (Kallisthenes *FGrHist* 124 F 11, cf. F 18); Xen. *Hell.* vi. 4. 3–15; Diod. xv. *l.* 2–5, 33. 2–3, 51. 1–56. 4; Nepos, *Ep.* 6. 4, 8. 3, 10. 2, *Pel.* 2. 4, 4. 2, *Agesilaus*, 6. 1, 7. 1; Paus. ix. 13. 3–14. 1; for the cavalry's dust-screen devised by Epameinondas, exaggerated estimates of numbers of troops, and other anecdotes, Polyain. ii. 3. 2, 3. 3, 3. 8, 3. 12, 3. 14, 3. 15; Frontin. *Str.* i. 2. 7, 11. 16, ii. 2. 12, iv. 2. 6; Busolt (1905); Kaupert (1926c); Westlake (1939); Pritchett (1965–92), i. 49–58; Buckler (1980b); Lazenby (1985), 151–62; Tuplin (1987); Hanson (1988), (1991), *passim*; C. D. Hamilton (1991), 202–14, 215; Hornblower (1994b), 37–8 and n. 79.
20. Hanson (1988).
21. Cawkwell (1983), 399.
22. Lazenby (1985), 14–16 and 176 n. 24.
23. Cawkwell (1983), 387, 397–8.
24. Lazenby (1985), 17.
25. A cavalryman, Eudikos, one of the Perioikoi, was killed in Boiotia with Agesilaos (378): Xen. *Hell.* v. 4. 39; Poralla (1985), no. 296.
26. Lazenby (1985), 16–20.
27. Ibid. 17.
28. Beloch (1886), 131–44.
29. Lazenby (1985), 162.

CHAPTER 29

1. Cf. Russell (1973), 68–9, 88; Babut (1969a), 318–24.
2. Rawson (1969), 89–91.
3. T. P. Wiseman (1993), 145–6.
4. Woodman (1988), 197–9; cf. Pelling (1986b), 187 = (1995), 353, (1990a), esp. 41–2, 51–2; Gill (1993), 38–87; Moles (1993), 88–121, esp. 114–18; T. P. Wiseman (1993), 122–46, esp. 127.

CHAPTER 30

1. Pelling (1990a), 38–43.
2. Brenk (1977), ch. 12.
3. Themistokles' interpretation of 'wooden walls' was similarly preferred (Hdt. vii. 141, 143. 2–3).
4. McQueen (1978); Cartledge (1987), 241, 411–12. For τρέσαντες in 331 see Diod. xix. 70. 5; Cartledge and Spawforth (1989), 24, 236–7.
5. Bordes (1982), 177.

6. David (1989), 14–15.
7. Lazenby (1985), 14–20.
8. Ibid. 21.
9. Cawkwell (1983), 391–3.
10. Bordes (1982), 176–9.
11. Wheeler (1988), 18, 26–8; cf. Stanton (1973), 351–8; Duff (1994), 59. See Introd., D.1(e).
12. Cartledge (1987), 179.
13. Ibid. 120.
14. Ibid. 261–2.
15. Cf. Diod. xv. 59. 3–4, where Agesilaos is more effective; for Diodoros' Lykomedes 'of Tegea' (xv. 59. 1), see xv. 62. 2 and Xen. *Hell.* vii. 1. 23: he was Mantineian.
16. Cartledge (1987), 262.

CHAPTER 31

1. The main extant accounts of Epameinondas' invasion are in *Pel.* 24. 1–5, Xenophon (*Hell.* vi. 5. 17–52; *Agesilaos,* 2. 24), Diodoros (xv. 62–7. 1), Nepos (*Epaminondas,* 7. 3–8, *Pelopidas,* 4. 3, *Agesilaus,* 6. 1–3), and the later Pausanias, who at ix. 13–15 preserves evidence from sources also perhaps available to Plutarch: Shrimpton (1971*b*); Buckler (1978), (1980*a*), 70–90; Bengtson (1983), 199–227; Cartledge (1987), 232–6; C. D. Hamilton (1991), 223–31; Tuplin (1993), 141–4; cf. Griffin (1982), 66–8.
2. For the chronology of Epameinondas' four invasions of the Peloponnese see J. Wiseman (1969).
3. Modern estimates are as low as 30,000: Lazenby (1985), 166, 203 n. 2; Cartledge (1987), 232.
4. Armstrong *et al.* (1992), 295, 301.
5. *BSA* 13 (1906–7), pl. 1, 11–19 M–L. Note orientation.
6. Two (241 B–C) are concerned more for Sparta than for their sons; cf. Lazenby (1985), 166.
7. Cf. 83. 3 for defenders on the roofs. Plutarch reports the heroism of an Argive woman who threw a tile from the roof and disabled Pyrrhos who was then killed (*Pyrrh.* 34. 2–3). Aeneas Tacticus says that when Sinope was under attack from Datames, sturdy women were dressed as men to defend it, and used pots and jugs to look like armour: but they were warned not to give themselves away by throwing anything (40. 4–5; for Datames, see Nepos, *Dat.* 4. 1–3; Hornblower (1982), 171–2).

CHAPTER 32

1. Armstrong *et al.* (1992), 293–310.
2. Cartledge and Spawforth (1989), 178–9.
3. Sparta: General Plan, *BSA* 13 (1906–7), pl. 1; Cartledge and Spawforth (1989), 215. For the Issorion see Fimmen (1916).
4. Cartledge (1987), 235.
5. Hammond and Griffith (1979), 615–19; Hornblower (1991), 258–9.
6. Hanson (1983), 150–1, (1989), 33–4; Foxhall (1993), 138–40, 142–3; cf. ch. 22. 10.
7. See David (1980), 299–303.
8. Devereux (1965), 35.
9. Cf. Cartledge (1987), 164.
10. David (1980), 304–5; Fuks (1962), 257 n. 69 = (1984), 243 n. 69.
11. *BSA* 13 (1906–7), General Plan L–N 11; Fimmen (1916).
12. Roobaert (1977); Talbert (1989), 24–5; Ducat (1990); Cartledge (1991), cf. (1985); Whitby (1992), (1994), 98–9.
13. David (1980), 305–7.
14. Ibid. 307.
15. Lazenby (1985), 166–7.
16. J. Wiseman (1969), 178–80.

CHAPTER 33

1. David (1979–80); Poralla (1985), no. 276; Schütrumpf (1987); Hodkinson (1993), 150 n. 1, (1994), 184, 207. Cf. ch. 26. 5.
2. Cartledge and Spawforth (1989), 42.
3. Hodkinson (1983), 243, (1989), (1994), 203.
4. Cawkwell (1976a), 80–4.
5. Lazenby (1985), 165–70.
6. Cartledge (1987), 406–7; he noting serious underlying strains, ibid. 407–12.
7. Cf. Cawkwell (1972), 274–5.
8. Xenophon delays mention of Lykomedes until he suggests that his growing confidence and popularity made the Thebans jealous (*Hell.* vii. 1. 23).
9. Buckler (1980a), 90–102.
10. Dindorf (1853); Cartledge (1979), 300; Lazenby (1985), 203 n. 7.
11. Cartledge (1987), 387.
12. Bos (1947), 180; Schneider (1912), 2214.
13. Jameson (1991), 198; Jackson (1991), 232.
14. Cf. Cartledge (1987), 131.

15. Frazier (1992), 4511; Fuhrmann (1964), 47; cf. ch. 16. 6.
16. Armstrong *et al.* (1992), 296 (route 1).
17. τὸ φῶς ὁρώσης and ἀντιβλέπειν; cf. n. 15 above.

CHAPTER 34

1. How and Wells (1912), ii. 199–200; Dover and Andrewes (1970), 218–19; Dipersia (1974); G. Shipley (1987), 108.
2. G. Shipley (1987), 161–4.
3. Ryder (1957), (1965); Cawkwell (1961), esp. 85–6, (1972); Roy (1971), (1994); Buckler (1980a), 100–8, 156, 185–208.
4. Diodoros reverses the role of the Messenians (xv. 82. 1).
5. Lazenby (1985), 165–9; Hornblower (1990c).
6. Oliva (1971), 196.
7. Hodkinson (1993), 148–9.
8. Cartledge (1987), 261, 401–2; C. D. Hamilton (1991), 252–3.
9. Wheeler (1988), 9–10 and n. 33. Cf. *Fab.* 7. 2 γνώμῃ καὶ προνοίᾳ, 'in judgement and foresight'.
10. Mosley (1971), 320, 324, 326, 329–30.
11. Waterhouse and Hope Simpson (1961); Armstrong *et al.* (1992), 296, 308 (routes 1 and 2).
12. Ibid. (route 1).
13. Tuplin (1979), 349.
14. Ibid. 350.
15. See n. 11.
16. 'The villain of a few pages earlier (19. 4) has now [at 31. 3–4] been transformed into a hero' (Westlake (1986a), 269).
17. Cartledge and Spawforth (1989), p. ix, after Mark Twain.
18. Poralla (1985), no. 397; cf. Aelian, *VH* vi. 3.
19. A similar exploit leading to the recovery of Gytheion in the first invasion (370–369; ch. 32. 5) is attributed to 'Isidas' by Polyainos (2.9, not 2. 19), cited as a 'doublet' by Poralla (1985), no. 399.
20. Poralla (1985), no. 734.
21. Cf. Buffière (1980), 83–4; Hanson (1989); Wheeler (1991), 143 with references; Ogden (1996), 119.

CHAPTER 35

1. Devine (1983); Buckler (1985); Westlake (1975); Bengtson (1983), 224 notes the legendary reports of Epameinondas' death but refers only to the delayed withdrawal of the spear. Death by the sword is delayed

until Epameinondas removes his hand from the wound (Paus. viii. 11. 7). The Spartan account, preferred by Plutarch, probably omitted the heroism of Epameinondas: it would be appropriately recorded in *Epameinondas*.

2. Cf. Buckler (1980*a*), 216; see above, ch. 34. 4 on Diod. xv. 82. 6.
3. Dioskourides is mentioned again at *Lyk*. 11, also in connection with an injury, the possible blinding of Lykourgos: *FHG* ii. 192.
4. Cartledge and Spawforth (1989), viii, 98, 163–4, 261 nn. 5–6.
5. For Kallikrates see Introd., F.3(*m*); above; for Antikrates see Poralla (1985), no. 99.
6. De Laix (1974), 21, 23; Huxley (1979), 51–2.
7. Hornblower (1982*a*), 105 n. 209, 109 n. 19, 201; Cartledge (1987), 325.
8. Cartledge (1987), 72–3, with inscriptional evidence for contributions to a war-fund (Meiggs and Lewis (1988), 67; Fornara (1983), 132; Matthaion and Pikoulas (1989), 77–124).

CHAPTER 36

1. See Hornblower (1982*a*), 170–82; Burn (1985); Bresciani (1985); Ray (1987), (1992); Cowley (1990); Lloyd (1994).
2. Satrap of Armenia rather than Mysia, probably a textual error at Diodoros, xv. 90. 3; see Hornblower (1982*a*), 176–8 and nn. 48, 58.
3. Cf. Pelling (1988*b*), 2.
4. See Hornblower (1982*a*), 173–5.
5. Ibid. 202, (1991), 231–2.
6. Ibid. 174–5.
7. Perlman (1976), 18–19. Cf. Briant (1977), 30–5 on Alexander.
8. Weiskopf (1989); Hornblower (1990*b*).
9. Leigh (1995).
10. Brink (1971), 215. Plutarch is not cited.
11. *FGrHist* 115 F 106a, 108, from Athenaeus, correspond to material in this chapter; see Ziegler (1973), ad loc. Bos (1947), ix, 195, refers to Athenaeus, xv. 676 D and emends to Theopompos.
12. Flower (1988), 124–5.

CHAPTER 37

1. Hammond (1986), 464; cf. Cartledge (1987), 209, 231; Will (1960).
2. Cawkwell (1976*a*), 274–5.
3. Hornblower (1991), 161, 202, 209.
4. That Chabrias acted independently of Athens is questioned (Pritchett

(1971–91), ii. 59): Athens was perhaps merely able to equivocate about the authorization of the expedition.

5. Hornblower (1982*a*) dates to the 380s or 360s the commemorative stone near Memphis that confirms the Athenian mercenaries (189 and n. 51, 202 and n. 158); Hicks and Hill (1901), no. 122.

6. Cartledge (1987), 328, citing Hicks and Hill (1901), no. 121 (= *IG*². 119); and 201, citing Tod (1948), no. 145 (= *IG*². 207*a*).

CHAPTER 38

1. Wheeler (1988), 31–2.

CHAPTER 39

1. Wheeler (1988), 26, 48.
2. Westlake (1986*a*), 271–2 and n. 22.

CHAPTER 40

1. See on ch. 35 for other financial references.
2. Pritchett (1971–91), i. 3–29; Andrewes (1981), 70–2, 96–9.
3. Unz (1986), 38; C. D. Hamilton (1982*b*).
4. Cawkwell (1976*a*), 63 n. 8, 76 and n. 51; Unz (1986), 29–37; Tuplin (1993), 202–3.
5. Unz (1986), 37–8 (Xen. *Hell*. iii. 2. 21, not 2. 1), 41–2; Tuplin (1993), 204.
6. Kienitz (1953), 95, 175–6; Hornblower (1982*a*), 174–5.
7. For a full discussion see Tuplin (1993), 201–5. D. H. Kelly (1975) puts Artaxerxes' death at 359/8, and suggests that it was in the absence of the successor Ochos (Artaxerxes III) after his father's death, that Agesilaos was able to defeat the Mendesian.
8. Kienitz (1953), 156–7; Cartledge (1987), 21; Tuplin (1993), 204–5.
9. Hamdorf (1964); Parker (1988); Cartledge (1988).
10. Cartledge (1987), 101.

EPILOGUE

1. Henderson (1989), 64, 66–85. Cf. Arist. *Poet*. 1451ᵃ16–19.

2. Aalders (1982), 28–36.
3. Pelling (1992), 19–31.
4. Ibid. 25.
5. Frazier (1992), 4535.

APPENDIX

ΑΓΗΣΙΛΑΟΥ ΚΑΙ ΠΟΜΠΗΙΟΥ ΣΥΓΚΡΙΣΙΣ

1. 1 Ἐκκειμένων οὖν τῶν βίων, ἐπιδράμωμεν τῷ λόγῳ ταχέως τὰ ποιοῦντα τὰς διαφοράς, παρ' ἄλληλα συνάγοντες. 2 ἔστι δὲ ταῦτα· πρῶτον ὅτι Πομπήιος ἐκ τοῦ δικαιοτάτου τρόπου παρῆλθεν εἰς δύναμιν καὶ δόξαν, αὐτὸς ὁρμηθεὶς ἀφ' ἑαυτοῦ καὶ πολλὰ καὶ μεγάλα Σύλλᾳ τὴν Ἰταλίαν ἀπὸ τῶν τυράννων ἐλευθεροῦντι συγκατεργασάμενος, Ἀγησίλαος δὲ τὴν βασιλείαν ἔδοξε λαβεῖν οὔτε τὰ πρὸς θεοὺς ἀμέμπτως οὔτε τὰ πρὸς ἀνθρώπους, κρίνας νοθείας Λεωτυχίδην, ὃν υἱὸν αὑτοῦ ἀπέδειξεν ὁ ἀδελφὸς γνήσιον, τὸν δὲ χρησμὸν κατειρωνευσάμενος τὸν περὶ τῆς χωλότητος. 3 δεύτερον, ὅτι Πομπήιος Σύλλαν καὶ ζῶντα τιμῶν διετέλεσε καὶ τεθνηκότος ἐκήδευσε βιασάμενος Λέπιδον τὸ σῶμα, καὶ τῷ παιδὶ Φαύστῳ τὴν αὑτοῦ θυγατέρα συνῴκισεν, Ἀγησίλαος δὲ Λύσανδρον ἐκ τῆς τυχούσης προφάσεως ὑπεξέρριψε καὶ καθύβρισε. 4 καίτοι Σύλλας μὲν οὐκ ἐλαττόνων ἔτυχεν ἢ Πομπηίῳ παρέσχεν, Ἀγησίλαον δὲ Λύσανδρος καὶ τῆς Σπάρτης βασιλέα καὶ τῆς Ἑλλάδος στρατηγὸν ἐποίησε. 5 τρίτον δ' αἱ περὶ τὰ πολιτικὰ τῶν δικαίων παραβάσεις Πομπηίῳ μὲν δι' οἰκειότητας ἐγένοντο· τὰ γὰρ πλεῖστα Καίσαρι καὶ Σκιπίωνι συνεξήμαρτε, κηδεσταῖς οὖσιν· 6 Ἀγησίλαος δὲ Σφοδρίαν μὲν ἐφ' οἷς Ἀθηναίους ἠδίκησεν ἀποθανεῖν ὀφείλοντα, τῷ τοῦ παιδὸς ἔρωτι χαριζόμενος ἐξήρπασε, Φοιβίδᾳ δὲ Θηβαίους παρασπονδήσαντι δῆλος ἦν δι' αὐτὸ τὸ ἀδίκημα προθύμως βοηθῶν. 7 καθόλου δ' ὅσα Ῥωμαίους δι' αἰδῶ Πομπήιος ἢ ἄγνοιαν αἰτίαν ἔσχε βλάψαι, ταῦτα θυμῷ καὶ φιλονικίᾳ Λακεδαιμονίους Ἀγησίλαος ἔβλαψε, τὸν Βοιώτιον ἐκκαύσας πόλεμον.

2. 1 Εἰ δὲ καὶ τύχην τινὰ τῶν ἀνδρῶν ἑκατέρου τοῖς σφάλμασι προσοιστέον, ἀνέλπιστος μὲν ἡ Πομπηίου Ῥωμαίοις, Ἀγησίλαος δὲ Λακεδαιμονίους ἀκούοντας καὶ προειδότας οὐκ εἴασε φυλάξασθαι τὴν χωλὴν βασιλείαν. 2 καὶ γὰρ εἰ μυριάκις ἠλέγχθη Λεωτυχίδης ἀλλότριος εἶναι καὶ νόθος, οὐκ ἂν ἠπόρησαν Εὐρυπωντίδαι γνήσιον καὶ ἀρτίποδα τῇ Σπάρτῃ βασιλέα παρασχεῖν, εἰ μὴ δι' Ἀγησίλαον ἐπεσκότησε τῷ χρησμῷ Λύσανδρος. 3 οἷον μέντοι τῇ περὶ τῶν τρεσάντων ἀπορίᾳ προσήγαγεν Ἀγησίλαος ἅμα μετὰ τὴν ἐν Λεύκτροις ἀτυχίαν, κελεύσας τοὺς νόμους ἐκείνην τὴν ἡμέραν καθεύδειν, οὐ γέγονεν ἄλλο σόφισμα πολιτικώτερον, οὐδ' ἔχομέν τι τοῦ Πομπηίου παραπλήσιον, ἀλλὰ τοὐναντίον οὐδ' οἷς αὐτὸς ἐτίθει νόμοις ᾤετο δεῖν ἐμμένειν, τὸ δύνασθαι μέγα τοῖς φίλοις ἐνδεικνύμενος. 4 ὁ δ' εἰς ἀνάγκην καταστὰς τοῦ λῦσαι τοὺς νόμους ἐπὶ τῷ σῶσαι τοὺς πολίτας, ἐξεῦρε τρόπον ᾧ μήτ' ἐκείνους βλάψουσι μήθ' ὅπως οὐ βλάψωσι λυθήσονται. 5 τίθεμαι δὲ κἀκεῖνο τὸ ἀμίμητον ἔργον εἰς πολιτικὴν ἀρετὴν τοῦ Ἀγησιλάου, τὸ δεξάμενον τὴν σκυτάλην ἀπολιπεῖν τὰς ἐν Ἀσίᾳ πράξεις. 6 οὐ γάρ, ὡς Πομπήιος, ἀφ' ὧν ἑαυτὸν ἐποίει μέγαν ὠφέλει τὸ κοινόν,

ἀλλὰ τὸ τῆς πατρίδος σκοπῶν τηλικαύτην ἀφῆκε δύναμιν καὶ δόξαν ἡλίκην οὐδεὶς πρότερον οὐδ᾽ ὕστερον πλὴν Ἀλέξανδρος ἔσχεν.

3. **1** Ἀπ᾽ ἄλλης τοίνυν ἀρχῆς, ἐν ταῖς στρατηγίαις καὶ τοῖς πολεμικοῖς, ἀριθμῷ μὲν τροπαίων καὶ μεγέθει δυνάμεων ἃς ἐπηγάγετο Πομπήιος, καὶ πλήθει παρατάξεων ἃς ἐνίκησεν, οὐδ᾽ ἂν ὁ Ξενοφῶν μοι δοκεῖ παραβαλεῖν τὰς Ἀγησιλάου νίκας, ᾧ διὰ τ ἄλλα καλὰ καθάπερ γέρας ἐξαίρετον δέδοται καὶ γράφειν ὃ βούλοιτο καὶ λέγειν περὶ τοῦ ἀνδρός. **2** οἶμαι δὲ καὶ τῇ πρὸς τοὺς πολεμίους ἐπιεικείᾳ διαφέρειν τὸν ἄνδρα τοῦ ἀνδρός. ὁ μὲν γὰρ ἀνδραποδίσασθαι Θήβας καὶ Μεσσήνην ἐξοικίσασθαι βουλόμενος, ἣν μὲν ὁμόκληρον τῆς πατρίδος, ἣν δὲ μητρόπολιν τοῦ γένους, παρ᾽ οὐδὲν ἦλθεν τὴν Σπάρτην ἀποβαλεῖν· ἀπέβαλε δὲ τὴν ἡγεμονίαν· **3** ὁ δὲ καὶ τῶν πειρατῶν τοῖς μεταβαλλομένοις πόλεις ἔδωκε καὶ Τιγράνην τὸν Ἀρμενίων βασιλέα, γενόμενον ἐφ᾽ ἑαυτῷ θριαμβεῦσαι, σύμμαχον ἐποιήσατο, φήσας ἡμέρας μιᾶς αἰῶνα προτιμᾶν. **4** εἰ μέντοι τοῖς μεγίστοις καὶ κυριωτάτοις εἰς τὰ ὅπλα πράγμασι καὶ λογισμοῖς προστίθεται πρωτεῖον ἀρετῆς ἀνδρὸς ἡγεμόνος, οὐ μικρὸν ὁ Λάκων τὸν Ῥωμαῖον ἀπολέλοιπε. **5** πρῶτον μὲν γὰρ οὐ προήκατο τὴν πόλιν οὐδ᾽ ἐξέλιπεν ἑπτὰ μυριάσι στρατοῦ τῶν πολεμίων ἐμβαλόντων, ὀλίγους ἔχων ὁπλίτας καὶ προνενικημένους ἐν Λεύκτροις· **6** Πομπήιος δέ, πεντακισχιλίοις μόνοις καὶ τριακοσίοις μίαν Καίσαρος πόλιν Ἰταλικὴν καταλαβόντος, ἐξέπεσε τῆς Ῥώμης ὑπὸ δέους, ἢ τοσούτοις εἴξας ἀγεννῶς ἢ πλείονας ψευδῶς εἰκάσας· **7** καὶ συσκευασάμενος τὰ τέκνα καὶ τὴν γυναῖκα αὐτοῦ, τὰς δὲ τῶν ἄλλων πολιτῶν ἐρήμους ἀπολιπὼν ἔφυγε, δέον ἢ κρατεῖν μαχόμενον ὑπὲρ τῆς πατρίδος ἢ δέχεσθαι διαλύσεις παρὰ τοῦ κρείττονος· ἦν γὰρ πολίτης καὶ οἰκεῖος· **8** νῦν δ᾽ ᾧ στρατηγίας χρόνον ἐπιμετρῆσαι καὶ ὑπατείαν ψηφίσασθαι δεινὸν ἡγεῖτο, τούτῳ παρέσχε λαβόντι τὴν πόλιν εἰπεῖν πρὸς Μέτελλον ὅτι κἀκεῖνον αἰχμάλωτον αὐτοῦ νομίζει καὶ τοὺς ἄλλους ἅπαντας.

4. **1** Ὃ τοίνυν ἔργον ἐστὶν ἀγαθοῦ στρατηγοῦ μάλιστα, κρείττονα μὲν ὄντα βιάσασθαι τοὺς πολεμίους μάχεσθαι, λειπόμενον δὲ δυνάμει μὴ βιασθῆναι, τοῦτο ποιῶν Ἀγησίλαος ἀεὶ διεφύλαξεν ἑαυτὸν ἀνίκητον· **2** Πομπήιον δὲ Καῖσαρ, οὗ μὲν ἦν ἐλάττων, διέφυγε μὴ βλαβῆναι, καθὸ δὲ κρείττων ἦν, ἠνάγκασεν ἀγωνισάμενον τῷ πεζῷ περὶ πάντων σφαλῆναι, καὶ κύριος εὐθὺς ἦν χρημάτων καὶ ἀγορᾶς καὶ θαλάττης, ἀφ᾽ ὧν διεπέπρακτ᾽ ἂν ἄνευ μάχης ἐκείνοις προσόντων. **3** τὸ δ᾽ ὑπὲρ τούτων ἀπολόγημα μέγιστόν ἐστιν ἔγκλημα στρατηγοῦ τηλικούτου. νέον μὲν γὰρ ἄρχοντα θορύβοις καὶ καταβοήσεσιν εἰς μαλακίαν καὶ δειλίαν ἐπιταραχθέντα, τῶν ἀσφαλεστάτων ἐκπεσεῖν λογισμῶν εἰκός ἐστι καὶ συγγνωστόν· **4** Πομπήιον δὲ Μάγνον, οὗ Ῥωμαῖοι τὸ μὲν στρατόπεδον πατρίδα, σύγκλητον δὲ τὴν σκηνήν, ἀποστάτας δὲ καὶ προδότας τοὺς ἐν Ῥώμῃ πολιτευομένους καὶ στρατηγοῦντας καὶ ὑπατεύοντας ἐκάλουν, ἀρχόμενον δ᾽ ὑπ᾽ οὐδενὸς ἔγνωσαν, πάσας δ᾽ αὐτοκράτορα στρατευσάμενον ἄριστα τὰς στρατείας, τίς ἂν ἀνάσχοιτο τοῖς Φαωνίου σκώμμασι καὶ Δομιτίου, καὶ ἵνα μὴ Ἀγαμέμνων λέγηται, παρ᾽ ἐλάχιστον ἐκβιασθέντα τὸν περὶ τῆς ἡγεμονίας καὶ ἐλευθερίας ἀναρρῖψαι κίνδυνον; **5** ὃς εἰ μόνον ἐσκόπει τὸ παρ᾽ ἡμέραν ἄδοξον, ὤφειλεν ἀντιστὰς ἐν ἀρχῇ διαγωνίσασθαι περὶ τῆς Ῥώμης, ἀλλὰ μὴ τὴν φυγὴν ἐκείνην

ἀποφαίνων στρατήγημα Θεμιστόκλειον, ὕστερον ἐν αἰσχρῷ τίθεσθαι τὴν ἐν Θετταλίᾳ πρὸ μάχης διατριβήν. 6 οὐ γὰρ ἐκεῖνό γε στάδιον αὐτοῖς καὶ θέατρον ἐναγωνίσασθαι περὶ τῆς ἡγεμονίας ὁ θεὸς ἀπέδειξε τὸ Φαρσάλιον πεδίον, οὐδ᾽ ὑπὸ κήρυκος ἐκαλεῖτο μάχεσθαι κατιὼν ἢ λιπεῖν ἑτέρῳ τὸν στέφανον, ἀλλὰ πολλὰ μὲν πεδία, μυρίας δὲ πόλεις καὶ γῆν ἄπλετον ἡ κατὰ θάλατταν εὐπορία παρέσχε βουλομένῳ μιμεῖσθαι Μάξιμον καὶ Μάριον καὶ Λεύκολλον καὶ αὐτὸν Ἀγησίλαον, 7 ὃς οὐκ ἐλάττονας μὲν ἐν Σπάρτῃ θορύβους ὑπέμεινε βουλομένων Θηβαίοις ὑπὲρ τῆς χώρας μάχεσθαι, πολλὰς δ᾽ ἐν Αἰγύπτῳ διαβολὰς καὶ κατηγορίας καὶ ὑπονοίας τοῦ βασιλέως ἤνεγκεν, ἡσυχίαν ἄγειν κελεύων, 8 χρησάμενος δὲ τοῖς ἀρίστοις ὡς ἐβούλετο λογισμοῖς, οὐ μόνον Αἰγυπτίους ἄκοντας ἔσωσεν, οὐδὲ τὴν Σπάρτην ἐν τοσούτῳ σεισμῷ μόνος ὀρθὴν ἀεὶ διεφύλαξεν, ἀλλὰ καὶ τρόπαιον ἔστησε κατὰ Θηβαίων ἐν τῇ πόλει, τὸ νικῆσαι παρασχὼν αὖθις ἐκ τοῦ τότε μὴ προαπολέσθαι βιασαμένους. 9 ὅθεν Ἀγησίλαος μὲν ὑπὸ τῶν βιασθέντων ὕστερον ἐπῃνεῖτο σωθέντων, Πομπήιος δὲ δι᾽ ἄλλους ἁμαρτὼν αὐτοὺς οἷς ἐπείσθη κατηγόρους εἶχε. 10 καίτοι φασί τινες ὡς ὑπὸ τοῦ πενθεροῦ Σκιπίωνος ἐξηπατήθη· τὰ γὰρ πλεῖστα τῶν χρημάτων ὧν ἐκόμιζεν ἐξ Ἀσίας βουλόμενον αὐτὸν νοσφίσασθαι καὶ ἀποκρύψαντα κατεπεῖξαι τὴν μάχην, ὡς οὐκέτι χρημάτων ὄντων. 11 ὃ κἂν ἀληθὲς ἦν, παθεῖν οὐκ ὤφειλεν ὁ στρατηγός, οὐδὲ ῥᾳδίως οὕτω παραλογισθεὶς ἀποκινδυνεῦσαι περὶ τῶν μεγίστων. ἐν μὲν οὖν τούτοις οὕτως ἑκάτερον ἀποθεωροῦμεν.

5. 1 Εἰς Αἴγυπτον δ᾽ ὁ μὲν ἐξ ἀνάγκης ἔπλευσε φεύγων, ὁ δ᾽ οὔτε καλῶς οὔτ᾽ ἀναγκαίως ἐπὶ χρήμασιν, ὅπως ἔχῃ τοῖς Ἕλλησι πολεμεῖν ἀφ᾽ ὧν τοῖς βαρβάροις ἐστρατήγησεν. 2 εἶθ᾽ ἃ διὰ Πομπήιον Αἰγυπτίοις ἐγκαλοῦμεν, ταῦτ᾽ Αἰγύπτιοι κατηγοροῦσιν Ἀγησιλάου. ὁ μὲν γὰρ ἠδικήθη πιστεύσας, ὁ δὲ πιστευθεὶς ἐγκατέλιπε καὶ μετέστη πρὸς τοὺς πολεμοῦντας οἷς ἔπλευσε συμμαχήσων.

BIBLIOGRAPHY

TEXTS

1. *Plutarch (of or including* Agesilaos*)*

Reiske, *Plutarchi Chaeronensis quae supersunt omnia Graece et Latine* (Leipzig, 1774–82).

Cl. Lindskog, *Plutarchi Vitae parallelae Agesilai et Pompeii* (Leipzig, 1906).

I. Bos, *Plutarchus' Leven van Agesilaus* (Groningen, 1947).

R. Flacelière and É. Chambry, *Plutarque: Vies*, viii: *Sertorius-Eumène—Agésilas-Pompée* (Paris, 1973).

M. Manfredini and L. Piccirilli, *Plutarque: le vite di Licurgo et di Numa* (Milan, 1980).

K. Ziegler, *Plutarchus. Vitae Parallelae*, iii/2 (Leipzig, 1973).

2. *The Oxyrhynchos Historian*

B. P. Grenfell and A. S. Hunt, *The Oxyrhynchus Papyri, Part V: Nos. 840–844* (London, 1908).

P. R. McKechnie and S. J. Kern, *Hellenica Oxyrhynchia* (Warminster, 1988).

M. Chambers, *Hellenica Oxyrhynchia* (Stuttgart, 1993).

3. *Xenophon (*Agesilaos *and* Hellenika*)*

L. Dindorf, Ξενοφῶντος Ἑλληνικά: *Xenophontis Historia Graeca* (Oxford, 1853).

G. E. Underhill and E. C. Marchant, *Xenophon: Hellenica* (Oxford, 1906).

C. Hude, *Xenophon: Hellenica* (Leipzig, 1930).

J. Hatzfeld, *Xénophon: Helléniques* (Paris, 1936).

P. Krentz, *Xenophon: Hellenika I–II. 3. 10* (Warminster, 1989).

——*Xenophon: Hellenika II. 3. 11–IV. 2. 8* (Warminster, 1995).

E. Luppino Manes, *L'Agesilao di Senophonte: tra commiato ed encomio* (Milan, 1991).

448 Bibliography

AALDERS H. WZN., G. J. D. (1973), 'De democratische ideologie en de tegenkrachten', *Lampas*, 6: 2–15.

——(1982), *Plutarch's Political Thought*, trans. M. A. Manekofsky (Amsterdam, Oxford and New York); originally published 1981.

ACCAME, S. (1951), *Ricerche intorno alla guerra corinzia* (Naples).

ADCOCK, F., and MOSLEY, D. J. (1975), *Diplomacy in Ancient Greece* (London).

ADKINS, A. W. H. (1960), *Merit and Responsibility: A Study in Greek Values* (Oxford).

ALFIERI TONINI, T. (1975), 'Il problema dei "neodamodeis" nell'ambito della società spartana', *RIL* 109: 305–16.

AMIT, M. (1971), 'The Boeotian Confederation during the Pentekontaetia', *Rivista storica dell'Antichità*, 1: 49–64.

ANDERSON, G. (1990), 'The Second Sophistic: Some Problems of Perspective', in Russell (ed.) (1990), 91–110.

——(1993), *The Second Sophistic: A Cultural Phenomenon in the Roman Empire* (London and New York).

ANDERSON, J. K. (1970), *Military Theory and Practice in the Age of Xenophon* (Berkeley).

——(1974a), 'The Battle of Sardis in 395 BC', *CSCA* 7: 27–53.

——(1974b), *Xenophon* (London).

——(1991), 'Hoplite Weapons and Offensive Arms', in Hanson (ed.) (1991), 15–37.

ANDREWES, A. (1938), 'Eunomia', *CQ* 32: 89–102.

——(1966), 'The Government of Classical Sparta', in Badian (ed.), *Ancient Society and Institutions: Studies Presented to Victor Ehrenberg on his 75th Birthday* (Oxford), 1–20.

——(1971), 'Two Notes on Lysander', *Phoenix*, 25: 206–26.

——(1978), 'Spartan Imperialism?', in Garnsey and Whittaker (eds.) (1978), 91–102, 302–6.

——(1981), Gomme *et al.* (1945–81), vol. v.

—— and DOVER, K. J. (1970), Gomme *et al.* (1945–81),vol. iv.

ANSON, E. M. (1985), 'Macedonia's Alleged Constitutionalism', *CJ* 80: 303–16.

ARMSTRONG, P., CAVANAGH, W. G., and SHIPLEY, G. (1992), 'Crossing the River: Observations on Routes and Bridges in Laconia from the Archaic to Byzantine Periods', *BSA* 87: 293–310.

ASHERI, D. (1961), 'Sulla legge di Epitadeo', *Athenaeum*, NS 39: 45–68.

——(1963), 'Laws of Inheritance, Distribution of Land and Political Constitutions in Ancient Greece', *Historia*, 12: 1–21.

——(1983), *Fra ellenismo e iranismo* (Bologna).

AUCELLO, E. (1964), 'Ricerche sulla cronologia della guerra corinzia', *Helikon*, 4: 29–45.

AUSTIN, M. M. (1993), 'Alexander and the Macedonian Invasion of Asia: Aspects of the Historiography of War and Empire in Antiquity', in Rich and Shipley (eds.) (1993), 197–223.

BABUT, D. (1969*a*), *Plutarque et le stoïcisme* (Paris).

——(1969*b*), *Plutarque: De la vertue éthique* (Paris).

——(1988), 'La part du rationalisme dans la religion de Plutarque', *ICS* 13. 2: 388–408.

BARBER, G. L. (1935), *The Historian Ephorus* (Cambridge).

BARBIERI, G. (1955), *Conone* (Rome).

BARRON, J. (1981), *Introduction to Greek Sculpture* (London).

BARROW, R. H. (1967), *Plutarch and his Times* (London).

BARTOLETTI, V. (1959), *Hellenica Oxyrhynchia* (Leipzig).

BATEMAN, J. J. (1958), 'Lysias and the Law', *TAPhA* 89: 276–85.

BECKER, C. L. (1959), 'What are Historical Facts?', in H. Meyerhoff (ed.), *Philosophy of History in Our Time* (New York).

BEISTER, H. (1970), *Untersuchungen zu der Zeit der thebanischen Hegemonie* (diss. Munich).

BELOCH, K. J. (1886), *Die Bevölkerung der griechisch-römischen Welt* (Leipzig).

——(1912–27), *Griechische Geschichte* (Berlin and Leipzig).

——(1921), 'Artabazos', *Janus*, i: 8–12.

BENGTSON, H. (1975), *Die Staatsverträge des Altertums II: Die Verträge der griechisch-römischen Welt von 700 bis 338 v. Chr.*, 2nd edn. (Munich).

——(1983), *Griechische Staatsmänner des 5. und 4. Jahrhunderts v. Chr.* (Munich), 184–98 (Agesilaos), 199–227 (Epameinondas).

BÉQUIGNON, Y. (1937), *La Vallée du Spercheios des origines au IVᵉ siècle* (Paris).

BERLIN, I. (1980), 'The Concept of Scientific History', in id., *Concepts and Categories* (Oxford), 103–42.

BERNINI, U. (1985), 'Il "progetto politico" di Lisandro sulla regalità spartana e la teorizzazione critica di Aristotele sui re spartani', *Studi ital. fil. class.* 3/78: 205–38.

BIELEFELD, E. (1964), 'Gott, Heros oder Feldherr?', *Gymnasium*, 71: 519–34.

BINTLIFF, J. L. (1985), 'Greece: The Boiotia Survey, Archaeological Field Surveys in Britain and Abroad', in F. Macready and F. H. Thompson (eds.), *The Society of Antiquaries: Occasional Paper* (London), 196–216.

—— and SNODGRASS, A. M. (1985), 'The Cambridge and Bradford Boeotian Expedition: The First Four Years', *JFA* 12: 123–61.

BLACKMAN, D. J. (1966), 'The Harbour at Perachora', *BSA* 61: 192–4 and pl. 42.

BLOCH, H. (1940), 'Herakleides Lembos and his *Epitome* of Aristotle's *Politeia*', *TAPhA* 71: 27–39.

BLOIS, L. DE (1992), 'Plutarch und die politische Philosophie der Griechen', *ANRW* II 36.5: 3384–404.

BLUNDELL, M. W. (1989), *Helping Friends and Harming Enemies: A Study in Sophocles and Greek Ethics* (Cambridge).

BOARDMAN, J. (1977), 'The Parthenon Frieze. Another View', in U. Hoeckmann and A. Krug (eds.), *Festschrift für Frank Brommer*, (Mainz), 39–49.

—— (1993) (ed.), *The Oxford History of Classical Art* (Oxford).

—— and FINN, D. (1985), *The Parthenon and its Sculptures* (London).

BOCKISCH, G. (1965), 'Ἁρμοσταί (431–387)', *Klio*, NF 46: 129–239.

—— (1974), 'Die sozial-ökonomische und politische Krise der Lakedaimonier und ihrer Symmachoi im 4. Jahrhundert v. u. Z.', in Welskopf (ed.), *Hellenische Poleis: Krise, Wandlung, Wirkung*, 3 vols. (Berlin), I: 199–230.

BOER, W. DEN (1954), *Laconian Studies* (Amsterdam).

—— (1974), 'Plutarchus' oogmerk als biograaf', *TG* 87: 365–78.

—— (1979), *Private Morality in Greece and Rome: Some Historical Aspects* (Mnemosne Suppl. 57: Leiden).

—— (1985), 'Plutarch's Philosophic Basis for Personal Involvement', in Eadie and Ober (eds.) (1985), 373–85.

BOMMELAER, J.-F. (1981), *Lysandre de Sparte: histoire et traditions* (Paris).

—— (1983), 'Le songe d'Agésilas: mythe ou rêve d'un mythe', *Ktèma*, 8: 19–26.

BORDES, J. (1982), *Politeia dans la pensée grecque jusqu'à Aristote* (Paris).

BÖRKER, CH. (1980), 'König Agesilaos von Sparta und der Artemis-Tempel in Ephesos', *ZPE* 37: 69–75.

BOS, I. (ed.) (1947), *Plutarchus' Leven van Agesilaus* (Groningen).

BOTHA, L. A. (1980), 'The *Hellenica Oxyrhynchia* and the Asiatic Campaign of Agesilaus' (diss. Univ. of South Africa).

—— (1988), 'The Asiatic Campaign of Agesilaus—the Topography of the Route from Ephesus to Sardis', *AC* 31: 71–80.

BOWERSOCK, G. (1969), *Greek Sophists in the Roman Empire* (Oxford).

BOWIE, E. L. (1970), 'The Greeks and their Past in the Second Sophistic', *Past and Present*, 46: 3–41, repr. in Finley (ed.), *Studies in Ancient Society* (London, 1974), 166–209.

BRADFORD, A. S. (1994), 'The Duplicitous Spartan', in Powell and Hodkinson (eds.) (1994), 59–85.

BREITENBACH, H. R. (1966), *Xenophon von Athen* (Stuttgart).

—— (1967), 'Xenophon', *RE*² ixB. 1569–2052.

——(1970), 'Hellenika Oxyrhynchia', *RE* Suppl. xii. 383–426.

BREMMER, J. M. (1981), 'Plutarch and the Naming of Greek Women', *AJP* 102: 425–6.

BRENK, F. E. (1975), The Dreams of Plutarch's *Lives*', *Latomus*, 34: 336–49.

——(1977), *In Mist Apparelled: Religious Themes in Plutarch's Moralia and Lives* (Leiden).

——and GALLO, I. (eds.) (1986), *Miscellanea Plutarchea: Atti del I. Convegno di studi su Plutarco* (Quaderni del Giornale filologico ferrarese 8: Ferrara).

BRESCIANI, E. (1985), 'The Persian Occupation of Egypt', in Gershevitch (ed.) (1985), 502–25.

BRIANT, P. (1977), *Alexandre le Grand* (Paris).

BRINGMANN, K. (1971), 'Xenophons Hellenika und Agesilaos: Zu ihrer Entstehungsweise und Datierung', *Gymnasium*, 78: 224–41.

——(1975), 'Die große Rhetra und die Entstehung des spartanischen Kosmos', *Historia*, 24: 513–38.

——(1980), 'Die soziale und politische Verfassung Spartas—ein Sonderfall der griechischen Verfassungsgeschichte?', *Gymnasium*, 87: 465–84.

BRINK, C. O. (1940), s.v. 'Peripatos', *RE* Suppl. vii. 899–949.

——(1971), *Horace on Poetry* (Cambridge).

BROCK, R. (1991), review of Woodman (1988), *LCM* 16. 8: 97–102.

BROMMER, F. (1967), *Die Metopen des Parthenon* (Mainz).

BRUCE, I. A. F. (1960), 'Internal Politics and the Outbreak of the Corinthian War', *Emerita*, 28: 75–86.

——(1961), 'The Democratic Revolution at Rhodes', *CQ*, NS 11: 166–70.

——(1963), 'Athenian Foreign Policy in 396–395 BC', *CJ* 58: 289–95.

——(1966), 'Athenian Embassies in the Early Fourth Century BC', *Historia*, 15: 272–81.

——(1967), *An Historical Commentary on the Hellenica Oxyrhynchia* (Cambridge).

BRUNT, P. A. (1975), 'Alexander, Barsine, and Heracles', *Riv. fil.* 103: 22–34.

——(1980), 'On Historical Fragments and Epitomes', *CQ*, NS 30: 477–94.

BUCHER-ISLER, B. (1972), *Norm und Individualität in den Biographien Plutarchs* (Noctes Romanae, 13; Bern and Stuttgart).

BUCK, R. J. (1972), 'The Formation of the Boeotian League', *CP* 67: 94–101.

——(1979), *A History of Boeotia* (Edmonton, Alta.).

——(1994), *Boeotia and the Boeotian League, 432–371 BC* (Edmonton, Alta.).

BUCKLER, J. (1971), 'Theban Treaty Obligations in IG II² 40: A Postscript', *Historia*, 20: 506–8.

BUCKLER, J. (1977), 'Plutarch and the Fate of Antalkidas', *GRBS* 18: 139–45.

——(1978), 'Plutarch on the Trials of Pelopidas and Epameinondas in 369 BC', *CP* 73: 36–42.

——(1979), 'The Re-establishment of the *Boiotarchia (378 BC)*', *AJAH* 4: 50–64.

——(1980a), *The Theban Hegemony, 371–362 BC* (Cambridge, Mass.).

——(1980b), 'Plutarch on Leuktra', *SO* 55: 75–93.

——(1982), 'Alliance and Hegemony in Fourth-Century Greece: The Case of Theban Hegemony', *Anc. World*, 5: 79–89.

——(1985), 'Epameinondas and the *Embolon*', *Phoenix*, 39: 134–43.

——(1992), 'Plutarch and Autopsy', *ANRW* II 33. 6: 4788–830.

BUFFIÈRE, F. (1980), *Éros adolescent: La pédérastie dans la Grèce antique* (Paris).

BURN, A. R. (1949), 'Helikon in History: A Study in Greek Mountain Topography', *BSA* 44: 313–23 and pl. 42.

——(1985), 'Persia and the Greeks', in Gershevitch (ed.) (1985), 292–391.

BURNETT, A. P. (1962), 'Thebes and the Expansion of the Second Athenian Confederacy: IG II² 40 and IG II² 43', *Historia*, 11: 1–17.

BUSOLT, G. (1905), 'Spartas Heer und Leuktra', *Hermes*, 40: 387–449.

BUTLER, D. (1962), 'Competence of the Demos in the Spartan Rhetra', *Historia*, 11: 385–96.

CAMERON, AVERIL (ed.) (1989), *History as Text: The Writing of Ancient History* (London).

CAMPAGNANO DI SEGNI, L. (1978), 'Commento a Plutarco, *Agide* 6. 1–2', *SCI* 4: 28–37.

CAMPBELL, D. A. (1988), *Greek Lyric* (Cambridge, Mass.), vol. ii.

CARGILL, J. (1981), *The Second Athenian League: Empire or Free Alliance?* (Berkeley and Los Angeles).

CARR, E. H. (1986), *What is History?* 2nd edn. (London).

CARTLEDGE, P. A. (1976a), 'Seismicity and Spartan Society', *LCM* 1.3: 25–8.

——(1976b), 'Did Spartan Citizens ever Practise a Manual *Technê?*', *LCM* 1.9: 115–19.

——(1977), 'Hoplites and Heroes: Sparta's Contribution to the Technique of Ancient Warfare', *JHS* 97: 11–27, repr. in K. Christ (ed.), *Sparta* (Darmstadt, 1986).

——(1978), 'Literacy in the Spartan Oligarchy', *JHS* 98: 25–37.

——(1979), *Sparta and Lakonia: A Regional History c. 1300–362 BC* (London).

——(1981), 'The Politics of Spartan Pederasty', *PCPhS*, NS 71: 17–36, repr. in A. K. Siems (ed.), *Sexualität und Erotik in der Antike*

(Darmstadt, 1988), 385–415.

——(1982), 'Sparta and Samos: A Special Relationship?', *CQ*, NS 32: 243–65.

——(1985), 'Rebels and Sambos in Classical Greece', in P. A. Cartledge and F. D. Harvey (eds.), *Crux: Essays Presented to G. E. M. de Ste. Croix on his 75th Birthday* (Exeter and London, 1985), 16–41.

——(1987), *Agesilaos and the Crisis of Sparta* (London).

——(1988), 'Yes, Spartan Kings Were Heroized', *LCM* 13.3: 43–4.

——(1991), 'Richard Talbert's Revision of the Spartan–Helot Struggle: A Reply', *Historia*, 40: 379–81.

——(1992), 'Early Lakedaimon: The Making of a Conquest-State', in Sanders (ed.) (1992), 49–55.

——(1993), *The Greeks: A Portrait of Self and Others* (Oxford).

——(1995), ' "We are all Greeks"? Ancient (especially Herodotean) and Modern Contestations of Hellenism', *BICS* 40 (NS 2): 75–82.

——and SPAWFORTH, A. J. S. (1989), *Hellenistic and Roman Sparta: A Tale of Two Cities* (London and New York).

CAUER, E. (1847), *Quaestiones de fontibus ad Agesilai historiam pertinentes* (Breslau), vol. i.

CAWKWELL, G. L. (1961), 'The Common Peace of 366/5 BC', *CQ*, NS 11: 80–6.

——(1963), 'Notes on the Peace of 375/4', *Historia*, 12: 84–95.

——(1972), 'Epaminondas and Thebes', *CQ*, NS 22: 254–78.

——(1973), 'The Foundation of the Second Athenian Confederacy', *CQ*, NS 23: 46–60.

——(1976a), 'Agesilaos and Sparta', *CQ*, NS 26: 62–84.

——(1976b), 'The Imperialism of Thrasybulus', *CQ*, NS 26: 270–7.

——(1979), introd. and notes to *Xenophon: A History of My Times*, trans. R. Warner (Harmondsworth).

——(1981a), 'Notes on the Failure of the Second Athenian Confederacy', *JHS* 101: 40–55.

——(1981b), 'The King's Peace', *CQ*, NS 31: 69–83.

——(1983), 'The Decline of Sparta', *CQ*, NS 33: 385–400.

——(1984), 'Athenian Naval Power in the Fourth Century', *CQ*, NS 34: 334–45.

——(1987), review of Cartledge (1987), *TLS*, 26 June, 699.

——(1989), 'Orthodoxy and Hoplites', *CQ*, NS 39: 375–89.

——(1994), 'The Deification of Alexander the Great: A Note', in I. Worthington (ed.), *Ventures into Greek History: Festschrift for N. G. L. Hammond* (Oxford), 292–306.

CEADEL, M. (1987), *Thinking about Peace and War* (Oxford).

CHAMBERS, M. (1993), *Hellenica Oxyrhynchia* (Stuttgart).

CHRIMES, K. M. T. (1949), *Ancient Sparta: A Re-examination of the*

Evidence (Manchester).

CHRISTIEN, J. (1974), 'La loi d'Epitadeus: un aspect de l'histoire économique et sociale à Sparte', *Rev. hist. de droit français et étranger*, 52: 197–221.

CLAUSS, M. (1983), *Sparta: Eine Einführung in seine Geschichte und Zivilisation* (Munich).

CLOCHÉ, P. (1918), 'La politique thébaine de 404 à 395', *Revue des études grecques*, 31: 315–48.

——(1949), 'Sur le rôle des rois de la Sparte', *Les Études classiques*, 17: 113–38, 343–81.

——(1952), *Thèbes de Béotie des origines à la conquête romaine* (Paris).

COBET, C. G. (1878), *Collectanea Critica* (Leiden).

CONNOR, W. R. (1968), *Theopompos and Fifth-Century Athens* (Cambridge and Washington, DC).

CONSTANZA, S. (1955), 'La synkrisis nello schema biografico di Plutarco', *Messana*, 4: 127–56.

COOK, J. M. (1962), *The Greeks in Ionia and the East* (London).

——(1983), *The Persian Empire* (London).

COOK, M. L. (1988), 'Ancient Political Factions: Boiotia 404–395', *TAPA* 118: 57–85.

COOK, R. M. (1962), 'Spartan History and Archaeology', *CQ*, NS 12: 156–8.

CORNELIUS, F. (1933), 'Die Schlacht bei Sardes', *Klio*, 26 = NF 8: 29–31.

COSTA, E. A. (1974), 'Evagoras I and the Persians c. 411–391 BC', *Historia*, 23: 40–56.

COURCELLE, P. (1974), *Connais-toi toi-même, de Socrate à Saint Bernard*, i (Paris).

COVENTRY, L. (1989), 'Philosophy and Rhetoric in the *Menexenus*', *JHS* 109: 1–15.

COWLEY, N. (1990), 'Africa in Plutarch: On References to Egypt, Carthage, Libya, Numidia and Mauretania, and their Literary Importance in the *Lives*', *Akroterion*, 35: 80–83.

COX, P. (1983), *Biography in Later Antiquity: A Quest for the Holy Man* (Berkeley and Los Angeles).

COZZOLI, U. (1978a), 'I fondamenti del κόσμος licurgico nel pensiero di Plutarco', *Cultura e scuola*, 66: 84–93.

——(1978b), 'Sparta e l'affrancamento degli iloti nel V e nel IV secolo', in id., *Sesta miscellanea greca e romana* (Rome), 213–32.

CROSS, R. C., and WOOZLEY, A. D. (1964), *Plato's Republic: A Philosophical Commentary* (London).

CRUSIUS, O. (1905), 'Sagenverschiebungen', *Sitzungsberichte der philos. und der hist. Klasse der Königlich Bayerischen Akad. der Wissenschaften*, 749–802.

DAVID, E. (1979a), 'The Conspiracy of Cinadon', *Athenaeum*, NS 57: 239–59.

——(1979b), 'The Pamphlet of Pausanias', *PP* 34: 94–116.

——(1979–80), 'The Influx of Money into Sparta at the End of the Fifth Century BC', *SCI* 5: 30–45.

——(1980), 'Revolutionary Agitation at Sparta after Leuktra', *Athenaeum*, NS 58: 299–308.

——(1981), *Sparta between Empire and Revolution, 404–243 BC* (New York).

——(1982–3), 'Aristotle and Sparta', *Anc. Society*, 13/14: 67–103.

——(1989), 'Laughter in Spartan Society', in Powell (ed.) (1989), 1–25.

——(1992), 'Sparta's Social Hair', *Eranos*, 90: 11–21.

DE LACY, P. (1952), 'Biography and Tragedy in Plutarch', *AJP* 73: 159–71.

DELBRÜCK, H. (1975), *History of the Art of War within the Framework of Political History*, trans. W. J. Renfrew (Lincoln, Nebr., and London; in German, Berlin, 1920).

DELEBECQUE, E. (1957), *Essai sur la vie de Xénophon* (Paris).

DEMAND, N. H. (1980), review of Dover (1978), *AJPh* 101: 121–4.

——(1982), *Thebes in the Fifth Century: Herakles Resurgent* (London).

——(1994), *Birth, Death, and Motherhood in Classical Greece* (Baltimore and London).

DENNISTON, J. D. (ed.) (1939), *Euripides: Electra* (Oxford).

DESIDERI, P. (1985), 'Ricchezza e vita politica nel pensiero di Plutarco', *Index*, 13: 391–405.

——(1986), 'La vita politica e culturale nell'Impero. Letture dei *Praecepta gerendae reipublicae* e dell'*An seni respublica gerenda sit* di Plutarco', *Athenaeum*, NS 64: 371–81.

——(1992), 'La formazione delle coppie nelle *Vite* plutarchee', *ANRW* II 33. 6: 4470–86.

DEVEREUX, G. (1965), 'La psychanalyse et l'histoire: une application à l'histoire de Sparte', *Annales ESC* 20: 18–20.

DEVINE, A. M. (1983), 'Embolon: A Study in Tactical Terminology', *Phoenix*, 37: 201–17.

DE VOTO, J. G. (1986), 'Agesilaos, Antalcidas and the Failed Peace of 392/91 BC', *Class. Phil.* 81: 191–202.

——(1988), 'Agesilaos and Tissaphernes near Sardis in 395 BC', *Hermes*, 116: 41–53.

DE WET, B. X. (1981), 'Aspects of Plutarch's Portrayal of Pompey', *Acta Class.* 24: 119–32.

DIHLE, A. (1956), *Studien zur griechischen Biographie* (*Abhandlungen der Akademie der Wissenschaften in Göttingen, ph.-hist. kl.*, 3 Folge, 37; Göttingen).

DILLON, J. (1988), 'Plutarch and Platonist Orthodoxy', *ICS* 13. 2: 357–64.

DINDORF, L. (1853), *Historia graeca xenophontea* (Oxford).

DIPERSIA, G. (1974), 'La nuova popolazione di Messene al tempo di Epaminonda', in M. Sordi (ed.), *Contributi dell'Istituto di storia antica,* ii: *Propaganda e persuasione occulta nell'Antichità* (Pubbl. dell'Univ. cattol. del Sacro Cuore, Sc. stor., 8; Milan), 54–61.

DONINI, P. L. (1986), 'Plutarco, Ammonio e l'Academia', in Brenk and Gallo (eds.) (1986), 97–110.

DOREY, T. A. (ed.) (1967), *Latin Biography* (London).

DOVER, K. J. (1974), *Greek Popular Morality in the Time of Plato and Aristotle* (Oxford).

—— (1978), *Greek Homosexuality* (London).

—— (1980), *Plato: Symposium* (Cambridge, repr. 1984).

—— (1982), review of den Boer (1979), *JHS* 102: 260–1.

—— (1988), *The Greeks and their Legacy, Collected Papers,* ii: *Prose Literature, History, Society, Transmission, Influence* (Oxford).

—— and ANDREWES, A. (1970) = Gomme *et al.* (1945–81), vol. iv.

DREIZEHNTER, A. (1975), 'Pompeius als Städtegründer', *Chiron,* 5: 213.

DREWS, R. (1962), 'Diodorus and his Sources', *AJPh* 83: 382–92.

—— (1963), 'Ephoros and History Written κατὰ γένος', *AJPh* 84: 244–55.

—— (1976), 'Ephoros κατὰ γένος Revisited', *Hermes,* 104: 497–8.

DUCAT, J. (1974), 'Le mépris des hilotes', *Annales ESC,* 29: 1451–64.

—— (1983), 'Sparte archaïque et classique: Structures économiques, sociales, politiques (1965–1982)', *REG* 96: 194–225.

—— (1990), *Les Hilotes* (*BCH,* Suppl. 20; Athens and Paris).

DUE, B. (1987), 'Lysander in Xenophon's *Hellenica*', *C&M* 38: 53–62.

DUFF, T. E. (1994), 'Signs of the Soul: Moralising in the *Parallel Lives* of Plutarch' (Ph.D. thesis, Cambridge).

—— (forthcoming) *Plutarch's Lives: Biographies as Moral Texts* (Oxford).

DUGAS, CH. (1910), 'La Campagne d'Agésilas en Asie Mineure (395): Xénophon et l'Anonyme d'Oxyrhynchos', *BCH* 34: 58–95.

DULL, C. J. (1975), 'A Study of the Leadership of the Boiotian League from the Invasion of the Boiotoi to the King's Peace' (diss. University of Wisconsin at Madison).

—— (1977), 'Thucydides i. 113 and the Leadership of Orchomenos', *CPh* 72: 305–14.

EADIE, J. W. and OBER, J. (eds.) (1985), *The Craft of the Ancient Historian: Essays in Honor of Chester G. Starr* (New York and London).

EBERT, J. (1972), *Griechische Epigramme auf Sieger an gymnischen und hippischen Agonen* (ASAW 63; Berlin).

EDELMANN, H. (1974), 'Volksmassen und Einzelpersönlichkeit im Spiegel von Historiographie und Publizistik des 5. und des 4. Jahrhunderts', *Klio*, NF 56: 415–44.

ELTON, G. R. (1967), *The Practice of History* (London).

ERBSE, H. (1956), 'Die Bedeutung der Synkrisis in den Parallel-biographien Plutarchs', *Hermes*, 84: 398–424, repr. in *Ausgewählte Schriften zur klassischen Philologie* (Berlin and New York, 1979), 478–505.

ERRINGTON, R. M. (1986), *Geschichte Makedoniens von den Anfängen bis zum Untergang des Königreiches* (Munich).

ESYE (1963/72), Νομοί Ἀρκαδίας, Ἀττικῆς, Βοιωτίας, Λαρίσης (Athens).

FARRELL, J. (1907–8), 'The Archaic Terracottas from the Sanctuary of Orthia', *BSA* 14: 48–72.

FIGUEIRA, T. J. (1984), 'Mess Contributions and Subsistence at Sparta', *TAPhA* 114: 87–109.

——(1986), 'Population Patterns in Late Archaic and Classical Sparta', *TAPhA* 116: 165–213.

FIMMEN, D. (1916), 'Issorion', *RE* ix/2. 2247.

FINLEY, M. I. (1968), 'Sparta', in J.-P. Vernant (ed.), *Problèmes de la guerre en Grèce ancienne* (Paris), 143–60 = 'Sparta and Spartan society', in id., *Economy and Society in Ancient Greece*, ed. B. D. Shaw and R. P. Saller (London, 1981), 22–40 = 'Sparta', in id., *Use and Abuse of History*, 2nd edn. (London, 1986), 161–77.

——(1977), *The World of Odysseus*, 2nd edn. (London).

——(1983), *Politics in the Ancient World* (Cambridge).

——(1985), *Ancient History: Evidence and Models* (London).

——and PLEKET, H. W. (1976), *The Olympic Games: The First Thousand Years* (London).

FLACELIÈRE, R. (1970), 'Héracles ou Héraclite?', in *Hommages à M. Delcourt* (Coll. Latomus, 114; Brussels), 207–10.

——(1979), 'La pensée de Plutarque dans les *Vies*', *Bull. Ass. G. Budé*, 264–75.

——and CHAMBRY, É. (1973), *Plutarque: Vies*, viii: *Sertorius-Eumène—Agésilas-Pompée* (Paris).

FLOWER, M. A. (1988), 'Agesilaos of Sparta and the Origins of the Ruler Cult', *CQ*, NS 38: 123–34.

——(1991), 'Revolutionary Agitation and Social Change in Classical Sparta', in Flower and Toher (eds.) (1991), 78–97.

——(1994), *Theopompos of Chios: History and Rhetoric in the Fourth Century BC* (Oxford).

——and TOHER, M. (eds.) (1991), *Georgica: Greek Studies in Honour of George Cawkwell* (*ICS Bulletin Supp.* 58; London).

FORNARA, C. W. (ed.) (1983), *Archaic Times to the End of the Peloponnesian War*, 2nd edn. (Cambridge).

FORREST, W. G. (1967), 'Legislation in Sparta', *Phoenix*, 21: 11–19.

——(1968), *A History of Sparta c.950–192 BC* (London).

——(1981), review of C. D. Hamilton (1979), *JHS* 101: 197–8.

FOSS, C. (1979), 'Explorations in Mount Tmolus', *CSCA* 11: 21–60.

FOSSEY, J. M. (1979), 'The Cities of the Kopaïs in the Roman Period', *ANRW* 17. 1: 48–72.

FOXHALL, L. (1993), 'Farming and Fighting in Ancient Greece', in Rich and Shipley (eds.) (1993), 134–45.

FRASER, P. M. (1996), *Cities of Alexander the Great* (Oxford).

FRAZIER, F. (1987), 'A propos de la composition des couples dans les *Vies Parallèles* de Plutarque', *RPh* 61: 65–75.

——(1988), 'A propos de la *philotimia* dans les *Vies*: quelques jalons dans l'histoire d'une notion', *RPh* 62: 109–27.

——(1992), 'Contribution à l'étude de la composition des *Vies* de Plutarque: l'élaboration des grandes scènes', *ANRW* 11 33. 6: 4487–535.

FROST, F. J. (1980), *Plutarch's Themistocles: A Historical Commentary* (Princeton).

FUHRMANN, F. (1964), *Les Images de Plutarque* (Paris).

FUKS, A. (1962), 'The Spartan Citizen-Body in Mid-Third Century BC and its Enlargement Proposed by Agis IV', *Athenaeum*, NS 40: 244–63, repr. in id. (ed.) (1984), *Social Conflict in Ancient Greece* (Jerusalem and Leiden), 230–49.

FUNKE, P. (1980), *Homónoia und Arché: Athen und die griechische Staatenwelt vom Ende des Peloponnesischen Krieges bis zum Königsfrieden (404–387/6)* (Historia Einzelschriften, 37; Wiesbaden).

FUSCAGNI, F. (1972), 'Le beotarchie di Pelopida e il numero dei beotarchi dopo la liberazione della Cadmea del 379', *RIL* 106: 415–33.

GARCÍA VALDÉS, M. (1990), 'Algunas sugerencias sobre la *Vida de Agesilao*', in Pérez Jiménez and Cerro Calderón (1990), 27–38.

GARLAN, Y. (1982), *Les Esclaves en Grèce ancienne* (Paris).

GARNSEY, P. D. A., and WHITTAKER, C. R. (eds.) (1978), *Imperialism in the Ancient World* (Cambridge).

GEIGER, J. (1974), 'Plutarch and Rome', *SCI* 1: 137–44.

——(1981), 'Plutarch's *Parallel Lives*: The Choice of Heroes', *Hermes*, 109: 85–104, repr. in Scardigli (ed.) (1995), 165–90.

——(1985), *Cornelius Nepos and Ancient Political Biography* (Historia Einzelschriften, 47: Stuttgart).

——(1988), 'Nepos and Plutarch: From Latin to Greek Political Biography', *ICS* 13. 2: 245–56.

GEORGIADOU, A. (1988), 'The *Lives* of the Caesars and Plutarch's Other *Lives*', *ICS* 13. 2: 349–56.

——(1992a), 'Bias and Character-Portrayal in Plutarch's *Lives* of

Pelopidas and Marcellus', *ANRW* II 33. 6: 4222–57.

—— (1992*b*), 'Idealistic and Realistic Portraiture in the *Lives* of Plutarch', *ANRW* II 33. 6: 4616–23.

GERSHEVITCH, I. (ed.) (1985), *The Cambridge History of Iran*, II: *The Median and Achaemenian Periods* (Cambridge).

GILL, C. (1983), 'The Question of Character Development: Plutarch and Tacitus', *CQ*, NS 33: 469–87.

—— (1984), 'The Ethos/Pathos Distinction in Rhetorical and Literary Criticism', *CQ*, NS 34: 149–66.

—— (1990), 'The Character–Personality Distinction', in Pelling (ed.) (1990*b*), 1–31.

—— (1993), 'Plato on Falsehood—Not Fiction', in Gill and Wiseman (eds.) (1993), 38–87.

—— and WISEMAN T. P. (eds.) (1993), *Lies and Fiction in the Ancient World* (Exeter).

GLUCKER, J. (1978), *Antiochus and the Late Academy* (Hypomnemata, 56; Göttingen).

—— (1988), 'Πρὸς τὸν εἰπόντα—Sources and Credibility of De Stoicorum Repugnantiis 8', *ICS* 13. 2: 473–89.

GÓMEZ ESPELOSÍN, F. J. (1990), 'Plutarco y la revolución social', in Pérez Jiménez and Cerro Calderón (eds.) (1990), 87–94.

GOMME, A. W. (1945) = Gomme *et al.* (1945–81), vol. i.

—— (1954), 'Who was Kratippos?', *CQ*, NS 4: 53–5.

—— (1956) = Gomme *et al.* (1945–81), vols. ii–iii.

—— ANDREWES, A., and DOVER, K. J. (1945–81), *A Historical Commentary on Thucydides*, 5 vols. (Oxford).

GOSSAGE, A. J. (1967), 'Plutarch', in Dorey (ed.) (1967), 45–77.

GRANIER, F (1931), *Die makedonische Heeresversammlung: Ein Beitrag zum antiken Staatsrecht* (Münchener Beiträge zur Papyrusforschung, 13; Munich).

GRANT, J. R. (1965), 'A Note on the Tone of Greek Diplomacy', *CQ*, NS 15: 261–6.

GRANT, M. (1990), *The Visible Past: Greek and Roman History from Archaeology (1960–1990)* (London).

GRAY, V. J. (1979), 'Two Different Approaches to the Battle of Sardis', *CSCA* 12: 183–200.

—— (1980), 'The Years 375 to 371 BC: A Case Study in the Reliability of Diodorus Siculus and Xenophon', *CQ*, NS 30: 306–26.

—— (1981), 'Dialogue in Xenophon's *Hellenica*', *CQ*, NS 31: 321–34.

—— (1987), 'The Value of Diodorus Siculus for the Years 411–386 BC', *Hermes*, 115: 72–89.

—— (1989), *The Character of Xenophon's Hellenica* (London).

GREENHALGH, P. (1980), *Pompey: The Roman Alexander* (London).

GREENHALGH, P. (1981), *Pompey: The Republican Prince* (London).

GRENFELL, B. P., and HUNT, A. S. (1908), *The Oxyrhynchus Papyri, Part V. Nos. 840–844* (London).

GRIFFIN, A. (1982), *Sikyon* (Oxford).

GRIFFITH, G. T. (1950), 'The Union of Corinth and Argos (392–386 BC)', *Historia*, 1: 236–56.

——(1978), 'Athens in the Fourth Century', in Garnsey and Whittaker (eds.) (1978), 127–44, 310–14.

GROTE, G. (1869), *History of Greece* (London), vols. ix–x.

GRUBE, G. M. A. (1935), *Plato's Thought* (London).

GUTHRIE, W. K. C. (1971), *The Sophists* (Cambridge).

HABICHT, C. (1970), *Gottmenschtum und griechische Städte* (Zetemata, 14[2]; Munich).

HACK, H. M. (1978), 'Thebes and the Spartan Hegemony, 386–382', *AJPh* 99: 210–27.

HALL, E. (1989), *Inventing the Barbarian: Greek Self-Definition through Tragedy* (Oxford).

——(1993), 'Asia Unmanned: Images of Victory in Classical Athens', in Rich and Shipley (eds.) (1993), 108–33.

HALLIWELL, S. (1990), 'Traditional Greek Conceptions of Character', in Pelling (ed.) (1990*b*), 32–59.

HALLOCK, R. T. (1985), 'The Evidence of the Persepolis Tablets', in Gershevitch (ed.) (1985), 588–609.

HAMDORF, F. W. (1964), *Griechische Kultpersonifikation der vorhellenistischen Zeit* (Mainz).

HAMILTON, C. D. (1970), 'Spartan Politics and Policy, 405–401 BC', *AJPh* 91: 294–314.

——(1972), 'The Politics of Revolution at Corinth, 395–386 BC', *Historia*, 21: 21–37.

——(1979), *Sparta's Bitter Victories: Politics and Diplomacy in the Corinthian War* (Ithaca, NY).

——(1982*a*), 'Agesilaos and the Failure of Spartan Hegemony', *Anc. World*, 5: 67–78.

——(1982*b*), 'Étude chronologique sur le règne d'Agésilas', *Ktèma*, 7: 281–96.

——(1991), *Agesilaus and the Failure of Spartan Hegemony* (Ithaca, NY).

——(1992), 'Plutarch's *Life of Agesilaos*', *ANRW* II 33. 6: 4201–21.

HAMILTON, J. R. (1969), *Plutarch, Alexander: a Commentary* (Oxford).

——(1973), *Alexander the Great* (London).

HAMMOND, N. G. L. (1954), 'The Main Road from Boeotia to the Peloponnese through the Northern Megarid', *BSA* 49: 103–22.

——(1986), *A History of Greece to 322 BC*, 3rd edn. (Oxford).

——and GRIFFITH, G. T. (1979), *A History of Macedonia 550–336* (Oxford), vol. ii.

HANSON, V. D. (1983), *Warfare and Agriculture in Classical Greece* (Pisa).

——(1988), 'Epameinondas, the Battle of Leuktra (371 BC), and the "Revolution" in Greek Battle Tactics', *CA* 7: 190–207.

——(1989), *The Western Way of War: Infantry Battle in Classical Greece* (London and New York).

——(ed.) (1991), *Hoplites: The Classical Greek Battle Experience* (London and New York).

HART, J. (1982), *Herodotus and Greek History* (London and New York).

HATZFELD, J. (1930), 'Notes sur la composition des Helléniques', *Revue de philologie*, 4 (56): 113–27, 209–26.

——(1933), 'Notes sur la chronologie des Helléniques', *REA* 35, 387–409.

——(1946), 'Agésilas et Artaxerxès II', *BCH* 70: 238–46.

——(1951), *Alcibiade: étude sur l'histoire d'Athénes à la fin du Ve siècle* (Paris).

HEFTNER, H. (1995), *Plutarch und der Aufstieg des Pompeius: Ein historischer Kommentar zu Plutarchs Pompeiusvita. Teil I: kap. 1–45* (Frankfurt am Main).

HENDERSON, J. (1989), 'Livy and the Invention of History', in Cameron (ed.) (1989), ch. 3.

HENNIG, D. (1974), 'Orchomenos', *RE* Suppl. xiv: 333–55.

HENRY, W. P. (1967), *Greek Historical Writing: A Historiographical Essay Based on Xenophon's Hellenica* (Chicago).

HERMAN, G. (1987), *Ritualised Friendship and the Greek City* (Cambridge).

HERSHBELL, J. P. (1992), 'Plutarch and Stoicism', *ANRW* II 36. 5: 3336–52.

HERTZBERG, G. F. (1856), *Das Leben des Königs Agesilaos II. von Sparta* (Halle).

HEURTLEY, W. A. (1923), 'Harbours of S. Boeotia', *BSA* 26: 38–45, pl. VII.

HICKS, E. L., and HILL, G. F. (1901), *A Manual of Greek Historical Inscriptions*, 2nd edn. (Oxford).

HINDLEY, C. (1994), '*Eros* and Military Command in Xenophon', *CQ*, NS 44: 347–66.

HIRSCH, S. W. (1985), *The Friendship of the Barbarians: Xenophon and the Persian Empire* (London and Hanover, NH).

HODKINSON, S. J. (1983), 'Social Order and the Conflict of Values in Classical Sparta', *Chiron*, 13: 239–81.

——(1986a), 'Land Tenure and Inheritance in Classical Sparta', *CQ*, NS 36: 378–406.

HODKINSON, S. J. (1986*b*), review of MacDowell (1986), *JHS* 106: 231–2.

——(1989), 'Inheritance, Marriage and Demography: Perspectives upon the Success and Decline of Classical Sparta', in Powell (ed.) (1989), 79–121.

——(1993), 'Warfare, Wealth, and the Crisis of Spartiate Society', in Rich and Shipley (eds.) (1993), 146–76.

——(1994), ' "Blind Ploutos"? Contemporary Images of the Role of Wealth in Classical Sparta', in Powell and Hodkinson (eds.) (1994), 183–222.

HOFMANN, N. B., rev. SZANTYR, A. (1965), *Lateinischer Syntax und Stilistik* (Munich).

HOLLADAY, A. J. (1977), 'Spartan Austerity', *CQ,* NS 27: 111–26.

——(1982), 'Hoplites and Heresies', *JHS* 102: 94–103.

——and GOODMAN, M. D. (1986), 'Religious Scruples in Ancient Warfare', *CQ,* NS 36: 151–71.

HOMANN-WEDEKING, E. (1965), 'Samos 1964', *Archäologischer Anzeiger*, 428–46.

HORNBLOWER, S. (1982*a*), *Mausolus* (Oxford).

——(1982*b*), review of Cargill (1981), *CR,* NS 32: 235–9.

——(1991), *The Greek World 479–323 BC*, 2nd edn. (London and New York).

——(1988), review of Hirsch (1985), *CR,* NS 38: 144.

——(1990*a*), review of Sancisi-Weerdenburg (ed.) (1987), *CR,* NS 40: 89–95.

——(1990*b*), review of Weiskopf (1989), *CR,* NS 40: 363–5.

——(1990*c*), 'When was Megalopolis Founded?', *BSA*, 85: 71–7.

——(1994*a*), ch. 3: 'Persia', ch. 8a: 'Asia Minor', in *CAH* 2nd edn., vol. vi.

——(ed.) (1994*b*), *Greek Historiography* (Oxford).

HOW, W. W., and WELLS, J. (1912), *A Commentary on Herodotus* (Oxford).

HUSSEY, E. (1972), *The Presocratics* (London).

HUXLEY, G. (1979), *On Aristotle and Greek Society* (Belfast).

——(1987), review of Symeonoglou (1985), *CR,* NS 37: 68–72.

INGENKAMP, H. G. (1992), 'Plutarch und die konservative Verhaltens-norm', *ANRW* II 33. 6: 4624–44.

JACKSON, A. H. (1991), 'Hoplites and the Gods: The Dedication of Captured Arms and Armour', in Hanson (ed.) (1991), 228–49.

JACOBY, F. (1950), 'The Authorship of the *Hellenica* of Oxyrhynchus', *CQ* 44: 1–11.

——(1923–55), *Die Fragmente der griechischen Historiker* (Berlin and Leiden).

JAMESON, M. H. (1991), 'Sacrifice before Battle', in Hanson (ed.) (1991), 197–227.

JEFFREY, L. H. (1990), *The Local Scripts of Archaic Greece*, rev. A. W. Johnston (Oxford).

JEHNE, M. (1991), 'Die Friedensverhandlungen von Sparta 392/1 v. Chr. und das Problem der kleinasiatischen Griechen', *Chiron*, 21: 265–76.

——(1994), *Koine Eirene: Untersuchungen zu den Befriedungs- und Stabilisierungsbemühungen in der griechischen Poliswelt des 4. Jahrhunderts v. Chr.* (Hermes Einzelschriften, 63; Stuttgart).

JENKINSON, E. M. (1967), 'Nepos—An Introduction to Latin Biography', in Dorey (ed.) (1967), 1–15.

JOHNSTON, A. E. M. (1967), 'The Earliest Preserved Greek Map, A New Ionian Coin Type', *JHS* 87: 92–3 and pl. 9.

JONES, C. P. (1966*a*), 'The Teacher of Plutarch', *HSCPh* 71: 205–15.

——(1966*b*), 'Towards a Chronology of Plutarch's Works', *JRS* 56: 61–74, repr. in Scardigli (ed.) (1995), 95–123.

——(1971), *Plutarch and Rome* (Oxford).

JUDEICH, W. (1892), *Kleinasiatische Studien: Untersuchungen zur griechisch-persischen Geschichte des IV. Jahrhunderts v. Chr.* (Marburg).

JÜTHNER, J. (1923), *Hellenen und Barbaren* (Leipzig).

KAGAN, K. (1961), 'Economic Origins of the Corinthian War', *PP* 16: 321–41.

——(1962), 'Corinthian Politics and the Revolution of 392 BC', *Historia*, 11: 447–57.

KAHN, C. H. (1963), 'Plato's Funeral Oration: The Motive of the *Menexenus*', *CP* 58: 220–34.

——(1976), 'Plato on the Unity of the Virtues', in W. H. Werkmeister (ed.), *Facets of Plato's Philosophy* (*Phronesis*, Suppl. 2; Assen and Amsterdam), 21–39.

KAHN, H. A. (ed.) (1994), *The Birth of European Identity: The Europe–Asia Contrast in Greek Thought 490–322 BC* (Nottingham).

KAHRSTEDT, U. (1922), *Griechisches Staatsrecht I: Sparta und seine Symmachie* (Göttingen).

KALLET-MARX, R. M. (1985), 'Athens, Thebes and the Foundation of the Second Athenian League', *CA* 4: 127–51.

KAUPERT, W. (1924–31), 'Sardes 395 v. Chr.', in J. Kromayer, G. Veith, et al., *Antike Schlachtfelder: Bausteine zu einer antiken Kriegsgeschichte*, iv (Ergänzungsband; Berlin), 261–89.

——(1926*a*), 'Sardes 395 v. Chr.', in Kromayer–Veith (1926), Blatt 4, Kärtchen 8–9.

——(1926*b*), 'Schlacht bei Koronea 394 v. Chr.', in Kromayer–Veith (1926), Blatt 5, Kärtchen 3.

KAUPERT, W. (1926c), 'Leuktra 371 v. Chr.', in Kromayer–Veith (1926), Blatt 5, Kärtchen 4–5.

KEAVENEY, A. (1982), 'Young Pompey: 106–79 BC', *Ant. Class.* 51: 111–39.

KEBRIC, R. B. (1976), 'Implications of Alcibiades' Relationship with the Ephor Endius', *Historia*, 25: 249–52.

——(1977) *In the Shadow of Macedon: Duris of Samos* (Historia Einzelschriften, 29; Wiesbaden).

KEEN, A. G. (1996), 'Lies About Lysander', in Cairns and Heath (eds.), *Papers of the Leeds International Latin Seminar*, 9 (Leeds), 285–96.

KELLY, D. H. (1975), 'Sources and Interpretations of Spartan History in the Reigns of Agesilaus II, Archidamus III and Agis III' (diss. Cambridge).

——(1978), 'Agesilaus' Strategy in Asia Minor, 396–5 BC', *LCM* 3: 97–8.

KELLY, T. (1985), 'The *Skutale*', in Eadie and Ober (eds.) (1985), 141–69.

KENNELL, M. M. (1995), *The Gymnasium of Virtue: Education and Culture in Ancient Sparta* (Chapel Hill, NC, and London).

KERFERD, G. B. (1981a), *The Sophistic Movement* (Cambridge).

——(ed.) (1981b), *The Sophists and their Legacy* (Hermes Einzelschriften, 44; Wiesbaden).

KIENITZ, F. K. (1953), *Die politische Geschichte Ägyptens vom 7. bis zum 4. Jhdt. vor der Zeitwende* (Berlin).

KIEPERT, H. (1844), *Atlas von Hellas* (Berlin).

——(1898), *Atlas Antiquus*, 12th edn. (Berlin).

KING, H. (1989), 'The Daughter of Leonides: Reading the Hippocratic Corpus', in Cameron (ed.) (1989), 11–32.

KIRK, G. S., RAVEN, J. E., and SCHOFIELD, M. (1983), *The Presocratic Philosophers: A Critical History with a Selection of Texts*, 2nd edn. (Cambridge).

KODER, J., and HILD, F. (1976), *Tabulo Imperii Byzantini: Hellas und Thessalia* (Vienna).

KRENTZ, P. (1995), *Xenophon: Hellenika II. 3. 11–IV. 2. 8* (Warminster).

KROMAYER, J., and VEITH G. (1926), *Schlachten-Atlas zur antiken Kriegsgeschichte: 120 Karten mit begleitendem Text, Vierte Lieferung: Griechenland* (Leipzig).

KRÖMER, D. (1971), *Xenophons Agesilaos: Untersuchungen zur Komposition* (diss. Augsburg).

KUKOFKA, D.-A. (1993), 'Die παιδίσκοι im System der spartanischen Altersklassen', *Philologus*, 137: 197–205.

LAIX, R. A. DE (1974), 'Aristotle's Conception of the Spartan Constitution', *JHPh* 12: 21–30.

LANE, E. A. (1933–4), 'Lakonian Vase-Painting', *BSA* 34: 99–189.

LANE FOX, R. (1973), *Alexander the Great* (London).

LANZILLOTTA, E. (1980), 'La politica spartana dopo la pace di Antalcida', *Miscell. greca e rom.* 7: 129–78.

LARMOUR, D. H. J. (1992), 'Making Parallels: *Synkrisis* and Plutarch's *Themistocles and Camillus*', *ANRW* II 33. 6: 4154–200.

LARSEN, J. A. O. (1925), 'Representative Government in the Panhellenic Leagues', *CP* 20: 313–29.

——(1954), 'The Judgment of Antiquity on Democracy', *CP* 49: 1–14.

——(1955*a*), 'The Boeotian Confederacy and Fifth Century Oligarchic Theory', *TAPhA* 86: 40–50.

——(1955*b*), *Representative Government in Greek and Roman History* (Berkeley, Los Angeles, and London).

——(1960), 'Orchomenos and the Foundation of the Boeotian Confederacy in 447', *CP* 55: 9–18.

——(1962), 'Freedom and its Obstacles in Ancient Greece', *CP* 57: 230–4.

——(1968), *Greek Federal States: Their Institutions and History* (Oxford).

——(1973), 'Demokratia', *CP* 68: 45–6.

LATICHEFF, B. (1882), 'Inscriptions de Narthakion', *BCH* 6: 356–63.

LAUNEY, M. (1987), *Recherches sur les armées hellénistiques*, 2nd edn. rev. Y. Garlan, P. Gauthier, C. Orrieux (BEFAR 169; Paris).

LAVERY, G. B. (1973/4), 'Training, Trade and Trickery: Three Lawgivers in Plutarch', *CW* 67: 369–81.

LAZENBY, J. F. (1985), *The Spartan Army* (Warminster).

——(1989), review of Cartledge (1987), *CR*, NS 39: 283–4.

——(1991), 'The Killing Zone', in Hanson (ed.) (1991), 87–109.

——(1993), *The Defence of Greece* (Warminster).

LEACH, J. (1978), *Pompey the Great* (London).

LEAKE, W. M. (1835), *Travels in N. Greece*, iii–iv: *Thessaly* (London).

LE CORSU, F. (1981), *Plutarque et les femmes dans les* Vies Parallèles (Paris).

LEGON, R. P. (1981), *Megara: The Political History of a Greek City-State to 336 BC* (Ithaca, NY).

LEHMANN, G. A. (1978), 'Spartas ἀρχή und die Vorphase des korinthischen Krieges in den Hellenica Oxyrhynchia', *ZPE* 28: 107–26; 30: 73–93.

LEIGH, M., 'Wounding and Popular Rhetoric at Rome', *BICS* 40 (NS 2): 195–215.

LENDON, J. E. (1989), 'The Oxyrhynchus Historian and the Origins of the Corinthian War', *Historia*, 38. 3: 299–313.

LENGAUER, W. (1979), *Greek Commanders in the Fifth and Fourth Centuries BC—Politics and Ideology: A Study of Militarism* (Warsaw).

LENK, B. (1936), 'Thrake: Stämme', *RE²* vi A: 404–7.

LEO, F. (1901), *Die griechisch-römische Biographie nach ihrer literarischen Form* (Leipzig; repr. Hildesheim, 1965).

LÉVY, E. (1976), *Athènes devant la défaite de 404: histoire d'une crise idéologique* (Paris).

——(1977), 'La Grande Rhétra', *Ktèma*, 2: 85–103.

——(1978), 'La monarchie macédonienne et le mythe d'une royauté démocratique', *Ktèma*, 3: 201–35.

——(1983), 'Les Trois Traités entre Sparte et le roi', *BCH* 107: 221–41.

LEWIS, D. M. (1958), 'The Phoenician Fleet in 411', *Historia,* 7: 392–7.

——(1977), *Sparta and Persia* (Leiden).

——(1994), ch. 2: 'Sparta as Victor', ch. 5: 'Sicily 412–368 BC', in *CAH*, 2nd edn., vol. vi.

LITTMAN, R. J. (1969), 'A New Date for Leotychidas', *Phoenix,* 23: 269–77.

——(1970), 'The Loves of Alcibiades', *TAPhA* 101: 263–76.

LLOYD, A. B. (1994), ch. 8e: 'Egypt', 404–332, *CAH*, 2nd edn., vol. vi.

LONGRIGG, J. (1980), 'The Great Plague of Athens', *History of Science,* 18: 209–25.

——(1985), 'A Seminal "Debate" in the Fifth Century BC', in A. Gotthelf (ed.), *Aristotle on Nature and Living Things* (Bristol), 277–87.

——(1988a), review of P. Brain, *Galen on Bloodletting* (Cambridge, 1986), *CR,* NS 38: 19–21.

——(1988b), 'Anatomy in Alexandria in the Third Century BC', *British Journal for the History of Science,* 21: 455–88.

——(1989), 'Presocratic Philosophy and Hippocratic Medicine', *History of Science,* 27: 1–39.

——(1993), *Greek Rational Medicine: Philosophy and Medicine from Alcmaeon to the Alexandrians* (London).

LONIS, R. (1980), 'La valeur du serment dans les accords internationaux en Grèce classique', *DHA* 6: 267–86.

LÓPEZ FÉREZ, J. A. (1990), 'Plutarco y la medicina', in Pérez Jiménez and Cerro Calderón (eds.) (1990), 217–27.

LOTZE, D. (1962), '*Μόθακες*', *Historia,* 11: 427–35.

——(1964), *Lysander und der Peloponnesische Krieg* (Abhandlungen der Sächsischen Akademie der Wissenschaften zu Leipzig, Phil.-hist. Klasse, 57; Berlin, DDR).

LUPPINO MANES, E. (1989), 'La traccia della biografia plutarchea di Agesilao: individuazione di una possibile indagine critica', *Misc. grec. e rom.* 14 (= Studi pubblicati dell'Istituto italiano per la storia antica, 42; Rome), 87–122.

——(1991) *L'Agesilas di Senofonte: tra commiato e encomico* (Milan).

LURIA, S. (1927), 'Zum politischen Kampf in Sparta gegen Ende des 5. Jahrhunderts', *Klio,* 21 = NS 3: 404–20.

MacDonald, A. (1972), 'A Note on the Raid of Sphodrias', *Historia*, 21: 38–44.

MacDowell, D. M. (1986), *Spartan Law* (Edinburgh).

McKechnie, P. R., and Kern, S. J. (eds.) (1988), *Hellenica Oxyrhynchia* (London).

MacKendrick, P. L. (1960), *The Mute Stones Speak: The Story of Archaeology in Italy* (London).

——(1962), *The Greek Stones Speak: The Story of Archaeology in Greek Lands* (New York).

McQueen, E. I. (1978), 'Some Notes on the Anti-Macedonian Movement in the Peloponnese', *Historia*, 27: 40–64.

Malkin, I. (1990), 'Lysander and Libys', *CQ*, NS 40: 541–5.

——(1994), *Myth and Territory in the Spartan Mediterranean* (Cambridge).

Manfredini, M., and Piccirilli, L. (1980), *Plutarco: Le vite di Licurgo et di Numa* (Milan).

Marasco, G. (1978), 'La leggenda di Polidoro e la ridistribuzione di terre di Licurgo nella propaganda spartana del III secolo', *Prometheus*, 4: 115–27.

——(1980), 'La retra di Epitadeo e la situazione sociale di Sparta nel IV secolo', *Ant. Class.* 49: 131–45.

Martin, H. (1960), 'The Concept of Prāotēs in Plutarch's *Lives*', *GRBS* 3: 65–73.

——(1961), 'The Concept of Philanthropia in Plutarch's *Lives*', *AJP* 82: 164–75.

——(1984), 'Plutarch, Plato and Eros', *CB* 60: 82–6.

Martin, J.-P. (1986), 'Plutarque: Un aspect de sa pensée et son temps', in J. M. Pailler (ed.), *Mélanges offerts à Michel Labrousse* (Toulouse), 59–78.

Martin, V. (1944), 'Le traitement de l'histoire diplomatique dans la tradition littéraire du IVᵉ siècle avant J.-C.', *Mus. Hel.* 1: 13–30.

Matthaion, A. P., and Pikoulas, G. A., "Ἔδον Λακεδαιμονίοις ποττὸν πόλεμον", Horos, 7 (1989), 77–124.

Meiggs, R., and Lewis, D. M. (1988), *A Selection of Greek Historical Inscriptions: To the End of the Fifth Century BC*, rev. edn. (Oxford).

Meyer, Eduard (1877), *Geschichte von Troas* (Leipzig).

——(1898–1956), *Geschichte des Altertums* (Stuttgart and Basel).

Meyer, Ernst (1965), 'Pras', *RE* Suppl. x. 651–2.

Michler, M. (1963), 'Die Krankheit des Agesilaos in Megara', *Sudhoffs Archiv f. d. Geschichte der Medizin und der Naturwissenschaften*, 47: 179–83.

Missiou-Ladi, A. (1987), 'Coercive Diplomacy in Greek Interstate Relations', *CQ*, NS 37: 336–45.

MITCHELL, L. G., and RHODES, P. J. (1996), 'Friends and Enemies in Athenian Politics', *G&R*, 2nd ser. 43: 11–30.

MOLES, J. L. (ed.) (1988), *Plutarch: The Life of Cicero* (Warminster).

——(1993), 'Truth and Untruth in Herodotus and Thucydides', in Gill and Wiseman (eds.) (1993), 88–121.

——(1994), 'Xenophon and Callicratidas', *JHS* 114: 70–84.

MOMIGLIANO, A. (1971*a*), *The Development of Greek Biography* (Cambridge, Mass.).

——(1971*b*), 'Second Thoughts on Greek Biography', *MKNA* 34: 245–57, repr. in *Quinto contributo alla storia degli studi classici e del mondo antico* (Rome, 1975), I. 33–47.

——(1977), *Essays in Ancient and Modern History* (Oxford).

——(1979), 'Persian Empire and Greek Freedom', in A. Ryan (ed.), *The Idea of Freedom: Essays in Honour of Isaiah Berlin* (Oxford), 139–51.

MOORE, J. M. (1975), *Aristotle and Xenophon on Democracy and Oligarchy* (London).

——(1983), *Aristotle and Xenophon on Democracy and Oligarchy* (London).

MORENO, L. A. G. (1992), 'Paradoxography and Political Ideals in Plutarch's *Life of Sertorius*', in Stadter (ed.) (1992*a*), 132–58.

MORETTI, L. (1953), *Iscrizioni agonistiche greche* (Rome).

——(1957), *Olympionikai: i vincitori negli antichi agoni olimpici* (Atti della Accademia Nazionale dei Lincei, Classe di scienze morali, storiche e filologiche, Memorie, ser. 8, vol. 8, fasc. 2 (Rome)).

MOSLEY, D. J. (1962), 'The Athenian Embassy to Sparta in 371 BC', *PCPS*, NS 8: 41–6.

——(1971), 'Diplomacy and Disunion in Ancient Greece', *Phoenix*, 25: 319–30.

——(1972), 'Theban Diplomacy in 371 BC', *REG* 85: 312–18.

MOSSMAN, J. M. (1988), 'Tragedy and Epic in Plutarch's *Alexander*', *JHS* 108: 83–93.

——(1991), 'Plutarch's Use of Statues', in Flower and Toher (eds.) (1991), 98–119.

MOXON, I. S., SMART, J. D., and WOODMAN, A. J. (eds.) (1986), *Past Perspectives* (Cambridge).

MUNN, M. H. (1987), 'Agesilaos' Boiotian Campaigns and the Theban Stockade of 378–377 BC', *CA* 6: 106–38.

——(1993), *The Defense of Attica. The Dema Wall and the Boiotian War of 378–375 BC* (Berkeley and Los Angeles).

MURRAY, O. (1972), 'Herodotos and Hellenistic Culture', *CQ*, NS 22: 200–13.

NELLEN, D. (1972), 'Zur Darstellung der Schlacht bei Sardes in den Quellen', *Anc. Soc.* 3: 45–54.

NIKOLAIDES, A. G. (1982–4), "Ὁ σκοπὸς τῶν βίων τοῦ Πλουτάρχου καὶ οἱ διάφορες συναφεῖς θεωρίες", Ἀρχαιογνωσία, 3: 93–114.

——(1986), 'Ἑλληνικὸς–βαρβαρικός: Plutarch on Greek and Barbarian Characteristics', WS 119 (NF 20): 229–44.

NINOU, K. (ed.) (1981), Archaeological Museum of Thebes (Athens).

NUTTON, V. (1971), 'L. Gellius Maximus, Physician and Procurator', CQ, NS 21: 262–72.

OAKESHOTT, M. (1962), 'The Activity of being a Historian', in id., Rationalism and Politics (London), 137–67.

OBER, J. (1985), Fortress Attica (Leiden).

OGDEN, D. (1996), 'Homosexuality and Warfare in Ancient Greece', in A. B. Lloyd (ed.), Battle in Antiquity (London), 107–68.

OLIVA, P. (1961), 'On the Problem of the Helots', Historia, 3: 5–34.

——(1966), 'Lycurgan Sparta', ŽAnt. 16: 123–34.

——(1967), 'Das lykurgische Problem', A. Ant. Hung. 15: 273–81.

——(1971), Sparta and her Social Problems (Amsterdam and Prague).

——(1975), 'Die Helotenfrage in der Geschichte Spartas', in J. Herrmann and I. Sellnow (eds.), Die Rolle der Volksmassen in der Geschichte der vorkapitalistischen Gesellschaftsformationen: Zum XIV. Historiker-Kongreß in San Francisco 1975 (Veröffentlichungen des Zentralinstituts für Alte Geschichte und Archäologie der Akademie der Wissenschaften der DDR, 7; Berlin), 109–15.

——(1981), 'Heloten und Spartaner', Index, 10: 43–54.

OLLIER, F. (1933–43), Le Mirage spartiate, 2 vols. (Paris).

——(1934) Xénophon: La République des Lacédémoniens (Annales de l'Université de Lyon, NS 2/47; Lyon and Paris).

PAGE, D. L. (1953), Corinna (London).

——(1962), Poetae Melici Graeci (Oxford).

——(1968), Lyrica Graeca Selecta (Oxford).

PAPAGIANNOPOULOS-PALAIOS, A. A. (1956–7), Κράνος χαλκοῦν ἐξ Ὀλυμπίας ἐνεπίγραφον Ὀρχομενίων ἀνάθημα Κορωνεία[θεν], Polemon, 6: 3–6.

PAPAHATZIS, N. (1969), Παυσανίου Ἑλλάδος περιήγησις (Athens), vol. v.

PARKE, H. W. (1945), 'Deposing of Spartan Kings', CQ 39: 106–12.

PARKER, R. T. (1988), 'Were Spartan Kings Heroized?', LCM 13. 1: 9–10.

PASCUAL GONZÁLEZ, J. (1990), 'Plutarco y su visión de la hegemonía tebana', in Pérez Jiménez and Cerro Calderón (eds.) (1990), 73–80.

PAUW, D. A. (1980), 'Impersonal Expressions and Unidentified Spokesmen in Greek and Roman Historiography and Biography', AC 23: 83–95.

PAVIS D'ESCURAC, H. (1981), 'Périls et chances du régime civique selon Plutarque', Ktèma, 6: 287–300.

PAYNE, H. (ed.) (1940), Perachora I (Oxford).

PAYRAU, S. (1971), 'Eirenika: Considérations sur l'échec de quelques tentatives panhelléniques au IVe siècle avant J.-C.', *REA* 73: 24–79.

PEARSON, L. (1968), 'Characterization in Drama and Oratory—*Poetics* 1450ᵃ20', *CQ*, NS 18: 76–83.

PELLING, C. B. R. (1979), 'Plutarch's Method of Work in the Roman *Lives*', *JHS* 99: 74–96, repr. in Scardigli (ed.) (1995), 265–312.

——(1980), 'Plutarch's Adaptation of his Source Material', *JHS* 100: 127–40, repr. in Scardigli (ed.) (1995), 125–54.

——(1986*a*), 'Synkrisis in Plutarch's *Lives*', in Brenk and Gallo (1986), 83–96.

——(1986*b*), 'Plutarch and Roman Politics', in Moxon *et al.* (eds.) (1986), 159–87, repr. in Scardigli (ed.) (1995), 319–56.

——(1988*a*), 'Aspects of Plutarch's Characterisation', *ICS* 13. 2: 257–74.

——(1988*b*), (ed.), *Plutarch: Life of Antony* (Cambridge).

——(1990*a*), 'Truth and Fiction in Plutarch's *Lives*', in Russell (ed.) (1990), 19–52.

——(ed.) (1990*b*), *Characterization and Individuality in Greek Literature* (Oxford).

——(1990*c*), 'Childhood and Personality in Greek Biography', in id. (ed.) (1990*b*), 213–44.

——(1992), 'Plutarch and Thucydides', in Stadter (ed.) (1992*a*), 10–40.

——(forthcoming), *Plutarco: Filopemene e Flaminino* (Milan).

PEPER, L. (1912), *De Plutarchi Epaminonda* (Wiede and Jena).

PÉREZ JIMÉNEZ, A. (1973), 'Actitudes del hombre de frente a la Tyche en las *Vidas Paralelas* de Plutarco', *Boletín del Instituto de Estudios Helénicos*, 7 (Barcelona), 101–10.

——and CERRO CALDERÓN, G. DEL (eds.) (1990), *Estudios sobre Plutarco: Obra y Tradición: Actas del I Symposion Español sobre Plutarco, Fuengirola, 1988* (Málaga).

PERLMAN, S. (1958), 'A Note on the Political Implications of Proxenia', *CQ*, NS 8: 185–91.

——(1964), 'The Causes and the Outbreak of the Corinthian War', *CQ*, NS 14: 64–81.

——(1968), 'Athenian Democracy and the Revival of Imperialistic Expansion at the Beginning of the Fourth Century BC', *CPh* 63: 257–67.

——(1976), 'Panhellenism, the Polis and Imperialism', *Historia*, 25: 1–30.

PERRY, B. E. (1965), *Babrius and Phaedrus* (Cambridge, Mass., and London).

PHILIPPSON, A. (1897), *Thessalien und Epirus: Reisen und Forschungen im nördlichen Griechenland* (Berlin).

PICCIRILLI, L. (1980), 'Cronologia relativa e fonti delle *Vitae Lycurgi et Numae* di Plutarco', in Φιλίας χάριν: *Miscellanea di studi classici in onore di Eugenio Manni*, 6 vols. (Rome), v. 1751–64.

——(1984), 'Dall'"anomia" all'"eunomia"', in *Sodalitas: scritti in onore di A. Guarino*, 9 vols. plus index (Naples), iii. 1031–6.

PLEZIA, M. (1982), 'Agesilaos und Timotheos: zwei Staatsmännerporträts aus der Mitte des IV. Jhs.', *ICS* 7: 49–61.

PLUMB, J. H. (1988), *The Making of an Historian: The Collected Papers of J. H. Plumb* (London).

PODLECKI, A. J. (1987), *Plutarch: Life of Pericles* (Bristol).

——and DUANE, S. (1992), 'A Survey of Work on Plutarch's Greek *Lives*, 1951–1988', *ANRW* II 33. 6: 4053–127.

POMEROY, S. B. (1994), *Xenophon, Oeconomicus: A Social and Historical Commentary* (Oxford).

PORALLA, P. (1985), *Prosopographie der Lakedaimonier bis auf die Zeit Alexanders des Großen*, 2nd edn., rev. A. S. Bradford (Chicago).

POWELL, A. (ed.) (1989), *Classical Sparta: Techniques behind her Success* (London and New York).

——and HODKINSON, S. (eds.) (1994), *The Shadow of Sparta* (London and New York).

PRENTICE, W. K. (1934), 'The Character of Lysander', *AJA* 38: 37–42.

PRITCHETT, W. K. (1965–92), *Studies in Ancient Greek Topography*, 8 vols. (Berkeley and Los Angeles).

——(1971–91), *The Greek State at War*, 7 vols. (Berkeley and Los Angeles).

PROIETTI, G. (1987), *Xenophon's Sparta: An Introduction* (*Mnemosyne*, Suppl. 98; Leiden).

PUECH, B. (1992), 'Prosopographie des amis de Plutarque', *ANRW* II 33. 6: 4831–93.

PURCELL, B. (1994), 'Television and the Great War', *History Today*, 44. 8: 9 12.

RAWSON, E. (1969), *The Spartan Tradition in European Thought* (Oxford).

RAY, J. D. (1987), 'Egypt: Dependence and Independence, 425–343 BC', in Sancisi-Weerdenburg (ed.) (1987), i. 70–95.

——(1992), 'Nectanebo: The Last Egyptian Pharaoh', *History Today, 42*: (February), 38–44.

REDFIELD, J. (1977/8), 'The Women of Sparta', *CJ* 73: 146–61.

REISKE, J. J. (1774–82), *Plutarchi Chaeronensis quae supersunt omnia Graece et Latine* (Leipzig).

RENOIRTE, TH. (1951), *Les 'Conseils politiques' de Plutarque* (Louvain).

RICE, D. G. (1974), 'Agesilaus, Agesipolis and Spartan Politics, 386–79 BC', *Historia, 23*: 164–82.

——(1975), 'Xenophon, Diodorus and the Year 379–378 BC: Reconstruction and Reappraisal', *YCS* 24: 95–130.

RICH, J., and SHIPLEY, G. (eds.) (1993), *War and Society in the Greek World* (Leicester–Nottingham Studies in Ancient Society, 4; London and New York).

RICHMOND, I. A. (ed.) (1951), *Handbook to the Roman Wall* (Newcastle upon Tyne).

RIEDINGER, J. C. (1993), 'Un aspect de la méthode de Xénophon: l'origine des sources dans les Helléniques III–VII', *Athenaeum*, 81: 517–44.

RILEY, M. (1977), 'The Purpose and Unity of Plutarch's *De genio Socratis*', *GRBS* 18: 257–73.

RÍOS FERNÁNDEZ, M. (1979), *Plutarco y Jenofonte: Paralelismo filológico entorno a Agesilao* (Seville).

——(1984), 'Los silencios de Jenofonte en el *Agesilao* de Plutarco', *Habis*, 15: 41–70.

ROBERT, L. (1935), 'Études sur les inscriptions et la topographie de la Gréce centrale', *BCH* 59: 398–402.

——(1963), *Noms indigènes dans l'Asie mineure gréco-romaine* (Paris).

——(1966), *Documents de l'Asie mineure méridionale: Inscriptions, monnaies et géographie* (Paris and Geneva).

ROBINSON, E. W. (1992), 'Oracles and Spartan Religious Scruples', *LCM* 17. 9: 131–3.

ROESCH, P. (1965), *Thespies et la confédération béotienne* (Paris).

——(1982), 'Athéna Itonia. Cultes et Associations', in id., *Études béotiennes* (Paris), 218–60.

ROMILLY, J. DE (1979), *La Douceur dans la pensée grecque* (Paris).

——(1988a), 'Rencontres avec Plutarque', *ICS* 13. 2: 219–29.

——(1988b), *Les Grands Sophistes dans l'Athènes de Périclès* (Paris), Eng. trans. J. Lloyd (Oxford, 1992).

RONNET, G. (1981), 'La figure de Callicratidas et la composition des "Helléniques"', *RPh* 55: 111–21.

ROOBAERT, A. (1977), 'Le danger hilote?', *Ktèma*, 2: 141–55.

ROY, J. (1971), 'Arcadia and Boeotia in Peloponnesian Affairs 370–362', *Historia*, 20: 569–99.

——(1994), ch. 7: 'Thebes in the 360s', *CAH*, 2nd edn., vol. vi.

RÜHL, F. (1913), 'Randglossen zu der Hellenika von Oxyrhynchos', *RhM*, NF 68: 161–201.

RUSSELL, D. A. (1966a), 'Plutarch: Alcibiades 1–16', *PCPhS* 12: 37–47, repr. in Scardigli (ed.) (1995), 191–207.

——(1966b), 'On Reading Plutarch's *Lives*', *G&R*, NS 13. 2: 139–54, repr. in Scardigli (ed.) (1995), 75–94.

——(1967), 'Rhetoric and Criticism', *G&R*, NS 14. 2: 130–44.

——(1973), *Plutarch* (London).

——(ed.) (1990), *Antonine Literature* (Oxford).

RYDER, T. T. B. (1957), 'The Supposed Common Peace of 366/5 BC', *CQ*, NS 7: 99–205.

——(1963*a*), 'Spartan Relations with Persia after the King's Peace: A Strange Story in Diodorus 15. 9', *CQ*, NS 13: 105–9.

——(1963*b*), 'Athenian Foreign Policy and the Peace Conference at Sparta in 371 BC', *CQ*, NS 13: 237–41.

——(1965), *Koine Eirene: General Peace and Local Independence in Ancient Greece* (Oxford).

SAHLINS, M. (1974), *Stone Age Economics* (London).

STE. CROIX, G. E. M. DE (1972), *The Origins of the Peloponnesian War* (London).

——(1981), *The Class Struggle in the Ancient Greek World* (London).

SAKELLARIOU, M. B. (1980), 'Panhellenism: From Concept to Policy', in M. B. Hatzopoulos and L. D. Loukopoulos (eds.), *Philip of Macedon*, (Athens, 1980), 128–45.

SALMON, J. B. (1984), *Wealthy Corinth: A History of the City to 338 BC* (Oxford).

SALMON, P. (1981), *Études sur la confédération béotienne (447–386)* (Brussels).

SALVIONI, L. (1982), '"Le Madri dell'ira" nelle *Vite* di Plutarco', *Giornale filologico ferrarese*, 5: 83–92.

SANCISI-WEERDENBURG, H. (ed.) (1987), *Achaemenid History*, i: *Sources, Structures and Synthesis* (Leiden).

SANDBACH, F. H. (1975), *The Stoics* (London).

——(1982), 'Plutarch and Aristotle', *ICS* 7: 207–32.

SANDERS, J. M. (ed.) (1992), *Φιλολάκων: Lakonian Studies in Honour of Hector Catling* (London).

SAUNDERS, T. J. (1973), 'Penology and Eschatology in Plato's *Timaeus* and *Laws*', *CQ*, NS 23: 232–44.

SCARDIGLI, B. (ed.) (1986), 'Scritti recenti sulle *Vite* di Plutarcho (1974–1986)', in Brenk and Gallo (eds.) (1986), 7–59.

——(1995), *Essays on Plutarch's Lives* (Oxford).

SCHACHTER, A. (1986), 'Prehistoric Hydraulic Systems', and 'Skourta Project', *Teiresias*, 16, Appendix: 'Boeotica', AB/4–6, 7–10.

SCHAPS, D. (1977), 'The Woman least Mentioned', *CQ*, NS 27: 323–30.

SCHNEEWEISS, G. (1979), 'History and Philosophy in Plutarch: Observations on Plutarch's *Lycurgus*', in G. W. Bowersock *et al.* (eds.), *Arktouros: Hellenic Studies Presented to B. M. W. Knox on the Occasion of his 65th Birthday* (Berlin and New York), 376–82.

——(1985), 'τὴν τοῦ ἀρίστου καὶ δοκιμωτάτου μνήμην ὑποδεχόμενος ἀεὶ τῇ ψυχῇ . . . Gegenstand und Absicht in den Biographien Plutarchs', in W. Suerbaum *et al.* (eds.), *Festschrift für Franz Egermann zu seinem 80. Geburtstag am 13. Februar 1985* (Munich), 147–62.

SCHNEIDER, K. (1912), 'Hahnenkämpfe', *RE* vii/2. 2210–15.

SCHÜTRUMPF, E. (1987), 'The *Rhetra* of Epitadeus: A Platonist's Fiction', *GRBS* 28: 441–57.

—— (1994), 'Aristotle on Sparta', in Powell and Hodkinson (eds.) (1994), 323–45.

SCHWARTZ, E. (1951), *Ethik der Griechen* (Stuttgart).

SCOTT-KILVERT, I. (1973), *The Age of Alexander: Nine Greek Lives by Plutarch* (Harmondsworth).

SEAGER, R. J. (1967), 'Thrasybulus, Conon and Athenian Imperialism 396–386', *JHS* 87: 95–115.

—— (1974), 'The King's Peace and the Balance of Power in Greece 386–362', *Athenaeum*, NS 52: 36–63.

—— (1977), 'Agesilaus in Asia: Propaganda and Objectives', *LCM* 2. 8: 183–4.

—— (1979), *Pompey: A Political Biography* (Oxford).

—— and TUPLIN, C. J. (1980), 'The Freedom of the Greeks of Asia: On the Origins of a Concept and the Creation of a Slogan', *JHS* 100: 141–54.

SERGENT, B. (1976), 'La représentation spartiate de la royauté', *RHR* 189: 3–52.

SHERWIN-WHITE, S. M. (1982), review of Cargill (1981), *JHS* 102: 269–71.

SHIPLEY, G. (1987), *A History of Samos 800–188 BC* (Oxford).

—— (1992), '*Perioikos:* The Discovery of Classical Lakonia', in Sanders (ed.) (1992), 211–26.

—— (1993), 'The Limits of War', in Rich and Shipley (eds.) (1993), 1–24.

SHRIMPTON, G. S. (1971*a*), 'Plutarch's *Life of Epaminondas*', *Pacific Coast Philology*, 6: 55–9.

—— (1971*b*), 'The Theban Supremacy in Fourth-Century Literature', *Phoenix*, 25: 310–18.

—— (1991), *Theopompos the Historian* (Montreal and London).

SINCLAIR, R. K. (1966), 'Diodorus Siculus and Fighting in Relays', *CQ*, NS 16: 249–55.

SMITH, R. E. (1948), 'Lysander and the Spartan Empire', *CP* 43: 145–56.

—— (1953–4), 'The Opposition to Agesilaos' Foreign Policy 394–371 BC', *Historia*, 2: 274–88.

SMITS, J. (1939), *Plutarchus' Leven van Lysander* (Amsterdam).

SORDI, M. (1968), 'Aspetti del federalismo greco arcaico: autonomia e egemonia nel κοινόν beotico', *Atene e Roma*, 13: 55–75.

—— (1973), 'La restaurazione della lega beotico nel 379–8 a.C.', *Athenaeum*, NS 51: 79–91.

SORUM, C. E. (1984), 'The Authorship of the *Agesilaus*', *PP* 217: 264–75.

SPAWFORTH, A. J. S. (1994), 'Symbol of Unity? The Persian-Wars

Tradition in the Roman Empire', in Hornblower (ed.) (1994*b*), 233–59.

SPENCE, I. G. (1993), *The Cavalry of Ancient Greece: A Social and Military History* (Oxford).

STADTER, P. A. (1965), *Plutarch's Historical Methods: An Analysis of the Mulierum Virtutes* (Cambridge, Mass.).

——(1975), 'Plutarch's Comparison of Pericles and Fabius Maximus', *GRBS* 16: 77–85, repr. in Scardigli (ed.) (1995), 155–64.

——(1984), review of F. W. J. Frost, *Plutarch's Themistocles: A Historical Commentary* (Princeton, 1980), *CJ* 79: 356–63.

——(1988), 'The Proems of Plutarch's *Lives*', *ICS* 13. 2: 275–95.

——(ed.) (1992*a*), *Plutarch and the Historical Tradition* (London and New York).

——(1992*b*), 'Paradoxical Paradigms: Lysander and Sulla', in id. (ed.) (1992*a*), 41–55.

STÄHLIN, F. (1924*a*), 'Larissa', *RE* xii/1. 849–71.

——(1924*b*), *Das hellenische Thessalien* (Stuttgart), 186–91.

——(1935), 'Narthakion', *RE* xvi/2. 1760–4.

STANTON, G. R. (1973), 'Sophists and Philosophers: Problems of Classification', *AJPh* 94: 350–64.

——(1982), 'Federalism in the Greek World', in G. H. R. Horsley (ed.), *Hellenika: Essays on Greek Politics and History* (North Ryde, NSW), 183–90.

STINTON, T. C. W. (1975), 'Hamartia in Aristotle and Greek Tragedy', *CQ*, NS 25: 221–54.

STRASBURGER, H. (1965), 'Poseidonius on Problems of the Roman Empire', *JRS* 55: 40–53, repr. 'Posidonius über die Römerherrschaft', in W. Schmittenner and R. Zoepffel (eds.), *Studien zur alten Geschichte* (Hildesheim, 1982), ii. 920–45.

STRAUSS, B. S. (1986), *Athens after the Peloponnesian War: Class, Faction and Policy, 403–386 BC* (London and Sydney).

STUBBS, H. W. (1950), 'Spartan Austerity: A Possible Explanation', *CQ* 44: 32–7.

SWADDLING, J. (1980), *The Ancient Olympic Games* (London).

SWAIN, S. (1988), 'Plutarch's *Philopoemen* and *Flamininus*', *ICS* 13/2: 335–47.

——(1989*a*), 'Character Change in Plutarch', *Phoenix*, 43: 62–8.

——(1989*b*), 'Plutarch: Chance, Providence and History', *AJP* 110: 272–302.

——(1990), 'Hellenic Culture and the Roman Heroes of Plutarch', *JHS* 100: 126–45, repr. in Scardigli (ed.) (1995), 229–64.

——(1992), 'Plutarchan Synkrisis', *Eranos*, 90: 101–11.

SYMEONOGLOU, S. (1985), *The Topography of Thebes from the Bronze Age to Modern Times* (Princeton).

TAGLIASACCHI, A. M. (1960), 'Plutarco e la tragedia greca', *Dioniso, 34:* 124–42.

TALBERT, R. J. A. (1989), 'The Role of the Helots in the Class Struggle at Sparta', *Historia,* 38: 22–40.

TAZELAAR, C. M. (1967), '*Paides kai epheboi:* Some Notes on the Spartan Stages of Youth', *Mnemosyne,* 4th ser. 20: 127–53.

THOMAS, C. G. (1974), 'On the Role of the Spartan Kings', *Historia,* 23: 257–70.

THOMPSON, W. E. (1973), 'Observations on Spartan Politics', *RSA* 3: 47–58.

——(1983), 'Isocrates on the Peace Treaties', *CQ,* NS 33: 75–80.

TIGERSTEDT, E. N. (1965–74), *The Legend of Sparta in Classical Antiquity,* 2 vols. (Stockholm).

TITCHENER, F. B. (1992), 'Critical Trends in Plutarch's Roman *Lives,* 1975–1990', *ANRW* II 33. 6: 4128–53.

TOD, M. N. (1948), *A Selection of Greek Historical Inscriptions,* II. *403–323 BC* (Oxford).

TODD, S. (1993), *The Shape of Athenian Law* (Oxford).

TOMLINSON, R. A. (1985), 'The Circular Building at Perachora', *BSA* 80: 261–79.

——and FOSSEY, J. M. (1970), 'Ancient Remains on Mount Mavrobouni, South Boeotia', *BSA* 65: 243–64.

TOSH, J. (1991), *The Pursuit of History: Aims, Methods and New Directions in the Study of Modern History,* 2nd edn. (London and New York).

TRITLE, L. A. (1992), 'Plutarch's *Life of Phocion:* An Analysis and Critical Report', *ANRW* II 33. 6: 4256–97.

TSIMPOUKIDES, D. (1987), *Ὁ Βιόγραφος Πλούταρχος* (Athens).

TUPLIN, C. J. (1977), 'The Athenian Embassy to Sparta, 372/1', *LCM* 2. 3: 51–6.

——(1979), 'Two Proper Names in the Text of Diodorus, Book 15', *CQ,* NS 29: 347–57.

——(1982), 'The Date of the Union of Corinth and Argos', *CQ,* NS 32: 75–83.

——(1984), 'Pausanias and Plutarch's Epaminondas', *CQ,* NS 34: 346–58.

——(1986), 'Military Engagements in Xenophon's *Hellenika*', in Moxon *et al.* (eds.) (1986), 37–66.

——(1987), 'The Leuctra Campaign: Some Outstanding Problems', *Klio,* NF 69: 72–107.

——(1993), *The Failings of Empire: A Reading of Xenophon: Hellenica 2. 3. 11–7. 5. 27* (Historia Einzelschriften, 76; Stuttgart).

TZANNETATOS, TH. S. (1960), "*Ὁ Πλούταρχος ὡς ἄνθρωπος καὶ ὡς* συγγραφεύς", *Parnassos*, 2. 1: 21–41.

UNDERHILL, G. E., and MARCHANT, E. C. (1906), *Xenophon: Hellenica* (Oxford).

UNZ, R. K. (1986), 'The Chronology of the Elean War', *GRBS* 27: 29–42.

VALGIGLIO, E. (1987), 'Ἰστορία e βίος in Plutarco', *Orpheus*, 3rd ser. 8: 50–70.

——(1992), 'Dagli "Ethica" ai "Bioi" in Plutarco', *ANRW* II 33. 6: 3963–4051.

VALK, M. VAN DER (1982), 'Notes on the Composition and Arrangement of the Biographies of Plutarch', in *Studi in onore di Aristide Colonna* (Perugia), 301–37.

VAN DE MAELE, S. (1987), 'La route antique de Megare à Thèbes par le défilé du Kambili', *BCH* 111: 191–205.

VANDERPOOL, E. (1978), 'Roads and Forts in Northwestern Attica', *CSCA* 11: 227–45.

VAUGHN, P. (1991), 'The Identification and Retrieval of the Hoplite Battle-Dead', in Hanson (ed.) (1991), 38–62.

VERMEULE, E. T. (1979), *Aspects of Death in Early Greek Art and Poetry* (Berkeley, Los Angeles, and London).

VERNIÈRE, Y. (1983), 'Masques et visages du destin dans les *Vies* de Plutarque', in F. Jouan (ed.), *Visages du destin dans les mythologies: Mélanges Jaqueline Duchemin, actes du colloque de Chantilly (1–2 mai 1980)* (Paris), 111–19.

VOURVERIS, K. I. (1966), Πλάτων καὶ βάρβαροι (Athens).

VRIESLAND, V. E. VAN (1961), *Agesilaos (ontleed aan Plutarchus)* (Amsterdam).

WALBANK, F. W. (1955), 'Tragic History: A Reconsideration', *BICS* 2: 4–14.

——(1960), 'History and Tragedy', *Historia*, 9: 216–34, repr. in id., *On Greek and Roman Historiography: Selected Papers* (Cambridge, 1985), 224–41.

WALCOT, P. (1996), 'Continuity and Tradition: The Persistence of Greek Values', *G&R*, NS 43: 169–77.

WALKER, E. M. (1908), 'Cratippus or Theopompus', *Klio*, 8: 356–71.

WALL, S. M., MUSGRAVE, J. H., and WARREN, P. M. (1986), 'Human Bones from a Late Minoan IB House at Knossos', *BSA* 81: 333–88, plates 21–37.

WALLACE, M. B. (1970), 'Early Greek *Proxenoi*', *Phoenix*, 24: 189–208.

WALSER, G. (1967), 'Griechen am Hofe des Grosskönigs', in Ernst Walder (ed.), *Festgabe Hans von Greyerz* (Bern), 189–202.

——(1975), 'Zum griechisch-persischen Verhältnis vor dem Hellenismus', *HZ* 220: 529–42.

WALSER, G. (1984), *Hellas und Iran* (Wege der Forschung; Darmstadt).

WALSH, W. H. (1967), *An Introduction to the Philosophy of History*, 3rd edn. (Hutchinson).

WARDMAN, A. E. (1967), 'Description of Personal Appearance in Plutarch and Suetonius: The Use of Statues as Evidence', *CQ*, NS 17: 414–20.

——(1971), 'Plutarch's Methods in the *Lives*', *CQ*, NS 21: 254–61.

——(1974), *Plutarch's Lives* (London).

WATERHOUSE, H. (1986), *The British School at Athens: The First Hundred Years* (London).

——and HOPE SIMPSON, R. (1961), 'Prehistoric Lakonia: II', *BSA* 56: 114–75.

WEISKOPF, M. (1989), *The So-Called 'Great Satraps' Revolt', 366–360 BC: Concerning Local Instability in the Achaemenid Far West* (Historia Einzelschriften, 63: Stuttgart).

WEIZSÄCKER, A. (1931), *Untersuchungen über Plutarchs biographische Technik* (Berlin).

WESENBERG (1980), 'Agesilaos im Artemision', *ZPE* 41: 175–80.

WESSELING, P. (1746), Διοδώρου τοῦ Σικελιώτου Βιβλιοθήκης Ἱστορικῆς τὰ σωζόμενα: *Diodori Siculi Bibliothecae Historicae libri qui supersunt* (Amsterdam).

WEST, S. (1988), 'Archilochus' Message-Stick', *CQ*, NS 38: 42–8.

WESTLAKE, H. D. (1935), *Thessaly in the Fourth Century* (London).

——(1938), 'Alcibiades, Agis and Spartan Policy', *JHS* 58: 30–40.

——(1939), 'The Sources of Plutarch's Pelopidas', *CQ*, 33: 11–22.

——(1966), 'Individuals in Xenophon's *Hellenica*', *Bulletin of the John Rylands Library*, 49: 246–69, repr. in id., *Essays on the Greek Historians and Greek History* (Manchester, 1969), 203–25.

——(1968), *Individuals in Thucydides* (Cambridge).

——(1975), 'Xenophon and Epaminondas', *GRBS* 16: 23–40.

——(1977), 'λέγεται in Thucydides', *Mnemosyne*, 4th ser. 40: 345–62.

——(1981a), 'The Decline and Fall of Tissaphernes', *Historia*, 30: 257–79.

——(1981b), review of Lengauer (1979), in *JHS* 101: 195–6.

——(1983a), 'Conon and Rhodes: The Troubled Aftermath of Synoecism', *GRBS* 24: 333–44.

——(1983b), 'The Progress of Epiteichismos', *CQ*, NS 33: 12–24.

——(1985a), 'Tissaphernes in Thucydides', *CQ*, NS 35: 43–54.

——(1985b), 'The Sources for the Spartan Debacle at Haliartus', *Phoenix*, 39: 119–33.

——(1986a), 'Agesilaos in Diodorus', *GRBS* 27: 263–77.

——(1986b), 'Spartan Intervention in Asia, 400–397', *Historia*, 35: 405–26.

WHEELDON, M. J. (1989), ' "True Stories": The Reception of Historiography in Antiquity', in Cameron (ed.) (1989), 33–63.

WHEELER, E. L. (1988), *Stratagem and the Vocabulary of Military Trickery* (*Mnemosyne*, Suppl. 108; Leiden).

——(1991), 'The General as Hoplite', in Hanson (ed.) (1991), 121–70.

WHITBY, MICHAEL (1992), review of Ducat (1990), *CR*, NS 42: 358–60.

——(1994), 'Two Shadows: Images of Spartans and Helots', in Powell and Hodkinson (eds.) (1994), 87–126.

WHITTAKER, J. (1969), 'Ammonius on the Delphic E', *CQ*, NS 19: 185–92.

WILAMOWITZ-MOELLENDORFF U. VON (1874), 'Abrechnung eines boiotischen Hipparchen', *Hermes*, 8: 431–41, repr. (1935–72), v (1). 245–55.

——(1889), 'Commentariolum Grammaticum I', *Index scholarum hibernarum Gryphiswaldiae*, 1879, 3–12, repr. (1935–72), iv. 583–96.

——(1935–72), *Kleine Schriften*, 6 vols. (Berlin).

WILL, E, (1960), 'Chabrias et les finances de Tachōs', *REA* 62: 254–75.

WILLIAMS, R. S. (1978), 'The Role of *Amicitia* in the Career of A. Gabinius (cos. 58)', *Phoenix*, 32: 195–210.

WISEMAN, J. (1969), 'Epaminondas and the Theban Invasions', *Klio*, NF 51: 177–99.

WISEMAN, T. P. (1979), *Clio's Cosmetics: Three Studies in Greco-Roman Literature* (Leicester).

——(1993), 'Lying Historians: Seven Types of Mendacity', in Gill and Wiseman (eds.) (1993), 122–46.

WOODMAN, A. J. (1988), *Rhetoric in Classical Historiography* (London and Sydney).

WOOZLEY, A. D. (1971), 'Socrates on Disobeying the Law', in G. Vlastos (ed.), *The Philosophy of Socrates* (New York), 299–318.

XANTHAKIS-KARAMANOS, G. (1979), 'The Influence of Rhetoric on Fourth Century Tragedy', *CQ*, NS 29: 66–76.

YAGINUMA, Y. (1992), 'Plutarch's Language and Style', *ANRW* II 33. 6: 4726–42.

ZIEGLER, K. (1951), 'Plutarchus von Chaironeia', *RE* xxi/1, 636–92; separately published, 2nd edn. (Stuttgart, 1964).

——(1973), *Plutarchus: Vitae Parallelae*, iii/2 (Leipzig).

ZINSERLING, G. (1965), 'Persönlichkeit und Politik Lysanders im Lichte der Kunst', *Wiss. Zeits. Jena*, 14: 35–43.

ZOEPFFEL, R. (1985), 'Geschlechtsreife und Legitimation zur Zeugung im alten Griechenland', in E. W. Müller (ed.), *Geschlechtsreife und Legitimation zur Zeugung, Histor. Ansichten III: Kindheit, Jugend, Familie* (Freiburg and Munich), 319–401.

INDEXES

In the following indexes, *bis* and *ter* denote, respectively, two and three separate discussions on a page; *passim* indicates a non-continuous discussion with no interruption longer than a page.

1. GENERAL INDEX

Modern scholars and ancient authors are not normally listed (for ancient, see mainly Index 3). Entries and subentries are alphabetized on a 'word-by-word' basis (e.g. 'competitive virtues' before 'competitiveness'), except for a few arranged chronologically (e.g. under Epameinondas). In a few entries concerning literary features, long strings of references have deliberately not been divided into subheadings (see e.g. 'chiastic patterns').

Page-numbers in italics refer to Maps.

Special abbreviations: 'A.' = Agesilaos; *Ages.* = Plutarch, *Agesilaos*; 'r.' = reigned.

2. SELECT INDEX OF GREEK WORDS

3. INDEX LOCORUM

4. INSCRIPTIONS